HARRY FIRST
A Global Vision for Competition Law

Foreword by Rochelle C. Dreyfuss

Editors

Darren Bush
Andrew I. Gavil
Spencer Weber Waller

Concurrences

Paris - New York - London

All rights reserved. No photocopying: copyright licences do not apply. The information provided in this publication is general and may not apply in a specific situation. The publisher accepts no responsibility for any acts or omissions contained herein. Enquiries concerning reproduction should be sent to the Institute of Competition Law, at the address below.

Copyright © 2025 by Institute of Competition Law
106 West 32nd Street, Suite 144 New York, NY, 10001, USA
www.concurrences.com
book@concurrences.com

First Printing, April 2025
978-1-954750-19-7 (Hardcover)
Library of Congress Control Number: 2025936599

Cover Design: Yves Buliard, www.yvesbuliard.fr
Book Design and Layout implementation: Nord Compo

Concurrences Books

Tributes

James F. Rill – A Life in Antitrust, *2024*
Eleanor M. Fox – Antitrust Ambassador to the World, *2021*
Herbert Hovenkamp – The Dean of American Antitrust Law, *2021*
Frédéric Jenny – Standing Up for Convergence and Relevance in Antitrust, (Vol. I & II), *2019 & 2021*
Albert Foer – A Consumer Voice in the Antitrust Arena, *2020*
Richard Whish – Taking Competition Law Outside the Box, *2020*
Douglas H. Ginsburg – An Antitrust Professor on the Bench (Vol. I & II), *2018 & 2020*
Wang Xiaoye – The Pioneer of Competition Law in China, *A. Emch, W. Ng (eds.), 2019*
Ian S. Forrester – A Scot without Borders (Vol. I & II), *A. Komninos (eds.), 2015*
William E. Kovacic – An Antitrust Tribute (Vol. I & II), *2013 & 2014*

Practical Books

Competition Law and the Challenges of Insular Economies – A Focus on French Polynesia and the Pacific Region, *J. Peyre, E. Silvestro, V. Terrien, T. Emen, Y. Lecornu (eds.), 2025*
Competition Inspections under EU Law, 2nd Edition, *N. Jalabert-Doury, 2025*
Navigating the DMA: Application Across National Jurisdictions, *G. Muscolo & A. Massolo (eds.), 2025*
Artificial Intelligence and Competition Policy, *A. Abbott, T. Schrepel (eds.), 2024*
State Aid & National Enforcement, *J. Derenne, D. Jouve, C. Lemaire, F. Martucci (eds.), 2024*
The 2023 U.S. Merger Guidelines: *A Review, Sean Sullivan (ed.), 2024*
Competition Inspections in 25 Jurisdictions 2nd Edition – A Practitioner's Guide, *N. Jalabert-Doury (ed.), 2024*
EU Antitrust Enforcement – Law, Economics, History, *Policy & Practice, Wouter P. J. Wils, 2024*
The EU Foreign Subsidies Regulation, *Andreas Reindl, Isabelle Van Damme, 2024*
Compendium of Antitrust Damages Actions – ICC – 2nd edition, *J.W.H. Denton AO, F. Brunet, S. Williams, C. Inthavisay (eds.), 2023*
Pharmaceutical Antitrust: An Analysis of US and EU Law, *M. Thill-Tayara, G. Gordon (eds.), 2023*
Innovation Paradox in Merger Control, *G. Gurkaynak, 2023*
Antitrust and the Digital Economy, *Y. Katsoulakos (ed.), 2023 (in collaboration with CRESSE)*
Judicial Review of Competition Cases, *D. Ginsburg, T. Eicke (eds.), 2023*
Competition Law Treatment of Joint Ventures, *B. Bleicher, N. Campbell, A. Hamilton, N. Hukkinen, A. Khan, A. Mordaunt (eds.), 2022 (in collaboration with the IBA)*
Information Exchange & Related Risks, *Z. Marosi, M. Soares (eds.), 2022 (in collaboration with the IBA)*
Rulemaking Authority of the US Federal Trade Commission, *D. Crane (ed.), 2022*
The International Competition Network at Twenty, *D. Anderson & P. Lugard (eds.), 2022*
Competition Case Law Digest – 5th Edition, *F. Jenny, N. Charbit (eds.), 2022*
Competition Inspections in 21 Jurisdictions – A Practitioner's Guide, *N. Jalabert-Doury (ed.), 2022*
Perspectives on Antitrust Compliance, *A. Riley, A. Stephan, A. Tubbs (eds.), 2022 (in collaboration with the ICC)*
Turkish Competition Law, *G. Gürkaynak, 2021*
Competition Law – Climate Change & Environmental Sustainability, *S. Holmes, D. Middelschulte, M. Snoep (eds.), 2021*
Merger Control in Latin America – A Jurisdictional Guide, *P. Burnier da Silveira, P. Sittenfeld (eds.), 2020*
Competition Inspections under EU Law – A Practitioner's Guide, *N. Jalabert-Doury, 2020*
Gun Jumping in Merger Control – A Jurisdictional Guide, *C. Hatton, Y. Comtois, A. Hamilton (eds.), 2019 (in collaboration with the IBA)*
Choice – A New Standard for Competition Analysis? *P. Nihoul (ed.), 2016*

PhD Theses

The Economics of Digital Markets – Essays in Theoretical and Empirical Industrial Organization, *E. Arnaud-Joufray, 2024*
Abuse of Platform Power, *F. Bostoen, 2023*
Reform of Chinese State-Owned Enterprises, *X. Bai, 2023*
Competition & Regulation in Network Industries – Essays in Industrial Organization, *J-M. Zogheib, 2021*
The Role of Media Pluralism in the Enforcement of EU Competition Law, *K. Bania, 2019*
Buyer Power, *I. Herrera Anchustegui, 2017*

General Interest

Why Competition? Voices from the Antitrust Community and Beyond, *D. Crane, D. Gerard, R. Tritell (eds.), 2024*
Competition Law Dictionary, *D. Healey, R. Whish, W. E. Kovacic, P. Trevisán (eds.), 2024*
The 5 Labours of Europe, *P.-E. Partsch, 2024*
Great Antitrust Enforcers, *W. E. Kovacic, 2023*
Competition – How to Speak Like an Expert, *E. Combe, 2023*
Women and Antitrust – Voices from the Field (Vol I & II), *E. Kurgonaite & K. Nordlander, 2020*

e-Book versions available for **Concurrences+** subscribers

Foreword

A Tribute to Harry First
Friend and Colleague

ROCHELLE C. DREYFUSS[*]
New York University School of Law

This book is a tribute to the many important contributions that Harry First has made to the field of antitrust law. I, however, offer a different perspective. I am not an antitrust scholar. But I know Harry well, as a mentor *par excellence*, an institutional bedrock, a gifted teacher, and the best colleague and friend one could have.

I first encountered Harry in his role as my mentor. He was chair of the personnel committee when I was hired as an assistant professor at NYU School of Law. He not only chose me for the faculty; he also assisted me through the difficult promotion and tenuring process. Together with Diane Zimmerman, we launched the Engelberg Center on Innovation Law and Policy and established the Colloquium on Innovation Policy. Harry and I also taught together many times, sometimes running the Colloquium, other times conducting seminars on a variety of topics, including on the interface between intellectual property (my area) and antitrust law. I have learned an enormous amount about teaching from watching Harry present complex materials, engage students, and provide them with detailed comments on their papers. Harry has turned at least one junior faculty member (me) into a decent instructor and many, many students into first-class lawyers.

Harry's contributions to NYU go far beyond establishing new institutes and courses. NYU was founded as a Law *Center* (rather than *School*), with the idea of combining the insights of scholarship with the experience of practice. Retaining that focus has not always been easy. As self-described high-level legal theorists joined the faculty, they began to discourage practitioner-oriented work. But Harry kept the Law Center's tradition alive through his work as counsel to

---

[*] Pauline Newman Professor of Law Emerita, New York University School of Law.

Loeb & Loeb, his service as chief of New York's Antitrust Bureau, and his writing and editorship of publications aimed at bench, bar, and lectern. His example has made it possible for newer colleagues to take time away from NYU to work in the government and at firms and to participate in the litigation of significant national issues. These experiences have made a mark on their scholarship and teaching, and have vastly improved their capacity to guide students.

Harry has helped NYU stay its course in other ways as well. What I have found most astonishing about Harry is his appreciation for the power of information and the grace and sophistication with which he has collected, used, deployed, and considered it. At some schools, issues churn and are never resolved dispositively.[1] But under Harry's watch, things never got out of hand at NYU. Even before computers, digitized content, and cloud storage, he managed to retain every report on Law School policy issued during his tenure and could whip a relevant document out at a moment's notice. His files kept track of where we had reached agreement and that allowed us to move things forward rather than continually revisit the past. The reports he so carefully preserved ensured that the faculty remained true to its commitments and guaranteed that similarly situated people were treated alike. In that manner, Harry helped make NYU diverse in every important way. People of differing backgrounds, viewpoints, fields, and approaches to scholarship all found the school an inviting place to spend a career. Harry and his files have had an institutional impact that NYU will surely find difficult to replace.

Harry's interest in information came to fruition in a seminar we taught together for several years. Startled by the growth in crimes related to the unauthorized use of patents, copyrights, trademarks, and trade secrets, I persuaded Harry – who had long been interested in the evolution of criminal law – to explore this phenomenon in a course. We called it Intellectual Property Crimes, but in truth, we looked at information crimes more generally. Harry started us off with old English cases about things like breaking into bales of woad and failing to deposit banknotes.[2] Through these cases, he demonstrated how the law has always responded to novel ways for misappropriating things, including things that suddenly become valuable enough to be worth misappropriating. His message was that as our society transitioned from the Industrial Revolution to a Knowledge Economy and information became a dominant form of wealth, it should be no surprise that law would begin to criminalize its unauthorized appropriation.

The problem then became deciding what types of appropriation ought to be considered crimes.[3] For intellectual property, the answer is not obvious. On the

---

[1] Sayre's Law states that the intensity of feeling tends to be inversely proportional to the value of the issues at stake. Rehashing grievances during faculty meetings is thus to be expected.

[2] The Carrier's Case, YB Pasch. 13 Edw. IV, f. 9, pl. 5 (1473); The King v. Bazeley, 168 Eng. Rep. 517 (Ex. Ch. 1799).

[3] An example of the struggle entailed by that enterprise is exemplified by the cases involving Sergey Aleynikov, *see, e.g.*, United States v. Aleynikov, 676 F.3d 71 (2d Cir. 2012).

one hand, exclusive rights over information create incentives to produce more information – music, books, marketing signals, manufacturing know-how, medicines, and the like. On the other hand, there are strong public interests in sharing information so that creative employees can change jobs and put their knowledge to the highest and best use, so that advances that improve social welfare are widely available, and so that the knowledge frontier can advance.[4] When civil liability is in issue, it has proved difficult to balance proprietary and public interests; criminalization makes the problem worse.[5] As readers of this volume know well, there are somewhat similar ambiguities in how to think about information usage in the antitrust arena. Sometimes sharing it is a crime, but sometimes the problem lies in refusing to deal.[6]

Indeed, as Harry and I searched for course materials, we found the question of criminalizing the taking and use of information to be slippery in every realm. In securities law, efficient markets rely on maximizing the distribution of firms' internal information, and indeed, public disclosure is sometimes required. Yet trading on inside information can be a crime.[7] Economic espionage may threaten U.S. industry, but punishing efforts to share technical advances can discourage international cooperation and lead to discriminatory treatment of scientists who trace their heritage to countries the U.S. considers to be commercial rivals.[8] Telling voters about a presidential candidate's involvement with a porn star would seem to be a breach of privacy. Still, paying to withhold that information may, in some circumstances, be criminal.[9]

Harry's background in white-collar crime was key to analyzing these issues.[10] His pedagogic technique was to continually pose the question: Villain or Hero?

---

[4] United States v. Nosal, 844 F.3d 1024 (9th Cir. 2016); Superseding Indictment, United States v. Aaron Swartz, No. 11-CR-10260-NMG, 2012 WL 4341933 (D. Mass. Sept. 12, 2012). *See also* Harry First, *Exploitative Abuses of Intellectual Property Rights*, in THE CAMBRIDGE HANDBOOK OF ANTITRUST, INTELLECTUAL PROPERTY, AND HIGH TECH 222 (Roger D. Blair and D. Daniel Sokol eds., 2017)

[5] Fogerty v. Fantasy, Inc., 510 U.S. 517 (1994); United States v. Reichert, 747 F.3d 445 (6th Cir. 2014).

[6] Harry First, *Bork and* Microsoft*: Why Bork Was Right and What We Learn About Judging Exclusionary Behavior*, 79 ANTITRUST L.J. 1017 (2014); Harry First, *Online Music Joint Ventures: Taken for a Song* (N.Y.U. L. & Econ. Rsch. Paper Series, Working Paper No. 04-006, Feb. 2004), https://papers.ssrn.com/sol3/papers.cfm?abstract_id=508685. *See also* HARRY FIRST & ANDREW I. GAVIL, THE MICROSOFT ANTITRUST CASES: COMPETITION POLICY FOR THE TWENTY-FIRST CENTURY (2014).

[7] Dirks v. SEC, 463 U.S. 646 (1983); United States v. O'Hagan, 521 U.S. 642 (1997); Salman v. United States, 580 U.S. 39 (2016).

[8] OFFICE OF THE NAT'L COUNTERINTEL. EXEC., FOREIGN SPIES STEALING US ECONOMIC SECRETS IN CYBERSPACE: REPORT TO CONGRESS ON FOREIGN ECONOMIC COLLECTION AND INDUSTRIAL ESPIONAGE, 2009-2011 (Oct. 2011), https://www.dni.gov/files/documents/Newsroom/Reports%20and%20Pubs/20111103_report_fecie.pdf; Rochelle Cooper Dreyfuss & Orly Lobel, *Economic Espionage as Reality or Rhetoric: Equating Trade Secrecy with National Security*, 20 LEWIS & CLARK L. REV. 419 (2016).

[9] Trump v. Vance, 941 F.3d 631 (2d Cir. 2019); Corinne Ramey & James Fanelli, *Donald Trump Found Guilty on All 34 Counts in New York Hush-Money Case*, WALL ST. J. (May 30, 2024), https://www.wsj.com/us-news/law/donald-trump-convicted-87a4e465.

[10] Harry First, *Business Crime and the Public Interest: Lawyers, Legislators, and the Administrative State*, 2 U.C. IRVINE L. REV. 871 (2012).

How should the law regard Daniel Ellsberg? Chelsea Manning? Edward Snowden?[11] Should the U.S. be allowed to extradite Kim Dotcom?[12] What should it have done to Julian Assange?[13] What is the difference between protecting national interests and liberating knowledge that "wants to be free," or between whistle-blowing and treason?[14] Harry's questions forced our students to think critically about law, relative power, morality, politics, economics, and social institutions. With his support, they contrasted civil and criminal approaches, the role of defenses and presumptions, and contemplated the impact of sentencing guidelines. He helped them to think normatively and to see the law on information as an instrument to be construed for the betterment of society.

Over this time, we and our spouses, Robert and Eve, became friends. Together, we have enjoyed many a meal, at our homes and at restaurants. We have shared the ups and downs of parenthood and grandparenthood; celebrated holidays and life-cycle events; explored museums and galleries, music and drama, and attractions both foreign and domestic. The four of us are now busy thinking through the challenges of retiring and aging.

Harry has excelled as a scholar of antitrust, criminal and information law; as a builder of institutions; as a colleague, teacher, and friend. He is truly First in multiple domains.

---

11   David D. Cole, *Assessing the Leakers: Criminals or Heroes?*, 8 J. Nat'l Sec. L. & Pol'y 107 (2015).

12   Bruce Zagaris, *U.S. Appellate Court Affirms Seizure of Kim Dotcom's Assets*, 32 Int'l Enf't L. Rep. 325 (2016).

13   Glenn Thrush & Megan Specia, *A Wish From All Sides to Move On Ends With Liberty for Assange*, N.Y. Times (June 29, 2024), https://www.nytimes.com/2024/06/29/us/politics/julian-assange-release-uk-us.html.

14   Bess Levin, *Trump Suggests Executing the Whistle-Blower's Sources Like "in the Old Days,"* Vanity Fair (Sept. 26, 2019), https://www.vanityfair.com/news/2019/09/trump-whistleblower-spies-treason?srsltid=AfmBOoroytSW95OVgffKqFhmCx8LRYNAqqCt7z_BbiKE4P2CVY5sNuki; 5 U.S.C. § 2302(b)(8).

Contributors

Adi Ayal
Bar Ilan University

Darren Bush
University of Houston Law Center

Stephen Calkins
Wayne State University Law School

Michael A. Carrier
Rutgers Law School

Peter C. Carstensen
University of Wisconsin Law School

Erika M. Douglas
Temple University, Beasley School of Law

Ariel Ezrachi
University of Oxford

Albert A. Foer
American Antitrust Institute

Eleanor M. Fox
New York University School of Law

Mark Glick
University of Utah

Jamie Ha
Econic Partners

Jonathan Jacobson
Wilson Sonsini Goodrich & Rosati

Wolfgang Kerber
University of Marburg

John B. Kirkwood
Seattle University School of Law

Robert H. Lande
University of Baltimore School of Law

Marina Lao
Seton Hall University School of Law

Ioannis Lianos
University College London

Gabriel A. Lozada
University of Utah

Melissa H. Maxman
Cohen & Gresser LLP

Barak D. Richman
The George Washington University Law School

Tadashi Shiraishi
University of Tokyo

Daniel Sokol
USC Gould School of Law

Erica Straus
Wayne State University Law School

Maurice E. Stucke
University of Tennessee

Sean P. Sullivan
University of Iowa College of Law

Simonetta Vezzoso
Trento University

Ronald F. Wick
Cohen & Gresser LLP

Diane P. Wood
American Law Institute

Angela Huyue Zhang
University of Southern California

Table of Contents

Foreword	I
Contributors	V
Table of Contents	VII
Harry First Biography & Publications	IX
Introduction	1

Part I: Harry First: The Man, The Mensch

Harry First & Noble Competition 11
Ariel Ezrachi and Maurice E. Stucke

Harry First and His Institutional Vision for Antitrust Law 19
Angela Huyue Zhang

Antitrust, Democracy, and "Being a Mensch" 31
Adi Ayal

Professor Harry First: Champion for Competitive
and Fair Markets 39
Diane P. Wood

Academic "Capture"? The Hidden Costs of Corporate Funding
in Competition Policy Research and Proposed Remedies.................... 55
Ioannis Lianos

Part II: What Comes First for Antitrust?

The High Costs of Not Prohibiting Anticompetitive Megamergers 101
Eleanor M. Fox

Remedies First 135
Melissa H. Maxman and Ronald F. Wick

Is Antitrust Law, Policy, or Politics? 147
Sean P. Sullivan

National Competition Policy and the Election of 2024 161
Albert A. Foer

First on Antitrust and Regulation: Symbiosis From Rail to Digital 185
Erika M. Douglas

Part III: The Statute Comes First

The FTC Act Section 5's Delegation Paradox 205
Marina Lao

The Clayton Act Does Not Contain or Permit an Efficiency Rebuttal 227
Darren Bush, Mark Glick, Robert H. Lande and Gabriel A. Lozada

Decoding the Meaning of "Any Section of the Country":
The Pabst-Blatz Saga 239
Peter C. Carstensen

The Other Side of Market Definition 263
Tadashi Shiraishi

Part IV: Getting to First Place – Microsoft and Other Players

Two Cheers for the Revolving Door 277
Stephen Calkins and Erica Straus

On Rabbis and Mentors 317
Barak D. Richman

Competition vs. Regulation 329
Jonathan Jacobson

Competition and Innovation: Incorporating a More Dynamic
Perspective into Enforcement 341
Wolfgang Kerber and Simonetta Vezzoso

High Prices and Pharmaceuticals 363
Michael A. Carrier

Microsoft v. Apple 377
John B. Kirkwood

What Have We Learned from the Scholarship Inspired
by the Microsoft Saga? 391
Jamie Ha and D. Daniel Sokol

Harry First

Biography & Publications

Biography

Harry First is the Charles L. Denison Professor of Law Emeritus at New York University School of Law, where he taught for more than forty years. During that time Professor First served as Co-Director of the Trade Regulation LL.M. Program and of the Competition, Innovation, and Information Law LL. M. Program. Professor First's teaching interests included antitrust, regulated industries, international and comparative antitrust, business crime, intellectual property crime, and innovation policy. From 1999-2001 he served as Chief of the Antitrust Bureau of the Office of the Attorney General of the State of New York. He was twice a Fulbright Research Fellow in Japan and taught antitrust as an adjunct professor at the University of Tokyo. Prior to joining the faculty of New York University School of Law, Professor First taught at the University of Toledo College of Law, practiced at the Antitrust Division of the United States Department of Justice, and served as a law clerk to Justice Samuel J. Roberts, Supreme Court of Pennsylvania.

Professor First is the co-editor of the casebook *Free Enterprise and Economic Organization: Antitrust* (7th Ed. 2014) (with John Flynn and Darren Bush), as well as a casebook on regulated industries (with John Flynn) and a casebook on business crime. Professor First's most recent scholarly work has focused on various aspects of antitrust enforcement and theory. These include: *The Microsoft Antitrust Cases: Competition Policy for the Twenty-first Century* (with Andrew I. Gavil) (MIT Press, 2014), winner of the Jerry S. Cohen Memorial Fund Writing Award for Antitrust Scholarship; "Merger Policy for a Platform Economy" (*ZweR [Journal of Competition Law]*, 2023); "Bespoke Antitrust," (*South Dakota Law Review*, 2023) (with Spencer Weber Waller); "Antitrust Remedies and the Big Tech Platform Cases," in *Washington Center for Equitable Growth, Judging Big Tech: Insights on applying U.S. antitrust laws to digital markets* (2022); "Excessive Drug Pricing as an Antitrust Violation" (*Antitrust Law Journal*, 2019); "Exploitative Abuses of Intellectual Property Rights" in *The Cambridge Handbook of Antitrust, Intellectual Property, and High Tech* (2017); "Philadelphia National Bank, Globalization, and the Public Interest" (*Antitrust Law Journal*, 2015) (with

Eleanor M. Fox); and "Antitrust's Democracy Deficit" (*Fordham Law Review*, 2013) (with Spencer Weber Waller), winner of the Institute of Competition Law's 2014 Antitrust Writing Award for Best General Antitrust Academic Article.

Professor First is a contributing editor of the *Antitrust Law Journal*, foreign antitrust editor of the *Antitrust Bulletin*, a member of the executive committee of the Antitrust Section of the New York State Bar Association, and a member of the advisory boards of the Institute for Consumer Antitrust Studies and of the American Antitrust Institute. He has received the Distinguished Public Service Award (2024) and the William T. Lifland Service Award (2017) from the New York State Bar Association Antitrust Section and a Lifetime Achievement Award from the Antitrust and Economic Regulation Section of the Association of American Law Schools (2024).

Publications
(as of April 2025)

Books

Antitrust in Emerging and Developing Countries (Institute of Competition Law 2d ed., 2016) (ed. with Eleanor M. Fox, Nicolas Charbit, Elisa Ramundo et al.)

Antitrust: Statutes, Treaties, Regulations, Guidelines, Policies (Foundation Press, 2014) (ed. with John J. Flynn and Darren Bush)

Free Enterprise and Economic Organization: Antitrust (Foundation Press 7th ed., 2014; 6th ed., 1983) (with John J. Flynn and Darren Bush)

The Microsoft Antitrust Cases: Competition Policy for the Twenty-first Century (The MIT Press, 2014) (with Andrew I. Gavil)

Working Within the Boundaries of Intellectual Property: Innovation Policy for the Knowledge Society (Oxford University Press, 2010) (ed. with Rochelle Dreyfuss and Diane Zimmerman)

Expanding the Boundaries of Intellectual Property: Innovation Policy for the Knowledge Society (Oxford University Press, 2001) (ed. with Rochelle C. Dreyfuss and Diane L. Zimmerman)

Revitalizing Antitrust in its Second Century: Essays on Legal, Economic, and Political Policy (Quorum Books, 1991) (ed. with Eleanor M. Fox and Robert Pitofsky)

Business Crime: Cases and Materials (Foundation Press, 1990 and Supp. 2003)

Free Enterprise and Economic Organization: Government Regulation (Foundation Press 6th ed., 1985) (with Louis B. Schwartz and John J. Flynn)

Problems in Antitrust (Foundation Press, 1983) (with Louis B. Schwartz and John J. Flynn)

Articles, Essays and Chapters in Collection

"Antitrust and Regulatory Alternatives: How the Past Points the Way to the Future," 11 J. Antitrust Enforcement 173 (2023)

"Bespoke Antitrust," 68 S.D. L. Rev. 468 (2023) (with Spencer Weber Waller)

"Merger Policy for a Platform Economy," 21 Zeitschrift für Wettbewerbsrecht 334 (2023)

"Panel One: How Did We Get Here? A Review of Major Antitrust Cases, Questions, and Controversies," 28 Fordham J. Corp. & Fin. L. 300 (2023) (with Jonathan Jacobson and Spencer Weber Waller)

"The Internet of Change: Foreword to the Symposium on the Google and Facebook Cases," 67 Antitrust Bull. 3 (2022) Abstract

"American Express, the Rule of Reason, and the Goals of Antitrust," 98 Neb. L. Rev. 319 (2019)

"Antitrust Analysis of NOPEC Legislation," 32 Loy. Consumer L. Rev. 83 (2019) (with Darren Bush)

"Excessive Drug Pricing as an Antitrust Violation," 82 Antitrust L.J. 701 (2019) Abstract

"General Principles Governing Criminal Liability of Corporations, Their Employees and Officers White Collar Crime: Business and Regulatory Offenses," L. J. Seminars Press (2017) Abstract

"Philadelphia National Bank, Globalization, and the Public Interest," 80 Antitrust L.J. 307 (2015) (with Eleanor M. Fox) Abstract

"Are the 'A's' in AAI Anachronistic? An Imaginary Interview with Bert Foer," 60 Antitrust Bull. 79 (2015) (with Eleanor M. Fox)

"Bork and Microsoft: Why Bork Was Right and What We Learn About Judging Exclusionary Behavior," 79 Antitrust L.J. 1017 (2014) Abstract

"Antitrust's Democracy Deficit," 81 Fordham L. Rev. 2543 (2013) (with Spencer Weber Waller) Abstract

"Business Crime and the Public Interest: Lawyers, Legislators, and the Administrative State," 2 UC Irvine L. Rev 871 (2012)

"Branch Office of the Prosecutor: The New Role of the Corporation in Business Crime Prosecutions," 89 N.C. L. Rev. 23 (2010) Abstract

"Lost in Conversation: The Compensatory Function of Antitrust," N.Y.U. L. & Econ. Rsch. Paper No. 10-14 (2010) Abstract

"No Single Monopoly Profit, No Single Policy Prescription?," 5 Competition Pol'y Int'l 199 (2009)

"Modernizing State Antitrust Enforcement: Making the Best of a Good Situation," 54 Antitrust Bull. 281 (2009) Abstract

"The Case for Antitrust Civil Penalties," 76 Antitrust L.J. 127 (2009) Abstract

"Netscape is Dead: Remedy Lessons from the Microsoft Litigation," N.Y.U. L. & Econ. Rsch. Paper No. 08-49 (2008) Abstract

"Strong Spine, Weak Underbelly: The CFI Microsoft Decision," N.Y.U L. & Econ. Rsch. Paper No. 08-17 (2008) Abstract

"Controlling the Intellectual Property Grab: Protect Innovation, Not Innovators," 38 Rutgers L.J. 365 (2007) Abstract

"'Market Power': Why Are We Asking? A Comment on 'Electricity and Market Power,'" 1 Env't & Energy L. & Pol'y J. 43 (2006)

"Microsoft and the Evolution of the Intellectual Property Concept," 2006 Wis. L. Rev. 1369 Abstract

"Re-framing Windows: The Durable Meaning of the Microsoft Antitrust Litigation," 2006 Utah L. Rev. 641 (with Andrew I. Gavil) Abstract

"Online Music Joint Ventures: Taken for a Song," N.Y.U. L. & Econ. Rsch. Paper No. 04-006 (2004) Abstract

"Book Review, John O. Haley, Antitrust in Germany and Japan: The First Fifty Years, 1947-1998," 61 J. Asian Stud. 183 (2002) Abstract

"Regulated Deregulation: The New York Experience in Electric Utility Deregulation," 33 Loy. U. Chi. L.J. 911 (2002) Abstract

"Delivering Remedies: The Role of the States in Antitrust Enforcement," 69 Geo. Wash. L. Rev. 1004 (2001) Abstract

"The Vitamins Case: Cartel Prosecutions and the Coming of International Competition Law," 68 Antitrust L.J. 711 (2001) Abstract

"Antitrust in Japan: The Original Intent," 9 Pac. Rim L. & Pol'y J. 1 (2000) Abstract

"Kokusaiteki hantorasto ho shiko no tenbo: gekiteki yuniraterarizumu [The Prospect for International Antitrust Law Enforcement: Aggressive Unilateralism]," 572 Kosei Torihiki [Fair Trade] 34 (1998)

"The Intersection of Trade and Antitrust Remedies," 12 Antitrust 16 (1997)

"Antitrust Enforcement in Japan," 64 Antitrust L.J. 137 (1995) Abstract

"Is Antitrust 'Law'?," 10 Antitrust 9 (1995) Abstract

"An Antitrust Remedy for International Price Predation: Lessons from Zenith v. Matsushita," 4 Pac. Rim L. & Pol'y J. 211 (1995) Abstract

"Lessons for Antitrust Enforcement: A Comparative Study of the United States and Japan," 28 Waseda U. Compar. L. Rev. 43 (1994)

"Response: Selling Antitrust in Japan," 7 Antitrust 34 (1993)

"The View from 1984: What Have We Learned in Five Years?," 22 Cornell Int'l L.J. 510 (1989) Abstract

"Structural Antitrust Rules and International Competition: The Case of Distressed Industries," 62 N.Y.U. L. Rev. 1054 (1987)

"Protecting Soft Property Through the Criminal Law: The Emerging View from the United States," 2 Nihon U. Comp. L. 1 (1985)

"Legal Aspects of Business Crime in the United States (Parts I and II)," 12 J. Japanese Inst. of Int'l Bus. L. 535 (1984)

"The Business of Legal Education," 32 J. Legal Educ. 201 (1982) Abstract

"Competition in the Legal Education Industry (II): An Antitrust Analysis," 54 N.Y.U. L. Rev. 1049 (1979) Abstract

"Competition in the Legal Education Industry (I)," 53 N.Y.U. L. Rev. 311 (1978) Abstract

"Book Reviews [Posner, Antitrust Law: An Economic Perspective]," 52 N.Y.U. L. Rev. 947 (1977)

"Legal Education and the Law School of the Past: A Single-Firm Study," 8 U. Tol. L. Rev. 135 (1976)

"Private Interest and Public Control: Government Action, The First Amendment and the Sherman Act," 1975 Utah L. Rev. 9

"Law For Sale: A Study of the Delaware Corporation Law of 1967," 117 U. Pa. L. Rev. 861 (1969)

Introduction

But First

DARREN BUSH[*]
University of Houston College of Law

ANDREW I. GAVIL[**]
Howard University School of Law

SPENCER WEBER WALLER[***]
Loyola University Chicago School of Law

1. We are proud to introduce this volume in honor of our friend and colleague, Harry First. It is a fitting addition to the series of Liber Amicorum collections already published by Concurrences paying tribute to the work of leading competition law scholars and enforcers throughout the world.[1]

2. During his distinguished career as a government enforcer and faculty member at the New York University School of Law, Professor First has consistently advocated for a humane and progressive vision of competition law and policy rooted in the search for true justice, and not merely wealth maximization. He was a public servant and a public-spirited scholar who has influenced thousands of students, judges, enforcers, and practitioners in the United States, Europe, and Asia.

---

[*] Leonard B. Rosenberg Professor of Law, University of Houston College of Law.
[**] Professor of Law, Howard University School of Law.
[***] John Paul Stevens Chair in Competition Law, Loyola University Chicago School of Law.
[1] *See* https://www.concurrences.com for a list of the other volumes in this series.

Introduction

3. Harry has been a leading scholar and teacher not just in competition law, but also in intellectual property, business crimes, and regulated industries. We pause to point out that Harry has always seen the interplay between regulation and antitrust. In his classes, Antitrust and Regulatory Alternatives, First's syllabus states: "Antitrust and Regulatory Alternatives I and II examine two different legal approaches for controlling private economic power – the antitrust laws, designed to establish and maintain competitive markets, and regulatory statutes, under which government agencies supervise entry, rates, and service." As First contemplated this binary world, he also recognized that the movement towards deregulation has alternated the interplay of antitrust and regulation. For example, in his piece "Regulated Deregulation," First notes the dramatic changes in electricity markets that seek to eliminate monopoly power through competition, but still require regulation for some key components.[2]

4. Harry also relished his time as a public servant. From 1999–2001, he served as chief of the Antitrust Bureau of the Office of the Attorney General of the State of New York, playing a leading role in the federal and state coalition of plaintiffs in the groundbreaking *Microsoft* antitrust litigation.[3]

5. We have each been privileged to work with Harry as co-authors of books, casebooks, articles for law reviews and peer-review journals, as well as shorter works. Our individual work has also benefitted from many hours of conversations, comments, and suggestions that Harry generously provided. Harry is a meticulous researcher and writer and has extraordinary academic integrity. He unmistakably loves a good legal argument about antitrust law, and we have all enjoyed many long calls deconstructing, debating, and then reconstructing our thoughts, arguments, and conclusions. We know there are thousands more people who have benefitted from their work with Harry in the classroom, academia, competition enforcement, or in practice.

6. Professor First's career is global in scope, both in terms of his writings covering issues in United States, European, and Japanese competition law and in terms of where he has taught. In addition to his decades at NYU School of Law, he also was twice a Fulbright Research Fellow in Japan and taught antitrust at the University of Tokyo. He has lectured around the world and argued for the respectful consideration of comparative competition law in the ongoing debates in the United States over the future of competition law and policy.

7. On a personal level, we have all benefitted from Harry's generous spirit as a friend, mentor, and co-author. As a collaborator, he brings deep knowledge, precise writing, a skill at organization, insight, and a wry

---

2   Harry First, *Regulated Deregulation: The New York Experience in Electric Utility Deregulation*, 33 Loy. U. Chi. L.J. 911 (2002).

3   The landmark opinion holding Microsoft liable for violations of sections 1 and 2 of the Sherman Act can be found at United States v. Microsoft Corp., 253 F.3d 34 (D.C. Cir. 2001).

sense of humor to any project where he serves as a co-author. Although he produced dozens of groundbreaking works as the sole author, he brought a special gift to any project as a co-author – that of a friend who also helped the work of others to shine. Harry First made any work of scholarship better as a co-author. He has collaborated with dozens of authors over his lengthy and distinguished career, many of whom have contributed to this volume.[4]

8. Each of the co-editors has enjoyed working with Professor First on very different types of projects. Professor Gavil worked with Harry on the 2014 book *The Microsoft Antitrust Cases*[5] exploring the seminal public and private competition litigation in the United States, the European Union, and other jurisdictions that set the gold standard for monopolization and abuse of dominance law in the tech sector and that continue to serve as a roadmap for the dozens of cases and investigations against today's dominant web platforms.

9. Professor Bush and Harry are co-authors of one of the leading casebooks on U.S. competition law, *Free Enterprise and Economic Organization: Antitrust*.[6] This casebook is unique in both its content and approach. The casebook traces its own lineage back to the work of Louis Schwartz and John Flynn, two of the important influences on Harry's own work.[7] The book is unique in how it advocates for a progressive vision of U.S. antitrust law, while at the same time skillfully educating the students on both sides of the ongoing debates on contemporary competition law and policy.

10. Finally, Professor Waller has co-authored with Professor First a series of articles on diverse topics. Among other topics, these works examine the relationship between antitrust and democracy,[8] an issue that is attracting increasing attention as part of the ongoing debate about connections between the abuse of economic and political power.

11. These are just a few of the ways that the editors are grateful for how Harry has touched our lives and careers. Professor First has made us better in what we do and happier for the chance to work with him at different stages in our careers. He is humble, proud of the work we did together and yet always happy to share credit. So too has he changed

---

4 For a listing of Professor First's principal publications, *see* https://its.law.nyu.edu/facultyprofiles/index.cfm?fuseaction=profile.publications&personid=19919.

5 ANDREW I. GAVIL & HARRY FIRST, THE MICROSOFT ANTITRUST CASES: COMPETITION POLICY FOR THE TWENTY-FIRST CENTURY (2014). *See also* Harry First & Andrew I. Gavil, *Re-framing Windows: The Durable Meaning of the* Microsoft *Antitrust Litigation*, 2006 UTAH L. REV. 641 (2006).

6 JOHN J. FLYNN, HARRY FIRST & DARREN BUSH, FREE ENTERPRISE AND ECONOMIC ORGANIZATION: ANTITRUST (7th ed. 2014); *See also* Darren Bush & Harry Fist, *Antitrust Analysis of NOPEC Legislation*, 32 LOY. CONSUMER L. REV. 83 (2019).

7 *See also* LOUIS B. SCHWARTZ, JOHN J. FLYNN & HARRY FIRST, PROBLEMS IN ANTITRUST (1983).

8 *See, e.g.*, Harry First & Spencer Weber Waller, *Antitrust's Democracy Deficit*, 81 FORDHAM L. REV. 2543 (2013). *See also* Harry First & Spencer Weber Waller, *Bespoke Antitrust*, 68 S.D. L. REV. 468 (2023).

for the better the multitudes of students, colleagues, professors, judges, and practitioners he has worked with throughout his career.

12. In this brief introduction, we discuss the scope of an extraordinary career through the lens of Harry as a friend, mentor, and colleague, and Harry as a scholar and teacher to provide a better context to the more than twenty essays that follow. Each of these chapters discusses a particular theme of Professor First's career or an issue suggested by Professor First from his body of scholarship or government service. Together, these chapters from leading scholars and practitioners provide a rich mosaic of Harry's many accomplishments and interests and the qualities that make Harry a very special person, teacher, scholar, lawyer, and friend.

13. This collection of essays starts with Harry First the human. It is a small sample of the lives he has touched and his influence across scholarly agendas, including those of the writers of this introduction. The lives he has touched, colleagues and students alike, are his largest legacy. In the words of his co-author, John J. Flynn, "Giants roam the earth."

I. Harry First: The Man, the Mensch

14. Ariel Ezrachi & Maurice Stucke speak of Harry First's collaborative approach as "Noble Competition." Harry's open-minded exploration and thoughts about competition policy, according to the authors, have "turned what could have been toxic zero-sum competition into noble competition."

15. Angela Zhang explores Harry First's contributions in aiding her research and writing on Chinese antitrust law, offering her perspective on his personal impact and mentorship.

16. Adi Ayal links the relationship of Harry First's decency as a human being to the goal of democracy. In "Antitrust, Democracy, and 'Being a Mensch,'" Ayal walks through the link between being a decent human being and the survival of democracy: "The essence of democracy has more to do with how losers are treated than increasing the size or the scope of the win."

17. Beyond Harry First being a brilliant and decent human being, Judge Diane Wood's chapter, "Professor Harry First: Champion for Competitive and Fair Markets," summarizes Harry First's importance in antitrust scholarship. Judge Wood notes Harry First's continued scholarly voice for over 45 years. She commences by noting Harry First's recognition that antitrust serves broader goals than mere consumer welfare, tempered by his international understanding of competition laws and goals. She notes his work spans into the interplay of antitrust and other areas of economic regulation, such as intellectual property and the regulation of the Internet.

18. Finally, in "Academic 'Capture'? The Hidden Costs of Corporate Funding in Competition Policy Research and Proposed Remedies," Ioannis Lianos extends Harry's work with Spencer Waller regarding academic capture – the notion that money influences economic expertise – both in terms of outright capture and its milder form, bias. Lianos pursues the various structural and market origins of bias and capture, and proposes some remedies to cure those ills.

II. What Comes First for Antitrust?

19. In "Antitrust First," Eleanor Fox contemplates what putting antitrust first would mean in terms of policies. Fox argues that the clear priority of putting antitrust first would be to target power and its abuse, eyes wide open. No more cartel "exemptions," such as OPEC. Defendant tactics to avoid and delay (for the sake of creating costs to the enforcers or perhaps waiting out an election) will be penalized. Economics will be valued, but tempered with an understanding of its limitations. Other factors apart from consumer welfare will be considered, including the impact of economic power on democracy. And reverence will be given to the interplay that Congress intended between federal, state, and private antitrust enforcement.

20. In "Remedies First," Melissa Maxman and Ronald Wick address Professor First's very practical approach to his jurisprudence, addressing remedies at the beginning of his analysis rather than proceeding on theory alone. It is one thing to seek to address a problem; it is another to be able to fashion a remedy that does not exacerbate it. In walking through Harry First's 21st-century writings, Maxman and Wick find wisdom and common themes in seeking to address the very real and thorny problem of remedies.

21. Sean Sullivan asks the question: "Is antitrust law, policy, or politics?" This is a question that Harry First posed this question initially in the heyday of Clinton antitrust enforcement, noting that antitrust had been moving away from law and into regulatory policy. Regulation takes many forms, including the increasing use of consent decrees. The downside, Harry First argued, was that it takes away from traditional antitrust enforcement. Sullivan explores this conundrum in light of the Biden administration, and raises concern about how antitrust has been moving toward capture by political interests.

22. Bert Foer continues this discussion of the integration of antitrust into other economic policies in "The Whole of Government Strategy for Competition Policy." He examines the need for coordination of the many governmental impacts on competition, focusing on President Biden's

innovative executive order and a comparison with the anticipated policies of a possible Trump administration.

23. Erika Douglas, in "First on Antitrust and Regulation: A Dual System From Rail to Digital," addresses the problem of the overlay of regulation and regulated industries with antitrust. Harry's antitrust courses, Antitrust and Regulatory Alternatives, teach us that antitrust and regulation are not just substitutes, but complements. Douglas picks up that theme by pointing out that where antitrust is supposed to yield, the expectation is that other regulators will take up the competitive objective. Alas, Douglas describes how that has not been so, which seems doomed to be repeated when we speak of the digital economy.

III. The Statute Comes First

24. Any discussion of policy should begin with the meaning of the statute. Marina Lao kicks off that discussion by arguing that nondelegation challenges to section 5 of the Federal Trade Commission (FTC) Act are without merit, as the FTC Act possesses an intelligible principle. The Act's text contains that principle "unfair methods of competition," and the legislative history and purpose of the Act make clear a polestar sufficient to ward off a nondelegation challenge. That is, unless Justice Gorsuch and others get their way.

25. Bob Lande, Mark Glick, Gabriel Lozada and Darren Bush discuss the legislative history of the Clayton Act and its amendments, arguing that there is no efficiencies defense or rebuttal, and that there should be no such defense or rebuttal in the Merger Guidelines. The danger of the Guidelines recognizing such a rebuttal is promoting the expansion of the doctrine even beyond where it is now.

26. Peter Carstensen decodes the "Meaning of 'Any Section of the Country'" in the context of the "Pabst-Blatz Saga," a case that spanned more than a decade. It is the leading SCOTUS decision to define the term "section of the country" in which competition may be lessened. The government's novel market (besides the state of Wisconsin, which made more sense) was the three-state market of Illinois, Wisconsin, and Michigan, a market Carstensen argues is nearly impossible to explain in contemporary market analysis terms. Carstensen engages in legal archaeology, using Antitrust Division documents to provide some insight into the origins of this market and draw conclusions as to how the Division's thinking evolved to a more economically oriented approach by the time of briefing in the Supreme Court.

27. Economics has permeated antitrust beyond Pabst, a notion that Tadashi Shiraishi describes in "The Other Side of Market Definition."

Shiraishi flips the script to focus on the uniqueness of relevant purchasers. In instances in which multiple segments of purchasers exist, Shiraishi argues there should be distinct relevant markets for analysis. Shiraishi reminds us that analytically identifying purchasers precedes identifying sellers, but that process is often opaque. Shiraishi seeks to elucidate the logical structure of market definition and elaborates on its implications for various antitrust issues, including submarkets, two-sided markets, exploitative abuse, the green deal in antitrust, and its international applications.

IV. Getting to First Place – Microsoft and Other Players

28. Any discussion of policy in antitrust requires a discussion of the players. Stephen Calkins tackles the controversial notion of the "Revolving Door" in antitrust enforcement, and notes that Harry First has been on both sides of that door multiple times, for the betterment of the public. Of course, Harry has not been on the side of private corporations, so working for the state Attorney General and for the Department of Justice (DOJ) is pretty much the same side of the door.

29. On the academic side of the door, Barak Richman, in his chapter "On Rabbis and Mentors," describes his interactions with Harry First in terms of his scholarship, in particular Richman's scholarship on professional associations as cartels. He notes Harry's contributions to his scholarship and thinking every step of the way in his career arc.

30. Jonathan Jacobson, in "New Economy Antitrust: from Microsoft to Google and Apple," continues a theme picked up in Sullivan's chapter about competition regulation and applies to firms that Jacobson views as increasing consumer welfare. Jacobson asserts that competition regulation, such as the Digital Markets Act and the Klobuchar bill, will harm firms creating consumer welfare. Jacobson reflects on passed economic regulation endorsing the move away from it.

31. Wolfgang Kerber and Simonetta Vezzoso's chapter, "Competition and Innovation: Incorporating a More Dynamic Perspective into Enforcement," raises the question of innovation – something often left out of consumer welfare considerations. They argue that antitrust must develop "innovation-specific assessment concepts and methods that are capable of complementing, and to some extent replacing, traditional static assessment frameworks."

32. In "High Prices and Pharmaceuticals," Mike Carrier discusses a troubling industry in terms of antitrust policy. High prices, according to Carrier, are often explained by antitrust violations and standard setting, the latter of which could facilitate lower prices, should reasonable licensing requirements come into play.

Introduction

33. In "Microsoft v. Apple," John Kirkwood describes the interrelationship between the *Microsoft* case and that against Apple. In effect, the DOJ's case against Microsoft allowed for Apple's growth. And, in proving Santayana was right about the lessons of history, the case against Apple has parallels to the case against Microsoft. Kirkwood eloquently details these developments.

34. Finally, in "What Have We Learned from the Scholarship Inspired by the Microsoft Saga?," Danny Sokol and Jamie Ha summarize the extensive scholarship that arose after the *Microsoft* case.

35. We hope you enjoy this tribute to an exceptional teacher, scholar, enforcer, and colleague in the global competition law and policy community whom we are also proud to call a friend.

PART I
Harry First: The Man, The Mensch

Harry First & Noble Competition

ARIEL EZRACHI[*]
University of Oxford

MAURICE E. STUCKE[**]
University of Tennessee

Abstract

Competition is often celebrated as the engine of progress, but its outcomes can range from toxic rivalry to cooperative excellence. This essay examines the concept of noble competition – where rivals strive for mutual improvement and societal benefit – and contrasts it with the detrimental effects of unregulated, toxic and zero-sum competition. Through the example of Professor Harry First, a leading antitrust scholar who exemplifies noble competition, the essay explores how ethical rivalry can inspire individual and collective growth. It also critiques the dangers of overreliance on competition as a cure-all, particularly in policy contexts like the Covid-19 pandemic, where unfettered competition exacerbated harm. By reorienting competition toward its nobler form, policymakers can address market failures and build systems prioritizing human dignity and democratic values.

---

[*] Slaughter and May Professor of Competition Law and Director of the Centre for Competition Law and Policy, University of Oxford.

[**] Douglas A. Blaze Distinguished Professor of Law, University of Tennessee College of Law; Affiliate of Baker School for Public Policy and Public Affairs; Research Fellow, Anderson Center for Entrepreneurship & Innovation, UT Haslam College of Business.

1. Why can scholarly debates be so acrimonious? As Samuel Johnson noted, the disputed topics are often of limited importance: "they involve neither property nor liberty; nor favour the interest of sect or party."[1] Add to the mix zero-sum status competition, where one scholar's rise in estimation means another scholar's decline. So, if disputes over inconsequential matters can make status-seeking scholars proud and angry, what happens when scholars debate topics of great importance, such as economic liberty and well-being? It follows that antitrust conferences and policy debates have the potential to be especially contentious, where scholars undercut their peers with the swiftness of the most experienced surgeon's scalpel.

2. That zero-sum rivalry is not inevitable. Indeed, whereas scholarly interactions can be characterized by intense competition and rivalry, they can also take the form of a competitive yet collaborative pursuit of the common goal of furthering knowledge. The shift from zero-sum rivalry to healthier competition often depends on the framing of the interaction and one's understanding of the tradeoffs at stake. In academic contexts, much depends on the individuals who set the tone for these exchanges.

3. Enter Professor Harry First, who belies the drift toward zero-sum competition and redirects it into healthier forms. At every conference, we saw how this leading antitrust scholar combined wit with insight to elevate the debate. His comments on other scholars' work were helpful and never harsh. And his graciousness continued over martinis after the conference.

4. As we note in our book *Competition Overdose*,[2] competition does not have to be zero-sum (or toxic). Often, there are alternatives, such as positive-sum, ethical competition, and the ideal form of competition, which we call *noble competition*. Noble competition is helping your rivals reach their full potential. Players compete fiercely but do so with deep societal and moral awareness. While seeking to prevail, each player knows her wider community and recognizes how her competitiveness can help her rivals be their best selves.

5. To us, Professor First embodied this noble competition. Indeed, many of us try to instill this noble competition in our children. We encourage them to work hard and compete – whether on the playing field, in the classroom, or in any other endeavor, from spelling bee to theater audition. But if we are thoughtful, we emphasize that values such as friendship, honesty, fairness, and responsibility should shape the way they compete. Ultimately, we try to communicate that any rivalry should serve some greater end and that whatever the outcome, the rivalry should build character and dignify and ennoble the participants.

---

1 Samuel Johnson, Preface to Shakespeare (1765), https://www.bartleby.com/lit-hub/hc/prefaces-and-prologues/105900.

2 Maurice E. Stucke & Ariel Ezrachi, Competition Overdose: How Free Market Mythology Transformed Us from Citizen Kings to Market Servants (2020).

6. To illustrate, suppose you have twins who compete in the same sport – let's say tennis. You would not wish one child to thrash or humiliate the other. Nor would you encourage a "win-at-all-costs" attitude. Instead, the athletic competition, if properly designed and overseen, would help build both children's character and make them feel good about themselves – and each other. As described by Craig Clifford and Randolph Feezell, two philosophy professors who also played and coached on the college level, competition can be understood as a "mutual striving for excellence,"[3] where each competitor helps the others elevate their performance. So, no matter which child prevails in the tennis match, the rivalry will have catalyzed levels of effort and execution that neither child would have been capable of without that spur. The reward, then, is not just being acclaimed as the winner; the reward also comes from the self-improvement and the camaraderie that result from the rivalry. In this light, noble competition, encompassing both self-mastery and cooperation, reduces the incentive to behave boorishly and unethically.

7. Of course, the goal is to win even in the most public-spirited, ethically informed competition. Our children will still be intent on beating their opponents. We will still cheer for our team. And wherever we work, we will still compete with other companies and perhaps our colleagues. As individuals, we are in it to win it. But as a societal ideal, noble competition provides us with a valuable compass.

8. Noble competition is possible on an individual level, as Professor First demonstrates. But importantly, it is also possible on a broader societal level. Just as Professor First's framing and signaling of a healthier form of competition can affect the behavior of others, so too can the government reorient rivalry toward a nobler form of competition. No doubt, noble competition, in its purest form, is often unachievable on a day-to-day basis. Still, the State can point us in the right direction and help us provide safeguards against the dangers of unfettered competition. It can ensure that incentives are carefully structured to prevent a spiraling zero-sum competition that harms all involved and encourages a form of rivalry that benefits society. When we reorient competition towards this ideal, then many of the dark sides of competition disappear. Policymakers, companies, and we – as voters, workers, and consumers – can redesign the competition game to bring out our best rather than worst traits.

9. But this nuance for many years was lost on policymakers, who previously touted competition per se as the magical elixir. Whatever illness our society suffered, competition was often the cure. Do we want a better education for our children? Create competition among public schools with charter schools. Better, more cost-effective prisons? Same principle. More efficient

---

3 CRAIG CLIFFORD & RANDOLPH FEEZELL, COACHING FOR CHARACTER: RECLAIMING THE PRINCIPLES OF SPORTSMANSHIP (1997).

health services? Same formula – increase choice and competitive pressure and limit government intervention. The competition elixir had several alluring features: First, competition seemingly worked well, regardless of the ethical scruples of its market participants. Judges, policymakers, and past economic theories (particularly of the old Chicago School bent) characterized competition as a pursuit where corporate and individual greed benefits society. When unleashed, the rugged pursuit of self-interest will deliver lower prices, more choices, and innovation. Second, competition was an organic, natural force. There were no distinctions among the types of competition, just competition per se. Third, this all-purpose, supposedly organic competition was cheap to administer: just unleash it, and it will work far better with any governmental intervention. The government still has a limited role (such as defining property rights, providing a well-functioning judiciary, reducing transaction costs and corruption, etc.), but the harm is typically ascribed to too much (rather than too little) government intervention.

10. This simplified vision, which views rivalry in all its forms as a magical cure for all of society's ills, ignores the imperfections of the competitive process. Competition will often yield excellent results and efficiencies but cannot be assumed to do so in all instances. External intervention and signaling are sometimes required to ensure that rivalry delivers the promised efficiency and welfare gains.

11. Indeed, a complex picture emerges when one looks at how the competition ideal has been promoted as a simple cure in the U.S. Overreliance on the competitive process and the idea that it will always deliver better prices, quality, and services ignores key market failures. One example concerns quality degradation, where increased competitive pressure without the necessary safeguard results in hidden decreases in quality control. We have all witnessed this process in recent years, from stories about significant shortcuts in food supply (such as the packaging of horse meat in Europe and its marketing as beef) to worrying stories about quality control in the manufacturing and servicing of airplanes. Another example concerns toxic rivalry that discounts wider societal effects. Consider, for instance, how competition between banks and lenders contributed to the 2008 financial crisis.

12. While often valuable, competition requires a guiding hand to ensure that it delivers on its promise. Otherwise, it can underperform and fail to truly advance societal welfare.

13. Indeed, many citizens feel uneasy about the results of unbridled neoliberal competition orthodoxy (even if we had not identified it as the cause of our problems). Despite the promise of prosperity, many work harder and longer but for less money, fewer or nonexistent benefits, and less security. And those low prices we paid often came with a price we did

not immediately see, such as offshoring manufacturing to countries with fewer labor and environmental protections. Often, we were spending less but getting much less. Our food has undeclared additives and dishonest labeling; our bargain airlines may be flying with dangerously low fuel loads. The list continues and leads to an alarming reality – instead of competition serving us, we serve it.

14. The Covid-19 pandemic that dominated much of our lives between 2020 and 2023 provides an interesting large-scale socio-political behavioral experiment in which the simplified competition ideology was pressure tested. Initially, there was unbridled competition in the U.S., where the states sought to outbid each other to acquire ventilators and protective equipment. As then-New York's Governor Andrew Cuomo noted, with so many states competing to buy the same commodity, "It's like being on eBay with 50 other states bidding on a ventilator." As California's governor added on the bidding, "it's the Wild, Wild West, there's no question about it." Such auctions may make sense for antiques and artworks, but not when doctors were left deciding who got to breathe and who did not. Absent a coordinated federal policy, this free-for-all competition enriched a few at the expense of many. At one point, New York paid nearly 15 times the regular price for masks as it sought to outbid other stricken states and nations. Rather than relying on the competition elixir, the federal government should have intervened earlier to secure the ventilators and protective gear on behalf of the states and deploy them accordingly.

15. At a fundamental level, the coronavirus also tested the assumption that market forces will always yield the right mix and quantity of products at the right price. While often true, market forces do not always deliver. Competition works well in making supply chains efficient by driving down costs. This looks good during ordinary times, until a major shock to the economy, like the pandemic, exposes the system's fragility. For example, competition, in squeezing out costs, discourages (rather than promotes) hospitals from having enough ventilators and protective masks for a pandemic. Consequently, some inefficiency (or redundancy) is needed, such as more ventilators, beds, and doctors. Sometimes, the government must require some inefficiencies (like having more regional banks than a few national banks, more supermarkets, bookstores, and retailers than relying on Amazon and a few club stores, and more regional seed providers than the Big Four that currently dominate private-sector research on both seeds and herbicides) to safeguard society in case one important player is taken out. The lesson is clear, albeit not always apparent. When our leaders unthinkingly outsource too many of their responsibilities to the competition elixir, they undermine the government's ability to ensure that markets will actually deliver, especially during times of crisis. No one else is tasked with this responsibility.

16. But, of course, the pandemic also revealed the triumph of humanity. The pandemic, while unleashing toxic competition, also unleashed noble competition, one infused with a social purpose other than maximizing shareholder value or personal gain. The race to find a vaccine, for example, led to unparalleled cooperation in a mutual striving for excellence. After discovering that "a ferret exposed to Covid-19 particles had developed a high fever – a potential advance toward animal vaccine testing," scientists at the University of Pittsburgh did not opt for the usual route for academics – publication in a prestigious journal. Instead, they shared their findings with other scientists on a World Health Organization conference call. As Paul Duprex, a virologist leading the university's vaccine research, said, "It is pretty cool, right? You cut the crap, for lack of a better word, and you get to be part of a global enterprise."[4]

17. The pandemic also revealed how we reacted to a highly stressful event. No doubt we saw incivility. But we also saw many altruistic acts around us, where self-interest was not only irrational but self-defeating. There was a greater recognition that we had to look beyond our immediate self-interest to save others (and possibly us).

18. So, this pandemic exposed the different kinds of competition in our society, what these different types of competition can (and cannot) provide, and how our policies can affect which type of competition we experience.

19. Moving back to the present, we are encouraged by policymakers who are starting to acknowledge that competition is not inherently and invariably good. It can range from toxic (think of the classic arms race) to zero-sum competition, positive-sum rivalry, and noble competition. Thus, the government has an important role in ensuring that we benefit from the right forms of competition. Too quickly in the past, governments were willing to remove regulatory protections that actually protected us from overdosing. Too often, they took the easy path of outsourcing challenges to the free market and then blamed it when it failed to deliver.

20. Finally, we must recognize what competition, even in its noblest form, can and cannot deliver. Competition may yield an efficient outcome but not necessarily a fair, just, or wise outcome. When our governments elevate competition and capitalism above other values, we end up with markets that do not necessarily serve society. Consider the following example of vaccine inequity.

21. In 2021, the heads of the International Monetary Fund, World Bank Group, World Health Organization, and World Trade Organization met with the CEOs of leading vaccine manufacturers to address vaccine inequity, where "despite adequate total global vaccine production in the

---

4 Matt Apuzzo & David D. Kirkpatrick, *Covid-19 Changed How the World Does Science, Together*, N.Y. TIMES (Apr. 1, 2020), https://www.nytimes.com/2020/04/01/world/europe/coronavirus-science-research-cooperation.html.

aggregate, the doses [were] not reaching low- and lower-middle-income countries in sufficient amounts."[5] Cooperation, rather than competition, was necessary to ensure an equitable distribution of these vaccines, especially when countries with high vaccination rates had "collectively pre-purchased over two billion doses in excess of what [was] required to fully vaccinate their populations."[6] Under the competition ideology, one would expect wealthier countries to outbid poorer countries for these vaccines and for vaccine manufacturers to maximize profits by selling their vaccines to those willing to pay the most. But it makes little sense from a moral and equitable perspective.

22. Those in wealthy countries might be less troubled by vaccine inequity. But now, suppose your country relied on competition rather than equity concerns to determine the allocation of the vaccine early on. Suppose the U.S. relied on competitive auctions to allocate the vaccine (instead of distributing it free of charge to higher-risk groups first). The Federal Reserve examined the state of wealth inequality in the U.S. in early 2024: "The top 10% of households by wealth had $6.9 million on average. As a group, they held 67% of total household wealth. The bottom 50% of households by wealth had $51,000 on average. As a group, they held only 2.5% of total household wealth."[7] Imagine, with this wealth inequality, if the U.S. relied on competition to allocate the vaccine. As the Federal Reserve report notes, "[k]nowing the current state of wealth inequality sheds light on opportunities to foster a more equitable economy where everyone can thrive."[8]

23. Professor Harry First evinces – both in his behavior and scholarship – that competition, whether in academia or beyond, need not be a rat race. Instead, we can aspire for a nobler form of competition (and a healthier society) that actually serves us and our children. There is another way. A path in which competition is promoted alongside other democratic values. Where governments recognize, as President Franklin D. Roosevelt articulated eighty years ago, the vital role they must play in providing what competition cannot – such as promoting freedom from want with a basic safety net.

---

5 World Trade Organization, Press Release, International Organizations, Vaccine Manufacturers Agree to Intensify Cooperation to Deliver COVID-19 Vaccines (Sept. 16, 2021), https://www.who.int/news/item/16-09-2021-international-organizations-vaccine-manufacturers-agree-to-intensify-cooperation-to-deliver-covid-19-vaccines.

6 *Id.*

7 Ana Hernández Kent & Lowell R. Ricketts, *The State of U.S. Wealth Inequality*, FED. RES. BANK OF ST. LOUIS (Oct. 22, 2024), https://www.stlouisfed.org/institute-for-economic-equity/the-state-of-us-wealth-inequality.

8 *Id.*

Harry First and His Institutional Vision for Antitrust Law

ANGELA HUYUE ZHANG[*]
University of Southern California

Abstract

Professor Harry First is a distinguished antitrust scholar and practitioner whose work extends beyond legal theory to the institutional forces that shape enforcement. This essay examines two of his major contributions: his analysis of Japan's antitrust framework, which emphasizes bureaucratic guidance over adversarial enforcement, and his critique of the "democratic deficit" in U.S. antitrust law, which highlights the concentration of decision-making power among technocrats. Additionally, Professor First has been a leading advocate for decentralized enforcement, particularly the role of state attorneys general in strengthening regulatory accountability. Beyond his scholarship, his mentorship and commitment to fostering the next generation of antitrust scholars have left a lasting impact on the field.

---

[*] Professor of Law, Gould School of Law, University of Southern California

Harry First and His Institutional Vision for Antitrust Law

1. Few figures in US antitrust scholarship possess the breadth of experience that defines Professor Harry First. He is not merely a scholar who theorizes from a distance, but a seasoned practitioner who has navigated the complex terrain of antitrust law from both public and private practice. This hands-on experience has left an indelible mark on his work, shaping not only his insights on antitrust theories but also his deep understanding of the forces that shape enforcement itself. Unlike many of his peers, Professor First's academic interest extends beyond the cases and statutes – he has a rare and enduring interest in the institutional machinery behind antitrust enforcement. His curiosity does not stop at US borders, either. He is among the few American scholars to develop a keen and sustained interest in the evolution of antitrust law in Asia, with a particular focus on Japan.

2. But what truly sets Professor First apart, beyond his considerable expertise in antitrust law, is his writing. His writing style is intellectual without being impenetrable, scholarly but never stuffy. It is a rare gift – one that allows his readers to chuckle while being guided toward profound and thought-provoking insights. In many ways, this blend of humor and rigor has made his work timeless. Many of his articles, penned decades ago, still hold practical relevance today, continuing to provoke, inform, and inspire a new generation of scholars and practitioners.

3. In what follows, I will explore two of Professor First's major contributions to the institutional analysis of global antitrust law: his examination of how regulatory culture and institutional design have shaped Japanese antitrust enforcement, and his critique of the democratic deficit in US antitrust law. Indeed, Professor First was among the first scholars to highlight Japan's unique regulatory culture, which, unlike the West's more adversarial approach to antitrust enforcement, focuses on bureaucratic guidance rather than legalistic punishment.[1] His insightful work revealed that antitrust enforcement in Japan is less about reprimanding market misdeeds and more about steering the economy in a particular direction.[2] This subtle yet profound distinction continues to set Japanese enforcement apart from its Western counterparts, where confrontational legal battles are the norm. In Japan, antitrust is not merely a tool for maintaining competitive markets; it is part of a broader framework of economic governance, where the state plays a guiding role rather than an antagonistic one.[3]

4. Professor First's critique of US antitrust law is equally compelling. In collaboration with Professor Spencer Waller, Professor First has illuminated

---

[1] Harry First, *Antitrust Enforcement in Japan*, 64 ANTITRUST L.J. 137 (1995).

[2] *Id.* at 144.

[3] *Id.* at 144–45.

what they call the "democratic deficit" in US antitrust enforcement – a structural imbalance that places too much power in the hands of technocrats and too little in the hands of elected officials or the public.[4] They argued that this overreliance on technocratic expertise has insulated antitrust law from democratic accountability, creating a system where key decisions are made by a small group of experts who are often free from meaningful oversight.[5]

5. Meanwhile, Professor First has long championed the importance of decentralized enforcement. He believes that concentrating antitrust power in a single agency, as exemplified by Japan's Fair Trade Commission (JFTC), often leads to bureaucratic inertia and weak enforcement.[6] In the United States, he has been an outspoken defender of state attorneys general, arguing that they play a vital role in antitrust enforcement.[7] His foresight has been particularly validated in recent years, as many states like California have led the charge in regulating data privacy and artificial intelligence, areas where federal efforts have stalled amid political gridlock. Professor First's work shows that decentralizing enforcement power not only enhances accountability but also fosters innovation in regulatory practices, ensuring more dynamic and responsive governance.

6. Beyond his scholarship, Professor First has been a dedicated mentor, investing his time and energy into the development of students and fellow academics. For many years, he and his colleagues at New York University Law School (NYU) organized conferences that welcomed and supported emerging antitrust and data privacy scholars, fostering a friendly environment of intellectual growth and collaboration. His generosity in mentoring is a testament to his belief in cultivating the next generation of antitrust thinkers and enforcers. In the final part of this essay, I will reflect on my personal experiences with Professor First and how his mentorship has profoundly shaped my scholarly path over the past fifteen years.

I. The Influence of Regulatory Culture and Institutional Design on Japanese Antitrust Law

7. In a field where regulatory culture was often overlooked, Professor First dissected Japan's unique blend of bureaucratic oversight and legal enforcement with precision. In his 1995 article "Antitrust Enforcement

---

4   Harry First & Spencer Weber Waller, *Antitrust's Democracy Deficit*, 81 FORDHAM L. REV 2543, 2544 (2013).
5   *Id.*
6   Harry First & Tadashi Shiraishi, *Concentrated Power: The Paradox of Antitrust in Japan*, in LAW IN JAPAN: A TURNING POINT 521 (Daniel H. Foote ed., 2007).
7   Harry First, *Modernizing State Antitrust Enforcement: Making the Best of a Good Situation*, 54 ANTITRUST BULL. 281 (2009).

in Japan," published in the *Antitrust Law Journal*, Professor First laid out a framework for understanding Japan's ambivalent relationship with antitrust law. "Two questions are often raised with regard to antitrust enforcement in Japan," he wrote. "The first is whether there has been any. The second is whether there is reason to expect that there would be any."[8]

8. It was a characteristically sharp observation, one that cut to the heart of Japan's unique regulatory landscape. Japan, at least on the surface, had a robust antitrust regime. But, as Professor First explained, while there was much enforcement, its practical impact was less clear. The problem, he suggested, was not rooted in Japan's business culture, as many observers might assume.[9] Instead, it lay in the country's regulatory culture, a force as powerful as it was misunderstood.[10]

9. Professor First described this regulatory culture as a spectrum, with two poles: "legalistic" on one end and "bureaucratic" on the other.[11] The United States, he argued, falls firmly within the legalistic tradition.[12] In such systems, regulation is driven by the protection of individuals from specific harmful acts.[13] "Such regulation is individual-case-oriented, fact-bound, and backward-looking," Professor First wrote, "[t]he decision-making model is a trial," where evidence is presented, decisions are methodically reasoned, and judgments are rooted in precedent.[14]

10. Japan, by contrast, operates in a bureaucratic mode.[15] Here, regulation is less concerned with specific violations and more focused on managing the welfare of the broader economy. "This type of regulation is group-oriented, theory-based, and forward-looking,"[16] Professor First explained, noting that "[t]he decision-making model is consensual."[17] This explains why in Japan, "[r]igorous justification for particular decisions is not only unnecessary but may be unwise."[18] This difference in approach meant that while antitrust laws existed, their enforcement was often subordinated to broader economic goals.

---

8   First, *supra* note 1, at 137.
9   *Id.* at 139-42.
10 *Id.* at 142.
11 *Id.*
12 *Id.* at 143.
13 *Id.*
14 *Id.*
15 *Id.*
16 *Id.*
17 *Id.*
18 *Id.*

11. When Professor First looked closely at the early cases brought by the JFTC, his findings were both revealing and unsettling.[19] He noted that the agency, rather than pursuing vigorous judicial enforcement, tended to resolve matters bureaucratically, often through settlements that sidestepped any form of judicial-style hearing.[20] Of the eight cases he examined, only one even reached the stage of a hearing.[21] This tendency toward quiet, administrative disposal reflected a deeper struggle within the JFTC – a regulatory body attempting to assert its authority in a bureaucracy that, for decades, had not only promoted cartels but aimed to control the very structure of Japan's postwar economy.[22]

12. Professor First's engagement with Japan's antitrust regime dates back decades, but his observations remain strikingly relevant. In early 2024, I was invited to give a talk at the JFTC in Tokyo. During discussions with Japanese officials, it became clear that the same problems Professor First had written about decades ago were still alive and well. I was struck by how deeply ingrained this regulatory culture remains, and yet equally impressed by how precisely Professor First had captured its essence so many years ago. Antitrust enforcement in Japan still exists within a framework where bureaucratic compromise often trumps legal confrontation, where the spirit of enforcement is more cooperative than adversarial.

13. Indeed, what Professor First identified in his research is not unique to Japan – it is part of a broader phenomenon in which regulatory culture profoundly shapes how antitrust laws are enforced, particularly in systems that rely on bureaucratic rather than legalistic models. China is another striking example. Like Japan, China's regulatory institutions are steeped in a bureaucratic tradition, where economic policy often takes precedence over strict legal enforcement.[23] Years ago, when I sent Professor First an early draft of my paper *Bureaucratic Politics and China's Anti-Monopoly Law*, his response was immediate and insightful. I guess he saw in my analysis of China similar dynamics to what he had encountered in Japan: a system where enforcement was less about punishing wrongdoers and more about managing the economy in a way that supported the state's broader goals. China's antitrust enforcement, much like Japan's, operates within a delicate balance. The regulatory agencies wield significant power, but that power is often exercised in the service of economic growth rather than strict legal accountability.[24]

---

19 *Id.* at 148–56.

20 *Id.* at 154.

21 *Id.*

22 *Id.*

23 Angela Huyue Zhang, Chinese Antitrust Exceptionalism: How the Rise of China Challenges Global Regulation 19–54 (2021).

24 Angela Huyue Zhang, High Wire: How China Regulates Big Tech and Governs Its Economy 109–15 (2024).

14. During the first decade of China's Anti-Monopoly Law, one of its most formidable enforcers was the National Development and Reform Commission (NDRC), a powerful body with deep roots in China's economic planning history. The agency, whose predecessor had overseen the country's price controls and centrally planned economy, carried forward many of the same heavy-handed regulatory tactics that had defined its earlier mandate.[25] Under the NDRC, antitrust enforcement became less a mechanism for ensuring competition and more a tool for exerting policy control and industrial policy, deeply intertwined with China's broader economic strategy.[26] The NDRC's approach was, in some ways, emblematic of the bureaucratic regulatory culture described by Professor First.

15. Indeed, the NDRC's aggressive and hectic enforcement actions in the early days of Chinese antitrust enforcement generated tremendous controversy.[27] The agency targeted multinationals with large fines for resale price maintenance or abuse of dominance practices, often in industries critical to China's national interests.[28] What followed was a growing backlash from the international business community, which saw these actions as protectionist measures thinly veiled as antitrust enforcement.[29] These tensions, simmering beneath the surface for years, ultimately helped fuel the larger trade conflict that would erupt between the United States and China in 2018.[30]

16. In addition to the question about regulatory culture, the other major institutional issue Professor First identified as holding back Japanese antitrust enforcement is its institutional design. In their 2007 article, *Concentrated Power: The Paradox of Antitrust in Japan*, Professor First and Professor Tadashi Shiraishi sought to unravel the persistent myth of weak antitrust enforcement in Japan.[31] The JFTC, Japan's central antitrust authority, had for decades been viewed as a regulatory body that seemed unwilling – or unable – to exercise its full authority.[32] As one commissioner put it, the JFTC had earned a reputation as "a watchdog that does not bite."[33]

17. Professor First and Professor Shiraishi argued that the JFTC's ineffectiveness was not a matter of mere reluctance but was, in fact, a consequence

---

25 Angela Huyue Zhang, *Bureaucratic Politics and China's Anti-Monopoly Law*, 47 CORNELL INT'L L.J. 671 (2014).

26 *Id.* at 694–99.

27 ZHANG, *supra* note 23, at 69.

28 *Id.* at 68–70.

29 *Id.* at 69–70.

30 Angela Huyue Zhang, *The U.S.-China Trade Negotiation: A Contract Theory Perspective*, 51 GEO. J. INT'L L.809 (2020).

31 First & Shiraishi, *supra* note 6, at 521.

32 *Id.* at 521–22.

33 *Id.* at 522.

of the very concentration of enforcement power within the agency.[34] Unlike in the United States, where private antitrust litigation plays a critical role in enforcement, Japan's system gave the JFTC a near monopoly over antitrust actions. Without a tradition of robust private litigation, the JFTC lacked the external pressure to refine its legal doctrines.[35] In their analysis, Professor First and Professor Shiraishi also noted that the JFTC tended to rely on informal enforcement mechanisms.[36] Decisions were rarely contested in court, leaving little room for judicial review or the evolution of nuanced legal standards.[37] Furthermore, the commission's tendency to issue overly broad rulings on antitrust violations, often without considering efficiency arguments, further weakened its effectiveness.[38] As they put it, the JFTC "has been a cause of the inadequate development of legal doctrines."[39]

18. What Professor First and Professor Shiraishi unraveled was, at its core, a profound and perennial question of institutional design: how should a country structure its antitrust enforcement to ensure both effectiveness and fairness? The issue seems deceptively straightforward. A single, centralized public enforcer would, on the surface, seem to offer the most coherence – one agency with a unified vision, eliminating the risk of conflicting interpretations or fragmented authority. But, as Professor First astutely observed, this concentration of power carries its own risks. Power consolidated in one agency can easily stagnate, becoming less responsive to change, more rigid in its processes, and less accountable to the public it is meant to serve.

19. This dilemma is not unique to Japan. When China introduced its Anti-Monopoly Law in 2008, it faced a similarly urgent question of institutional design. However, unlike Japan, which entrusted enforcement to a single body, China opted for a fragmented system, dividing responsibilities among three agencies – each with its own history and approach to regulation. The result was a quagmire of coordination challenges. These agencies often interpreted the law differently, followed different procedures, and sometimes issued inconsistent decisions.[40] This fragmentation also sparked bureaucratic competition, with some agencies such as the NDRC engaging in overzealous enforcement to assert dominance in the regulatory space.[41] Professor First's broader question – whether to centralize

---

34 *Id.*

35 *Id.* at 528–29.

36 *Id.* at 530.

37 *Id.*

38 *Id.*

39 *Id.* at 528–30.

40 Angela Huyue Zhang, *The Enforcement of the Anti-Monopoly Law in China: An Institutional Design Perspective*, 56 ANTITRUST BULL. 630, 639–44 (2011).

41 Zhang, *supra* note 25, at 692–700.

antitrust enforcement or disperse it across multiple bodies – remains deeply relevant. The risks of concentrating power in a single agency are well known, from regulatory capture to bureaucratic inertia. Yet, the inefficiencies of fragmentation could also pose significant challenges, as illustrated in the Chinese example.

II. The Democratic Deficit in US Antitrust Enforcement

20. One of Professor First's most profound contributions to antitrust scholarship is his exploration of the democratic deficit in US antitrust enforcement. In a 2013 article co-authored with Professor Waller, Professor First ventured into largely uncharted territory, dissecting how institutional failures within the US antitrust framework have weakened enforcement over time.[42] This widely cited article has since inspired many prominent thinkers in the field, including Lina Kahn,[43] Frank Pasquale,[44] Jonathan Baker[45] and many more.

21. Professor First and Professor Waller zeroed in on the growing imbalance within the institutions responsible for enforcing antitrust policy. "The institutional aspects of [the US] antitrust enterprise," they observed, had become "increasingly out of balance."[46] They argued that "too much control" had been placed "in the hands of technical experts," who often pursued "self-referential goals" with little "political [oversight or] economic accountability."[47] In their critique, Professor First and Professor Waller identified three key institutions shaping US antitrust enforcement: the courts, Congress, and public enforcers. Their first target was the judiciary, which, they argued, had effectively overstepped its boundaries, often exercising what amounted to "legislative power" in antitrust matters, all while ignoring the constraints Congress had set.[48] This unchecked judicial power, they noted, had largely escaped public scrutiny – a quiet but profound shift in how antitrust law was being interpreted and enforced.[49]

22. Professor First and Professor Waller then turned their focus to a lesser-discussed actor of US antitrust enforcement: the jury. In America, juries are only required in antitrust suits seeking damages or in criminal cases,

---

42 First & Waller, *supra* note 4.

43 Lina M. Khan, *Amazon's Antitrust Paradox*, 126 YALE L.J. 710, 743 (2016); *see also* Lina Khan & Sandeep Vaheesan, *Market Power and Inequality: The Antitrust Counterrevolutions and Its Discontents*, 11 HARV. L. & POL'Y REV. 235, 275 (2017).

44 Frank Pasquale, *Privacy, Antitrust, and Power*, 20 GEO. MASON L. REV. 1009, 1024 (2013).

45 Jonathan B. Baker, *Finding Common Ground Among Antitrust Reformers*, 84 ANTITRUST L.J. 705, 730 (2022).

46 First & Waller, *supra* note 4, at 2544.

47 *Id.*

48 *Id.* at 2548.

49 *Id.* at 2552.

and even then, jury trials have become a rarity as most cases are settled or dismissed before reaching trial.[50] Yet, despite their infrequent presence, a deep-rooted hostility toward juries persists in antitrust law, driven by the fear that a "populist jury" that "hates big business" will also lack sufficient understanding of economics.[51] The implications of this hostility go far beyond a mere procedural preference. Professor First and Professor Waller saw this trend as part of a broader shift that recasts antitrust enforcement as a technocratic endeavor, best left to federal agencies and economic experts.[52] In distancing juries from antitrust cases, they are concerned that the law risks becoming more insulated from public participation, furthering the notion that enforcement should be handled by a cloistered group of specialists rather than by representatives of the public.[53]

23. Their third criticism was directed squarely at Congress. They argued that lawmakers had become too preoccupied with trivial matters, while being scared off by the technocratic wall that antitrust professionals had carefully constructed around the field.[54] This insulation, they noted, had left Congress hesitant to engage with substantive antitrust issues.[55] To address this democratic deficit, Professor First and Professor Waller proposed five reforms aimed at reinvigorating Congress's role in shaping competition policy.[56] One of their key suggestions was for Congress to require federal agencies to report periodically on any changes in enforcement strategies, budget priorities, or shifts in judicial interpretation of antitrust law.[57] This would restore a measure of accountability, ensuring that agencies could not operate unchecked by the legislative branch.[58] They also advocated for Congress to introduce mechanisms ensuring that when blue-ribbon commissions conduct sweeping studies on competition policy, their recommendations are formally introduced into the legislative process.[59]

24. Last but not least, Professor First and Professor Waller defended state enforcement, emphasizing its crucial role in public antitrust enforcement.[60] As the professors pointed out, "From the point of view of democratic accountability, the criticism of the state attorneys general is deeply ironic

---

50 *Id.* at 2553.
51 *Id.*
52 *Id.* at 2555.
53 *Id.*
54 *Id.* at 2558.
55 *Id.*
56 *Id.* at 2560.
57 *Id.*
58 *Id.*
59 *Id.*
60 *Id.* at 2561.

because nearly all the state attorneys general are elected officials."[61] Professor First, a staunch advocate of decentralized enforcement, has long championed the idea that dispersing power across multiple enforcers is far preferable to centralizing authority in a single agency.[62]

25. More than a decade has passed since Professor First and Professor Waller published their seminal critique, and yet their insights remain strikingly relevant. In recent years, both federal agencies and states have ramped up antitrust enforcement, particularly against Big Tech. However, despite these renewed efforts, antitrust authorities have faced considerable obstacles in the courts. Judges, clinging to decades of non-interventionist precedents, have often struck down or limited the scope of enforcement actions.[63] The much-publicized congressional hearings on Big Tech, followed by a flurry of legislative proposals, raised hopes that real reform might be on the horizon.[64] Yet, despite the high drama of the hearings and a cascade of proposed bills, the results have largely fallen short. The technocratic wall that has long insulated antitrust law from serious congressional scrutiny remains intact, with Congress showing little appetite for substantive reform. Indeed, Congress has yet to pass any meaningful antitrust legislation targeting Big Tech – except, notably, for the law aimed at regulating TikTok, which itself emerged more from national security concerns than a genuine push to rein in monopolistic power.[65]

26. Professor First's insights into state enforcement also proved remarkably prescient, particularly as the role of states in shaping US technology law has grown in recent years. While Congress has repeatedly failed to pass comprehensive federal legislation on key issues such as data privacy, states have stepped in to fill the gap. Thus far, twenty US states have enacted their own privacy laws, forming a mosaic of regulations that is slowly but surely reshaping the legal landscape.[66] Not only have states been at the forefront of data regulations, but they have also moved swiftly to address emerging technologies like artificial intelligence (AI). While Washington has seen extensive debate over the need for federal AI legislation, these discussions have largely stalled amid complex economic and geopolitical concerns. Meanwhile, state governments, less hindered by the gridlock of

---

61 *Id.* at 2562.

62 First, *supra* note 7, at 282.

63 Jonathan B. Baker, *What About the Supreme Court? The Lurking Threat to US Antitrust Reform*, 11 J. ANTITRUST ENFORCEMENT 154 (2023).

64 Cecilia Kang & David McCabe, *House Lawmakers Condemn Big Tech's 'Monopoly Power' and Urge their Breakups*, N.Y. TIMES (Oct. 6, 2020), https://www.nytimes.com/2020/10/06/technology/congress-big-tech-monopoly-power.html.

65 Bobby Allyn, *President Biden Signs Law to Ban TikTok Nationwide Unless It Is Sold*, NPR (Apr. 24, 2024), https://www.npr.org/2024/04/24/1246663779/biden-ban-tiktok-us.

66 F. Paul Pittman, Hope Anderson & Abdul M. Hafiz, *US Data Privacy Guide*, WHITE & CASE (July 2, 2024), https://www.whitecase.com/insight-our-thinking/us-data-privacy-guide.

national politics, have become laboratories for innovation in law. In the past year, states such as Colorado and California have already started releasing their own regulations to oversee AI, once again stepping into the void left by federal indecision.[67] This trend toward state-led governance underscores the very decentralization that Professor First championed throughout his career. His belief that a dispersed network of enforcers – not a single, centralized authority – would foster both democratic accountability and regulatory experimentation is playing out in real time. By empowering states to act independently, the United States has allowed for diverse approaches to regulatory challenges, creating a dynamic legal landscape that adapts more readily to the rapid pace of technological change.

III. Professor First as a Mentor

27. I first connected with Professor First in 2009, when I submitted an article to the *Antitrust Bulletin* on the institutional design challenges with Chinese antitrust enforcement. Professor First, who served as an editor at that time, rejected my article. Yet, his rejection felt like anything but a dismissal. It was more of an invitation – an intellectual challenge to sharpen my thinking, refine my arguments, and dig deeper into my analysis. His comments were meticulous, thoughtful, and pointed. He did not simply critique the weaknesses in my argument; instead, he laid out a clear path for improvement, providing a roadmap for how the paper could be elevated. I took his advice to heart, revised the article, and resubmitted it. In the end, he published what became my first essay in antitrust law.

28. After completing my JSD in 2011, I entered the academic "meat market," the notoriously competitive job market for aspiring professors. Recommendations were considered crucial for the application process, but I hesitated to ask Professor First for a letter. After all, we had never met in person – our only connection was through my submission to the *Antitrust Bulletin*. Still, I reached out, unsure of what to expect. To my surprise, Professor First readily agreed. Despite only knowing me through my writing, he was willing to vouch for me. I never saw the letter, but from what I heard, it was glowing. His willingness to support me, based solely on my work, meant so much to me. It was a gesture that not only spoke to his generosity but also to his commitment to nurturing young scholars, even those he had not yet met in person.

29. In 2013, I landed my first academic position at King's College London, where I finally had the chance to dedicate myself to writing and researching

---

67 Stuart D. Levi, Ken D. Kumayama, William E. Ridgway, Mana Ghaemmaghami & MacKinzie M. Neal, *Colorado's Landmark AI Act: What Companies Need to Know*, Skadden (June 24, 2024), https://www.skadden.com/insights/publications/2024/06/colorados-landmark-ai-act; Arsen Kourinian, *California Passes New Generative Artificial Intelligence Law Requiring Disclosure of Training Data*, Mayer Brown (Sept. 30, 2024), https://www.mayerbrown.com/en/insights/publications/2024/09/california-passes-new-generative-artificial-intelligence-law-requiring-disclosure-of-training-data.

antitrust law. Unlike many in the field, I did not focus on the core antitrust doctrines. Instead, I became fascinated by the role institutional factors play in shaping antitrust enforcement in China. Over the years, my research expanded to examine the influence of bureaucratic politics, media, and even geopolitics on antitrust enforcement practices. Whenever I had a new antitrust paper, I would send it to Professor First, and without fail, he would take the time to read it, offering succinct, insightful feedback and always a word of encouragement. His support not only validated my work but gave me the confidence to pursue these issues further. As a junior scholar, that kind of validation was invaluable. It was not just that Professor First thought my research was important – it was that he showed me, time and again, that it had practical relevance. His mentorship was a source of confidence at a critical time in my career.

30. When I published my second book, *High Wire: How China Regulates Big Tech and Governs Its Economy*, I had the distinct privilege of presenting it at NYU's U.S.-Asia Law Institute. Professor First, ever generous with his time, graciously agreed to serve as a commentator alongside Professor Eleanor Fox, another scholar I deeply admire. True to form, Professor First's feedback was extremely insightful and penetrating. He did not simply skim through the book; he read it with painstaking attention, filling it with Post-its and meticulous notes. Once again, I was struck by the depth of his intellectual engagement and his commitment to nurturing ideas from young scholars.

IV. Conclusion

31. As the field of antitrust law continues to evolve, the relevance of Professor First's work only grows. His analyses of regulatory culture and institutional design remain central to understanding not just antitrust enforcement in Japan and the United States, but the broader challenges of global governance in an increasingly interconnected world. Whether through his dissection of bureaucratic systems in Japanese antitrust enforcement or his calls for greater democratic accountability in US antitrust law, Professor First's work challenges us to rethink how laws are enforced, who wields that power, and, ultimately, in whose interest the system operates.

32. But Professor First's impact extends far beyond the pages of antitrust law or the sharpness of his legal commentary. His true legacy, I believe, will live on in the careers of the many scholars he has mentored over the years. His influence on my own career has been nothing short of profound, and I am committed to carrying forward that same spirit of generosity and mentorship in my own work. In every sense, he exemplifies what it means to be a scholar – not just through his contributions to the field, but through the lives he has touched and the scholars he has guided.

Antitrust, Democracy, and "Being a Mensch"

ADI AYAL[*]
Bar Ilan University

Abstract

"Being a Mensch" is a deeply personal compliment, bestowed upon someone who truly sees others as complete human beings, inherently worthy of respect and consideration. A "mensch" (literally, a human being) internalizes others' needs and wants, and feels a deep personal need to help them out – beyond mere self-interest or utility. In this paper, I delve into the attributes involved, and how the spirit of antitrust and democracy are deeply intertwined with "being a mensch". While competition is often seen as a self-interested dynamic focused (mainly) on price, I argue for respect of the dynamism and variety that tell more about the observer than the observed. I argue that democracy is founded on considerate behavior and respect for others' individuality – even (and perhaps especially) when we vehemently disagree with them. Connecting between antitrust, democracy, and basic human decency, I hope to shed light on why these things matter, and how much they have in common.

---

[*] PhD Law, PhD Economics. Comments and discussion are welcome! Adi.ayal@biu.ac.il.

1. At a conference dedicated to Harry First, Dan Rubinfeld, and Eleanor Fox, a common theme that the participating academics kept mentioning about the honorees was how they embodied "being a mensch."[1] In Yiddish, "mensch" literally means "a human being," but in popular parlance, it is understood as a deep and indefinable description focusing on character: a trustworthy, moral, decent human being. Not a saint, but what good people should aspire to, and some actually achieve. It is usually accompanied by a thoughtful facial expression and a nod of the head conveying respect and admiration for the "human being" being discussed. This broad accolade was used to describe the innumerable ways in which all three consistently did more than what is required (or expected) of them, how they reached out and helped those who could not repay them, and how they behaved in ways that most of us hope we would be able to emulate, given the chance.

2. Harry, Dan, and Eleanor reaped such praise because of who they are, not because of what they know – somewhat out of character for an academic conference. While primarily a personal trait, I will argue that "being a mensch" is deeply connected to the spirit of antitrust as a field and to competition as a mechanism, especially within the context of democratic institutions – something common to the writing of all three.[2] The "mensch" quality, once understood and applied, symbolizes what competition is really about, and how the law should (and should not) intervene. I hope to show that "being a mensch" resonates not only with respect for competition on the merits, but with the underlying principles of democratic institutions. In order to do this, I will delve into the underlying characteristics that make up "a mensch," using the language of economics and competition. Hopefully, I will be able to show not only that Harry, Dan, and Eleanor were justifiably praised, but that their field and their character intertwine. Perhaps we shall even gain a glimpse into the effervescent "spirit of antitrust" that many of us allude to.

I. What Is a "Mensch"?

3. If asked to describe what they mean by "mensch," most academics participating in the conference could point to a positive demeanor, a respect for differing views, and a willingness to listen and give others a chance – even when the listener already thinks they are wrong. They might stress the

---

1 New York University Law School (Sept. 29, 2023), https://www.law.nyu.edu/news/antitrust-merger-guidelines-conference-nyu-law.

2 *E.g.*, ROBERT P. INMAN & DANIEL L. RUBINFELD, DEMOCRATIC FEDERALISM: THE ECONOMICS, POLITICS, AND LAW OF FEDERAL GOVERNANCE (2020); Harry First & Spencer Weber Waller, *Antitrust's Democracy Deficit*, 81 FORDHAM L. REV. 2543 (2013); Eleanor M. Fox, *Antitrust and Democracy: How Markets Protect Democracy, Democracy Protects Markets, and Illiberal Politics Threatens to Hijack Both*, 46 LEGAL ISSUES ECON. INTEGRATION 317 (2019).

importance of true curiosity, one that is accompanied by avoiding dogmatic belief or a need to be right (or at least appear to be right). They might point to the importance a mensch ascribes to acknowledging mistakes and fallibility – including their own. The resulting behavior, such as giving others a chance and lending a helping hand, when possible, are implementations of this underlying character, but attitude matters no less than action.

4. True respect for the competitive process is similar. It requires overcoming the human tendency to simplify and dichotomize. It follows from avoiding clear hierarchies of value, and allowing multiple "conceptions of good" to thrive.[3] Competition is about letting different people choose different things for different reasons. It entails respect for things we do not know and cannot plan for, while understanding that allowing everyone to "put in their two cents" will create a diversity of ideas and implementations. Respect for competition is about allowing the public to create (or pay for) what they value, and the belief that this will increase overall utility, both measured and otherwise.

5. When economists describe the benefits of competition, they usually focus on two effects: competitive pressure incentivizing the production of better and cheaper goods, and the search for new and lucrative markets leading to innovation in new goods and services – serving segments previously unattended to. The former focuses on how to better produce homogenous goods, while the latter relates to heterogeneity and differences in taste and circumstances. While both are important, homogenous goods are more useful in theory than in practice. Most producers work very hard to create (or convince the public of) differences between what they sell and what is offered by their competitors, as product differentiation allows for higher profitability and stronger customer loyalty.[4]

6. Differentiation is not merely an economic phenomenon, or one pertaining to finding niche markets or consumers more sensitive to product attributes than price. Differentiation relies on people having diverse wants and needs, and on economic actors striving to fulfill these wants, rather than forcing consumers to "make do" with what already exists. In other words, differentiation in economics is the result of a true respect for diversity and the right to pursue happiness in multiple and personal ways. A view that people should be served where they are, rather than forced into a single uniform conception of "what is right" or "what is good."

---

3   Some focus on democracy as a procedural rather than substantive issue, specifically in order to avoid even a theoretical need to choose among competing values, *e.g.*, JOHN RAWLS, POLITICAL LIBERALISM (1993). For our purposes here, we need not go this far. It is enough to "agree to disagree" and seek a way to live together, even when conceptions of good differ. The mensch would probably choose a narrow answer, one which opposing sides could agree to, even without solving the philosophical question of what democracy truly is.

4   *E.g.*, "When product differentiation exists, each firm will possess some market power as a result of the uniqueness of its product," ANDREU MAS-COLELL, MICHAEL D. WHINSTON & JERRY R. GREEN, MICROECONOMIC THEORY 395 (1995).

7. Some take "competition" to mean striving to overcome others or push them out of the way, but antitrust aficionados understand this is but a small part of the game. Most of the competitive process is about understanding the needs of others, seeking knowledge and extrapolating, and hoping to fulfill others' wants (so that they may wish to buy the product or service in question). Even in the "cutthroat" stage, competitors are mostly producing and researching and taking care of financing and logistics – the work of making and selling. First-year textbooks might focus on the intersection of one demand curve and one supply curve, but we all understand this is a very focused (and limited) lens, with which to examine one issue *ceteris paribus*.[5] Of course, in reality, other things are rarely equal...

II. Democracy as Considerate Behavior

8. Democracy might be described in a similar manner. Some focus on the end result of political parties and competition for votes. But this is a somewhat superficial description of one of the results of democracy, not its essence. Political competition that results in a majority winning power, which is then used to exclude the minority, may be a side effect of the need for structured decision-making within public institutions – but it is far from its aim. For example, imagine a vote being held in which 51% gain power and use it to externalize the costs of their preferences onto the losing 49%. This could be called "majority rule," and it might be better than the reverse – but these are far from the only options. When competition for power is framed as a win-lose game, and opposing parties are framed as competing for the right to wield power, it is easy to fall into the trap of basking in the glory of the win – or lamenting the loss. But democratic institutions are structured to protect the rights of those who have little power and cannot protect themselves. The essence of democracy has more to do with how losers are treated than increasing the size or the scope of the win.[6]

9. As a structural issue, this aspect of democracy is embodied in immutable rights that are assured and promised to all, regardless of their relative power or ability to protect themselves. It also underlies the idea that multiple conceptions of good and ways of life can coexist in a diverse society, that for some to achieve their goals and implement their ideals should not

---

5 *See, e.g.*, Robert S. Pindyck & Daniel L. Rubinfeld, Microeconomics (9th ed., 2018), ch. 3.

6 Again, one may think of Rawls, especially as formulated in A Theory of Justice (1971), but we need not go to the extreme of his *maximin* principle to accept the basic premise that political minorities deserve, and are entitled to, protection. The extent of this protection, and what societies owe their citizens, will obviously be debated. The mensch, though, would probably argue that focusing on the minorities' rights is important, but not sufficient. One should take into account individual ability and willingness to respect the other, even when their request stems from a need or a difficulty, rather than a justifiable claim. In other words, a mensch favors offering voluntary assistance and sees both sides gaining from such an interaction. Utilizing rights and legal protection are an important second-best safeguard, to be used when needed, but not preferred.

come at the expense of others' needs and preferences. In economic terms, we might see this as a form of differentiation, or multi-faceted interaction between complex people who simultaneously belong to different groups.

10. Differentiation allows for heterogeneous goods to be sold side-by-side, satisfying different forms of preferences and allowing competing value systems to thrive. In economics, we model this by focusing on defined markets and submarkets, using the language of local optima. In democracy, we focus on multiple levels of decision-making, allowing local and national policies to differ, and ensuring that even within small polities, different people will be allowed their way of life, inasmuch as they can without interfering with others doing the same. The language of externalities and their minimization is useful throughout.

11. Democracy is about allowing people to self-govern, while maintaining limits on the externalities imposed on others, who should not be impeded in their own self-governing. Ideally, one should not pay the price for another's freedom, though we all understand this as an ideal, unrealistic yet still worth striving for. Like antitrust, democracy focuses more on process than result, with both relying on competition among different players with different preferences to achieve a commonly beneficial outcome. In both cases, the end result hoped for is not merely the "better" one according to some pre-specified prioritization, but the variety that is invariably produced when different people simultaneously try to reach their (different) goals.

12. "Being a mensch" is intimately related to this love of diversity, this respect for differences between people. It does not entail giving up your opinion, or what you want to achieve. It is about including others in your decision – what economists might call internalizing externalities (and others might call conscientiousness).[7]

13. A mensch realizes that our actions affect others, and that those others deserve respect and consideration. They view others as important, and have an inner need to avoid harming others, or benefiting at others' expense. At the same time, a mensch realizes that self-interest is no less legitimate or important than other-regarding behavior, and they do not deprive themselves of individual goals. A mensch likes to help, but does not forgo their own conception of good or their personal preferences. In short, a mensch respects competition and democracy as processes of interaction between people with inherent value, not as merely a method of assigning power or attaining efficiency.

14. Being a mensch can also have beneficial effects beyond the direct interaction between those involved, creating positive externalities with the potential of shifting to an equilibrium better for all. A beautiful example can be found

---

[7] With obvious reference to Pigou, some take this further, and argue that internalization can be thought of as a social means of creating better citizens, facilitating cooperation as well as efficiency. *See, e.g.*, Robert Cooter, *Expressive Law and Economics*, 27 J. LEGAL STUD. 585 (1998).

in a paper by Salop and Moresi, expanding on the well-known "Tit for Tat" strategy.[8] Modeling societal interaction, they imagine a space where many people congregate to find partners for a one-on-one win/lose game of prisoner's dilemma.[9] In their conception, each round of the game begins with individuals seeking partners, then playing a one-round simultaneous-action prisoner's dilemma. After observing the result, players choose whether to stick with their current partner (or seek a new one) for another round of the same game. A well-known result is that one-shot prisoner's dilemma leads both players to choose the "defect" option – creating a loss for both. In the Salop and Moresi framework, any trust potentially created by having multiple rounds into an infinite future is overpowered by one's incentive to defect and reap immediate rewards, followed by seeking another (new) partner for the next round – who might be similarly exploited. Enter the mensch.

15. The model introduces a new type of player, one who is "righteous." A "righteous" player always cooperates and is unable to defect. Seemingly, this sets them up to suffer constant defection, except for one tactic they have at their disposal – leaving and seeking a new partner for the next round. This "Quit for Tat" strategy causes them to suffer no more than one defection from any partner, as they will stay and play again with whoever cooperated with them – but will leave immediately after losing to a defecting partner.

16. Salop and Moresi ask how many of these "righteous" players are necessary in order to induce an equilibrium in which not only the righteous cooperate, but other self-interested players will as well. In other words, they ask when the righteous (or mensch-like) action creates incentives for others to behave similarly.

17. Solving the model shows that a small minority of righteous players can influence the behavior of many self-interested players, leading to everyone cooperating all the time. This stems from the self-interested players preferring long-term cooperation over short-term defection, specifically because the righteous will suffer defection only once – then leave. Whenever two righteous players meet, they will cooperate and stay together. This dilutes the population such that with every additional round, the ratio of righteous players available for new partners drops – until the chance of meeting one all but disappears. In other words, self-serving behavior self-selects for future self-serving partners. Repeated enough times, even the most self-serving will find that exploiting another's generosity is a losing proposition.

---

8   The original formulation from Robert Axelrod & William D. Hamilton, *The Evolution of Cooperation*, 211 SCIENCE 1390 (1981) was expanded upon by Serge Moresi & Steven Salop, *A Few Righteous Men: Imperfect Information, Quit-for-Tat, and Critical Mass in the Dynamics of Cooperation*, in ECONOMICS FOR AN IMPERFECT WORLD: ESSAYS IN HONOR OF JOSEPH E. STIGLITZ 183 (Richard Arnott, Bruce Greenwald, Ravi Kanbur & Barry Nalebuff eds., 2003).

9   Thus, they envision people seeking social interaction, against a backdrop of difficult circumstances, naturally tilted *against* successful cooperation.

18. Observe how the righteous in this model mirror the mensch discussed here. Both are kind and generous, and both have limits. In the model, the righteous leave after being exploited – but will continue to offer cooperation in the future (to new partners, from whom the righteous have not yet suffered defection). Like the mensch, they have an inner need to behave morally, but a self-serving defense mechanism to protect themselves from subjugation. Like the mensch, they affect others not only through direct interaction, but also through a form of osmosis through social dynamics. In both cases, societies where enough people behave morally cause many others to do the same, albeit based on incentives rather than principles.

19. Being a mensch means recognizing the humanity of others, seeing and accepting their imperfections. A mensch looks beyond another's faults, and sees *them* – as a whole, as imperfect, as valuable. A mensch strives to meet others on their own level, meet them in their imperfections without letting judgment interfere with empathy. This is not to say that judgment is lacking, or that "anything goes," but a mensch understands the other is more than their faults and is able to work with others while recognizing that even bad behavior is but one aspect and does not negate the person as a whole. A mensch is able to connect to another's feelings and situation, even when their experience differs.

20. Like choice in democratic decision-making or in market competition, such "taking as a whole" or "focusing on the good or useful" allows for beneficial cooperation or deal-making, even when the other is lacking. Just as we buy from people (or firms) without condoning all their actions, and just as we vote for politicians without supporting all their policies, mensch-like qualities facilitate competition on many levels. We focus not on what the other "deserves," but on what they can offer. A mensch goes one step further, focusing on the good and worthy. Similar to Dworkin's "interpretation in the best light possible", a mensch hopes to see the other's best. This does not negate judgment, or the human need to punish or even extract vengeance when offended. Still, the mensch will experience inner turmoil when hoping for another's suffering. While the wicked deserve castigation, they are not purely evil, and the mensch sees the good even while experiencing the bad.

III. A Personal Note

21. I first met Harry First when he graciously invited me to present at the Next Generation of Antitrust Scholars conference, engaging and fostering young aficionados of the field. Since then and over the years, I have observed how he loves a good argument, while always maintaining respect for (and the respect of) his counterparts. Dan Rubinfeld was my teacher, advisor, and mentor. I was fortunate to learn from him, observing the care

and precision of his thinking, while tremendously benefiting from his generosity and care. Eleanor Fox has been described by many in the field as caring and smart and kind, opening doors to diverse thought and ideas – her own and others'. All three embody the spirit of academia, but even more so – the spirit of antitrust.

22. The spirit of antitrust is about belief in the democratic system of competition on the merits: in goods, in services, and in ideas. It is about allowing diversity, about maintaining and ensuring it even when the benefits may flow to someone else. Scholars and courts focus on price effects, on output decisions, on efficiency – since this is the language of economics. Money is often used as a metric, "letting the market take its course", but we all understand that much more is going on. Prices, among economists, are one vector among many that can live within a mathematical model. If we could measure utility, we would, but life is more complex than our measurements allow. We often forget that the mathematics of economics allow for many parameters, while in reality we can only measure a few. And we exhibit a quantification bias, by which we overemphasize what can be counted or measured, because measurement allows us unidimensional thinking, focusing on what can be maximized. And economists do love to maximize…

23. Of course, we know that in truth we are optimizing, sometimes satisficing, in an imperfect world, and choosing among realistic alternatives – not the ideal.[10] But the tools of antitrust require narrowly defining what is relevant, often at the expense of what truly matters.[11]

24. Academics understand how imperfect our knowledge is.[12] Still, judges need to make clear decisions, and lawyers are driven to make stark arguments. The spirit of antitrust is remembering that opinions have weaknesses, like people. That the need for implementation requires simplifications – but these are not the whole of the matter. We do not discard tools because of their imperfections; we engage and understand them in order to give them credit where possible and to learn from them, while striving for their improvement.

25. For three of the greats of antitrust to celebrate the culmination of their careers with praise from colleagues – not just for their scholarship but for their character – is special, perhaps extraordinary. I believe that I speak on behalf of many others, who wish to thank Dan, Harry, and Eleanor for what they did and who they are, giving us all an opportunity to see that even while engaging in academic competition, and even when prestige and reputation are somewhat limited resources, it is possible to be a mensch.

---

10 Herbert A. Simon, *Rationality as Process and as Product of Thought*, 68 AM. ECON. REV. 1 (1978).

11 Louis Kaplow, *Why (Ever) Define Markets*, 124 HARV. L. REV. 437 (2010).

12 Even when academics become policymakers, some still maintain modesty regarding how sure we can be of the benefit antitrust creates. Or in the words of one recent chief economist of the Antitrust Division: "[N]o comprehensive study yet exists that quantifies the benefits (or costs) of our current antitrust policies compared to other possible policy regimes." Dennis W. Carlton, *Does Antitrust Need to be Modernized?*, 21 J. ECON. PERSP. 155, 174 (2007).

Professor Harry First: Champion for Competitive and Fair Markets

DIANE P. WOOD[*]

American Law Institute

The University of Chicago

U.S. Court of Appeals for the Seventh Circuit (ret.)

Abstract

Harry First has been a thoughtful and independent member of the competition-law scholarly community for many years. This article details the positions he has taken on important issues within the field, and how they have (or have not) fit in with the prevailing common wisdom of the time. Specifically, Professor First never lost sight of the original purposes of the antitrust laws, which at least in some eyes suffer from some internal contradictions. But that is often true of legislation, and so there is nothing unusually disturbing about its being true of U.S. antitrust law. It was this fidelity to the law, during the years when the classical Chicago School model was in vogue, that inspired much of his work. He also recognized how much can be learned from comparative competition law, whether that of the European Union, that of Japan, or that of other countries. We are greatly in his debt for his clear-eyes assessments of these systems, and in today's world, his global perspective is more important than ever.

---

[*] Director, American Law Institute; senior lecturer in law, The University of Chicago; circuit judge (ret.), U.S. Court of Appeals for the Seventh Circuit.

1. What a roller coaster antitrust law has ridden over the course of Professor Harry First's career! In 1966, the year he earned his B.A. from the University of Pennsylvania, most respected scholars agreed that the Sherman Act prescribes rules for market transactions, but that those rules exist against the backdrop of political choices and are intended to implement broader social goals. Carl Kaysen and Donald Turner wrote in 1959 that the drafters of the antitrust laws sought both to protect the competitive process and to assure "equal opportunity and equal access for small business for noneconomic reasons," including keeping in check the social power of big business.[1] Richard Hofstadter made much the same point, writing in 1965 that "[t]he political and social arguments against monopoly were pressed [by the drafters of the Sherman Act] with greater clarity than the economic argument and with hardly less fervor."[2]

2. During the same era – the mid-1960s – the Supreme Court handed down decision after decision that reflected this philosophy. It defined relevant markets narrowly and it worried about exclusionary practices. This led it to strike down many arrangements that would have passed muster in later years. Examples include *United States v. Grinnell Corp.*,[3] which found in 1966 that the defendant had violated Sherman Act section 2's monopolization prohibition in its operation of a national network of accredited central station services; *United States v. General Motors Corp.*,[4] which in the same year struck down the defendant's effort to control the locations at which its dealers sold its cars; *United States v. Topco Associates, Inc.*,[5] which in 1972, in the name of Sherman Act section 1, barred small grocery stores from banding together to create a jointly owned private label in the hope of enhancing their ability to compete more effectively against the large chain stores; and the now-infamous 1967 decision in *Utah Pie Co. v. Continental Baking Co.*,[6] holding that the Robinson-Patman Act[7] forbade Utah Pie from competing by lowering its prices aggressively. And this list is illustrative only: the conclusion is inescapable that the antitrust laws were marching to a different drummer during that period, easily extending through 1969, the year when Professor First graduated from Penn's Law School.

3. That is not, however, where antitrust stayed. Powerful intellectual forces were afoot that advocated a radically different reading of the statutory language and a far more modest scope for the laws. Those forces were assisted by the

---

[1] See CARL KAYSEN & DONALD F. TURNER, ANTITRUST POLICY: AN ECONOMIC AND LEGAL ANALYSIS 19 (1959).
[2] RICHARD HOFSTADTER, *What Happened to the Antitrust Movement?*, *in* THE PARANOID STYLE IN AMERICAN POLITICS AND OTHER ESSAYS 196–98 (1965), reprinted in HBPW TRADE REGULATION (4th ed.) at 10.
[3] 384 U.S. 563 (1966).
[4] 384 U.S. 127 (1966).
[5] 405 U.S. 596 (1972).
[6] 386 U.S. 685 (1967).
[7] 15 U.S.C. § 13.

delphic nature of the statute, whose terms have always been undefined. As enacted, section 1 of the Sherman Act made it a misdemeanor to participate in any "contract, combination in the form of trust or otherwise, or conspiracy [] in restraint of trade or commerce" in interstate or foreign commerce.[8] Section 2 condemned (also originally as a misdemeanor) "[e]very person who shall monopolize, or attempt to monopolize, or combine or conspire with any other person or persons [] to monopolize" any part of interstate or foreign commerce.[9] But what is a "restraint of trade," as opposed to the normal kind of forbearance that accompanies every contract? Assuming that "monopolization" occurs only when a firm has "too much" power in a market, what share of a properly defined market should trigger concern? Twenty percent? Fifty percent? Seventy? One hundred? And how, if at all, is the verb "to monopolize" different from the noun "monopolist"? There is plenty of room for interpretation as one seeks to answer those questions.

4. Beginning quietly in the 1950s at the University of Chicago Law School, an intellectual movement that would profoundly change both the legal academy's and the courts' understanding of the antitrust laws for several generations took root. It began in classrooms and workshops, spearheaded by such giants as Aaron Director and Edward Levi (later president of the University of Chicago and attorney general of the United States), but it soon grew beyond those people and that institution. Legal superstars, including Richard Posner, Robert Bork, and Frank Easterbrook, to name just a few, joined with Nobel Prize-winning economists such as Ronald Coase, George Stigler, and Gary Becker to develop a consumer-welfare-based antitrust doctrine. They urged that the law not only should, but did, cover only practices that are likely to lead to higher prices or lesser output (or the monopsony equivalent), thereby leading to a deadweight loss for the economy. The Chicago School adherents argued that it is impossible at the same time to pursue consumer welfare, so understood, and to pursue egalitarian goals – that is, to protect the position of "small dealers and worthy men"[10] in the market (assuming realistically that the latter would often be unable to meet or beat the low prices others were offering).

5. Although the triumph of the Chicago School was never complete in the academy – Professor First's career is proof enough of that point – it did not take long for the consumer-welfare advocates to prevail before one of their most important audiences: the Supreme Court of the United States. Gone were concerns about the fairness of business practices; exclusion

---

[8] 15 U.S.C. § 1. Violations of section 1 are now felonies, *see* the Antitrust Procedures and Penalties Act, Pub. L. No. 93-528, § 3, 88 Stat. 1708 (1974); and such violations can also be pursued in private civil litigation, *see* 15 U.S.C. § 15 (treble damages); *id.* § 26 (injunctive relief).

[9] *Id.* § 2. The same law that upgraded criminal section 1 violations to felony status did the same for violations of section 2, *see supra* note 8. That said, it is exceedingly rare to see a criminal section 2 prosecution.

[10] *See* United States v. Trans-Missouri Freight Ass'n, 166 U.S. 290 (1897), stating that the antitrust law covered restraints that had the effect of driving such people out of business.

from a marketplace was seen as merely the logical result of tough competition. The Court transformed a phrase from a much-maligned 1950s-era merger case, *Brown Shoe Co., Inc. v. United States*,[11] proclaiming that "[i]t is competition, not competitors, which the [Sherman] Act protects," into a mantra that today accompanies almost every rejection of an antitrust challenge to an exclusionary course of conduct. In so doing, the Court followed the approach to the antitrust laws most prominently advocated by Robert Bork in his pivotal book, *The Antitrust Paradox*.[12]

6. Rivers of ink have spilled over this book – whether it accurately captures the concerns of the drafters of the laws, whether those concerns can legitimately be summarized as a "consumer welfare" prescription, whether it is unduly insouciant about exclusionary practices that drive rivals out of markets, whether it brushes aside the problem of oligopoly too readily, and much more. This is not the place to explore all that.[13] What is important here is that Professor First resisted the pressure to follow the crowd. He has been a forceful voice for a more nuanced antitrust law – one that not only condemns practices that harm consumer welfare, such as price-fixing, market allocations, bid rigging, and mergers to monopoly, but also curbs practices that qualify as an abuse of a dominant or monopolistic position, practices that unfairly exclude rivals from the marketplace, and practices that amount to a significant step toward competitive harm (the so-called incipiency violations), even if that harm has not yet come to pass.

7. One cannot summarize a career as rich as Professor First's in one contribution to a *Festschrift*, but it is possible to point to some highlights. In that spirit, four subjects he has tackled struck me as particularly significant: (i) how should exclusionary behavior be approached; (ii) is there any way to hold monopolists responsible for abusive prices that overcharge consumers; (iii) how should antitrust respond to the tech giants (Alphabet, Amazon, Apple, Meta, and Microsoft); and (iv) is there any room for an international agreement on antitrust principles, or are the differences among nations and regions simply too great?

I. Exclusionary Practices

8. Professor First normally does not leave his readers guessing about what he really thinks. In an article entitled "Bork and *Microsoft*: Why Bork Was Right and What We Learn about Judging Exclusionary Behavior,"[14]

---

11 370 U.S. 294, 344 (1962).

12 ROBERT H. BORK, THE ANTITRUST PARADOX: A POLICY AT WAR WITH ITSELF (Free Press 1993) (1978).

13 These questions are explored from numerous points of view in a symposium sponsored by the *University of Chicago Law Review*. *See Symposium: Reassessing the Chicago School of Antitrust Law*, 87 U. CHI. L. REV. 263 (2020).

14 Harry First, *Bork and* Microsoft: *Why Bork Was Right and What We Learn about Judging Exclusionary Behavior*, 79 ANTITRUST L.J. 1017 (2014).

however, he teases with a title that might make one think that he was on Bork's side. But the joke does not last for long: he opens instead with the flat statement "Robert Bork nearly killed antitrust."[15] After finishing the article, the reader realizes that the truth lies somewhere in the middle. Despite the fact that Bork surely did mean to kill a great deal of antitrust doctrine that he found to be profoundly mistaken, in the end this article posits that Bork played a role in reinvigorating the law of exclusionary practices. He did so despite his powerful argument in *The Antitrust Paradox* that antitrust had gotten utterly out of hand in many ways, including by inspiring serious efforts in both the courts and Congress to deconcentrate oligopolies that were managing to survive without any hint of agreement among firms in the industry (none successful); advocacy of price caps for monopolists that were enjoying their ability to charge supracompetitive prices; and a host of business practices such as tying arrangements, exclusive dealing, and price discrimination were viewed with a beady eye by courts that characterized them as per se illegal, thereby putting a firm thumb on the liability side of the scale. Mergers of all kinds were routinely banned, whether horizontal, vertical, or conglomerate, with post-merger market structures that would universally be viewed as benign today.

9. What many of these "extreme" positions had in common was their focus on exclusionary acts. Bork urged that the antitrust laws should stop worrying about exclusion and let the market correct that type of abuse of power. That was never Professor First's position, causing one to wonder why the two may have converged in their assessment of the government's case in the late 1990s against Microsoft. Why, in other words, did Bork agree with Professor First that the Microsoft litigation was "rock solid"?

10. Perhaps the answer is that in his earlier writings, Bork mistook something that is rare – an exclusionary practice that harms competition – for something that is nonexistent. By the 1990s, however, he was a practicing lawyer, after his time on the Yale Law School faculty, his service as solicitor general of the United States from 1973 until 1977, and his years as a circuit judge on the U.S. Court of Appeals for the District of Columbia Circuit (1982 to 1988). He was renowned as one of the leading spokespersons for the "Chicago School" of antitrust analysis. Nevertheless, he chose to advocate alongside the government for the proposition that Microsoft had illegally acquired and maintained its dominance in the browser market through the use of anticompetitively exclusionary practices. As Professor First points out,[16] Bork explained himself in a White Paper that he issued in July 1998, where he analyzed why Microsoft's efforts to integrate its own browser, Internet Explorer, into the Windows operating system and

---

15 *Id.* at 1017.

16 *See* First, *supra* note 14, at 1030–36.

thereby push its competitor Netscape out of the market were not just exclusionary, but anticompetitively so. Professor First explained why that analysis was sound.

11. The government's case against Microsoft was all about exclusionary practices; it was never a case that attacked monopoly power as an evil in itself. Firms invest in exclusionary practices because they are hoping for a positive return on that investment – the power to charge supracompetitive prices and keep rivals at bay. And in the *Microsoft* case, as in many, the resources available to the two sides – predator and prey – were asymmetric.

12. Few people other than Microsoft would have contested the proposition that Microsoft had monopoly power in the PC operating system market at the pertinent time: it had 97% of original equipment manufacturer installations. The real action in the case centered on the evaluation of Microsoft's market tactics: was it just engaged in tough but fair competition, or was it violating Sherman Act section 2? Here is Professor First's take on that question:

> Bork argues that Microsoft had waged an "exclusionary war" along two lines. One was to build the browser into the operating system and not allow the OEMs to remove it. The other was to use a "complex web of restrictive agreements" to block the entry or growth of rivals. To reach his conclusion that this conduct was exclusionary or predatory, Bork then uses the approach he adopted in *The Antitrust Paradox*. He looks at the purpose and effect of the conduct, the potential for efficiency gains, the costs of the tactics to Microsoft, and the potential profitability of predation.[17]

13. In coming to these conclusions, Bork relied on Microsoft's internal documents as evidence of forbidden intent, as well as on the lack of any discernible efficiency justification for Microsoft's course of conduct.

14. The *Microsoft* case breathed new life into the exclusionary-act branch of antitrust law. The D.C. Circuit ultimately agreed with the government (and Bork) that Microsoft had monopoly power, and that it had unlawfully used that power to exclude Netscape and others from the market.[18] The exclusionary effect was hard to deny. Both Microsoft's contracting practices and the way that it integrated Internet Explorer into Windows lacked any efficiency justification and excluded rivals. Microsoft did all this with a proven intent to exclude.

15. Professor First distilled "four valuable lessons" from all this.[19] First, "exclusionary conduct exists," and "[e]xclusionary practices are properly

---

17   *Id.* at 1031–32 (footnote omitted).
18   United States v. Microsoft Corp., 147 F.3d 935 (D.C. Cir. 1998).
19   First, *supra* note 14, at 1042.

within the bounds of antitrust enforcement."[20] Second, it is possible, though not necessarily easy, to distinguish exclusionary conduct from "hard competition." That task will usually require a deep dive into the facts and the relevant economic theory. Third, "intent is useful," though Professor First cautions that there may be more possibilities than just the dichotomy between specific intent to exclude and acceptable competitive behavior. Finally, "institutions matter,"[21] especially the courts and the marketplace. Bork argued in the end that structural remedies were preferable to behavioral remedies (though he largely lost that battle), because courts are ill-suited to monitor business practices.

16. Perhaps to remind the reader that the acknowledgment of exclusionary conduct as within the scope of Sherman Act section 2 is just the beginning of the analysis, not the end, Professor First ends his article by highlighting a few key issues still up for grabs:

   – Should coerced agreements be more suspect than bargained-for agreements, because the former are less likely to reflect efficiency considerations?

   – What constitutes an efficiency justification?

   – Clarify that exclusion is bad not only because it produces or protects monopoly profits, but also because it dampens innovation.[22]

17. Swimming against the general current on both sides of the aisle, Professor First draws the lesson that once the rhetoric is swept aside, Bork was taking just as political a view of the antitrust laws as anyone else; he posits that there is less distance between Bork's "Chicago" views and mainstream antitrust than is often supposed:

   > Bork favored the still valid antitrust philosophy of free entry, open markets, and vigorous competition. What antitrust advocate could quarrel with this philosophy? Bork quite properly feared the misuse of government power to exclude competitors. But the Sherman Act's passage primarily reflected concern about private economic power. Reclaiming exclusion as a key problem in antitrust would go a long way to addressing that concern. It would even be consistent with Bork's still valid view of antitrust's philosophy.[23]

18. Perhaps this is the rapprochement that the current resurgence of interest in antitrust needs to pursue, if it is to succeed in its effort to make antitrust effective and relevant to 21st-century markets.

---

20   *Id.*

21   *Id.*

22   *Id.* at 1043.

23   *Id.* at 1044–45 (footnotes and quotation marks omitted).

II. Abusive High Prices

19. The question whether high prices alone should be enough to prove a violation of section 2 has bedeviled antitrust scholars practically since the statute was passed. On the one hand, the monopolistic (or cartel) overcharge is the starting point for any damages remedy in an antitrust case. Although some would argue that the real harm from monopoly is the deadweight loss that accompanies monopolistic pricing, many others view the transfer of wealth from the consumer to the monopolist as equally concerning. On the other hand, as Judge Learned Hand put it so eloquently in the *Alcoa* decision,[24] "the [Sherman] Act does not mean to condemn the resultant of those very forces which it is its prime object to foster: *finis opus coronat*. The successful competitor, having been urged to compete, must not be turned upon when he wins."[25] Other countries and regions, notably the European Union, have not been as reluctant to deem excessive prices a violation of their abuse-of-dominance rules – indeed, article 102 of the Treaty on the Functioning of the European Union specifies that one prohibited abusive practice is "directly or indirectly imposing unfair purchase or selling prices."[26]

20. For a long time, it appeared that U.S. law was settled on the proposition that more is needed: despite the arguments that could be mustered in favor of the European approach, courts and Congress alike thought that the greater evil would be interference with market forces, and that those same market forces could be counted on eventually to undermine whatever monopoly prices existed in the market.[27] Of late, however, there has been a new round of criticism of this laissez-faire attitude, and Professor First has been at the forefront of those new voices. His article on drug pricing, "Excessive Drug Prices as an Antitrust Violation,"[28] is a case in point.

21. The article begins with some well-known anecdotes about ballooning drug price increases measured in orders of magnitude.[29] It then notes

---

[24] United States v. Aluminum Co. of America, 148 F.2d 416 (2d Cir. 1945).

[25] *Id.* at 430.

[26] Consolidated Version of the Treaty on the Functioning of the European Union, art. 102, May 9, 2008, 2008 O.J. (C 115) 89.

[27] *See, e.g.*, Pacific Bell Telephone Co. v. linkLine Communications, Inc., 555 U.S. 438, 447–48 (2009), *see also* Frédérique Daudret-John & François Souty, *Price Squeeze: The US Supreme Court, in a ruling which reversed a lower court following US DOJ amicus brief arguments, confirms and extends its conservative line of decisions rejecting private claims and thus limiting antitrust suits and gives further precisions on its previous rulings on the relationships between competition law and telecommunications sector regulation regarding "price squeeze" aimed at driving out competitor of the market* (Pacific Bell Telephone), Concurrences no. 2-2009, art. No. 25909; Verizon Communications, Inc. v. Law Offices of Curtis V. Trinko, LLP, 540 U.S. 398, 407 (2003), *see* Frédérique Daudret-John & François Souty, *United States of America: The US Supreme Court rules on the current relationship between antitrust law and sectoral regulation in the telecommunications sector* (Trinko), Concurrences no. 1-2004, art. no. 1603.

[28] Harry First, *Excessive Drug Pricing as an Antitrust Violation*, 82 Antitrust L.J. 701 (2019).

[29] *Id.* at 701 n.1.

that among the many solutions people have proposed that would curb or restrain those prices, antitrust is conspicuously absent from the list,[30] aside from its role in the reverse-payment phenomenon that sometimes arises when a branded pharmaceutical product goes generic.[31] Professor First thinks that antitrust should not be dismissed so easily. He acknowledges that the "conventional wisdom is that the U.S. antitrust laws do not forbid high prices *simpliciter*,"[32] but he then posits that "we are not forever condemned to that result."[33] This is not as foreign a concept as it may seem at first glance, he contends. For example, the common law imposed duties of reasonable pricing in what it called the public or common callings, such as innkeepers, carriers, ferrymen, and surgeons. Later, as public electric, water, and gas utilities developed – all areas that were thought to be natural monopolies and thus not suitable for antitrust regulation – regulatory agencies were created to ensure fair pricing. Other efforts to control high prices have included outright wage and price controls (now universally maligned), such as those imposed during the Nixon administration[34] and rent-control laws in many cities.

22. Professor First acknowledges that the Supreme Court has said that "the mere possession of monopoly power, and the concomitant charging of monopoly prices, is not only not unlawful; it is an important element of the free-market system."[35] But, with lawyerly precision, he contends in the drug-pricing article that the Court has never explicitly said that excessive pricing *cannot* satisfy the monopolistic conduct requirement. He distinguishes *linkLine* as a case in which the wholesale-level firm had no duty to deal at all, and so the price term was irrelevant and, in any event, was not alleged to be predatory. He finds ambiguity in *Alcoa*. There, the Court focused on "the exclusionary impact of Alcoa's price squeeze on downstream competition in the aluminum sheet market."[36] That reliance on exclusion made it unnecessary to reach the "price alone" issue; presumably, he is arguing that everything the Court had to say about the need for more than high prices was *dicta*.

23. Although Professor First's position is quite unorthodox, he offers interesting support for it. For example, he notes that in standard essential

---

30 *Id.* at 702–703.

31 *See, e.g.*, FTC v. Actavis, Inc., 570 U.S. 136 (2013), *see* Jean-Christophe Roda, *United States: The U.S. Supreme Court issues a landmark decisions in relation to "reverse payment" settlements and rules that such agreements should be subject to "rule of reason" analysis (*Actavis*)*, CONCURRENCES no. 3-2013, art. no. 54214

32 First, *supra* note 28, at 704.

33 *Id.*

34 *See* Exec. Order No. 11,615 (Aug. 15, 1971), issued pursuant to the Economic Stabilization Act of 1970 and imposing a 90-day freeze on wages and prices in an effort to control inflation.

35 *Trinko*, 540 U.S. at 407.

36 First, *supra* note 28, at 714, citing *Alcoa*, 148 F.2d at 430–31.

patent (SEP) cases, courts regularly create mechanisms to ensure that the holder of the SEP charges only a reasonable licensing fee for those who wish to use the patent. This is known as the FRAND standard (fair, reasonable, and non-discriminatory); it openly evaluates royalty rates to ensure that the patent holder receives no more than fair compensation, not whatever the market would bear. Another area in which the law takes into account possible price effects is merger enforcement. If, post-merger, the new firm would be able to raise prices without losing too many customers, the authorities will challenge that transaction and seek either to stop it altogether or to restructure the business entity so that competition can be preserved. In short, Professor First rightly points out that pricing level considerations do sneak into U.S. antitrust doctrine now and again. Why not in section 2 cases, too, given the harm to consumers that results from excessive prices?

24. Many would answer that question by saying that it is just too hard to pick a perfect price level – the Goldilocks point where it is not so high as to be abusive, and not so low as to be predatory. Professor First has an answer for them, too. He suggests, using the drug market as his example, that control of abusive pricing should occur only if a rule-of-reason-style methodology indicated that such a measure was suitable. He points to several factors that are especially telling. The first assumes that there has been an acquisition that was not challenged. If, after that acquisition, the price of one or more drugs spikes, then action to lower the price to its pre-existing level might be appropriate. He gives the example of Daraprim, which cost $13.50 per tablet before the company that made it was sold to Turing Pharmaceuticals, but after the acquisition the price shot up to $750 per tablet. This is as clear an example as one could find for "testing a Section 2 theory based on excessive pricing as exploitative conduct, improperly transferring surplus from consumers to producers."[37] Perhaps things would have been different if Turing had offered some pro-competitive or efficiency justification for the increase, but nothing of the sort was in the record.

25. Another sign of exploitation the article suggests is a pattern of gradual price increases in a brand-protected market such as the one for EpiPens – auto-injector devices used for emergency treatment of a violent allergic reaction known as anaphylaxis. Over the course of a decade or so, the price of these vital devices increased at a rate that could not be explained by anything but a desire to squeeze as much out of consumers as possible. In 2007, a two-pack of EpiPens sold for $100; by 2016, the price for the same two items was $600. Before condemning the owner's actions, Professor First would conduct a full rule-of-reason analysis of the pricing, the structural barriers to competition in the market, and

---

37   First, *supra* note 28, at 728.

possible efficiencies. Perhaps everything is compatible with the antitrust laws, but perhaps it is not. But, as Professor First points out, in a world where high prices get a pass, we will never know.

III. Antitrust and the Tech Giants

26. There can be little doubt that a great deal of the renewed interest in antitrust stems directly from the growth of the "Tech Giants" – Alphabet (i.e., Google), Amazon, Apple, Meta (i.e., Facebook), and Microsoft. This is not the first time scholars and practitioners alike have wondered whether the old 1890 antitrust laws have met their match. Granted, antitrust litigation no longer moves at the glacial pace that characterized the 1950s and 1960s – notoriously, it took more than 20 years to resolve all the issues that arose out of Procter & Gamble's 1957 acquisition of Clorox.[38] The Microsoft litigation, discussed earlier, moved like lightning in comparison.[39] Filed in 1998, it was largely resolved three years later, in 2001, although disputes over the scope of the consent decree dragged on for quite a while. And the efficiency of the administrative or judicial process is highly relevant, as there is little point in a challenge that depends on market conditions that have disappeared by the time the challenge has been adjudicated. Put differently, if the market will correct itself before the law can intervene, intervention by courts or administrative agencies is unnecessary.

27. But once again, Professor First has pointed out that the real picture is more complicated, and that it would be an overreaction to think that such a pessimistic view of the capacity of the law is always warranted. Not every case is a hard case, and the very existence of enforcement actions has a powerful effect on business compliance programs and general understandings of what is permissible and what is not. It is fair to wonder, as Professor First has, whether the stark increase in concentration in industry after industry in the United States can be traced directly to the fact that the government did not file a single section 2 case between its 1998 complaint in *Microsoft* and the new round of challenges that

---

38 Procter & Gamble (P&G) acquired Clorox in 1957. FTC v. Procter & Gamble Co., 386 U.S. 568 (1967). The FTC challenged the acquisition under section 7 of the Clayton Act right away. *See* Procter & Gamble v. FTC, 358 F.2d 74, 76 (6th Cir. 1966). A hearing examiner for the Commission held extensive hearings. Initially, the examiner found that the acquisition violated the law. On appeal, the Commission set aside that finding and remanded for further fact findings. The examiner obliged, and on the second appeal to the Commission it found that the acquisition violated the law (by now it was 1962). P&G then appealed to the Sixth Circuit, which in 1966 ruled in P&G's favor. But that did not end the case, because the Supreme Court granted the Commission's petition for a writ of certiorari and in 1967 reversed the 6th Circuit and found that the acquisition violated the law. After that, follow-on private litigation took place, as the antitrust laws permit. That litigation was not resolved until 1981, when on its second trip to the Ninth Circuit, the court held that the record supported a finding that Purex was not injured by the effects of the acquisition (which had long since been unwound) and that the district court did not abuse its discretion by refusing to reopen the record.

39 *See* 252 F.3d 34 (D.C. Cir. 2001).

began roughly in 2020. This "desert," he contends, has created its own problems. It is far easier to take prophylactic action against mergers that are likely to lead to substantial market power than it is to fix the problem afterward. If a given merger takes the market from six active participants to five, that too poses serious problems. That is true even if the remaining five firms refrain from entering into horizontal agreements on price or output. Oligopoly is one of the most persistent problems in antitrust. It is largely unreachable, because the lack of anything resembling an agreement prevents the use of Sherman Act section 1, and the unlikelihood of a successful attempt to monopolize rules out the use of Sherman Act section 2.

28. The government does, however, have one powerful tool at its disposal: the ability to obtain injunctive relief against anticompetitive practices. And government suits for preliminary injunctions move along at a much faster pace than a private action for damages. A host of problems are off the table when the government is the plaintiff: no one needs to worry about antitrust standing;[40] no one has to anticipate perverse incentives that might exist if a rival tried to use the antitrust laws themselves as an exclusionary device;[41] and the economic complexities of computing damages are off the table. What the United States does not have, in contrast with the EU, is the ability to impose civil fines on monopolists. That is simply a feature of the statutes in force in both places. One could argue that fines are unsatisfactory because the target firm may view them as just a cost of doing business, but the fines that the European Commission has been levying against Google, for instance, seem large enough to get any firm's attention.[42]

29. The final case that Professor First has discussed in his writings is one that represents the application of the antitrust laws to a more traditional market – financial services. The case is *Ohio v. American Express Co.*,[43] which he brands as "one of the worst opinions ever written by the

---

[40] *See* Brunswick Corp. v. Pueblo Bowl-O-Mat, Inc., 429 U.S. 477, 489 (1977) (private plaintiff must "prove… injury of the type the antitrust laws were intended to prevent and that flows from that which makes defendants' acts unlawful"); Associated Gen. Contractors v. California State Council of Carpenters, 459 U.S. 519, 539 (1983) (no standing for union that was neither a competitor nor a consumer in the market in which trade was restrained).

[41] *See, e.g.*, Cargill, Inc. v. Monfort of Colorado, Inc., 479 U.S. 104, 116–17 (1986) (rejecting a competitor's claim that its loss of profits to a competitor is cognizable under the antitrust laws in a suit by that competitor, but rejecting the argument of the government urging the Court to adopt a strict rule denying competitors standing to challenge acquisitions on predatory pricing theories).

[42] Barron's reports that the EU's biggest fine ever was the €4.3 billion assessed against Google for abusing the dominant position of its Android Mobile operating system. *See EU's Five Biggest Antitrust Fines on Big Tech*, BARRON'S (Mar. 4, 2024), https://www.barrons.com/news/eu-s-five-biggest-antitrust-fines-on-big-tech-62979fed. That was later reduced to €4.125 billion – still a hefty sum. And that was not its only fine against Google. It also fined it €2.4 billion in a case focusing on Google's shopping service. *Id.* Meanwhile, the Commission fined Apple €1.8 billion in a case involving its music streaming services. *Id.*

[43] 585 U.S. 529 (2018), *see* Walid Chaiehloudj, *United States: The US Supreme Court rules that the credit card market is a multisided market and that anti-steering clauses do not have anticompetitive effects on this market (*American Express*)*, CONCURRENCES no. 4-2018, art. no. 88296.

Supreme Court."[44] Readers will recall that the case involved the legality of American Express's rules forbidding merchants that subscribed to its credit card from steering their own customers to alternate credit cards (Visa, MasterCard, Discover) that charged a lower processing fee to the merchant. This created a two-sided market, where each side depended on the other's performance. One side was the relationship between Amex and the merchants, who, as noted, had to pay a fee to Amex for credit processing services, and the other side was the relationship between the merchants and their retail customers, who wanted the convenience of paying with the credit card(s) they carried. Taking both sides of that market into account, the Supreme Court found nothing anticompetitive about Amex's rules. Over the dissent of four Justices, the Court found that the United States had failed to prove any anticompetitive effects from Amex's antisteering rules. It also commented that the price charged on either side of the market reflected only the pertinent demand elasticity, not market power. The majority concluded with the argument that plaintiffs had not offered any evidence that the price of credit-card transactions undertaken with the antisteering rules in place was any higher than it would have been in the absence of such rules.[45]

30. To put it bluntly, Professor First found this to be nonsense. He stated that there were "a lot of reasons to criticize [the decision], including the fact that it was just factually untrue. Amex raised their fees to merchants by quite a lot – billions – and never passed a penny on to consumers on the 'other side.'"[46] In his view, the Court simply defined away any problem with Amex's practices. The only remaining question was (and is) whether the Supreme Court will limit the *Amex* decision to platforms such as credit-processing services and consumer card usage, or if it will take an expansive view under which almost all markets have some two-sided features.

IV. International Antitrust Rules?

31. Perhaps one of the reasons why Professor First has always understood that it is possible to have a competition law that takes into account not only consumer welfare but also anticompetitively exclusionary practices is his engagement with the international aspect of this field. He is particularly well versed in the Japanese Antimonopoly Law, passed in 1947 in

---

44 Harry First et al., *Panel One: How Did We Get Here? A Review of Major Antitrust Cases, Questions, and Controversies*, 28 Fordham J. Corp. & Fin. L. 300, 317 (2023).

45 585 U.S. at 547–48.

46 First et al., *supra* note 44, at 317.

the immediate aftermath of Japan's defeat in World War II.[47] The common wisdom told a story in which the Japanese law was pushed onto Japan by the American occupation forces, and that its lackluster enforcement was a result of the fact that it was a poor fit for Japanese culture. Professor First resists that tale. Insisting on the relevance of original intent, both for Japan and for the United States, he sets the stage with a rich set of materials about both the business and regulatory culture that prevailed in Japan before the war, going all the way back to the 17th-century shogunate. Japan's pre-war economy was dominated by the zaibatsu, powerful conglomerates that participated in a wide variety of markets. Cartels were also commonplace, as was an industrial policy that emphasized exports.

32. That was backdrop for the devastation of the Japanese economy that followed the war. Eager to rebuild, Japan was willing to participate in discussions with the United States about economic issues, including the development of an antitrust law. The article goes on to provide a detailed history of the drafting of the Antimonopoly Law, with an emphasis on the genuine Japanese contributions during that process. In the end, Professor First contends, "Japan's government was able to move from the original proposal, an ambitious U.S.-style piece of legislation, to one that was more suited to Japan's economic ideas and its view of the proper roles of government and free markets in controlling economic decisions."[48] In so doing, it passed a law that openly embodied goals "in terms broader than economic efficiency" – it also reflected a political philosophy based on freedom of choice.[49] Included within this idea was a commitment to prohibit "conduct that might exclude firms from markets."[50]

33. At the end of the article, Professor First offers a critical thought about the prospect of any future international antitrust regime. Substantive agreement is plainly important, but perhaps even more critical is an understanding of how the institutions of competition-law enforcement operate.[51] A set of substantive rules that work well, for example, when a government agency is the only entity authorized to intervene, may not work as well if private enforcement stands side-by-side with government measures, as it does in the United States.

34. He made a related point in an article about the international *Vitamins* cartel.[52] There, he rejected the idea that a formal international agreement

---

47 *See* Harry First, *Antitrust in Japan: The Original Intent*, 9 Pac. Rim L. & Pol'y. J. 1, 2 & n.4 (2000) (note 4 gives the full citation to the law from the Japanese sources).

48 *Id.* at 68.

49 *Id.* at 29.

50 *Id.*

51 *Id.* at 71.

52 Harry First, *The Vitamins Case: Cartel Prosecutions and the Coming of International Competition Law*, 68 Antitrust L.J. 711 (2001).

was necessary for the achievement of an effective world trading system in which competition laws are observed.[53] The reason why is simple: such a system is already evolving, he argues, "even without the formal adoption of legal principles and without the establishment of any new enforcement mechanism."[54] It is a system based on implicit consensus and explicit effective enforcement. This system has been strengthened, I would add, by the efforts of the voluntary International Competition Network (a body that had yet to come into existence at the time of the *Vitamins* article). In this matter, as in many others, Professor First has supported a position that was somewhat unpopular for a time, but that ultimately won the day.[55]

35. Apart from the areas I have discussed thus far, there is much more that Professor First has contributed that must be left with a quick nod. He has worried, for example, about a "democracy deficit" that has slowly grown.[56] "The modern Supreme Court," he points out, "has come to be unmoored from any sense of legislative direction of judicial decision making when it comes to interpreting the antitrust laws."[57] (One may wonder whether the Supreme Court's enthusiasm for the common-law method of developing this area will survive its recent insistence that agencies exercise only those powers clearly delegated to them.[58]) Congress's disengagement may have allowed political influences to fade, and as the political salience of the field has diminished, antitrust has quietly become a technocracy. Maybe this is fine, but Professor First does not think so. He posits that there may be a vital link between free people and free markets. Centuries ago, the common law worried about a person's exclusion from the market because such a person might become a "charge" on society. Perhaps they were on to something.

36. Another of Professor First's ideas that must await further development is his suggestion that the one-size-fits-all antitrust law we presently have might not be up to the job. Instead, writing with Professor Spencer Weber Waller, he has suggested that the time might be right for "bespoke"

---

53   *Id.* at 712.

54   *Id.*

55   The World Trade Organization and other bodies worked for years to see if they could develop a multilateral agreement on competition before finally moving on to other approaches. *See, e.g.*, Sanoussi Bilial & Marcelo Olarreaga, *Competition Policy and the WTO: Is There a Need for a Multilateral Agreement?* (Eur. Inst. of Pub. Adm., Working Paper 98/W/02, 1998), http://aei.pitt.edu/600/1/98w02.pdf.

56   First, *supra* note 28, at 701.

57   Harry First & Spencer Weber Waller, *Antitrust's Democracy Deficit*, 81 FORDHAM L. REV. 2543, 2548–49 (2013).

58   *E.g.*, Biden v. Nebraska, 143 S. Ct. 2355 (2023) (striking down Secretary of Education's student loan forgiveness program); West Virginia v. EPA, 597 U.S. 697 (2022) (striking down EPA's emissions caps on greenhouse gases); Loper Bright Enterprises v. Raimondo, 144 S. Ct. 2244 (2024) (overruling Chevron and thus eliminating court's duty to defer to certain agency interpretations of law), *see* Logan Breed, Chuck Loughlin & Ilana Kattan, *The US Supreme Court overturns Chevron deference doctrine removing the requirement that courts defer to agency interpretations of ambiguous statutes (*Loper Bright / Raimond*)*, E-COMPETITIONS June 2024, art. no. 119498.

antitrust.⁵⁹ This goes somewhat counter to the idea that antitrust law has been flexible enough to weather profound changes in the economy, from the railroad era, through the Great Depression and World War II, to the Internet revolution of more recent years. (It is hard to believe that the iPhone was introduced in early 2007, just 17 years ago. One source estimates that as of 2023, there are 16.8 billion mobile devices worldwide.⁶⁰) Some would argue, however, that the challenges posed by the digital world demand tailored solutions, and that there are threats to the rule of law itself that require more focused attention. On the other hand, Professor First points out that bespoke antitrust law might be inefficient and might pose its own threats to the integrity of the law. For now, it is fair to say that he is not pushing for this approach.

V. Conclusion

37. The beauty of academic freedom lies in the ability to think for oneself, put ideas out in the marketplace, and see how they fare. Sometimes they will be mainstream, but sometimes, as Professor First's long arc of antitrust scholarship shows, they will be more in the nature of the loyal opposition. Professor First's contributions to the field of antitrust have illustrated that independence of thought. He is not one to jump on the nearest bandwagon, whether it is driven by people with whom he is ideologically aligned or those with whom he has significant disagreements. He has given us a provocative and helpful perspective on this vital area of the law, and fortunately he will continue to do so for a long time to come.

---

59   Harry First & Spencer Weber Waller, *Bespoke Antitrust*, 68 S. Dak. L. Rev. 468 (2023).

60   *See* Frederica Laricchia, Number of mobile devices worldwide 2020–2025, Statista (Mar. 10, 2023), https://www.statista.com/statistics/245501/multiple-mobile-device-ownership-worldwide/.

Academic "Capture"? The Hidden Costs of Corporate Funding in Competition Policy Research and Proposed Remedies

IOANNIS LIANOS[*]

University College London

Abstract

This paper examines how corporate funding influences competition policy research across both forensic economics applications and academic research settings, ultimately shaping competition law design and implementation. The analysis builds on the premise that competition economics encompasses two distinct but increasingly interrelated communities: forensic economists working in public and private sectors who apply economic principles to concrete competition law enforcement cases, and academic economists who generate broadly applicable economic knowledge through theoretical work, empirical studies, and experimental methods. The analysis then proceeds in four parts. First, it traces the emergence of economic experts and consultants as a distinct profession, explaining how this development brought issues of bias in economic research to the forefront, initially within forensic economics presented

---

[*] Professor of Global Competition Law and Public Policy and co-director Centre for Law, Economics and Society, UCL Faculty of Laws; member of the UK Competition Appeal Tribunal; senior fellow, CeBIL, University of Copenhagen. The author received funding in 2024 through the Novo Nordisk Foundation Grant for a scientifically independent International Collaborative Bioscience Innovation & Law Programme (Inter-CeBIL programme – grant no. NNF23SA0087056) for research on bioscience innovation and law. The author has no other conflict of interest to declare. Any views expressed are personal. Many thanks to Todd Davies and Filippo Lancieri for excellent comments. The paper partly draws on Ioannis Lianos, *"Judging Economists": Economic Expertise in Competition Litigation: A European View*, in THE REFORM OF EC COMPETITION LAW: NEW CHALLENGES 185 (Ioannis Lianos & Ioannis Kokkoris eds., 2010).

in litigation. Second, it examines various forms of expert bias, extending beyond the market for applied economic expertise in competition regulation to encompass the broader marketplace of competition economics ideas. Third, it explores how these biases may stem not only from market dynamics but also from the concentrated structure of competition economics expertise, considering both supply and demand factors, as well as strategic efforts to influence competition policy discourse. Finally, it evaluates existing tools for containing bias and capture in forensic economics expertise markets and in the marketplace of knowledge in competition economics and proposes regulatory reforms for the future, including mandatory funding disclosure by large corporate funders and a matching of funds requirement to align corporate incentives with the public interest in unbiased research.

I. Introduction

1. The 2007 financial crisis triggered severe criticism of the economics profession on two fronts: its failure to predict the impending economic collapse and its role in enabling the crisis through decades of advocating deregulation.[1] Despite these general criticisms, the mid to end-2000s marked the high period of the dominance of mainstream (neoclassical and neoliberal) economics in competition law enforcement, not only in the United States, where they played a prominent role since at least the early 1980s,[2] but also in Europe and other parts of the world.[3] The 2010s witnessed, however, a mounting criticism of mainstream neoclassical economics' normative role in competition law. This criticism centred on two key failures: competition economics' ineffectiveness in addressing rising economic concentration and market power,[4] and its contribution to what Harry First termed "antitrust's democracy deficit."[5]

2. In a seminal piece published in 2013, Professor Harry First and his co-author, Professor Spencer Weber Waller, noted how the antitrust system was captured by lawyers and economists "advancing their own self-referential goals, free of political control and economic accountability."[6] This self-interested

---

[1] See, inter alia, David Colander et al., *The Financial Crisis and the Systemic Failure of the Economic Profession*, 21 CRITICAL REV. 249 (2009); Angus Deaton, *Rethinking My Economics*, IMF F&D MAG. 20 (Mar. 2024), https://www.imf.org/en/Publications/fandd/issues/2024/03/Symposium-Rethinking-Economics-Angus-Deaton.

[2] Harry First, *Is Antitrust "Law"?*, 10 ANTITRUST 9 (1995).

[3] See, inter alia, Lars-Hendrik Röller, *Economic Analysis and Competition Policy Enforcement in Europe*, in MODELLING EUROPEAN MERGERS 11 (Peter A. G. van Bergeijk & Erik Kloosterhuis eds., 2005); Giorgio Monti, *EC Competition Law: The Dominance of Economic Analysis?*, in THE DEVELOPMENT OF COMPETITION LAW 3 (Roger Zäch, Andreas Heinemann & Andreas Kellerhals eds., 2010).

[4] THOMAS PHILIPPON, THE GREAT REVERSAL: HOW AMERICA GAVE UP ON FREE MARKETS (2019); JAN EECKHOUT, THE PROFIT PARADOX: HOW THRIVING FIRMS THREATEN THE FUTURE OF WORK (2021). A different criticism came from the right, with the so-called dynamic Schumpeterian approaches: *see* J. Gregory Sidak & David Teece, *Dynamic Competition in Antitrust Law*, 5 J. COMPETITION L. & ECON. 581 (2009). See also Herbert Hovenkamp, *The Looming Crisis in Antitrust Economics*, 101 B.U. L. REV. 489 (2021).

[5] Harry First & Spencer Weber Waller, *Antitrust's Democracy Deficit*, 81 FORDHAM L. REV. 2543 (2013).

[6] *Id.* at 2544.

activity has morphed the law into an "unbalanced system" that "puts too much control in the hands of technical experts, moving antitrust enforcement too far away from its democratic roots."[7] These calls for a more democratic antitrust, eventually leading to new directions as to the role of technocracy in setting and/or implementing the goals of competition law, have not been isolated; indeed, the interaction of democracy with competition law became a topic of intense debate among competition law, but also economics, scholars.[8]

3. The push to realign antitrust law with democratic institutions stems largely from eroding public trust in technocrats who stand accused of hijacking competition law to serve their own interests (and to increase their rents).[9] This scepticism has been fuelled by the emergence of a lucrative global market for technical (mostly economic) expertise in competition law, which has expanded to more than 130 jurisdictions worldwide. The role these relatively few experts deemed qualified to intervene in highly complex antitrust cases play in law enforcement and policy-design has motivated research on their role in shaping competition policy and their influence over its implementation, thus fuelling the concerns expressed about the "democratic deficit" of antitrust.[10] It also raises the spectre of their "capture" by the same corporate interests competition laws aim to regulate.[11] As Zingales astutely noted a decade ago, "why academic economists think that the regulators are generally captured, while they cannot stand even the thought that this might happen to one of them?"[12]

4. The alleged "capture" of antitrust policy by consultants and corporate-funded academic experts has garnered significant media attention, with numerous press reports highlighting anecdotal evidence of this concerning

---

7   *Id.*

8   *See, inter alia,* Ioannis Lianos, *Polycentric Competition Law*, 71 CURRENT LEGAL PROBS. 161 (2018); Daniel A. Crane, *Antitrust as an Instrument of Democracy*, 72 DUKE L.J. ONLINE 21 (2022); Elias Deutscher, *The Competition-Democracy Nexus Unpacked – Competition Law, Republican Liberty, and Democracy*, 41 Y.B. EUR. L. 197 (2022); Viktoria H. S. E. Robertson, *Antitrust, Big Tech, and Democracy: A Research Agenda*, 67 ANTITRUST BULL. 259 (2022); Todd Davies & Spencer Cohen, *Error Costs, Platform Regulation, and Democracy* (UCL Rsch. Paper Series, No. 2/2025, Sept. 15, 2024), https://ssrn.com/abstract=4888631.

9   A separate but connected argument is the ideological drive for the use of a certain kind of economics in competition law enforcement, exemplified by the rise of the Chicago School that has led to a decline of antitrust enforcement in the US: Filippo Lancieri, Eric A. Posner & Luigi Zingales, The Political Economy of the Decline of Antitrust Enforcement in the United States (Mar. 20, 2023), https://ssrn.com/abstract=4011235.

10 Most recently, *see* Jonathan B. Baker, *How Economists Influence Antitrust: The Contributions of Tim Bresnahan, Janusz Ordover, Steve Salop, and Bobby Willig*, J. ANTITRUST ENF'T (2024), jnae049, https://doi.org/10.1093/jaenfo/jnae049.

11 *See* the "capture theory that views economic analysis as produced and deployed in the interests of big business," as exposed by Baker, *supra* note 10, and the references included. There is a broader concern about the influence of economic oligarchy on the production of knowledge: *see* Emma Saunders-Hastings, *Plutocratic Philanthropy*, 80 J. POL. 149 (2018); Marianne Bertrand, Matilde Bombardini, Raymond Fisman, Brad Hackinen & Francesco Trebbi, *Hall of Mirrors: Corporate Philanthropy and Strategic Advocacy*, 136 Q. J. ECON. 2413 (2021). Regulatory capture by corporate interests is a well-known field in economics literature: *see* MANCUR OLSON, THE LOGIC OF COLLECTIVE ACTION: PUBLIC GOODS AND THE THEORY OF GROUPS (1965); George J. Stigler, *Theory of Economic Regulation*, 2 BELL J. ECON. & MGMT. SCI. 3 (1971), also discussed by Luigi Zingales, *Preventing Economists' Capture, in* PREVENTING REGULATORY CAPTURE: SPECIAL INTEREST INFLUENCE AND HOW TO LIMIT IT 124 (Daniel Carpenter & David A. Moss eds., 2013).

12 Zingales, *supra* note 11, at 151 (noting the parallelism between the forces used to explain regulatory capture and those that can capture economists).

trend,[13] comments by the economic profession,[14] but also from the leadership of competition enforcement institutions.[15] More generally, the risk of biases of different sorts, particularly material bias, has been a recurrent theme, not just in competition economics but more generally regarding research in economics,[16] but also in other fields.[17] However, the distinctive prominence of economic analysis in antitrust law, combined with economists' leadership in redefining the field's objectives since the 1980s, has fundamentally transformed both the production and governance of competition-related economic knowledge.

5. Research on the role of economists in competition law has so far focused on the contribution of individuals, mostly academic economists, who have also been active in the enforcement of competition law, as enforcers and consultants to competition agencies or private parties.[18] The emergence of forensic economics and its associated market for competition expertise has profoundly reshaped both the academic study of competition economics and the development of competition law and policy, though this transformation has received insufficient scholarly attention. As competition law has increasingly embraced a "more economic approach," forensic economists' methodologies, research questions, and operational concepts have extended their influence well

---

13 *See, inter alia*, Brody Mullins & Jack Nicas, *Paying Professors: Inside Google's Academic Influence Campaign*, WALL ST. J. (July 14, 2017), https://www.wsj.com/articles/paying-professors-inside-googles-academic-influence-campaign-1499785286; *See Google Academics Inc.*, TECH TRANSPARENCY PROJECT (July 11, 2017) https://www.techtransparencyproject.org/articles/google-academics-inc; Mark Bridge, *Google Pays Academics Millions for Key Support*, TIMES (July 13, 2017), https://www.thetimes.com/article/google-pays-academics-millions-for-key-support-tnb3zgbxp; Noam Scheiber, *When Scholars Collaborate With Tech Companies, How Reliable Are the Findings?*, N.Y. TIMES (July 12, 2020), https://www.nytimes.com/2020/07/12/business/economy/uber-lyft-drivers-wages.htm; Daisuke Wakabayashi, *Big Tech Funds a Think Tank Pushing for Fewer Rules. For Big Tech*, N.Y. TIMES (July 24, 2020), https://www.nytimes.com/2020/07/24/technology/global-antitrust-institute-google-amazon-qualcomm.html; Brody Mullins, *The Hidden Life of Google's Secret Weapon*, WALL ST. J. (June 6, 2024), https://www.wsj.com/us-news/law/google-lawyer-secret-weapon-joshua-wright-c98d5a31; Peter Cory, *For Economists, Defending Big Business Can Be Big Business*, N.Y. TIMES (Sept. 20, 2024), https://www.nytimes.com/2024/09/20/opinion/economists-conflict-interest-kanter.html; James Panichi & Ryan Cropp, *Antitrust's Big Tobacco Moment*, INSIDE STORY (Sept. 25, 2024), https://insidestory.org.au/antitrusts-big-tobacco-moment. Citing these studies does not provide support or endorsement of their allegations regarding specific individuals or institutions, nor does it take position on the veracity of the facts put forward. Its purpose is only to describe the mounting concerns expressed by the media regarding corporate funding of academia involved in competition law enforcement.

14 *See, inter alia*, Zingales, *supra* note 11; Tommaso Valletti, *What Have the Consultants Ever Done for Us?* PROMARKET (Feb. 28, 2024) https://www.promarket.org/2024/02/28/what-have-the-consultants-ever-done-for-us/; Tommaso Valletti, Debate: *'Doubt Is Their Product' – The Difference between Research and Academic Lobbying*, PUB. MONEY & MGMT. 1 (2024), https://doi.org/10.1080/09540962.2024.2404249.

15 Assistant Attorney General Jonathan Kanter Delivers Remarks for the Fordham Competition Law Institute's 51st Annual Conference on International Antitrust Law and Policy (Sept. 12, 2024), https://www.justice.gov/opa/speech/assistant-attorney-general-jonathan-kanter-delivers-remarks-fordham-competition-law-0.

16 John P. A. Ioannidis, T. D. Stanley & Hristos Doucouliagos, *The Power of Bias in Economic Research*, 127 ECON. J. F236 (Oct. 2017), https://doi.org/10.1111/ecoj.12461; John Ioannidis & Chris Doucouliagos, *What's to Know about the Credibility of Empirical Economics?*, 27 J. ECON. SURVS. 997 (2013).

17 *See, inter alia*, Lisa Bero, *When Big Companies Fund Academic Research, the Truth Often Comes Last*, THE CONVERSATION (Oct. 2, 2019), https://theconversation.com/when-big-companies-fund-academic-research-the-truth-often-comes-last-119164; Sheldon Krimsky, *Do Financial Conflicts of Interest Bias Research?: An Inquiry into the "Funding Effect" Hypothesis*, 38 SCI. TECH. & HUM. VALUES 566 (2013).

18 *See* Baker, *supra* note 10.

beyond litigation, penetrating deeply into economic research performed at universities and public research centres. This evolution has effectively dissolved the traditional boundaries between the commercial market for economic expertise and the broader intellectual marketplace of competition economics knowledge through the operation of various feedback loops, corporate funding of academic research offering such a feedback loop mechanism.[19]

6. This study examines how the structure of these markets (the one for economic forensic expertise and the one for competition economics research), the links between them and the professional aspirations of some of the actors in the field have contributed to what Harry First and his co-author identified as competition law's democratic deficit. Capture by vested interests of the marketplace of knowledge/economic discourse in competition law and economics exemplifies this democratic deficit, the democratic ideal of self-government and autonomy being essential features of academia and scientific research.

7. The study does not question the need for the law to open up cognitively to social sciences, including the most recent advances in economics. This dynamic cognitive openness should be an important feature of competition law. It should not, however, compromise the goals of the law as set by the underlying social contract (as the law is normatively closed). Additionally, there should be democratic accountability regarding the choice of the economic theories and methodologies put forward in the enforcement of the law.[20] Building on First's foundational scholarship on the democracy/antitrust intersection, the study argues for reclaiming this democratic self-governing space of academia and knowledge production in competition policy research by restricting efforts of academic capture by the industry. While this analysis primarily addresses competition economists, its implications extend to other forms of expertise, including legal scholarship. The study honours First's academic legacy and extends his crucial insights into the relationship between antitrust and democracy.

8. The purpose of this work is to document and problematize the corporate funding of competition policy research, either in the field of its application (forensic economics) or in that of its generation (mostly academic research done in universities). My purpose is not to criticize the use of economic evidence and knowledge within the enforcement of the law, nor to chastise individual economists, most of them decent people motivated

---

19   See Ioannis Lianos, *The Emergence of Forensic Economics in Competition Law: Foundations for a Sociological Analysis* (CLES Working Paper Series No. 5/2012, Sept. 1, 2012), https://ssrn.com/abstract=2197025.

20   The need to combine cognitive/epistemic openness and normative closure has been a recurrent feature of my work: *see* IOANNIS LIANOS, LA TRANSFORMATION DU DROIT DE LA CONCURRENCE PAR LE RECOURS À L'ANALYSE ÉCONOMIQUE (2007); Ioannis Lianos, *Lost in Translation? Towards a Theory of Economic Transplants*, 62 CURRENT LEGAL PROBS. 346 (2009).

by noble goals.[21] Rather, adopting a sociological approach to analyse the different markets for economic expertise, the study points out the mechanisms by which the rising influence of corporate interests in the production and dissemination of knowledge concerning competition law enforcement may lead to these markets not functioning well. Follow suggestions for ways to improve the practice of competition policy and law enforcement to prevent or limit such alleged "capture," particularly the implementation of mandated disclosure of industry funding of competition research imposed not only on those funded but crucially on corporate funders, and a funding matching requirement restructuring the entire research funding ecosystem to align corporate incentives with the public interest in unbiased research.

9. The analysis proceeds in four parts. First, it traces the emergence of economic experts and consultants as a distinct profession, explaining how this development brought issues of bias in economic research to the forefront, initially within forensic economics. Second, it examines various forms of expert bias, extending beyond the market for applied economic expertise in competition regulation to encompass the broader marketplace of competition economics ideas. Third, it explores how these biases may stem not only from market dynamics but also from the concentrated structure of competition economics expertise, considering both supply and demand factors, as well as strategic efforts to influence competition policy discourse. While grounding its theoretical framework in the sociology of professions and knowledge, this study leaves empirical validation for future research.[22] Finally, it evaluates existing tools for containing bias and capture in forensic economics expertise markets and in the marketplace of knowledge in competition economics and proposes regulatory reforms for the future. The last section concludes.

II. The Professional Project of Forensic Economics and Their Influence in the Production of Knowledge in Competition Economics

10. One may distinguish between two marketplaces: the marketplace for economic ideas (principally academia) and that for forensic economic expertise and advice (principally consultants). My initial hypothesis is therefore that there are two distinct sub-communities in industrial organization economics: forensic economists working in the private or public sector, applying economic ideas to concrete real problems of competition law

---

21 Zingales, *supra* note 11, at 151, seems to also depart from this premise.
22 On this, *see* IOANNIS LIANOS, THE MAKING OF COMPETITION LAW AND ECONOMICS (forthcoming 2025).

enforcement, and academic economists, producing economic knowledge of general application (useful for a variety of contexts), through introspection, theoretical digressions, empirical analysis, experiments, etc.

11. This section articulates the role of forensic economics in competition law enforcement, exploring the structure of the market for economic expertise that has emerged in recent years. It then explores the knowledge ecosystem in competition economics through a market framework, mapping the relationships between "buyers" and "sellers" of competition economic analysis. While using market terminology to describe intellectual exchange might seem reductive, this metaphor serves a practical purpose: it illuminates the complex interactions between two traditionally distinct domains – forensic economics and the academic production of knowledge in competition economics – and reveals how ideas, influence and power flow between key stakeholders in both domains, the two forming now an almost unified strategic field of action.

1. Forensic Economics

12. While consulting economists have acted as witnesses in United States (US) antitrust trials since at least the 1920s, they have only done so regularly since the 1960s.[23] Connor observes that the first refereed economic journal articles explaining some of the methods used by economists in antitrust litigation were published in the late 1960s and 1970s.[24] The field of "forensic economics" is a more recent occurrence. Forensic economics extends beyond antitrust and has been defined as "the analysis of the participation of economists in the litigation process."[25] The primary focus of forensic economics is the measurement and valuation of economic loss (damage)[26] and, in the competition law/regulatory context, building theories of harm and efficiency justifications for business conduct.[27]

---

23 Ioannis Lianos, *"Judging Economists": Economic Expertise in Competition Litigation: A European View*, in THE REFORM OF EC COMPETITION LAW: NEW CHALLENGES 185 (Ioannis Lianos & Ioannis Kokkoris eds., 2010).

24 John M. Connor, *Forensic Economics: An Introduction With Special Emphasis on Price Fixing*, 4 J. COMPETITION L. & ECON. 31 (2008); Maarten Pieter Schinkel, *Forensic Economics in Competition Law Enforcement*, 4 J. COMPETITION L. & ECON. 1 (2008).

25 Thomas R. Ireland, *The Interface between Law and Economics and Forensic Economics*, 7 J. LEGAL ECON. 60, 64 (1997). Remark, however, the broader definition provided by Eric Zitzewitz, *Forensic Economics*, 50 J. ECON. LITERATURE 731 (2012) https://www.aeaweb.org/articles?id=10.1257/jel.50.3.731.

26 *See*, for instance, MARK L. BERENBLUT & HOWARD N. ROSEN, LITIGATION ACCOUNTING: THE QUANTIFICATION OF ECONOMIC DAMAGES (1995); ROBERT L. DUNN, RECOVERY OF DAMAGES FOR LOST PROFITS (4th ed. 1992); COMMERCIAL DAMAGES: A GUIDE TO REMEDIES IN BUSINESS LITIGATION (Charles L. Knapp ed., 1993); ALBERT N. LINK, EVALUATING ECONOMIC DAMAGES: A HANDBOOK FOR ATTORNEYS (1992); GERALD MARTIN, DETERMINING ECONOMIC DAMAGES (7th ed. 1995); GORDON V. SMITH & RUSSELL L. PARR, VALUATION OF INTELLECTUAL PROPERTY AND INTANGIBLE ASSETS (2nd ed. 1994); LITIGATION ECONOMICS (Patrick A. Gaughan & Robert J. Thornton eds., 1993); Robert Thornton & John Ward, *The Economist in Tort Litigation*, 13 J. ECON. PERSP. 101, 101 (1999).

27 For a recent discussion, *see* Jan Broulík, *What Is Forensic Economics?* in ECONOMICS IN LEGAL REASONING 83 (Péter Cserne & Fabrizio Esposito eds., 2020).

13. In the last three decades, economists have increasingly been involved in competition authorities' cases and are frequently called to testify as experts in court proceedings, either invited by the parties or, more rarely, appointed by the courts.[28] In their study on the development of forensic competition economics in Europe and in the US, Damien Neven[29] and Jonathan Baker[30] noted the increasing importance of forensic economic evidence in several steps of competition law litigation. Neven offers a valuable analysis of how the market for competition law economic expertise has evolved from its earlier reliance on individual academic experts in industrial organization (IO), who provided occasional consulting between the 1960s and the late 1980s, to today's landscape dominated by large corporate consultancies that systematically concentrate and deploy economic expertise. This structural transformation reflects a fundamental shift in how economic advice is organized and delivered in competition law enforcement, moving from an ad hoc, academically oriented model to an institutionalized, corporate-driven approach that brings together diverse economic expertise under unified professional service firms.[31] He observes that:

> [W]ith the implementation of the merger regulation in 1990, demand for economic advice seems to have risen. NERA opened an office in London in 1984 and London Economics was set up in 1986. Lexecon (Ltd) was set up in January 1991 and up until the mid-nineties, Lexecon, London Economics and NERA were the main suppliers with a total amount of fees around £2.5 million in 1995. This turnover corresponds to EU[-]related competition work but also to competition work in national jurisdictions. UK[-]related work accounts for the vast majority of the latter. The market for EU[-]related advice grew rapidly in the late nineties, as the number of merger notifications (as well as other types of cases) grew but also following the preparation and implementation of the notice on market definition [adopted by the European Commission]. This notice, inspired by the US practice, used economic concepts explicitly. . . . For the following ten years, total turnover grew at some 25–30% per year, reaching about £24 million in 2004.[32]

---

28   See Phillip E. Areeda, *Are Economists Taking Over*, in ANTITRUST POLICY IN TRANSITION: THE CONVERGENCE OF LAW AND ECONOMICS 23 (Eleanor M. Fox & James T. Halverson eds., 1984); William E. Kovacic, *The Influence of Economics on Antitrust*, 30 ECON. INQUIRY 294 (1992); Fred S. McChesney, *The Role of Economists in Modern Antitrust: An Overview and Summary*, 17 MANAGERIAL & DECISION ECON. 119 (1996); THE ROLE OF THE ACADEMIC ECONOMIST IN LITIGATION SUPPORT (Daniel Jonathan Slottje ed., 1999), especially Jeffrey K. MacKie-Mason & Richard A. Pfau, *Inducements to Advocacy: The Economist as Independent Expert*, at 207, and Frederic M. Scherer, *Economic Consulting, Fire Fighting, and Similar Adventures*, at 129; Lianos, *supra* note 23; Jan Broulík, Economics in Legal Decision-Making (2017) (Doctoral thesis, Tilburg University).

29   Damien J. Neven, *Competition Economics and Antitrust in Europe*, 21 ECON. POL'Y 742 (2006).

30   Jonathan B. Baker, *The Case for Antitrust Enforcement*, 17 J. ECON. PERSP. 27 (2003).

31   This is not picked up by other studies on the role of economists in competition law enforcement, such as Baker, *supra* note 10, who examines the role of specific economists on antitrust enforcement but does not engage with the role of economic consultancies.

32   Neven, *supra* note 29, at 748.

14. These estimations, from 2006, were based on assumptions that economic consultancy fees would amount to about 15% of the total amount of legal fees, this percentage being, more-or-less, similar in Europe and the US. Connor notes that antitrust economic consulting in the US must have exceeded $800 million per year in the late 1990s.[33] Writing in 2024, Valletti estimates that the competition law and economics-related business of the top three economic consultancies "is worth well above $1 billion per year."[34] The industry has also moved towards global consolidation, with a small number of global consultancy firms with operations in Europe and the United States, and increasingly globally, and some smaller boutique firms in important national jurisdictions around the world. Neven notes that the market structure in the market for forensic economic expertise on competition issues is "characterized by the presence of three firms with global (or at least transatlantic) operations" and highlights that "[i]n this respect, economic consultancy seems to have followed the same path as legal advice, both moves being triggered by clients with operations and antitrust filings across jurisdictions."[35]

15. More recent reports put the broader economic consulting services market to around $22–30 billion turnover in 2024 (revenue collected for economic consulting services globally),[36] which is still a fraction of the global consulting services market evaluated to be around $220 billion in 2023[37] and forecasted to increase to around 290 billion in 2030.[38] The specific segment for forensic economics and antitrust consulting may represent a smaller portion, as mentioned by some authors, possibly in the range of $1 billion per year, depending on the volume of antitrust cases and regulatory activity in different jurisdictions.

16. Some economic consultancy services are very well-known for providing forensic economics services in the field of competition and antitrust law. The main firms include NERA Economic Consulting, Charles River Associates (CRA), Compass Lexecon, RBB, The Brattle Group, Economists Incorporated, Analysis Group, OXERA, and PwC Economics. The annual survey GCR100 for 2023 lists three "elite" economic consultancies active in competition economics expertise/advice,

---

[33] Connor, *supra* note 24.

[34] *See* Valletti, *What Have the Consultants Ever Done for Us*, *supra* note 14.

[35] Neven, *supra* note 29, at 750.

[36] *See*, for instance, ECONOMIC CONSULTING SERVICES MARKET SIZE & GROWTH – 2025 GLOBAL REPORT, KENTLEY INSIGHTS (Feb. 2025), https://www.kentleyinsights.com/economic-consulting-services-market-size-growth-report/.

[37] Other estimates are higher. *See*, for instance, Raphael Bohne, *Consulting Industry Worldwide – Statistics & Facts*, STATISTA (Sept. 3, 2024), https://www.statista.com/topics/8112/global-consulting-services-industry/ (noting that the management consulting market size in the US was valued at approximately 374 billion U.S. dollars in 2023)

[38] *See*, for instance, *Consulting Services Market Size, Share, Industry Analysis, Trends, Growth, 2030*, ZION MKT. RSCH., https://www.zionmarketresearch.com/report/consulting-services-market

eight "outstanding," nine "highly recommended," and four "recommended." These firms concentrate most, if not all, of the turnover (and revenues) for the market for economic expertise/advice in competition investigations and litigation. From a reputational perspective, we can therefore observe a clear hierarchy between a small group of economic consultancies dominating the market for economic expertise/advice in competition economics.[39] Competition economics forms a sizable part of the activity of these firms, with, according to the same GCR statistics, 30% to 100% of their economists' staff being specialized and active in competition economics.

17. In terms of headcount, GCR100 notes that the three "elite" economic consultancies employ 1,241 economists specialized in competition economics, while the eight "outstanding" consultancies operate with 1,716 competition economists. In total, the number of competition economists employed by the 24 economic consultancies listed in the GCR100 amounts to 3,422 economists active in competition economics, the top 5 firms in terms of employment (as identified by the GCR100) employing more than 55% of all the economists active in competition law enforcement in the economic consultancy sector.

18. Competition economists working as in-house consultants are not included in these figures, but it is not infrequent that large corporations, such as Google, Microsoft, Amazon, IBM and Goldman Sachs, employ chief economists with economic teams to reflect on competitive strategy, and also provide support with regulatory and competition law enforcement issues whenever these arise.[40]

19. The market for competition economics consulting exhibits clear oligopolistic features, dominated by a few global firms capable of serving multinational clients across multiple jurisdictions. Entry barriers are substantial, requiring not only expertise in IO economics, but also experience working with lawyers, knowledge of competition law procedures, established credibility, and extensive professional networks. These firms engage in mutual monitoring of pricing and services, typically aligning their fee structures with those of major law firms in the field, enabling them to maintain significant profit margins.[41]

---

39 *See GRC100 2024*, GRC, https://globalcompetitionreview.com/survey/gcr-100/24th-edition.

40 *See*, for instance, the appointment of Professor Hal Varian as chief economist of Google in 2002.

41 Neven, *supra* note 29, at 750. The profit margins of economic consultancies range between 15% and 30%, which is still lower than top-tier law firms' margins, which in the London, New York and Brussels legal markets, see their margins be between 30% to 50% or more. *See* Paul Hodkinson, *The UK Law Firms With the Highest Profit Margin*, Law.com (June 7, 2024), https://www.law.com/international-edition/2024/06/07/the-uk-law-firms-with-the-highest-profit-margin/?slreturn=2024102275854; Bruce MacEwen, *How Profitable Are Law Firms? Really*, Adam Smith, Esq. (June 27, 2014), https://adamsmithesq.com/2014/06/how-profitable-are-law-firms-really/; Pat Walls, *How Profitable Is a Law Firm? (Updated for 2024)*, Starter Story (Oct. 5, 2024), https://www.starterstory.com/ideas/law-firm/profitability. *See also* PWC, Facing the Future with Confidence, PwC Law Firm's Survey 2021 (2021) at 10 (noting that the top 10 law firms' profitability in 2021 was 38%, close to the record 40% reported in 2014).

20. An important factor to consider is the parallel development of a concentrated market structure for economic consultants in competition economics and a concentrated market of a small circle of multinational law firms on the legal side. The corporatization of forensic economics, with the emergence of multinational economic consultancies specialized in support services for competition litigation, is more pronounced in the application of IO economics to competition and regulatory litigation than in other areas of practice regarding economic expertise. The distinctive role of forensic competition economics extends beyond providing mere evidence, as economic analysis serves a fundamental normative function in competition law. This dual purpose – both evidential and normative – distinguishes forensic competition economists as a unique professional community, separate from both general forensic economists and academic economists.

21. IO and competition economists have been integrated into the public authorities involved in the monitoring of competition and/or enforcement of competition law, probably to a larger extent than in other areas of regulation, such as environmental regulation, employment discrimination, or even IP and trademark offices. Neven noted that in 2004, there were 83 professionals with a background in economics and around 184 with a background in law (hence roughly a ratio of 1 to 2) at the European Commission, up from a ratio of one economist to seven lawyers in the early 1990s.[42] To this, one could add the establishment in 2003 of the position of chief economist of the European Commission, with a team consisting of 25–30 PhD economists in 2024.[43] In his study, Neven estimated that there were more than 100 professional economists working with the US Department of Justice (DOJ) Antitrust Division and the US Federal Trade Commission (FTC). The numbers have since increased considerably, with approximately 80 PhD-holding applied microeconomists working at the Bureau of Economics at the US FTC in 2024,[44] in addition to a number of non-PhD economists working in other Bureaus of the US FTC, and more than 50 microeconomists at the Experts Analysis Group at the DOJ Antitrust Division.[45] As is noted in the most recent Organisation for Economic Co-operation and Development (OECD) Competition Trends covering competition law enforcement between 2015 and 2022 in 77 jurisdictions, competition authorities' staff (all categories) amounted to 9,228 individuals in 2022. The percentage of economists to the whole expert staff varies from jurisdiction to jurisdiction, going from around 8% to more than 50% in some jurisdictions.

---

42 Neven, *supra* note 29, at 751.

43 *See Chief Competition Economist*, Eur. Comm'n, https://competition-policy.ec.europa.eu/chief-competition-economist_en.

44 *See Economist Recruiting*, Fed. Trade Comm'n, https://www.ftc.gov/about-ftc/bureaus-offices/bureau-economics/careers-ftc-bureau-economics/economist-recruiting.

45 *See About EAG*, Dep't of Just., https://www.justice.gov/atr/about-eag#:~:text=Along%20these%20lines%2C%20EAG%20can,various%20institutions%20with%20various%20specializations.

22. We may therefore conclude that the expansion of economic consultancies worldwide and the increasing recruitment of economists by number of national competition authorities in Europe, Asia, Latin America and Australia during the last five years may put the figure of forensic economists, working in the private sector or governmental bureaucracies, to a figure of more than 5,000 people.[46] The large and growing size of the sector, coupled with its important and strategic role in competition litigation, adds to the importance of understanding the systemic biases that may be present among its actors.

2. The Marketplace of Economic Knowledge

23. Focusing on this market for professional (forensic) economics services for competition investigations and litigation may seem reductionist, as it does not take into account the broader marketplace of ideas that may impact on or influence not just the evaluation of the available evidence in a specific case in front of a competition authority or court, but more generally the public discourses about market economy,[47] the dominant paradigm of competition economics that would guide decision-makers in their activity, the subsequent policy discussion, and also the prevailing consensus in the way "proper" competition economics should be done.

24. Academic economists have been traditionally considered the most prominent contributors to the marketplace of ideas. The leading role they play in this marketplace results from the fact that they manage the main academic journals of the discipline in which research on competition economics and IO is published (the *American Economic Review*, the *RAND Journal of Economics*, the *Journal of Competition Law & Economics*, the *Review of Industrial Organization*, the *International Journal of Industrial Organization, Econometrica*), as well as their participation as reviewers in these journals. Peer review also plays an important role in the progression of the academic career (e.g. promotions, grant applications). As academic economists are primarily responsible for the transmission of the values and principles of the discipline to their students during their formative undergraduate years, and the training of both professional and junior academic economists, through the provision of graduate and doctoral education, they hold a central role in determining the overall academic consensus and the boundaries of the discipline of competition economics/ Industrial organization[48] and in the selection of the prevalent methodologies and conceptual frameworks.

---

46 According to the author's calculations. Note that the Antitrust Section of the American Bar Association had in recent years an average membership of 15,000, some of which are economists.

47 Marion Fourcade, Étienne Ollion & Yann Algan, *The Superiority of Economists*, 29 J. ECON. PERSP. 89 (2015).

48 In the sense of "boundary work" as mentioned by SHEILA JASANOFF, THE FIFTH BRANCH: SCIENCE ADVISERS AS POLICYMAKERS 13 (1998).

25. Unlike the concentrated market for forensic competition expertise, the broader marketplace for economic knowledge in competition appears, at first sight, more diverse and decentralized. Although estimating the exact number of economists working as faculty in universities globally can be challenging due to variations in data reporting and definitions of "economist," the US Bureau of Labor Statistics estimates that there were 12,210 economists in 2023 in the US teaching courses in economics or combining teaching and research in the post-secondary sector.[49] There are no equivalent numbers for Europe and other parts of the world. It is not possible to identify how many of these economists are in full-time positions as well as the number of economists teaching and researching competition economics or other neighbouring fields in economics. Although academic economists studying competition policy are distributed across numerous institutions – with over 230 US universities alone offering graduate economics programmes that include industrial organization, econometrics, and competition policy courses – a select few programmes with international prestige wield disproportionate influence over knowledge production in economics in general, and competition economics in particular.

26. Usually, IO (competition) economics and microeconomics is taught in all, or most, undergraduate economics programmes, which means that there should be some teaching capacity in the area, in addition to any specific investment made in building research capacity in the area, as has been done by some universities, the most prominent example being the Toulouse School of Economics (TSE).[50] There are 275 academic institutions in the area of industrial competition that are listed in the top 10% of institutions globally, thus indicating that there are 2,759 institutions overall that are active in this area.[51] The Association of Competition Economics (ACE),[52] the largest association regrouping economists working in the public and private sector in Europe, often gathers between 250 and 300 participants in its annual conference,[53] probably the most attended competition economists' event in Europe.

27. Public institutions or bureaucracies may also employ economists active in the marketplace of ideas, including research foundations, such as the National Bureau of Economic Research, ministerial departments involved in competition policy but also in-house economists in publicly owned business entities,

---

49   *See Occupational Employment and Wage Statistics*, U.S. BUREAU OF LAB. STAT., https://www.bls.gov/oes/2023/may/oes251063.htm.

50   *See Top 10% Institutions and Economists in the Field of Industrial Competition, as of January 2025*, IDEAS, https://ideas.repec.org/top/top.com.html.

51   Although only 1,571 authors, which means that many of these authors may be affiliated with more than one institution: *see id.*

52   *See* https://www.competitioneconomics.org.

53   Communication of the author with the president of the ACE, Dr Hans Zenger.

which may participate to the marketplace of ideas through publications (academic articles, reports) or participation in conferences and public events.

28. In recent years, as competition law enforcement has seen its remit expand in multiple jurisdictions, we have witnessed the involvement of competition economists in a number of international organizations, research foundations, think-tanks, non-profits and other non-governmental organizations involved or interested in competition policy and competition law enforcement, such as the OECD, the United Nations Conference on Trade and Development (UNCTAD), the World Bank, the International Monetary Fund (IMF), the American Antitrust Institute, the Open Markets Institute, the Institute for Policy Integrity, the Progressive Policy Institute, the International Centre for Law and Economics, the Heritage Foundation, the Cato Institute, the George Mason's University's Mercatus Center, the Competitive Enterprise Institute, and lobby groups, such as the American Chamber of Commerce, the Internet Association, the Information Technology Industry Council, and the Business Roundtable. These employ or are associated with an increasing number of competition economists, although their number tends to be rather limited in comparison to the other constituents of the competition economics marketplace of ideas.

29. Although the supply side of this "marketplace" of ideas seems at first sight decentralized, it is important to acknowledge the importance of academic reputation, first concerning the different teaching programmes and their faculty, which may provide a significant competitive advantage in terms of their influence in the marketplace of ideas (measured by the number of their citations in publications in the top 5 journals[54]), and second of a few economists academic "stars" that play a hub role for the production of academic research[55] or of a handful of leading and impactful research programmes/centres or research networks globally.[56] This shows the existence of significant geographic disparities and differentials of influence in the marketplace of ideas.[57] Although these results come from empirical research on all areas of economics and not just competition economics, it is reasonable to expect such concentration and differential impact to take place also in this context. Similarly, international organizations,

---

54 For a discussion, Daniel S. Hamermesh, *Citations in Economics: Measurement, Uses, and Impacts*, 56 J. ECON. LITERATURE 115 (2018).

55 Sanjeev Goyal, Marco van der Leij & Jose Moraga-Gonzalez, *Economics: An Emerging Small World*, 114 J. POL. ECON. 403 (2006).

56 *See* the discussion on "citation networks" in Ali Sina Önder & Maarco Terviö, *Is Economics a House Divided? Analysis of Citation Networks*, 53 ECON. INQUIRY 1491 (2015).

57 *See* Florentin Glötzl & Ernest Aigner, *Six Dimensions of Concentration in Economics: Evidence from a Large-Scale Data Set*, 32 SCI. CONTEXT 381 (2019) (showing that articles in which authors from the US or Canada participated received 72% and those with Western European authors 24% of all citations among articles published between 1980 and 2014); Ernest Aigner, Jacob Greenspon & Dani Rodrik, The Global Distribution of Authorship in Economics Journals (Feb. 2024), https://drodrik.scholar.harvard.edu/sites/scholar.harvard.edu/files/dani-rodrik/files/global_distribution_of_authorship_021724.pdf.

such as the OECD, the IMF, the World Bank, UNCTAD, or old and well-respected research foundations and think-tanks, may benefit from an institutional reputation that may provide more opportunities for impact on the marketplace of ideas to the economists that are affiliated to them.

3. From Separate Reward Mechanisms to a Unified Field?

30. The reward mechanisms for each of these two markets are not the same. In the market for services of economic expertise/advice, the experts are usually hired by companies or by law firms involved in competition investigations or litigation with the purpose of providing expert evidence that supports them in their allegations and argumentation, and their remuneration is part of the litigation costs or the costs for legal compliance, which, of course, are more significant if the party in question has been successful in the specific litigation or matter to be resolved by a competition authority. The reputation and overall competence of the expert (as this results from a past successful record) and/or the specific issues raised in the economic consultancy in question (as this may require industry or methods-based specialization) play an important role in their positioning in this market and may lead to the payment of hefty consultancy fees.

31. In the marketplace for ideas for economics of competition policy and enforcement, the principal actors are academics with institutional affiliations with universities and public research centres. These earn a salary, which is sometimes supplemented with other sources of income, either royalties from publications or side consultancy work.[58] This is sometimes provided in the context of a forensic competition economics consultancy to which they may contribute a small or a more significant part of their time. It is possible that the income generated by consultancy and professional services-related activities might be more significant than the academic salary and royalties from publications.[59] However, the reward system in science is managed by the scientific community itself. This does not exclude the intervention of the market mechanism at a second stage, after the social reward structure of collegiate science took place, "picking up" the disclosed knowledge or information brought in by the open science phase in order to develop new products and services in the forensic market for economic expertise.

32. Reputation may be a significant drive for activity in the putative marketplace of ideas, as it may lead to academic promotion and an increase of the academic salary, offering because of this reputation further opportunities

---

58 See Zingales, *supra* note 11, at 125 (on the reasons behind the capture of economists, including career incentives and opportunities in consulting and careers outside academia).

59 For instance, it was reported that in some cases, the academic salary can be less than 25–30% of the income generated by different sorts of consultancy services. See Mullins, *supra* note 13 (reporting for an annual salary of around $400,000 and consultancy income during the same period of more than $1 million).

for other lucrative activities, either with monetary compensation, such as consultancies for the private and/or the public sector, royalties from publications, invitations to fee-paying lectures or with non-monetary compensation, such as esteem by peers. High-status economists, particularly editors of prestigious economic journals,[60] are also taken more seriously than other economists, leading to a rich-get-richer effect.[61] This high esteem may lead to appointments in prestigious academic positions or learning societies, government positions, more extensive media presence, participation in international conferences and events, etc. There is important empirical research on how reward systems shape behaviour in academic science, through different conduits, such as motivation, cultural socialization, psychological contract, marketplace and system effects.[62] The existence of different reward systems may therefore influence the strategies of the various actors involved in each of these markets.

33. Reward systems are institutionalized to respond to demand factors that are theoretically different in each of the two "markets." Demand for forensic competition economics services is usually driven by corporations that are involved in competition authorities' investigations (including merger activity), litigation in courts, or corporate compliance to competition legislation. Due to the asymmetrical character of competition law, and the fact that it is principally enforced against relatively large or quite powerful corporations, the demand in this market is driven by these large economic players and their interests. Although the development of private enforcement and class actions has been a feature of US antitrust law for decades, leading to the emergence of other market players in the demand side of this market for professional economic expertise/advice, such as consumers and smaller undertakings, damages actions for infringement of competition law have not taken off significantly in other jurisdictions so far. Hence, there is a risk that the interests of large corporations drive the market for economic expertise in competition policy and enforcement.

34. In light of the fact that most of the publication and other intellectual activities by economists following their formal training are geared towards enhancing their employment opportunities in top academic institutions, the main demand factor influencing the marketplace of ideas is, in principle, the employment market for academic economists, where mostly public educational institutions, such as universities and research centres, are

---

60 See Zingales, *supra* note 11, at 125 (noting the crucial role of journal editors in the process of producing and disseminating economic knowledge and the risk that "if a few editors are captured, this effect spreads out through the entire profession").

61 Mohsen Javdani & Ha-Joon Chang, *Who Said or What Said? Estimating Ideological Bias in Views Among Economists*, 47 CAMBRIDGE J. ECON. 309 (2023).

62 KerryAnn O'Meara, *Inside the Panopticon: Studying Academic Reward Systems*, in 26 HIGHER EDUCATION: HANDBOOK OF THEORY AND RESEARCH 161 (John C. Smart & Michael B. Paulsen eds., 2011).

active. In view of the importance of the peer-review process in academic selection, the final users of academic research are first and foremost other academics in the specific field that is the primary audience for the research, also in view of the gatekeeping function they exercise regarding access to prestigious academic journals for publication and thus their control over access to a broader audience for one's research work. This autonomy and self-reference constitute defining characteristics of academia as a self-governed social subsystem that operates following rules it has mostly set for itself.[63] An important driving force for knowledge production in academia is also public funding of academic research, universities and research centres being traditionally seen as key players in national innovation systems.[64]

35. However, external factors, such as industry funding of research, have become prominent characteristics of scientific production during the last three decades, leading some to even argue that this leads to new modes of knowledge production and a different social contract for science.[65] Recent research has highlighted that scientific knowledge is increasingly the product of trans-disciplinary collaboration and takes place in a heterogeneous environment, where not only universities but also the public and the private sector contribute to knowledge production. Gibbons et al. employed the term of Mode 2 knowledge to distinguish science produced in a "context of application," according to a "dialogic process" that incorporates multiple societal interests and institutions, such as universities, research centres, corporations and consultancies.[66] Mode 2 knowledge is profoundly contextualized: for example, the traditional peer review systems of Mode 1 science are supplemented by additional criteria of economic, political, social, and cultural nature. Mode 2 knowledge does not substitute but only complements Mode 1 knowledge. Nevertheless, its standards of validity are different. Some authors even claim that Mode 2 knowledge production illustrates a shift from "quality control" to "quality monitoring," a concept permitting the inclusion of new peers, such as users and lay persons, in the evaluation of knowledge and awarding greater consideration to the instrumental concerns of scientific knowledge, in the context of its application.[67]

---

63 *See*, for instance, the seminal work of Michael Polanyi, *The Republic of Science: Its Political and Economic Theory*, 1 MINERVA 54 (1962).

64 *See* NATIONAL INNOVATION SYSTEMS: A COMPARATIVE ANALYSIS (Richard R. Nelson ed., 1993).

65 David H. Guston & Kenneth Keniston, *Introduction: The Social Contract for Science*, in THE FRAGILE CONTRACT: UNIVERSITY SCIENCE AND THE FEDERAL GOVERNMENT 1 (David H. Guston & Kenneth Keniston eds., 1994).

66 MICHAEL GIBBONS, CAMILLE LIMOGES, HELGA NOWOTNY, SIMON SCHWARTZMAN, PETER SCOTT & MARTIN TROW, THE NEW PRODUCTION OF KNOWLEDGE: THE DYNAMICS OF SCIENCE AND RESEARCH IN CONTEMPORARY SOCIETIES (1994).

67 Sven Hemlin & Søren Barlebo Rasmussen, *The Shift in Academic Quality Control*, 31 SCI. TECH. & HUM. VALUES 173 (2006).

36. This is particularly significant in view of the rise of industry funding of academic research, particularly in competition economics, while the share of public funding for universities and academic research is decreasing. Although, due to the lack of transparency in the industry funding of academic research in competition economics, it is not possible to establish with certainty the relevant figures, anecdotal evidence that became public shows that these are quite significant and could therefore constitute an important part of the funding of academic research in the area,[68] eventually with the purpose of influencing the academic agenda in the discipline,[69] thus eventually merging the two initially separate systems of reward put in place. The fact that some of the major actors in academic competition economics are also active in the market for consulting raises the question about the interactions between these two markets and the influence large corporations may exercise on the scientific production in competition economics, through corporate funding of academic research but also through the oligopsony they benefit in the demand for economic expertise/advice services.

37. Dasgupta and David have clearly shown that changes brought to the underlying reward system of science will have particular implications on the "autonomy" of the scientific process, "in the sense of the scientific community's self-governance and control over the research agenda."[70] Others, like Wible, have developed a complements view of the organization of the scientific process, with market and nonmarket institutions being separate institutions but also fulfilling the "dual nature of the scientific enterprise": a unique nonmarket structure and a "secondary science" relying on markets.[71]

38. The distinction between academic economists and forensic economists is not something specific to economics. Krohn distinguished three types of research situations, depending on the reward structure and the time spent for non-research activities:

    1. Academic basic research: scientist were hired to perform limited non-research duties, and obtained outside support for (presumably) theoretical research of their own choice.

---

68 Olivia Solon, *Google Spends Millions* on *Academic Research* to *Influence Opinion, Says Watchdog*, THE GUARDIAN (July 13, 2017), https://www.theguardian.com/technology/2017/jul/13/google-millions-academic-research-influence-opinion. Some of the empirical research on funding for economics, in general and not only competition economics, is only reporting public funding: *see* MIKE MARIATHASAN & RAMON MARIMON, RESEARCH FUNDING FOR ECONOMICS IN EUROPE (Report of the Eur. Econ. Ass'n Standing Comm. on Rsch. & the Academic Careers Observatory of the Max Weber Programme, Eur. Univ. Inst., 2011).

69 Marianne Bertrand, Matilde Bombardini, Raymond Fisman & Francesco Trebbi, *Tax-Exempt Lobbying: Corporate Philanthropy as a Tool for Political Influence* (NBER Working Paper 24451, 2018), https://www.nber.org/papers/w24451 (noting how firms deploy their charitable foundations as a form of tax-exempt influence seeking); Luigi Zingales, *Towards a Political Theory of the Firm*, 31 J. ECON. PERSP. 113 (2017).

70 Partha Dasgupta & Paul A. David, *Towards a New Economics of Science*, 23 RSCH. POL'Y 487, 505 (1994).

71 JAMES R. WIBLE, THE ECONOMICS OF SCIENCE: METHODOLOGY AND EPISTEMOLOGY AS IF ECONOMICS REALLY MATTERED 172 (1998).

2. Open-applied research: scientists were hired to perform limited non-research duties and obtained outside support for (presumably) practical research of their own choice.

3. Bound-applied research; scientists were hired to work full-time on problems related to the purposes of their employing organizations.[72]

39. Forensic competition economists (working in the public or private sector) are situated across the pole that goes from "bound-applied research" to "open-applied research," as some of them are also active academics, while academic economists concentrate at the pole of "academic basic research," with some being occasional consultants and could thus be included in the "open-applied research" category. The intermediary category of academics that are also acting as forensic economists is of particular importance for our study, as they might act as communicators of the values of each pole to the other, and indicate that the reward systems of the market for professional services in competition economics may sometimes be imbricated with that of the marketplace of ideas, establishing the possibility of feedback loops with regard to the positioning (and subsequent rewards) of an actor active in both markets. After identifying two distinct markets for economic knowledge – one for professional services in competition cases and another for competition economics knowledge – and establishing how both markets sometimes involve the same actors and therefore share some form of indirect interaction, eventually merging their separate rewards systems and challenging their autonomy, I now turn to explore how different forms of "bias" may impact on the quality dimension of competition in these two markets.

III. Building the Externality Story: Bias and Conflict of Interest Affecting Forensic and Academic Competition Economics

40. Providing professional advice to a party in the context of an adversarial process of decision-making or litigation has been long recognized as being a possible source of bias in the analysis provided.[73] Economic evidence is often presented by experts employed by the parties and providing advice on the economic merits of the case. These represent "persistent communities of practice outside the legal domain" but linked to it.[74]

---

72 ROGER G. KROHN, THE SOCIAL SHAPING OF SCIENCE 115 (1971).

73 On the role of expert witnesses, *see* Learned Hand, *Historical and Practical Considerations Regarding Expert Testimony*, 15 HARV. L. REV. 40 (1901). To the view that party experts' role was to educate or translate economic knowledge to the judge (or the jury), some have opposed the characterization of experts as "advocates." For a discussion, *see* Lianos, *supra* note 23.

74 DÉIRDRE DWYER, THE JUDICIAL ASSESSMENT OF EXPERT EVIDENCE 6 (2008).

To the extent that they provide services to their clients, there is an inherent risk of bias, something the legal system recognizes, as it has imposed on these experts, in addition to their duty to their clients, a "duty to the court."[75]

41. Exploring the judicial assessment of expert evidence in general, Déirdre Dwyer mentions three categories of interest that may cause some form of expert bias and therefore may give rise to expert disagreement: personal interest, financial interest, and intellectual interest.[76] These may exist "externally to the instant litigation," what she calls "predisposition," or arise in direct relation to the litigation, which she calls "involvement."[77] Personal bias may arise because of moral opinions or personal relations when the expert is associated with one of the parties (family, member of a professional organization, etc.). Financial interest originates when "the expert is employed by the party on an ongoing basis, beyond the scope of immediate litigation."[78]

42. Intellectual predisposition or involvement results from the fact that the expert shares a particular theory or, for instance, participates in a specific school of thought, which will influence their expertise. Expert bias may be "conscious," "where the expert chooses to adapt her opinion in order to favour one of the parties,"[79] or "unconscious," where the expert's opinion is trapped to a specific heuristic or schema, that of a specific theory or scientific discipline, for example. Déirdre Dwyer concludes that "to remove competing expert evidence does not of itself remove the problems of expert disagreement and bias," but simply "remove[s] the issue from the sight of the tribunal."[80] The adversarial process may exacerbate the risk of expert bias because of financial interest defended by each party's expert, although it could be useful to reduce the risk of intellectual bias. The asymmetry of knowledge between experts and judges or juries may also exacerbate the risk of biased expertise.[81]

43. Reputation effects may dissuade the expert from behaving opportunistically and from providing biased information, particularly if the expert is a repeat player in this market for professional economic advice. Credibility

---

[75] According to Part 33.2 Civil Procedure Rules, "An expert must help the court to achieve the overriding objective by giving objective, unbiased opinion on matters within his expertise." Part 35.3 Civil Procedure Rules: "This duty overrides any obligation to the person from whom he has received instructions or by whom he is paid."

[76] DWYER, *supra* note 74, at 76.

[77] *Id.* at 163

[78] *Id.* at 167.

[79] *Id.* at 172.

[80] *Id.* at 178

[81] As noted by Richard A. Posner, *The Law and Economics of the Economic Expert Witness*, 13 J. ECON. PERSP. 91, 93 (1999), experts may hide behind "an impenetrable wall of esoteric knowledge" and therefore can easily mislead judges and juries.

is an important asset that the expert has an interest in preserving in order to operate in the market of legal expertise and maintain the value of theirservices. The market for experts may, in this case, have a disciplining effect in ensuring that the expertise has the required quality. Nevertheless, it is possible that the disciplining effect of the market may not work well. The expert might adopt a strategy of signalling an intellectual interest to secure continuous employment by a certain category of clients. For example, an expert may adopt a theoretical starting point that is generally positive to defendants or plaintiffs in a particular industry or area of law. It is often the case that parties shop around to identify the experts that will be the most favourable to their cause. The prospect of a continuous flow of cases from clients with a high risk of repeated litigation (e.g. dominant firms, particularly in the IT technology sector) may well motivate experts to specialize in a specific kind of argument as a signal to potential clients in order to attract employment. In this case, the market for expertise will not operate as a disciplining mechanism but rather as an inducement to intellectual interest and expert bias.

44. The growing scepticism over the role of expert witnesses and more generally expertise in litigation with the emergence of the expression "junk science" or pseudo-science exemplifies how the perceived bias of experts may be a persistent problem, not only for them, but also for all actors in this market for professional services, thus producing externalities. The term "junk science" was used by Peter Huber to refer to "the science of things that aren't so"[82] science that is based on bad data and spurious inferences. The definition of the boundaries of "junk science" as opposed to "good science" is ambiguous. On which side of the boundary would idiosyncratic or minority views fall? What are the criteria that apply in setting the boundaries in the first place?

45. A remarkable shortcoming of the concept of "junk science" is also that it totally ignores the broader social context in which scientific research is produced and is based on an idealistic conception of science. Recent theories of the philosophy of science, as well as empirical observations, emphasize the role of social context and socialization as an instrument of consensus formation in scientific communities.[83] Scientists work in the context of paradigms or research programmes, which may operate under different assumptions or prior beliefs. The concept of "junk science" does not take into account the plurality of scientific discourse and the possibility that opinions that are now at the fringe may become part of the mainstream among the scientists of the specific group. Others have put forward the expression "snake oil" economics to indicate how sometimes "sophisticated" mathematical

---

82 Peter W. Huber, Galileo's Revenge: Junk Science in the Courtroom 24 (1991).

83 Gary Edmond & David Mercer, *Trashing "Junk Science"* 1998 Stan. Tech. L. Rev. 3, 6 (2008).

models are used to make tendentious arguments without proper support by the facts in the relevant industry.[84]

46. One of the sources of the problem of expert bias is that parties are interested in bringing forward experts that would be favourable to their cause. Judges and juries are aware of this strategic objective and may eventually ignore the expert's testimony. The side effect may be that good quality scientists are dissuaded from participating as experts in legal proceedings in order to avoid tarnishing their public image by appearing in court. This issue is related to one of the strongest manifestations of conscious financial interest by the expert, leading to expert bias: the risk that expert witnesses become "hired guns" for the parties that employ them. "Hired guns" are driven in their testimony by the successful outcome of the case (for their employers) rather than by the loyalty and independent judgment they owe to their science/field. Their motivations can be diverse: ensure a continuous working relation with one of the parties, particularly if this party is involved in a great amount of litigation or any other personal benefit by defending views that are not the result of independent (in motives) study and research.

47. The problem of "hired guns" illustrates the paradox of the position of scientific expert witnesses in modern litigation. The dominant conceptualization of expert witnesses' role relies on a principal/agent model, with the judge being the principal. Experts have a duty to the court to act as honest representatives of their academic fields. Their role as educators and translators of scientific knowledge assumes that they would place themselves outside the actual (legal) controversy Nonetheless, at the same time, expert witnesses are hired by one of the parties and they participate in an adversarial procedure and may therefore be tempted to put forward sophist arguments to confuse the principle for their own benefit. One could therefore oppose the dominant conception of the scientific expert witnesses as representatives of their field to that of the experts acting as advocates. . . .[85] The development of the field of forensic expertise and the professionalization of the role of expert witnesses, with the establishment of multinational corporations specializing in economic expertise, underlines the ongoing transformation of the role of economic expert witnesses. There is a risk that the duty of the experts to their employer may overstep the duty they owe to the court, the administrative authority, or eventually their academic institutions.

48. If material bias is an important issue affecting the quality of expertise in the market for competition economics advice, the prevalence of industry

---

[84] Simon Bishop, *Snake-Oil with Mathematics is Still Snake-Oil: Why Recent Trends in the Application of So-Called "Sophisticated" Economics Is Hindering Good Competition Policy Enforcement*, 9 EUR. COMPETITION J. 67 (2013).

[85] Lianos, *supra* note 23.

funding in some areas of competition economics may similarly also affect the quality (impartiality) of academic work in the marketplace of ideas. Drawing on the work of Robert Merton on the reward system of open science,[86] one could argue the specificity of the academic community of economists with regard to the community of forensic economists, which is not marked by openness (there is an inherent bias that only the results that could be positive to the client are publicly shared). Furthermore, as explained in section II above, the structure of rewards in these two markets is different. In the marketplace of ideas, it is not expected, as is probably more the case in the market for economic expertise for litigation, that economists will put forward views and arguments with the sole purpose of satisfying their clients and attracting industry funding. As Herman describes, "more problematic... is the possibility that... a segment of the [academic economists] profession will shift views to satisfy the market demand," those receiving grants and serving as consultants and witnesses "gradually" coming "to accept the premises of those funding them or whose views and interests they are paid to represent."[87] Corporate-funded conferences can serve as amplification chambers for specific viewpoints, potentially influencing participants – especially junior researchers eager to present at prestigious venues – who may not recognize the subtle shaping of academic discourse. In this context, as Herman writes, "[t]his mobilization of bias suggests the possibility that the entire drift of the science – its principles and their refinements appropriate to special applications – may be decisively shaped by market forces,"[88] further accentuating the "credibility crisis" in economics.[89]

49. Any material bias in the marketplace of ideas may thus lead to a larger negative externality, as it may affect the integrity of the autonomous and self-governed system of academia, or at least its perception as such. A possible externality is the intrusion of the market for economic expertise/advice in the organization of knowledge production in academia, and more generally the marketplace of ideas. Of essence to the concept of "marketplace of ideas," by analogy to the economic concept of free market, is the idea of intellectual competition, the intellectual exchange that occurs between the different participants to this "marketplace" being grounded to the freedom of speech, the best ideas rising to the top. Diversity of ideas and competition "on the merits" between them is therefore of essential importance for the marketplace of ideas to work.

50. This dimension shows that the negative externality of blurring the distinction between the reward system of academic economics and that for

---

[86] ROBERT K. MERTON, THE SOCIOLOGY OF SCIENCE: THEORETICAL AND EMPIRICAL INVESTIGATIONS (1979), ch. 4.

[87] Edward S. Herman, *The Institutionalization of Bias in Economics*, 4 MEDIA, CULTURE & SOC'Y 275, 284 (1982).

[88] *Id.* at 285.

[89] *See* Ioannidis et al., *supra* note 16 (describing the "credibility crisis" in economics).

forensic economics in the market for economic expertise may expand beyond the simple issue of the misalignment of incentives between the agent (academic) and its principle (the academic community or the public at large) and affect the integrity of the competitive process of knowledge production in economics. Wible emphasizes the need to preserve this institutional and epistemic diversity, noting that "a variety of qualitatively differentiated organizations are essential for resolving epistemic scarcity. Humanity cannot depend on just one institution like the market or even the primacy of one institution among others. We cannot put all our organizational 'eggs' into one institutional basket."[90] Calls for epistemic diversity have also been recently made in competition economics literature. Oliver Budzinski, among others, has highlighted the risks of "monoculture" in competition economics and proposed "theory pluralism" of competition policy paradigms as being an essential prescription for public policy in this area.[91] "Sustainable pluralism of competition theories" should thus serve as an imperative for science and public policy.

51. Material bias is not the only source of negative externalities in this context. There has been significant research in economics about ideological bias, and how this may affect public discussion of competition economics-related issues.[92] There is also significant literature on the impact of ideology in economics,[93] and that of schools of economic thought in defining the agenda of competition law enforcement.[94]

52. Barrios et al. use the terminology of "conflict of interest" to portray multiple factors that may affect the "trustworthiness" of the scientific belief formation process, and which may influence a researcher's prior beliefs towards the conclusion reached in the specific output.[95] In addition to material (financial) conflicts of interest, the authors cite professional interest resulting from motivated interest to arrive to a specific conclusion because of career or academic conflicts, thus affecting the integrity

---

90 WIBLE, *supra* note 71 at 174–75.

91 Oliver Budzinski, *Pluralism of Competition Policy Paradigms and the Call for Regulatory Diversity* (Philipps-University of Marburg Volkswirtschaftliche Beitraege No. 14/2003, 2003), http://papers.ssrn.com/sol3/papers.cfm?abstract_id=452900; Oliver Budzinski, *Monoculture versus Diversity in Competition Economics*, 32 CAMBRIDGE J. ECON. 295 (2008).

92 Herman, *supra* note 87; Gilles Saint-Paul, *The Possibility of Ideological Bias in Structural Macroeconomic Models*, 10 AM. ECON. J.: MACROECONOMICS 216 (2018); Javdani & Chang, *supra* note 61; John Barrios, Filippo Lancieri, Joshua Levy, Shashank Singh, Tommaso Valletti, & Luigi Zingales, *The Conflict-of-Interest Discount in the Marketplace of Ideas* (Stigler Ctr. New Working Paper Series No. 348, Oct. 2024).

93 THOMAS PIKETTY, CAPITAL AND IDEOLOGY (2020).

94 *See*, for instance, Einer Elhauge, *Harvard, not Chicago: Which Antitrust School Drives Recent Supreme Court Decisions*, 3 COMPETITION POL'Y INT'L 59 (2007), http://papers.ssrn.com/sol3/papers.cfm?abstract_id=1010769; Joshua Wright, *The Robert Court and the Chicago School of Antitrust: The 2006 Term and Beyond*, 3 COMPETITION POL'Y INT'L 24 (2007), https://papers.ssrn.com/sol3/papers.cfm?abstract_id=1028028; Alberto Pera, *Changing Views of Competition, Economic Analysis and EC Antitrust Law*, 4 EUR. COMPETITION J. 127 (2008).

95 Barrios et al., *supra* note 92, at 1.

of scientific findings, data conflicts to the extent that privileged access to private data may enhance the influence of vested interests in the direction of the results, or political (ideological) conflicts, emerging when a researcher's political ideology aligns with specific results.[96]

53. Following empirical analysis based on survey results, the authors put forward the thesis that the presence of certain conflicts of interest may lead to discounting the value of the research in the eyes of a group of selected academic economists, a group of ordinary academic economists, and the general public. According to the authors, the value of the research in the intellectual marketplace is determined by its ability to shift people's priors,[97] the conflict of interest discount being the "percentage reduction in the value of a paper due to the presence of a conflict of interest."[98] The results reported indicate that a considerable number of research papers published present conflicts of interest, these reducing trust in the results by around 30% on average.[99] This discount is higher in the presence of material bias resulting from corporate funding and data access facilitation by corporations than in the presence of ideology and partisan affiliation-related bias. The authors also note that although ideology and career incentives are more evenly distributed, and therefore cancel each other out, the same cannot be said for financial support/funding that remains unbalanced in favour of large companies (and thus shows a pro-defendant bias) and it is even more unbalanced regarding access to data, in view of the important data harvesting and processing asymmetry between Big Tech platforms and other businesses (or even public authorities).

54. In conclusion, theoretical research and empirical evidence indicate the existence of considerable negative externalities affecting both the market for forensic economic expertise and the intellectual marketplace, from conflicts of interest and different forms of bias. In the absence of specific mechanisms to address the "distrust deficit" created by these conflicts, internalizing the negative externalities, the presence of these conflicts of interest may lead to a "systemic problem in which the negative externalities of conflicted research affect the entire academic community."[100] This "misalignment" of private and public incentives leads to "an overproduction of conflicted papers from a societal perspective" and calls for measures addressing such biases. Before, however, addressing possible remedies, it is important to explore the nature of these externalities.

---

96 *Id.* at 1–2.
97 *Id.* at 8.
98 *Id.* at 4.
99 *Id.*
100 *Id.* at 42.

IV. The Theoretical Hypothesis of the Strategic Nature of These Externalities Examined

55. Arguing for pluralism may seem to be a valid goal in the context of academic economics, but it may be difficult to transpose this discussion to the field of the market for forensic economic expertise. Would, for instance, emphasis on pluralism lead the courts or the competition authorities to choose a minority theory instead of a majority one, the two theories being equal from the point of view of explanatory power, for the simple reason that choosing a dominant theory would be considered as a reduction of pluralism in the marketplace of ideas? On what practical basis should this choice for pluralism be made? Would that require the artificial preservation of failing research programmes for the simple sake of pluralism? These difficult questions show that any analysis of pluralism should focus on the consideration of the selection process and in particular the reasons that led to the emergence of biased non-pluralistic results in the first place.

56. The concept of a "dominant" paradigm in economic thought extends beyond mere description of prevalent theoretical frameworks. This terminology illuminates how knowledge production in academia is shaped by external power dynamics. The dominance of certain economic paradigms often stems not from their inherent theoretical superiority but from the leveraging of influence from adjacent social spheres – particularly the market for economic expertise and private research funding. This interplay between academic economics and external power structures raises important questions about the autonomy of economic thought and the mechanisms through which certain theoretical perspectives achieve and maintain their dominant status.[101]

57. It is obvious that if the selection process, which can be conceived as applied practical reason, worked well, there would be no "dominant" paradigm, in the sense that the representatives of all "research programmes" and "paradigms" would feel confident that their positions are equally taken into consideration in adjudicating each case, according to the merits and fit of their arguments and theory *to the facts in question*. The lack of trust in the selection process could thus be explained by the fact that there is the perception that actors behave strategically. These actors can be internal to academia ("research programmes," "schools of thought," "paradigms") or external to it (e.g. corporations funding research). Several structural market features illuminate potential sources of leverage in shaping economic paradigms. The highly concentrated nature

---

[101] I refer here to the concept of dominance as envisaged by Michael Walzer, in the sense that some actors may control a social good (here economic power), whose control commands a wide range of other goods, presumably in other spheres of social activity, thus blurring or collapsing the necessary boundaries that should exist in the structuration of society along different "spheres of justice": MICHAEL WALZER, SPHERES OF JUSTICE: A DEFENSE OF PLURALISM AND EQUALITY (1983).

of the forensic economic expertise market, combined with the oligopsonistic power wielded by corporate clients, creates conditions where certain theoretical perspectives may be privileged over others. To the extent that the same (useful to the defence) arguments come up again and again in litigation, and judges become more familiar with those modes of thought compared to other arguments, this may facilitate their eventual acceptance and lead to change in the interpretation of the law.[102] Furthermore, the strategic positioning of major funding entities in competition economics research within the broader marketplace of ideas provides insight into which actors possess both the means and motivations to exercise such intellectual leverage. These market dynamics help explain the mechanisms through which particular economic paradigms achieve and maintain their dominant position in academic discourse.

58. The hypothesis to empirically examine is therefore whether the concentrated structure of the market for economic expertise, and intentional strategies followed by the actors present in this market (either as sellers of expertise or as buyers of it), may affect the process of scientific knowledge production in competition economics and thus the marketplace of economic discourse about competition matters, which in turn also influences the process of forensic economic expertise, as this often relies on argumentation drawn from academic economic studies in the area. It is relevant in this context to note that, in contrast to other disciplines, in which forensic scientists and academic researchers form distinct scientific communities, the leading forensic competition economists are academics who actively participate in theoretical economic debates. Consequently, it may be expected that the emergence of a market for economic experts, and its structure, will impact the research agenda of certain areas in economics (e.g. industrial organization) linked to competition policy. The empirical validation, or not, of this hypothesis forms part of ongoing work by the author of this study.

59. However, it is already possible to put forward some theoretical arguments drawing on the sociology of professions and sociological literature to support the intuition behind this hypothesis.

60. In some of her recent work, renowned sociologist of professions Magali Larson has focused on the relations between knowledge and power, preferring the terminology of "discipline" rather than the narrower concept of "profession."[103] For Larson, the monopolization of a specific discourse constitutes the means through which power is exercised. This discursive monopoly is granted if the profession, transformed into

---

102 I am thankful to Todd Davies for making this point.

103 Magali Sarfatti Larson, *In the Matter of Experts and Professionals, or How Impossible Is to Leave Nothing Unsaid, in* THE FORMATION OF THE PROFESSIONS: KNOWLEDGE, STATE AND STRATEGY 24, 37 (Rolf Thorstendahl & Michael Burrage eds., 1990).

a discipline, succeeds in presenting its theoretical apparatus as scientific, that is, empirical, objective, disinterested, and methodologically rigorous. Larson notes that university departments constitute the core regions where professional discourse develops.[104] The links between the communities of academic economists and forensic economists in competition economics guarantee the semblance of neutrality of the produced knowledge, conceived as a strategy for exercising power. But what is the social space in which interactions, transactions and eventually power are exercised?

61. Bourdieu and Wacquant also understand each social field of practice as a competitive game or a field of struggles in which social agents strategically interact in the quest to maximize their positions.[105] The stakes of this competitive game will be the accumulation of capital. Capital can take four forms: economic (e.g. money, assets), cultural (e.g. knowledge), social (e.g. networks, affiliation) and symbolic (e.g. credentials). Moving the analogy of the field further, it is possible to conceive the social arena of competition law and economics as a specific strategic action "field,"[106] entangling multiple markets (e.g. the market for competition economics expertise/advice, the marketplace of ideas about competition), on which different players (forensic economists, lawyers, academic economists, regulators, judges) develop strategies. Each of them competes with one other for the acquisition of symbolic and, consequently, economic and social capital. Despite their different dispositions and strategies, these actors should be conceived as being entangled in a mutual process of influence that contributes to the ongoing co-construction of the "field."

62. It follows that focusing the analysis on the emergence of the profession of forensic economists without examining the complex relations forensic economists develop with other actors they interact with, and the field's topologies of power, may profoundly misunderstand their strategies and miss the important changes that take place in their dispositions – their specific *doxa* – when internalizing the specific economic and social conditions that characterize the field in which they are active.

63. As Sheila Jasanoff explains in her work, "[s]cience carried out in non-academic settings may be subordinated to institutional pressures that critically influence researcher's attitudes to issues of proof and evidence" and "in turn affect the packaging and presentation of scientific results."[107] An important difference between pure and mandated science, respectively

---

104 *Id.* at 37–38.

105 Pierre Bourdieu & Loïc J. D. Wacquant, An Invitation to Reflexive Sociology 127 (1992).

106 A "strategic action field" is "a constructed mesolevel social order in which actors (who can be individual or collective) are attuned to and interact with one another based on shared (which is not to say consensual) understandings about the purposes of the field, relationships to others in the field (including who has power and why), and the rules governing legitimate action in the field": Neil Fligstein & Doug McAdam, A Theory of Fields 9 (2012).

107 Sheila Jasanoff, The Fifth Brand: Science Advisers as Policymakers 78 (1990).

academic economics and forensic economics, resides in the definition of standards by which each is evaluated. Jasanoff rightly notes that "[a]cademic research, on the whole, works within established scientific paradigms, subject to relatively well-negotiated prior understandings about what constitutes good research methodology. . . . Instead, the guidelines for validating science in the regulatory context tend to be fluid, controversial and arguably more politically motivated than those applicable to university-based research."[108]

64. This indirect reference to the different ethos of "ordinary" science has resolutely a Mertonian taste. The assumption is that the "regulatory science" of economics will fulfil four sets of institutional imperatives: universalism with its requirement of objectivity and impartiality, communism with its aversion to secrecy, disinterestedness with its emphasis on competition and testability, and organized scepticism with its opposition to crystallization.[109] One could identify in the efforts of "regulatory science" to integrate peer review processes and strict scrutiny by experts of the verifiability of results, an attempt to emulate the institutional imperatives of "ordinary" or "academic science."[110] It is well known that the Mertonian conception of disinterestedness advocates a fundamental distinction between the ethos of the scientist and the professional ethos: "The scientist does not stand vis-à-vis a lay clientele in the same fashion as do the physician and lawyer for example. The possibility of exploiting the credulity, ignorance, and dependence of the layman is thus considerably reduced."[111] In the Mertonian conception of science, rewards for scientists are "largely honorific, since even today, when science is largely professionalized, the pursuit of science is culturally defined as being primarily a disinterested search for truth and only secondarily a means of earning a livelihood."[112] Merton went even further by warning that "[t]o the extent that the scientist-layman relation does become paramount, there develop incentives for evading the mores of science."[113] The intervention of an external authority, outside the realm of the process of scientific discovery, is, thus, seen as a major anomaly to the Mertonian framework of impartial science.[114]

65. Ironically, Merton's concern over the influence of the external authority on the definition of norms of scientific validity seems to describe well the situation of competition economics: this time it is the market for economic

---

108 *Id.* at 79.

109 Robert K. Merton, *The Ethos of Science* (1942), *in* ROBERT K. MERTON, ON SOCIAL STRUCTURE AND SCIENCE 267 (1996).

110 JASANOFF, *supra* note 107. On the importance of peer review in science, *see* Robert K. Merton, *The Reward System of Science* (1957), *in* MERTON, *supra* note 109, at 296.

111 Merton, *supra* note 109, at 275.

112 Merton, *supra* note 110, at 303–304.

113 Merton, *supra* note 109, at 275.

114 Robert K. Merton, *Science and the Social Order* (1938), in MERTON, *supra* note 109, at 280.

advice that interacts with the scientific process, and not political authorities or the State in general, as was feared by Merton in the late 1930s. This concern was also expressed by Mannheim, who referred to these extra-theoretical factors that are not driven by the "inner dialectic" of the thought.[115] The "Strong Programme" in sociology of knowledge will also not disagree with the view that social interests, in particular "vested professional interests," influence the standards and conventions of science.[116]

66. In his research, Coats also examined the significance of the professionalization process of economics and the interrelationships between the various economics professions (academic, government economists, business).[117] Drawing on the Strong Programme in sociology of knowledge,[118] Coats explained how "[t]he rise of professionalism, both within the academic community and in society at large, represented an effort by new specialist groups to gain social status and market power."[119] In this context, he describes the "academization" of economics, the university becoming "the principal intellectual and social context for the advancement of scientific economics" in the late 19th century as an important milestone in this strategy,[120] but he also notes that the rapid growth of non-academic opportunities, in particular in government in the 1930s, may have affected the content of economic thought produced, its methodology and its standards of validity.

67. The influence of social networks and power relations on competition economics is now widely acknowledged, significantly shaping both research agendas and the emergence of dominant theoretical frameworks in the marketplace of ideas. A particularly notable dynamic exists in the complex interplay between forensic economics and academic discourse. The boundary between courtroom expertise and scholarly debate is increasingly porous, with expert witness interactions extending well beyond legal proceedings into academic journals, conferences, and research networks like SSRN.

68. This integration serves a strategic purpose: the development and defence of particular theoretical positions in academic forums become an integral component of establishing legitimacy for courtroom arguments. Such academic validation carries special significance due to the judiciary's inherent scepticism toward expert testimony. Competition authorities (and courts) may accord greater weight to peer-reviewed economic literature than to

---

115 KARL MANNHEIM, IDEOLOGY AND UTOPIA: AN INTRODUCTION TO THE SOCIOLOGY OF KNOWLEDGE (1929).
116 DAVID BLOOR, KNOWLEDGE AND SOCIAL IMAGERY 170 (2nd ed. 1991).
117 A.W. BOB COATS, THE SOCIOLOGY AND PROFESSIONALIZATION OF ECONOMICS (1993).
118 DAVID BLOOR, KNOWLEDGE AND SOCIAL IMAGERY (1976).
119 COATS, *supra* note 117, at 138.
120 *Id.* at 40.

expert witness reports, creating a feedback loop where forensic economic arguments seek legitimation through academic channels.

69. This dynamic reveals a subtle irony: judicial scepticism toward expert testimony has inadvertently strengthened the connection between forensic and academic economics, as parties strategically leverage scholarly discourse to enhance the credibility of their positions. The result is an intricate ecosystem where legal, academic, and market forces continuously interact to shape the evolution of competition economics thought. The legal system emerges as a crucial strategic ally in the ongoing intellectual contests between competing academic networks in economics. This alliance operates through a sophisticated feedback mechanism: the legal system's normative authority ensures that dominant economic paradigms fundamentally shape legal interpretation and application, both in specific cases and through analogical reasoning in subsequent litigation. Once a research paradigm becomes juridified, by being incorporated into the law as an economic transplant,[121] this may lead to path dependence in academic research, as research that contributes to this now juridified research paradigm is more easily accepted than research that challenges it. The resultant interdependence between academic economic discourse and the forensic expertise market creates lucrative opportunities for academic economists who also serve as consultants.

70. Empirical research has demonstrated that legal system adoption of particular economic frameworks serves as a powerful determinant of success in the intellectual competitions between rival economic networks. This process generates a stabilizing effect for mainstream economic thought, as legal recognition provides both legitimacy and durability to specific theoretical approaches. The integration of economic reasoning into legal doctrine thus functions not merely as a validation mechanism but as an institutional force that reinforces and perpetuates particular economic paradigms. This dynamic reveals how the intersection of legal authority and economic expertise creates a self-reinforcing cycle: dominant economic theories shape legal interpretation, which in turn cements their position within both academic discourse and forensic practice, ultimately generating sustained economic returns for practitioners aligned with these prevailing paradigms.[122]

71. Current changes in scientific practice with a more systematic industry funding of economic research challenge the traditional conception of knowledge production as being located primarily in scientific institutions, such as universities, or the public sector (government), and structured by scientific disciplines. Whatever the name given to this description of

---

121 Lianos, *supra* note 20.
122 Yuval P. Yonay, The Struggle Over the Soul of Economics (1998).

the evolution of knowledge production[123] – Mode 2, "post-normal science," "Triple-Elix" and "post-academic science" – the general question of validity of the knowledge produced in this context is an issue generally not examined. As Ziman observes, the "meta-scientific spotlight has shifted to ethical issues," but *in fine* more general questions of validity of established scientific theories or the weight that should be given to a highly unorthodox scientific opinion, or an opinion produced outside the academic environment, remain largely unexplored.[124]

72. Recent efforts to discuss the standards of validity of such "contextualized science" have not been convincing. Nowotny, Scott and Gibbons[125] argue that knowledge is produced in a new heterogeneous public space than the university, what they call "the agora," where society and science meet, and note the evolution in terms of standards of validity from reliable knowledge to "socially robust knowledge," the latter being "relational" and "process oriented." However, no clear explanation is provided on what distinguishes this type of social robustness from the scientific robustness required for Mode 1 knowledge produced in the traditional setting of the university. Of particular interest is also that the claim of expertise is based not only on scientific reputation but also on the ability of the expert to "orchestrate" the many heterogeneous and context-specific knowledge dimensions that are involved in this fuzzier process of knowledge production.

73. This literature and the analysis of the way the consultancy industry in forensic economics is organized demonstrate fundamental structural links between the forensic economic expertise market and the marketplace of ideas in competition economics, evidenced through both actor interdependencies and strategic alignments across these domains. Market conditions and power dynamics in each sphere inevitably influence the other due to this structural integration, with dominant actors able to orchestrate resources across both markets. This influence extends beyond immediate market outcomes to shape the very foundations of the field, including the epistemological standards that define valid economic analysis and "good science" in competition economics.

74. Large digital platforms occupy a uniquely influential position in competition economics through their dual role as major consumers of forensic services and significant funders of academic research. This strategic positioning stems from their global involvement in antitrust investigations and litigation, coupled with their substantial funding of academic research in competition economics. This dual market presence enables these platforms

---

123   See, for a literature review, Laurens K. Hessels & Harro van Lente, *Re-Thinking New Knowledge Production: A Literature Review and a Research Agenda*, 37 RSCH. POL'Y 740 (2008).

124   JOHN M. ZIMAN, REAL SCIENCE: WHAT IT IS, AND WHAT IT MEANS 17 (2002).

125   HELGA NOWOTNY, PETER B. SCOTT & MICHAEL T. GIBBONS, RE-THINKING SCIENCE: KNOWLEDGE AND THE PUBLIC IN AN AGE OF UNCERTAINTY (2001).

to effectively orchestrate substantial resources and shape the production of knowledge and discourse in competition economics.

75. Their distinctive positioning across both the academic funding and forensic services markets facilitates their growing dominance in the broader field of competition law and economics. This concentration of influence raises significant concerns about potential conflicts of interest and their impact on the intellectual marketplace. The ability to simultaneously influence both academic research directions and forensic economic analysis creates risks for the independent development of competition theory and practice.

76. Addressing these power dynamics becomes crucial for preserving the integrity of both the marketplace of ideas and the forensic competition economics market. Without appropriate safeguards, the selection process for superior theories and arguments may be compromised by the outsized influence of these digital platforms. This situation calls for structural interventions to ensure that theoretical and analytical developments in competition economics emerge from genuine scholarly discourse rather than being shaped by the strategic interests of dominant market players.

V. Tools for the Containment of Conflicts of Interest

77. A number of procedural and substantive law reforms were introduced in order to limit the risk of partisanship in the market for economic forensic expertise services, including the development of hybrid mid-adversarial, mid-consultative expert witness procedures, admissibility standards for expertise, greater involvement of "neutral" or impartial (judge-appointed) experts in the process.[126] These reforms were all based on the assumption that through these tools, expertise can become "objective." In the received view, expertise cannot be normative or involve value judgments. As is rightly explained by Gary Edmond, "[t]ypically, objectivity is equated with qualities such as independence, impartiality and neutrality. Good science, so this story goes, derives its authority from being evidence-based, efficacious, communal, critical and driven by a powerful method. These characteristics, which are often seen as dimensions of scientific (or mechanical) objectivity, purportedly function to liberate science from a range of contaminants, such as subjectivity, personal interests, partisanship, fraud, speculation, bias, gratuitous assumptions and so forth."[127] Emphasizing the specific role of judges or competition authorities as gatekeepers in this process would therefore lead to an increase in the amount of processing in the presence of conflicting expert testimony.

---

126 For a discussion, *see* Lianos, *supra* note 23.

127 Gary Edmond, *After Objectivity: Expert Evidence and Procedural Reform*, 25 SYDNEY L. REV. 131 (2003).

1. The Gatekeeping Role of Judges in the Market for Forensic Economics

78. The *Daubert* principle for the admissibility of economic evidence in US civil procedure provides a specific theory for consideration in clear-cut cases of "junk science" where there is no doubt that the theory presented is totally unfounded or the expert is not qualified, and judges move to exclude evidence from consideration by the jury.[128] Similar, although less strict, admissibility rules apply in the UK,[129] and have occasionally given rise to an extensive analysis of the qualifications and possible conflicts of interest of expert witnesses, even if there is no jury trial and all competition-related litigation is heard by a specialized tribunal.[130] Such procedural rules show that there is some recognition that reputational costs in the market for forensic economic expertise or the adversarial process may not be enough to deal with most cases of biased expertise, hence the need to regulate any possible conflicts of interest *ex ante*. However, excluding the expertise from being considered may not be an adequate solution for most cases, where there is a suspicion of structural, intellectual, material or other biases, but the expert is otherwise competent and has the required qualifications. Litigation-driven or materially biased research would most likely satisfy the Daubert criteria and will then be assessed in equal terms with independent academically created research.[131] However, it is expected that decision-makers will consider, to the extent they have that information, the material (and other) conflicts of interest in evaluating and weighing the sufficiency of evidence provided by the expert.[132] This may lead to procedures that will attempt to exclude all external factors from the academic discipline-related discussion between expert witnesses, for instance by removing the parties' lawyers, at least momentarily, from the cross-examination of experts to ensure the academic nature of the discussion. The expert "hot tub" procedure, developed by the Australian Competition Tribunal

---

128 Daubert v. Merrell Dow Pharmaceuticals, Inc., 509 U.S. 579 (1993).

129 *See*, for instance, BSkyB Limited and Sky Subscribers Services Limited v. HP Enterprise Services UK Limited (formerly Electronic Data Systems Limited) and Electronic Data Systems LLC (formerly Electronic Data Systems Corporation) [2010] EWHC 86 (TCC); British Telecommunications v. Office of Communications (BCMR), Case No. 1260/3/3/16 (2017) (CAT), ¶ 87; Lexon (UK) Limited v. Competition and Markets Authority, Case No. 1344/1/12/20 (2021) (CAT); Royal Mail Group Limited v. DAF Trucks Limited and Others, Case Nos 1284/5/7/18, 1290/5/7/18 (2023) (CAT), ¶¶ 25 & 235.

130 *See*, for a discussion, John Davies & Lau Nilausen, Technicians or Master-Economists? The Role of Testifying Economists in Competition Litigation (June 2023), https://www.catribunal.org.uk/sites/cat/files/2023-11/Paper%20-%20The%20Role%20of%20Testifying%20Economists%20in%20Competition%20Litigation%20%28Compass%20Lexecon-Davies-Lau%29.pdf.

131 Nicola Giocoli, *Rejected! Antitrust Economists as Expert Witnesses in the Post-Daubert World*, 42 J. Hɪs. Ecᴏɴ. Tʜᴏᴜɢʜᴛ 203 (2020).

132 On the role of the standard of proof and the analysis of the expert's possible conflict of interest in analysing the sufficiency of evidence, *see* Lianos, *supra* note 23.

in the 1970s,[133] and emulated in the UK,[134] aims to maintain the basic principles of the adversarial system while at the same time orchestrating a more "neutral" interaction among experts.

2. Self-Regulation and Disclosure Policies

79. Professional self-regulation has emerged as one approach to managing conflicts of interest in forensic economics, particularly through the establishment of ethics frameworks by key professional organizations. The National Association of Forensic Economics (NAFE), established in 1988, and the American Academy of Economic and Financial Experts (AAEFE), formed in 1989, have both developed ethical guidelines aimed at preserving professional integrity. These organizations' ethics statements emphasize crucial principles, including the rejection of predetermined positions in litigation, avoidance of ethically questionable assignments, prohibition of contingent compensation, and mandatory disclosure of received or anticipated benefits. By establishing these guidelines, these professional bodies attempt to standardize ethical practices in forensic economic analysis through voluntary compliance mechanisms.[135] The American Economic Association (AEA) has also issued a policy with detailed rules about disclosure concerning the sources of financial support for the research.[136]

80. The competition law and economics academic community's commitment to disclosure is exemplified by the Academic Society for Competition Law (ASCOLA)'s Declaration of Ethics, adopted by its general assembly in New York in 2018. This declaration establishes three foundational principles: independence and objectivity in research, transparency in funding sources, and fairness in presenting academic findings. Through detailed disclosure requirements, the declaration provides a structured framework for maintaining academic integrity in competition law scholarship, representing a significant step toward standardizing ethical practices in the field.[137] The Declaration was accepted as good practice by some of the leading academic

---

133 Gary Edmond, *Secrets of the 'Hot Tub': Expert Witnesses, Concurrent Evidence and Judge-led Law Reform in Australia*, 27 CIV. JUST. Q. 51, 58 (2008); Maureen Brunt, *Antitrust in the Courts: The Role of Economics and of Economists*, *in* INTERNATIONAL ANTITRUST LAW & POLICY: FORDHAM CORPORATE LAW 1998 357, 364–66 (Barry Hawk ed., 1999).

134 Part 35.7 of the UK Civil Procedure Rules. Its first application in the UK was in the Streetmap v. Google [2016] EWHC 253 (Ch), ¶ 47. *See* Penny Coombs, *The England & Wales High Court dismisses a claim for abuse of dominance brought against a Big Tech firm by an online map provider and holds that an alleged harmful effect of a pro-competitive innovation by a dominant company must be significant in the market to constitute an abuse (*Streetmap / Google*)*, E-COMPETITIONS Feb. 2016, art. no. 111655.

135 *Statement of Ethical Principles*, AAEFE, http://aaefe.org/Documents/AAEFE_Ethical_Principles.pdf. *See also*, for a similar effort, *Statement of Ethical Principles and Principles of Professional Practice*, NAFE, https://nafe.net/ethics/. Note that the AAEFE has a stronger disclosure statement than NAFE, requiring that such disclosure "should be in sufficient detail to allow identification of specific sources relied upon, and replication of the analytical conclusions by a competent economist with reasonable effort."

136 *See Disclosure Policy*, AEA, https://www.aeaweb.org/journals/policies/disclosure-policy, and the examples of disclosure provided in https://www.aeaweb.org/journals/policies/disclosure-policy/disclosure-examples.

137 *See Declaration of Ethics*, ASCOLA, https://ascola.org/declaration-of-ethics/.

journals in the area of competition law and policy.[138] Additional approaches put forward include the "naming and shaming" of experts that are captured, the sharing of the data code as well as of the disclosure agreements that may limit the use of data provided by corporations, and the mandatory disclosure of expert testimonies, even when a case is settled, so as to enable peer-review and critical engagement with the content of the expertise.[139]

3. Disclosure Rules With Some Form of Sanctioning

81. The persistent emergence of non-disclosure cases and the proliferation of opaquely funded research centres in competition law and policy suggest, however, the inadequacy of self-regulatory approaches. Despite established ethical guidelines, the same corporate entities continue to fund research through complex, often obscured networks, indicating that reliance on individual authors' ethical compliance and self-regulation has failed to address the significant negative externalities of corporate funding. This pattern demonstrates that voluntary disclosure of material conflicts of interest, however well-intentioned, proves insufficient to safeguard academic integrity in this field.

82. Barrios et al. highlight fundamental flaws in assuming that research users can effectively discount conflicted research. Their analysis identifies two critical issues. First, incomplete or absent disclosure enables biased research to erode trust in the entire field, creating negative externalities that damage the credibility of non-conflicted work. Second, current academic evaluation systems fail to incorporate conflict of interest considerations when assessing research impact. Publication metrics, whether based on raw publication counts, citation numbers, or journal prestige, typically weigh conflicted and non-conflicted research equally, offering no mechanism to apply appropriate discounting in career advancement decisions.[140] This leads, according to these authors, to the result that "the marketplace of ideas overvalues conflicted research."[141] Rather than advocating for an outright ban on corporate funding or conflicted research, Barrios et al. propose a nuanced approach to managing its impact on academic credibility. Their recommendations centre on two key mechanisms: implementing systematic discounting of conflicted research in academic evaluations and promotions, and establishing more rigorous transparency requirements for data access agreements between

---

138 This includes the *Journal of Competition Law & Economics*, the *Journal of Competition Law & Practice* and the *Journal of Antitrust Enforcement*. *See*, for a discussion, Alfonso Lamadrid & Pablo Ibáñez Colomo, *On Disclosure and Conflicts of Interests: Three Years Later, We Are in a Better Place*, CHILLIN'COMPETITION (July 29, 2020) https://chillingcompetition.com/2020/07/29/on-disclosure-and-conflicts-of-interests-three-years-later-we-are-in-a-better-place.

139 Zingales, *supra* note 11, at 146–47.

140 Barrios et al., *supra* note 92, at 43.

141 *Id.*

academics and private sector providers. This approach acknowledges the reality of corporate funding while seeking to mitigate its potential negative effects on research trustworthiness through institutional reforms and enhanced disclosure requirements.[142]

4. Mandated Disclosure Sunshine Regulation for Corporate Funders

83. Another avenue for addressing corporate influence in academic research recognizes the fundamental connection between market power and the above-mentioned negative externalities. This approach acknowledges how dominance in both the professional economic expertise market and the marketplace of ideas can shape research outcomes. Whether through the buying or selling of expert services in competition matters, or through the industry's strategic demand for favourable research, positions of economic power directly influence the creation and dissemination of knowledge in competition economics. Concentrated industries may hire a large portion of academic expertise in their field and exercise control over what those academics publish through agreements governing the use of the data they provide them. Understanding these power dynamics in both professional and academic spheres provides essential context for developing effective regulatory responses.[143]

84. This further step will justify the move towards some form of asymmetric sunshine regulation imposed on corporations and business groups for which there is now public information on their systematic effort to influence academic research in competition policy,[144] and which are also, in view of pending investigations and litigation, active in the use of forensic competition economics experts.

85. Disclosure requirements regarding payments to consultants, experts, and academic institutions are well-established within various regulated industries in the US, operating through both federal and state mechanisms. At the federal level, the Securities and Exchange Commission (SEC) mandates publicly traded companies, including telecommunications firms, to submit detailed financial information through annual Form 10-K filings, which may also encompass comprehensive reporting of consultant-related expenses. Additionally, these companies must file Form 8-K to report significant events, including major consulting contracts or expert engagements.

86. In the telecommunications sector specifically, the Federal Communications Commission (FCC) implements parallel disclosure requirements through Form 499-A, which requires service providers to report detailed financial

---

142 *Id.* at 39–41.

143 *See also id.* at 42 (noting that in concentrated industries or academia, career concerns may exert significant pressures on people to skew their results, this highlighting "a major cost of industrial concentration," which is the fact that it "ultimately destroys the diversity of ideas in the marketplace of knowledge").

144 *See* the media references in footnote 12 above.

information, including payments to contractors and consultants. While companies also typically disclose expenditure information in their annual shareholder reports, these documents generally provide less granular detail about specific payment allocations and rarely include exhaustive lists of funded consultants, experts, or research institutions.

87. At the state level, telecommunications companies face additional disclosure obligations through reporting requirements established by state public utility commissions (PUCs). These state-level annual reports often parallel federal disclosure requirements but may demand more specific financial details, including payments to consultants and experts. PUCs can also mandate project-specific disclosures, particularly for major infrastructure initiatives or regulatory proceedings, requiring detailed documentation of expenditures on external expertise and consulting services.

88. Despite these various disclosure requirements, payments to academics and consultants often remain partially obscured in corporate financial reporting. In SEC filings like Forms 10-K and 8-K, such expenditures may not meet the materiality threshold for explicit disclosure, particularly when individual payments are modest relative to a company's overall spending. Companies frequently categorize these expenses under broad classifications such as "professional fees" or "consulting expenses" in their financial statements, especially when dealing with routine, recurring payments of relatively small magnitude for their scale of operations. This aggregation practice is particularly evident in cases where multiple payments occur throughout the year, as could be demonstrated by available public records of corporate funding patterns. Furthermore, disclosure limitations may be reinforced by legal constraints, including confidentiality agreements and EU General Data Protection Regulation (GDPR), which can restrict the publication of specific payment amounts and engagement details.

89. A first step towards more transparency, and also in order to enable the systematic use of the conflict-of-interest discount in promotion and other evaluation procedures (e.g. grants, academic positions), would be to impose a clear duty of disclosure to some large corporate funders, which, due to the position of economic power they enjoy, may attempt to leverage this position in the marketplace of ideas. The Digital Markets Act (DMA) may provide the tool to impose such disclosure duties to gatekeepers, in a similar vein as the information requirements imposed on them under article 14 DMA, which require them to inform the Commission about any intended concentration, where the merging entities or the target of concentration provide core platform services or any other services in the digital sector.[145] This duty of disclosure

---

[145] This proposal thus only covers gatekeepers in core platform services, but not other powerful firms in other industries (pharmaceuticals, agriculture, etc.). The reason for that is that the sheer economic power of digital platforms in many markets, their control of data resources and also publicly available information about corporate funding of academic research identify them as the appropriate personal scope for this legislative

will not only apply to the part of the gatekeeper's business that has been designated as a core platform service; it will also extend to all the activities of the undertaking within the meaning of article 5(1) of Regulation (EC) 139/2004, but also to funding by business entities in the gatekeeper's relevant ecosystems that, to their knowledge, have a similar purpose. This broad information obligation will guarantee that the gatekeeper takes an active role in monitoring the relevant activities of its ecosystem, in the same way as this is envisioned in the context of the corporate sustainability due diligence directive for responsible corporate behaviour across companies' global value chains.[146]

90. A future revision of the DMA could establish comprehensive disclosure obligations for gatekeepers' academic and research funding activities. This expanded framework would require annual reporting of all payments for consulting and professional services to academics and research centres, either directly or indirectly through industry groups and foundations. The disclosure requirements would encompass both monetary compensation and in-kind benefits, such as data access privileges, conference participation support, and travel accommodations. Following models established by professional organizations like the AEA and the ASCOLA, these disclosures would need to include detailed explanations of payment amounts and underlying rationales for significant engagements. To ensure accessibility and transparency, all disclosures would be centralized and publicly available through a dedicated portal on the European Commission's website.

91. To establish a comprehensive historical record of corporate funding in academia, the disclosure requirements should include a retrospective component covering at least the preceding decade of payments and funding arrangements. This lookback provision is particularly important given the documented evidence of corporate funding dating back to 2005–2006, and acknowledges the extended timeframe typically involved in academic research and publication processes. Verification of these disclosures would be conducted by auditors seconded from national tax authorities to the European Commission, who would be granted unrestricted access to relevant corporate financial records, including books, accounts, and vouchers. The European Commission would integrate this funding transparency data into its annual DMA implementation reports required under article 35, ensuring ongoing public accountability and oversight of corporate influence in academic research.

---

initiative. Once experience has accumulated, similar schemes mandating disclosure could also be extended to other industries for powerful actors.

146 Directive (EU) 2024/1760 of the European Parliament and of the Council of 13 June 2024 on Corporate Sustainability Due Diligence and Amending Directive (EU) 2019/1937 and Regulation (EU) 2023/2859, 2024 O.J. (L 2024/1760).

92. This centralized disclosure framework would represent a significant shift from the current fragmented system, which relies primarily on individual academics' voluntary compliance with ethical guidelines. By monitoring corporate funding at its source and empowering the European Commission with substantial enforcement authority, the new approach would ensure systematic oversight and accountability. This transition from a discretionary, decentralized model to a mandatory, centralized system acknowledges that effective transparency requires both comprehensive monitoring capabilities and meaningful enforcement mechanisms. The Commission's authority to impose substantial remedies and sanctions for non-compliance under the DMA would provide the necessary incentives for corporate funders to maintain accurate and complete disclosure records.[147] Access to gatekeepers' comprehensive financial records would serve multiple regulatory objectives beyond mere transparency. Such access would enable Commission staff to develop deeper insights into gatekeepers' operational strategies, particularly regarding their influence on academic discourse. This broader visibility would be further enhanced by the Commission's inspection powers under article 23 DMA, which could uncover internal documents revealing undisclosed long-term commitments and strategic initiatives. The combination of regular financial disclosure requirements and targeted inspection capabilities would create a more complete picture of how gatekeepers leverage their resources to shape academic and policy discussions.

5. Matching of Funding Requirement Imposed to Corporate Funders

93. While mandatory disclosure represents a step toward addressing the negative externalities of industry-funded academic research, its effectiveness relies on potentially optimistic assumptions about information processing by end users. The proposed approach assumes that knowledge of funding sources will enable readers to appropriately discount research findings through conflict-of-interest considerations. However, this assumption may prove unrealistic in practice. Even with full transparency about funding sources and research programmes, end users may struggle to properly evaluate and contextualize research findings, particularly in an environment increasingly dominated by industry-funded studies. This challenge is further compounded by the considerable "communication power"[148] of digital platforms and social media, which can amplify and promote research findings regardless of their funding sources. In this context, it would be important to ensure that any algorithms used to promote content

---

[147] The usual sanctions of the DMA will apply as for infringements of the information requirements under art. 14 DMA.

[148] MANUEL CASTELLS, COMMUNICATION POWER (2013).

on the platform are applied according to objective and non-discriminatory criteria, with regard to the content in terms of academic views.[149]

94. The mere identification of funded scholars and programmes, without explicit negative implications, may prove insufficient to enable meaningful discounting of potentially biased research in an increasingly crowded intellectual marketplace. Mere disclosure requirements fail to address the historical trust deficit created by years of cross-subsidization between unfunded and industry-funded research. A more comprehensive solution would involve restructuring the entire research funding ecosystem to align corporate incentives with the public interest in unbiased research. This could be achieved through two alternative approaches. First, requiring all corporate funding to flow through objective, competitive processes overseen by public research foundations or the European Research Council (ERC), thereby limiting potential distrust in the selection process itself. Alternatively, implementing a matching requirement where corporations must provide equivalent funding for independent research projects for every euro spent on industry-directed research. Under this approach, if a corporation invests €10 million in regulatory science research advancing its interests, it must contribute an equal amount to independent projects selected through peer review processes managed by academic institutions such as the AEA or ASCOLA.

95. This matching mechanism would help restore balance between industry-funded and independent research. Furthermore, the framework should explicitly promote academic diversity by ensuring that a portion of the matching funds benefits researchers from developing and emerging economies. This provision acknowledges that these scholars often lack access to robust public research funding systems and are consequently underrepresented in academic discourse. By expanding participation beyond traditional research centres/institutes, this approach would enhance the representation of diverse stakeholder perspectives in academic discussions.

96. The proposed matching requirement, while seemingly ambitious, would be narrowly targeted to regulatory science research rather than encompassing all corporate-funded academic work. This focused approach recognizes the unique significance of "regulatory science,"[150] particularly in competition law, where economic theories and interpretations can significantly influence market dynamics and regulatory outcomes. The strategic value of regulatory science research makes it an especially powerful lever for dominant firms seeking to shape policy discourse and legal interpretations

---

149 With the exception, of course, of the protective legal provisions against "hate speech" and the spreading of illegal content, under the Digital Services Act.

150 Sheila Jasanoff, *The Practices of Objectivity in Regulatory Science*, in SOCIAL KNOWLEDGE IN THE MAKING 307 (Charles Camic, Neil Gross & Michèle Lamont eds., 2011).

in their favour. By limiting the matching requirement to regulatory science, the proposal acknowledges that corporate funding of technical or commercial research serves different purposes and warrants different treatment. This targeted intervention is justified by the need to correct the longstanding imbalance created by years of unregulated corporate influence in regulatory science, where economic and legal theories can be strategically deployed to reinforce market dominance and potentially limit intellectual diversity in competition policy discourse.

VI. Conclusion

97. The landscape of competition economics has undergone significant transformation with the emergence of a market for forensic expertise and increased industry funding of academic research. This evolution has introduced considerable risks of "capture" of competition policy research by powerful vested interests. The phenomenon has gained particular prominence amid ongoing competition investigations and litigation against major digital platforms, which have attracted attention for their extensive funding and support of research aligned with their interests and preferred policy directions.

98. The growing concentration of industrial power has intensified the problem of conflicts of interest and material bias, a challenge that has existed since the expert witness emerged as an independent actor in litigation during the first half of the 20th century, but has intensified in recent years in the field of competition economics as a result of industrial concentration, also in the market for forensic competition economics, and the rise of Big Tech. While the analysis primarily focuses on competition economics, its implications extend to other forms of expertise, including legal scholarship, to which similar principles (in terms of mandated disclosure and matching) should also apply.

99. Initially, the adversarial process and reputational considerations in the forensic expertise market were deemed sufficient safeguards against excessive expert bias, whether material or ideological. However, the distinction between the forensic economic expertise market and the broader marketplace of competition economics knowledge has become increasingly nebulous. Key actors frequently operate across both domains as part of the applied economic knowledge field in competition matters. This overlap creates a complex web of interdependencies between forensic economists, academics, companies under investigation, and corporate funders. Dominant players in the forensic competition economics market or concentrated industries, such as Big Tech, providing academic funding can leverage their influence across the entire field of competition economics, leading to significant negative externalities.

100. These externalities manifest primarily as a "trust deficit" – a burden imposed by conflicted research on non-conflicted research and researchers. This dynamic results in an overproduction of biased research and an underproduction of unbiased work. Moreover, it threatens to reduce the diversity of economic discourse, potentially compromising research quality and undermining academia's independence, self-governance, and autonomy as a distinct institution promoting valuable social activity, thus contributing to the "democratic deficit" of competition law as identified by Harry First in his co-authored work.

101. In response to these challenges, judges and competition authorities have developed increasingly stringent gatekeeping roles, in addition to the duty the experts have to the court, either by excluding conflicted research or by scrutinizing its evidential sufficiency more carefully. This evolution suggests that mere disclosure and reliance on adversarial processes and reputation mechanisms may be insufficient safeguards. While ensuring appropriate disclosure in academic economics might provide necessary transparency and help align public goals (as these were identified by the social contract of the specific polity) with private incentives, it perhaps expects too much from knowledge users in their ability to identify and appropriately discount conflicted research.

102. A more robust approach might involve incorporating the conflict of interest discount into promotion procedures and career development activities, thereby internalizing the negative externality and reshaping actor incentives. However, such measures may prove inadequate in addressing poor disclosure practices or reversing the existing legacy of corporate funding and influence on academic research in competition economics. Once intellectual positions and concepts stemming from conflicted research become established, they acquire independent momentum and become embedded in academic consensus, requiring significant time and effort to dislodge.

103. The implementation of mandated disclosure of industry funding imposed on gatekeepers emerges as a potentially superior solution. This approach could be particularly relevant in the context of the information requirements imposed on gatekeepers by the DMA. Furthermore, requiring transfer payments from industry to non-conflicted research could help counterbalance the risk that corporate influence poses to the diversity of economic discourse in the knowledge marketplace. Such measures would help preserve the integrity and independence of academic research while ensuring a more balanced and diverse scholarly debate in competition economics, thus contributing to the reversal of the "democratic deficit" of competition law.

PART II
What Comes First for Antitrust?

# The High Costs of Not Prohibiting Anticompetitive Megamergers

ELEANOR M. FOX[*]
New York University School of Law

Abstract

Megamergers can have large payoffs – especially to the executives and financial intermediaries. They can also entail large harms to competition and huge inefficiencies. When planned megamergers have significant anticompetitive aspects, they are nearly always approved with spin-offs and other conditions. This chapter argues that anticompetitive megamergers present a seriously overlooked enforcement problem at the point of remedies. Incentives facing enforcers to clear the merger with agreed remedies to protect their country are not aligned with an optimal solution to protect the world from the global anticompetitive effects. Moreover, anticompetitive megamergers tend to impose disparate costs on developing countries, which are often the loci of greatest harms and least power to prevent them. This article demonstrates in detail the misalignment of incentives through the window of the Bayer/Monsanto merger. It proposes solutions that would nudge national authorities to consider global mergers' harms and benefits holistically and to recognize when a simple prohibition is in the interests of their own jurisdiction as well as the interests of the world.

---

[*] Eleanor Fox is Walter J. Derenberg Professor of Trade Regulation Emerita, New York University School of Law. She dedicates this article to her dear friend and colleague, Harry First, who has given so much to the academy and the profession; to antitrust theory and to antitrust law enforcement; and who has been, for almost half a century, a most generous and supportive colleague. She thanks her research team on this article – Jackson K. Maxwell, NYU Law 2024; Emmett Tabor, NYU Law 2025; and Albin Quan, NYU Law 2025 – for their extraordinary research and drafting. She thanks Andrew Gavil, who, as editor of this article, contributed important insights.

I. Introduction

1. Megamergers can have large payoffs – especially to the executives and financial intermediaries.[1] They can also entail large harms to competition and huge inefficiencies. When planned megamergers have significant anticompetitive aspects and are challenged by the competition authorities, they are nearly always approved with spin-offs and other conditions. This chapter, dedicated to my dear colleague Harry First, who has been centrally concerned with the effectiveness of antitrust enforcement for all of his illustrious career,[2] argues that anticompetitive megamergers present a seriously overlooked enforcement problem at the point of remedies. Incentives facing enforcers to clear the merger with agreed remedies are not aligned with optimal solutions to protect competition in the world.

2. The US, EU, and a handful of other major jurisdictions vet the megamerger. Then, each agency negotiates with the merging parties for "fixes" that will notionally cure the anticompetitive aspects in their jurisdiction. The fixes are usually a combination of spin-offs and behavioral injunctions. Then, the merger problems are in effect handed over to scores of smaller or younger jurisdictions for each to do what it will and can to counter the looming anticompetitive effects facing its people. Some twenty to thirty jurisdictions may churn up their antitrust machines to examine the merger, consider anticompetitive aspects on their territories, and order relief – which may be spin-offs, separations, and conditions. Mandatory injunctions often require a stream of supply, access, or non-discriminatory treatment. They draw on the scarce resources of small agencies, often requiring years of supervision. The remedies usually do not fully restore the lost competition. Oftentimes, they are band-aids applied by small agencies to satisfy their publics that they have done something significant to "control" the giant merger. Often, the harm from the merger is greater in developing countries than in the developed jurisdictions that "went first" in the queue of enforcers because developing country markets are more fragile and their people are more vulnerable. Developing country authorities, while facing more serious competition problems, are less able

---

1   They are usually expected to benefit shareholders and consumers. But research shows that mergers rarely result in efficiencies or gains for consumers, and often result in inefficiencies. *See* Nancy L. Rose & Jonathan Sallet, *The Dichotomous Treatment of Efficiencies in Horizontal Mergers: Too Much? Too Little? Getting It Right*, 168 U. Pa. L. Rev. 1941 (2020); Mark Glick, Robert H. Lande & Darren Bush, *The Efficiency Rebuttal in the New Merger Guidelines: Bad Law and Bad Economics*, 38 Antitrust 20, 23 (2024).

2   Professor First's concerns with effective enforcement, including effective remedies, are illustrated in the following articles: Harry First, *Netscape Is Dead: Remedy Lessons from the Microsoft Litigation* 17–19, 22–24 (N.Y.U. Ctr. for L., Econ. & Org., Working Paper No. 08-49, 2008); Harry First, *Antitrust Remedies and the Big Tech Platform Cases*, in Judging Big Tech: Insights on Applying U.S. Antitrust Laws to Digital Markets 10 (Laura Alexander ed., 2022); Harry First, *Digital Platforms and Competition Policy in Developing Countries*, in Eleanor M. Fox Liber Amicorum: Antitrust Ambassador to the World 253 (Nicolas Charbit & Sébastian Gachot eds., 2021). Also, with Professor Andrew Gavil, Professor First made an important contribution to the scholarship on remedies in their book, Andrew I. Gavil & Harry First, The Microsoft Antitrust Cases: Competition Policy for the Twenty-first Century 235–79 (2014).

to handle competition problems, and have no practical power to prohibit a global merger even if by rights (i.e., good antitrust analysis) the merger should be prohibited.[3]

3. Megamergers that fit within this category are numerous. Four prominent examples are *Bayer/Monsanto*, *Dow Chemical/DuPont*, *AB InBev/SABMiller*, and *Holcim/Lafarge*.[4] If an antitrust expert were charged with devising an optimal resolution for the world, counting all of the costs and benefits to competition/efficiency/innovation globally and locally, that expert is likely to have sympathetically considered a clean and decisive prohibition of the merger. Given that we have no global competition law or framework and that incentives work at a national level, the incentives to do what is right for global welfare are misaligned. The serious chance to prohibit globally anticompetitive mergers is a missed opportunity, probably inflicting high and unnecessary costs on localities and the world.

4. This article identifies the unnecessary costs and missed opportunities for more effective competition policy regarding megamergers in view of the misaligned incentives. It uses one prominent transaction, *Bayer/Monsanto*, as a window. It then – drawing on both the capabilities of the International Competition Network and developments in Africa – presents a modest proposal for correcting the misalignment.

5. It proceeds as follows: Part II describes the *Bayer/Monsanto* merger and its probable effects on competition. Part III describes the process and outcomes of vetting the merger in the two most mature jurisdictions, the US and the EU. Part IV describes the same process and resolutions in the rest of the world. Part V analyzes incentives and their misalignment. Part VI recommends how the dynamic might be changed toward a holistic assessment.

II. Through the Window of *Bayer/Monsanto* – The Merger

6. In June 2018, Bayer, a German agrochemicals company and inventor of aspirin, paid US$63 billion to take over Monsanto, the number one producer of seeds and traits – one of the largest deals of the decade.[5]

---

3   *See* Liberty Mncube, Laurie Binge & Helen Kean, *Local competition assessment of global mergers – playing golf with one hand? A focus on South Africa and remedies sought*, in Conference *Competition law and developing countries: Overarching themes from Africa, cartels and corruption, and mergers*, Concurrences no. 2-2020, art. no. 94272 www.concurrences.com/94272, at 31, available at https://drive.google.com/file/d/1IQIHFCpB1lDUuL-fXaeyeTYbUSGHyTgO/view and copy on file with author; Reena Das Nair and Simon Roberts, *Sustainability and Competition in Eastern and Southern Africa*, in Research Handbook on Sustainability and Competition Law 457, 459–64 (Julian Nowag ed., 2024), https://www.elgaronline.com/edcollchap-oa/book/9781802204667/book-part-9781802204667-35.xml.

4   *See* Mncube et al., *supra* note 3, highlighting *Bayer/Monsanto*, *Dow/DuPont*, and *Holcim/Lafarge*; Das Nair & Roberts, *supra* note 3.

5   Press Release, Bayer, Bayer Closes Monsanto Acquisition (June 7, 2018), https://www.bayer.com/media/en-us/bayer-closes-monsanto-acquisition.

By August 2019, the *Wall Street Journal* reported that *Bayer/Monsanto* "ranks as one of the worst corporate deals in recent memory."[6] Scholars conducting a retrospective study reported: "[T]his was eventually one of the most value-destructive transactions ever experienced…"[7] A major culprit was harm to public health caused by Monsanto's blockbuster pesticide Roundup, found to cause cancer by jury verdicts within weeks after the closing of the deal.[8] But also, the deal threatened competition across the globe. The "fix" of divestiture of competitively overlapping assets largely to BASF may have merely entrenched an oligopoly.[9] Also, research analysts estimate that Bayer's final purchase price entailed a premium over value by about 18% – which translates into a higher cost base, usually elevating prices.[10] Meanwhile, the costs of completing the acquisition and divestitures and monitoring the divestitures were huge, as were the avoidable costs of multiple jurisdictions' closer scrutiny necessitated by their individual adversarial contexts.

7. This part describes the acquisition and its expected harms to competition, looking prospectively from the time of the announcement of the plan to merge.

1. The Transaction

8. The *Bayer/Monsanto* merger combined two of the largest global producers of agriculture seeds, traits, and agrochemicals during a wave of consolidation in the industry.[11] This industry was already dominated by a Big Six group of companies: Monsanto, Bayer, BASF, Syngenta,

---

6 Ruth Bender, *How Bayer-Monsanto Became One of the Worst Corporate Deals – in 12 Charts*, WALL ST. J. (Aug. 28, 2019, 10:12 AM), https://www.wsj.com/articles/how-bayer-monsanto-became-one-of-the-worst-corporate-dealsin-12-charts-11567001577.

7 Georgios Ritsos-Kokkinis, Case Study: The Bayer-Monsanto Acquisition Deal iii (Aug. 2020) (M.Sc. dissertation, Tilburg University), http://arno.uvt.nl/show.cgi?fid=153166. *See* Maurice E. Stucke & Allen P. Grunes, An Updated Antitrust Review of the Bayer-Monsanto Merger (The Konkurrenz Group, Mar. 6, 2018), annexed to *Farmers Overwhelmingly Oppose Bayer Monsanto Merger*, FARM AID BLOG (Mar. 8, 2018), https://www.farmaid.org/issues/corporate-power/farmers-overwhelmingly-oppose-bayer-monsanto-merger/.

8 Ritsos-Kokkinis *supra* note 7, at 7–12. Monsanto's herbicides also hurt farmers by ruining their crops. Johnatan Hettinger, *'Buy It or Else': Inside Monsanto and BASF's Moves to Force Dicamba on Farmers*, INVESTIGATE MIDWEST (Dec. 4, 2020), https://investigatemidwest.org/2020/12/04/buy-it-or-else-inside-monsanto-and-basfs-moves-to-force-dicamba-on-farmers/.

9 *See* ANDREW NIXON & KELDON BESTER, FROM PLOW TO PANTRY: MONOPOLY IN THE CANADIAN FOOD SYSTEM (2024), https://antimonopoly.ca/wp-content/uploads/2024/10/CAMP-Report-Monopoly-in-the-Canadian-Food-System.pdf. *Also see* Ritsos-Kokkinis, *supra* note 7, at 2 ("Agriculture supply industry has been markedly consolidated after three major mergers, with the Bayer-Monsanto merger being the largest. The other two mergers were Dow-DuPont and Syngenta–ChemChina (2017). Now, 'approximately 61% of the global seeds and pesticide production is concentrated in these three enormous entities.'" (quoting B. RAJESH KUMAR, WEALTH CREATION IN THE WORLD'S LARGEST MERGERS AND ACQUISITIONS: INTEGRATED CASE STUDIES 283 (2019)).

10 Ritsos-Kokkinis, *supra* note 7 at 29, 51 ("The average promised premium over the fundamental price of 21.93% is substantially higher than the average maximum justified premium of 3.85%, meaning that Bayer eventually overpaid an estimated stunning 18.08% over Monsanto's fundamental price.")

11 *See generally* OECD, CONCENTRATION IN SEED MARKETS: POTENTIAL EFFECTS AND POLICY RESPONSES 13 (2018), https://doi.org/10.1787/9789264308367-en [hereinafter "OECD Report"].

Dow Chemical, and DuPont.[12] The industry was consolidating further through the announced mergers of *Dow Chemical/DuPont*[13] and *Syngenta/ChemChina*.[14] After the *Bayer/Monsanto* deal and spinoffs were completed, the industry was dominated by the Big Four: Bayer, BASF, Corteva (the result of the *Dow Chemical/DuPont* merger), and Syngenta/ChemChina.[15]

9. A 2018 report by the Organisation for Economic Co-operation and Development (OECD) identified two root reasons for the consolidation.[16] First, "[h]igh fixed costs, in particular for R&D, create pressure for 'horizontal' mergers that combine firms with activities in the same domains."[17] Second, "technological and commercial complementarities between seeds, GM [genetically modified] technology, and crop protection chemicals create incentives for 'non-horizontal' mergers between companies active in these different domains."[18] The report further notes that "[a] new complementarity may be emerging today with digital technologies and precision agriculture."[19] It was in these key agricultural input markets – seeds and traits, agrochemicals, and the burgeoning field of digital agriculture services – that the *Bayer/Monsanto* merger raised anticompetitive concerns by joining together significant competitors.

2. The Markets: Seeds and Traits, Agrochemicals, and Digital Agriculture

10. Bayer and Monsanto competed in the development and sale of agricultural seeds and GM seed traits, which give crops herbicide tolerance and insect or disease resistance.[20] Developing seeds involves breeding the genetic bases of specific crops and infusing specific seed traits to increase crop productivity and sustainability.[21] The importance of these inputs has led

---

12 *Id.* at 17.

13 *See* Press Release, DuPont, DuPont and Dow to Combine in Merger of Equals (Dec. 11, 2015), https://www.investors.dupont.com/news-and-media/press-release-details/2015/Dupont-And-Dow-To-Combine-In-Merger-Of-Equals/default.aspx#!.

14 *See* Press Release, Syngenta, Syngenta Shareholders Accept ChemChina Offer (May 5, 2017), https://www.syngenta.com/en/company/media/syngenta-news/year/2017/syngenta-shareholders-accept-chemchina-offer.

15 *See* Keith Fuglie, *Two Companies Accounted for More Than Half of Corn, Soybean, and Cotton Seed Sales in 2018–20*, U.S. DEP'T OF AGRIC., ECON. RSCH. SERV. (Oct. 2, 2023), https://www.ers.usda.gov/data-products/chart-gallery/gallery/chart-detail/?chartId=107516.

16 OECD Report, *supra* note 11, at 13.

17 *Id.*

18 *Id.*

19 *Id.*

20 *See* European Commission, Press Release IP/17/2762, Mergers: Commission Opens In-Depth Investigation Into Proposed Acquisition of Monsanto by Bayer (Aug. 22, 2017), https://ec.europa.eu/commission/presscorner/detail/en/IP_17_2762 (describing Bayer and Monsanto's activities in breeding and licensing seeds and traits).

21 *See* COMPETITION COMMISSION OF SOUTH AFRICA [CCSA], IMPACT ASSESSMENT REPORT ON THE BAYER MONSANTO MERGER 14 (March 2023) ("There are three critical inputs for competitiveness in a seed breeding business namely, a deep, diverse and strong pool of genetics (i.e. the germplasm), advanced breeding technologies[,] and biotech trait development.").

to a "highly integrated relationship between agricultural biotechnology and seed firms."[22] Firms will use their own traits or license the traits of other firms to breed seeds and produce new seed varieties.[23]

11. Bayer and Monsanto also competed in the market for agrochemicals, such as herbicides, fungicides, insecticides, and treatments applied directly to seeds.[24] This is a highly regulated industry; extensive time and resources are needed to fulfill various safety and efficacy tests before products make it to market.[25] Agrochemical products are developed from active ingredients, which can take 30 years to properly research, develop, and commercialize.[26] Consequently, the US Department of Justice (DOJ) described the relevant seeds/traits and agrochemicals markets as having "extraordinarily high" barriers to entry.[27]

12. According to 2013 estimates, the Big Six already controlled 75% of the global agrochemical market and 63% of the commercial seed market.[28] With the Bayer/Monsanto combination, three companies (ChemChina/Syngenta, DuPont/Dow, and Bayer/Monsanto) were poised to control "60 percent of the world's patented *seeds* and 64% of world's pesticides/herbicides[.]"[29] Even after the spinoffs to BASF mandated by the settlement, scholars estimate that now the Big Four firms retained control of "around 70% of the global pesticides market and around 60% of the global seed market."[30] Concentration is probably even greater for seed traits, where competition from regional firms is minimal.[31]

---

22 Ioannis Lianos, Alexey Ivanov & Dennis Davis, Global Food Value Chains and Competition Law 132 (2022).

23 *See id.*

24 *See id.* at 133.

25 *Id.* at 134.

26 *Id* at 134–35.

27 Complaint ¶ 62, United States v. Bayer AG, Monsanto Company, and BASF SE, Case 1:18-cv-01241 (D.D.C. May 29, 2018), https://www.justice.gov/atr/case-document/file/1066656/dl?inline.

28 *See* ETC Group, Breaking Bad: Big Ag Mega-Mergers in Play; Dow + Dupont in the Pocket? Next: Demonsanto?, 115 ETC Group Communiqué (Dec. 2015), at 4, https://www.etcgroup.org/files/files/etc_breakbad_23dec15.pdf.

29 Ioannis Lianos & Dmitry Katalevsky, Merger Activity in the Factors of Production Segments of the Food Value Chain: A Critical Assessment of the *Bayer/Monsanto* Merger 12 (Ctr. for L., Econ. & Soc'y, Pol'y Paper Series 2017/1, 2017), https://discovery.ucl.ac.uk/id/eprint/10045082/1/Lianos_cles-policy-paper-1-2017.pdf (emphasis added).

30 Jennifer Clapp, *The Problem With Growing Corporate Concentration and Power in the Global Food System*, 2 Nature Food 404, 405 (2021); *see also* Keith O. Fuglie et al., Research Investments and Market Structure in the Food Processing, Agricultural Input, and Biofuel Industries Worldwide 35 (Econ. Rsch. Report No. 130, U.S. Dept. of Agriculture, Econ. Res. Serv. 35, 2011), https://papers.ssrn.com/sol3/papers.cfm?abstract_id=2027051 ("In 2009, the top four companies accounted for 54 percent of the global commercial seed market (including public sector commercial seed), and the top eight companies accounted for 63 percent of total commercial seed sales... In 1994, these shares were 21 percent and 29 percent, respectively.")

31 *See* OECD Report, *supra* note 11 at 150 ("For GM traits, market concentration appears much higher than for seed markets. While several medium-sized regional players are active in seed markets, the market for GM traits is dominated almost exclusively by large multinational firms (Monsanto, Bayer, Syngenta, DowDuPont).").

13. At the time of the transaction, both Bayer and Monsanto were developing digital agriculture solutions, which entail the "collection of data and information about farms with the aim of providing tailored advice or aggregated data to farmers."[32] The market for these software solutions was growing.[33]

3. Concerns Regarding Competitive Effects of the Merger

14. The primary anticompetitive concern with the deal was the elimination of head-to-head competition between Bayer and Monsanto in several of the key markets. As expressed by the European Commission, the combination of Bayer and Monsanto "could reduce competition in a number of different markets resulting in higher prices, lower quality, less choice and less innovation."[34] The US DOJ similarly emphasized that "the proposed merger would likely result in higher prices, lower quality, and fewer choices across a wide array of seed and crop protection products."[35]

15. Among seed offerings, Bayer and Monsanto were key global competitors in the sale of GM cotton, canola, and soybean seeds, as well as non-GM vegetable seeds.[36] Likewise, among agrochemical herbicides, Bayer's "Liberty" product (that paired with its herbicide-resistant LibertyLink cotton, canola, and soybean seeds) was one of the few non-selective competitors to Monsanto's blockbuster "Roundup" system, and both companies sold overlapping pesticide products in certain markets.[37] The parties also provided competing agrochemical seed treatments – Monsanto had recently developed and brought to market a treatment that protected crops from nematode worms, for which Bayer was the main competitor.[38] According to the US DOJ, the expected

---

32 European Commission, *supra* note 20.

33 *See* Tim Sparapani, *How Big Data and Tech Will Improve Agriculture, From Farm to Table*, FORBES (Mar. 23, 2017, 12:18 PM), https://www.forbes.com/sites/timsparapani/2017/03/23/how-big-data-and-tech-will-improve-agriculture-from-farm-to-table/#7da2a8655989 ("The software market for these sorts of precision farming tools (such as yield monitoring, field mapping, crop scouting and weather forecasting) is expected to grow 14% by 2022 in the United States alone. Researchers suggest the full-scale adoption of these technologies could mean an increase in farm productivity unseen since mechanization.").

34 European Commission, *supra* note 20.

35 Press Release, U.S. Dep't of Just., Justice Department Secures Largest Negotiated Merger Divestiture Ever to Preserve Competition Threatened by Bayer's Acquisition of Monsanto (May 29, 2018), https://www.justice.gov/opa/pr/justice-department-secures-largest-merger-divestiture-ever-preserve-competition-threatened.

36 *See* Complaint, *supra* note 27, ¶¶ 2, 6.

37 *See id.* ¶ 3 ("Today, Bayer's weed-control systems are the only competitive alternatives to Monsanto's Roundup Ready systems in cotton, canola, and soybeans."); European Commission, *supra* note 20 ("[T]he Commission will further assess both Monsanto's activities in biological pesticide products that would compete with Bayer's existing portfolio of chemical pesticide products, and the parties' overlapping activities in products that tackle varroa mites, a parasite affecting bee colonies in Europe.").

38 *See* Complaint, *supra* note 27, ¶ 4.

price effects from lost competition in these markets would raise costs by "hundreds of millions of dollars per year" for farmers and consumers.[39]

16. Another horizontal concern was the elimination of potential competition in the research and development (R&D) of new seeds, traits, and agrochemical products.[40] Bayer and Monsanto had both invested significant resources in research pipelines for future innovation in GM traits and seed treatments, "spurring each other to work faster and invest more to improve their offerings and develop new products."[41] In fact, in 2016, "Bayer spent more on seeds-related research and development as a percentage of sales than any of the other Big Four."[42] According to the US DOJ, the proposed combination would "eliminate this competition to develop new products that farmers will depend on for decades into the future."[43]

17. The transaction may have raised additional horizontal concerns in smaller, younger, or less developed jurisdictions. For instance, as the number of significant firms competing in the same global markets consolidated across the various product lines, there would be more "multimarket contact" between these firms, increasing the risk of higher prices from coordinated effects.[44] Additionally, limited seed choices for farmers raised environmental and resiliency concerns outside of the scope of traditional market analysis.[45]

18. In some markets, enforcers were concerned with potential vertical harms from the transaction as well. As noted by the US DOJ, the combined dominance of Bayer and Monsanto in seed treatment licensing "would give the combined company the incentive and ability to harm its seed rivals by raising the price of those seed treatments – a key input for genetically modified seeds."[46] For instance, the merged company could have the incentive and ability to limit sales of Bayer's corn rootwood pest seed treatment to rival sellers of

---

39 See id. ¶ 59.

40 See id. ¶ 4 ("Bayer and Monsanto also compete head-to-head to develop the next generation of transformative products...").

41 Id.

42 See id. ¶ 60.

43 Id.; see also European Commission, Press Release IP/18/2282, Mergers: Commission Clears Bayer's Acquisition of Monsanto, Subject to Conditions (Mar. 21, 2018), https://ec.europa.eu/commission/presscorner/detail/en/IP_18_2282 (noting that divestiture of Bayer's agrochemical R&D was necessary as "this research forms part of the race to find challenger products for glyphosate.").

44 See OECD Report supra note 11, at 94 ("Mergers between firms active in different regions or different products could facilitate collusion by increasing the degree of 'multimarket contact'. Firms competing across several markets may find it easier to collude, as both the benefits of collusion and the costs of deviating are greater." (citation omitted)). See also NIXON & BESTER, supra note 9.

45 Some farmers plant multiple seed varieties to provide resilience in the event that any particular variety fails due to environmental or pest pressures. Limited seed choice results in "path dependency" for farmers, who become locked into a narrow set of main crops with greater genetic uniformity. See USDA, MORE AND BETTER CHOICES FOR FARMERS: PROMOTING FAIR COMPETITION AND INNOVATION IN SEEDS AND OTHER AGRICULTURAL INPUTS 37, 63 (2023), https://www.ams.usda.gov/sites/default/files/media/SeedsReport.pdf ("Genetic uniformity lends a high degree of performance and predictability to crop systems, but also means that the entire maize industry might be at an increased risk of novel pathogens or climatic stressors.").

46 Complaint, supra note 27, ¶ 5.

Monsanto's corn seed.[47] The European Commission was likewise interested in "whether competitors' access to distributors and farmers could become more difficult if Bayer and Monsanto were to bundle or tie their sales of pesticide products and seeds, notably with the advent of digital agriculture."[48]

19. A final consideration is whether the principal divestiture – to BASF – would create additional competition concerns. BASF, a European multinational, was the largest chemical producer in the world. Prior to the divestiture, BASF was apparently the sole firm positioned to enter the highly concentrated seed and trait market.[49] This market reality was acknowledged in the DOJ's Competitive Impact Statement on the merger and settlement.[50] Thus, prior to the transaction and spinoff, BASF may have been the only force exerting a moderating effect on seed prices through threat of future entry. Absent the transaction and spinoff to BASF, some commentors have suggested that BASF may have entered the seed market as a competitor (similar to Bayer's entry in 2002[51]), driving additional price competition that would benefit farmers and consumers.[52]

4. Justifications from Efficiencies of the Merger

20. The parties claimed that the merger would drive efficiencies from cost savings including the consolidation of R&D budgets, fueling greater levels of innovation.[53] Following a meeting with then President-elect Trump, the Bayer and Monsanto CEOs released a joint statement. The statement read:

---

47 *See id.* In recent years since the transaction closed, the Independent Professional Seed Association has accused Bayer/Monsanto of using their "dominant position [in trait licensing] along with contracts and agreements with the rest of the industry to control pricing and the rules of engagement in non-competitive and unhealthy way." *See* Independent Professional Seed Association, Comment on "Competition and the Intellectual Property System: Seeds and Other Agricultural Inputs," (June 15, 2022), www.regulations.gov/comment/AMS-AMS-22-0025-0061.

48 European Commission, *supra* note 20. The Commission later announced that "the in-depth investigation did not confirm any of these concerns." European Commission, *supra* note 43.

49 As noted by a letter signed by five US state attorney generals, at the time of the transaction "[t]he seed markets were already so concentrated that there [was] only one possible buyer of the divestiture assets." Comments of the Attorneys General of California, Iowa, Massachusetts, Mississippi, and Oregon on the Proposed Final Judgment at 5, United States v. Bayer AG, Monsanto Company, and BASF SE, Case 1:18-cv-01241 (D.D.C. May 29, 2018).

50 *See* Competitive Impact Statement at 31–32, United States v. Bayer AG, Monsanto Company, and BASF SE, Case 1:18-cv-01241 (D.D.C. May 29, 2018) ("[I]f BASF is unable to acquire the assets, simply divesting the package to another purchaser would not preserve competition.").

51 *See* Fuglie et al., *supra* note 30, at 30 ("Bayer, another Big 6 firm, only entered the seed market in 2002 with the acquisition of Aventis Crop Science; by 2009, it ranked sixth in global seed sales.").

52 *See* Lianos, *supra* note 22, at 176 ("[T]he ultimate result is that there will be one less major competitor in an industry that already has very high barriers to entry… [the] divestiture eliminates BASF from being a potential new entrant. BASF was and continues to be… a major producer of agricultural chemicals for treating seeds and, thus, it had a significant basis upon which it could have effectively entered into this industry by itself.").

53 *See* Sylvie Bonny, *Corporate Concentration and Technological Change in the Global Seed Industry*, 9 Sustainability 1632, 1649 (2017); Brian C. Albrecht, Dirk Auer, Eric Fruits & Geoffrey A. Manne, *Doomsday Mergers: A Retrospective Study of False Alarms* 24 (Int'l Ctr. for L. & Econ. White Paper 2023-03-22, 2023), https://laweconcenter.org/wp-content/uploads/2023/03/Doomsday-Mergers-FINAL.pdf ("Among the primary benefits of the merger have been increased efficiency and cost savings. By combining the resources and expertise of both companies, the newly merged company is better positioned to invest in research and development, improve yields, and reduce costs for farmers.").

"The driving force behind the Bayer-Monsanto combination is increasing and accelerating innovation to help growers around the world address challenges like climate change and food security. This becomes increasingly important as we all work together to feed a growing population in a sustainable way."[54] The statement claimed that the "combined company expects to spend approximately $16 billion for R&D in agriculture over the next six years."[55] A white paper by two scholars argued that this type of R&D combination generates real procompetitive benefits because "[m]erged companies – especially in the agriculture industry, where firms frequently rely on other companies' innovation to develop their own products – are better able to coordinate investment decisions (instead of waiting to see what the other company produces), avoid duplication of research, adapt to changing conditions and the unanticipated course."[56] The paper asserted that past agricultural consolidation had translated into consumer welfare enhancements through technological advancements that increased crop yield and reduced operational costs.[57] In theory, "[v]ertical efficiencies such as reduced transactions costs and coordination achieved by exploiting the complementarities between traits and traited seed assets can also reduce costs."[58] There is some evidence that cost savings did follow the integration of Monsanto, although it is unclear if these translated into lower prices.[59]

21. Others suggest reasons to doubt the magnitude of any efficiency gains from the Bayer/Monsanto combination and to doubt its potential to advance rather than to suppress innovation. A US Department of Agriculture (USDA) study of seed company consolidations between 1994 and 2009 found no association between the merger and a permanent increase in research investments.[60] Likewise, analysis by the American Antitrust Institute suggested that consolidation did not necessarily drive innovation.[61] Ultimately, enforcers such as the US DOJ found that the

---

54   *Joint Statement: Monsanto, Bayer CEOs Meet With New Administration*, MARKETSCREENER (Jan. 17, 2017, 12:01 PM), https://www.marketscreener.com/quote/stock/MONSANTO-13589/news/Joint-Statement-Monsanto-Bayer-CEOs-meet-with-new-administratiom-23707490/.

55   *Id.*

56   Geoffrey A. Manne & Allen Gibby, *A Brief Assessment of the Procompetitive Effects of Organizational Restructuring in the Ag-Biotech Industry* 7 (Int'l Ctr. for L. & Econ. Antitrust & Consumer Prot. Rsch. Program, White Paper 2017-2, May 9, 2017), https://laweconcenter.org/images/articles/icle-ag_mergers_short_paper_final.pdf (financial support from the agricultural industry acknowledged).

57   *Id.* at 11–14.

58   Diana L. Moss, *Transgenic Seed Platforms: Competition Between a Rock and a Hard Place?* 15 (Am. Antitrust Inst. White Paper, Oct. 23, 2009), https://www.justice.gov/sites/default/files/atr/legacy/2010/02/24/254998b.pdf.

59   *See* Angus Liu, *Beleaguered Bayer Adds $1.8B to Cost-Cutting Goal Amid COVID-19 Slowdowns*, FIERCEPHARMA (Oct. 1, 2020), https://www.fiercepharma.com/pharma/bayer-expands-restructuring-plan-for-1-8b-cost-cuts-amid-covid-19-slowdowns.

60   FUGLIE ET AL., *supra* note 30, at 14–15 ("Greater concentration was not associated with a permanent rise in R&D intensity in these input industries.").

61   *See* Am. Antitrust Inst., Proposed Merger of Monsanto and Bayer 3–4 (2017), https://www.antitrustinstitute.org/wp-content/uploads/2018/08/White-Paper_Monsanto-Bayer_7.26.17_0.pdf ("While the precise nature of the relationship has not been fully explored in agricultural biotechnology, we can say that the largest

merger was "unlikely to generate verifiable, merger-specific efficiencies that would offset the proposed acquisition's likely anticompetitive effects in the relevant markets."[62]

III. The Process of Vetting the Merger – The Most Mature Jurisdictions

22. Bayer announced its signed agreement to acquire Monsanto on September 14, 2016, with an expected closing by the end of 2017.[63] Bayer committed to a reverse antitrust break-up fee of USD $2 billion if the deal did not go through.[64] The transaction was officially notified to the United States on December 12, 2016,[65] and to the European Commission on June 30, 2017.[66] From the start there was close cooperation – including information-sharing between the US and EU authorities, and with other interested authorities, including Australia, Brazil, Canada, and South Africa.[67] The Chinese and Indian competition authorities also cooperated.[68] In spring 2018, both the US and the European Commission cleared the transaction subject to a divestiture package valued at US$9 billion[69] to BASF.[70] Final judgment was entered in the US on February 8, 2019, following a Tunney Act hearing to affirm that the settlement was in the public interest, as required by US law.[71]

---

companies have probably engaged in M&A to proactively or reactively cope with the pressures of continued innovation. Monsanto and Bayer may well raise arguments that the proposed merger is necessary to maintain or generate new innovation. We encourage the DOJ to be particularly sceptical of any such claims."). *See also* Das Nair & Roberts, *supra* note 3, at 461. While control over government regulatory policies was apparently not expressed as a concern of the merger, Das Nair and Roberts report, in observing the increasing concentration in the global food value chain, including seeds: "One of the largest [firms in the concentrated global seed market], Monsanto, ... has been found to have a strong influence on government policies." *Id.* at 459–60. They also observe: "Firms with substantial market power may also [in addition to hindering innovation] be able to set private standards ..." *Id.* at 461.

62 Complaint, *supra* note 27, ¶ 63.

63 Press Release, Bayer and Monsanto to Create a Global Leader in Agriculture (Sept. 14, 2016) https://www.bayer.com/sites/default/files/2020-11/Ad-hoc_2016-09-14_e.pdf.

64 *Id.*

65 *See U.S. v. Bayer AG, et al.*, U.S. Dep't of Just. (last modified June 30, 2019), https://www.justice.gov/atr/case/us-v-bayer-ag-and-monsanto-company (listing December 22, 2016, as the "Case Open Date").

66 Case M.8084, Bayer/Monsanto, Prior Notification of a Concentration, 2017 O.J. (C 222) 6, https://eur-lex.europa.eu/legal-content/EN/TXT/PDF/?uri=CELEX:52017M8084.

67 European Commission, *supra* note 20.

68 European Commission, *supra* note 43.

69 Dan Mangan, *US Forces Germany's Bayer to Shed $9 Billion in Ag Business in Biggest Ever Antitrust Sell-off*, CNBC (May 29, 2018, 12:00 PM), https://www.cnbc.com/2018/05/29/bayer-will-sell-basf-9-billion-in-assets-to-allow-monsanto-purchase.html.

70 Case M.8084, Bayer/Monsanto, 2018 O.J. (C 459) 10, https://eur-lex.europa.eu/legal-content/EN/TXT/PDF/?uri=CELEX:52018M8084(02); Proposed Final Judgment, United States v. Bayer AG, No. 1:18-cv-01241 (D.D.C. Feb. 8, 2019), https://www.justice.gov/atr/case-document/file/1066676/dl?inline.

71 Hearing pursuant to the Antitrust Procedures and Penalties (Tunney) Act. U.S. Explanation of Consent Decree Procedures, United States v. Bayer AG, No. 1:18-cv-01241 (D.D.C. May 29, 2018), https://www.justice.gov/opa/press-release/file/1066641/dl; Proposed Final Judgment, *supra* note 70

1. United States

23. The US DOJ Antitrust Division opened its investigation of the transaction on December 22, 2016.[72] In the following 17 months, the DOJ investigated and conferred with the parties to discuss their concerns. The merging parties assembled a package of remedies, chiefly involving the sale of assets to BASF, which as noted was the largest chemical producer in the world.[73] The antitrust officials reached agreement with the merging parties on an acceptable package – the largest divestiture ever negotiated by the DOJ.[74] Then, as is the practice, the DOJ drafted the Complaint[75] and Proposed Final Judgment[76] tailored to its refined appreciation of the harms and how they would be addressed by the relief. The DOJ's Competitive Impact Statement[77] stated the expected harms and how the agreed remedies would avert them. The DOJ filed these documents with the District Court for the District of Columbia on May 29, 2018,[78] the same day that the European Commission closed its investigation and approved divestiture sales to BASF.[79]

24. Under the terms of the settlement, Bayer was required to divest its "cotton, canola, soybean, and vegetable seed businesses, as well as [its] Liberty herbicide business," all of which competed with Monsanto prior to the merger.[80] Moreover, in view of the fact that Bayer and Monsanto had been competing "to develop new products and services, the settlement require[d] the divestiture of certain intellectual property and research capabilities, including 'pipeline' R&D projects."[81] In order to allay concerns stemming from vertical integration, Bayer also agreed to divest various "assets relating to its seed treatment businesses," including intellectual property associated with the Poncho, VOTiVO, and TWO.0 brands, as well as the ILeVO and COPeO seed treatments.[82] The DOJ settlement differed from the divestitures ordered by the European Commission in two significant respects. First, the DOJ settlement required Bayer to divest only two lines of non-selective

---

72 *See supra* note 65.

73 *See* Alexander H. Tullo, *C&EN's Global Top 50 Chemical Companies of 2017*, C&EN (July 30, 2018), https://cen.acs.org/business/finance/CENs-Global-Top-50-chemical/96/i31 (listing BASF as the world's largest chemical firm by sales in 2017).

74 U.S. Dep't of Just., *supra* note 35.

75 Complaint, *supra* note 27.

76 Proposed Final Judgment, *supra* note 70.

77 Competitive Impact Statement, *supra* note 50.

78 *See supra* notes 75–77.

79 *See infra* note 188.

80 U.S. Dep't Just., *supra* note 35.

81 *Id.*

82 Competitive Impact Statement, *supra* note 50, at 23–25.

herbicide research (as opposed to three),[83] and the DOJ settlement contained no provisions regarding glyphosate-based pesticide products.[84]

25. These divestiture assets were to be sold to BASF.[85] While BASF was "an experienced chemical company with a substantial crop protection business," the DOJ was concerned that BASF, as an independent competitor, would not have "the same innovation incentives, capabilities and scale" as Bayer, absent further divestitures.[86] Consequently, Bayer was required to divest "additional complementary assets... including, most notably, Bayer's nascent 'digital agriculture' business."[87] The total divestitures were valued at about US$9 billion.[88] Moreover, BASF had "a one-year window after closing to identify any additional assets that are reasonably necessary to ensure the continued competitiveness of the divested business," subject to the DOJ's discretion.[89]

26. In addition to the divestitures, the Proposed Final Judgment included provisions "aimed at ensuring that the assets [were] handed off in a seamless and efficient manner."[90] These provisions required Bayer to support BASF's new businesses. Thus, Bayer had "to transfer existing third-party agreements and customer information to BASF, as well as to enter transition services agreements ensuring that BASF can continue to serve customers immediately upon completion of the divestitures."[91] Also, the judgment instructed that Bayer shall, at BASF's option, supply broad acre seed treatments and isoxaflutole to BASF at cost.[92] BASF could require Bayer to enter into two-year tolling agreements relating to "the formulation, filling, and packaging of" glufosinate ammonium and divested seed treatments, as well as two-year tolling agreements relating to the active ingredients used in clothianidin seed treatments and the fluopyram active ingredient.[93] BASF could "hire all of the personnel from Bayer needed to support" the divested businesses.[94]

---

83 *See* United States v. Bayer AG, 2019 U.S. Dist. LEXIS 63566, at *12, *14, *27–28 (D.D.C. Feb. 8, 2019); *infra* notes 115–116 and accompanying text.

84 *See Bayer AG*, 2019 U.S. Dist. LEXIS 63566.

85 U.S. Dep't Just., *supra* note 73.

86 *Id.*

87 *Id.*

88 *Id.*

89 Competitive Impact Statement, *supra* note 50, at 18.

90 *Id.* at 17.

91 *Id.* These transition services agreements included a one-year commitment to provide IT services and support, as well as a one-year agreement "to distribute on BASF's behalf products containing glufosinate ammonium, clothianidin, *Bacillus firmus* strain I-1582, or fluopyram outside the United States." Proposed Final Judgment, *supra* note 70, at 25–26.

92 *Id.* at 22–23.

93 *Id.* at 23–25.

94 *Id.* at 18.

27. To monitor compliance with the terms of the Proposed Final Judgment, the DOJ appointed Judge Michael B. Mukasey.[95] As monitoring trustee, Judge Mukasey was charged with reviewing the implementation of a firewall compliance plan (to prevent sharing of competitively sensitive information), investigating claimed breaches of any transition services, supply, or tolling agreements, filing monthly compliance reports with the DOJ, and conducting semi-annual audits of compliance with firewall provisions.[96] Judge Mukasey was to serve in this capacity until the divestitures were finalized and the required transition services, supply, and tolling agreements had all expired, subject to the DOJ's discretion.[97]

28. After the Complaint, the Proposed Final Judgment, and the Competitive Impact Statement were published in the *Federal Register*, the DOJ received fourteen comments.[98] These included comments by several state attorneys general arguing that the proposed divestitures were insufficient to eliminate anticompetitive effects from the merger.[99] First, the attorneys general were concerned that "[t]he breakneck speed of consolidation in the agricultural chemicals sector has prevented regulators from understanding the effects of one mega-merger on agriculture before the next mega-merger is completed."[100] Second, they expressed concern that divested assets were going to an insufficiently experienced buyer.[101] Third, "[a] BASF failure to successfully operate a leading, dominant seed business would result in a Bayer/Monsanto monopoly...." This is because the markets had become so consolidated that "there [was] only *one* possible buyer of the divestiture assets. According to [the DOJ], '... if BASF is unable to acquire the assets, simply divesting the package to another purchaser would not preserve competition.'"[102] Further, with a successful BASF, the market might be collusive given that Bayer and BASF were previously in a cartel together.[103] Finally, the merger could be expected to reduce R&D spending, especially given that the merging parties listed savings on R&D as a "synerg[y]."[104] The DOJ responded to these and other comments on January 29, 2019, asserting *inter alia* that "[t]he United States

---

[95] Memorandum of Points and Authorities in Support of Unopposed Motion of the United States to Appoint Monitoring Trustee at 1, United States v. Bayer AG, Case 1:18-cv-01241 (D.D.C. Feb. 8, 2019).

[96] Proposed Final Judgment, *supra* note 70, at 22–28, 33–35, 36–37.

[97] *Id.* at 22–28, 36.

[98] Response of Plaintiff United States to Public Comments on the Proposed Final Judgment at 3, United States v. Bayer AG, Case 1:18-cv-01241 (D.D.C. Feb. 8, 2019).

[99] Comments of the Attorneys General of California, Iowa, Massachusetts, Mississippi, and Oregon on the Proposed Final Judgment in *United States v. Bayer AG, Monsanto Company, and BASF SE*, Case 1:18-cv-01241 (D.C. Cir. May 29, 2018) (2018), https://www.justice.gov/file/976741-0/dl?inline=.

[100] *Id.* at 4.

[101] *See id.* at 4–5.

[102] *Id.* at 5 (quoting Competitive Impact Statement, *supra* note 50, at 31–32).

[103] *Id.* at 5–7.

[104] *Id.* at 8.

crafted the remedy specifically taking into account BASF's existing assets and capabilities."[105] The Court of Appeals for the D.C. Circuit entered final judgment approving the settlement on February 8, 2019,[106] more than two years after the DOJ began investigating the transaction.

2. European Union

29. On August 22, 2017, the European Commission reported that it "ha[d] opened an in-depth investigation" (a Phase II investigation).[107] Phase II was opened 53 days after receiving notice of the transaction and eight months after the DOJ investigation began.[108] Although the parties had already submitted commitments to address some of the Commission's initial concerns, the Commission had found these commitments "insufficient to clearly dismiss its serious doubts as to the transaction's compatibility with the EU Merger Regulation."[109] Announcing the Phase II investigation, the Commission identified anticompetitive concerns in markets for pesticides, seeds, and traits.[110] Furthermore, given that "the merged entity would hold both the largest portfolio of pesticid[e] products and the strongest global market positions in seeds and traits," the Commission announced concern that the merged entity might foreclose rivals' access "to distributors and farmers" by bundling or tying its "sales of pesticide products and seeds, notably with the advent of digital agriculture."[111] Over the next seven months, the Phase II investigation would involve assessment of "more than 2,000 different product markets" and review of "2.7 million internal documents,"[112] resulting in a half-dozen deadlines and extensions.[113]

30. During Phase II, the parties submitted a complex list of divestiture commitments.[114] Two complex divestiture packages were initially offered "worth well over €6 billion" in total.[115] The first package of assets, to be sold to an unspecified buyer, was specific to Bayer's vegetable seeds business,

---

105 Response of Plaintiff United States to Public Comments on the Proposed Final Judgment, *supra* note 98, at 14.

106 *Bayer AG*, 2019 U.S. Dist. LEXIS 63566.

107 *See* European Commission, Press Release IP/17/2762, Mergers: Commission Opens In-Depth Investigation Into Proposed Acquisition of Monsanto by Bayer (Aug. 22, 2017), https://ec.europa.eu/commission/presscorner/detail/en/IP_17_2762.

108 Case M.8084, Bayer/Monsanto, Initiation of Proceedings, 2017 O.J. (C 286) 1, https://eur-lex.europa.eu/legal-content/EN/TXT/PDF/?uri=OJ:C:2017:286:FULL.

109 European Commission, *supra* note 107.

110 *Id.*

111 *Id.*

112 European Commission, *supra* note 43.

113 *See M.8084 Bayer/Monsanto*, EUROPEAN COMMISSION (last visited Sept. 5, 2024), https://competition-cases.ec.europa.eu/cases/M.8084 (noting four deadline suspensions and two deadline extensions between August 22, 2017, and March 31, 2018).

114 European Commission, *supra* note 43.

115 *Id.*

including the Nunhems brand and R&D projects. The second, to be sold to BASF, contained the other seven areas of competitive overlap: (i) Bayer's broadacre crop seeds business, including oilseed, rape, cotton, soybean, wheat, and R&D projects; (ii) Bayer's glufosinate pesticide business, including the Liberty and Basta brands; (iii) Bayer's three separate lines of non-selective herbicide research; (iv) Bayer's seed treatment business, including NemaStrike assets; (v) a sole license of Bayer's digital agriculture business and R&D; (vi) Bayer's global broadacre traits business, including R&D projects, subject to numerous geographic carveouts;[116] and (vii) Bayer's glyphosate-based pesticide products within the European Economic Area.[117]

31. The European Commission cleared the merger subject to the proposed conditions on March 21, 2018, more than two months before the US DOJ would file its complaint and proposed final judgment on May 29, 2018.[118] The Commission emphasized the importance of international cooperation in its review, stating that "[t]he Commission has cooperated very closely with a number of competition authorities on this case, including among others the US [DOJ] as well as … the Australian, Brazilian, Canadian, Chinese, Indian and South African competition authorities."[119] The Commission found that, after accounting for the proposed structural remedies, the resultant concentrations were compatible with the internal market within the meaning of article 3(1)(b) of the Merger Regulation.[120]

32. Following the release of the Commission's conditional approval, the parties submitted a request on April 6, 2018, to modify their commitments. It first requested to replace the original seed treatment divestment of Monsanto's NemaStrike assets with the sale of Bayer's Poncho, Poncho/VOTiVO, Poncho/VOTiVO 2.0, ILeVO, and COPeO businesses instead.[121] It also requested to replace the sole license of Bayer's digital agriculture business with a "full divestment to BASF of the same assets, with a limited licence back to Bayer."[122] The Commission accepted both modifications on April 11, 2018.[123]

33. The case was closed on May 29, 2018, the same day the DOJ filed its complaint and final judgment, following an independent assessment of BASF

---

116 The broadacre traits sale was subject to numerous carveouts where Monsanto had limited presence, including for hybrid rice in Asia; hybrid cotton, mustard, and millet in India; cotton in South Africa; R&D regarding sugarcane in Brazil; and R&D regarding sugar beet in Europe.

117 Case M.8084, Bayer/Monsanto, Decision on the Implementation of Commitments – Purchaser Approval, C(2018) 3557 final, https://ec.europa.eu/competition/mergers/cases1/202150/M_8084_8063669_13738_3.pdf.

118 European Commission, *supra* note 43.

119 *Id.*

120 *Id.*

121 Decision on the Implementation of Commitments – Purchaser Approval, *supra* note 117, at 2.

122 *Id.* at 3.

123 Case M.8084, Bayer/Monsanto, Modification of Commitments, C(2018) 2208 final, at 5, https://ec.europa.eu/competition/mergers/cases1/202150/M_8084_8063748_12985_9.pdf.

as the divestment buyer by Mazars LLP.[124] Based on Mazars' assessment, the Commission approved the sale of both divestiture packages to BASF, finding that "BASF has sufficient financial resources, proven expertise and the incentive to maintain and develop the [Divestment Packages] as a viable and active competitive force in competition with the Parties and other competitors."[125] The Commission noted that sale to BASF would allow BASF to "become a globally integrated crop protection, seed and trait player" that could compete with "Bayer-Monsanto and other players, including in particular DowDuPont and ChemChina-Syngenta, at a global level."[126]

34. In both the US and EU proceedings, Bayer and Monsanto were represented by distinguished law firms and economist teams, with several law partners at the helm, teams of associates, and distinguished economic experts and their support staff.[127] Indeed, Sullivan & Cromwell, representing Bayer, and Arnold & Porter, representing Monsanto, were awarded for the top deal of the year by *Global Competition Review*.[128]

IV. The Process of Vetting the Merger – The Rest of the World

35. On the eve of the merger plan, Bayer and Monsanto announced that they planned to seek approval in 30 jurisdictions.[129] My research team uncovered investigations in 24 jurisdictions in addition to the US and the EU. Many of the jurisdictions ordered relief. This part summarizes 19[130] of these investigations in alphabetical order of jurisdiction, with COMESA, a regional economic community, discussed separately. In the next part, we observe patterns across the investigations.

---

124 Decision on the Implementation of Commitments – Purchaser Approval, *supra* note 117, at 26.

125 *Id.* at 13, 20.

126 *Id.* at 8.

127 This included Sullivan & Cromwell (Bayer's counsel), Arnold & Porter (Monsanto's counsel), and Compass Lexecon (economic support). *See S&C's Antitrust Team Takes Top Honors for Work on Bayer's $66 Billion Acquisition at 2019 GCR Awards*, SULLIVAN & CROMWELL LLP (Apr. 1, 2019), https://www.sullcrom.com/About/News-and-Events/Highlights/2019/April/SCs-Antitrust-Team-Takes-Top-Honors-for-Work-on-Bayers-66-Billion-Acquisition-at-2019-GCR-Awards; *Arnold & Porter's $66 Billion Monsanto Deal Wins Global Antitrust 'Matter of the Year' and 'Merger Control Matter of the Year – Europe' GCR Awards*, ARNOLD & PORTER (Mar. 29, 2019), https://www.arnoldporter.com/en/perspectives/news/2019/03/ap-monsanto-deal-wins-matter-of-the-year; *Bayer/Monsanto Merger*, COMPASS LEXECON (May 29, 2018), https://www.compasslexecon.com/cases/bayer-monsanto-merger/.

128 *Bayer/Monsanto/BASF Wins Matter of the Year at GCR Awards 2019*, GCR (Mar. 27, 2019), https://globalcompetitionreview.com/article/bayermonsantobasf-wins-matter-of-the-year-gcr-awards-2019.

129 Drew Harwell, *Bayer and Monsanto to Merge in Mega-Deal that Could Reshape World's Food Supply*, WASH. POST (Sept. 14, 2016, 10:26 AM), https://www.washingtonpost.com/news/business/wp/2016/09/14/bayer-and-monsanto-merge-in-mega-deal-aimed-at-domi-worlds-food-supply/#.

130 This number includes several jurisdictions where my research team found evidence that an investigation was taking place – for instance, because a different jurisdiction's press release mentioned cooperation with that jurisdiction – but could not locate further information regarding the investigation. These jurisdictions were Japan, Macedonia, Montenegro, South Korea, and Tanzania.

1. Country Summaries

A. *Argentina*

36. Argentina's competition authority (CNDC) was notified of the transaction on March 31, 2017.[131] The CNDC studied the transaction and wrote a 79-page report to the Secretary of Interior Commerce. The report stated that the divestments ordered by foreign authorities failed to resolve increasing horizontal concentrations in nonselective herbicides, selective herbicides for soy, corn, wheat, and barley, and inoculants and growth promoters.[132] The report discussed an unresolved vertical relationship involving Bayer's insecticides/fungicides, which were used as inputs in Monsanto's sorghum and corn seed treatments.[133] It then analyzed each of the overlaps. Some were apparently significant. For example, in the domestic selective herbicide market for soy, the merger would result in a Herfindahl-Hirschman Index (HHI) of 2538, with a delta of 700.[134] Nonetheless, the report concluded that there would be sufficient competition from other market participants to mitigate increases in concentration and vertical foreclosure concerns.[135] The Secretary of Interior Commerce authorized the transaction on February 1, 2019.[136]

B. *Australia*

37. The Australian Competition and Consumer Commission (ACCC) commenced its investigation of the *Bayer/Monsanto* merger on February 16, 2017.[137] The investigation closed a year later, on March 22, 2018. The ACCC spent 54 days reviewing the transaction.[138] After taking account of "Bayer's commitments to the European Commission," the ACCC identified two issues specific to the Australian market.[139] First, the ACCC examined the possibility that Bayer could anticompetitively bundle its seed treatments with Monsanto's cotton traits. It satisfied the concern, however, finding

---

131 Ignacio Werner, Secretario, Secretaría de Comercio Interior, Resolución [Resolution] 2019-7-APN-SCI#MPYT 1 (2019), https://www.argentina.gob.ar/sites/default/files/conc1438.pdf.

132 Roberta Marina Bidart, Vocal, Comisión Nacional de Defensa de la Competencia et al., Dictamen Firma Conjunta [Joint Signature Opinion] IF-2018-64234286-APN-CNDC#MPYT ¶ 87 (2018), https://www.argentina.gob.ar/sites/default/files/conc1438.pdf. Please note that the report to the Secretary is attached to the same file after the Secretary's decision and a note from the CNDC regarding the report.

133 *Id.* ¶ 88.

134 *Id.* ¶¶ 103–104 tbl.3.

135 *Id.* ¶¶ 102, 114, 122, 129.

136 WERNER, *supra* note 138, at 1, 10.

137 *Bayer AG – Proposed Acquisition of Monsanto Company*, ACCC, https://www.accc.gov.au/public-registers/mergers-registers/public-informal-merger-reviews-register/bayer-ag-proposed-acquisition-of-monsanto-company (last visited Sept. 1, 2024).

138 *Id.*

139 *Id.*

that "there were sufficient constraints that would limit the ability of the merged entity to do this."[140] Second, the ACCC "considered the decision of Bayer," shortly before announcement of the merger, "to cancel a program to develop cotton seed for sale in Australia."[141] "Based on the investigation, including information provided by Bayer, the ACCC considered that the closure of the breeding program was not connected to the proposed acquisition."[142] Accordingly, in the shadow of the EU divestitures, it found no violation in Australia.[143]

C. Brazil

38. The Administrative Council for Economic Defense (CADE) was notified of the transaction on February 20, 2017.[144] CADE and the merging parties signed a settlement agreement on February 15, 2018.[145] The agreement required divestment of Bayer's LibertyLink traits, Bayer's R&D related to soybean, canola, and cotton traits, Bayer's soybean business, various elements of Bayer's seeds and traits businesses, and Bayer's glufosinate-ammonium business.[146] All of these divestitures appear to have been global in scale, apart from one condition applying only within Brazil, which was redacted.[147] The agreement also stipulated various behavioral remedies to allay vertical concerns, including nondiscriminatory licensing of nonselective herbicides and traits, a commitment to not use most-favored-nation clauses in agreements with BASF, and a commitment to not abusively tie or bundle products after the merger.[148]

---

140 *Id.*

141 *Id.*

142 *Id.*

143 Bayer was represented by Dr. Wolfgang Hellmann of Johnson Winter Slattery. *Dr. Wolfgang Hellmann*, then of JOHNSON WINTER SLATTERY, https://cdn.jws.com.au/documents/ACCC-informal-merger.pdf.

144 *See Pesquisa Processual [Procedural Research] 08700.001097/2017-49*, CONSELHO ADMINISTRATIVO DE DEFESA ECONÔMICA, https://sei.cade.br/sei/modulos/pesquisa/md_pesq_processo_exibir.php?0c62g27-7GvPsZDAxAO1tMiVcL9FcFMR5UuJ6rLqPEJuTUu08mg6wxLt0JzWxCor9mNcMYP8UAjTVP9dxRfPBcVZL75c3cw1WpT8oTjt8Mkys2jy9EeDvPBuurj_6bX3A (last visited Sept. 1, 2024) (listing February 20, 2017, as the date of a document entitled "Notification of Concentration Act") (electronic translation).

145 *Acordo em Controle de Concentrações [Merger Control Agreement] – ACC*, CONSELHO ADMINISTRATIVO DE DEFESA ECONÔMICA (Feb. 15, 2018), https://sei.cade.gov.br/sei/modulos/pesquisa/md_pesq_documento_consulta_externa.php?DZ2uWeaYicbuRZEFhBt-n3BfPLlu9u7akQAh8mpB9yM6Fdz47Y-sUcBKSTlBUdG9yg5c7bgTkCZlTGdAXK5PSPVGTKQAT3cG-lupL9MBbWekC_F7ghsMMzs-NrSP58ap5B.

146 *Id.* ¶¶ 53, 57, 61.

147 *See id.*

148 *Id.* ¶¶ 63–65, 70. Bayer was represented by twenty-one attorneys affiliated with the Magalhães e Dias law firm. Procuração dos Representantes Legais da BAYER [Power of Attorney for BAYER Legal Representatives] 2–3 (June 21, 2016), https://sei.cade.gov.br/sei/modulos/pesquisa/md_pesq_documento_consulta_externa.php?DZ2uWeaYicbuRZEFhBt-n3BfPLlu9u7akQAh8mpB9yOyRwawf5hsHhDxOpyCitOCaSorRh1rB-iL43EO9BMNts_dSNjT7jiUAG4SL00uHvGSNykrPpBBdVniHZCERVlVj. Monsanto was represented by eight attorneys from Franceschini e Miranda. Procuração dos Representantes Legais da MONSANTO

D. Canada

39. The Canadian Competition Bureau started reviewing the merger before April 4, 2017.[149] After one of "the longest merger reviews ever undertaken in Canada,"[150] the Bureau entered into a consent agreement with the merging parties on May 30, 2018.[151] The agreement required Bayer to divest its canola seeds and traits business, glufosinate-ammonium business, business assets related to the Centurion and Select herbicides and the Amigo adjuvant in Canada, digital farming business in Canada, soybean seeds and trait business, carrot seeds business, and "seed treatment business related to the nematicidal products VOTiVO and ILeVO."[152] Upon buying divested assets, BASF would be required to divest some of its own assets, including the Clearfield herbicide tolerance trait.[153]

E. Chile

40. The Chilean competition authority (FNE) was notified of the transaction on October 3, 2017, and began investigating on December 18, 2017.[154] On May 25, 2018, the chief of the Division of Mergers submitted a report recommending that the FNE approve an agreement with the merging parties, with conditions.[155] The conditions included Bayer agreeing to

---

[Power of Attorney for MONSANTO Legal Representatives] 3–4 (Dec. 5, 2016), https://sei.cade.gov.br/sei/modulos/pesquisa/md_pesq_documento_consulta_externa.php?DZ2uWeaYicbuRZEFhBtn3BfPLlu9u7akQAh8mpB9yPjDnOhDVcaSf4k7U-hqcFYqqARxeM0kTixvuEpF1zzuDS7wm9z1veipFIR-IUGGjNtpahQqkjME8uKzH7UJewvJ.

149. *See* John Pecman, Comm'r of Competition, Competition Bureau Can., Promoting Competition, Innovation and Growth in Saskatchewan and all of Canada, Remarks at the Saskatchewan Economic Summit (Apr. 4, 2017), https://www.canada.ca/en/competition-bureau/news/2017/03/promoting_competitioninnovationandgrowthinsaskatchewanandallofca.html ("You may be aware of our ongoing reviews of the Agrium/Potash Corp, Dow/DuPont and Bayer/Monsanto mergers.").

150. *Bayer Successfully Obtains Approval from Canadian Competition Bureau for Highly Anticipated Acquisition of Monsanto*, STIKEMAN ELLIOTT (June 29, 2018), https://www.stikeman.com/en-ca/kh/competitor/Bayer-successfully-obtains-approval-from-Canadian-Competition-Bureau.

151. *Bayer AG's Acquisition of Monsanto Company*, GOV'T OF CAN. (Jan. 20, 2022), https://competition-bureau.canada.ca/bayer-ags-acquisition-monsanto-company.

152. *Id.*

153. *Competition Bureau Statement Regarding BASF's Purchase of Assets from Bayer AG Following Its Acquisition of Monsanto Company*, GOV'T OF CAN. (Jan. 20, 2022), https://competition-bureau.canada.ca/competition-bureau-statement-regarding-basfs-purchase-assets-bayer-ag-following-its-acquisition. Bayer was represented by attorneys from Stikeman Elliott, led by Susan Hutton and Paul Collins. STIKEMAN ELLIOTT, *supra* note 150. Monsanto was represented by attorneys from Davies, including John Bodrug, Elisa Kearney, and Alysha Manji-Knight. *Bayer AG Acquires Monsanto Company for US$63 Billion*, DAVIES (June 11, 2018), https://www.dwpv.com/en/Insights/News/Announcements/2018/Bayer-AG-Acquires-Monsanto. BASF was represented by Anthony Baldanza, Huy Do, and Tony Di Domenico from Fasken Martineau DuMoulin. *Bayer AG Divests $9B Agriculture Business to BASF*, LEXPERT (last visited Sept. 1, 2024), https://www.lexpert.ca/big-deals/bayer-ag-divests-9b-agriculture-business-to-basf/352190.

154. Report from Felipe Cerda Becker, Jefe División de Fusiones [Mergers Division Chief], to Fiscal Nacional Económico [National Economic Prosecutor] regarding the merger between Bayer AG and Monsanto Company 2 (May 25, 2018), https://www.fne.gob.cl/wp-content/uploads/2018/06/inap1_F97_2017.pdf.

155. *Id.* at 1–2.

divest its global ammonium-glufosinate business and global vegetable seeds business.[156] The merging parties agreed to several behavioral remedies surrounding the sale of RoundUp in Chile for five years, including prohibitions on volume discounts, exclusive dealing, and bundling arrangements.[157] The FNE approved the merger subject to the same conditions on May 29, 2018.[158]

F. *China*

41. In China, the Ministry of Commerce (MOFCOM) was notified of the transaction on December 5, 2016, and re-notified on February 9, 2017.[159] MOFCOM launched a preliminary investigation on February 24, 2017, and the merger was approved with conditions on March 13, 2018.[160] The conditions included: divestiture of Bayer's global vegetable seeds business, divestiture of Bayer's global non-selective herbicide business, divestiture of Bayer's global corn, soybean, cotton, and oilseed trait businesses, and an interoperability requirement such that "Chinese agricultural software and application developers [may] connect their digital agriculture software and application programs to the digital agriculture platform of Bayer, Monsanto and the [merged] entity" on fair, reasonable, and non-discriminatory (FRAND) terms.[161]

G. *Costa Rica*

42. The Costa Rican competition authority (COPROCOM) was notified of the transaction on March 16, 2017.[162] COPROCOM approved the transaction without conditions on June 13, 2017.[163] The 22-page decision analyzes how the merger would increase concentration. For instance, the report

---

156 *Id.* at 24–26.

157 *Id.* at 27–28.

158 Memorandum from Felipe Irarrázabal Philippi, Fiscal Nacional Económico [National Economic Prosecutor] regarding the merger between Bayer AG and Monsanto Company 1, 3 (May 29, 2018), https://www.fne.gob.cl/wp-content/uploads/2018/06/aprob54a_F97_2017.pdf.

159 MOFCOM Announcement No. 31 of 2018 on Anti-Monopoly Review Decision Concerning the Conditional Approval of Concentration of Undertakings in the Case of Acquisition of Equity Interests of Monsanto Company by Bayer Aktiengesellschaft Kwa Investment Co., Ministry of Comm. (Mar. 15, 2018, 2:33 PM), http://english.ccpitbj.org/web/static/articles/catalog_2c94bbf02fd8b281012fd8de94480004/article_ff8080816203500c01626006cdcd0117/ff8080816203500c01626006cdcd0117.html.

160 *Id.*

161 *Id.* Elizabeth Wang led a team at Compass Lexecon, which was responsible for drafting an economic report to submit to MOFCOM. The team "work[ed] closely with John Ren from T&D Associates and Chen Ma from Han Kun Law offices." *Bayer/Monsanto Merger*, Compass Lexecon (May 29, 2018), https://www.compasslexecon.com/cases/bayer-monsanto-merger/.

162 Marcela Gómez et al., Voto [Vote] No. 44-2017, Expediente [File] No. 019-17-CE 1 (2017), https://www.coprocom.go.cr/resoluciones/2017/VOTO-44-2017-CE-BAYER-MONSANTO.pdf.

163 *Id.* at 1, 23.

discusses limited horizontal overlaps in the domestic herbicide market as well as various domestic seeds markets.[164] The largest increase in market share as a result of the merger appeared to be in the melon seeds market, where Bayer and Monsanto each had a 12% share pre-merger.[165] COPROCOM ultimately concluded that the merger would not be anticompetitive.[166]

H. *Ecuador*

43. The Ecuadorian competition authority (SCPM) was notified of the transaction on November 10, 2016, and approved the merger with a condition on October 16, 2017.[167] The condition prohibits the merging parties from producing, introducing, or commercializing genetically modified organisms (GMOs), and it prohibits "the application of modern, risky, and experimental biotechnologies, in order to protect Ecuador's genetic heritage and prevent the entry of GMOs into the country."[168] The brief (seven-page) decision does not analyze or discuss market characteristics or potential anticompetitive effects.[169] Thus, the authority uses its competition powers to protect the environment.

I. *India*

44. The Competition Commission of India (CCI) was notified of the merger on July 8, 2017, and subsequently published a 99-page order approving the merger subject to certain conditions on June 14, 2018.[170] The order required that Bayer divest its global glufosinate-ammonium business, its global broad acre crop seeds and traits business (with limited carveouts), and its global vegetable seeds business.[171] Monsanto was required to divest its stake in Mahyco, a company active in the domestic seed sector.[172] The

---

164 *Id.* at 12–16.

165 *See id.* at 12–15 (cataloging the shares of each company doing business in the domestic herbicide, insecticide, and fungicide markets, as well as different seed markets).

166 *Id.* at 22.

167 Dr. Marcelo Ortega Rodríguez, Presidente [President] et al., Superintendencia de Control del Poder de Mercado [Superintendence of Market Power Control], Expediente [File] No. SCPM-CRPI-0024-2017 1, 6–7 (2017), https://www.sce.gob.ec/sitio/wp-content/uploads/2020/10/SCPM-024-2017-16oct-2017.pdf.

168 *Id.* at 2 (translated by Jackson Maxwell, J.D., 2024, New York University School of Law).

169 The decision names four government officers who were involved in the process, and Bayer was represented by Dr. Diego Pérez Ordoñez. *Id.* at 1.

170 Competition Comm'n of India, Order under Section 31(7) of the Competition Act, 2002, Combination Registration No. C-2017/08/523 (notified on June 14, 2018), https://www.cci.gov.in/images/caseorders/en/order1654513106.pdf.

171 *Id.* at 52–59.

172 *Id.* at 59–60.

order also stipulated an "unprecedented" swath of behavioral remedies,[173] which would be binding for a term of seven years.[174] These included[175] licensing traits and non-selective herbicides on FRAND and non-exclusive terms, data-sharing with rival digital farming platforms, nondiscrimination with respect to licensing terms (i.e., if a new licensee is offered better terms, the same terms shall be offered to other licensees), a prohibition on exclusionary bundling, and a prohibition on exclusive distribution channels for the supply of agricultural products.[176]

J. Kenya

45. The Competition Authority of Kenya unconditionally approved the merger, following an analysis that "revealed it would not affect competition negatively nor raise any negative public interest issues."[177]

K. Mexico

46. The Mexican competition authority (COFECE) was notified of the transaction on February 27, 2017, and cleared the merger with conditions on May 24, 2018.[178] The 128-page decision required Bayer to divest its domestic nonselective herbicides business (Finale Ultra), its global cotton seeds and traits business, and its Nunhems México vegetable seeds business to BASF.[179]

---

173 Malina McLennan, *Bayer/Monsanto Secures Post-Closing Clearance in India*, GLOB. COMPETITION REV. (June 21, 2018), https://globalcompetitionreview.com/article/bayermonsanto-secures-post-closing-clearance-in-india (quoting Rahul Rai, Partner at AZB & Partners in Mumbai); *see id.* at 61–66.

174 Competition Comm'n of India, *supra* note 170, at 61.

175 *Id.* at 61–65.

176 G. R. Bhatia, Abdullah Hussain, Kanika Chaudhary Nayar, Rudresh Singh, and Divye Sharma of Luthra & Luthra Law Offices represented Bayer. *Luthra and Luthra Law Offices India*, FACEBOOK (May 24, 2018), https://www.facebook.com/llpartners/posts/779967628794257/?_rdr. A team of ten attorneys, a consultant, and an economist from Shardul Amarchand Mangaldas & Co advised Monsanto. Ani, *SAM Advises Monsanto on Securing CCI Approval Bayer AG*, BUS. STANDARD (May 23, 2018), https://www.business-standard.com/article/news-ani/sam-advises-monsanto-on-securing-cci-approval-bayer-ag-118052300534_1.html.

177 COMPETITION AUTH. OF KENYA, ANNUAL REPORT & FINANCIAL STATEMENTS 2016/2017 94 (2017), https://www.cak.go.ke/sites/default/files/annual-reports/FY%202016-2017%20CAK%20Annual%20Report.pdf. John Oxenham and Andreas Stargard of Primerio advised Monsanto and were assisted by local counsel. *Primerio's Merger Team First to Obtain Clearances on Bayer's $66 Billion Monsanto Acquisition*, AFRICAN ANTITRUST & COMPETITION L. (Apr. 2, 2019), https://africanantitrust.com/2019/04/02/gcr-matter-of-the-year-2019-awarded-to-ag-deal-with-significant-african-dimension/.

178 Alejandra Palacios Prieto, Comisionado Presidenta [Commissioner President] et al., Resolución [Resolution], Expediente [File] CNT-024-2017 1, 126–28 (2018), https://www.cofece.mx/cfcresoluciones/docs/concentraciones/v5898/7/4312994.pdf.

179 *Id.* at 119–26.

L. *Paraguay*

47. The Paraguayan competition authority (CNC) was notified of the transaction on November 10, 2016, opened a second-stage investigation four days later, and unconditionally authorized the merger on February 28, 2017, following a recommendation from the director of the investigation.[180] The decision is short and cursory. It repeatedly notes that there was insufficient information to analyze substitutability.[181] The CNC nonetheless concluded that the merger was not problematic because there were additional competitors even in narrowly defined candidate markets.[182]

M. *Philippines*

48. The Philippine Competition Commission (PCC) decided to take no action against the merger on December 1, 2017.[183] "[O]n the basis of information obtained from the parties and other sources to date," the Mergers & Acquisitions Office concluded that the merger would "not result in a substantial lessening of competition on the relevant market..."[184] This conclusion was based on apparent "limited substitutability of the products of the parties in the market for non-selective herbicides,"[185] "sufficient competitive constraints from other market participants on the merged firm post-[t]ransaction in the markets for vegetable seeds and non-selective herbicides," and the apparent unlikelihood that "tying or bundling of the merged firm's products... [would] result in foreclosure of the affected product markets..."[186]

N. *Russia*

49. In November 2016, the Federal Antimonopoly Service (FAS) "arrived at a conclusion when reviewing the deal in Russia that the transaction could create significant risks for competition."[187] A year later, "Bayer filed a lawsuit in the Moscow Arbitration Court demanding that the FAS['] decision

---

180 Fabrizio Castiglioni S., Miembro del Directorio [Board Member], Comisión Nacional de la Competencia [National Competition Commission], Resolución [Resolution] 2/2017 1, 7 (2017), https://drive.google.com/file/d/1_3HaU-dAUXqRwNnshuGsblrCh6STRjxs/view.

181 *Id.* at 4, 6.

182 *Id.* at 6. Bayer was represented by Nestor Loizaga Franco and Frabrizio Franco Lopez Moreira. *Id.* at 1.

183 Arsenio M. Balisacan, Chairman, Philippine Competition Comm'n, et al., Commission Decision No. 35-M-012/2017 1–2 (2017), https://www.phcc.gov.ph/storage/pdf-resources/1678155613_M-012.2017_Bayer-AG_Commission-Decision.pdf.

184 *Id.* at 1.

185 *Id.*

186 *Id.*

187 *Russian Antitrust Watchdog Approves Bayer-Monsanto Deal*, TASS (Apr. 20, 2018), https://tass.com/economy/1000874.

to extend consideration of the deal should be declared illegal," with a preliminary hearing scheduled for April 11, 2018.[188] Bayer presumably dropped the legal case after the FAS approved the merger with conditions in April 2018.[189] The conditions included the following behavioral remedies, which are targeted at protecting and enabling Russia's domestic industry: (i) "transfer to Russian companies of the molecular means of selection and germplasm needed to create new varieties and hybrids," (ii) "obligations to provide Russian companies engaged in the development of agricultural software and applications with non-discriminatory access to digital farming platforms, including access to [relevant] data," and (iii) "the creation of a plant biotechnology research centre in the Russian Federation, which will provide practical training for Russian specialists."[190]

O. *Serbia*

50. The Serbian Commission for Protection of Competition (CPC) was notified of the transaction on September 29, 2016.[191] The CPC unconditionally approved the transaction on November 3, 2016.[192] The short (ten-page) decision approving the merger includes a seemingly cursory analysis of potential competitive effects. The analysis notes that there are many other sellers in Serbian seeds markets and cites the merging parties' findings of "significant and long-lasting" efficiencies.[193]

P. *South Africa*

51. The Competition Commission was notified of the transaction on February 1, 2017, and approved the merger with conditions on May 3, 2017.[194] Following an application from the merging parties, the Competition

---

188 *Id.*

189 *See* Russian Federation, Start-ups, Killer Acquisitions and Merger Control 5, Contribution at the 133rd OECD Competition Committee meeting (June 11, 2020), https://one.oecd.org/document/DAF/COMP/WD(2020)27/en/pdf.

190 OECD, Merger Control in Dynamic Markets – Contribution from the Russian Federation, DAF/COMP/GF/WD(2019)56 4–5 (Nov. 20, 2019), https://one.oecd.org/document/DAF/COMP/GF/WD(2019)56/en/pdf; *see* Russian Federation, *supra* note 189, at 5. ALRUD Law Firm and the National Research Institute Higher School of Economics assisted Bayer during the review process. Vassily Rudomino, Ksenia Tarkhova & Alexander Nazarov, *Bayer/Monsanto Transaction: Brand New Approach of FAS Russia to Merger Control*, KLUWER COMPETITION LAW BLOG (July 11, 2018), https://competitionlawblog.kluwercompetitionlaw.com/2018/07/11/bayermonsanto-transaction-brand-new-approach-fas-russia-merger-control/.

191 Dr. Miloje Obradović [Др Милоје Обрадовић], Predsednik Komisije [President of the Commission], Komisija Za Zaštitu Konkurencije [Commission for the Protection of Competition], Broj: [Number:] 6/0-02-687/2016-9 2 (2016), https://kzk.gov.rs/kzk/wp-content/uploads/2016/11/687-Bayer.pdf.

192 *Id.* at 1.

193 *Id.* at 9–10 (electronic translation).

194 Sipho Ngwema, Head of Commc'ns, The Competition Comm'n of S. Afr., Commission Conditionally Approves Bayer and Monsanto Transaction 1 (2017), https://www.compcom.co.za/wp-content/uploads/2017/01/Commission-Conditionally-Approves-Bayer-Transaction-Final.pdf.

Tribunal held hearings. It took seriously the anticompetitive aspects of the merger in South Africa. Ultimately, after a year of investigation and adjudication, it conditionally approved the merger.[195] The conditions included: divestiture of Bayer's "entire global Liberty Link trait technology and the associated Liberty[-]branded agro-chemicals business... as well as Bayer's [South African] Cotton Seed Business."[196] The Tribunal also imposed a behavioral remedy, requiring the divestiture buyer "to commercialise the divested products in South Africa, or alternatively... license the divested business to a South African third party to commercialise should the [buyer] be unable to do so."[197] Finally, the Tribunal imposed a "public interest condition requiring the provision of a 25% discount on sales of maize seeds and the 'Poncho' value offering to small emerging farmers in South Africa."[198] In March 2023, the Commission published a report assessing the impacts of these conditions and concluded that they were generally successful.[199] However, due to regulatory environmental obstacles, other components of the agreed-upon divestiture package could not be made. This has brought the case back to the Tribunal.[200]

52. At the time that the *Bayer/Monsanto* merger came before the South African Competition Commission, the Commission's chief economist was Liberty Mncube. Three years later, Dr. Mncube, with coauthors Laurie Binge and Helen Kean, wrote an article ("Local Competition Assessment of Global Mergers – Playing Golf with one Hand?") explaining how South Africa was seriously handicapped in designing appropriate remedies in *Bayer/Monsanto* (and other global mergers such as *Dow/DuPont* and *Holcim/Lafarge*). Thus:

> When it comes to evaluating global mergers, the South African competition authorities have found themselves unable to prohibit mergers with clear anticompetitive or negative public interest effects.... In situations where the most effective remedy would be a merger prohibition... the competition authorities have tended to choose a less effective local remedy. One reason for this could be a concern that

---

195 See Chantelle Benjamin, Commc'ns Officer, Competition Tribunal, *Merger of Global Firms Bayer AG and Monsanto Company Granted Subject to Divestiture of Bayer's Cotton Business*, COMPETITION TRIBUNAL (May 11, 2018), https://www.comptrib.co.za/open-file?FileId=51183 ("Date of release: 11 May 2018.... The Competition Tribunal has approved a merger between Bayer... and Monsanto....").

196 *Id.*

197 *Id.*

198 JASON APROSKIE & TESSA BLEAZARD, COMPETITION COMM'N S. AFR., IMPACT ASSESSMENT REPORT ON THE BAYER MONSANTO MERGER 5 (2023), https://www.compcom.co.za/wp-content/uploads/2023/07/ERB-Bayer-Monsanto-Impact-Study-Assessment_NonConfidential.pdf.

199 *See id.* at 6–7.

200 *BASF SE Germany and the Divestment Business of Bayer AG (Liberty Link Technology Business, Liberty Business and Seed Treatment Business)*, COMPETITION TRIBUNAL (last visited Sept. 2, 2024), https://www.comptrib.co.za/case-detail/20421. John Oxenham and Andreas Stargard of Primerio advised Monsanto and were assisted by local counsel. AFRICAN ANTITRUST & COMPETITION L., *supra* note 177.

prohibiting a global merger because of purely local concerns would be clumsy (and disproportionate). Another potential reason, perhaps even more important, is the concern that such a prohibition could lead to the merged firm simply withdrawing from South Africa. . . .[201]

Q. *Turkey*

53. The Turkish Competition Authority opened a Phase II investigation of the transaction on May 15, 2017.[202] Following the European Commission's conditional approval of the merger, the Competition Board found that the conditions stipulated by the European Commission would "eliminate the horizontal and vertical overlaps in the relevant markets in Turkey" and therefore did not violate Turkey's merger control law.[203]

R. *Ukraine*

54. The Antimonopoly Committee of Ukraine (AMCU) approved the merger with two behavioral conditions.[204] The first condition was to not "engage in input foreclosure by unreasonably restricting access to the relevant markets of crop protection products, seeds for vegetables and row crops or by eliminating competitors from these markets."[205] The second condition required the merged entity "to submit to the AMC[U] copies of all agreements relating to distribution of [the same] products in Ukraine" for three years.[206]

S. *Common Market for Eastern and Southern Africa (COMESA)*

55. The Common Market for Eastern and Southern Africa (COMESA)[207] is a regional economic community. It comprises 21 member states, from

---

201 Mncube et al., *supra* note 3, at 31.

202 M. Togan Turan & Derya Genç Paksoy, *Turkish Competition Board Approves Acquisition of Bayer by Monsanto*, THOMSON REUTERS PRAC. L. (June 1, 2018), https://uk.practicallaw.thomsonreuters.com/w-014-9195?comp=pluk&transitionType=Default&contextData=(sc.Default)&firstPage=true&OWSessionId=893a0b5b03714051a599e381478cc2fd&skipAnonymous=true.

203 *Id.*

204 OECD, Annual Report on Competition Policy Developments in Ukraine – 2017, DAF/COMP/AR(2018)30 14–15 (Oct. 31, 2018), https://amcu.gov.ua/storage/app/uploads/public/611/40b/175/61140b175e5be045339390.pdf.

205 Anastasia Usova & Nataliya Kovalyova, *Record-Breaking Fines and Top Trends in Ukrainian Merger Control*, KLUWER COMPETITION L. BLOG (May 30, 2019), https://competitionlawblog.kluwercompetitionlaw.com/2019/05/30/record-breaking-fines-and-top-trends-in-ukrainian-merger-control/.

206 *Id.*

207 *The Common Market for Eastern and Southern Africa*, COMESA (last visited Sept. 2, 2024), https://www.comesa.int/.

Egypt to Zambia to Eswatini.[208] It is the flagship regional economic community in Africa and is grooming its position to be a sturdy pillar for the African Continental Competition Protocol when it becomes operational.

56. The COMESA Competition Commission was notified of the transaction on February 16, 2017.[209] In June of that year, it decided to take no action on the merger.[210] The Commission disposed of the case in two one-sentence paragraphs. The decision states, under the heading "Competition Analysis": "The CID (Committee Responsible for Initial Determination) established that the merger is not likely to substantially prevent or lessen competition in the relevant markets and is not likely to be contrary to public interest…"[211]

2. Observations

57. While the US and EU enforcers were the highest profile actors, the rest of the world did not just sit on the sidelines. Competition authorities in Brazil, Canada, Chile, China, India, Mexico, Russia, South Africa, and Ukraine all imposed their own remedies aimed at preserving competition or enhancing technical capabilities in their jurisdictions. India provides a particularly interesting example, pairing global divestitures with a wide swath of behavioral remedies over a relatively long (seven-year) timeline.[212] Some of these behavioral remedies, such as regulations on licensing terms and data-sharing with rival digital farming platforms, were bound to entail significant monitoring costs if conscientiously pursued. Divestiture remedies, too, were predictably costly for enforcers, who would have to have explored: Is the divestiture buyer capable of replenishing the lost competition? Will its business be robust and make a difference? Might the divestiture buyer fall into a cozy oligopoly? Does the divestiture itself create new competition problems – such as when BASF bought canola seeds and

---

208 *What is COMESA*, COMESA (last visited Sept. 2, 2024), https://www.comesa.int/what-is-comesa/ (noting COMESA's "21 Member States").

209 Commissioner Langa, Chairperson, COMESA Competition Comm. et al., *Decision of the Thirty Third Committee Responsible for Initial Determination on the Application for Authorisation of the Acquisition of Monsanto Company by Bayer Aktiengesellschaft* 2 (COMESA Competition Comm'n Staff Paper No. 2017/06/JB06, 2017), https://www.comesacompetition.org/wp-content/uploads/2014/10/Decision-Bayer_Monsanto-Merger-Transaction.pdf.

210 *Id.* at 3. *See Antitrust and Developing Economies in an Era of Crises: Webinar #1: Growing Cross-Border Challenges and New Life for Public Interests and Industrial Policy Synthesis*, CONCURRENCES (Oct. 27, 2020), https://www.concurrences.com/en/events/antitrust-and-developing-economies-in-an-era-of-crisis-webinar-1-growing-cross. John Oxenham and Andreas Stargard of Primerio advised Monsanto and were assisted by local counsel. AFRICAN ANTITRUST & COMPETITION L., *supra* note 177.

211 Langa et al., *supra* note 209, at 3. "[T]he Commission reached its decision based on the large number of players in the market, including DuPont, BASF, Arysta, and Dow…" (summary of remarks of Willard Mwemba, then head of mergers at COMESA, at panel discussion, Oct. 27, 2020, Concurrences, *supra* note 210).

212 *See supra* notes 171–175.

traits in Canada,[213] and corn and sugar beet seed treatments and non-selective herbicides in the EEA?[214]

58. Several jurisdictions appeared predisposed towards the merger. Competition authorities in Argentina, Costa Rica, Paraguay, and Serbia all published analyses acknowledging that the merger could have anticompetitive effects through increased horizontal concentration and/or vertical foreclosure but dismissed these effects as insignificant and/or counteracted by claimed efficiencies.[215] None of their published analyses included a factual basis for dismissing the concerns or for embracing the parties' claims of efficiencies and their balance of the trade-offs.[216] Ecuador's decision did not even analyze possible anticompetitive effects, but it seemed to welcome the opportunity to issue conditions that could help protect the environment and the people from GMOs and "risky… experimental biotechnologies."[217]

59. A sympathetic stance towards unconditionally clearing the merger without much investment in investigation and analysis could have several explanations. It could be associated with corruption or poor management. But choosing not to commit significant resources to reviewing the merger may have been perfectly rational for conscientious enforcers in young and small jurisdictions. First, "[s]mall jurisdictions can rarely make a credible threat to prohibit the conduct of a foreign firm,"[218] especially against two enormous multinational firms. Were the Paraguayan competition authority to unilaterally impose significant restrictions on the merger (let alone enjoining it entirely), Bayer may simply have exited from Paraguay, a country with a GDP of less than Harvard University's endowment.[219] The costs of complying with Paraguay's demands would

---

213 Consequently, the Canadian Commissioner of Competition required another divestiture "to a purchaser acceptable to the Commissioner." A search of the Competition Bureau's website reveals no further updates, suggesting that such a purchaser may not yet have been found. *See* Competition Bureau Statement Regarding BASF's Purchase of Assets from Bayer AG Following Its acquisition of Monsanto, Gov't of Can. (Jan. 20, 2022), https://competition-bureau.canada.ca/competition-bureau-statement-regarding-basfs-purchase-assets-bayer-ag-following-its-acquisition.

214 Decision on the Implementation of Commitments – Purchaser Approval, *supra* note 117. As a consequence of the overlap with the divestiture buyer, the Commission's approval of BASF as a purchaser depended on BASF's commitment to divest its own overlapping assets, eventually selling its Trunemco nematicidal seed treatment business to Nufarm in February 2019. https://nufarm.com/uscrop/2019/02/19/nufarm-acquires-trunemco-nematode-management-seed-treatment-from-basf/.

215 *See supra* 131–37, 162–166, 181–183, and 191–193 and accompanying text.

216 *Id.*

217 *See supra* notes 168–169 and accompanying text.

218 Michal S. Gal, *Antitrust in a Globalized Economy: The Unique Enforcement Challenges Faced by Small and Developing Jurisdictions*, 33 Fordham Int'l L.J. 1, 31 (2009); Mncube et al., *supra* note 3.

219 *See Paraguay*, CIA, https://www.cia.gov/the-world-factbook/countries/paraguay/ (Aug. 7, 2024) (estimating that Paraguay had a nominal GDP of US$42.956 billion in 2023); Sarah Wood, *15 National Universities with the Biggest Endowments*, U.S. News (Oct. 2, 2024, 4:48 PM), https://www.usnews.com/education/best-colleges/the-short-list-college/articles/10-universities-with-the-biggest-endowments (reporting that Harvard University had an endowment of over US$50 billion at the end of fiscal year 2022).

probably exceed the gains from trading in Paraguay.[220] Second, investigating large multinationals might be not only a formidable task but a poor use of small enforcers' resources. Conducting a thorough investigation of a merger such as *Bayer/Monsanto* would have required gathering and assimilating evidence from foreign sources and witnesses or experts, on top of mustering domestic market information. Thorough enforcement against a lawyered-up giant like Bayer would probably cost more than the agency's budget.[221] Third, as may have been the case in Paraguay,[222] enforcers in small and/or developing jurisdictions face legal obstacles to obtaining relevant information.[223] This is, in part, a function of the rules of confidentiality, which might preclude one (small) jurisdiction's building on the knowledge base of another.[224]

60. In sum, the world apart from the US and EU may take a credible role in enforcement against anticompetitive megamergers, and some of the larger countries – especially the BRICS countries – may make the investment, but the numerous smaller jurisdictions in harm's way face daunting challenges in both investigating and proceeding. They may go through the motions of vetting the merger. (Their law usually requires them to.) They may impose a small condition or none at all, and they inevitably clear the merger.

V. The Misalignments of Incentives – The Discounting of "Fix-it" Risks

61. Through the window of *Bayer/Monsanto*, we get insight into the structure of incentives of the competition authorities in ordering appropriate relief in the case of anticompetitive megamergers. Since inferences are drawn from data about only one globally anticompetitive megamerger, the observations that follow might be taken as hypotheses.

---

220 *See* Gal, *supra* note 218, at 31: "Consider an example of an international merger that has no negative welfare effects on the large jurisdictions. . . . [T]he gains from trade within [the small country] are limited. Accordingly, the firm would most likely choose to exit the small country... if the small jurisdiction imposed significant restrictions." (footnote omitted).

221 It should go without saying that enforcement against a megamerger would be much more expensive than enforcement against a smaller company. *See id.* at 33–34 ("[S]mall and developing jurisdictions often have limited resources to combat anticompetitive conduct... This problem is even more pronounced in international antitrust cases..." (footnote omitted)).

222 *See supra* note 181 and accompanying text.

223 *See* Gal, *supra* note 218, at 35 ("Oftentimes [small jurisdictions'] authorities cannot receive the relevant factual information from those authorities that have prosecuted the firms because of secrecy issues.").

224 *See also id.* ("For example, the New Zealand Competition Authority considered bringing a case against the Vitamins cartel after it was prosecuted elsewhere. However, it could not obtain the pertinent information because the [DOJ] was prevented, under its plea bargain agreement with the relevant firms, from disclosing the relevant information. In this case, the U.S. authority made a strategic decision to limit the number of possible world-wide prosecutions against the cartel in order to ensure that it be brought to trial in the United States." (footnotes omitted)).

62. The *Bayer/Monsanto* merger, which was one in a rapid series of megamergers in the sector of agriculture, seeds and fertilizers that consolidated the Big Six into the Big Four, posed serious competition problems in food markets across the world. If it raised the price of fertilizers, pesticides, and seeds, it would harm the food supply globally. If it further consolidated the industry, it could make the global food chain more susceptible to shocks of disease and war. If it degraded the lines of plant traits and significantly reduced the traits, it would also harm the environment. If it enhanced the mechanisms to exploit the already challenged farmers and independents, it would weaken their durability. If the fix-it remedies failed to replace the lost competition and created new competition problems, it would further undermine the market.

63. The *Bayer/Monsanto* merger appeared to pose all these problems, all over the world. The most severe harms were likely to fall on developing countries. Especially in developing countries, the farmers were likely to be overcharged for fertilizer, seeds, and chemicals, and they themselves were and are uniquely exposed to the shocks of climate change and shrinking arable land. The developing country markets and the infrastructure to support them are so fragile that the people – who are some of the poorest in the world – commonly pay the highest price for food in the world.[225]

64. This review of the competition authorities' actions suggests the following four points.

　　1. Institutional incentives to prevent competition harm from globally anticompetitive mergers are not conducive to producing the best outcomes. They do not support serious consideration of the choice of prohibition as the first best remedy.

　　2. The mismatch is facilitated by the following four conditions:

　　　　(i) There is an existing practice for competition authorities to clear mergers with spinoffs to eliminate direct overlaps, often with conditions to support the divestiture buyer. The merging parties have a strong incentive to reach such a settlement. They can retain the heart of their advantage from the deal, spin off dispensable assets, and promise to support divestiture buyers. Competition authorities may be too easily persuaded that the "fixes" proposed by the parties will cure the competition risks and not entail high costs of supervising the performance of the conditions; they may be too easily persuaded to overlook competition problems at the core of the merger and to discount high risks of failure of the fix-it plan.[226] (For the US, this was not true of the Biden administration enforcers.)

---

225 *See* Rob Vos, Joseph Glauber, Soonho Kim & Will Martin, *Despite Improved Global Market Conditions, High Food Price Inflation Persists*, IFPRI Blog (Dec. 4, 2023), https://www.ifpri.org/blog/despite-improved-global-market-conditions-high-food-price-inflation-persists/; Das Nair & Roberts, *supra* note 3.

226 *See* John Kwoka & Spencer Waller, *Fix It or Forget It: A "No-Remedies" Policy for Merger Enforcement*, Antitrust Chron. (Summer 2021), https://papers.ssrn.com/sol3/papers.cfm?abstract_id=3915083.

(ii) In elaboration of the biases: In contemplating the remedies proposed by the parties, competition authorities appear inclined to discount the strength and importance of the competition that will be lost, the likelihood that the divestiture purchaser will fill the slack, the additional competition problems that may arise from the relief itself, and the costs of monitoring the divestitures and other conditions – a task likely to last for many years.[227]

(iii) Once a settlement is reached, the competition authority has an incentive to promote it and may appear to lose objectivity in the face of evidence of its insufficiency.[228] Once the agencies accept the settlement and publicize their "success," their public-facing work is done. For the merger parties, they are "all in" in supporting the deal; they want it to happen. Multi-million dollar break-up fees increase their commitment to get the deal through and thus their incentive to persuade the authorities of the virtues of a settlement suitable to them.

(iv) Once the remedy deal is made, the interests of the merging parties and the agencies become aligned, rather than adversarial. They share an incentive to defend the settlement in response to objectors.[229] In the US, the DOJ must get approval of the settlement from a court in a Tunney Act proceeding.[230] The DOJ drafts the Complaint only after the settlement is reached. In drafting the Complaint, the DOJ has the incentive to articulate the merger's threatened harms in terms of the relief already accepted.

3. The "vision" line of the agencies is nationalistic. They do what is good for their jurisdiction (if not also for themselves). Russia is the least subtle example in the *Bayer/Monsanto* story. It tends to impose affirmative conditions that will, for example, transfer technology to itself.[231] No country, including the home of the merging firms (often the US), has the incentive to prevent the merger from inflicting harm on those outside of its jurisdiction. Indeed, the home country may profit from squeezing farmers and small suppliers abroad. The outsiders in the line of harm from megamergers are commonly

---

227 *Id.*

228 *See* Kari Bode, *The Dish 'Fix' for the T-Mobile-Sprint Merger Seems More Shortsighted Than Ever*, THE VERGE (July 21, 2021, 5:00 AM), https://www.theverge.com/2021/7/21/22585761/dish-t-mobile-att-sprint-competition-editorial.

229 *See* New York v. Deutsche Telekom, 439 F. Supp.3d 179 (S.D.N.Y. 2020); U.S. Dep't of Just., Press Release, Justice Department Welcomes Decision in New York v. Deutsche Telekom, the T-Mobile/Sprint Merger (Feb. 11, 2020), https://www.justice.gov/opa/pr/justice-department-welcomes-decision-new-york-v-deutsche-telecom-t-mobilesprint-merger.

230 *See* description of the Tunney Act, *supra* note 71.

231 *See* the summary of Russia's treatment of *Bayer/Monsanto* above, *supra* notes 187–190. *See also* the summary of Chinese remedies, *supra* note 161.

developing countries. After the US and EU do what is good for them, the other countries are on their own. These other countries, whose people may be the biggest targets of harm, are usually resource-constrained in contemplating a full litigation challenge to a megamerger, as well as powerless to stop transactions that are bad for their people and their markets.[232]

4. In developing and emerging markets, BRICS countries and smaller, younger jurisdictions might be distinguished. The BRICS may devote resources to megamergers that threaten harm to them. They may impose conditions and even minor spinoffs, but they do not prohibit these mergers and may not have the practical power to do so. The smaller and younger jurisdictions may devote their very scarce resources to the megamerger and clear it – even where harm may lurk in their markets.[233]

VI. Is There a Better Way? – Recommendations

65. The two biggest problems can be summarized as:
    - The incentives and the momentum are such that competition authorities do not give sufficient sympathetic attention to prohibiting globally anticompetitive megamergers.
    - The result is huge costs from the unnecessary loss of competition and from the crafting, monitoring and supervision of the second-best remedies – to the extent the remedies are supervised at all; and if they are not supervised, the costs of the unmet promises to restore competition. The costs are especially high for developing countries, which lack the power and capacity to protect themselves.

66. Solutions require changing the perspective from solely national to also world welfare, and seeking a structure that would do so. This objective was a "futuristic" recommendation of the International Competition Policy Advisory Committee (ICPAC) to the US attorney general and assistant attorney general (James Rill and Paula Stern, chairs)(2000), envisioning the possibility, sometime in the future, of a "coordinating jurisdiction [that] could then design remedies to address the concerns of all interested jurisdictions."[234] The project would require transparency,

---

232 *See* discussion *supra* notes 218–224.
233 *See* Argentina, *supra* notes 138–143; Costa Rica, *supra* notes 162–166; Paraguay, *supra* notes 181–183; Serbia, *supra* notes 191–193.
234 INT'L COMPETITION POL'Y COMM. ADVISORY COMM. TO THE ATT'Y GEN. & ASSISTANT ATT'Y GEN. FOR ANTITRUST, FINAL REPORT 85 (2000), https://www.justice.gov/atr/final-report. *See also* Eleanor Fox & Janusz Ordover, *The Harmonization of Competition and Trade Law: The Case for Modest Linkages of Law and Limits to Parochial State Action*, in COMPETITION POLICY IN THE GLOBAL ECONOMY: MODALITIES FOR CO-OPERATION 364–366

including recognition at the agency level of the tendency to discount the lost competition and the costs of "fix-it" remedies as compared with prohibitions.

1. How Can We Nudge Global Vision?

A. *A Mechanism – A New Equilibrium on the Horizon*

67. Serendipity has brought us a possible mechanism that could change the dynamic. In Africa, a competition protocol for all of Africa has been approved and is pending ratification.[235] It will, when operational, provide a vehicle for Africa to engage with continent-wide and world restraints, including megamergers that hurt Africa. Africa has been a missing link at the "international competition table."

68. Imagine, after the African Continental Competition protocol is operational, a collaboration of national authorities to assess the next megamerger that threatens significant global harm. Vetting the merger, the head of the African Competition Commission sits at the international table with the heads of competition of the US, EU, BRICS, Latin America, Australia/New Zealand and Asia, with others as desired, representing the interests of the world.[236] If the (net) harms to the world are substantial, the enforcers may agree that the best and right remedy is a prohibition, and they may "go home" with the courage of their convictions to prohibit the merger under their national laws.

B. *An Ombuds-Team*

69. Much needed is an ombudsman or "ombuds-team" appointed to study each future megamerger in the context of the global market and write an expert report on the merger and possible remedies from the viewpoint of world benefits and harms. A second report would be required after the merging parties offer fix-it remedies.

C. *Appreciation*

70. Meanwhile and at the least, we need a bolder, clear-eyed view of the benefits of prohibition versus the benefits of ad hoc nationally-tailored spinoffs and conditions proffered to counteract the threatened global harms.

(Leonard Waverman, William S. Comanor & Akira Gotō eds., 1996) (arguing that "national solutions may be cut from too narrow a cloth" and that world welfare is the proper standard for global mergers).

235 *See AfCFTA Protocol on Competition Policy: Factsheet*, TRALAC (Oct. 5, 2023), https://www.tralac.org/resources/infographic/16150-afcfta-protocol-on-competition-policy-factsheet.html.

236 This is more than a collective action problem. The synergistic global effects are greater than and different from the sum of the national parts.

Remedies First

MELISSA H. MAXMAN[*]
Cohen & Gresser LLP

RONALD F. WICK[**]
Cohen & Gresser LLP

Abstract

This article pays tribute to Professor Harry First, a distinguished legal scholar whose contributions to antitrust law have profoundly influenced both academic discourse and practical litigation strategies. Renowned for his pragmatic approach, Professor First emphasized the importance of addressing remedies early in antitrust analysis, advocating for a focus on the real-world needs of litigants rather than solely on theoretical constructs. The article reviews his 21st-century scholarship, highlighting key works such as "The Case for Antitrust Civil Penalties" and "The Microsoft Antitrust Cases: Competition Policy for the Twenty-first Century," which illustrate his commitment to integrating empirical data with practical legal frameworks. It discusses his insights on the necessity of civil penalties in monopolization cases and the implications of his findings for contemporary antitrust challenges, particularly in the context of Big Tech. Ultimately, the article underscores Professor First's legacy as a pioneer of a remedy-focused approach in antitrust law, advocating for a shift towards practical solutions that align legal outcomes with the broader goals of competition policy.

---

[*] Melissa H. Maxman is the Managing Partner of Cohen & Gresser LLP's Washington, D.C. office.

[**] Ronald F. Wick is a Partner at Cohen & Gresser LLP's Washington, D.C. office.

1. Professor Harry First, the Charles L. Denison Professor of Law Emeritus at NYU Law School, will be remembered for many things: his many years of insights on contemporary antitrust issues, his casebooks, his time in public service, the countless students and fresh legal scholars he has mentored, his good cheer and clear thinking and self-deprecating wit.

2. But we will always remember his jurisprudence for his practical overlay on antitrust theory. His jurisprudence, always grounded in the real world, asks scholars to think less about the best theoretical answer to a thorny problem and more about the actual needs and desires of litigants. Consistent with this approach is his promotion of addressing remedies at the beginning of the analysis rather than proceeding on theory alone. As litigators who for decades have looked at the world through the lens of attempting to achieve results that will satisfy our real-life clients rather than get to the "right answer," Professor First's approach to scholarship is not only wise: It is invaluable. In fact, for us, it is why civilizations create legal frameworks in the first place: to enable citizens to settle their inevitable differences without violence.

3. When reviewing the scholarship of someone who has been writing for as long as Professor First has, a trajectory becomes clear. This article will limit its analysis to his 21st-century writings because a more expansive review would require more space than this tribute allows. But first, a little "modern history."

I. Late 20th Century Academic Scholarship Debate

4. In the late 20th century, legal scholarship was engaged in a debate between the majority view that law schools should teach "pure theory,"[1] which was criticized as "impractical," and a competing argument that legal scholarship should be more relevant to practitioners, producing "practical" scholarship.[2] Of course, the highest accolade bestowed upon a law professor would be to be relied on and cited by a court – the higher the court, the better.[3]

---

[1] See, e.g., George L. Priest, *Social Science Theory and Legal Education: The Law School as University*, 33 J. LEGAL EDUC. 437, 441 (1983) (arguing that law schools "will of necessity" transform themselves into universities, "comprised of a set of miniature graduate departments in the various disciplines"); George L. Priest, *The Increasing Division Between Legal Practice and Legal Education*, 37 BUFF. L. REV. 681 (1988).

[2] See Harry T. Edwards, *The Growing Disjunction Between Legal Education and the Legal Profession*, 91 MICH. L. REV. 34, 35 (1992) (arguing that law professors "considered themselves academics first and lawyers only by the sheerest of happenstance" and that "most faculty members (and certainly most of the youngest and most ambitious) were generally disdainful of the practice of law.")

[3] A 1991 study found that law reviews are seldom cited by the federal courts of appeals. Louis J. Sirico, Jr. & Beth A. Drew, *The Citing of Law Reviews by the United States Courts of Appeals: An Empirical Analysis*, 45 U. MIAMI L. REV. 1051 (1991).

5. Less than fifteen years later, a truce had been struck between these competing doctrines. Law school education in the early 21st century embraced a balance between the theoretical and doctrinal approaches. Professor First's scholarship followed this pattern, and his writings are full of concrete examples examining the kinds of theories useful to frontline litigators like us.[4]

II. Professor First's 21st Century Antitrust Scholarship

6. The importance of remedies, and Professor First's practical approach to them, becomes clear even in a cursory review of his major writings. In "The Case for Antitrust Civil Penalties,"[5] Professor First began, "When it comes to remedying illegal monopolization, U.S. antitrust law would seem to provide every remedy in the book."[6] But he noted that there was one key missing remedy that is widely used outside the United States: civil penalties. He went on to argue that civil penalties are a weapon that could and should be used to deter, compensate, and remediate violations of section 2.[7] While acknowledging that "[c]ivil fines are not the remedial cure-all," he noted, pragmatically, that in setting civil fines at an appropriately high level depending on the financial condition of the violator, "incentives matter. How much they matter is another story."[8]

7. Professor First considered the potential application of civil penalties to different categories of antitrust violations, formulating compelling arguments against them in most types of cases. Cartel enforcement, he contended, is already done through the criminal justice system, which has a moral component. Adding a civil penalty would "cloud[] the message" of "opprobrium" conveyed by a criminal conviction, thereby blunting its deterrent impact.[9] Moreover, because civil cases are easier to litigate and settle than criminal cases, Professor First expressed concern that a civil fine case might be an "attractive nuisance" to prosecutors that would come at the expense of criminal enforcement.[10]

8. Professor First suggested that the case for civil fines might be stronger in monopolization cases. Given the relative paucity of government enforcement cases and obstacles to private section 2 litigation, Professor First

---

4   See Alex M. Johnson, Jr., *Think Like a Lawyer, Work Like a Machine: The Dissonance Between Law School and Law Practice*, 64 S. Cal. L. Rev. 1231 (1991).

5   Harry First, *The Case for Antitrust Civil Penalties*, 76 Antitrust L.J. 127 (2009).

6   *Id.*

7   *Id.* at 143–53.

8   *Id.* at 166.

9   *Id.* at 146.

10 *Id.*

noted that "one would be hard-pressed to argue that current penalties are adequately deterring corporations from violating Section 2."[11] Since monopolization is rarely, if ever, prosecuted criminally, there would be no criminal deterrence message for a civil fine to undermine, unlike in cartel cases. And given the complexities involved in fashioning remedies – particularly behavioral remedies – in a monopolization case, a sufficiently large civil fine would shift the burden from the court to the defendant to identify the behavioral changes necessary to avoid future violations.[12] Professor First also acknowledged, however, that section 2 jurisprudence leaves businesses with guidance that is "often unclear."[13] Accordingly, there is reason for concern that "the addition of a fine on top of uncertain liability may produce uncertain deterrent effects as business people try to stay further from the liability line."[14]

9. So, Professor First suggested two categories of monopolization cases as a starting point for the use of civil fines. One category was "systemic conduct" cases, such as *Microsoft*, which challenge a "systemic effort to maintain monopoly" as opposed to specific business practices.[15] Such cases, he argued, are difficult both to try, because of the widespread nature of the conduct, and to remedy, because targeting specific behavior invites the monopolist to switch to a different set of practices to maintain its monopoly. The other category was "no efficiency justification" cases, in which "there is no case to be made that the conduct provides social benefit," such as *Walker Process* patent fraud cases.[16] In both categories of cases, he reasoned, there is substantial concern that injunctive relief, or even private damages, may not provide sufficient deterrence, yet little reason for concern that civil fines would result in over-deterrence.[17]

10. We choose this article as a starting point not because the argument over the relative benefit or detriment of civil fines is still a pressing issue today, but because fifteen years ago, the trajectory of Professor First's jurisprudence was already picking up the mantel of practical scholarship, which necessarily starts with remedies. His civil fines proposal reflected a real-world analysis of the impact of the available remedies on different types of anticompetitive conduct, taking into account how the antitrust laws are enforced today, where they are falling short, and how to address those shortcomings without undermining the remedies already in place.

---

11 *Id.* at 148.
12 *Id.* at 152.
13 *Id.* at 148.
14 *Id.*
15 *Id.* at 154.
16 *Id.* at 160; *see* Walker Process Equip., Inc. v. Food Mach. & Chem. Corp., 382 U.S. 172 (1965).
17 *Id.* at 165–66.

11. Professor First once remarked in a conversation with us that the best way to address a legal problem for a client is to start at the end – where does the client want to end up, and how does it want to get there? – and then examine what remedies are available under the law to achieve the client's goals. When starting on a case, a practitioner should start with how to get to where the client wants to go and what legal avenues are available to get there. By weaving this imperative into his teaching, Professor First enabled his students to come away with both an understanding of the theoretical scaffolding and a process by which to use it to achieve the desired outcome.

III. The *Microsoft Book*

12. As other articles in this *Liber amicorum* have discussed in more depth, Professor First coauthored with Professor Andrew Gavil a seminal 2014 book, *The Microsoft Antitrust Cases: Competition Policy for the Twenty-first Century* (hereinafter *Microsoft Book*).[18] It has been described as the most "comprehensive, thoughtful, and authoritative assessment"[19] of the large "family of antitrust cases we call 'Microsoft' [cases]."[20] Notably, the introduction stated that one of its primary goals was to "use the *Microsoft* cases – public, private, domestic, and international – to illuminate and evaluate the institutional and *remedial* dimensions of contemporary antitrust enforcement."[21] Indeed, the last three chapters of the book are devoted to addressing the topic of remedies.[22]

13. One of the undersigned authors was fortunate to have participated in the private civil class actions transferred by multidistrict litigation (MDL) to Judge Frederick Motz in the U.S. District Court for the District of Maryland,[23] representing three European software designers (two British and one Swiss) who sued as class representatives for non-U.S. companies injured by Microsoft's anticompetitive actions in the United States. Our clients designed the software for the slot machines used by Bally's Casinos in Las Vegas and alleged that they were harmed by being precluded from using Unix/Linux software on Microsoft hardware.

---

18 ANDREW I. GAVIL & HARRY, THE MICROSOFT ANTITRUST CASES: COMPETITION POLICY FOR THE TWENTY-FIRST CENTURY (2014) (hereinafter MICROSOFT BOOK).

19 European Commission's former Director-General for Competition Philip Lowe, praise for MICROSOFT BOOK (back cover).

20 Professor Herbert Hovenkamp, praise for MICROSOFT BOOK (back cover).

21 MICROSOFT BOOK at 5 (emphasis added).

22 Chapter 7 is entitled "The Challenge of Remedy," *id.* at 235; Chapter 8 is entitled "In Praise of Institutional Diversity," *id.* at 281, and Chapter 9 is entitled "Lessons from the *Microsoft* Cases," *id.* at 309.

23 In re Microsoft Corp. Antitrust Litig., 237 F. Supp. 2d 639 (D. Md. 2002).

14. At the time, there was a circuit split as to whether non-U.S. plaintiffs had standing to sue in the U.S. under the Sherman Act. Consistent with Fourth Circuit precedent, Judge Motz granted Microsoft's motion to dismiss the international plaintiffs early in the case.[24] After the Fourth Circuit denied Judge Motz's certification for interlocutory appeal of his decision,[25] the case was being briefed on final appeal just as the U.S. Supreme Court issued its seminal *Empagran* case.[26] *Empagran* held that foreign plaintiffs did, indeed, have standing to sue a U.S. corporation under the Sherman Act in the U.S. federal courts where the foreign injury was not independent of the domestic effects.[27] Thus, in 2004, Microsoft entered into a confidential settlement with the individual foreign plaintiffs (no class had yet been certified), likely because Microsoft did not want to be the first test case of *Empagran*'s reach.[28]

15. As a result of this participation in the private civil suits against Microsoft, this author was invited to review a pre-publication of the *Microsoft Book* at the Tenth Annual Loyola University of Chicago School of Law Antitrust Colloquium in 2010.[29] This review was limited to Chapter 5, "Private Litigation in the United States,"[30] and was predictably focused on the international aspect of the case. Following the review, Professors First and Gavil graciously – and, we believe, accurately – added a reference to the important (albeit rarely invoked) international implications of the case.[31] While acknowledging that there was at least one empirical area they could not include in their book, Professors First and Gavil nevertheless were willing to point out to a careful reader that the legal implications of the *Microsoft* cases were so far-reaching that not even the most comprehensive review could address all of them in detail.

16. Perhaps the most instructive overarching conclusions of the book – again, from the perspective of frontline antitrust litigators rather than theorists – are in the book's final chapter, "Lessons from the *Microsoft* Cases,"[32] and more particularly, "Were the Remedies Adequate?"[33]

---

24   In re Microsoft Corp. Antitrust Litig., 127 F. Supp. 2d 702, 714–17 (D. Md. 2001).

25   *Id.*

26   F. Hoffman-La Roche Ltd. v. Empagran S. A., 542 U.S. 155 (2004). *See* John M. Nannes, Shepard Goldfein & C. Benjamin Crisman, *The US Supreme Court blocks foreign plaintiffs from bringing price-fixing cartel claims (*Hoffman-LaRoche / Empagran*)*, e-Competitions June 2004, art. no. 45646.

27   *F. Hoffman-La Roche Ltd. v. Empagran S. A.*, 542 U.S. 155 (2004).

28   *Empagran* has subsequently been narrowly interpreted by lower courts and, over the past two decades, has largely been an impediment to foreign plaintiffs' standing to sue under the Sherman Act.

29   *See also* Microsoft Book, Acknowledgements at viii (acknowledging the usefulness of the comments given at the colloquium).

30   *Id.* at 133.

31   *Id.* at 165–66 and endnote 70 to Chapter 5 (noting that the issues raised by foreign plaintiffs beyond the scope of this chapter).

32   *Id.* at 309.

33   *Id.* at 322–27.

and "Did Antitrust Enforcement Dull Microsoft's Innovative Edge?"[34] From the undersigned authors' perspective two decades later, Microsoft has improved its reputation to that of a better corporate citizen, particularly when compared to the conduct subsequently alleged by the Department of Justice (DOJ) and the Federal Trade Commission (FTC) in cases against Google[35] and Amazon,[36] among others.[37] Antitrust observers' opinions diverge as to whether the changes were brought about by the court-imposed remedies themselves, or by the transaction costs Microsoft has weighed against the potential benefits in a traditional cost/benefit analysis. Nevertheless, the ultimate result is that Microsoft is widely perceived to have ceased its prior abuse of dominant advantage – at least in part because it no longer enjoys monopoly market share and thus cannot do so, whereas other large technology firms can.[38] The *Microsoft Book* wisely noted that it is not clear precisely which remedies created this effect and which were not as useful, because "there were no benchmarks established at the start of the case whereby any of the measures ultimately ordered or agreed upon could be evaluated."[39] Nevertheless, the authors noted that the "*Microsoft* cases may have taught us about the design of remedies and what criteria we should use to judge their efficacy."[40] They continued, aptly, that "[a]ntitrust enforcement didn't hobble Microsoft; Microsoft got into antitrust trouble when it fell behind its rivals and tried to use its market power to exploit the characteristics of the industry to slow its rivals and buy time to catch up."[41]

17. It is in this context that we initially had the opportunity to get to know Professor First and his 21st-century practical antitrust approach. The detail, care, and accuracy with which the book recounted the details of the day-to-day litigation slog were impressive.

18. It was a privilege to be able to add in a small way to the book's carefully collected empirical data. Professor First was courteous as always, showing genuine interest in the details pertaining to clients who simply happened to be in the right place at the right time. From this opportunity, we developed an easy working relationship, as the book's approach was entirely consistent with the practical need to satisfy clients.

---

34   *Id.* at 327–30.

35   United States v. Google LLC, No. 1:20-cv-03010 (D.D.C. 2020).

36   FTC v. Amazon.com, Inc., No. 2:23-cv-0932 (W.D. Wash. 2023).

37   FTC v. Facebook, Inc., No. 1:20-cv-03590-JEB; Epic Games, Inc. v. Apple Inc., 559 F. Supp. 3d 898 (N.D. Cal. 2021).

38   *See, e.g.*, MICROSOFT BOOK at 323.

39   *Id.* at 322.

40   *Id.*, citing David A. Heiner, Microsoft: *A Remedial Success?*, 78 ANTITRUST L.J. 329 (2012).

41   *Id.* at 327.

IV. Post Microsoft Scholarship

19. Following the *Microsoft Book*, Professor First's scholarship continued to focus on empirical data that he interpreted in a practical, remedy-focused way. In April 2018, he published a short yet charming piece entitled "Woodstock Antitrust," which he dubbed a precursor to the much-maligned yet now in-vogue "Hipster Antitrust" of today. He noted that "both labels connect antitrust to a broader social movement, each of its time. . . . [B]oth labels are indicative of those unusual times when antitrust comes out of the legal and technical shadows to have broader political and social salience."[42] Professor First dated "Woodstock Antitrust" to the 1970s, arguing that it was set aside when Ronald Reagan was elected in 1980.[43]

20. Over 40 years later, the Biden administration's embrace of "Hipster Antitrust" has become a metaphor for jettisoning the old Chicago School "consumer welfare standard," which focuses on lowering consumer prices even at the potential expense of longer-term discouragement of competition and innovation, the two hallmarks of a healthy market. Supporters such as Professor First have worked to transform "Hipster Antitrust" from a pejorative term to a positive one, applauding its long-term rather than short-term economic vision. Focusing on remedies at the outset of any antitrust case, Professor First was a pioneer of ushering in a new practical approach that embraces the real world and the theoretical world at the same time.

21. In May 2023, Professor First authored "Antitrust Remedies and the Big Tech Platform Cases" (hereinafter "Big Tech Platforms").[44] It brought together many of the theories he had promoted during the course of his career. As he put in the paper's abstract,

> Remedies often get overlooked in discussions of antitrust litigation, treated almost as an afterthought. When remedies have been part of the antitrust debate the focus has often been on an after-the-fact assessment of their effectiveness, or on the general question whether there should be a preference for conduct or structural remedies, or sometimes on what remedies would be a good idea in a specific important case currently under litigation.[45]

22. Professor First's insights on the tendency to overlook remedies in the early stages of an antitrust case are apt. It is not surprising, he argues,

---

42 Harry First, *Woodstock Antitrust*, CPI ANTITRUST CHRON., Apr. 2018, at 2.

43 *Id.*

44 Harry First, *Antitrust Remedies and the Big Tech Platform Cases* (N.Y.U. Sch. of Law, Pub. L. & Legal Theory Rsch. Paper Series, Working Paper No. 23-33, 2024), https://ssrn.com/abstract=4324570 (hereinafter *Big Tech Platforms*).

45 *Id.*

because legal logic naturally backloads the remedies issue; one cannot "decide what remedies to impose before one knows whether they need to be imposed."[46] Liability thus "appropriately" tends to "take center stage. . . . But that shouldn't make the remedy discussion less critical."[47]

23. As is his fashion, Professor First began by explaining the theoretical underpinnings of the problem, starting with case law going back to the first half of the 20th century.[48] He analyzed the three policy goals traditionally at the core of remedies: deterrence, compensation, and remediation.[49] He then analyzes how these goals were considered by the D.C. Circuit in the *Microsoft*[50] litigation, which was all too familiar to him.

24. This discussion is where practical realism takes over. While the trial court agreed with the government's case fairly quickly and found that Microsoft violated section 1 and section 2 of the Sherman Act, the design of remedies ultimately slowed the proceedings down such that intervening events dramatically impacted the outcome. The many months that passed while a remedy was being hammered out by the parties, ultimately requiring discovery and a trial, meant that the presidential election of 2000 came and went. The case, originally brought by the Clinton Justice Department, ended up being completed by a much more defendant-friendly Bush administration. By the time the case was heard on appeal by the D.C. Circuit, more than six years had passed since Microsoft had engaged in its anticompetitive conduct. The D.C. Circuit "reflected" that its decision on a remedy was impacted by the "practical matter of... the temporal dimension of this case."[51] Noting that the six years that had passed were "a virtual eternity" in the fast-paced computer industry, the focus of any remedy would of necessity be on the deterrent objectives rather than the remedial aspects, because as a practical matter, the issue of restoring any lost competition had become moot.[52]

25. Thus, because of several inescapable realities, the *Microsoft* remedy ended up being behavioral rather than structural. First, the change in administration meant that the Justice Department no longer sought a structural remedy. This set up an unusual conflict between the Bush administration and several of the co-plaintiff states, which continued to seek a structural

---

46   *Id.* at 11.

47   *Id.*

48   *Id.* at 13–17.

49   *Id.*

50   United States v. Microsoft Corp., 147 F.3d 935 (D.C. Cir. 1998).

51   United States v. Microsoft Corp., 253 F.3d 34, 48–49 (D.C. Cir. 2001). *See* James Burling, Michelle D. Miller & John Christie, *The US Court of Appeals for the District of Columbia Circuit partially upholds a ruling that a Big Tech company abused its PC operating systems monopoly but reverses the District Court's breakup remedy (Microsoft)*, e-Competitions June 2001, art. no. 120159.

52   *Id.*

remedy. Ultimately, however, the futility of a structural remedy due to the passage of time prevailed.[53]

26. Professor First's article summarized several teachings of the *Microsoft* case, all of which influenced his analysis of how today's courts should handle challenges to Big Tech actions.[54] He noted that the liability trial record will largely set the stage for the remedy, and that the practical realities of the times will determine "what works."[55] Courts will focus on forward-looking remedies firmly anchored in the violations proven at trial, making it all the more important for remedies – and their possible implementation – to be considered at the beginning of a case. Plaintiffs, Professor First argued, should frame remedies in terms of goals and benchmarks rather than limit themselves to the usual directives of an injunction, where the defendant is told what not to do and sometimes what to do.[56]

27. Professor First then applied these lessons to the pending government cases against Google[57] and Facebook.[58] As of this writing, the court in the *Google* case has found that Google did, indeed, abuse its monopoly power,[59] and the remedy phase of the case is pending,[60], Discovery is still ongoing in the cases against Facebook[61] and Amazon.[62] Drawing from the experience in the *Microsoft* case, Professor First concluded that a more successful approach to designing a remedy in each case, assuming liability is found, would be to "frame the remedy in terms of the goals of the litigation and to provide benchmarks by which the defendant could show a court that it was achieving the goals. This approach would call on the government to think about what it wants to achieve in the litigation": "once the goal is articulated, it would be up to the defendant to figure out the best way to achieve it, a bottom-up approach."[63] Such an approach would be in lieu of a "top-down" approach, in which the government enforcer draws up "an injunction intended to stop" the particular offending practices.[64] While Professor First acknowledged that there are myriad practical impediments to implementing the "goals approach," its

---

53 *Big Tech Platforms* at 20–23.
54 *Id.* at 25.
55 *Id.*
56 *Id.* at 12, 25.
57 United States v. Google, LLC, No.1:20-cv-03010-APM (D.D.C. Jan. 15, 2021) (amended complaint).
58 FTC v. Facebook, Inc., No. 1:20-cv-03590-JEB (D.D.C. Sept. 9, 2020).
59 United States v. Google LLC, No. 1:20-cv-03010 (D.D.C. Aug. 5, 2024)
60 United States v. Google LLC, No. 1:20-cv-03010 (D.D.C. Dec. 20, 2024).
61 FTC v. Facebook, Inc., No. 1:20-cv-03590-JEB (D.D.C. Sept. 9, 2020).
62 FTC v. Amazon.com, Inc., No. 2:23-cv-0932 (W.D. Wash. 2023).
63 *Big Tech Platforms* at 31–32.
64 *Id.* at 31.

benefit would be that it would end "the dissonance between what the court orders and what is hoped to be gained from the antitrust litigation."[65]

28. The Big Tech cases, given the complexities of the conduct alleged and the difficulties inherent in remedying anticompetitive conduct in rapidly emerging markets, will test the ability of our antitrust laws to regulate industries that have seemingly limitless impact on commerce. As these cases move forward, we have a hunch that Professor First's practical scholarship will inform not only the courts' consideration of remedial measures in cases where liability is found, but also the strategies of some of the litigants. As they frame their liability cases, they could do worse than to heed the legacy for which Professor First is known: Remedies First.

---

65 *Id.* at 32.

Is Antitrust Law, Policy, or Politics?

SEAN P. SULLIVAN[*]
University of Iowa College of Law

Abstract

Thirty years ago, Harry First posed a simple but provocative question: Is antitrust law or is it policy? Today, I wish to revisit and expand upon that inquiry. Recent events have introduced a third dimension to consider: what if antitrust is politics? I position recent developments – like the resurgence of populist antitrust rhetoric, renewed political interest in antitrust enforcement, and sweeping changes in administrative practices – within antitrust's historic expression as a shifting combination of law, policy, and politics. From this vantage point, I argue that the recent movement toward political control is cause for concern.

---

[*] Professor of Law & Bauma Faculty Fellow in Law, University of Iowa College of Law.

I. Introduction

1. Thirty years ago, Harry First posed a simple but provocative question: Is antitrust *law* or is it *policy*?[1] The question was motivated by developments taking place in antitrust enforcement in the early 1990s. The agencies were making greater use of consent decrees and crafted remedies than ever before.[2] Broad, forward-looking guidance, particularly in the form of economic commentary, was seen to be crowding out the evolution of antitrust through judicial decisions of litigated cases.[3] Changes like these drove Harry to question what exactly antitrust was supposed to be. The depth of this question, and the non-obviousness of its answer, made the work an instant treasure.

2. Harry's argument embraced both positive and normative considerations. The positive considerations were conspicuous and empirical. The question – What *is* antitrust? – demanded a trip to the trenches. What were the agencies doing? How were disputes getting resolved? What was the published record of what was illegal and likely to be opposed? Normative considerations tiptoed more gently into the argument. Harry did not try to answer anything as broad as what antitrust optimally should be. Instead, he tackled a narrow and pragmatic question: Were changes in antitrust enforcement heading in a good direction?

3. In a brief but persuasive analysis, Harry concluded that antitrust was drifting toward regulatory policy.[4] He cautioned that this change was not costless. It traded concrete precedent and law for abstract expressions of transient policy positions. Harry predicted that the drift toward policy would eventually sap the strength of antitrust.[5] He recommended a reverse course in the direction of law and legalistic enforcement.[6]

4. Today, I want to revisit Harry's question. Excuses for returning to the subject can be found throughout the changes that have taken place in antitrust over the past decade. The reemergence of populist antitrust rhetoric,[7] the sudden spike in political attention to antitrust law,[8] and the sweeping changes that have taken place in administrative practices under the Biden administration[9] all invite a fresh look at the question: What exactly is antitrust supposed to be?

---

1 Harry First, *Is Antitrust "Law"?*, 10 ANTITRUST 9 (1995).

2 *See id.*

3 *See id.*; A. Douglas Melamed, *Antitrust: The New Regulation*, 10 ANTITRUST 13 (1995).

4 First, *supra* note 1, at 9; *see also* Melamed, *supra* note 1346 at 13.

5 First, *supra* note 1, at 11–12.

6 *Id.* at 12.

7 *See infra* notes 51–54 and accompanying text.

8 *See infra* notes 55–58 and accompanying text.

9 *See infra* notes 59–67 and accompanying text.

5. Returning to Harry's question also presents an opportunity to expand its scope. The law-policy continuum that Harry explored in 1995 is insufficient for mapping recent developments. Instead, I pose a generalization of Harry's question: Is antitrust *law*, is it *policy*, or is it *politics*?

II. Law, Policy, and Politics

6. Why does it matter if antitrust is law, policy, or politics? It matters because each of these categories represents a distinct approach to regulation. The categories overlap, to be sure, but they are not the same. They do not promise similar results. And movement from one category to another is not costless for enforcement outcomes.

1. Law and Legalistic Regulation

7. Harry identifies "legalistic regulatory culture" as focusing on the protection of individuals against harmful acts.[10] Law is "individual-case oriented" in this understanding, as well as "fact bound, and backward looking."[11] In a legalistic approach to regulatory enforcement, substantive law is developed and applied through the litigation of specific disputes, each in a unique factual context. Enforcement standards emerge from the iterative application of precedent to concrete facts, one case at a time.

8. One wrinkle in this definition of legalistic regulation is that it seems to focus on adjudication to the exclusion of legislation. Specific and detailed statutes are also a source of law and would rank as legalistic regulatory culture if they existed in antitrust. Harry's focus on adjudication reflects the obvious point that the brevity and vagueness of the antitrust statutes relegate the development of substantive enforcement standards to adjudication, not legislation.

9. But there are other wrinkles. Law in the common law tradition has never been exclusively about what happened in the past. As soon as precedential effect is given to judicial decisions, those decisions become as much about social policy, and the regulation of future behavior, as about responding to past acts.[12] So, even in a purely adjudicated context, the game is not exclusively about the identification and resolution of past injuries.[13]

---

10 First, *supra* note 1, at 9.

11 *Id.*

12 *See* Frederick Schauer, *Precedent*, 39 STAN. L. REV. 571, 572–75 (1987) (discussing the forward-looking effect and considerations in precedential decisions); *see also* Frederick Schauer, *Do Cases Make Bad Law?*, 73 U. CHI. L. REV. 883 (2006).

13 Remedies are forward-looking as well. The Holmesian view of legal remedies as nothing more than prices to be paid for engaging in certain acts finds intuitive application in antitrust's imposition of trebled damages as a way of disincentivizing anticompetitive price elevation. Oliver Wendell Holmes, *Path of the Law*, 10 HARV. L. REV. 457, 462 (1897) ("The duty to keep a contract at common law means a prediction that you must pay damages if you do not keep it – and nothing else.").

The backdrop of potential legislative override also muddies the distinction between adjudication and politics. The substance of legalistic regulation, as Harry identifies it, always exists at the pleasure and peril of legislative coalitions.

10. Still, these overlaps conceded, the functional implications of a legalistic approach to regulatory enforcement are distinct enough to justify focusing on law as one paradigmatic mode of regulation. Just as Harry's definition focuses on the resolution of individual disputes with private consequences, a legalistic regulatory culture directs attention to concrete questions like what the defendants have done in a particular case, rather than abstract matters like optimal behavior or status considerations like the social or political standing of the respective litigants.[14] Law grows haphazardly in this approach, but its growth is contained by the sober influences of concrete facts and the need to do justice between real people in real cases.

2. Policy and Bureaucratic Regulation

11. As a counterpoint to law, Harry identifies "bureaucratic regulatory culture" as focusing on broader policy questions like "how the economy should be structured and run."[15] This policy-based approach to regulation is "group oriented, theory based, and forward looking."[16] It is regulatory policy of a technocratic variety. One imagines expert agency staffers debating, promulgating, and enforcing rules and policies in a process of regular communication and cooperation with regulated populations.

12. This definition recalls the distinction between legislation and agency rulemaking.[17] Agencies empowered to develop rules and enforce laws – particularly under vague empowering statutes – inevitably exercise a great deal of regulatory discretion. The need for transparency in the exercise of that discretion motivates forward-looking announcements. Guidance documents, policy statements, and advisories are the bread and butter of bureaucratic regulation.

13. Here, again, we must not overstate the distinction. Bureaucratic regulatory authority arises from empowering legislation and is exercised against a backdrop of political oversight and punctuated judicial review.[18] Even expert and specialized agency staff are constrained to roam within a

---

14 Today, this narrowed focus is enforced by rules of evidence. *See, e.g.*, FED. R. EVID. 402 (requiring evidence to be legally relevant to be admissible); FED. R. EVID. 403 (providing for discretionary exclusion on the basis of unfair prejudice), FED. R. EVID. 404 (prohibiting character and propensity reasoning).

15 First, *supra* note 1, at 9.

16 *Id.*

17 *See, e.g.*, Gary Lawson, *Delegation and Original Meaning*, 88 VA. L. REV. 327, 335–53 (2002) (explaining this distinction in the context of the nondelegation doctrine).

18 *See* Sean P. Sullivan, *Powers, But How Much Power? Game Theory and the Nondelegation Principle*, 104 VA. L. REV. 1229 (2018).

field bounded by statutes and ultra vires review.[19] On the political side, opportunities for manipulation and intrusion into agency policymaking abound.[20]

14. But, despite these caveats, the identification of bureaucratic policymaking as a distinct mode of regulation is again helpful in thinking about enforcement consequences. Bureaucratic regulatory enforcement is likely to be both broader and narrower than legalistic enforcement. At the broad end, substantive rules and policies are often abstract and forward-looking – think guidance documents and policy statements, for example. At the narrow end, close communication between regulators and regulated parties invites out-of-court resolutions of disputes. Negotiated remedies and consent decrees can be tailored so tightly to individual facts that they leave no generalizable principles behind.[21]

15. Policy-based regulation is also more flexible than law. Opportunities for changing substantive rules and enforcement approaches are more frequent and less constrained than they would be in a legalistic context.[22]

3. Politics and Populist Regulation

16. Unexplored in Harry's formulation – but important for considering current events – is what we might call "political regulatory culture." Here, substantive laws and enforcement norms arise from political influences, like changing presidential administrations. Regulations reflect the influence of political coalitions and voter interests, not judicial interpretations or technocratic expertise. This description of political regulation overlaps with some articulations of populism.[23] It contemplates the vesting of enforcement authority in non-experts, unconstrained by the moderating influences of precedent or technical rigor, and beholden only to transient coalitions in a democratic context.

17. This definition of political regulation borrows from several literatures. The discontinuous translation of voter preferences into political outcomes is well studied in research on voting and majority rules.[24] Studies of populism and movement politics also contribute to understanding political regulation.[25]

---

19   *Cf.* Loper Bright Enterprises v. Raimondo, 144 S. Ct. 2244 (2024); W. Virginia v. Env't Prot. Agency, 597 U.S. 697 (2022).

20   *Cf.* R. Douglas Arnold, *Political Control of Administrative Officials*, 3 J.L. Econ. & Org. 279, 280–81 (1987) (listing many ways that Congress may react to agency exercises of discretion).

21   *See* First, *supra* note 1, at 11.

22   *Cf.* Frederick Schauer, *Why Precedent in Law (And Elsewhere) Is Not Totally (Or Even Substantially) about Analogy*, 3 Persp. Psych. Sci. 454 (2008) (noting that decision-making under the constraint of binding precedent is distinct even from reasoning by analogy outside the common law decision space).

23   *See, e.g.*, Sheri Berman, *The Causes of Populism in the West*, 24 Ann. Rev. of Pol. Sci. 71 (2021).

24   *See generally* W. D. Wallis, The Mathematics of Elections and Voting (2014).

25   *See, e.g.*, Nicola Lacey, *Populism and the Rule of Law*, 15 Ann. Rev. of L. & Soc. Sci. 79, 80-81 (2019) (collecting works that study the recent emergence of populist movements in Europe and North America).

18. Political actors are, of course, responsible for both creating and executing laws in the U.S. constitutional framework, and so it is little wonder that political regulation overlaps both legal and bureaucratic regulation. Bureaucratic agencies are funded, monitored, and often run by politicians and political appointees.[26] Judges, too, are appointed and funded through the political process.[27] At a philosophical level, all force of law ultimately derives from some degree of public support for legally imposed duties and prohibitions.[28]

19. But distinguishing political regulation from law and policy is still helpful. The distinction drawn here underlies constitutional separation of powers principles,[29] a common justification for which is the need to moderate the changes in law that would result from unconstrained political passions.[30] We are also focused on a specific subset of political regulation. Nothing prevents a political body from delegating authority and then stepping back to allow expert agency staff to decide how to exercise that authority – what we would call bureaucratic regulatory culture.[31] Our concern, here, is the direct assumption of control over enforcement by inexpert politicians and their immediate appointees.[32]

20. If policy is more flexible than law, then politics is more flexible than policy. Apart from constitutional protections and the need to answer to voting bases, political coalitions face the least constraints of all on how they may change rules and redirect enforcement priorities.

---

26 *See supra* note 20 and accompanying text.

27 *See generally* Michael D. Gilbert, *Judicial Independence and Social Welfare*, 112 MICH. L. REV. 575 (2014) (discussing sources of judicial dependence on politics).

28 *Cf.* KEN BINMORE, NATURAL JUSTICE (2011).

29 *See, e.g.*, Mistretta v. United States, 488 U.S. 361, 371–72 (1989) (asserting that the nondelegation principle – which separates valid delegations of lawmaking authority from invalid delegations of legislative power – is "rooted in the principle of separation of powers that underlies our tripartite system of Government").

30 *Cf.* Rice v. Foster, 4 Del. 479, 486 (1847) ("In every government founded on popular will, the people, although intending to do right, are the subject of impulse and passion; and have been betrayed into acts of folly, rashness and enormity, by the flattery, deception, and influence of demagogues. A triumphant majority oppresses the minority; each contending faction, when it obtains the supremacy, tramples on the rights of the weaker: the great aim and objects of civil government are prostrated amidst tumult, violence and anarchy; and those pretended patriots, abounding in all ages, who commence their political career as the disinterested friends of the people, terminate it by becoming their tyrants and oppressors.").

31 In theory, the constitutional nondelegation doctrine limits what authority Congress can delegate to administrative agencies. *See* Sullivan, *supra* note 18. Many of the principles underlying this doctrine appear equally offended by delegations of lawmaking authority to the judiciary, however. Margaret H. Lemos, *The Other Delegate: Judicially Administered Statutes and the Nondelegation Doctrine*, 81 S. CAL. L. REV. 405 (2008). And having rarely doubted their own power to interpret the antitrust statutes, it would be at best awkward for courts to apply this doctrine strictly against the federal antitrust agencies.

32 *Cf.* Barak Orbach, *Antitrust Populism*, 14 N.Y.U. J. L. & BUS. 1, 8 (2017) (describing populist anti-intellectualism as "the willingness of populists to seek endorsement of low-information audiences, rejection of facts and criticism, common use of conspiracy theories, and targeting of intellectuals as 'corrupt elites'").

III. The Law-Policy-Politics Triangle

21. The regulatory parameter space that is coming into focus is not a collection of discrete categories or even a continuum between poles; it is the surface of a triangle with law, policy, and politics at its points. Substantive law and enforcement norms can share features of all three approaches simultaneously. Indeed, antitrust and its ancestral expressions have long done exactly this, albeit with different loadings of law, policy, and politics over time.

1. Antitrust as Law

22. We need not devote much effort to defending the idea that antitrust is law. Every indication is that it has been seen this way for a very long time. Blackstone's Commentaries, for example, indicate prohibitions on combinations in restraint of trade and monopoly long before the 1800s.[33] The common law antecedents of U.S. antitrust law include decisions like *Mitchel v. Reynolds*,[34] decided in 1711, and *Darcy v. Allen*,[35] decided in 1602 – though misreadings of the latter seem to have been more influential than the decision itself.[36] The eventual codification of antitrust law in the Sherman Act, Clayton Act, and Federal Trade Commission Act cinches the matter.

23. But while antitrust has never lacked the trappings of law, neither has it ever managed to work itself clean of policy tensions or political influence. From the start, it has always been *law and* these other things.

2. Antitrust as Policy

24. Blackstone's recitation of prohibitions on restraints of trade and monopolies places these offenses alongside similarly severe offenses such as "regrating" (which seems to have involved what we now call "retailing"),[37] "engrossing" (which similarly seems to have involved bulk purchasing with intent to resell),[38] and "forestalling" (which seems to have involved out-of-market purchasing, perhaps with intent to evade price controls).[39]

---

[33] WILLIAM BLACKSTONE, 4 COMMENTARIES ON THE LAWS OF ENGLAND: IN FOUR BOOKS ch.12, at 158–59 (15th ed., A. Strahan, 1809).

[34] 24 Eng. Rep. 347 (K.B. 1711).

[35] 77 Eng. Rep. 1260 (K.B. 1602).

[36] *See* Harold Evans, *The Supreme Court and the Sherman Anti-Trust Act*, 59 U. PA. L. REV. 61, 62–63 (1910); William F. Dana, *"Monopoly" under the National Anti-Trust Act*, 7 HARV. L. REV. 338 (1894).

[37] BLACKSTONE, *supra* note 33, at 158.

[38] *Id.*

[39] *Id.*; *see also* William L. Letwin, *The English Common Law Concerning Monopolies*, 21 U. CHI. L. REV. 355, 369 (1954) ("[T]he offense was generally understood quite literally as buying commodities before they had been carried into the actual market place or before the market had officially opened."). *But see* R. H. Britnell, *Forstall,* Forestalling and the Statute of Forestallers, 102 ENG. HIST. REV. 89 (1987) (interpreting forestalling as something closer to reselling at a markup).

The latter prohibitions sound strange to modern ears, but reflect the depth to which competition policy was once regulated by powerful guilds and local governments. William Letwin summarizes the situation succinctly:

> [T]he common law did not always defend freedom of trade and abhor monopoly. For a long time it did quite the opposite: it supported an economic order in which the individual's getting and spending were closely controlled by kings, parliaments, and mayors, statutes and customs, and his opportunities limited by the exclusive powers of guilds, chartered companies, and patentees.[40]

25. Between long apprenticeship requirements, limits on what trades could be practiced where, and prohibitions on buying and selling outside of regulated marketplaces,[41] the early competitive landscape was severely regulated. Entrusting the oversight of these matters to interested parties may not have been the wisest competition policy of all time, but it was competition policy nonetheless, and the laws that empowered these policymakers placed antitrust's ancestral footing deep into the policy point of the triangle.

26. It has rarely ventured far from that start. In the United States, the Sherman Act had only begun to be enforced in major cases when dissatisfaction with its operation agitated lawmakers into action.[42] Congress could have responded with specific legislation to correct perceived inadequacies in judicial application of the Sherman Act. It did so to some extent with the passage of the Clayton Act, though creative license is needed to call the provisions of that act "specific legislation." More tellingly, Congress opted to create the Federal Trade Commission (FTC) as an agency empowered to develop and use its expertise to regulate competition in the detail that statutory provisions lacked.[43] Subsequent decades saw the growth of expertise and policy-oriented regulatory structures within both the FTC and the Antitrust Division of the Department of Justice (DOJ).

27. A distinguishing feature of policy-oriented antitrust is its adaptability to advances in economic reasoning. Judges, too, can incorporate new thinking into their decisions.[44] But not at the speed or scope with which policy can be revised and rewritten in a bureaucratic context. This is not always a good thing. The episodic emergence of protectionist agendas

---

40   Letwin, *supra* note 39, at 355.

41   *See id.* at 364–66.

42   *See, e.g.*, Standard Oil Co. of New Jersey v. United States, 221 U.S. 1 (1911).

43   *See* GERARD C. HENDERSON, THE FEDERAL TRADE COMMISSION: A STUDY IN ADMINISTRATIVE LAW AND PROCEDURE, 16–27, 33–36 (1924) (describing the origins of the FTC).

44   *See* Kimble v. Marvel Entm't, 576 U.S. 446, 461–62 (2015) (reasoning that in antitrust cases "the Court's rulings necessarily turn[] on its understanding of economics" and thus that "to overturn [earlier] decisions in light of sounder economic reasoning [is] to take them on [their] own terms" (internal quotation marks removed)). *See also* Jean-Christophe Roda, *USA: The U.S. Supreme Court refuses to apply the rule of reason, inspired by antitrust law, to patent law in a case related to the payment of post-expiration royalties (Kimble/Marvel Entertainment)*, CONCURRENCES no. 3-2015, art. no. 75265.

in U.S. competition policy aptly illustrates the downside risk of policy-oriented regulation.[45] But often the flexibility of the policy approach is a clear advantage – as when the efficacy of enforcement is increased by the rapid integration of new economic techniques and modes of thinking.

3. Antitrust as Politics

28. Politics has also been a part of antitrust from the start. The early history of prohibitions on monopolization was not about high prices or economic waste; it was about ensuring that only selected political bodies enjoyed the right to grant monopoly protections. Edward Adler puts it like this:

> The statute of 21 James I, which is often erroneously assumed to have prohibited monopolies was of a political nature and was aimed at abuses of the royal prerogative. The Act itself expressly provides that it shall not be prejudicial to any grant of privilege, power or authority whatsoever theretofore made or confirmed by an act of Parliament, nor was it to be prejudicial to the grants, charters or customs of the City of London or any town. . . .[46]

29. Letwin similarly describes early oscillations in the strength of prohibitions on combinations in restraint of trade as mainly explained by shifting political sympathies toward the opposing interests of laborers and employers.[47]

30. In the United States, the influence of politics on antitrust is even clearer. Each of the major antitrust statutes emerged during a period of intense political focus on business practices and the state of competition. Public interest in antitrust enforcement fueled these legislative exercises, and populist rhetoric plasters the legislative record of the antitrust statutes. The vagueness of the statutory prohibitions is perhaps explained by the characteristically inconsistent and superficial rhetoric of populist antitrust movements.[48]

31. More than law and policy, however, the influence of politics in antitrust has changed over the decades. Reasonable people can debate whether antitrust's political salience began to fade in the 1920s, 1960s, or 1980s. Regardless, the distance between antitrust enforcement and politics expanded over the

---

[45] Ugly examples include the facilitation of collusion and promulgation of rules designed to dampen competition. *See, e.g.*, Margaret C. Levenstein and Valerie Y. Suslow, *Cartel Bargaining and Monitoring: The Role of Information Sharing, in* THE PROS AND CONS OF INFORMATION SHARING 43, 62 (Mats Bergman ed., Stockholm: Konkurrensverket 2006) ("During the 1920s the Federal Trade Commission helped many industry associations to form with the express intention of stemming 'cutthroat competition.'").

[46] *See* Edward A. Adler, *Monopolizing at Common Law and under Section Two of the Sherman Act*, 31 HARV. L. REV. 246, 258 (1917).

[47] Letwin, *supra* note 39, at 379–81.

[48] *See* Herbert Hovenkamp, *Whatever Did Happen to the Antitrust Movement?*, 94 NOTRE DAME L. REV. 583, 585–89 (2018) (discussing the conceptual deficiencies that are typical of movement antitrust rhetoric).

twentieth century. Writing in 2008, Daniel Crane described political interest in antitrust as all but evaporated:

> Since the Chicago School revolution in the 1970s, federal antitrust enforcement has become considerably less democratic and more technocratic. It has become increasingly separated from popular politics, insulated from direct democratic pressures, delegated to industrial-policy specialists, and compartmentalized as a regulatory discipline. Presidents no longer pay it attention, the major political parties' platforms no longer mention it, and the public does not follow it.[49]

32. But, as Barak Orbach muses, "the populist style has always been common and is here to stay."[50] The recent reemergence of populist antitrust attitudes in politics illustrates this point precisely.

IV. Antitrust Today: A Positive Appraisal

33. In 1995, Harry argued that antitrust was drifting toward the policy point of the law-policy-politics triangle. Today, I argue that it is careening toward the political point. I do not suppose that this is a highly controversial claim, but evidence of the hard turn toward politics is readily available at any rate.

34. One place to see this change is in the recent spike in populist antitrust rhetoric and the concomitant jump in public attention to antitrust. Concerns about economic bigness have swept back into the conversation.[51] Magazine articles celebrate the efforts of "anti-monopoly" crusaders and lament each setback in their struggle to control tech giants, self-evidently bad.[52] Commentators bewail lax merger enforcement, which they say has emboldened "unprecedented concentrations of economic and political power."[53] The telling point in these claims is not that they appear to be empirically unsupported;[54] it is that empirical support seems not to have been considered important in the first place.

---

49 Daniel A. Crane, *Technocracy and Antitrust*, 86 TEX. L. REV. 1159, 1160 (2008).

50 Orbach, *supra* note 32, at 8.

51 *See, e.g.*, TIM WU, THE CURSE OF BIGNESS: ANTITRUST IN THE NEW GILDED AGE (2018); AMY KLOBUCHAR, ANTITRUST: TAKING ON MONOPOLY POWER FROM THE GILDED AGE TO THE DIGITAL AGE (2021); ZEPHYR TEACHOUT, BREAK 'EM UP: RECOVERING OUR FREEDOM FROM BIG AG, BIG TECH, AND BIG MONEY (2020).

52 *E.g.*, Eric Cortellessa, *The White House Is Pushing Congress to Rein in Big Tech Before the GOP Takes Over the House*, TIME (Nov. 18, 2022), https://time.com/6235180/tech-antitrust-bills-white-house-congress.

53 Open Markets Institute, Comment Letter on Request for Information on Merger Enforcement 3 (Apr. 21, 2022), https://www.regulations.gov/comment/FTC-2022-0003-1123.

54 *See, e.g.*, D. Daniel Sokol & Sean P. Sullivan, *Coordinated Effects and the Half-Truth of the Lax Enforcement Narrative*, CPI ANTITRUST CHRON., July 2023 (critiquing the empirical foundation for lax enforcement claims); Nolan McCarty & Sepehr Shahshahani, *Testing Political Antitrust*, 98 N.Y.U. L. REV. 1169 (2023) (testing and failing to find support for claims of a relationship between economic concentration and lobbying power).

35. Another way to track movement toward political regulation is in the intensity of political focus on antitrust issues. Antitrust enforcement polls well[55] and is thus a popular talking point for politicians. Are new merger guidelines a credible strategy for combating inflation?[56] No. But that does not stop the message from resonating with voters. The flurry of recent bills seeking to revamp antitrust law is a more serious example of political interest in taking control of antitrust. Bills like the American Innovation and Choice Online Act[57] and the Open App Markets Act[58] propose to change antitrust enforcement in fundamental ways – and have, at times, seemed close to becoming law.

36. Finally, increased political influence over antitrust is easy to spot in executive statements and the actions of agency leaders. Little needs to be said about the political content of presidential remarks instructing the antitrust agencies to abandon the failed experiment of prior decades of enforcement norms.[59] The FTC's subsequent withdrawal of support for the 2020 Vertical Merger Guidelines – barely a year after their publication – is also difficult to read as anything other than political influence. The explanation that withdrawal was needed to address "flawed provisions" in the document is otherwise puzzling on its face, since little but the composition of the administration had changed in the intervening months.

37. Replacement of the 2010 Horizontal Merger Guidelines is a closer call. At more than a decade since publication, the 2010 guidelines had reached an age where they would have been due for revision or replacement even during prior decades of political detachment.[60] But the substance of the 2023 revision, which includes things like a sudden deemphasis of economic theory,[61] rejection of decades of stability in market definition,[62] and substitution of dated judicial rhetoric for empirically grounded predictions

---

55 *See* Taylor Orth, *Most Americans oppose monopolies and support antitrust laws*, YouGov (Nov. 6, 2023), https://today.yougov.com/economy/articles/47798-most-americans-oppose-monopolies-and-support-antitrust-laws.

56 Tobias Burns, *White House says new antitrust rules will help fight inflation*, THE HILL (Dec. 18, 2023), https://thehill.com/business/4366250-white-house-new-antitrust-rules-inflation.

57 S. 2992 (as reported by S. Comm. on the Judiciary, Mar. 2, 2022).

58 S. 2710 (as reported by S. Comm. on the Judiciary, Feb. 17, 2022).

59 Press Release, White House, Remarks by President Biden at Signing of an Executive Order Promoting Competition in the American Economy (July 9, 2021), https://www.whitehouse.gov/briefing-room/speeches-remarks/2021/07/09/remarksby-president-biden-at-signing-of-an-executive-order-promoting-competition-in-theamerican-economy.

60 *See, e.g.*, U.S. DEP'T OF JUST. & FED. TRADE COMM'N, HORIZONTAL MERGER GUIDELINES (Apr. 2, 1992); U.S. DEP'T OF JUST. & FED. TRADE COMM'N, HORIZONTAL MERGER GUIDELINES (Apr. 8, 1997); U.S. DEP'T OF JUST. & FED. TRADE COMM'N, HORIZONTAL MERGER GUIDELINES (Aug. 19, 2010).

61 *See* Eleanor M. Fox, *Awakening Merger Control: The New U.S. Merger Guidelines*, in THE 2023 U.S. MERGER GUIDELINES: A REVIEW 85 (Sean P. Sullivan, ed., 2024).

62 *See* Gregory J. Werden, *Market Delineation under the New Merger Guidelines: Gerrymandering Redux*, in THE 2023 U.S. MERGER GUIDELINES: A REVIEW 171 (Sean P. Sullivan, ed., 2024).

about competitive effects,⁶³ is hard to reconcile with the general stability of law and economic reasoning since 2010. These changes are, of course, easily explained by the enforcement interests of the Biden administration and its appointed agency leaders.

38. Similar shifts can be seen in other aspects of enforcement. Rejection of the consumer welfare standard is not explained by any intervening change in law or economic theory – but is a touchstone of the current populist movement in antitrust.⁶⁴ A moratorium on public speaking by FTC staff is very nearly the opposite of technocratic policymaking and transparent communication with the public.⁶⁵ Withdrawal of policy statements and exercises in novel substantive rulemaking are acts that could be explained as policy-oriented antitrust enforcement, but that take on political tones when implemented in adversarial and procedurally objectionable ways.⁶⁶ The same goes for monopolization suits brought against major tech companies. Even if these challenges are fully grounded in law and economics, their consistency with the political messaging of the Biden administration⁶⁷ raises questions about political motivation that simply would not arise in a less politicized antitrust regime.

V. Antitrust Today: A Normative Critique

39. Writing 30 years ago, Harry concluded his inquiry into the state of antitrust with a warning about the direction things were headed. He cautioned that the drift toward regulatory policy was not costless, and he recommended a return to more legalistic enforcement norms.⁶⁸ Today, I would like to conclude with a similar warning. The turn toward political control of antitrust harbors more risks than might be apparent. I believe antitrust should turn back from its rapid course toward politics, while it still can.

---

63   See Sean P. Sullivan, *The Evolution (and Devolution) of Market Structure Reasoning*, in THE 2023 U.S. MERGER GUIDELINES: A REVIEW 147, 167–69 (Sean P. Sullivan, ed., 2024).

64   See Jonathan Kanter, Antitrust Enforcement: The Road to Recovery, Remarks as Prepared for Delivery at the University of Chicago Stigler Center (Apr. 21, 2022), https://www.justice.gov/opa/speech/assistant-attorney-general-jonathan-kanter-delivers-keynote-university-chicago-stigler.

65   Leah Nylen & Betsy Woodruff Swan, *FTC staffers told to back out of public appearances*, POLITICO (July 6, 2021), https://www.politico.com/news/2021/07/06/ftc-staffers-public-appearances-498316.

66   *See, e.g.,* Dissenting Statement of Commissioners Noah Joshua Phillips and Christine S. Wilson Regarding the Commission's Rescission of the 2020 FTC/DOJ Vertical Merger Guidelines and the Commentary on Vertical Merger Enforcement (Sept. 15, 2021), https://www.ftc.gov/system/files/documents/public_statements/1596388/final_vmgs_phillips_wilson_dissenting_statement_for_posting.pdf (objecting to the process by which the Commission withdrew support for the 2020 Vertical Merger Guidelines); Dissenting Statement of Commissioner Melissa Holyoak, Joined by Commissioner Andrew N. Ferguson, In the Matter of the Non-Compete Clause Rule (June 28, 2024), https://www.ftc.gov/system/files/ftc_gov/pdf/2024-6-28-commissioner-holyoak-nc.pdf (objecting to the process by which the Commission promulgated a blanket rule prohibiting non-compete clauses).

67   See Eric Cortellessa, *Biden Calls for Antitrust Laws to Rein in Big Tech After Schumer Blocked Last Effort*, TIME (Feb. 7, 2023), https://time.com/6253755/biden-big-tech-state-of-the-union-2023.

68   First, *supra* note 1, at 11–12.

40. I do not mean this warning to sound hyperbolic. Politics has been a part of antitrust from the earliest days of its English law heritage. Populist sentiments are baked into the legislative history of all the major antitrust statutes. And while the recent spike in political intervention strikes a sharp contrast to antitrust enforcement under, say, the Obama administration, that may be because political attention to antitrust was abnormally low in recent decades. In short, my point is not that political control of antitrust is abnormal or even that it is necessarily undesirable.

41. My point is that movement in the political direction is not costless – and that the costs of recent escalations in political control may be greater than many realize. A few examples will help to illustrate the dangers we are courting.

42. First, we run the risk of dissipating accumulated trust and confidence in the policy positions of the federal antitrust agencies. This is because the effectiveness of any rule, law, or policy declines when it lacks stable and predictable expression. Policy statements have weight proportionate to their durability. Guidelines command respect and reliance when they describe stable and predictable principles and practices. Anything that casts doubt upon the durability and reliability of agency communications diminishes the value of those communications – in a way that may take decades to reverse.

43. This light casts shadows when trained upon things like the FTC's rushed withdrawal of support for the 2020 Vertical Merger Guidelines. Like all guidelines, the 2020 guidelines had flaws and areas in need of improvement. But while unceremonious withdrawal may have achieved the short-run goals of agency leaders – eliminating language that failed to align with their ideology and enforcement expectations – the long-run costs of this retraction may be felt for years to come. Confidence in the merger guidelines declines – and *should* decline – when those guidelines are treated as disposable at will.

44. Second, we run the parallel risks of increasing substantive uncertainty, vesting too much discretion in short-term political appointees, and decreasing the protective influence of the rule of law in antitrust. A predictable response would say that antitrust is so famously flexible and uncertain that these concerns have little significance in this field. But that gets things precisely backward. The flexibility and vagueness of antitrust law make substantive stability and predictability more important here than elsewhere. Without strong tethers, discretion over antitrust enforcement becomes tantamount to royal prerogative.

45. To be blunt, while I suspect that supporters of the Biden administration's antitrust program have felt quite comfortable entrusting the Biden administration's agency leaders with discretion to rewrite antitrust rules and enforcement norms, I am less sure that they would like to see this

same degree of substantive discretion exercised by future administrations of different political persuasion. But seeds that are planted today will grow tomorrow. And if today's agency leaders are free to cast aside past policy statements, guidance documents, and enforcement procedures, then what chance do their own contributions stand of lasting through future administrations? If current enforcement decisions bear even the slightest appearance of being motivated by prior prejudice or political considerations, then what politically motivated targeting by future presidential administrations might this precedent one day come to support?

46. Finally, increased politicization of antitrust risks decreasing the long-term efficacy of antitrust enforcement. Movements fade; politicians live one election at a time. In past decades, antitrust has been steered against a distant horizon by career staffers with the experience needed to see far into the future. But in a time of intense political control, the relevant time horizon is short, the measure of success is immediate, and the future consequences of exciting strategies are considered a matter of secondary importance, if they are considered at all.

47. None of this should be taken as a denial that there are good things about the recent political disruption. Nobody could seriously claim that antitrust had ascended to a state of perfection before the recent turmoil. And few would deny that the Biden administration has identified real problems with enforcement or that it has improved antitrust thinking in important ways. But disruption is best embraced in sprints, and the long-run integration of new approaches and ideas is a task better suited to policy-oriented bureaucratic regulation than it is to either law or political control. It is, in my view, time for quiet confidence and depth to return to antitrust enforcement. The pomp and flash and headlines have done all that they can usefully do.

National Competition Policy and the Election of 2024

ALBERT A. FOER[*]
American Antitrust Institute

Abstract

Written during the late stages of the presidential campaign between Harris/Walz and Trump/Vance in August, 2024, this chapter depicts three models for managing broadly-defined national competition policy: (1) the New Deal model of relatively random and minimal interventions by the White House in the competition-related policies of government agencies; (2) the innovative whole-of-government approach applied via an executive order of President Joe Biden, which deeply, systematically, and transparently engaged the White House in coordination and guidance of both executive branch and independent federal regulatory agencies; and (3) an authoritarian populist model based on pre-election statements of Donald Trump and his supporters. By the time of publication, the reader will both know that Donald Trump was elected to his second term as president and should be able to evaluate the extent to which his management of competition policy appears to be consistent with the projected authoritarian populist model.

> Intellectual property law is out of control.... I propose... an aphorism: "It is innovation, not innovators, which the [intellectual property] Acts protect."
>
> Harry First[1]

---

[*] Founder, former president, and senior fellow, American Antitrust Institute (AAI). The author thanks the following for their comments on a draft: Eleanor Fox, Robert Lande, David Lawsky, Donald Resnikoff, Randy Stutz, Jeffrey Weinberg, and Arthur Wilmarth. The article is not intended to represent the views of AAI or of the above readers.

[1] The first footnote of course belongs to Harry First, *Controlling the Intellectual Property Grab: Protect Innovation, Not Innovators*, 38 RUTGERS L.J. 365 (2007). This was an AAI symposium on the boundaries between antitrust and trade regulation. Harry was a key advisor to the American Antitrust Institute for all the years in which I was its president. He and his colleague at NYU and the AAI, Eleanor Fox, another recipient of a Concurrences *Festschrift*, contributed a jovial imaginary interview with me about the AAI in 60 ANTITRUST BULL. 79 (2015).

I. The Nature of a National Competition Policy

1. This article raises the implications of the Biden administration's whole-of-government strategy for systematizing the manifold ways the national government regulates competition in comparison to the unsystematic authoritarian populist strategy that appears to be planned by Donald Trump as he campaigns for re-election in the November 2024 presidential election.

2. For a long time, before the rest of the world caught up with us, there was only antitrust. Today, one sees both "antitrust" and "competition policy" in the domestic and foreign literature. In Europe, the reach of competition policy includes mergers and state aids that distort competition, while "antitrust" covers cartels, collaborations, and dominance. In the U.S., under the Biden innovative administration, we have for the first time an executive order on national competition policy, which established a Council on Competition Policy and designated positions within the National Economic Council (NEC) to oversee the work between presidentially led twice-a-year Competition Council meetings.[2]

3. In my expansive usage, "competition policy" involves any decision by the government or its various agencies and agents that affects how the concept of competition (whatever that may mean with particularity) is or is not applied to rivalrous relations within civil society. Antitrust (essentially limited to the antitrust and fair competition statutes enforced by the Department of Justice (DOJ) – an executive department – and the Federal Trade Commission (FTC) – an independent regulatory agency) is today but a subset of competition policy.

4. Let me be clear: *competition itself comes in many degrees, depending, for example, on the extent to which efficiency is emphasized vis-à-vis other values such as safety, reliability, redundancy, privacy, universal service, liberty, equality, fairness, and justice.* Often, the situation-appropriate balance of values is stated in legislation, such as the Sherman Act or a sectoral regulatory statute that requires "the public interest" or even "competition" to be taken into account. These statutory instructions often tend to be vague, leaving it up to administrators and courts to interpret through regulations, guidelines, and judicial opinions. There is no single conception of competition that can be derived from the various interpretations that have been and will likely remain in play not only around the world, but even within the U.S., which sees itself as the traditional homeland of antitrust.

5. The public may not comprehend the importance of competition policy as a factor in everyday life or the functioning of government. To set

---

2   Exec. Order No.14,036, 86 Fed. Reg. 36989 (July 9, 2021).

the scene, here are some examples of when competition policy is being applied:

- Tax law or regulation promotes or restrains merger decisions or provides a comparative advantage or disadvantage to certain industries.
- Labor law affects how private companies compete with one another in the compensation of employees or other costs of doing business.
- Communications law affects competition between television content providers or between TV and other means of communication.
- Transportation law affects intra-modal or intermodal competition.
- Intellectual property law affects standard setting in high-tech industries.
- Civil procedure rules affect private class actions, altering the incentives for competitors' treatment of consumers and of one another.
- Intellectual property law provides an inventor with an exclusive right, not subject to direct competition.
- Trade law imposes a tariff or quota that creates a competitive disadvantage on imported or exported products.
- An agency subsidizes a particular industrial policy, class of businesses or category of people.

6. In short: a huge proportion of the actions that governments take (or determine not to take) affect how companies, industries, and even non-profit organizations compete.

7. The diversity of arenas for competition policy to be established in the U.S. itself is exacerbated by the existence of separate competition laws in each state, as well as a fragmented central government that contains an executive branch (including departments and agencies), a legislative branch, and a judicial branch. All of these play a role in establishing the circumstances under which competition takes place. These mundane observations lead one to understand that *there is no single "competition policy" universally applicable, but only a multitude of possibilities for which appropriate balances must be reached in particularistic contexts* that are themselves subject to change over time not only due to political elections, but also to ideological movements, cultural and technological change, and our knowledge of economics and social sciences. Competition policy is the quintessential regulatory moving target.

8. Diversity is furthered by the role of international trade. There has never been a central authority for resolution of differences that may occur as varying national competition policies may lead to conflicting consequences.

9. The question I intend to focus on in this paper is how the U.S. government can best bring transparency, intentionality, and coherence to the task of reconciling diverse views of the various governmental players

toward competition and regulation.³ The immediate context for this discussion is the U.S. presidential election of 2024. The following sections will develop three different models, two of which, New Deal antitrust and President Biden's whole-of-government strategy, can be summarized based on experience. The third, authoritarian populism, is admittedly hypothetical, being based on public documents and statements presented during Donald J. Trump's 2024 campaign to regain the presidency from the Democrats.⁴

II. The New Deal Era of Decentralized Competition Policy, Silos with Random and Ad Hoc Interventions

10. The Sherman Act had become the primary competition law before the twentieth century, but the overall role of federal regulation was itself relatively minor until after World War II. During World War I, the Great Depression, and World War II, various national strategies were enforced to greatly reduce the role of antitrust-regulated competition within the economy, either by making the entire economy secondary to national security or by the creation of an "associational" regime in which big business, organized labor, and government collaborated closely to try to escape the Great Depression, effectively generating cartels rather than effective market competition.⁵ When these deviations from competitive capitalism failed to fill the perceived need, the resilience of antitrust reasserted itself during the so-called Second New Deal.⁶

---

3   One might ask, why do we want coherence? Partly because it is better than incoherence, which is to say, chaos. Coherence implies thoughtfulness rather than randomness. But how much weight we should give to coherence is a question I won't resolve other than to suggest that consistency is not essential to coherence. Too much coherence in itself may be inconsistent with the various advantages of competition. *See* ROBERT SOUTHEY, GOLDILOCKS AND THE THREE BEARS (1837).

4   Information on which this paper is based was gathered until September 1, 2024, after the Republican Platform, the Republican National Convention, and the issuance of the Heritage Foundation's Project 2025 (MANDATE FOR LEADERSHIP: THE CONSERVATIVE PROMISE (2023)). What is "populism"? It is a political strategy that is critical of elites, a form of identity politics, and antipluralist. According to Jan-Werner Müller, "[p]opulist governance exhibits three features: attempts to hijack the state apparatus, corruption and 'mass clientelism' (trading material benefits or bureaucratic favors for political support to citizens who become the populists' 'clients'), and efforts systematically to suppress civil society. Of course, many authoritarians will do similar things. The difference is that populists justify their conduct by claiming that they alone represent the people: this allows populists to avow their practices quite openly." JAN-WERNER MÜLLER, WHAT IS POPULISM? 2-4 (2016). *Also see* JOHN B. JUDIS, THE POPULIST EXPLOSION: HOW THE GREAT RECESSION TRANSFORMED AMERICAN AND EUROPEAN POLITICS (2016). The Trump/Vance team declares itself populist.

5   *See* ALAN BRINKLEY, THE END OF REFORM: NEW DEAL LIBERALISM IN RECESSION AND WAR 5 (1995) (associationalism was advocated since World War I by those who advocated cartelistic arrangements within major industries to curb the destabilizing impact of competition – arrangements in which the government would play a modest, largely uncoercive role). Business historian Thomas K. McCraw described the attitude embodied in the early New Deal's National Recovery Act as "[i]f the remedy of cooperation required a suspension of the antitrust laws, then so be it." THOMAS K. MCCRAW, PROPHETS OF REGULATION 211 (1984).

6   FED. TRADE COMM'N, BUREAU OF COMPETITION, OFF. OF SPECIAL PROJECTS, NATIONAL COMPETITION POLICY: HISTORIANS' PERSPECTIVES ON ANTITRUST AND GOVERNMENT-BUSINESS RELATIONSHIPS IN THE UNITED STATES (1981).

11. Perhaps it is not too much to say that the economic policies of the Second New Deal were invigorated following upon the large-scale and well-publicized Temporary National Economic Committee, which examined the failings of non-market strategies and opened the door for the appointment by Franklin Delano Roosevelt of Thurman Arnold as assistant attorney general (AAG) for antitrust and his headlined enforcement of the Sherman Act.[7]

12. During the New Deal, the Democratic regime expanded on regulatory initiatives of the Progressive Era, serving up the well-known alphabet soup of administrative agencies, thereby bringing a multitude of industries under the auspices of federal agencies. Each was provided by Congress with its own mission, a high degree of independence, and with limited guidance, if any, as to the role that competition was intended to play in the government's enforcement agenda.

13. I choose to describe this as a "silo" model because there was little systematic oversight centrally directing how competition and other values would be reconciled. Heads of agencies were appointed by the President, for the most part, and some served in the President's cabinet, so if the President wanted to talk directly to cabinet heads about competition, he could – but this would have been rare.[8] Generally, the policies of cabinet agencies, and even more so of the new independent regulatory agencies, were left to their internal leadership. Under the *Chevron* doctrine, the federal courts gave deference to the independence of the regulatory agencies.[9] When a dispute between agencies arose, it might be resolved on an ad hoc basis with the help of the White House (generally lacking its own expertise in antitrust or competition policy). While cabinet officials reported to the President, their degree of independence varied, but independent agencies were supposedly independent, and their members could not be fired (except for cause) during their statutory term, once their leaders had received the President's nomination and the Senate's confirmation.

---

7   *See, e.g.*, ELLIS HAWLEY, THE NEW DEAL AND THE PROBLEM OF MONOPOLY: A STUDY IN ECONOMIC AMBIVALENCE (1966); BRINKLEY, *supra* note 5; SPENCER WEBER WALLER, THURMAN ARNOLD: A BIOGRAPHY (2005); RUDOLPH J. R. PERITZ, COMPETITION POLICY IN AMERICA, 1888–1992: HISTORY, RHETORIC, LAW (rev. ed. 2000).

8   An interesting example was the effort of President Reagan's top officials to stop DOJ's then-pending *AT&T* case, which would ultimately lead to the dramatic breakup of the phone company's monopoly. The showdown came at a meeting in which Bill Baxter, the AAG for antitrust, stood up for the case and Reagan backed away. STEVE COLL, THE DEAL OF THE CENTURY: THE BREAKUP OF AT&T (1986).

9   Under *Chevron* deference, Chevron U.S.A., Inc. v. Natural Resources Defense Council, Inc., 467 U.S. 837 (1984), judges must respect an agency's reasonable interpretation of the statutes it administers. *Chevron* is discussed favorably in DAVID S. TATEL, VISION: A MEMOIR OF BLINDNESS AND JUSTICE 255 (2024). For most of the New Deal era, the job of federal judges was "not to decide whether the rule the agency picked was the one they'd have chosen themselves. Instead, a statute called the Administrative Procedure Act requires courts to respect an agency's scientific judgments unless it acts 'arbitrarily and capriciously' – administrative-law speak for 'totally irrationally.'" Judge Tatel wrote that "arbitrary and capricious" review and *Chevron* deference are "important principles of judicial restraint that keep unelected judges from second-guessing agency decision-making." *Id.* In my discussion of the authoritarian populism model, I will stress how the Roberts Supreme Court's opinions on these principles affects the powers of the three branches of federal government in terms of the possible centralization of presidential power over the economy. *See* text at note 35 *et seq.*

14. During the New Deal era, the two antitrust agencies, the DOJ Antitrust Division and the FTC, developed internal "competition advocacy" units responsible for following the work of other regulatory agencies and offering intermittent non-binding advice with respect to the competitive implications of pending policies. These efforts were usually understaffed and not well appreciated by the agencies being lectured to. In the case of the relationship between antitrust and international trade, the differences were not merely that one agency, the FTC, had a mission to increase domestic competition, while the other, the International Trade Commission (ITC), had a mission to decrease foreign competition in the U.S. market; it was also that those who staffed and led the two agencies tended to come up through separate occupational sociologies of trade and antitrust, establishing their separate "priors" and self-protecting prejudices.[10]

15. This is not to deny that during the course of the New Deal and Post-New Deal silo model, occasional efforts were made to take a big-picture approach toward competition. One technique was in the Office of Management and Budget's (OMB) Circular A-19, "a tool used by every modern president to ensure that the Administration has one coordinated position, the president's position, on authorizing legislation."[11] Although this coordination process for legislation applies to all departments and agencies, it does not apply to the rules of independent regulatory agencies.

16. Another tool was the occasional blue-ribbon study commission.[12] For example, an executive branch effort of the Carter administration to promote the goal of more competition to the regulatory agencies through a blue-ribbon panel called the National Commission for the Review of Antitrust Laws and Procedures (NCRALP).[13] A DOJ (rather than congressional) initiative, NCRALP held hearings and ultimately concluded that competition should play a larger role in regulatory decisions, thereby providing ammunition to Congress to support a burgeoning deregulation movement. In effect, it blessed a movement toward less stringent economic regulation that was already underway as the Chicago School

---

[10] See the American Antitrust Symposium, *Trade and Antitrust: Is Rapprochement Desirable? Is It Possible?*, 47 N.Y.L. SCH. L. REV. 131 (2003).

[11] Jeffrey A. Weinberg, *The View from the Oval Office: Understanding the Legislative Presidency*, 24 J. LEGIS. STUD. 395, 398 (2018). A-19 is at https://www.whitehouse.gov/wp-content/uploads/2017/11/Circular-019.pdf. OMB is also responsible for Circular A-4, which provides guidance on how agencies should develop legislatively required regulatory impact analyses, including competitive impacts, for economically significant rules. The 2003 predecessor was updated and expanded by the Biden administration in November 2023, and after March 1, 2024, applies to all proposed rules, direct final rules, and interim final rules. After January 1, 2025, it will apply to other final orders. A-4 addresses some of the challenges in marrying competition policy with other regulatory mandates (like fairness, access, diversity, etc.).

[12] See Albert A. Foer, *Putting the Antitrust Modernization Commission into Perspective*, 51 BUFF. L. REV. 1029 (2003) (describes the 1938–1941 Temporary National Economic Commission, the 1955 Attorney General's National Committee to Study the Antitrust Laws, the 1969 White House Task Force on Antitrust Policy, the 1979 National Commission for the Review of Antitrust Laws and Procedures, the 1998 International Competition Policy Advisory Committee, and the 2002 Antitrust Modernization Commission).

[13] REPORT TO THE PRESIDENT AND THE ATTORNEY GENERAL OF THE NATIONAL COMMISSION FOR THE REVIEW OF ANTITRUST LAWS AND PROCEDURES (1979).

(based on maximizing efficiency) began to displace the older Harvard School (based more on inferences from industrial structure).[14] NCRALP disbanded after issuing its report and left no institutional residue to ensure coherence within the overall administration. In later Republican administrations, deregulation (which was supposed to benefit consumers as well as businesses) began to morph into a movement for privatization, an effort to reduce the role of government in the economy.

17. Another factor of importance was the emergence of international adoption of antitrust laws as first only a very few, and then, rather explosively, many nations adopted competition policy laws, especially after the Soviet Union fragmented late in the twentieth century and markets replaced central planning around the world. This made some reasonably similar rules for markets and trade ever more imperative. The U.S. participated in the formation and implementation of the International Competition Network (ICN) in 2001, eventually bringing together, in an innovative voluntary venture lacking even a central office, now over 130 nations with different cultures, economic and political histories, and governmental experiences.[15] For the U.S. to play a leading role, it had to come to terms with the varieties of competition policy becoming prevalent in the world, and particularly to understand that there are many different "best practices" for competition policies. Many of the ICN countries came with "strong government" histories and devoted their "competition" resources to a variety of regulatory issues, including consumer protection or, in some nations, other policies that may have been of greater benefit to the state or its officials than to consumers or the public.

18. DOJ had long maintained a foreign commerce section, reflecting its executive branch's interests in international affairs. At the FTC, the growth of international competition policy led to the creation of a new office focused on international competition policy, which combined expertise in consumer protection issues with antitrust. In other words, there grew increasing recognition that traditional consumer protection issues and traditional antitrust issues were often two sides of the same coin, sometimes involving tradeoffs.

19. Some might argue that I have overlooked the important battle between the Harvard School and the Chicago School that took place in the late 1970s, in which the earlier "structure-behavior-performance" model of industrial organization economics was displaced by an efficiency-based

---

14 *See* MARC ALLEN EISNER, ANTITRUST AND THE TRIUMPH OF ECONOMICS: INSTITUTIONS, EXPERTISE, & POLICY CHANGE (1991). *Also see* Eisner's REGULATORY POLITICS IN TRANSITION (1993) and BINYAMIN APPELBAUM, THE ECONOMISTS' HOUR: FALSE PROPHETS, FREE MARKETS, AND THE FRACTURE OF SOCIETY (2019).

15 THE INTERNATIONAL COMPETITION NETWORK AT TEN: ORIGINS, ACCOMPLISHMENTS AND ASPIRATIONS (Paul Lugard ed., 2011), and *International Competition Network*, WIKIPEDIA, https://en.wikipedia.org/wiki/International_Competition_Network (last visited Aug. 17, 2024).

model of neoclassical economics.¹⁶ This ongoing controversy involved the important questions of how to analyze particular microeconomic problems about marketplace competition, and especially how much weight to give to the concentration of markets and industries versus the importance of efficiency-driven competition, which sought low prices at the expense of growing concentration; but it did not create any new institutions for providing overall coherent executive control over the entire government. For that, we now turn to the administration of President Joe Biden.

III. The Biden Whole-of-Government Model

20. Why might a decentralized national government believe more centralized and systematic management of competition policy would be desirable? Elsewhere, I have set out the following possibilities:[17]

    – Perhaps most important, an incoming administration might believe that (a) more or (b) less or (c) a different kind of attention should be a high priority of the overall government. An Executive Order (or "EO") is a relatively quick way of focusing the machinery of a new or reorienting government without going through Congress.

    – Decision-making is often fragmented, with the potential for conflicting outcomes. For example, the Federal Communications Commission (FCC) and the DOJ may disagree on the consequences of a proposed FCC regulation regarding telecommunications.

    – Jurisdictions that affect marketplace competition often overlap. At the heart of antitrust enforcement, for example, there are two separate federal agencies, state enforcement agencies, and private litigation.

    – Some federal agencies are legally independent from the executive branch and might be difficult to coordinate in the name of a national economic policy. It is sometimes difficult for the private sector to predict, e.g., whether a merger will be challenged, if DOJ and FTC (an independent agency) set inconsistent guidelines.

    – Relevant expertise regarding a pending governmental decision may be lodged in numerous niches that too infrequently are provided a timely opportunity to weigh in.

---

16   EISNER, ANTITRUST AND THE TRIUMPH OF ECONOMICS, *supra* note 14, is a good source on the takeover by the Chicago School. A briefer study is TIM WU, THE CURSE OF BIGNESS, ANTITRUST IN THE NEW GILDED AGE (2018).

17   Albert A. Foer, *The Bridge from Chicago to Biden: The American Antitrust Institute in Perspective*, 53 U. BALT. L. REV. 195, 208–209 (2024).

- Clarity may be lacking as to who the authorized decision-maker is and who must (or may) be consulted in a timely manner. Who should be "in the room where it happens"?

- With all the possible targets for governmental action, it may be unclear what the priorities should be for spending the public's limited time and money.

- Where conflicting values must be balanced, some general guidance may be needed, for example, on how much competitive efficiency might be traded off for greater privacy, reliability, fairness, etc.

- There may be a basic conflict between domestic and international consequences of an action, without clear guidance as to which considerations should prevail.

- Predictions are of fundamental importance to competitors, investors, and the executors of competition policy – with the need for better-coordinated procedures for reaching consensus within government on likely consequences, taking into account timely inputs from all knowledgeable perspectives.

- In theory, the entire government, like a symphony orchestra, should be playing from the same sheet music regarding economic policies as basic and far-reaching as competition policy.[18]

- A coordinated approach to competition policy provides guidance to the processes of personnel administration.

21. The idea of a whole-of-government strategy for competition policy was first presented late in the Obama administration with the expectation that Hillary Clinton would carry it forward after her election. Instead, Trump was elected and the idea was dropped.[19] Biden signed his EO on July 9, 2021. Institutionally, it created an office within the National Economic Council to staff a new White House Competition Council composed of cabinet-level officials and relevant agency heads.[20] The EO included a list of some 72 projects that it assigned to various units of government, requiring reports to be prepared under deadlines. President Biden himself was present at all six meetings of the Competition Council, convening twice

---

18 An orchestra, like the government, is made up of different instruments with different roles, each playing its own music. Conflict is built into the system for good reasons, but cooperation of the players is essential.

19 *See* Exec. Order No. 13,725, 81 Fed. Reg. 23417 (Apr. 15, 2016). The Trump administration formally rejected the Obama EO. Joe Biden, Obama's vice president, was presumably aware of the EO and several people in the Biden White House or involved in Biden's transition planning had worked on the Obama EO.

20 Technically, executive orders can only be enforced by the President against the executive agencies. The Competition EO attempted to get around this by including heads of relevant independent agencies within the Competition Council and urging independent leaders to go along with the program. According to Jeffrey Weinberg, a former career-long OMB official, this may have been the first time an executive order attempted to include independent agencies (conversation with the author, Aug. 6, 2024).

a year through March 2024. At the most recent meeting, the President announced the launch of a new Strike Force to crack down on unfair and illegal pricing.[21]

22. According to people involved at the White House and within the government, the role of the President served two important purposes. One was to highlight to the public the President's personal concern with his administration's work on particular issues, such as inflation, junk fees, gas and pharmaceutical prices. The other, and perhaps more important in terms of impact, was to require all of the relevant government agencies to pay more attention to the competitive effects of their decisions. In practice, there was agreement that this seemed to mean that when the Antitrust Division or the FTC weighed in on a regulatory matter, their intervention carried more weight than in the past.[22]

23. "Personnel is Policy" is often the case. The Biden EO carried with it the appointment of leaders to carry it out. Significantly, the AAG of the DOJ Antitrust Division (Jonathan Kanter) and the chair of the FTC (Lina Khan) were known as strong advocates of antitrust enforcement, particularly in the important high-tech arena. Tim Wu, a Columbia University law professor who had written books on the telecommunications industry and competition policy, was appointed as a special advisor to the President for technology and competition policy within the National Economic Council.[23] He reported to Brian Deese, who had been a high-level economic policy advisor in the Obama administration. All four were seen as favored by the progressive wing of the Democratic Party. After the 2022 mid-term elections, Wu and Deese moved on and several key supporters of antitrust enforcement left their Judiciary Committee seats in the House, the point being that there is a possibility that the personnel and the political support for a whole-of-government strategy will likely change even during the course of a single presidential administration. Continuity between administrations is a more important question to be addressed later in this paper.

24. A primary question for organizing a whole-of-government strategy is "who is to be excluded from the table?" In the Biden EO, states and the private sector were immediately excluded and little was initially expected of the financial regulators or of international trade, but as time went by, these interests played a larger role, which would not have been foreseen by readers of the EO, which set out initial topics and tasks.

---

[21] White House, Readout of the Sixth Meeting of the White House Competition Council, https://www.whitehouse.gov/briefing-room/statements-releases/2024/03/06/readout-of-the-sixth-meeting-of-the-white-house-competition-council/.

[22] I base this on ongoing discussions on and off the record from the beginning of the Biden administration with a variety of people in the White House, participating regulatory agencies, and others in positions to have observations, who are not named as readers in footnote *.

[23] TIM WU, THE MASTER SWITCH: THE RISE AND FALL OF INFORMATION EMPIRES (2011) and WU, *supra* note 16.

For instance, as the Biden administration put increased emphasis on industrial policy and protectionist trade policies, the special trade representative was brought into the Competition Council, where Ambassador Tai made an effort to assure that trade competition policy "must row in the same direction" as the other agencies.[24] She announced that the shift in trade as in antitrust must move away from a narrow focus on benefits for consumers. The new trade policy would "place[] workers at its center to reflect the reality that the consumer who enjoys the low prices of imported goods is also a worker who must withstand the downward pressures that come from competing with workers in other parts of the world toiling under exploitative conditions." This effort to coordinate competition policy and trade policy, whether one agrees with the new policies or not, represents an explicitly new development in overall coherence. It reverses much of the Chicago School's free trade emphasis on efficiency by also recognizing such non-efficiency values as resiliency, worker protection, more *inclusive prosperity* at home and abroad, and represents a labor-oriented departure from globalization and free trade.

25. Initially, government interests in banking and finance were only represented in the White House Competition Council by the Consumer Financial Protection Bureau, and not the Federal Reserve, Federal Deposit Insurance Corporation (FDIC), and other financial regulators. Large questions of industry structure, such as the separation between banking and capital markets, or the separation of banking and commerce, or smaller ones, such as access to capital by small and medium-sized businesses, are not mentioned, nor are possible interventions by the DOJ, in particular, in the workings of the government in the face of financial emergencies, which in the past have resulted in rapid and perhaps unnecessarily substantial increases in the concentration of the financial industry.[25] The Biden EO encouraged the DOJ and the federal banking agencies to "adopt a plan... for the revitalization of merger oversight under the Bank Merger Act and the Bank Holding Company Act." Citing the EO's call "for bank antitrust policy to better reflect today's market realities and support a more resilient banking system," Antitrust Chief Jonathan Kanter's speech in June 2023 clearly indicated a shift toward

---

24 Ambassador Katherine Tai was appointed to the White House Competition Council on Sept. 29, 2023. The quotes in the text are from June 2023 and may be found at https://ustr.gov/about-us/policy-offices/press-office/speeches-and-remarks/2023/june/ambassador-katherine-tais-remarks-national-press-club-supply-chain-resilience. It has long been controversial in the U.S. and Europe as to whether competition policy should be targeted at benefitting workers independently or at their role as consumers. Here is one area where Biden's policy seems to be making an important policy break with the past. DG Competition in Brussels rejected such a change.

25 Jeremy C. Kress, *Reviving Bank Antitrust*, 72 Duke L.J. 519–598, 528 (2022) (proposing "a roadmap for reviving bank antitrust" and urging "authorities to reject a narrow focus on consumer prices in favor of a more comprehensive analysis of the numerous nonprice harms that bank consolidation threatens to impose on society").

more vigorous engagement of the DOJ in the blocking of anticompetitive bank mergers.[26]

26. As planners consider the future of the whole-of-government strategy, it would make sense to think through the range of trade and financial issues that might be brought under the umbrella in order to develop a more truly coherent strategy. Future meetings of the White House Competition Council could, for example, feature a presidential message bringing the issue of competition in banking to national attention. At the same time, it must be acknowledged that the "whole" of government might be too large and complicated to bite off with a small central staff, a president with limited time and energy, and the perhaps inelegant fact that all policies cannot have the same priority in a four-year administration. Furthermore, there is a question of how large a staff in the White House is desirable, in terms of when too much centralization of power is legally and practically unhealthy.

27. Ambassador Tai's declaration that now "all of us working in these spaces must row in the same direction" raises an important question about the difference between coordination and consistency. National competition policy benefits from coordination but cannot and should not demand total consistency. Rather, *each category of government activity that affects the nature of competition demands its own appropriate reconciliation of values and interests.* While retailing, for example, can generally be highly competitive and a kind of area in which vigorous antitrust enforcement can incorporate a reasonable balance of competition and cooperation, with an emphasis on the former, the sectors in which Congress has created additional values – such as safety (transportation), reliability (electricity), privacy (finance), transparency (securities), and universal service (communications) – will necessarily demand explicit incorporation of additional values. The White House will need to respect any relevant statutory guidance on incorporating such values provided by the other branches of government. Not incidentally, *there is no guarantee that even the best management of competition policy will bring the best applications of policy.*

28. The institutional future of a whole-of-government approach is still totally unclear.[27] What role will it play, if any, in the presidential administration that will be elected in 2024? Wide swings over time and between administrations in antitrust enforcement and other regulatory priorities create uncertainty, which probably affects investment decisions at home

---

26 Assistant Attorney General Jonathan Kanter Delivers Keynote Address at Brookings Institution's Center on Regulation and Markets Event "Promoting Competition in Banking" (June 20, 2023), https://www.justice.gov/opa/speech/assistant-attorney-general-jonathan-kanter-delivers-keynote-address-brookings-institution.

27 I am not attempting in this paper to evaluate either Biden's or the prior Trump's record on antitrust/competition policy enforcement. In most instances, it takes substantial time and scrutiny to determine how successful a record has been achieved. For examples of well-developed case studies, *see* the series of THE ANTITRUST REVOLUTION volumes by John Kwoka and Lawrence White.

and abroad and makes it difficult for other countries to know what to expect from the U.S. If such swings are institutionally configured to affect the entirety of the government for at least four years, the effects will be vastly multiplied. Recognizing that politics is largely about economic power and the distribution of benefits, it seems unlikely that there is a single model for a durable whole-of-government institution. Dynamic forces will continually be at play. On the other hand, for political parties to commit to a whole-of-government approach to competition policy could make explicit future directions with greater internal coherence and external predictability than we have often had in the past.

29. Would putting this task into the hands of party platform committees angling toward a general election add some moderating dynamic, or would it just push toward the extreme differences between the parties? Do platform committees have the time and expertise found within the government? What impact do party platforms actually have once the party is in power? Or, perhaps, should any White House "executive order" for a whole-of-government strategy require prior approval of Congress? No, that would be trenching on executive authority and unrealistic in terms of political compromise and timing, as well as presenting a challenge to the political interests of congressional committees. But some sort of congressional input, maybe by select committee, tailored to the particular whole-of-government plan might be a useful check on major deviations from statutory intent or other kinds of centralized overreaching.

30. Another potential strategy for dealing with overly sharp swings in policy could be to embed within each sectoral agency a very small civil service cadre of experts in competition policy who can become a government-wide sub-community and help ensure an ongoing level of expertise and commitment to working cooperatively with the NEC to find the best combination of competition, cooperation, and other policies identified in statutes, regulations, and specific agency missions. How to actually do this is obviously a complicated matter. One consideration is that the concept of "experts in competition policy" ignores the great variety of actual policy biases inherent in the term: for instance, do we mean the expertise of the Cato Institute, of the Heritage Foundation, of the AAI, of Open Markets or other advocacy groups? Do we mean the expertise of a particular school of economists, of business school academics, of lawyers (antitrust lawyers? tax lawyers? trade lawyers?) The history of competition policy reflects the array of possible experts.

31. Should it be anticipated that the makeup of this cadre would evolve over time within a framework of the career civil service or political appointments? On the one hand, we need something like a "deep state" to moderate the pace and extremes of change within a dynamic middle. And on the other hand, we need a degree of concern that too much centralization can exacerbate the problem of "capture" by an industry or interest group

that has occurred from time to time within regulatory agencies. We will need experience to answer some of these questions, but even more, we will need closer scrutiny of the whole-of-government idea by journalists and academics than it has received thus far.

32. This much is clear to me: on the one hand, more central guidance from the White House is a worthwhile institutional experiment and competition policy is a plausible choice for a topic at this time, deserving more attention as an institutional reform than it has thus far garnered. But there is also another hand to consider: too much centralization has dangers that could, under unprincipled or extreme leadership, exacerbate the inevitable divergences from administration to administration. In the worst case, it could become a facilitator of centrally administered crony capitalism and undermine civil service morale, if we are not very careful.

33. One suggestion to minimize the downside risks would be to specify as clearly as possible what kinds of White House interventions must be avoided. Most White House administrations have provided guidelines to their direct employees on when they can and cannot intervene or micromanage, but as the role of the White House in competition policies grows, the potential for excessive centralization also grows. Where should the line be drawn between such possibilities as selecting an industry or region for subsidies that will provide it a competitive advantage, targeting an industry for antitrust investigation (as when the previous Trump administration for political reasons of opposition to a legal drug brought a series of antitrust investigations against small marijuana-producing companies, all of which had to be abandoned),[28] targeting a particular company, instructing an enforcement agency to bring or dismiss a suit or prosecution, or shaping a remedy (as in the case of Microsoft after it was found guilty of monopolizing but before the remedy had been imposed[29])?

IV. An Authoritarian Populist Model for Competition Policy

1. Some Background on Sources

34. During the presidential campaign of 2024, a new model began to take shape, having roots in candidate and former President Donald Trump's speeches, those of his Vice Presidential nominee J. D. Vance, the Republican Party's platform, and the Heritage Foundation's Project 2025. Although the 900+ page Project 2025 did make one single mention

---

[28] *See* Betsy Woodruff Swan and Leah Nylen, *DOJ Document Defends Scrutiny of Marijuana Mergers*, POLITICO (June 24, 2020), https://www.politico.com/news/2020/06/24/doj-document-defends-scrutiny-of-marijuana-mergers-338430.

[29] *See* the history of the remedy in the historic *Microsoft* case in ch. 4, *Concluding the Windows 95/98 Case: Appeal and Settlement, in* ANDREW I. GAVIL AND HARRY FIRST, THE MICROSOFT ANTITRUST CASES: COMPETITION POLICY FOR THE TWENTY-FIRST CENTURY 89 (2014).

of a whole-of-government approach in an area unrelated to competition policy, there were no similar ideas in any of the collected GOP (Republican Party) materials or its application to competition policies. One must therefore piece together the elements of the management of a Trump competition policy by focusing on proposals that are likely to affect competition.

35. A further word on two sources is in order. First, the GOP platform, "Make America Great Again!" (MAGA), was approved by the GOP convention on July 8, 2024.[30] It is relatively brief and does not specifically mention antitrust, competition policy, consumer protection or even competition itself – except vaguely in the context of healthcare and prescription drug costs and protecting American workers against foreign competition. The platform contains many promissory statements; however, that would likely have substantial direct implications for competition policy.

36. Project 2025 is the detailed playbook produced by the right-wing Heritage Foundation. Similar projects had been prepared by Heritage in advance of previous elections, but as this report became public, critics immediately reacted to the fact that many close associates of Donald Trump were involved in writing and approving the document, containing numerous proposals that were rapidly denounced as extreme by Democrats and non-MAGA Republicans. Commonly cited examples include blaming the Federal Reserve for the business cycle and proposing to abolish it; eliminating full employment from the Fed's mandate; merging the bank regulatory agencies; moving from an income tax to a consumption tax; reducing the corporate tax rate and the capital gains tax rate; abolishing the Department of Education and the Commerce Department's Economic Development Administration; recommending that Americans be paid more for working on Sunday; closing the borders and deporting large numbers of undocumented immigrants; further regulating pregnancy and abortion; unleashing the fossil fuel industry and loosening environmental rules; a rollback of diversity policies; and, perhaps most important for our purposes, dismantling the so-called administrative state, substituting political loyalists for neutral career civil servants.[31]

37. Trump attempted to distance himself from the production of Project 2025, claiming he had nothing to do with it and that it does not speak

---

30 Among other sources, the platform is provided by NPR Politics at 2024-gop-platforrm-july-7-final. It has been noted that the frequent and random use of capital letters in the document seems to reflect the style that Donald Trump typically uses in his tweets on social media. Also, the proposal for eliminating all taxes on tips for hospitality workers, caddies and drivers seems attributable to Trump personally. I cannot restrain myself from opining that it is a terrible idea, and I am disappointed that Kamala Harris has adopted the general idea, even though we do not know if she intends to include caddies and trucks, buses, or Uber drivers.

31 *See, e.g.*, Stephanie Lai, *Project 2025, Explained: What It Says and What Trump Says About It*, Bloomberg (July 18, 2024).

for him or the Republican Party.[32] Others noted that the president of the Heritage Foundation, Kevin Roberts, is a rumored candidate to be Trump's chief of staff in a second term.[33] At the end of July, apparently under pressure from the Trump campaign, it was announced that Paul Dans, director of Project 2025 at the Heritage Foundation and a former Trump administration personnel official, was departing. People familiar with the situation were reported to be saying that his departure has not established a transition away from influencing the Trump agenda, stressing that an arm of Project 2025 will remain in operation to provide Trump, should he be elected, with a database of more than 20,000 applicants for potential political appointments.[34]

38. To the extent that some parts of Project 2025 overlap with the platform and that there is a good chance that many of the people who worked on Project 2025 or who are in its personnel database will hold political positions in a second Trump administration, it does not seem unfair to employ proposals in Project 2025 in the process of predicting what a Trumpian approach to managing competition policy might entail. Nor does it seem unfair to identify this as the basis for describing an authoritarian populist model.

2. The New and Influential Context of the Supreme Court

39. In constructing an authoritarian populist model, it is necessary to recognize its relationship to the current Supreme Court.[35] At this time in American history, a conservative wing of the Court appointed by former President Trump and Republican predecessors has a solid majority, which is likely to continue into the next administration. While there is no guarantee that this Court will always uphold the interests of Donald Trump,

---

[32] Isaac Arnsdorf and Josh Dawsey, *Project 2025 Is Ending Its Policy Work after Attacks Angered Trump*, WASH. POST, July 31, 2024, at A7. Franco Ordoñez, *Project 2025's Director Steps Down, but the Think Tank Says Work Will Go on*, NPR (July 30, 2024, 6:44 PM ET), https://www.npr.org/2024/07/30/g-s1-14455/project-2025-trump-heritage. For a summary of economic effects being projected just from the tariff and deportation proposals, *see* Thomas B. Edsall, *You Want Policies? Trump's Got Policies*, N.Y. TIMES (Aug. 28, 2024), https://www.nytimes.com/2024/08/28/opinion/trump-tariffs-deportation-economy.html ("Trump tariffs and mass deportation, taken together, would be the largest adverse supply shock ever inflicted on the American economy. They would in all likelihood generate a combination of inflation and depression America has never before seen.") In the Great Depression, the country abandoned the Sherman Act and the idea of competition to the concept of cooperation between government, labor, and management, only to return to a competition-based economy after this system failed to save the economy. Edsall asks what would Trump do when things go sour, answering: "The historical pattern is for dictators then to find scapegoats to blame. . . . Whom will Trump pick as his scapegoats?".

[33] Kyler Alvord, *What Is Project 2025? Inside the Far-Right Plan Threatening Everything from the Word 'Gender' to Public Education*, PEOPLE (July 11, 2024, 4:53 PM EDT), https://people.com/what-is-project-2025-inside-far-right-plan-trump-presidency-8622964. The *Washington Post* reported that in April 2022, Trump shared a private flight with Roberts to a Heritage conference where Trump delivered a keynote address that gestured to Heritage's forthcoming policy proposals, saying: "They're going to lay the groundwork and detail plans for exactly what our movement will do." Isaac Arnsdorf, Josh Dawsey & Hannah Knowles, *Trump Took Private Flight with Project 2025 Leader in 2022*, WASH. POST, Aug. 8, 2024, A1.

[34] Arnsdorf & Dawsey, *supra* note 32.

[35] For a definition of populism, *see supra* note 4.

there is also no strong reason for Trump to believe that it will not. The majority's landmark opinion in *Trump v. United States* that makes it unlikely that a president can be criminally responsible for "official acts" while in office must be seen as broadly protecting the next president's decisions on economic matters from successful challenge, because such matters will arguably leave much room for discretion that can be papered as official and presumptively immune.[36]

40. The elimination of the *Chevron* doctrine in another landmark Roberts' Court opinion seems at first to shift much of administrative law from the expert agencies to the courts.[37] A partisan-divided Congress, such as we currently have, will make it more difficult to override a Supreme Court decision interpreting an existing law and will likely find it difficult to legislate more detailed and prescriptive new laws, a task made more difficult even if compromises can be found by the fact that much regulatory work involves complex science and technology, whose futures cannot be predicted in detail by legislators much less by generalist judges who are being invited to substitute their own opinions. Given the number of district court judges (and pending bipartisan bills to greatly expand the number), national uniformity of regulations and enforcement will become much more difficult to obtain.

41. This may augur a power shift not merely to the judiciary or to Congress, but to more use of executive orders by a president not particularly worried about ignoring the established law. (The constitutional question left ambiguous by the Supreme Court is whether it would be an official act to issue an executive order that is patently illegal. For instance, could the President create an EO that establishes a clear monopoly to benefit the President's own close relative?)

42. An additional consideration is the 2024 case of *Snyder v. United States*, holding that a federal anti-corruption law does not make it a crime for state and local officials to accept a gratuity for acts they have already taken.[38] This is indicative of a trend of the Supreme Court to narrowly

---

36 On July 1, 2024, a divided Supreme Court ruled that former presidents can never be prosecuted for actions relating to the core powers of their office, and that there is at least a presumption that they have immunity for their official acts more broadly. Trump v. United States, 603 U.S.__ (2024).

37 Chevron U.S.A., Inc. v. Natural Resources Defense Council, Inc., 467 U.S. 837 (1984) gave rise to the *Chevron* doctrine, under which, if Congress had not directly addressed the question at the center of a dispute, a court was required to uphold the agency's interpretation of the statute, as long as it was reasonable. On June 28, 2024, by a 6-3 vote, the justices rejected the doctrine, calling it "fundamentally misguided." Loper Bright Enterprises v. Raimondo, 603 U.S.__ (2024). *See* Amy Howe, *Supreme Court Strikes Down Chevron, Curtailing Power of Federal Agencies*, SCOTUSBLOG (June 28, 2024, 12:37 PM), https://www.scotusblog.com/2024/06/supreme-court-strikes-down-chevron-curtailing-power-of-federal-agencies/; *see also* Logan Breed, Chuck Loughlin & Ilana Kattan, *The US Supreme Court overturns Chevron deference doctrine removing the requirement that courts defer to agency interpretations of ambiguous statutes (*Loper Bright / Raimond*)*, E-COMPETITIONS June 2024, art. no. 119498.

38 Snyder v. United States, 603 U.S.__ (2024). *See* Abbie VanSickle & Adam Liptak, *Corruption Law Allows Gifts to State and Local Officials, Supreme Court Rules*, N.Y. TIMES (June 26, 2024), https://www.nytimes.com/2024/06/26/us/politics/supreme-court-corruption-bribery.html. The ruling would seem to require the government to establish a corrupt intent to reward a public official before they act, including agreeing with

interpret anti-corruption laws. One implication of this line of reasoning might be that if the President promised a post-action payoff to a state attorney general for opening an antitrust investigation against a local newspaper critical of the President, neither the briber nor the bribee could be punished.

43. Moreover, the Supreme Court has, in a series of opinions, reduced the significance of the concept of *stare decisis* – that precedents are generally respected – to an unpredictable role.[39] The Roberts Court has also created a new doctrine that welcomes the nation's many federal courts to overturn any reformist regulatory change that it decides amounts to a "major question" beyond the legislative language, to be determined by the court.[40]

44. Finally, the Roberts Court has applied the free speech clause of the First Amendment as being so protective of corporate speech that it has become more difficult for laws and regulations (which are necessarily communications and may often constrain some communications) to be upheld.[41]

45. Together, these holdings may well shift power from regulators to courts, or perhaps to Congress, or to the President. They create a legalistic framework facilitating regulatory abuse.

3. The Trumpian Authoritarian Populism Model[42]

46. In this new legal context, the first thing to notice is that Project 2025 and the GOP platform look toward strengthening the role of the President.

---

the official to pay them after the deed is done. The implications for other relevant laws, such as the Foreign Corrupt Practices Act, are now unclear.

39 *Stare decisis* means the ordinary course of courts standing by precedents. However, the role of stare decisis in giving predictability to the law was called into question by the Supreme Court's overturning of state abortion laws in Dobbs v. Jackson Women's Health, 597 U.S. 215 (2022) and a New York gun control laws in New York State Rifle & Pistol Association, Inc. v. Bruen, 597 U.S. 1 (2022). *See, e.g.*, Devin Dwyer, *After Roe Ruling, Is 'Stare Decisis' Dead? How The Supreme Court's View of Precedents Evolving*, ABC NEWS (June 24, 2022, 12:20 PM), https://abcnews.go.com/Politics/roe-ruling-stare-decisis-dead-supreme-court-view/story?id=84997047.

40 West Virginia v. EPA, 597 U.S. 697 (2022) established the first significant use of the major questions doctrine by the Supreme Court, which stated that "there are extraordinary cases in which the history and the breadth of authority that the agency has asserted, and the economic and political significance of that assertion, provide a reason to hesitate before concluding that Congress meant to confer such authority" (internal quotation marks and brackets omitted).

41 *See* Albert A. Foer, *Civil Liberties and Competition Policy: A Personal Essay Dedicated to John J. Flynn*, 56 ANTITRUST BULL. 731, 759 (2011); ADAM WINKLER, WE THE CORPORATIONS: HOW AMERICAN BUSINESSES WON THEIR CIVIL RIGHTS (2018). The Court's evolving emphasis on the Free Exercise Clause, rather than the Establishment Clause, may bring to the fore many situations in which religion becomes a factor in marketplace competition. *See* Tim Wu, *The First Amendment Is Out of Control*, N.Y. TIMES (July 2, 2024), https://www.nytimes.com/2024/07/02/opinion/supreme-court-netchoice-free-speech.html.

42 Populism is a political strategy that is critical of elites, an antipluralist form of identity politics. "Populist governance exhibits three features: attempts to hijack the state apparatus, corruption and 'mass clientelism' (trading material benefits or bureaucratic favors for political support to citizens who become the populists' 'clients'), and efforts systematically to suppress civil society. Of course, many authoritarians will do similar things. The difference is that populists justify their conduct by claiming that they alone represent the people: this allows populists to avow their practices quite openly." MÜLLER, *supra* note 4, at 2–4. *Also see* JUDIS, *supra* note 4. The Trump/Vance team declares itself populist. Harris/Walz may adopt a few populist policies, but they are not anti-elite and have shown no signs of trying to hijack the state apparatus.

They will do this by essentially wrecking the civil service as we have known it, returning it to the days in which everyone with any position of influence in the government was deemed a political appointee, subject to firing for insufficient loyalty to the political leadership and its ideology.[43]

47. In his first term, President Trump tried unsuccessfully to use "Schedule F" to turn many traditional civil service jobs into political appointments, thus attempting to reduce the role, for instance, of neutral, non-political experts in reaching decisions that impact the role of competition.[44] A principal personnel proposal in Project 2025 is to screen as many as 20,000 candidates for Schedule F jobs, pre-vetting them before the November election, with personal loyalty to Trump and a commitment to an antiliberal ideology as the key filters. As political scientist Damon Linker has written:

> Instead of building on or modestly adjusting what the federal government has done since the beginning of the 20th century, they aim to overturn the very structure of the modern state, gutting the professional, merit-based civil service in favor of a patronage-based system that would hire and promote loyalists and right-wing ideologues.[45]

48. The objective is not to make the government function more efficiently in the public interest, but to reduce the size of the government through actions by the chief executive and his loyalist political appointees.

49. How could this pertain to competition policy? Much of Project 2025 focuses on proposals for managing specific agencies of the federal government, especially in regard to their competition-affecting policies for fuel, energy, and the environment. In these and other cases, the emphasis is not on implications for the role of competition, but on how to repeal Biden's reformist policies. The emphasis is on expanding hierarchical control over government personnel. Chapter 2 of Project 2025 was written by Russ Vought, who served in President Trump's cabinet as director of the OMB. He proposes to steeply increase the number of important officials, currently civil servants, who would become classified as political appointees. He also proposes that regulatory and OIRA

---

43 Chapter 2 of Project 2025 proposes techniques for dismantling the so-called administrative state, in part by making it easier to fire federal government workers and replacing them with political appointees.

44 A Schedule F appointment was a job classification in the excepted service of the United States federal civil service that existed briefly at the end of the Trump administration during 2020 and 2021. It would have contained policy-related positions, removing their civil service protections and making them easy to fire. It was never fully implemented, and no one was appointed to it before it was repealed at the beginning of the Biden administration. *Schedule F Appointment*, WIKIPEDIA, en.wikipedia.org/wiki/Schedule_F_appointment. For those seeking more information about the Schedule F experiment, including examples of commentary since Project 2025 was announced, this Wikipedia article is a resource as to the proposal's controversiality.

45 Damon Linker, *Trump's Most Radical Plan: The Schedule F proposal would seize the administrative state for right-populist ends*, PERSUASION (July 31, 2024), https://www.persuasion.community/p/trumps-most-radical-plan. Linker is a senior lecturer in the Department of Political Science at the University of Pennsylvania, who writes the Substack newsletter *Notes from the Middleground*.

reviews should be required of the historically "independent" agencies.⁴⁶ These perhaps overlookable, seemingly technical changes, which had been proven controversial and were rejected by prior administrations, would go a long way in politicizing decisions that could be expected to affect competition throughout the economy.

50. Competition policy in the regulatory agencies tends to be established in the course of issuing and enforcing rules and regulations. In the modern administrative state, this depends on detailed staff work by experts in regulatory economics and many other technical disciplines. Politics may always enter at some point into the structuring of decisions, but raw politics and corruption tend to be constrained by procedures, transparency, and the impact of carefully prepared neutral staff work. Political leadership and oversight are essential to the democratic system, but when politics reaches too far into the administrative process, it will more likely lead to poor substantive decisions, political cronyism, and outright corruption. Corruption has been a noted problem in the management of competition in countries with an authoritarian history.⁴⁷

51. We next hone in on the Project 2025 chapters on the Justice Department and the FTC, where one might anticipate more discussion of the role of competition in the economy. There is a surprising vacuum.

52. In the chapter on the Justice Department, *there is no reference whatsoever to the Antitrust Division or its work*. There is no statement that either the DOJ or the FTC would continue their traditions of offering comments on competitive effects of pending policies and decisions. There are no statements regarding whether policies toward mergers would become more lenient or intellectual property rights would "trump" antitrust issues, as under the first Trump regime.⁴⁸

53. Although the Project 2025 chapter on the FTC discusses competition policy to a limited extent, it is ambivalent on the only specific agenda item considered, namely, whether very large companies such as tech giants should be attacked by competition enforcers. *The author notes two opposing views but proposes no particular policies.*⁴⁹

---

46 Project 2025 at 46, 49. OIRA is the Office of Information and Regulatory Affairs.

47 *See, e.g.*, Yuhua Wang, *Institutions and Bribery in an Authoritarian State*, 49 Stud. Compar. Int'l Dev. 217 (2014), https://scholar.harvard.edu/files/yuhuawang/files/wang_2014.pdf. (This study implies that firms operating in a weak property rights regime rely on political connections as a substitute for formal legal protection.) The ICN has long been concerned with how to minimize the element of corruption in the management of competition policy.

48 The bipartisan position on intellectual property was reversed in the Trump administration. Prior administrations tried to balance incentives for innovation against the detriment to competition caused by a patent's temporary but long-term exclusionary guarantee. Another example of a political impact on antitrust during the previous Trump regime: the opening of investigations of ten small marijuana businesses, on the basis of antipathy to marijuana rather than a competitive problem, all of which had to be closed for lack of evidence. *See supra* note 28.

49 Project 2025, ch. 30. The author is Adam Candeub, a professor of law and director of the Intellectual Property, Information & Communications Law Program at Michigan State University College of Law.

54. There is no policy recommendation reflecting any concern about corporate greed, cartel behavior, mergers, concentration or monopoly power. This certainly suggests that the current Republican leaders are not particularly interested in antitrust enforcement or influence on regulators. Do they want to make antitrust and competition enforcement disappear, or do they want to capture them through a personnel takeover based on political loyalty to the President?

55. Here we might bring in the reports that J. D. Vance, the Republican vice presidential candidate, has, to the concern of many Republicans, spoken favorably about FTC Chairperson Lina Khan, citing her as "one of the few people in the Biden administration that I think is doing a pretty good job."[50] One cannot help but wonder what would happen if an elected President Trump were to adopt a whole-of-government competition policy program and put Vice President Vance in charge. It is doubtful, of course, that Lina Khan could qualify for a continuing role as chair, on ideological or loyalty grounds, or indeed, whether Vance himself would qualify.

56. The GOP platform itself does not speak specifically to the DOJ or the FTC, but it offers numerous promises that would likely involve decisions reflecting competition policies, such as: "slash regulations that stifle Jobs, Freedom, Innovation and make everything more expensive"; "bring our critical Supply Chains back home"; "end market-distorting restrictions on Oil, Natural Gas, and Coal"; "end Democrats' unlawful and unAmerican Crypto crackdown"; "defend the right to mine Bitcoin, and ensure every American has the right to self-custody of their Digital Assets, and transact free from Government Surveillance and Control";[51] "repeal Joe Biden's dangerous Executive Order that hinders AI innovation";[52] "enhance partnerships with the rapidly expanding

---

50 THE ECONOMIST, July 20, 2024, at 19. In Vance's forward to a book by Heritage Foundation President Kevin Roberts, DAWN'S EARLY LIGHT: TAKING BACK WASHINGTON TO SAVE AMERICA (2024), Vance writes, in what he says may jar conservatives: "A private company that can censor speech, influence elections, and work seamlessly with intelligence services and other federal bureaucrats deserves the scrutiny of the Right, not its support. Roberts not only gets this at an instinctive level; he can articulate a political vision to engage in that scrutiny effectively." Alex Shephard, *Read J.D. Vance's Violent Foreword to Project 2025 Leader's New Book*, THE NEW REPUBLIC (July 30, 2024), https://newrepublic.com/article/184393/jd-vance-violent-foreword-kevin-roberts-project-2025-leader-book. *Also see* Michelle Goldberg, *JD Vance Just Blurbed a Book Arguing That Progressives Are Subhuman*, N.Y. TIMES (Aug. 7, 2024), https://www.nytimes.com/2024/08/05/opinion/jd-vance-fascism-unhumans.html. The book, titled *Unhumans*, is praised by Vance. In her review, Goldberg quotes Vance in a 2021 alt-right podcast as arguing that Republicans, upon taking power, should purge their opponents. Trump, the quote said, should "fire every single midlevel bureaucrat, every civil servant in the administrative state, replace them with our people."

51 An effect of this promise would seem to be to allow businesses to hide important business data from access by regulators, which, among other law enforcement issues, would make it more difficult to gather data essential to the analysis and enforcement of competition in markets.

52 To clarify, this is not a reference to the EO on competition policy. *See* White House, Executive Order on the Safe, Secure, and Trustworthy Development and Use of Artificial Intelligence (Oct. 30, 2023), https://www.whitehouse.gov/briefing-room/presidential-actions/2023/10/30/executive-order-on-the-safe-secure-and-trustworthy-development-and-use-of-artificial-intelligence/. Section 5 is titled "Promoting Innovation and Competition" and relates primarily to modernizing immigration pathways for experts in AI and other critical and emerging technologies, and to mitigate patent risks. Section 5.3 specifically discusses "promoting competition" and provides: "In particular, the Federal Trade Commission is encouraged to consider, as it

Commercial Space sector"; "promote homeownership through Tax Incentives"; "eliminate Taxes on Tips for millions of Restaurant and Hospitality Workers"; "support baseline Tariffs on Foreign-made goods"; "promote Choice and Competition" for healthcare and prescription drug costs; "canceling Biden's Electric Vehicle and other [auto industry] Mandates, and preventing the importation of Chinese vehicles"; "banning companies that outsource jobs from doing business with the Federal Government"; and "protecting American Workers from unfair Foreign Competition."

57. It seems fair to say that after reading the platform and the 2025 Project, we are left with little or no guidance as to desired antitrust policies or any concern about coordinating competition policy within the cut-down regulatory agencies that are to be staffed primarily by Trump loyalists and right-wing ideologues. The stray comments of Vance are vague and may or may not carry any weight with Trump.

58. There does seem to be one major competition policy, however, that drives the Republican competition agenda: protectionism. This primary "America First" economic policy includes the imposition of substantial universal tariffs and the exclusion or disadvantaging of imported products, components, and labor. The overall result will be to reduce competition in the U.S., the raising of prices at home and perhaps an escalating trade war as foreign nations naturally retaliate, which seemingly contradicts the platform's emphasis on fighting against inflation.[53]

59. The reduced role of foreigners in our economy, due to anti-immigration policies that are central to the platform and the 2025 agenda,[54] will lead to shifts in the labor market, with differential competitive impacts, perhaps most notably among small businesses, agriculture, and high-tech companies. At the same time, one should take note that the Project 2025 Report recognizes substantial controversy in regard to free trade, and *refrains from taking a position*, presenting both the protectionist views of Peter Navarro and the pro-trade views of Kent Lassman.[55]

---

deems appropriate, whether to exercise the Commission's existing authorities, including its rulemaking authority under the Federal Trade Commission Act, 15 U.S.C. 41 *et seq.*, to ensure fair competition in the AI marketplace and to ensure that consumers and workers are protected from harms that may be enabled by the use of AI."

[53] Chapter 1 of the platform is titled "Defeat Inflation and Quickly Bring Down All Prices." For an alarming assessment of the impacts of Trump's proposal to deport 11 million immigrants, *see* Eduardo Porter, *Trump's Deportation Plan Would Be Nearly Impossible to Implement*, Wash. Post (Aug. 26, 2024), https://wapo.st/3Mqt6pO.

[54] Chapter 5 of the platform is titled "Protect American Workers and Farmers from Unfair Trade."

[55] Project 2025, ch. 26 on trade. *See, e.g.*, Robert L. Borosage, *Will the Heritage Foundation's Project 2025 Turn Trumpism Into a Governing Agenda?*, The Nation (Feb. 8, 2024), https://www.thenation.com/article/politics/will-the-heritage-foundations-project-2025-turn-trumpism-into-a-governing-agenda/ ("Heritage, however, remains conflicted on signature Trump economic heresies. On trade, a chapter by Peter Navarro, Trump's former trade director, making the case for managed trade is countered by one reiterating the traditional doctrine. The chapter on the Federal Trade Commission can't reconcile the conservative antipathy to antitrust actions with the new fears of concentrated social-media platforms that allegedly suppress free speech.").

60. What can we predict about an authoritarian populism model for managing competition? Very simply, it would be the most highly centralized presidency in modern peacetime American history, without the rule of law protections inherent in the traditionally decentralized and largely apolitical management of the various arenas of competition regulation. Like everything else in this model, it will depend on President Trump's volatile and transactional nature, making prediction difficult for the private sector, and holding the potential for crony capitalism in which political loyalty outweighs the other usual measures for success in the marketplace.

V. Conclusion: The Election of 2024 and the Management of Competition

61. The 2024 election outcome may be known by the time this is published, and the candidates' issues relating to the management of the economy may have become clarified. As I write in late August 2024, the Democratic candidates, Harris and Walz, have not, to my knowledge, taken public positions on whether they intend to continue, modify, or reject the Biden executive order, but the '24 Democratic Party platform, written prior to Biden's announcement that he will not run for re-election, speaks clearly and favorably about the Competition Council's efforts and says: "Democrats will keep working to make the American economy more competitive for businesses and workers across sectors. . . ."[56] While there are elements of populist rhetoric in Kamala Harris' support of some China-focused tariffs, industrial policy, anti-price gouging, and removing taxes on tips, these are minor compared to Trump/MAGA's proposals and will still need to be formulated in as-yet-unrevealed detail. The Republican candidates have not taken positions directly relating to a national competition policy or specified detailed reactions to competition-related components of the Heritage Foundation's tome.

---

56 '24 Democratic Party Platform at 23, https://democrats.org/wp-content/uploads/2024/08/FINAL-MASTER-PLATFORM.pdf. Harris had much experience as California's attorney general dealing with both antitrust and competition policy questions. *See Honoring Kathleen Foote's Antitrust Career in the California Attorney General's Office*, CAL. LAW'S ASS'N (Apr. 2024), https://calawyers.org/antitrust-unfair-competition-law/honoring-kathleen-footes-antitrust-career-in-the-california-attorney-generals-office/. Former DOJ antitrust chief Bill Baer told a reporter, "As best I can tell, she was quite supportive [as California attorney general] of a vigorous antitrust enforcement at the state level." Early reports on Harris's campaign, he said, suggest that she "has been relatively quiet about how she would approach antitrust issues if she were to win the White House against Donald Trump." Rebecca Picciotto, *Kamala Harris Has a Murky Antitrust Record*, CNBC (Aug. 1, 2024, 1:20 PM EDT), https://www.cnbc.com/2024/08/01/kamala-harris-joe-biden-corporate-regulation-antitrust-election.html. Picciotto also writes, "Wall Street dealmakers… believe [Harris] is a clean slate on antitrust regulation and a prime opportunity to loosen the Biden antitrust regime." For a show of the Democratic Party progressive wing's concerns that a Harris administration may be less supportive of competition policy than Biden, *see* Matt Stoller, *It's Unclear What Kamala Harris Thinks About Corporate Power. But the Signs Are Worrisome*, N.Y. TIMES (Aug. 7, 2024), https://www.nytimes.com/2024/08/07/opinion/kamala-harris-google-antitrust.html. A noted concern has been that several wealthy Democrats with high-tech interests have been reported to be urging Harris to distance herself from Biden's aggressive competition policies. *See* Alexander Bolton, *Harris Caught in Fight between Donors, Progressives over Big Tech Power*, THE HILL (Aug. 16, 2024), https://thehill.com/homenews/campaign/4830326-kamala-harris-lina-khan-ftc-tech-companies/.

62. This article has been about the overall management of competition wherever it occurs within the federal government. It has not focused on the content of a competition policy, which has a long history of changeability. Management is not everything. Appropriate policies could be developed without overall coordination and guidance from the White House, and terrible policies could be well coordinated and centrally controlled. What we can predict about the significance of the 2024 election is this: if the Democrats win the White House in November, there are strong indications that the de facto rules for the coordination of federal competition policies will be generally pro-competition and aggressive antitrust interpretation and enforcement will generally continue, more or less, in the work begun by the Biden administration. Alternatively, if the Republicans win, competition policy will be largely based on protection of certain classes of competitors, in a populist Trumpian way, meaning highly dependent on the ad hoc discretion of former President Trump, a transactionally focused figure whose drive for power will be reflected in a new centralization of authority exercised through a personal demand for intense political loyalty that drills deeper into the "deep state" than at any time since a modern civil service transformed government away from a corruption-plagued patronage system. There will be a smaller government with less regulation, but businesses will be at risk of suffering from political disfavor. Transactional concerns will trump systematic, expert-led theory and analysis. Both doing business and living with business will be very different from the past.

First on Antitrust and Regulation: Symbiosis From Rail to Digital

Erika M. Douglas[*]

Temple University, Beasley School of Law

Abstract

This essay reflects on Professor Harry First's lifelong contributions to theories of antitrust law and regulation, and the continued relevance of his insightful work to digital competition policy. Over his distinguished career, Harry's polymathic writing has vividly explored the interrelationships between antitrust and regulation, in areas as far afield as the history of New York electricity deregulation, grain handling, rail, the power and limits of antitrust remedies, and digital regulation. His collective works carry a clear message: at its heart, U.S. competition policy relies on a hybrid system of both antitrust law and industry-specific regulation to maintain competitive markets. Effective competition policy and law demand symbiosis between antitrust and regulation, both at institutional and substantive levels.

---

[*] Associate Professor, Temple University, Beasley School of Law. The author thanks Darren Bush and Harry First for their time and thoughtful reading of earlier drafts of this article. All errors and omissions are my own.

1. This essays explores how this duality has been upset, at times, by judicial intervention, deregulatory cycles and institutional power allocation in competition enforcement. It finds that despite these disruptions, Harry's wisdom endures from rail to digital. As the U.S. grapples with the newest dilemmas of digital power and competition, the best solutions will emphasize his hybrid approach in substantive law and institutional roles.

2. The year was 1970. A young Harry First had just received a fateful early assignment as a lawyer for the Department of Justice (DOJ). As part of the Appellate Division, his task was to review decisions with an impact on government agency interests. The matter on his desk, *American International Drive-away v. U.S. & ICC*, involved the now-defunct Interstate Commerce Commission (ICC). At the time, the ICC was a powerful transportation regulator tasked with promoting "safe, adequate, economical, and efficient service" and "foster[ing] sound economic conditions in transportation."[1]

3. The appellant in the case, American International Drive-away, was a freight carrier challenging the ICC's refusal to allow its new entry into the market for "drive-away" services. These services involved interstate carriage of consumers' vehicles, often back and forth from vacation destinations such as California and Florida.[2] At the time, the operators of drive-away services required a certificate of public convenience and necessity from the ICC before they could lawfully transport cars on interstate highways.[3]

4. One might have expected Harry and the DOJ to lend their support to the ICC, as a fellow government agency. A rebel who had found his cause, Harry instead recommended that the DOJ Antitrust Division join the other side in the *AI Drive-away* case, arguing in favor of competition in the market.

5. The ICC's rationale for denying the certificate was, in short, that incumbent companies could simply expand their business to offer similar services, and so new entry was not necessary or in the public interest.[4] Several decisions around the time of *AI Drive-away* illustrate the ICC's problematic exercise of public interest powers in this manner, which served to limit competition in the drive-away business and beyond.[5] The ICC was on a mission

---

1 National Transportation Policy Act of 1940, ch. 722, tit. I, § 1, 54 Stat. 899 (1940), amending the Interstate Commerce Act, 49 U.S.C. §§ 1, 301, 901, 1001, 123 (1970).

2 American International Drive-away v. U.S. & I.C.C., Civ. No. C-70-1591-WTS (N.D. Cal. 1970). The company went by the name AAA Drive-away. Harry, with his unfailing sense of humor, dubs this "an early version of search optimization," since the company chose this name to garner top placement in the alphabetical yellow page listings. Phone Interview with Harry First and the author, Aug. 23, 2024. *See also* I.C.C. v. AAA Con Drivers Exchange, Inc. 340 F.2d 820, 821–23 (2d Cir. 1965) (describing the concept of drive-away services for vehicles).

3 *AAA Con Drivers Exchange, Inc.*, 340 F.2d at 823–24 (describing the ICC's power to issue certificates of public convenience under the Interstate Commerce Act, and the legislative requirement that such a certificate be obtained from the agency for the interstate transportation of motor vehicles).

4 American International Drive-away v. U.S. & I.C.C.

5 *See, e.g.*, Auto Drive-Away Co. of Hialeah, Inc. v. I.C.C., 360 F.2d 446, 447 (5th Cir. 1966); I.C.C. v. Interstate Auto Shippers, Inc., 214 F. Supp. 473, 476 (S.D.N.Y. 1963), *aff'd sub nom.* I.C.C. v. Interstate Auto Shippers, Inc., 323 F.2d 367 (2d Cir. 1963) (confirming the ICC's "broadly comprehensive" powers to require such certificates); I.C.C. v. Dudgeon, 213 F. Supp. 710, 712 (S.D. Cal. 1961) (same).

to prevent new drive-away services from operating without a certificate, and regularly sought injunctions against new competitors that entered the market.[6] In one case, incumbent firms were collectively abusing the ICC's administrative processes to keep competition out, forming a cartel that jointly opposed the issuance of any new certificates.[7]

6. Always the competition advocate, Harry argued the ICC should instead exercise its public interest powers to encourage competition, and should have permitted AI Drive-away to enter the market.[8] This was not just an upstart young lawyer's view – his boss at the time agreed to this defense of competitive markets.[9] He was even willing to let Harry make the oral argument in San Francisco, on one important condition: that he obtain a haircut. A DOJ slip from 1970 assigns Harry the case for argument, but only if "you get a haircut before going into court."[10]

7. This demand for a haircut evokes a different Harry than we know and admire today, but the *AI Drive-away* case foreshadowed an essential part of his intellectual legacy: Harry's outstanding contributions to theories of interaction between antitrust law and regulation. This essay reflects on Harry First's lifelong work on antitrust and regulation, and the continued relevance of his insights today to pressing dilemmas of digital regulation, competition and power.[11] His collective works carry a clear message: regulation and antitrust both play necessary roles in maintaining competitive markets, and effective competition policy must reflect this at institutional and substantive levels. Through insightful articles and books, and his longstanding courses at NYU School of Law, Antitrust and Regulatory Alternatives I and II, Harry emphasizes the combined relevance of antitrust and regulation to ensuring competitive markets, framing the U.S. approach as a dual or "hybrid" system of regulation and antitrust.[12]

8. Over his distinguished career, Harry's polymathic writing has lavished detail on areas as far afield as the history of New York electricity deregulation,[13]

---

6   *See* sources cited *supra* note 5.

7   California Motor Transp. Co. v. Trucking Unlimited, 404 U.S. 508, 510–11 (1972) (subjecting to antitrust scrutiny a conspiracy among incumbent highway carriers to oppose any new applications and transfers of certificates of public convenience in ICC proceedings, using the regulatory processes to keep competition out of the industry).

8   Interview with Harry First, *supra* note 2.

9   *Id.*

10 *See* Appendix A, Department of Justice Routing Slip, American International Drive-away v. U.S. & I.C.C., Civ. No. C-70-1591-WTS (N.D. Cal, 1970), Sept. 17, 1970.

11 Harry First, *Regulated Deregulation: The New York Experience in Electric Utility Deregulation* [hereinafter First, *Regulated Deregulation*], 33 Loy. U. Chi. L.J. 911 (2002) (tracing the challenges of deregulation of electric utilities in New York state); Harry First, *Antitrust and Regulatory Alternatives: How the Past Points the Way to the Future*, 11 J. Antitrust Enf't 173 (2023) [hereinafter First, *Antitrust and Regulatory Alternatives*] (tracing the relationship between antitrust and regulation in grain handling and storage, rail regulation and electric power regulation).

12 First, *Antitrust and Regulatory Alternatives*, *supra* note 11, at 177.

13 First, *Regulated Deregulation*, *supra* note 11.

grain handling,[14] the power and limits of antitrust remedies,[15] and digital regulation.[16] While too extensive to catalog in this short essay, his work thematically explores an array of subtle relationships between regulation and antitrust law, interrogates the substantive and institutional impacts and realities of deregulation, and deploys those insights to inform new or changing regulation and antitrust remedies. Harry champions the legitimacy of reasoned public intervention, and has pushed to revive antitrust, as well as regulation, in eras when one or the other was allowed to fade. In fact, Harry's calls to reassert antitrust as a tool of political and public control over corporate power foreshadowed the progressive movement now seizing antitrust law, a decade before such thinking took hold.[17] His more recent work reaffirms this view that "[r]egulation should not be a dirty word" as "antitrust and regulation can work together to control powerful network monopolies, allowing competition in markets where possible and providing regulatory supervision where the economics demand a single provider."[18]

9. The ICC, the very agency at issue in *AI Drive-away*, provides the ideal starting point to understand Harry's view of antitrust and regulation as twin flames. In 1887, Congress established the ICC, the first-ever federal regulatory agency, as a response to deep concern over the corporate power and misdeeds of railroads.[19] Three years later, Congress added the Sherman Antitrust Act (the Sherman Act), a much more general statute intended to control corporate trusts across the economy.[20] As Harry describes, these were the earliest beginnings of the hybrid system in U.S. law, which employs both widely applicable antitrust law and industry-specific regulation to control monopoly power.[21]

10. From the earliest Sherman Act cases, this hybrid approach spawned questions of reconciliation between antitrust law and ICC regulation of competition.

---

14 First, *Antitrust and Regulatory Alternatives*, *supra* note 514, at 173 (addressing the history of grain regulation, competition and Munn v. Illinois, 94 U.S. 113 (1877)).

15 ANDREW I. GAVIL & HARRY FIRST, THE MICROSOFT ANTITRUST CASES: COMPETITION POLICY FOR THE TWENTY-FIRST CENTURY (2014).

16 Eleanor M. Fox and Harry First, *We Need Rules to Rein in Big Tech*, CPI ANTITRUST CHRON. (Oct. 2020) at 1–5.

17 Harry First, *Bring Back Antitrust*, THE NATION (May 15, 2008), https://www.thenation.com/article/archive/bring-back-antitrust/ (observing that "there is a general perception today that businesses have slipped the traces of public control and that unregulated market forces will not ensure a just, or even efficient, economy. It is time to push the reset button, time to reassert the legitimacy of public intervention" through antitrust law).

18 First, *Antitrust and Regulatory Alternatives*, *supra* note 11, at 177.

19 AM. BAR ASS'N, SEC. OF ANTITRUST LAW, FEDERAL STATUTORY EXEMPTIONS IN ANTITRUST LAW (2007) at 193 (noting federal oversight of rail by the ICC since 1887 (citing Interstate Commerce Act, ch. 104, 24 Stat. 379 (1887)). The ICC was established in part to address complaints by shippers that railroads were setting their rates in an anticompetitive manner. *Id.*

20 The Sherman Antitrust Act, 15 U.S.C. §§ 1–38.

21 First, *Antitrust and Regulatory Alternatives*, *supra* note 11, at 174–75 (describing the creation of the ICC and its shared history with the Sherman Act).

In 1892, the U.S. Attorney accused eighteen competing railroads of colluding on rates and rules for their members under the auspices of the Trans-Missouri Freight Association.[22] The Association's agreements had been filed with the ICC, which was empowered to regulate certain business practices in rail. The U.S. Attorney looked through this veneer of regulatory filing to see the agreements for what they truly were – a Sherman Act section 1 violation.[23] It filed suit to dismantle the Association and end this price fixing.[24] The Supreme Court agreed with the government, interpreting the Sherman Act broadly to reinforce the importance of competition across all industries.[25] Although the ICC regulated the railroads, the agency did not require the collusive rail agreements at issue. Since this left no actual inconsistency between the rail regulation and antitrust law, the Supreme Court concluded that "both statutes may stand."[26] In the decades that followed, antitrust law continued to apply alongside rail regulation in several significant cases.[27]

11. This symbiosis between antitrust and regulation remained on display in major Supreme Court cases throughout the 1960s, such as *Otter Tail Power Co. v. United States*.[28] At the time of the *Otter Tail* case, the electric power industry was undergoing a massive technological and economic change from which there emerged a large array of new, independent power plants.[29] However, these new suppliers were stymied in their efforts to compete at the downstream retail level by monopolies or near-monopolies over the physical grids for power transmission.[30] Otter Tail, which held such a monopoly, was refusing to transmit power from alternative suppliers to municipalities that had terminated their agreements with Otter Tail, which had the effect of preventing these municipalities from using other power suppliers.[31] The DOJ alleged that Otter Tail was violating section 2 of the Sherman Act by refusing to either interconnect to supply power at wholesale or to transmit power on behalf of other wholesalers

---

22 United States v. Trans-Missouri Freight Ass'n, 166 U.S. 290 (1897).

23 *Id.*; 15 U.S.C. § 1.

24 *Trans-Missouri Freight Ass'n* 166 U.S. at 299.

25 *Id.* at 325 ("We see nothing, either in contemporaneous history, in the legal situation at the time of the passage of the [antitrust] statute, in its legislative history, or in any general difference in the nature or kind of these trading or manufact[ur]ing companies from railroad companies, which would lead us to the conclusion that it cannot be supposed the legislature, in prohibiting the making of contracts in restraint of trade, intended to include railroads within the purview of that act.")

26 *Id.* at 315.

27 First, *Antitrust and Regulatory Alternatives*, *supra* note 11, at 175 (noting the significant Northern Securities Co. v. United States, 193 U.S. 197 (1904) and United States v. Terminal Railroad Ass'n, 224 U.S. 383 (1912) cases applying antitrust law to railway companies).

28 410 U.S. 366 (1973).

29 First, *Antitrust and Regulatory Alternatives*, *supra* note 11, at 176.

30 *Id.*

31 *Otter Tail Power Co.*, 410 U.S. at 370–77.

so the towns could use a different supplier.³² It argued that Otter Tail's refusals to deal were an attempted or actual abuse of monopoly power that foreclosed competitor entry into retail power markets.³³

12. Otter Tail countered that its transmission business was regulated under the Federal Power Act, and thus its refusals to deal were shielded from antitrust scrutiny.³⁴ The Supreme Court majority pointedly disagreed. The Court encouraged the broad application of antitrust law even in regulated industries, invoking *U.S. v. Philadelphia National Bank* for the proposition that "[r]epeals of the antitrust laws by implication from a regulatory statute are strongly disfavored, and have only been found in cases of plain repugnancy between the antitrust and regulatory provisions."³⁵ Since there was no actual conflict between the antitrust remedial order – which required Otter Tail to interconnect or transmit power – and the regulator's similar power to order interconnection, there was no implied antitrust immunity arising from the regulatory scheme.³⁶ Antitrust law applied in full force. The Court dismissed Otter Tail's concern over potential future conflicts between the Federal Power Commission's rulings – which might, in theory, deny interconnection at the same time antitrust required it – leaving such conflict for "as, if and when" an actual case or controversy occurred.³⁷ The Supreme Court concluded that Otter Tail violated antitrust law by using its dominance in transmission to foreclose competitive entry into retail power markets.³⁸

13. This longstanding duality in antitrust and regulation, as emphasized in Harry's work, can be upset by various forces that threaten the functioning of this hybrid U.S. system. This essay examines several of these factors: judicial intervention to limit antitrust in regulated industries, deregulatory cycles, and the allocation of institutional power to enforce competition laws.

14. Over the last 15 years or so, judicial decisions have begun to shrink the shared ground between antitrust and regulation. The Supreme Court has increasingly cast antitrust as unnecessary where regulation exists, at least in certain industries.³⁹ In *Verizon Communications Inc. v. Law Offices of*

---

32 *Id.* at 368.

33 *Id.*

34 *Id.* at 372.

35 *Id.* (citing United States v. Philadelphia Nat'l Bank, 374 U.S. 321, 350–51 (1963)).

36 *Id.* Nor was there a conflict in the other terms of the antitrust remedy that ordered Otter Tail to transmit power from other wholesalers to the municipalities (called "wheeling"), and distinguishing from interconnection involving wholesale from Otter Tail itself, because the Federal Power Commission held no power to order wheeling, only interconnection. *Otter Tail*, 410 U.S. at 376–77 (noting lack of Commission authority under the Federal Power Act to order wheeling, as distinguished from its power to order interconnection under the same Act).

37 *Id.* at 377.

38 *Id.*

39 *See, e.g.*, Credit Suisse Securities (USA) LLC v. Billing, 551 U.S. 264 (2007), *see also* Stacey Chubbuck, *The US Supreme Court Finds Implied Antitrust Immunity in Regulated Securities Industry Related Claims (Credit Suisse Securities / Billing)*, E-COMPETITIONS June 2007, art. no. 44418; Verizon Communications Inc. v. Law

Curtis V. Trinko, the Court considered the defendant's refusal to deal with competitors, and declined to extend antitrust liability for such refusals into the highly regulated area of telecommunications.[40] Even though the Telecommunications Act of 1996 contains an antitrust saving clause that states nothing in the Act modifies or supersedes the application of antitrust law, the Court found this provision served only to preserve existing antitrust liability.[41] It did not speak to the wisdom of expanding antitrust liability into new areas of telecommunications regulation, the issue before the Court. The Court concluded that "[w]hen there exists a regulatory structure designed to deter and remedy anticompetitive harm, the additional benefit to competition provided by antitrust enforcement will tend to be small, and it will be less plausible that the antitrust laws contemplate such additional scrutiny."[42]

15. A few years later, the Court continued this trend in *Credit Suisse Securities (USA) LLC v. Billing*. Instead of requiring an actual conflict with the regulation for antitrust immunity, as in *Otter Tail*, the Court in *Credit Suisse* demanded only the risk that antitrust law might clash with the regulatory regime, finding such a risk adequate to block antitrust scrutiny of regulated conduct in securities regulation.[43] This lightened the judicial requirement to find implied antitrust immunity, at least where the regulatory statute is silent on the congressional intention to overlap with antitrust law. The Court's views in *Trinko* and *Credit Suisse* created new room, willingness and potential to push antitrust out of regulated spaces.[44]

16. This more recent view – that antitrust may be superfluous in regulated spaces – is a risky one. It creates the potential for unintended gaps in which neither antitrust nor regulation polices anticompetitive conduct. Such gaps can arise in a number of ways. Scholar Howard Shelanski observes a particular instance of this during economic cycles of deregulation, which he argues are prone to creating voids in competition policy.[45] When Congress repeals industry-specific competition regulation,

---

Offices of Curtis V. Trinko, LLP, 540 U.S. 398 (2004), *see also* Veronica Kayne, William J. Kolasky, Doug Melamed, Thomas Mueller, Ali Stoeppelwerth, Leon B. Greenfield, Robert B. Bell & James W. Lowe, *The US Supreme Court limits the antitrust liability in the telecommunications sector, affecting a competitor's access to a rival's network (*Verizon / Trinko*)*, E-COMPETITIONS Jan. 2004, art. no. 120421.

40   *Trinko*, 540 U.S. 398.

41   *Id.* at 399 ("nothing in this Act... shall be construed to modify, impair, or supersede the applicability of any of the antitrust laws" (quoting The Telecommunications Act of 1996, 47 U.S.C. § 152)).

42   *Id.* (declining to extend antitrust liability to conduct already regulated by telecommunications law).

43   *Credit Suisse*, 551 U.S. at 282-83 (finding the SEC needed to be able to make securities regulatory judgments free from the disruption of conflicting judgments that might be voiced by courts exercising jurisdiction under the antitrust laws and declining to apply antitrust scrutiny to conduct already regulated by securities law).

44   At least in telecommunications and securities law, *see* Samuel N. Weinstein, *Financial Regulation in the (Receding) Shadow of Antitrust*, 91 TEMP. L. REV. 447, 466–67 (2019) (finding claims of antitrust immunity based on *Credit Suisse* have not often been successful in areas of regulation beyond securities).

45   Howard Shelanski, *Antitrust and Deregulation*, 127 YALE L.J. 1922 (2018).

he contends that hurdles to antitrust law re-entering those deregulated spaces continue to persist.[46] This includes the judicial doctrine created by *Trinko* and *Credit Suisse*, which limits the application of antitrust law in certain regulated industries.[47] As a common law construct, these limits on antitrust are slow to change, even as the regulation they rely upon is repealed. To avoid such dynamically arising gaps, Shelanski calls for stronger antitrust enforcement during periods of regulatory repeal or scaling back, to enable antitrust law to serve as a backstop against anticompetitive conduct in newly deregulated industries.[48]

17. In a recent article, I argue that unintended gaps in competition oversight can arise not only from such changes in the substantive law, but also from the institutional design of enforcement powers.[49] Beyond the usual antitrust enforcers (the DOJ and the Federal Trade Commission (FTC)), there are several other federal regulatory agencies that hold significant statutory powers to ensure competition. A recent executive order from the Biden administration lists thirteen agencies or executive departments that administer "industry-specific fair competition and anti-monopolization laws" beyond general antitrust law.[50] For example, the Federal Maritime Commission (FMC), a federal agency that regulates ocean-borne transportation between the U.S. and foreign countries,[51] holds significant statutory powers over competition. The Shipping Act requires that ocean carriers file many types of agreements with the FMC, including agreements among carriers on prices, allocation of markets, shipping volumes, information and facilities sharing, "exclusive, preferential or cooperative" arrangements, and other agreements to "control, regulate, or prevent competition in international ocean transportation."[52] As antitrust readers will note, such agreements among competitors have great potential to limit competition, and would ordinarily be subject to close

---

46   *Id.* at 1944–55.

47   *Id.* at 1943–44.

48   *Id.*

49   Erika M. Douglas, *Antitrust Abandonment*, 42 Yale J. On Reg. 1 (2025).

50   Promoting Competition in America's Economy, Exec. Order No. 14,036, 86 Fed. Reg. 36987 (July 9, 2021), §§ 2(c), (e) (in addition to the Federal Trade Commission, identifying agencies that administer "similar authorities" related to competition as the Department of the Treasury, the Department of Agriculture, the Department of Health and Human Services, the Department of Transportation, the Federal Reserve System, the Securities and Exchange Commission, the Federal Deposit Insurance Corporation, the Federal Communications Commission, the Federal Maritime Commission, the Commodity Futures Trading Commission, the Federal Energy Regulatory Commission, the Consumer Financial Protection Bureau, and the Surface Transportation Board).

51   Power under the Shipping Act was initially granted to the FMC's precursor agency, the Shipping Board within the Department of Commerce. The Shipping Board later became the redundantly named Shipping Board Bureau, then the U.S. Maritime Commission, the Federal Maritime Board and, eventually, the Federal Maritime Commission. Edward Mansfield, *The Federal Maritime Commission*, in The Politics of Regulation 69 (James Q. Wilson ed., 1984).

52   46 U.S.C. §§ 40301–40303 (requiring that all agreements by or among ocean common carriers and/or marine terminal operators for the specified activities be filed with the Commission, including agreements to fix rates or conditions of service; pooling cargo revenue; allocating ports or sailings; limiting the volume or character of cargo or passengers to be carried; engaging in exclusive or preferential arrangements; or controlling or preventing competition).

antitrust scrutiny. Instead, the Shipping Act exempts these agreements from general antitrust law once they are filed with the FMC.[53]

18. This exclusion of general antitrust law leaves the FMC as the only agency with the power to police anticompetitive conduct related to ocean carrier agreements. In a quasi-substitute for general antitrust law, the Shipping Act grants the FMC the exclusive power to challenge certain agreements among ocean shippers that are "likely, by a reduction in competition," to result in either "an unreasonable reduction in transportation service" or "an unreasonable increase in transportation cost."[54]

19. The problem is that the FMC never uses this statutory power. It has held the power to challenge anticompetitive agreements under the modern Shipping Act for almost 40 years, yet has never once brought a case against the powerful ocean shipping carriers that dominate shipping markets.[55] These industry-specific antitrust enforcement powers go unused. Meanwhile, general antitrust law and its enforcers are barred from intervening by the Shipping Act statutory exemption.

20. This inaction is hard to explain away, as ocean shipping bears several hallmarks of an industry that merits antitrust scrutiny. During the period of the FMC's non-enforcement, the shipping industry has seen dramatic consolidation, and it is now more concentrated than ever. Sixteen of the top 20 global shipping carriers have combined into just three alliances,[56] down from approximately 360 conferences around the world in the early 1970s, and four alliances as recently as 2016.[57] The combined market share of these alliances is approximately 96% of transpacific export shipments, and almost 88% of imports.[58] Contrast this with the period from 1996 to 2011, when the leading three alliances operated only about 30% of global container shipping.[59] To be fair, concentration in shipping is not itself an antitrust law violation, and it has also been driven by legal, technological, and economic changes in the industry. Still, the recent concentration

---

53 46 U.S.C.A. § 40302(a) (setting out the filing requirement and statutory exceptions). Operation under a listed agreement that is *not* filed with the FMC is itself a violation of the Shipping Act.

54 46 U.S.C.A. § 41307(b)(1). This section also provides for the FMC to challenge agreements that "substantially lessen competition" in the purchasing of covered services, which is defined to involve port services. *Id.*; 46 U.S.C.A. § 40102 ("covered services"). The FMC also has the supporting powers to investigate and hold hearings regarding any potential violations of section 41307, as well as to issue certain reparations. 46 U.S.C.A. §§ 41302–41305 (empowering the FMC to investigate potential violations of the Act of its own volition, to hold hearings and to require reparations).

55 Douglas, *supra* note 50 at 20-23.

56 Letter from Renata B. Hesse, Acting Assistant Att'y Gen., Dept. of Just. Antitrust Div., to Sec'y, Fed. Maritime Comm'n 2 (Sep. 19, 2016).

57 Chris Sagers, *The Demise of Regulation in Ocean Shipping: A Study in the Evolution of Competition Policy and the Predictive Power of Microeconomics*, 39 Vand. J. Transnat'l L. 779, 790 n.41 (2006).

58 Fed. Mar. Comm'n, 61st Annual Report for Fiscal Year 2022 21 (2023) (noting the three global alliances of shipping carriers have a combined market share of 87.6% in the transpacific import trade and approximately 96% of the transpacific export trade).

59 White House Fact Sheet, Lowering Prices and Leveling the Playing Field in Ocean Shipping (Feb. 28, 2022).

levels in ocean shipping are high enough to be presumed likely to risk substantially lessening competition in antitrust law.[60] For years, antitrust enforcers have expressed concern over anticompetitive conduct in ocean shipping, with open criticism from the DOJ of the FMC's "monitoring and reporting" approach as inadequate to ensure competition among carriers.[61]

21. The FMC is not alone in this "antitrust abandonment" of its statutory powers to police competition.[62] Several other federal regulators hold antitrust-like powers that lie fallow, unused, or nearly so, for decades or more in concentrated industries where competition oversight seems appropriate. The Surface Transportation Board (STB), an independent federal transportation agency and successor to the ICC,[63] holds an array of powers to stop anticompetitive conduct in regulated rail. This includes powers to grant mandatory rail track access to competitors,[64] and the power to prevent dominant firms from charging unreasonable rates for rail carriage,[65] among others. The STB has never issued an order mandating such rail access.[66] It has stymied the review of unreasonable rates charged by dominant railways by making the process so onerous and expensive that it goes largely unused.[67]

22. The U.S. Department of Agriculture (USDA), too, holds significant statutory powers to fight anticompetitive acts in the meatpacking industries pursuant to the Packers and Stockyards Act.[68] The USDA's powers

---

60 Letter from Renata B. Hesse, *supra* note 57; U.S. Dep't of Just. & Fed. Trade Comm'n, Merger Guidelines § 2.1 (Dec. 18, 2023) (discussing presumptions of substantial lessening of competition based on industry concentration).

61 Letter from Renata B. Hesse, *supra* note 57, at 7 ("Monitoring and periodic reporting requirements, such as those the FMC has required of shipping alliances in the past, are insufficient to preserve competition in the container shipping market.").

62 Douglas, *supra* note 50 at 5 (identifying and labelling the problem of "antitrust abandonment" as a pattern of long-term, unexplained disuse by industry regulators of their antitrust-like enforcement powers).

63 Prior to the STB's creation, the ICC held many similar powers over rail regulation. The Interstate Commerce Commission Termination Act of 1995, Pub. L. No. 104-88, 109 Stat. 803 (eliminating the ICC and creating the STB in its stead). Am. Bar Ass'n, Sec. of Antitrust Law, *supra* note 19, at 193 (noting federal oversight of rail by the ICC since 1887 (citing Interstate Commerce Act, ch. 104, 24 Stat. 379 (1887)).

64 49 U.S.C. § 11102(c) ("The [STB] may require rail carriers to enter into reciprocal switching agreements, where it finds such agreements to be practicable and in the public interest, or where such agreements are necessary to provide competitive rail service."). When subject to an order for "reciprocal switching," the host railway must transport the rail cars of another company, such as a competitor, over its tracks up to an interchange point with that competitor's railway.

65 49 U.S.C. §§ 10701, 10704, 10707.

66 Douglas, *supra* note 50 at 37-38 (finding that, in the history of the STB as an agency, these antitrust-like powers have rarely or, in some cases, never been used).

67 *Id.*

68 Packers and Stockyards Act of 1921, Pub. L. No. 67-51, 42 Stat. 159, § 202(c)-(e) (enumerating various unlawful practices with respect to "livestock, meats, meat food products, or livestock products in unmanufactured form, or for any live poultry dealer with respect to live poultry"); *id.* § 202(f) (prohibiting conspiracies to divide territories, apportion sales, or fix prices) and 202(g) (prohibiting conspiracies to engage in the conduct prohibited in section 202(a)–(e)). While this discussion focuses on the subsections of section 202 that expressly relate to competition, it is worth noting that this provision contains other subsections that do not require competitive effects on their face, and so read more in consumer protection than antitrust law. *See* Packers & Stockyards Act §§ 202(a) and (b) (prohibiting unfair, deceptive practice and "undue or

were modeled on antecedent antitrust laws,[69] and feature similar prohibitions on "restraining commerce" or "creating a monopoly,"[70] as well as conspiracies, combinations or agreements to engage in such acts.[71] As written, these provisions in the Packers and Stockyards Act's have the potential to reach even more anticompetitive conduct than general antitrust law.[72] However, the USDA rarely brings antitrust complaints.[73]

23. Each of these antitrust-like provisions exists on paper, but is marked by a history of disuse by the FMC, STB and USDA. In these instances of "antitrust abandonment," the primary problem is not the law as written, nor its interpretation by the judiciary.[74] The issue is that regulators do not use their significant competition powers. This can create unintended gaps in antitrust oversight, particularly in areas of industry where statutory exceptions bar general antitrust law from applying to regulated conduct. The DOJ and FTC, whose mandates are to pursue competitive markets, are statutorily barred from acting, while the regulators that have the power to act do not use it to ensure competition. Neither antitrust law nor regulation ends up being applied in economically important, concentrated areas of these industries.

24. This pattern of antitrust abandonment by industry regulators is but one of the issues that can arise when antitrust law is pushed out of regulated spaces. Antitrust abandonment, much like the eras of deregulation observed by Shelanski or judicial interpretations that push antitrust out of regulated industries as in *Credit Suisse* and *Trinko*, creates a problematic space in which neither antitrust law nor regulation acts to ensure

---

unreasonable preference or advantage[s]"). The USDA has often taken the position these provisions do not require anticompetitive effects for a violation, though courts have reached differing conclusions on whether such effects are required for these subsections. *See* Fair and Competitive Livestock and Poultry Markets, 89 Fed. Reg. 53886 (proposed June 28, 2024) (to be codified at 9 C.F.R. 201) (taking the position that competitive effects need not be proven for a section 202(a) violation, but acknowledging that some courts have required proof of harm to competition for section 202(a) violations, while others have expressly rejected such a requirement).

69 Jackson v. Swift Eckrich, Inc., 53 F.3d 1452, 1460 (8th Cir. 1995) ("PSA has its origins in antecedent antitrust legislation and primarily prevents conduct which injures competition . . . .").

70 Packers and Stockyards Act § 202(c)-(e) (enumerating various unlawful practices with respect to "livestock, meats, meat food products, or livestock products in unmanufactured form, or for any live poultry dealer with respect to live poultry").

71 *Id.* § 202(f) (prohibiting conspiracies to divide territories, apportion sales, or fix prices) and 202(g) (prohibiting conspiracies to engage in the conduct prohibited in section 202(a)-(e)).

72 Swift Co. v. United States, 308 F.2d 849, 853 (7th Cir. 1962) ("The legislative history showed Congress understood the sections of the Packers and Stockyards Act under consideration were broader in scope than antecedent legislation such as the Sherman Antitrust Act, sec. 2 of the Clayton Act, 15 U.S.C.A. § 13, sec. 5 of the Federal Trade Commission Act, 15 U.S.C.A. § 45 and sec. 3 of the Interstate Commerce Act, 49 U.S.C.A. § 3.").

73 Douglas, *supra* note 50 at 47-52 (finding minimal enforcement of section 202(c)-(g) from the 1930s through 1957, occasional enforcement thereafter, and no claims in recent years, with the caveat of some transparency issues with the USDA's enforcement record). These USDA powers are distinguishable from those of the FMC and the STB in that the Attorney General shares certain enforcement power under the Packers and Stockyards Act. For beef packers or swine contractors, the USDA can either bring the case itself through an administrative pathway, or refer cases to the Attorney General. Packers and Stockyards Act § 404.

74 Douglas, *supra* note 50 at 56-59 (defining "antitrust abandonment").

competition. Each of these forces upsets the hybrid system of regulation and antitrust law long emphasized in Harry's work.

25. This abandonment by regulators of their antitrust enforcement powers also tends to undermine assumptions made in *Credit Suisse* and *Trinko* about the interface between regulation and antitrust law. Both cases rely on the premise that industry regulators will carry out their competition functions, which, in turn, is thought to make antitrust extraneous and perhaps even harmful to apply within the ambit of regulatory oversight. Put differently, the reasoning in these cases strongly implies that only antitrust *or* regulation is necessary to achieve competition, because whomever the sole enforcer is, they will act to ensure competitive markets.[75] The history above of antitrust abandonment by industry regulators, though, suggests that such assumptions about enforcement are often not true. Agencies in regulated rail, ocean shipping and meat packing are *not* carrying out their competition enforcement functions. Policymakers and courts should not assume that regulation necessarily eliminates the need for antitrust oversight.

26. Finally, when regulators disregard or underemphasize their responsibilities for competition this way, it can create cross-institutional tensions. Such antitrust abandonment has, at times, driven the DOJ into the adversarial and somewhat awkward position of fighting other regulatory agencies to ensure competition, much like the agency took against the ICC in *AI Drive-away* where this essay began. For example, during the late 1970s, the DOJ was the primary author of "protest filings," through which third parties could force the FMC to hold hearings on potentially anticompetitive agreements among ocean carriers, which the FMC was otherwise refusing to do.[76] The head of the FMC complained that "[t]he Justice Department has taken upon itself to protest every agreement that's filed... [and] would like to see us abolished."[77]

27. The DOJ also vociferously opposed the Surface Transportation Board on rail mergers throughout much of the 1990s.[78] When the STB approved the merger of the Union Pacific and Southern Pacific railways in 1996,[79] the DOJ publicly called it "the most anticompetitive rail merger ever

---

75 Shelanski, *supra* note 45, at 1943 (*Credit Suisse* and *Trinko* "render antitrust and regulation more like substitutes and less like complements").

76 Mansfield, *supra* note 52, at 60 (observing a 1977 DOJ estimate of "fourteen or fifteen" protests and a total of 28 docketed agreements for the year).

77 *Id.* at 61.

78 Salvatore Massa, *Are All Railroad Mergers in the Public Interest? An Analysis of the Union Pacific Merger with Southern Pacific*, 24 Transp. L.J. 413, 441-42 (1997) (observing the STB's disregard for DOJ opposition to mergers during the 1990s). The STB's passivity on rail merger enforcement has led to calls for the DOJ to take over its merger review powers. *See, e.g.*, Transp. Rsch. Bd., Special Report 318: Modernizing Rail Regulation 204 (2015) (recommending that the power to approve rail mergers be transferred to the DOJ).

79 Surface Transportation Board, Union Pacific/Southern Pacific Merger, 1 S.T.B. 233 (1996).

proposed."[80] The deal was one of the largest horizontal rail mergers ever proposed, and sought to combine companies with extensive parallel rail tracks in several geographic areas, against the backdrop of an already-concentrated industry that was unlikely to be subject to new entry.[81] Much like Harry's argument in *AI Drive-away*, the DOJ claimed that the merger failed to meet the public interest standard that the STB was statutorily required to apply because the deal was likely to have significant, anticompetitive effects in rail transportation.[82] The DOJ doubted the merging parties' failing-firm style justifications, and criticized the STB's conditions on the merger (such as "trackage" rights for competing firms to run trains) as inadequate to preserve competition.[83] The STB still approved the merger, despite being required by Congress to give "substantial weight to any recommendations of the Attorney General."[84] A few years later, though, the STB began to concede it was "seriously concerned" about the competitive consequences of the previously approved mergers and the effects of industry consolidation.[85] Perhaps too little too late, the STB imposed a moratorium in 2001 that barred any further railroad consolidation.[86]

28. This discussion of staid industries like shipping and rail may seem, like the *AI Drive-away* case, historical artifacts. The truth is that Harry's work on regulation and antitrust could not be more relevant today. His insights on antitrust and regulation apply to the newest of industries as much as the old. One of the most pressing debates in U.S. policy today asks whether and how to regulate digital competition.[87] Should the U.S. enact a new competition regulatory regime in digital markets?

---

80   Anne K. Bingaman, Assistant Att'y Gen., Antitrust Div., DOJ, Testimony Before the STB (July 1, 1996) 2 (observing that the approval will "result in a monopoly in many markets and a rail duopoly throughout the West – forever.").

81   *Id.*

82   *Id.*

83   1 S.T.B. at 350 (summarizing the DOJ's submissions).

84   49 U.S.C. § 11324(d); Massa, *supra* note 80, at 441–42 (observing the STB's disregard for DOJ opposition to mergers during the 1990s).

85   Pub. Views on Major Rail Consolidations, 4 S.T.B. 560 (2000) ("We at the Board, like members of the shipping public, are seriously concerned about the competitive consequences of this level of industry restructuring . . . .").

86   The moratorium was initially temporary, then permanent. *See* Major Rail Consolidation Procedures, 66 Fed. Reg. 32582 (June 15, 2001), https://www.federalregister.gov/documents/2001/06/15/01-14984/major-rail-consolidation-procedures. The moratorium was upheld in W. Coal Traffic League v. Surface Transp. Bd., 216 F.3d 1168 (D.C. Cir. 2000).

87   William E. Kovacic, *Adaptable Platforms for Platform Regulation: The Role of the Federal Trade Commission*, 7 J. L. & INNOVATION 106, 107-110 (2024) (observing the debate over regulatory intervention to address competition issues involving information services platforms, and the range of policy tools that could be used, including "the remedial powers contained in the United Kingdom's markets investigation regime, the adoption of prescriptive trade regulation rules, and the establishment of new "*ex ante*" regulatory mechanisms, such as the European Union's Digital Markets Act")

If so, which agencies should enforce those new laws?[88] The European Union recently passed sweeping, new digital regulation of large technology platforms,[89] putting an even finer point on these monumental questions for the U.S. Several recent legislative proposals would create special rules for digital competition,[90] and the newest presidential administration in 2025 is likely to see a continued emphasis on digital. This digital regulatory debate is intertwined with antitrust law because, in the absence of such regulation, antitrust enforcers are playing a prominent role in pushing for digital competition, bringing major litigation against Google,[91] Meta,[92] Apple,[93] and Amazon.[94]

29. As Harry points out in a recent article, these dilemmas of competition in digital markets are "remarkably familiar."[95] Networks with a tendency toward monopoly have long been the subject of both regulatory oversight and antitrust concern, as the above legal history of mature industries demonstrates. This echoes in the modern European experience regulating digital markets, which suggests that antitrust litigation battles can only do so much to rein in the power of large technology companies. After major antitrust cases against Google, Apple and other technology giants, the EU has come around to the need for additional digital regulation, and strong privacy laws to work alongside antitrust in ensuring digital competition.

30. The best answers on digital regimes come in the form of dual systems that lean on regulation and antitrust, understanding the strengths and weaknesses of each. Antitrust is a valuable legal tool, but it has limits. While antitrust is skilled at combatting monopoly power and highlighting harm from specific practices or market structures,[96] it is less suited

---

88   This debate has led to an array of digital regulatory bills, most notably the American Innovation and Choice Online Act (Klobuchar), S. 2992, 117th Cong. (2021–2022) (seeking to improve digital competition by prohibiting covered platforms from materially restricting interoperability with rivals); Augmenting Compatibility and Competition by Enabling Service Switching (ACCESS) Act, H.R. 3849, 117th Cong. (2021–2022) (mandating interoperability with large social media services to promote competition); Open App Markets Act, S. 2710, 117th Cong. (2021–2022) (requiring that covered companies allow interoperability with competing apps and app stores).

89   Regulation (EU) 2022/1925 on Contestable and Fair Markets in the Digital Sector and Amending Directives (EU) 2019/1937 and (EU) 2020/1828, 2022 O.J. (L 265) 1 (the "EU Digital Markets Act"); Regulation (EU) 2022/2065 on a Single Market for Digital Services and Amending Directive 2000/31/EC, 2022 O.J. (L 277) 1 (the "EU Digital Services Act").

90   *See, e.g.*, Digital Platform Commission Act of 2022, S. 4201, 117th Cong. §§ 4(b), 5(b) (2021–2022) (emphasizing competition in the purposes of the new digital regulator; empowering the regulator to create rules on interoperability); American Choice and Innovation Online Act, H.R. 3816, 117th Cong. § 4 (2021–2022) (prohibiting large digital platforms from restricting interoperability with competitors).

91   Complaint, United States et al. v. Google, LLC, No. 1:20-cv-03010 (D.D.C. Oct. 20, 2020).

92   Substitute Amended Complaint for Injunctive and Other Equitable Relief, Fed. Trade Comm'n. v. Meta Platforms, Inc. (previously known as Facebook), No. 1:20-cv-03590 (D.D.C. Sept. 8, 2021).

93   Complaint, United States of America v. Apple Inc., No. 2:24-cv-04055 (D.N.J. Mar. 21, 2024).

94   Complaint, Fed. Trade Comm'n. et al. v. Amazon.com, Inc., No. 2:23-cv-01495 (W.D. Wash. Nov. 2, 2023).

95   First, *Antitrust and Regulatory Alternatives, supra* note 11, at 177.

96   *Id.*

to ongoing, prescriptive supervision of corporate conduct. To overcome these limits, antitrust must work hand-in-hand with industry regulation, the latter being better suited to oversee mandated access and to address technical problems that require ongoing supervision.[97]

31. Harry understood these limits of antitrust law better than anyone, as a foremost authority on the *Microsoft* litigation in the U.S. and internationally. Settled in the early 2000s, the *U.S. v. Microsoft* litigation was the most significant monopoly case of its generation.[98] The DOJ and states won the war in proving that Microsoft had violated the Sherman Act, but the real battle lay in the design and implementation of remedies for this misconduct, which required innovative and quasi-regulatory approaches.[99]

32. This history, too, seems poised to repeat. The DOJ has just claimed a major victory in its case against Google for its anticompetitive search practices, *U.S. v. Google*.[100] The case was the first bet-the-farm government monopolization trial since the *U.S. v. Microsoft* liability-phase litigation ended in 2001. In August 2024, Judge Amit P. Mehta of the District Court of Columbia ruled that "Google is a monopolist," and its actions to maintain a monopoly in certain search and search advertising markets violated section 2 of the Sherman Act.[101] The Court and the DOJ now face the enormous task of determining a suitable remedy.[102]

33. The lessons that Andrew Gavil and Harry draw from the remedies in *Microsoft* remain apt advice for the *Google* remedies today.[103] After careful scrutiny of the remedies and their implementation in the U.S. and the EU Microsoft litigation, Gavil and First conclude that "antitrust's comparative advantage is in designing remedies with incentives for competition, not in predicting future events."[104] As an important corollary, they suggest conduct decrees should rely "less on commanding particular actions" and focus primarily on incentives for reaching remedial goals or results.[105] This is because the more complex the technical and business environment, the more challenging it often is for the government and

---

97 *Id.*

98 253 F.3d 34, 59 (D.C. Cir. 2001).

99 *See* GAVIL & FIRST, *supra* note 15, ch. 7, 259 (devoting a chapter to the "the challenge of remedy," and finding that while antitrust remedies can engage in regulatory-type interventions under certain conditions, governments and private parties in various jurisdictions "struggled with the challenges of remedying Microsoft's monopolizing conduct" in several ways); Harry First, *Netscape is Dead: Remedy Lessons from the Microsoft Litigation* (N.Y.U. L. & Econ. Rsch. Paper No. 08-49, 2008).

100 United States v. Google LLC, No. 1:20-cv-3010 (D.D.C. Aug. 5, 2024) (mem.).

101 *Id.* at 4 (summarizing the findings on monopolization). Google is appealing this finding.

102 *See* Plaintiff's Proposed Remedy Framework, United States v. Google LLC., No. 1:20-cv-3010 (D.D.C. Oct. 8, 2024).

103 GAVIL & FIRST, *supra* note 15.

104 *Id.* at 237.

105 *Id.*

the courts to dictate the actions necessary to achieve a desired remedial outcome. This was true for operating systems and browsers at the time of *Microsoft*, and it remains true today for the technologically complex online search and search advertising markets in *U.S. v. Google*.

34. Finally, Harry's writing speaks not only to these issues of substantive law in digital, but also to important yet overlooked matters of institutional design.[106] The effective selection and legislative empowerment of an enforcer or enforcers of digital regulation will have great bearing on the regulation's success (if such regulation should come to pass). While some legislative proposals would appoint the FTC as the most logical agency to enforce new digital rules, others seek to create a new digital regulator.[107] Harry emphasizes that "[i]f we are to make progress on a hybrid system [in digital regulation]… we will need to take on the task of institutional design. Congress either needs to create a new regulator or to settle the issues surrounding the FTC's powers and structure so that it can do the regulatory job."[108] Other leading scholars share his latter sentiment that Congress must act to clarify the FTC's powers if the agency is to address digital competition with any force.[109]

35. This view on institutional design for the digital era is reinforced by history recounted above. Whomever the regulator, antitrust law should continue to apply alongside any new digital regulation that comes to pass. Exemptions or exclusions from general antitrust law for regulated activity would recreate the risk of antitrust abandonment by industry regulators, leaving the potential for gaps if digital regulators fail to enforce antitrust-like provisions, as they have in the past for more staid industries. Judicial interpretations that shield regulated digital conduct from antitrust in the absence of a true conflict, as in *Credit Suisse*, would be a mistake to the extent they assume regulatory vigilance in competition enforcement. Such approaches remove the backstop antitrust supplies to competition regulation in digital markets and disintegrate the dual system that has so long characterized the U.S. approaches to ensuring competition. Instead, antitrust and regulation should be cast as overlapping

---

[106] Harry First, *Antitrust and Regulatory Alternatives*, *supra* note 11, at 178 (emphasizing the importance of institutional design to digital regulation, including the decision on whether to empower a new agency or clarify the FTC's power to act as a digital enforcer, and lamenting that "at the moment almost no one [in Congress] seems to be paying attention to either solution").

[107] *See, e.g.*, Digital Platform Commission Act of 2022, S. 4201, 117th Cong. (2021–2022); Digital Platform Commission Act of 2022, H.R. 7858, 117th Cong. (2021–2022) (creating a new digital regulatory agency). *But see* American Choice and Innovation Online Act, H.R. 3816, 117th Cong. § 4 (2021–2022) (proposing to establish a new bureau within the Federal Trade Commission (an existing federal agency) to regulate "digital markets," rather than a new agency); Kovacic, *Adaptable Platforms for Platform Regulation: The Role of the Federal Trade Commission supra* note 89, 130-33 (arguing that with the right legislative empowerment, the FTC could serve as the enforcer for new digital regulation).

[108] First, *Antitrust and Regulatory Alternatives*, *supra* note 11, at 177.

[109] Kovacic, *supra* note 89 (examining the FTC's suitability to serve as a digital regulator based on the history of the agency, and observing that if the FTC is to take on a regulatory role in digital, congressional action should empower the agency in specific ways related to the application of its powers and rulemaking).

complements, applying alongside each other at least until the point of plain repugnancy. Such overlap has characterized the European approach, where new digital regulations apply in conjunction with antitrust law.[110]

36. Harry's lifetime of insightful writing on antitrust and regulation has bestowed these insights for the ages on generations of policymakers, scholars, and students. His work vividly demonstrates the interrelationships between antitrust and regulation, portraying their nexus as variable, complex and dynamic, and at the same time longstanding, durable, and thoroughly necessary. At its heart, the U.S. system of competition policy and law relies on a duality in which both antitrust law and industry-specific regulation play essential roles. As the U.S. grapples with digital power and competition policy today, the best solutions will take heed of Harry's wisdom to focus on a hybrid approach both in substance and institutions. His views, shaped from the era of *AI Drive-away*, continue to resonate in modern law, as does the importance of obtaining a haircut before a big day in court.

---

110 Digital Markets Act, *supra* note 91, art. 1(6) (providing that the regulation is "without prejudice" to the application of the major provisions in EU competition law).

VI. Appendix A

```
Form DJ-96a                DEPARTMENT OF JUSTICE
(Rev. 6-22-66)                  ROUTING SLIP
```

TO:	NAME	DIVISION	BUILDING	ROOM
1.	Mr. First	AT	Main	3410
2.				
3.				
4.				

- [ ] SIGNATURE   - [ ] COMMENT   - [ ] PER CONVERSATION
- [ ] APPROVAL   - [ ] NECESSARY ACTION   - [ ] AS REQUESTED
- [ ] SEE ME   - [ ] NOTE AND RETURN   - [ ] NOTE AND FILE
- [ ] RECOMMENDATION   - [ ] CALL ME   - [ ] YOUR INFORMATION
- [ ] ANSWER OR ACKNOWLEDGE ON OR BEFORE _____
- [ ] PREPARE REPLY FOR THE SIGNATURE OF _____

REMARKS

Re: American International Driveaway v. U.S. & I.C.C., N.D. Calif., Civ. No. C-70-1591-WTS
Reviewer: Mr. Shapiro

This case is assigned to you for briefing and, on condition that you get a haircut before going into court, for argument.

FROM: NAME	BUILDING & ROOM	EXT.	DATE
Howard E. Shapiro	Main 3118	2413	9/17/70

PART III
The Statute Comes First

The FTC Act Section 5's Delegation Paradox

MARINA LAO[*]

Seton Hall University School of Law

Abstract

During the Biden administration, the FTC promulgated a "Noncompete Rule" categorically banning "noncompetes" as an unfair method of competition in violation of Section 5 of the FTC Act. This was preceded by its issuance of a new Section 5 Policy Statement embracing a reading of "unfair methods of competition" that reaches beyond the Sherman Act. Though this reading is consistent with congressional intent, it departs from the courts' usual construction of Section 5 as largely coextensive with the Sherman Act. The ultimate success of these bold initiatives, should they be continued under the new Trump administration, depends in part on their potential vulnerability to challenges based on the nondelegation doctrine and other related theories. This paper makes the case that Congress's directive to the FTC to prevent "unfair methods of competition" does not violate the nondelegation doctrine under the current intelligible principle test. The outcome, however, may well be different under the stricter doctrine proposed by Justice Gorsuch in his dissent in Gundy v. United States. The implications of finding a nondelegation violation are profound, and some who wish to severely limit agency discretion but avoid other monumental consequences may seek to minimize them by suggesting that the doctrine would somehow not affect federal courts' ability to "interpret" Section 5 in case-by-case decisions. This paper explains why such a theory is indefensible. Delegations to the federal judiciary raise similar

---

[*] Professor of Law, Seton Hall University School of Law. I am extremely grateful to Michael Coenen, Harry First, and Spencer Waller for their invaluable comments. I also thank Ben Cooper (Seton Hall Law 2026) for his excellent research assistance.

separation-of-power concerns as delegations to agencies, and thus the doctrine should apply equally to both. Moreover, even if it were possible to finesse the doctrine to favor delegations to the judiciary over agencies, that result would paradoxically raise more of the democratic concerns on which the nondelegation doctrine is grounded, since courts are less politically accountable than agencies. It would also be directly contrary to congressional intent in the case of the FTC Act.

I. Introduction and Background

1. The Biden administration had been clear from the start about its intention to pursue an ambitious antitrust agenda. One of its professed policy goals, expressed in the President's July 2021 executive order, was to reorient antitrust policy toward prioritizing worker welfare.[1] Whereas in the past, antitrust law focused mostly on cases where concentration or the suppression of competition adversely affected downstream product markets, antitrust enforcers also started targeting anticompetitive employer conduct and firm mergers (that tend to hurt workers by depressing wages, limiting worker mobility, inhibiting workers' economic freedom to switch jobs, or reducing competition in labor markets).[2] Demonstrations of harm to downstream markets or a reduction in the quantity of inputs purchased, often expected in traditional antitrust analysis but difficult to prove in these types of cases, were not demanded.[3]

2. The administration's antitrust leaders were in fact making progress on their promised policy agenda in this and other areas.[4] The agencies' newly revised Merger Guidelines, for example, in a departure from earlier guidelines, expressly included consideration of a proposed merger's likely impact on workers in the relevant labor markets.[5] Employer no-poach agreements were

---

1 Exec. Order 14036, 86 Fed. Reg. 36987, 36992 (July 9, 2021) (underscoring the importance of competition in labor markets and calling on the Federal Trade Commission (FTC) to "exercise the FTC's statutory rulemaking authority under the Federal Trade Commission Act to curtail the unfair use of non-compete clauses and other clauses or agreements that may unfairly limit worker mobility."). *See also* U.S. Dep't of Treasury, The State of Labor Market Competition (Mar. 2022) ("Treasury Report on Labor Market Competition") (summarizing the prevalence and impact of uncompetitive firm conduct in labor markets).

2 Treasury Report on Labor Market Competition, *supra* note 1 (describing the harms to workers from concentration and the weakening of competition).

3 *See* C. Scott Hemphill & Nancy L. Rose, *Mergers that Harm Sellers*, 127 Yale L.J. 2078, 2079 (2018) (making the case that harm to workers – in an input market – is an actionable harm without the need to show harm to downstream markets, or to show a reduction in the quantity of inputs (i.e., workers) transacted).

4 The agencies have adopted broader enforcement policies in other areas as well, including in the policing of the power of Big Tech. Recently, the Department of Justice (DOJ) Antitrust Division won its much-watched monopolization case against Google in federal district court. U.S. v. Google, 2024 WL 3647498 (finding that Google violated section 2 of the Sherman Act through anticompetitive exclusionary practices, resulting in foreclosure, in the market for general search services).

5 U.S. Dep't of Just. & Fed. Trade Comm'n, Merger Guidelines (Dec. 18, 2023), Guideline 10, https://www.justice.gov/d9/2023-12/2023%20Merger%20Guidelines.pdf. Under Guideline 10, in determining whether to challenge a proposed merger as anticompetitive, antitrust enforcers will now also examine "whether workers face a risk that the merger may substantially lessen competition for their labor." *Id.* at 26.

sometimes prosecuted criminally, rather than civilly (and rarely at that).[6] But the initiative that has drawn the most attention, and immediate legal challenge, was the Federal Trade Commission (FTC or "Commission")'s promulgation of a rule (the "Noncompete Rule") on May 7, 2024, categorically banning employers' use of noncompete agreements as "unfair methods of competition"[7] (with a few minor exceptions) under the first prong of section 5 of the Federal Trade Commission Act.[8] Noncompetes are contract terms imposed by employers on workers prohibiting them from working for competing firms after leaving the employer.[9]

3. Because a categorical ban effectively classifies noncompetes as per se section 5 violations, while the legal standard applied to most Sherman Act antitrust claims is the rule of reason, the FTC was evidently relying on a reading of "unfair methods of competition" under section 5[10] that is independent of, and broader than, the interpretation of the Sherman Act under prevailing antitrust doctrines. This deviates from the courts' usual construction of section 5, since the mid-1970s, as largely coextensive with the primary antitrust statutes,[11] the Sherman Act[12] and the Clayton Act.[13] (References hereafter to the Sherman Act in this paper will include the Clayton Act for convenience.) The agency paved the way for this step by

---

6   In late 2020, the DOJ Antitrust Division brought its first criminal no-poach case, followed in quick succession by several additional cases. U.S. v. Jindal, No. 4:20-cr-00358 (E.D. Tex. 2020) (jury acquittal, Apr. 2022); U.S. v. Surgical Care Affiliates LLC, No. 3:21-cr-00011-L (N.D. Tex. 2021) (voluntary dismissal of indictment, Nov. 2023); U.S. v. Hee, No. 2:21-cr-00098 (D. Nev. 2021) (plea agreement, Oct. 2022); U.S. v. DaVita, No. 1:21-cr-00229 (D. Colo. 2021) (jury acquittal, Apr. 2022); U.S. v. Manahe, No. 2:22-cr-00013 (D. Me. 2022) (jury acquittal, Mar. 2023); U.S. v. Lopez, No. 2:23-cr-00055 (D. Nev. 2023) (case pending). Though the DOJ has not yet won a conviction – it has secured one plea agreement – the agency has prevailed in pretrial proceedings, establishing that no-poach agreements that are effectively horizontal market allocations may be per se illegal, if proven. And Jonathan Kanter, head of the Antitrust Division, has stated that he is committed to staying the course and continuing to bring criminal no-poach cases. *See* Bryan Koenig, *DOJ Antitrust Head Calls No-Poach Prosecutions 'Righteous'*, Law360 (Mar. 31, 2023), https://www.law360.com/articles/1592488.

7   Fed. Trade Comm'n, Non-Compete Clause Rule, 89 Fed. Reg. 38342 (May 7, 2024) (to be codified at 16 C.F.R. pt. 910), https://www.govinfo.gov/content/pkg/FR-2024-05-07/pdf/2024-09171.pdf.

8   15 U.S.C. § 45(a)(1) ("Unfair methods of competition in or affecting commerce, and unfair or deceptive acts or practices in or affecting commerce, are hereby declared unlawful."). The second prong, prohibiting "unfair or deceptive acts or practices" (UDAP), implicates the consumer protection mandate of the FTC, not its competition mandate. This paper is confined to the FTC's mandate to prevent "unfair methods of competition" – the competition-protection prong – and does not discuss UDAP.

9   A Texas district court recently set aside the Noncompete Rule nationwide in a grant of summary judgment to plaintiffs in a case challenging the Rule. Ryan LLC v. Fed. Trade Comm'n, 2024 WL 3879954 (N.D. Tex.). *See* Anna Aryankalayil, Eileen M. Cole, Andrew Cook, Craig Falls, James McQuade, Amy Ray & Mike Delikat, *The US District Court for the Eastern District of Texas issues a preliminary injunction staying the effective date of the FTC's worker non-compete rule (*Ryan / FTC*)*, e-Competitions July 2024, art. no. 119003. However, it will be surprising if the issues are not ultimately addressed by an appellate court or the Supreme Court.

10   The original 1914 FTC Act did not include proscriptions against UDAP. That was added in the 1938 Wheeler-Lea amendments. Wheeler-Lea Act, Pub. L. No. 447, 52 Stat. 111 (1938). In this paper, all references to "section 5" are limited to "unfair methods of competition" – the FTC's competition mandate – and do not include UDAP under its consumer protection mission.

11   *See* William E. Kovacic & Marc Winerman, *Competition Policy and the Application of Section 5 of the Federal Trade Commission Act*, 76 Antitrust L.J. 929, 933-40 (2010).

12   15 U.S.C. §§ 1, 2.

13   15 U.S.C. § 18.

issuing a new Policy Statement Regarding the Scope of Unfair Methods of Competition Under Section 5 of the Federal Trade Commission Act[14] ("Section 5 Policy Statement") that explicitly embraced an understanding of the statute that reaches beyond the Sherman Act.[15] The issuance of this more expansive Section 5 Policy Statement suggests that the agency likely hoped to bring more "standalone" section 5 cases – that is, cases not premised on the Sherman Act – to target conduct (like noncompetes) that threatens the marketplace with harms to its market participants, including workers, but may fall short of a Sherman Act violation.[16]

4. The ultimate success of these efforts, should they be continued under the new FTC leadership, depends on many factors. But one that particularly stands out is the nondelegation doctrine, which sets constitutional limits on Congress's ability to confer policymaking authority on other branches of government.[17] In its current form, the "intelligible principle" test for this doctrine is undemanding and unlikely to impede more novel FTC initiatives.[18] However, if the current Supreme Court elevates the test or replaces it altogether with a formulation designed to severely "rein in" the so-called administrative state, as it has signaled it would,[19] the doctrine could greatly reduce what the FTC can hope to accomplish.[20]

---

14   Fed. Trade Comm'n, Policy Statement Regarding the Scope of Unfair Methods of Competition Under Section 5 of the Federal Trade Commission Act, Commission File No. P221202 (Nov. 10, 2022) ("Section 5 Policy Statement"), https://www.ftc.gov/system/files/ftc_gov/pdf/P221202Section5PolicyStatement.pdf.

15   *Id.* at 2 ("[T]he text, structure, and history of Section 5 reaches more broadly than the antitrust laws.").

16   The FTC has already taken a few steps in this direction. For example, in January 2023, the FTC announced consent settlements with three companies involving noncompete agreements brought as standalone section 5 cases. *In re* Prudential Security, Inc., File No. 221-0026 (Jan. 4, 2023), https://www.ftc.gov/system/files/ftc_gov/pdf/2210026prudentialsecuritycomplaint.pdf; *In re* O-I Glass, Inc., File No. 211-0182 (Jan. 4, 2023), https://www.ftc.gov/system/files/ftc_gov/pdf/21101820-iglasscomplaint.pdf; *In re* Ardagh Group S.A., File No. 211-0182 (Jan. 4, 2023), https://www.ftc.gov/system/files/ftc_gov/pdf/2110182ardaghcomplaint.pdf.

17   Another important factor is the so-called major questions doctrine. *See* West Virginia v. EPA, 142 S. Ct. 2587 (2022) (invoking the major questions doctrine to strike down the Environmental Protection Agency (EPA)'s assertion of authority to implement a certain regulatory policy, on the theory that it related to a "major question" and major questions required "clear congressional authorization," which was not shown). As transformed in *West Virginia*, especially by Justice Gorsuch's concurrence, the major questions doctrine could be construed indirectly what proponents of an aggressive nondelegation doctrine want to accomplish directly – substantially restricting Congress's authority to delegate policy decisionmaking authority to the Executive. *See* Michael Coenen, The Shaky Structural Foundations of the New Nondelegation Doctrine at 12–15 (draft on file with author). I do not examine the major questions doctrine here but have analyzed it in connection with the Noncompete Rule in another paper. *See* Marina Lao, *The Major Questions Doctrine, FTC Rulemaking, and Rulemaking on Non-Compete Clauses*, 11 J. ANTITRUST ENF'T 223 (2023), https://ssrn.com/abstract=4429124. For analysis of the major questions doctrine post-*West Virginia*, *see, e.g.*, Daniel T. Deacon & Leah M. Litman, *The New Major Questions Doctrine*, 109 VA. L. REV. 1009 (2023); Louis J. Capozzi III, *The Past and Future of the Major Questions Doctrine*, 84 OHIO ST. L.J. 191 (2023).

18   Except twice in 1935, courts have not struck down any statute as an unconstitutional delegation. The two exceptions are: Pan. Refin. Co. v. Ryan, 293 U.S. 388, 433 (1935), and A.L.A. Schechter Poultry Corp. v. U.S., 295 U.S. 495, 542 (1935).

19   *See* Gundy v. United States, 139 S. Ct. 2116, 2131–48 (2019) (Gorsuch, J., dissenting), *id.* at 2131 (Alito, J., concurring); *infra* Part II-3.

20   The Supreme Court's recent overturning of *Chevron*, in Loper Bright Enterprises, Inc. v. Raimondo, 144 S. Ct. 2244 (2024), however, should not have much impact on the FTC, because the agency has not historically relied on *Chevron* deference in the context of its competition mission. *See* Logan Breed, Chuck Loughlin & Ilana Kattan, *The US Supreme Court overturns* Chevron *deference doctrine removing the requirement that courts defer to agency interpretations of ambiguous statutes* (Loper Bright / Raimond), E-COMPETITIONS

5. This paper first examines the delegation risk and makes the case that a nondelegation challenge to section 5 should not succeed because the directive to the FTC to prevent "unfair methods of competition"[21] easily satisfies the intelligible principle test. Under an intelligible principle analysis, the focus should not be exclusively on the four words "unfair methods of competition," but should encompass the purpose of the legislation, its factual background, and the "statutory context."[22] Together, these factors should help supply the necessary congressional guidance, as discussed below. If the doctrine is subsequently transformed in the direction proposed by Justice Gorsuch in his *Gundy* dissent, then the outcome may be more uncertain.[23]

6. The potential implications of finding a nondelegation violation, however, are so profound that they should give pause to even a conservative Supreme Court intent on crushing agency authority. Because the doctrine is rooted in the Constitution, finding a violation would invalidate the offending statutory provision and remove the agency's ability to enforce it entirely. It could call into question the legitimacy of over a hundred years of relevant agency adjudications and Article III court decisions, and leave a vacuum in the field until Congress finds the political will to pass new legislation that the Court deems appropriately written.

7. One could claim that this dire result can be avoided on the theory that a violation of the doctrine would only preclude the *FTC* from relying on section 5 to determine which types of business practices are unfair methods of competition or how the determinations should be made. It would not preclude federal *courts* from essentially performing that function through "interpreting" section 5 in case-by-case decisions. But that argument is disingenuous. If Congress is deemed not to have provided sufficient guidance for the agency to apply a specific statutory provision, then it necessarily cannot have provided sufficient guidance for courts to interpret that same provision. The same reasoning would also apply under Justice Gorsuch's proposed new nondelegation doctrine imposing stricter limits. If it is considered policymaking (unconstitutional) – rather than "fill up the details" (constitutional) – when the FTC determines which practices are unfair methods of competition, then it should be equally unconstitutional when federal courts make that determination. So, unless courts are not part of the nondelegation equation, that argument does not seem coherent.

8. I argue that, despite the dearth of legal scholarship or case law on the issue, the nondelegation doctrine does apply to the judiciary as much

---

June 2024, art. no. 119498.

21   15 U.S.C. § 45(a).
22   Big Time Vapes, Inc. v. FDA, 963 F.3d 436, 443 (5th Cir. 2020).
23   *See infra* Part II-3.

as it does to the executive branch, including administrative agencies. The federal judiciary is one of the three branches of government, and there is no reason why the constitutional principles that underlie the nondelegation doctrine do not apply with equal force to it.

9. Also, given the fundamental value of democracy to our system of government, it is difficult to justify a default to judicial delegation – which is the effective outcome if the Court removes an agency's authority to give content to a statute on grounds of unconstitutional delegation and assumes the function itself under the guise of interpreting the law in deciding cases. If anything, delegation to agencies rather than to the judiciary is preferable in many respects. Agency administrators are more politically accountable than judges and also have more subject-matter expertise. Additionally, preferring judicial over agency delegation is particularly difficult to justify when Congress consciously intended for an agency, not the courts, to fill in the content of a legislative scheme within the parameters (however fuzzy) it set, as it did in section 5.

II. The FTC's Competition Mission and the Nondelegation Doctrine

10. Turning first to the general principles of the nondelegation doctrine and their application to the FTC's section 5 competition mandate: the relevant statutory text states that "unfair methods of competition" are unlawful,[24] and that the Commission is "empowered and directed to prevent" them.[25] Violation of the doctrine was one of the claims made by petitioners challenging the Noncompete Rule.[26] The argument was that "[u]nder the statutory language at issue here, there is no intelligible principle to direct the Commission's determination of what constitutes an unfair method of competition, and when and what sort of regulation is appropriate in response."[27]

11. On August 20, 2024, a Texas district court, in *Ryan v. FTC*, set aside the Noncompete Rule nationwide, holding that the agency lacks substantive competition rulemaking authority and that, even if such authority exists,

---

24   15 U.S.C. § 45(a)(1).

25   15 U.S.C. § 45(a)(2).

26   The main claim asserts that section 6(g) of the FTC Act, which grants the FTC rulemaking authority, only covers procedural rules, not substantive competition rules. *See, e.g.*, Complaint at 15–17 (Count One), Ryan LLC v. Fed. Trade Comm'n (*"Ryan* Complaint"), No. 3:24-cv-00986 (N.D. Tex. 2024); Complaint at 32–36, Chamber of Comm. v. Fed. Trade Comm'n (*"Chamber of Commerce* Complaint"), No. 6:24-cv-00148 (E.D. Tex. 2024). I have argued elsewhere that section 6(g) should be interpreted to grant the FTC authority to promulgate not only procedural rules, but also substantive competition rules, and will not repeat those arguments here. *See* Lao, *supra* note 17. For a recent collection of writings on the subject, *see* RULEMAKING AUTHORITY OF THE US FEDERAL TRADE COMMISSION (Daniel A. Crane ed. 2022).

27   *Ryan* Complaint ¶ 7; *see also Chamber of Commerce* Complaint ¶¶ 20, 100.

the Rule was arbitrary and capricious;[28] the decision did not address the plaintiffs' alternative claim that the statute itself is unconstitutional under the nondelegation doctrine. The FTC has appealed the ruling to the Fifth Circuit Court of Appeals.[29] While we do not know whether the nondelegation issue, or indeed the case, will eventually reach the Supreme Court (and whether the Court would address the issue if it did), the doctrine will almost certainly continue to be litigated if the FTC plans to bring the types of cases that it had not historically brought, based on distinctive section 5 principles. Five of the Justices currently serving on the Supreme Court have in recent years criticized the current nondelegation test and signaled their intention to reform it to sharply limit agencies' policymaking powers.[30] This will likely encourage more nondelegation challenges, and the Court's eventual revisit of the doctrine.

12. In the context of section 5, the unconstitutional delegation argument is generally that the statutory phrase "unfair methods of competition" is too open-ended and subjective, and thus lacks an intelligible principle to guide the Commission in its determination of what constitutes an unfair method of competition.[31] I disagree with this view. Analysis of a nondelegation claim should be informed not only by the statutory text, but also by the statute's purpose, the circumstances that led to its enactment, and other context.[32] In the case of section 5, these considerations should all add up to sufficient congressional guidance to the FTC.

1. The Nondelegation Doctrine's General Principles

13. Article I of the U.S. Constitution vests all legislative powers in Congress[33] – powers that Congress may not delegate to any other branch

---

28 Ryan LLC v. Fed. Trade Comm'n, 2024 WL 3879954 (N.D. Tex. 2024). The order granting summary judgment did not address the plaintiffs' nondelegation claim.

29 The FTC's opening brief was filed on January 2, 2025. *See* Ryan LLC v. Fed. Trade Comm'n, 2025 WL 50577 (5th Cir.). It should be noted that a district court in Pennsylvania considered a similar challenge in another case and declined to enjoin the Noncompete Rule in July 2024, holding that the plaintiff was unlikely to succeed on any of its claims, including the nondelegation claim. ATS Servs. LLC v. Fed. Trade Comm'n, 2024 WL 3511630, at *18–19 (E.D. Pa. 2024). Unsurprisingly, given the Texas district court's ruling setting aside the Rule nationwide in *Ryan*, the plaintiff in *ATS Tree Servs.* voluntarily dismissed the action on October 4, 2024.

30 *See Gundy*, 139 S. Ct. at 2131 (Alito, J. concurring) (concurring with decision but would support reconsidering the doctrine); *id.* at 2131–48 (Gorsuch, J., dissenting) (joined by Roberts and Thomas) (severely criticizing the intelligible principle test). Justice Kavanaugh, who did not participate in *Gundy*, also called for replacing the intelligible principle test in an individual statement he issued shortly after *Gundy* in a denial of certiorari in Paul v. United States, 140 S. Ct. 342 (2019) (Kavanaugh, J. statement respecting denial of certiorari).

31 *See Ryan* Complaint ¶ 1 (alleging that section 5's phrase "unfair methods of competition" is "open-ended" and "provides no intelligible principle to guide the agency or constrain its policy preferences, in violation of the Constitution's restriction on the delegation of legislative powers."); *id.* ¶ 7 (claiming that "[u]nder the statutory language [unfair methods of competition], there is no intelligible principle to direct the Commission's determination of what constitutes an unfair method of competition, and when and what sort of regulation is appropriate in response").

32 *Big Time Vapes, Inc.*, 963 F.3d at 443; Tomac, Tax. of Mich. v. Norton, 433 F.3d 852, 866 (D.C. Cir. 2006).

33 U.S. Const. art. I, § 1.

of the government.³⁴ At the same time, it has long been understood that "in our increasingly complex society… Congress simply cannot do its job absent an ability to delegate power under broad general directives."³⁵ Some measure of lawmaking outside of Congress is therefore necessary, even desirable.³⁶ But there are constitutional limits to how much lawmaking authority Congress can confer on others, and the point of the nondelegation doctrine is to set those limits.

14. To operationalize the doctrine, the Supreme Court held long ago that if Congress sets forth "by legislative act an intelligible principle to which the person or body authorized [to legislate] is directed to conform, such legislative action [would not constitute] a forbidden delegation of legislative power."³⁷ In practice, even though Congress has passed numerous statutes giving agencies tremendous lawmaking-like authority with little guidance, the Supreme Court has only twice sustained an unconstitutional delegation challenge.³⁸ But it has occasionally relied on the doctrine to give "narrow constructions to statutory delegations that might otherwise be thought to be unconstitutional."³⁹

15. Recently, a majority of the Justices now serving on the Supreme Court went further and signaled their intention to replace the existing intelligible principle test with a formulation that would sharply constrain the policymaking powers of regulatory agencies. In *Gundy v. United States*, although a plurality of Justices voted to uphold the statute in question against a nondelegation challenge, three dissenting Justices (Gorsuch, Roberts, and Thomas) criticized the ineffectiveness of the intelligible principle test in limiting agency authority,⁴⁰ and Justice Alito, who concurred in the judgment, indicated a willingness to reconsider the doctrine going forward.⁴¹ Justice Kavanaugh, who did not participate in *Gundy*, also called for replacing the test in an individual statement

---

34 *See, e.g.*, Whitman v. Am. Trucking Ass'ns, Inc., 531 U.S. 457, 472 (2001) (stating that the text of art. I, § 1 vesting all legislative powers in Congress "permits no delegation of those powers").

35 Mistretta v. United States, 488 U.S. 361, 372 (1989). *See Whitman*, 531 U.S. at 472.

36 *See, e.g.*, Thomas W. Merrill, *Rethinking Article I, Section 1: From Nondelegation to Exclusive Delegation*, 104 COLUM. L. REV. 2097, 2153–54 (2004) (discussing the common argument that delegations are necessary given the demands of modern government).

37 J.W. Hampton, Jr. & Co. v. United States, 276 U.S. 394, 409 (1928).

38 *See* Kristin E. Hickman, *Nondelegation as Constitutional Symbolism*, 89 GEO. WASH. L. REV. 1979, 1081 (2021). The two exceptions were *Schechter*, 295 U.S. at 541–42 and *Pan. Refin. Co.*, 293 U.S. at 433.

39 *Mistretta*, 488 U.S. at 373 n.7. *See also* Nat'l Cable Television Ass'n v. U.S., 415 U.S. 336, 342 (1974). The Supreme Court has also recently adopted a new version of the so-called major questions doctrine, which, in its application, reads statutes narrowly to avoid nondelegation problems. *See West Virginia; see also supra* note 17 and *infra* note 101.

40 139 S. Ct. at 2138–42 (Gorsuch, J., dissenting) (criticizing the intelligible principle test and proposing a new approach).

41 *Id.* at 2130–31 (Alito, J., concurring) (concurring with the decision upholding the statute but expressing support for future reconsideration of the doctrine).

he issued in a denial of certiorari in *Paul v. United States*[42] shortly after *Gundy*.

16. In the most recent case presenting a nondelegation issue to the Supreme Court, *SEC v. Jarkesy*,[43] the Court passed on the opportunity to reexamine the doctrine. The Fifth Circuit in that case had set aside a federal statute as unconstitutional under three theories, one of which was the nondelegation doctrine.[44] The Supreme Court affirmed on the first ground – the violation of the appellee's Seventh Amendment right to a jury trial – but did not address the nondelegation theory,[45] which therefore leaves the Fifth Circuit's holding on the doctrine good law in that Circuit. This is significant as it was the first case since 1935 where the nondelegation doctrine had been successfully invoked, suggesting potentially a more demanding doctrine going forward, even under the prevailing intelligible principle standard.

2. "Intelligible Principle" and Section 5's "Unfair Methods of Competition" Delegation

17. The basic nondelegation argument with respect to section 5 points to its text – "unfair methods of competition" – and argues that it is too subjective and open-ended to provide adequate guideposts (or intelligible principles) to help the agency determine which business practices constitute unfair methods of competition.[46] Because an analysis of a nondelegation claim should consider not only the statutory text at issue but also the statute's purpose, its factual background, and the statutory context,[47] an examination of these factors, as well as an understanding of section 5's evolution over the years, would be helpful.

A. *Purpose, Background, and Context of Section 5*

18. It is undisputed that Congress, in 1914, established the FTC and passed the FTC Act[48] in reaction to *Standard Oil Co. v. United States*.[49] Specifically, the Supreme Court in *Standard Oil* applied a rule-of-reason standard to evaluate the legality of the company's alleged anticompetitive conduct under the Sherman Act, the primary (then, the only) antitrust law. Though the Court did find a violation in that case, Congress

---

42 140 S. Ct. 342 (2019) (Kavanaugh J., statement respecting denial of certiorari).
43 144 S. Ct. 2117 (2024).
44 Jarkesy v. SEC, 34 F.4th 446 (5th Cir. 2022).
45 *SEC v. Jarkesy*, 144 S. Ct. at 2138.
46 *Ryan* Complaint ¶¶ 1, 62.
47 *Big Time Vapes, Inc.*, 963 F.3d at 443.
48 Federal Trade Commission Act, 15 U.S.C. §§ 41–58, as amended.
49 Standard Oil Co. v. United States, 221 U.S. 1 (1911).

feared that the rule-of-reason approach would fail to capture many "practices that seriously interfere with competition,"[50] and consequently passed the FTC Act specifically to bolster and supplement the Sherman Act.[51] Authority to implement the Act was then conferred on the newly created FTC.

19. Congress, therefore, left no doubt whatsoever that section 5 was designed to extend beyond the reach of the Sherman Act;[52] the relevant legislative record is replete with statements evidencing that intent. There were, for example, statements from members of Congress lamenting that the Sherman Act's rule of reason, articulated in *Standard Oil*, would permit courts "to test each restraint of trade by the economic standard which the individual members of the court may happen to approve."[53] Other congressional members stated that while the Sherman Act may be adequate to address monopoly, it was inadequate "for the regulation of competition."[54] Still others added that the new legislation was intended to protect against "unfair and oppressive competition," listing examples;[55] "to reach unfair, dishonest, crooked, oppressive, coercive acts;"[56] and to stop monopolies in their "incipiency."[57] Another member opined that "the distinction between close bargaining and oppression"[58] can help draw the line between fairness and unfairness. Concluding, reasonably, that a granular definition could quickly become outdated, Congress chose to adopt the short, open language in question and to delegate authority to the FTC to complete the legislative scheme.

B. *The Evolution of Section 5*

20. Before the mid-1970s, consistent with congressional intent, the FTC enforced section 5 expansively, beyond the confines of the Sherman Act,

---

50   S. Rep. No. 1326, 62d Cong., 3d Sess., at 10 (1913) ("the Cummins Report").

51   *See* 51 Cong. Rec. 12146 (1914) (statement of Sen. Hollis) ("The Sherman Act is adequate for the abolition of monopoly; it is, however, but imperfectly adequate for the regulation of competition. The present Congress is charged with the duty of supplying the defect in the law"); H.R. Rep. No. 63-1142, at 19 (1914) (Conf. Rep.).

52   *See* 51 Cong. Rec. 11236 (1914) (statement of Sen. Cummins) (stating that the purpose of section 5 was "to make some things punishable, to prevent some things, that cannot be punished or prevented under the antitrust law"); *id.* at 12024 (statement of Sen. Newlands) (explaining that the new Act was designed to be broader and would "have such an elastic character that it [would] meet every new condition and every new practice that may be invented with a view to gradually bringing about monopoly through unfair competition.").

53   Cummins Report, *supra* note 50, at 12.

54   Statement of Sen. Hollis, *supra* note 51.

55   H.R. Rep. No. 63-1142, at 2.

56   51 Cong. Rec. 13117 (1914) (statement of Sen. Reed).

57   *Id.* at 13118 (statement of Sen. Reed).

58   51 Cong. Rec. 8979 (statement of Sen. Murdock).

and the Supreme Court mostly upheld its subsequent actions.[59] Notably, in *FTC v. Brown Shoe Co.*, the Supreme Court agreed with the FTC's position that the exclusive dealing agreements in question violated section 5 regardless of whether they violated the Sherman Act[60] (which they most likely did not).[61] In *FTC v. Sperry & Hutchinson Co.*, the Supreme Court said that section 5 encompasses not only conduct prohibited by the Sherman Act, but also conduct that violates the spirit of that law.[62] In *Atlantic Refining Co. v. FTC*, the Court held that all that is needed to find a section 5 violation is to "discover conduct that 'runs counter to the public policy declared in the' Act."[63] And, in *FTC v. Cement Institute*, the Court suggested that section 5 can be used to address tacit coordination scenarios, which are difficult to reach under section 1 of the Sherman Act because the requisite concert of action is arguably missing.[64]

21. Beginning in the mid-1970s, influenced by the Chicago School's laissez-faire inclinations, courts became increasingly skeptical of antitrust intervention in general and, in the context of section 5, consistently ruled against the FTC in its standalone section 5 cases – that is, cases not premised on prevailing concepts of the Sherman Act.[65] (Note, however, that even then, the Court would typically acknowledge that section 5 is not confined to the Sherman Act.)[66] The agency, after a few high-profile appellate court losses,[67] mainly acquiesced and retreated to the safe space of premising section 5 on Sherman Act doctrine, which the Court had also narrowed considerably.[68]

---

59 *See, e.g.*, Atlantic Refining Co. v. Fed. Trade Comm'n, 381 U.S. 357, 369 (1965) (holding that all that is necessary is to "discover conduct that 'runs counter to the public policy declared in the' Act" and "there are many unfair methods of competition that do not assume the proportions of antitrust violations"); Fed. Trade Comm'n v. Sperry & Hutchinson Co., 405 U.S. 233, 239–44 (1972) (stating that section 5 reaches conduct that violates the spirit, if not the letter, of the Sherman Act); Fed. Trade Comm'n v. Cement Institute, 333 U.S. 683, 708 (1948) (holding that conduct that falls short of violating the Sherman Act may violate section 5); Pan Am. v. United States, 371 U.S. 296, 306–308 (1963) ("[Section 5] was designed to bolster and strengthen antitrust enforcement."); Fed. Trade Comm'n v. R. F. Keppel & Bro., Inc., 291 U.S. 304, 310 (1934) (finding that "unfair methods of competition" are not limited to practices "which are forbidden at common law or which are likely to grow into violations of the Sherman Act"). For a fuller list of early Supreme Court cases endorsing application of section 5 to reach beyond the Sherman Act, *see* Section 5 Policy Statement, *supra* note 14, at 1 n.3.

60 Fed. Trade Comm'n v. Brown Shoe Co., 384 U.S. 316, 322 (1966) (endorsing the FTC position that the exclusive dealing agreements violated section 5 regardless of whether they violated the Sherman Act).

61 The exclusive dealing agreements in question were terminable at will and involved a very small number of market participants. *Id.*

62 *Sperry & Hutchinson Co.*, 405 U.S. at 239–44.

63 *Atlantic Refining Co.*, 381 U.S. at 369.

64 *Cement Institute*, 333 U.S. at 709.

65 *See generally* Kovacic & Winerman, *supra* note 11, at 940–42 (describing the courts' unwillingness to sustain the FTC's section 5 cases that went beyond Sherman Act theories and doctrines).

66 *See, e.g.*, Boise Cascade Corp. v. Fed. Trade Comm'n, 637 F.2d 573, 581 (9th Cir. 1980); E.I. du Pont de Nemours & Co. v. Fed. Trade Comm'n ("*Ethyl*"), 729 F.2d 128, 136–37 (2d Cir. 1984).

67 *Boise Cascade Corp.*; Official Airline Guides, Inc. v. Fed. Trade Comm'n, 630 F.2d 920 (2d Cir. 1980); *Ethyl*.

68 *See* Kovacic & Winerman, *supra* note 11, at 937–39 (discussing the contraction in Sherman Act doctrines beginning in the late 1970s and providing likely explanations).

22. Under former Chair Lina Khan, recently succeeded by Chair Andrew Ferguson, the Commission emerged from this prior position of self-restraint and began to pursue a more ambitious competition policy – one that relied on the agency's expansive approach to section 5 taken in its earlier years. The Commission's Section 5 Policy Statement and its promulgation of the Noncompete Rule were among the first agency actions taken in that direction. The success of these efforts, assuming their continuation under new FTC leadership, will depend in part on how vulnerable they are to challenges under the nondelegation doctrine (or the related "major questions doctrine").

C. *"Intelligible Principle" and Section 5*

23. So far, the nondelegation arguments made by challengers to the FTC's Noncompete Rule do not actually contend that the agency has *no* authority to regulate unfair methods of competition. Rather, the claim seems to be that even if the delegation is viewed as constitutional in the context of agency adjudication, it violates the doctrine and is unconstitutional with respect to rulemaking.[69] But such an argument is puzzling. If the statutory phrase "unfair methods of competition" provides adequate guideposts to satisfy the doctrine for purposes of adjudication, it is unclear how it would be insufficient to support rulemaking.

24. Petitioners challenging the Noncompete Rule cited *Schechter*,[70] one of the only two cases that had found a nondelegation violation,[71] in support of that dubious claim. *Schechter* condemned the National Industrial Recovery Act's delegation of authority to the President to set codes of "fair competition."[72] And it contrasted that delegation with the (presumably permissible) delegation in the FTC Act to a quasi-judicial body to determine what constituted "unfair methods of competition" "in the light of particular competitive conditions and of what is found to be a specific and substantial public interest."[73] This language on its own, indeed, can be construed to support a contention that the distinguishing factor between the two scenarios was that the former involved rules while the latter involved adjudications. But the *Schechter* Court also specifically stated that "the difference between the code plan of the Recovery Act and the scheme of the [FTC] Act lies not only in procedure but in *subject matter*."[74]

---

69 See *Ryan* Complaint ¶ 62.
70 *Id.* ¶¶ 61–63.
71 *Schechter*, 295 U.S. 495.
72 *See id.*
73 *Id.* at 533; *see also id.* at 531–36.
74 *Id.* at 533–34 (emphasis added).

25. And it further said that the term "fair competition" used in the Recovery Act has "a much broader range and a new significance" as compared to "unfair methods of competition" used in the FTC Act.[75]

25. Another fuzzy nondelegation claim with respect to section 5 and the Noncompete Rule seems to be that it is the categorical prohibition of non-competes – without having to show actual harm to competition or the lack of procompetitive effects – that violates the nondelegation doctrine.[76] Stated differently, the argument is that it is the reliance on standalone section 5 principles, separate from the Sherman Act, that gives rise to the unconstitutional delegation. But such an argument is also puzzling. If the phrase "unfair methods of competition" lays out an intelligible principle for section 5, then the agency should have latitude to make policy choices – whether it be to hew strictly to the Sherman Act or to expand beyond it – subject to the usual judicial review. It is unclear why, if an intelligible principle is found for the former, it would not also be found for the latter.

26. So, the issue is simply whether section 5 lays out an intelligible principle to permit agency determinations on what constitutes an unfair method of competition. If an intelligible principle exists, then it should support both adjudication and rulemaking. And it should also support not only cases reliant on the Sherman Act, but also cases that the agency may develop premised on its standalone section 5 principles.

27. Overall, the weak point for the agency in the nondelegation analysis is section 5's open-ended phrase "unfair methods of competition," which is not accompanied by any explanatory text or definition. However, when this text is informed by additional information gleaned from the statute's rich legislative record,[77] section 5 should easily pass the intelligible principle test.[78] And if the conclusion is that the delegation under section 5 is constitutional, then the Commission should have full discretion, subject to the usual judicial review, to make policy choices about what types of business practices constitute unfair methods of competition, including the decision to develop distinctive standalone section 5 principles to expand its reach beyond the Sherman Act.

3. Justice Gorsuch's Proposed New Nondelegation Doctrine

28. But what if the Supreme Court repudiates the intelligible principle test and adopts Justice Gorsuch's analysis in his *Gundy* dissent, which has now won the support of four other Justices serving on the Court? In *Gundy*, though

---

75 *Id.* at 534.

76 *See Chamber of Commerce* Complaint ¶ 100.

77 *See Big Time Vapes, Inc.*, 963 F.3d at 443.

78 *See supra* notes 49–58 and accompanying text.

a plurality found that the challenged statute "easily passes constitutional muster" under the intelligible principle test,[79] Justice Gorsuch (joined by Chief Justice Roberts and Justice Thomas) strongly dissented. The dissent proposed a new nondelegation doctrine that would permit Congress to delegate authority to another branch of government only to "fill up the details" of a regulatory scheme (not make policy decisions);[80] to engage in various forms of "fact-finding;" and to make policy with respect to matters implicating the President's inherent Article II powers.[81] And whether the delegation involves policymaking (impermissible) or "fill up the details" (permissible) depends on the "importance" of the subject,[82] with no clarity on the measure of "importance." Though Justice Alito did not join in the dissent and concurred in the *Gundy* judgment for case-specific reasons, he voiced support for reconsidering the existing intelligible principle test.[83] And Justice Kavanaugh, who did not participate in *Gundy*, made a point of expressing his interest in future reconsideration of the doctrine following "Justice Gorsuch's scholarly analysis of the Constitution's nondelegation doctrine."[84]

29. Should Justice Gorsuch's approach to the nondelegation doctrine become law, defending section 5 against a delegation-based attack could be more of a challenge. It is not crystal clear whether Congress's charge to the FTC to identify and prohibit unfair methods of competition would be seen as empowering the agency to make policy decisions or merely fill up the details. In all probability, the regulation of unfair methods of competition would be considered a subject of "importance," thus involving policymaking, and thus qualifying as unconstitutional under Justice Gorsuch's proposed new doctrine.

4. Implications of Finding a Nondelegation Violation

30. Consider, however, the implications of such a conclusion. An unconstitutional finding means that the statute granting the authority is invalidated, and the agency has *no* authority to regulate in that area entirely. In the context of section 5, that means the FTC would have no ability at all to do what it has been doing since 1914 – identifying and prohibiting unfair methods of competition, however the lines were drawn over the years. It could call into question the legitimacy of over a hundred years of relevant agency adjudications and Article III court decisions, which is cause for serious reflection. And, even if courts recognize the integrity

---

79   *Gundy*, 139 S. Ct. at 2129.

80   *Id.* at 2136 (Gorsuch, J., dissenting) ("[W]e know that as long as Congress makes the policy decisions when regulating private conduct, it may authorize another branch to fill up the details.") (internal quotations omitted).

81   *Id.* at 2136–37 (Gorsuch, J., dissenting).

82   *Id.* at 2136 (Gorsuch, J., dissenting).

83   *Id.* at 2130–31 (Alito, J., concurring in the judgment).

84   *Paul*, 140 S. Ct. at 342 (Kavanaugh, J. statement respecting denial of certiorari).

31. of the accumulated jurisprudence, and the section is effectively voided only going forward, a vacuum in the field would be left unless and until Congress passes new legislation that courts consider appropriately worded.

31. Perhaps it might be suggested that no void would result because *courts* may continue to effectively make policy through "interpreting" the law. But that argument is perplexing, unless the nondelegation doctrine has no application to judicial delegations. For if Congress is deemed not to have laid out an intelligible principle in the statute to guide the agency in filling in the content, logically it cannot have provided the requisite intelligible principle to enable courts to interpret the law in accordance with Congress's intentions. "Interpreting" the law without an intelligible principle is essentially creating law, which should also be unconstitutional if the nondelegation doctrine, as I argue below, applies with equal force to delegations to courts.

III. Section 5's Delegation Paradox

32. Although there are few cases and little discussion in the literature concerning ceding lawmaking authority to the judiciary, courts are a part of the delegation picture. The doctrine should apply as much to delegations to federal courts as it does to delegations to federal administrative agencies, because delegations to both types of entities trigger similar separation-of-powers concerns. There may be some contexts in which a more relaxed nondelegation doctrine is justified with respect to delegations to courts rather than to federal agencies – namely, where Congress's delegation implicates courts' "inherent powers."[85] But that argument should have no application in the context of the FTC Act, since it is difficult to see any link between that Act and an area over which federal courts have independent authority. In any case, even assuming that it is possible in certain cases to rationalize permitting judges (but not agencies) to exercise policy judgments to give meaning to a vague statute, on the theory that courts are simply "interpreting" the law, the result would be paradoxically worse than the original problem.

1. Delegation to Courts and the Nondelegation Principle

33. With a few notable exceptions,[86] the literature on nondelegation, like case law,[87] focuses almost entirely on delegation of lawmaking authority to agencies. But Congress has in fact long delegated authority to courts as well,

---

85 *See* Alexander Volokh, *Judicial Non-Delegation, the Inherent-Powers Corollary, and Federal Common Law*, 66 EMORY L.J. 1391 (2017).

86 Only a few articles have addressed judicial nondelegation. *See* Margaret H. Lemos, *The Other Delegate: Judicially Administered Statutes and the Nondelegation Doctrine*, 81 S. CAL. L. REV. 405 (2008); Andrew S. Oldham, *Sherman's March (In) to the Sea*, 74 TENN. L. REV. 319 (2007); Aaron Nielson, *Erie as Nondelegation*, 72 OHIO ST. L.J. 239 (2011); Volokh, *supra* note 85.

87 The few judicial nondelegation cases tended to involve statutory authorization to courts to promulgate rules governing their own procedures. *See* Wayman v. Southard, 23 U.S. (10 Wheat) 1, 42 (1825); Chandler v. Judicial Council, 398 U.S. 74, 86 n.7 (1970); Sibbach v. Wilson & Co., Inc., 312 U.S. 1, 9–10 (1941).

even if its delegations to the judiciary have been less explicit than its delegations to agencies. When Congress passes broad open-ended laws such as the Sherman Act – which condemns in section 1 "[e]very contract... in restraint of trade,"[88] without further definition or explanation – it is effectively empowering courts (in the case of the Sherman Act) to create a body of antitrust law based on the phrase "restraints of trade" in the course of deciding cases brought under that statutory provision.[89] To assert that courts are merely "finding" the law, not creating it, in that context would vastly overstretch the notion of "finding" or interpreting the law.

34. Subscribers to a formalist model of adjudication[90] may argue that there is a difference between authorizing courts to discern the meaning of a vague statute and authorizing agencies to do the same. With respect to delegation to the judiciary, the formalist argument would likely be that Congress is merely empowering courts to *discover* (not make) the law, on the theory that there is a true meaning encoded in any statute that a court can find.[91] This then differs from delegations of power to agencies, where a vague statute effectively empowers agencies to make policy judgments.

35. The ultra-formalism of this argument seems outdated – though there is language in Chief Justice Robert's *Loper Bright* opinion suggesting a receptiveness to it.[92] Legal realists have long rejected the notion that common law is more "discovered" than made by judges in adjudication.[93] Their critique of formalism relating to common law should carry over to judicial decisionmaking involving broad or vague statutes. The idea that there is a true meaning embedded in every statute that a court can ferret out through regular tools of statutory construction, without resorting to making policy judgments, seems contrary to a reasonable view of what judges do.[94]

---

88   15 U.S.C. § 1.

89   *See generally* Oldham, *supra* note 86.

90   Under a formalist model of judicial decisionmaking, courts "discover" rather than "make" common law. *See* Frederick Schauer, *Do Cases Make Bad Law?*, 73 U. Chi. L. Rev. 883, 885 (2006) ("Common law decisionmaking was widely understood prior to the twentieth century as the process of discovering the rules and principles immanent in the existing law, such discovery being assisted by logical deductions from earlier cases as well as the less deductive but no less constrained application of that mysterious array of skills then and now known as 'legal reasoning.'"); Thomas W. Merrill, *The Common Law Powers of Federal Courts*, 52 U. Chi. L. Rev. 1, 64 (1985).

91   *See* Lemos, *supra* note 86, at 430–31 (discussing and disagreeing with the view that courts and agencies should be seen as dealing differently with statutory ambiguity, with courts "merely giving effect to Congress's will... not making law themselves.").

92   *Loper Bright*, 144 S. Ct. at 2266 (stating that "statutes, no matter how impenetrable do – in fact, must – have a single, best meaning. That is the whole point of having written statutes; 'every statute's meaning is fixed at the time of enactment.'... [C]ourts use every tool at their disposal to determine the best reading of the statute and resolve the ambiguity.").

93   *See* Lemos, *supra* note 86, at 423–25 (describing legal realists' critique of the formalist model, which argued that "common law was not something judges found but something that judges *made*, using the same sorts of policy judgments that legislators rely on when making law.").

94   *See* Harry T. Edwards, *The Role of a Judge in Modern Society: Some Reflections on Current Practices in Federal Appellate Adjudication*, 32 Clev. St. L. Rev. 385, 425 (1983–84) (acknowledging that judges often have "no choice but frankly to exercise [their] discretion and interpret a contested provision as [they] see fit.").

36. Overall, relying on courts to give content to a broad statute through legal decisionmaking is conceptually no different than Congress's grant of lawmaking-like authority to agencies. In both instances, Congress cedes some of its lawmaking functions to one of the other two branches of government. It requires the delegate to engage in the type of policy-making judgment that Congress relies on when it makes laws. And the constitutional principles that underlie the nondelegation doctrine should apply to both situations.

37. Margaret Lemos, one of the few legal scholars who have written on the issue, has persuasively argued that the focus of the nondelegation doctrine and the intelligible principle requirement "is not on the characteristics of Congress's chosen delegate, but on Congress itself and the choices it must make."[95] In other words, whether there is unconstitutional delegation does not depend on who (the agency, the Executive, or the judiciary) has been delegated the authority. Rather, it turns on Congress's action: how much and what authority it has delegated and whether some guideposts were provided to guide the delegate's policymaking. Aaron Nielson has similarly argued that it is common sense that "[j]ust as Congress cannot delegate unbridled power to the Executive Branch, Congress also cannot delegate unbridled power to the Judicial Branch."[96]

38. It is true, as Alexander Volokh has rejoined, that there may be contexts in which statutory delegations to courts should be viewed differently (more relaxed treatment) than delegations to agencies.[97] Volokh notes that Article III confers certain inherent powers on courts with respect to certain matters, notably to make rules over the courts' internal procedures,[98] and to make federal common law in areas of "unique[] federal interests."[99] And, in those contexts, the statutes at issue could be viewed as merely affirming or clarifying the courts' inherent powers, rather than Congress delegating *new* powers.

39. While this argument has merit in some contexts, the FTC Act does not appear to fit into the few categories for which a less demanding doctrine is warranted for judicial delegation than for agency delegation. The Act cannot be viewed as a corollary to an inherent power of federal courts: it obviously does not pertain to procedural judicial rulemaking; nor is it possible to credibly claim that the Act involves "uniquely federal interests." After

---

95 Lemos, *supra* note 96, at 436.

96 Nielson, *supra* note 86, at 239. Nielson argues that the nondelegation doctrine, in fact, explains the well-known *Erie* doctrine. On this reading, it is constitutionally no more acceptable for Congress to empower federal courts to make federal common law in cases not involving unique federal interests than it is for Congress to authorize agencies to make law without the benefit of an intelligible principle for guidance. *See id.* at 275–82.

97 Volokh, *supra* note 85.

98 *Id.* at 1426–28.

99 *Id.* at 1429–33

all, states have long had state antitrust statutes, as well as laws governing unfair competition, popularly called the "baby FTC Acts."[100] It follows, then, that the FTC Act cannot be construed as simply clarifying or supporting some inherent power of federal courts. And, if section 5's grant of power to the FTC to identify and prevent unfair methods of competition is potentially deemed unconstitutional under Justice Gorsuch's proposed test (should it become law), then it should be equally unconstitutional for the judiciary to assume that role for itself ostensibly through interpreting the law in deciding cases.

2. Defaulting to Judicial Delegation

40. To escape the implications of striking down section 5 as unconstitutional, the Court might attempt to give effect to the doctrine's core concerns through limiting the delegation with a narrow construction of the statute. The Court has adopted this narrow-construction avoidance strategy in several cases.[101] In the context of section 5, this path would probably involve construing section 5 as coextensive with the Sherman Act, covering no more than the proscriptions of that statute and governed by the same narrow antitrust doctrines. It would disallow the FTC from treating a business practice – for example, the use of noncompetes – as a per se section 5 violation based on the practice's aggregate negative effects on competitive conditions alone, without following the rule of reason developed in Sherman Act jurisprudence. It would, for instance, preclude the Commission, even with strong empirical evidence of the practice's aggregate pernicious effect on market conditions, from condemning the practice unless there is evidence of the actor's market power and of actual harmful effects on the specific relevant market, as required under prevailing Sherman Act doctrine for most antitrust cases.

41. This result, however, would paradoxically favor courts over an expert agency in the making of what are essentially policy judgments, not legal decisions. The application of section 5 would effectively default to the courts' value judgments, particularly the Supreme Court's, regarding whether and to what degree microeconomic theories and consumer welfare maximization principles should control section 5 analysis, whether

---

100 *See* Justin J. Hakala, Follow-On State Actions Based on the FTC's Enforcement of Section 5, Appendix A (2008) (unpublished) (providing a full index of state "little FTC Acts" and their characteristics), https://papers.ssrn.com/sol3/papers.cfm?abstract_id=1283261.

101 *See Nat'l Cable Television Ass'n*, 415 U.S. at 341–42; FPC v. New Eng. Power Co., 415 U.S. 345, 351 (1974); *Mistretta*, 488 U.S. at 373 n.7. A plurality of Justices also adopted this approach in Industrial Union Dep't v. American Petroleum Institute, 448 U.S. 607 (1980) (plurality opinion) (generally known as the "*Benzene*" case). It should be noted that Justice Gorsuch seems to read *Benzene* as consistent with the major questions doctrine, and he views the major questions doctrine as a clear statement rule intended to ensure that statutes are construed narrowly to avoid nondelegation problems. *See West Virginia*, 142 S. Ct. at 2619–20 (Gorsuch, J., concurring); Coenen, *supra* note 17, at 12–15. If the major questions doctrine is thus read, then the Supreme Court has already started adopting a nondelegation doctrine along the path that Justice Gorsuch laid out in his dissent in *Gundy*.

the goals of section 5 should be identical to that of the Sherman Act, and whether and how different policy trade-offs should be made. In other words, courts would effectively be empowering themselves to set the metes and bounds of the FTC's section 5 authority by way of their rulings on the Sherman Act. There is, however, no support for this default. If anything, delegation to courts, as compared to delegation to agencies, raises more of the democratic concerns on which the nondelegation doctrine is grounded.

3. Judicial Lawmaking Versus Agency Lawmaking

42. Finessing the doctrine such that policymaking delegation essentially defaults to the judiciary is in fact worse than the current "hands-off" approach toward delegation to agencies.[102] First, the nondelegation doctrine and the intelligible principle requirement are rooted in notions of democratic accountability, and agencies are politically more accountable than courts.[103] Second, agencies have expertise in their respective areas, whereas courts do not.[104] Third, in most instances, as in the case of the FTC Act, Congress consciously wanted the agency to be tasked with giving content to the law in question, and specifically conferred the authority to do so on the agency, not the courts.[105] Given these factors, it is hard to justify any solution that would prefer courts over agencies in the fashioning of policy.

43. First, regarding accountability, the nondelegation doctrine is based largely on American concerns about democracy and accountability, and the risks to those values when unbridled lawmaking power is placed in the hands of those with no political accountability. Both chambers of Congress are directly accountable to the American voters who elect them, which is the source of legitimacy for their legislative authority in the first place. Given this grounding of the doctrine, to the extent that some measure of lawmaking outside of Congress is inevitable, delegating that authority to the body that is more politically accountable would be more logical. And, as between agencies and the courts, agencies are much more democratically accountable than the courts, through their relationship with the President and Congress, a relationship that courts do not have.

---

102 *See* Lemos, *supra* note 86.

103 *See, e.g.*, Kisor v. Wilkie, 588 U.S. 558, 571–72 (2019) (stating that agencies, unlike courts, "have political accountability, because they are subject to the supervision of the President, who in turn answers to the public."); *see also* David Braff, Mitchell Eitel & Rodgin Cohen, *The US Supreme Court declines to overrule the principle of deference to agencies' interpretations of their regulations but clarifies limitations on its scope* (Kisor / Wilkie), e-Competitions June 2019, art. no. 96929; Free Enter. Fund v. Public Co. Acct. Oversight Bd., 561 U.S. 477, 499 (2010); Pauley v. BethEnergy Mines, Inc., 501 U.S. 680, 696 (1991).

104 *See Kisor*, 588 U.S at 571 ("Agencies (unlike courts) have 'unique expertise,'... relevant to applying a regulation 'to complex or changing circumstances.'") (internal citation omitted); *Loper Bright*, 144 S. Ct. at 2298 (Kagan, J., dissenting) (noting that "agencies often know things about a statute's subject matter that courts could not hope to... Agencies are staffed with 'experts in the field' who can bring their training and knowledge to bear...").

105 *See supra* Part II-2-A.

44. As the Supreme Court itself noted, "[A]gencies (… unlike courts) have political accountability, because they are subject to the supervision of the President, who in turn answers to the public."[106] And administrative law scholars generally agree.[107] Congress also retains meaningful control over agencies through its appropriations authority,[108] and the Senate's "advice and consent" role under the Appointments Clause.[109] Congress also has the ability to conduct oversight hearings and to engage informally with agency policymakers.[110] Through these and other control mechanisms, both formal and informal, Congress can restrain agency policies that depart from Congress's policy intentions.

45. Courts, in contrast, have far fewer checks. While Congress and/or the President, and indeed the public, can and often do criticize the work of the courts, they cannot do much beyond that because of the protection of life tenure for federal judges. Of course, Congress can overrule decisions with which it disagrees by passing new legislation, but that rarely happens. It could also in theory reduce funding for courts, but that is also unlikely to occur. In light of that, it would be ironic if the nondelegation doctrine is effectively used to prefer delegations to the less accountable branch of government, the judiciary, over the much more accountable agencies.

46. Second, equally important on the issue, agencies tend to possess expertise in the areas that they have been charged with regulating while courts do not.[111] Agencies often have experts on their staff and accumulate substantial specialized knowledge.[112] Also, since decisions that must be made typically involve questions of policy, not of law, an agency's expertise puts them in a far better position, relative to courts, to make them.[113] In the case of the FTC, the Commission additionally enjoys a panoply of powers conferred by Congress, including the power to collect market data from market participants and conduct sector studies.[114] In other

---

[106] *Kisor*, 588 U.S. at 571–72. *See also Loper Bright*, 144 S. Ct. at 2299 (Kagan, J., dissenting) ("Agencies are 'subject to the supervision of the President, who in turn answers to the public.'").

[107] *See, e.g.,* Thomas W. Merrill, *Judicial Deference to Executive Precedent*, 101 YALE L.J. 969, 978–79 (1992) (noting that "agency decisionmaking is always more democratic than judicial decisionmaking because all agencies are accountable (to some degree) to the President, and the President is elected by the people.").

[108] U.S. CONST. art I, § 9, clause 7 (the Appropriations Clause).

[109] U.S. CONST. art. II, § 2, clause 2 (the Appointments Clause).

[110] *See* Harry First & Spencer Weber Waller, *Antitrust's Democracy Deficit*, 81 FORDHAM L. REV. 2543 (2013); Lemos, *supra* note 86, at 449.

[111] *See Kisor*, 588 U.S. at 571.

[112] Lemos, *supra* note 86, at 445.

[113] *See id.* at 426, 445–46.

[114] 15 U.S.C. § 46(b).

words, the agency has valuable investigatory tools that give it a further advantage over generalist courts.[115]

47. Another related factor that should favor delegations to agencies over courts is that agency policymaking is more accessible and responsive to the public, and therefore more democratic, than judicial policymaking through case decisions. When agencies formulate policies, they are often bound by detailed, often statutorily required, procedures designed to solicit and respond to input from the public. For example, the rulemaking process under the Administrative Procedure Act (APA) requires publication of a detailed notice of the proposed rulemaking, and provides "an opportunity [to all interested persons] to participate... through submission of written data, views, or arguments."[116] The agency must then incorporate into its final rule "a concise general statement of [its] basis and purpose,"[117] which is generally interpreted to mean that the agency "must respond in a reasoned manner to [comments submitted] that raise significant problems."[118] Furthermore, agency actions are subject to judicial review.[119] In contrast, when courts formulate policy through case decisions, they essentially hear only from the parties to the case and their *amici*, and then make their judgments. Furthermore, those judgments are not subject to review from another branch of government.

48. Third, where it is clear that Congress consciously intended for an agency to supply the content of a legislative scheme, within broad parameters Congress has set, there is even less justification for preferring judicial over agency delegation. In the case of section 5, there is no doubt whatsoever that Congress purposefully turned to the FTC, not the courts, for assistance in giving meaning to that statutory provision.[120] It was concerned with the Supreme Court's approach to the Sherman Act in *Standard Oil*. And, in direct response to that concern, Congress passed the FTC Act to supplement the Sherman Act, specifically empowering and charging the newly created agency with elucidating the meaning of section 5. Given the clarity of Congress's intentions, it is difficult to justify courts taking for themselves the policymaking authority that Congress had clearly assigned to an agency.

---

115 For a contrary view, *see* Daniel A. Crane, *Debunking Humphrey's Executor*, 83 GEO. WASH. L. REV. 1836, 1856–58 (2015) (contending that the FTC is not uniquely expert and has no more expertise than the DOJ Antitrust Division, an executive branch agency).

116 5 U.S.C. § 553.

117 *Id.*

118 Reytblatt v. U.S. Nuclear Reg. Comm., 105 F.3d 715, 722 (D.C. Cir. 1997). *See also* Thompson v. Clark, 741 F.2d 401, 409 (D.C. Cir. 1984) (suggesting a reason for requiring agencies to respond to comments is to ensure that they have read and considered them).

119 5 U.S.C. § 702 ("A person suffering legal wrong because of agency action, or adversely affected or aggrieved by agency action... is entitled to judicial review thereof.").

120 *See supra* Part II-2-A.

IV. Conclusion

49. One of the bold initiatives undertaken by the FTC in its pursuit of a broader antitrust agenda was the promulgation of the Noncompete Rule categorically banning noncompetes as "unfair methods of competition" under section 5 of the FTC Act. That rule, in turn, relied on the agency's new, more expansive, Section 5 Policy Statement, one that explicitly embraced a broader approach to section 5 consistent with original congressional intent. The ultimate success of these efforts depends on many factors, including their vulnerability to potential challenges under the nondelegation doctrine (or the related "major questions doctrine").

50. This paper examines the delegation risk and argues that a nondelegation challenge to section 5 should not succeed because the statute should easily satisfy the intelligible principle test. If that test is replaced by Justice Gorsuch's version of the nondelegation doctrine in his *Gundy* dissent, the outcome could be less certain. Because of the profound implications of finding a statute unconstitutional, those intent on "reining in" the FTC through reliance on the nondelegation doctrine might attempt to avoid the dire fallout by arguing that the doctrine would preclude only the *FTC* from exercising policy discretion, not the courts from "interpreting" the statute in legal decisionmaking.

51. The nondelegation doctrine, however, should apply to the judiciary just as it does to administrative agencies. Furthermore, even assuming that it is possible to rationalize a default to judicial delegation (by courts removing an agency's policymaking authority while assuming that role for themselves in ostensible legal decisionmaking), that result would be paradoxically worse than the original problem. It would favor courts over agencies in the making of what are essentially policy, not legal, decisions, when there is little justification in most cases for that preference. If anything, the democracy grounding of the nondelegation doctrine should lean in the opposite direction, as agencies have more political accountability and subject-matter expertise than the federal judiciary. Moreover, in the specific case of the FTC Act, defaulting to the courts would be distinctly contrary to Congress's intentions, which were explicitly expressed in the Act's rich legislative record.

The Clayton Act Does Not Contain or Permit an Efficiency Rebuttal

DARREN BUSH[*]
University of Houston Law Center

MARK GLICK[**]
University of Utah

ROBERT H. LANDE[***]
University of Baltimore School of Law

GABRIEL A. LOZADA[****]
University of Utah

Abstract

This chapter demonstrates that there is not now, and there should not be, an efficiency rebuttal, defense or exception in merger cases. A textualist analysis demonstrates that it does not exist in the plain words of the antimerger statute, which prevents mergers that "may be substantially to lessen competition, or to tend to create a monopoly." The legislative history of section 7 shows only a scant concern for merger efficiency, certainly nothing that would justify otherwise anticompetitive mergers. The overwhelmingly dominant goal of the Clayton Act

---

[*] Darren Bush is Leonard B. Rosenberg Professor of Law, University of Houston Law Center.
[**] Mark Glick is a professor of economics and adjunct professor of law at the University of Utah.
[***] Robert Lande is Venable Professor of Law Emeritus, University of Baltimore School of Law.
[****] Gabriel A. Lozada is a professor of economics at the University of Utah. The authors thank Cherie Correlli and Joshua Rodriguez for research assistance.

and its Celler-Kefauver amendment was to prevent the possible formation of market power because the merger would transfer wealth from purchasers to the firm acquiring market power. This concern was so strong that Congress wanted to prevent the rise of this market power in its incipiency. Possible efficiencies from mergers should not be permitted to thwart congressional intent. This chapter is a short version of an article scheduled to appear in the Antitrust Bulletin by the same authors, titled, "The Merger Efficiency Defense: No Legal Basis and a Bad Idea".

1. Section 7 of the Clayton Act does not and should not contain an efficiency rebuttal, a claim that cost savings or other efficiencies from the combination of the two merged firms make the merger beneficial. Yet the claim persists in both many lower court analyses, as well as in the Department of Justice Antitrust Division and Federal Trade Commission merger guidelines and enforcement practices. The 2023 Merger Guidelines were right to eliminate it for "may… tend to create a monopoly" cases.[5] The Guidelines and the courts should go further and eliminate it for all merger cases because it is not justified by the words or legislative history of the statute

2. This chapter will demonstrate that, as a matter of statutory interpretation, there is no legal basis for an efficiency rebuttal. This analysis consists of two parts. Part I argues that textualist analysis demonstrates that there is no efficiency rebuttal (or defense or exception) contained in the words of the statute. It is simply not there. The Clayton Act forbids all mergers that "may be substantially to lessen competition, or to tend to create a monopoly."[6] The statute does not contain an efficiency rebuttal, exception or defense of any kind.

3. It would have been simple for Congress to include an efficiencies defense in section 7 of the Clayton Act, as it did when it enacted the Robinson-Patman amendment to the Clayton Act.[7] Section 7's lack of an explicit efficiencies defense should dispositively decide the efficiency defense question to a textualist,[8] but we nevertheless separately analyze each of the two parts of section 7's prohibition against mergers that "may be substantially to lessen competition, or to tend to create a monopoly" on this issue. Neither analysis justifies an efficiency rebuttal.

---

5 U.S. Dep't. Just. & Fed. Trade Comm'n, Merger Guidelines § 3.3 (Dec. 18, 2023), https://www.justice.gov/atr/2023-merger-guidelines ("Cognizable efficiencies that would not prevent the creation of a monopoly cannot justify a merger that may tend to create a monopoly"). We applaud the 2023 Merger Guidelines for eliminating an efficiency rebuttal for mergers that tend to create a monopoly.

6 *See* Pub. L. No. 63-212, 38 Stat. 730 (1914).

7 For example, Congress could have written a law that said, "Notwithstanding this prohibition, if the merging parties can demonstrate that their merger will produce efficiencies, the merger will be permitted." Or the law could have read, "If the merging parties can demonstrate that the merger will produce significant efficiencies, these efficiencies will be traded off against any market power effects the merger would be likely to produce." But Congress chose not to do this.

8 Antitrust enforcers can, of course, use their discretion to decline to challenge those few mergers they believe likely to produce significant cost savings but unlikely to produce serious market power effects.

4. Part II argues that, beyond textualism, the legislative history of section 7 provides little or no evidence of congressional concern for efficiencies. Section 7's legislative history demonstrates the primary goal was to prevent the incipient formation of market power through mergers.[1] Congress's main concern was a fear that the merging firm would engage in supracompetitive pricing, thereby unfairly acquiring wealth from consumers (purchasers).

5. Our search of the legislative history of the Clayton Act and Celler-Kefauver amendment uncovered no explicit or implicit evidence of a congressional concern with the allocative inefficiency arising from monopoly pricing. Moreover, the view of the Amendment's proponents, and thus of the majority in Congress, was that blocking mergers that may lead to market power probably would help, not hurt, corporate efficiency by preserving competitive pressure.

I. Textualist Reasons to Drop the Efficiency Rebuttal

6. Section 7 of the Clayton Act lacks any textual support for the notion of an efficiency rebuttal. Textualism is a method of statutory analysis that starts with, and in almost all cases ends with, the precise words of a statute.[2] It gives the words and phrases in the statute the plain, fair, straightforward and ordinary meanings they had when the statute was enacted, and almost always ignores everything else, including laws' legislative history.[3] Courts should not create exceptions that are not in the text of the law,[4] and should not impose their own policy preferences into a statute.[5] A majority of current Supreme Court Justices often use textualism to interpret statutes.[6]

---

[1] *See* Robert H. Lande, *Wealth Transfers as the Original and Primary Concern of Antitrust: The Efficiency Interpretation Challenged*, 34 HASTINGS L.J. 65, 80–142 (1982) (arguing that Congress passed the antimerger laws, and the Sherman and FTC Acts, primarily to prevent wealth transfers from purchasers to firms with market power goals).

[2] *See* ANTONIN SCALIA & BRYAN A. GARNER, READING LAW: THE INTERPRETATION OF LEGAL TEXTS (2012).

[3] *Id.* at 34–37. "Words must be given the meaning they had when the text was adopted." *Id.* at 78. Debra Cassens Weiss, Scalia Weighs in on Posner's Controversial Book Review, Calls Posner's Assertion 'a Lie,' ABA J. (Sept. 18, 2012), https://www.abajournal.com/news/article/scalia_weighs_in_on_a_controversial_book_review ("To say that I used legislative history is simply, to put it bluntly, a lie."). The authors of this article are not textualists, but they recognize that many members of the Supreme Court often use textualism.

[4] *See* Bostock v. Clayton County, 140 S. Ct. 1731, 1749 (2020) (quoting SCALIA & GARNER, *supra* note 6, at 101) ("[U]nexpected applications of broad language reflect only Congress's 'presumed point [to] produce general coverage – not to leave room for courts to recognize ad hoc exceptions.'").

[5] Scalia believed that judges should not insert their own policy preferences into a statute's interpretation because:
> [E]ven if you think our laws mean not what the legislature enacted but what the legislators intended, there is no way to tell what they intended except the text. Nothing but the text has received the approval of the majority of the legislature and of the President, assuming that he signed it rather than vetoed it and had it passed over his veto. Nothing but the text reflects the full legislature's purpose. Nothing.

Antonin Scalia & John F. Manning, *A Dialogue on Statutory Constitutional Interpretation*, 80 GEO. WASH. L. REV. 1610, 1612 (2012).

[6] Justice Kagan stated, "we are all textualists now." Harvard Law School, *The 2015 Scalia Lecture Series: A Dialogue with Justice Elena Kagan on the Reading of Statutes*, YOUTUBE, at 08:29 (Nov. 25, 2015). For a case in which all of the Justices used textualist analysis, *see Bostock*.

7. A textualist approach to the merger efficiency rebuttal question simply means that we should plainly and straightforwardly read the Clayton Act and ask whether an efficiency rebuttal, defense, or exception appears in the words of the statute. It does not. The Clayton Act forbids all mergers that "may be substantially to lessen competition, or to tend to create a monopoly."[7] The statute does not contain an efficiency rebuttal of any kind.

8. It would have been simple for Congress to include an efficiencies defense in section 7 of the Clayton Act.[8] Congress knew how to write one when it wanted one because the 1936 Robinson-Patman Act amendment to the Clayton Act does contain an efficiencies defense. Although section 2 of this statute forbids price discrimination whose effect "may be substantially to lessen competition or tend to create a monopoly"[9] (the exact language contained in section 7!), section 2 also provides an explicit efficiency defense, if the defendant can show that its pricing was caused by a lower "cost of manufacture, sale, or delivery."[10]

9. Because Congress in 1936 included an efficiencies defense in section 2 of the Clayton Act, but did not do so when it enacted section 7 of the Clayton Act in 1914 or when it passed the Celler-Kefauver amendment in 1950, section 7's lack of an explicit efficiencies defense should dispositively decide the efficiency defense question to a textualist. It is not in the statute. Therefore, judges should not allow one even if they personally consider it to be sound public policy.[11]

10. Despite this conclusion, each of the two parts of section 7's prohibition against mergers that "may be substantially to lessen competition, or to tend to create a monopoly" could be analyzed separately on this issue. Neither analysis justifies an efficiency rebuttal.

1. The "Tend to Create a Monopoly" Clause of Section 7

11. To a textualist, the "or to tend to create a monopoly" clause is clear. The plain reading of this text precludes an efficiencies defense if the merger may "tend to create a monopoly" with no consideration as to whether that

---

7   See Pub. L. No. 63-212, 38 Stat. 730 (1914).

8   For example, Congress could have written a law that said, "Notwithstanding this prohibition, if the merging parties can demonstrate that their merger will produce efficiencies, the merger will be permitted." Or the law could have read, "If the merging parties can demonstrate that the merger will produce significant efficiencies, these efficiencies will be traded off against any market power effects the merger would be likely to produce." But Congress chose not to do this.

9   See Robinson-Patman Act, 15 U.S.C. § 13 (1936).

10 The Robinson-Patman Act, 15 U.S.C. § 13, section 3(A) reads:
    It shall be unlawful for any person engaged in commerce... to discriminate in price between different purchasers of commodities of like grade and quality... and where the effect of such discrimination may be substantially to lessen competition or tend to create a monopoly in any line of commerce... Provided, That nothing herein contained shall prevent differentials which make only due allowance for differences in the cost of manufacture, sale, or delivery resulting from the differing methods or quantities in which such commodities are to such purchasers sold or delivered...

11 Antitrust enforcers may use their discretion to decline to challenge those few mergers they believe likely to produce significant cost savings but unlikely to produce serious market power effects.

monopoly[12] would be likely to be "efficient" (to lower costs, or increase innovation, quality, service or consumer choice).

12. In one of the most famous antitrust articles, Prof. Williamson showed that a merger could result in a monopoly that would raise prices, but that if the merger lowered the resulting monopoly's costs sufficiently, the monopoly could be net efficient in the Potential Pareto sense (if one unjustifiably ignores the welfare of input suppliers).[13] The Chicago School embraced this analysis, and concluded that mergers producing monopolies were fine so long as they are net efficient.[14] Moreover, if the merger led to cost savings that were enormous, they could even prevent prices from rising despite the resulting increase in market power.[15]

13. But the plain language of section 7 forbids all mergers that would even tend to create a monopoly, let alone actually create one – regardless of whether the resulting monopoly might have low costs, and without even examining whether prices were predicted to rise, fall, or remain stable, or whether innovation would rise or fall. Perhaps the simple, plain language of this clause of section 7 is what caused the writers of the 2023 Merger Guidelines to say that the enforcers would not recognize an efficiencies defense for mergers that "may... tend to create a monopoly."[16]

2. The "May Be Substantially to Lessen Competition" Clause of Section 7

14. Could an efficiencies defense arise under the "may be substantially to lessen competition" clause? A textualist analysis of this issue should center around what the word "competition" meant in the English language dictionaries and legal dictionaries from the 1900–1950 period that

---

12 Monopoly should be defined by a textualist the way it was defined by dictionaries and other sources of the period, as a market owned or controlled by a single firm. Justice Scalia provided a list of English Language dictionaries and legal dictionaries of the period that he considered "useful and authoritative," *see* SCALIA & GARNER, *supra* note 6, at 419, 422. All of these sources defined "monopoly" essentially the same, as:

   1. "Exclusive possession of the trade in some article of merchandise; the condition of having no competitor in the sale of some commodity.... In generalized sense.... Exclusive possession, control, or exercise of something." *Monopoly*, A NEW ENGLISH DICTIONARY ON HISTORICAL PRINCIPLES 624 (vol. VI pt. II 1908) (subsequently published in 1933, under the title *The Oxford English Dictionary*).

   2. "[E]xclusive control of the supply of any commodity or service in a given market; hence, often, in popular use, any such control of a commodity, service, or traffic in a given market as enables the one having such control to raise the price of a commodity or service materially above the price fixed by free competition." *Monopoly*, WEBSTER'S SECOND NEW INTERNATIONAL DICTIONARY 1587 (1936) (1936 printing has been used in lieu of the 1934 printing due to extremely limited availability).

13 *See* Oliver E. Williamson, *Economies as an Antitrust Defense: The Welfare Tradeoffs*, 58 AM. ECON. REV. 18 (1968).

14 *See* Timothy J. Muris, *The Efficiency Defense Under Section 7 of the Clayton Act*, 30 CASE W. RES. L. REV. 381 (1980).

15 *See* Alan A. Fisher, Frederick I. Johnson & Robert H. Lande, *Price Effects of Horizontal Mergers*, 77 CAL. L. REV. 777 (1989).

16 MERGER GUIDELINES, *supra* note 1, § 3.3 ("Cognizable efficiencies that would not prevent the creation of a monopoly cannot justify a merger that may tend to create a monopoly").

Justice Scalia considered "useful and authoritative."[17] These definitions have not changed in more than a century. They are:

- "The action of endeavouring to gain what another endeavours to gain at the same time; the striving of two or more for the same object; rivalry"[18]

- "The act of seeking or endeavoring to gain what another is endeavoring to gain at the same time; common contest or striving for the same object; strife for superiority; rivalry"[19]

- "Act of competing, esp. of seeking, or endeavoring to gain, what another is endeavoring to gain at the same time; common strife for the same object; strife for superiority; emulous contest; rivalry"[20]

- "The act or proceeding of striving for something that is sought by another at the same time; a contention of two or more for the same object or for superiority; rivalry. . . ."[21]

15. Every one of these dictionaries[22] defines competition in terms of rivalry; of acts of rivalry. None used an economic definition of competition (let alone an economic definition of "perfect competition," which is *complete lack* of rivalry, since all firms take prices as given). None defined less "rivalry" as having lower costs.

16. Suppose a merger would reduce the number of rivals in a market from four down to three. Under a straightforward definition of "rivalry," a textualist should clearly conclude that the amount of rivalry (i.e., competition) in the market would decrease, even if the merged firm would experience lower costs, because three firms "compete" less – engage in less rivalry – than four firms.

17. Suppose, for example, a market had four firms in it, with market shares of 40%, 30%, 15% and 15%. Suppose the two 15% firms wanted to merge, and claimed the merger would lead to tremendous cost savings, enabling the resulting firm to better compete with the two larger firms in the market. In this possibly "enhanced rivalry" scenario, it could be argued that an efficiencies defense should be allowed in "may be substantially to lessen competition" merger cases.[23]

---

17   See SCALIA & GARNER, *supra* note 6, at 419, 422.

18   *Competition*, A NEW ENGLISH DICTIONARY ON HISTORICAL PRINCIPLES 720 (vol. II 1893) (subsequently published in 1933, under the title *The Oxford English Dictionary*).

19   *Competition*, THE CENTURY DICTIONARY AND CYCLOPEDIA 1145 (vol. II 1906).

20   *Competition*, WEBSTER'S SECOND NEW INTERNATIONAL DICTIONARY 545 (1936) (1936 printing has been used in lieu of the 1934 printing due to extremely limited availability).

21   *Competition*, FUNK & WAGNALLS NEW STANDARD DICTIONARY OF THE ENGLISH LANGUAGE 542 (1943).

22   Scalia also recommended legal dictionaries of the period, but none contain a different definition.

23   Daniel Farber and Bret McDonnell assert that in some types of cases, a textual analysis of section 7 should permit an efficiency rebuttal. *See* Daniel A. Farber & Brett H. McDonnell, "*Is There a Text in this Class?" The Conflict Between Textualism and Antitrust*, 14 J. CONTEMP. LEGAL ISSUES 619, 645 (2005). Their argument's economic underpinnings, however, are flawed. First, they assume that only the merger can improve rivalry and

18. For a textualist, however, this possibility of "enhanced rivalry" should not be enough to offset the fundamental point that Congress chose not to include an efficiencies defense in section 7, so the courts should not invent or allow one. As noted, Congress included an efficiencies defense in another part of the Clayton Act, but not in section 7. If a court allowed an efficiencies defense in section 7 cases, this would mean it was inserting its own policy preferences into the law – which is the opposite of textualism.

19. Nonetheless, some have sought to alter the meaning of this text to include economic notions such as consumer welfare. In particular, Robert Bork famously argued that the text and the legislative history of the antitrust laws support such a notion. That argument is in part the basis for finding an efficiency rebuttal in the text and legislative history. We thus explore that next.

3. Robert Bork's Efficiency Argument

20. Robert Bork wrote in his celebrated article on the legislative history of the antitrust laws:[24]

> The polar models employed by these statutes are thus "competition" and "monopoly." These are models developed by economists rather than sociologists and appear therefore to frame a law to which economic analysis, and not much else, is relevant. As models, competition and monopoly indicate different outcomes for resource allocation. The preference for competitive rather than monopolistic resource allocation is most clearly explained and firmly based upon a desire to maximize output as consumers value it. *The language of the statutes, then, clearly implies a consumer welfare policy.*

21. We strongly disagree with the last sentence because the sentences that precede it are problematic at best.

22. The second sentence is a *non sequitur* because while it is true that economists model monopoly, that does not mean that monopoly has no important effects outside of those in economic models. Moreover, Bork's sentence leaves completely unanswered the question, "Whose economic models?" Those of institutional economists like Thorstein Veblen would view the effects of monopoly with a much wider lens than the model of Alfred Marshall.[25]

---

not internal development or other measures. This is often incorrect. Second, Farber and McDonnell assert that the merger can result in a more efficient firm that may reduce the ability of the competitors in the market to engage in cartel behavior. We consider this pure speculation. For example, in their review article of cartel literature, Levenstein and Suslow find that there is no empirical evidence that mergers reduce cartel activity, but they do find that the number of firms in a market is an important indicator of the probability of successful collusion. Margaret C. Levenstein and Valerie Y. Suslow, *What Determines Cartel Success?* 44 J. ECON. LIT. 43 (2006).

24 Robert H. Bork, *The Goals of Antitrust Policy*, 57 AM. ECON. REV. 242 (1967) 244–45 (emphasis added).

25 *See generally* THORSTEIN VEBLEN, THE THEORY OF BUSINESS ENTERPRISE (1904); THORSTEIN VEBLEN ABSENTEE OWNERSHIP AND BUSINESS ENTERPRISE IN RECENT TIMES (1923).

23. As was shown, Bork's notion that the goal is output maximization is completely divorced from the language of the statutes, and in particular of the merger statutes. Rather than looking at the text, Bork seeks some deeper "explanation" of the text; he wants to infer the "desire" of its authors; and Bork locates this explanation, this desire, in economic theory.

24. We have shown that Bork's notion of economic theory is not embodied in the text of the statutes. Between World War I and the 1960s, courts saw no reason to grope for an "explanation" of the statutes, let alone an explanation that would be found in economics textbooks. What motivated Bork was his belief that the statutes *should* reflect economic theory. And not just any economic theory: he thought they should reflect the one particular narrow economic theory that he was familiar with and thought made sense. Part II will demonstrate that economic theory did not motivate the statutes' authors. Nor should it, we argue later.

II. The Legislative History of the Antimerger Laws: No Support for an Efficiency Rebuttal

25. Searching legislative history unearths little support for an efficiency rebuttal in the Clayton Act. By contrast to textualism, a traditionalist approach to statutory interpretation analyzes a law's legislative history and purpose and interprets the law accordingly, especially in cases where the statutory language is ambiguous.[26] This analysis shows that when Congress debated the antimerger laws, it showed almost no concern with missed or foregone efficiencies from mergers.

26. Our search of the legislative history of the Clayton Act and its later amendment, the Celler-Kefauver Act, reveals no explicit or implicit evidence of a congressional concern with the allocative inefficiency arising from monopoly pricing.[27] Nor have scholars advocating a strong efficiency orientation to the legislation produced any such evidence.[28]

27. There was, however, a small amount of congressional attention to the possible effects of the legislation on the productive efficiency of firms.

---

26 A traditional analysis of a statute including its legislative history, one that relies upon the congressional debates and committee reports, is often called a "purposivist" analysis today. *See* Jeffrey A. Pojanowski, *Statutes in Common Law Courts*, 91 Tex. L. Rev. 479, 483, 503 (2013).

27 *See* Fisher et al., *supra* note 19, at 785–88 ("Moreover, Congress was surely unaware of even an intuitive version of the concept of allocative inefficiency in 1914 when it approved the Clayton Act; the notion that this concept could have caused Congress to pass the antimerger laws is hardly credible. Although economists had dramatically increased their understanding of allocative efficiency by 1950 when Congress enacted the Celler-Kefauver amendment, the legislative history of this bill contains absolutely no mention of this concept." *Id.* at 788) (footnotes omitted).

28 For the most comprehensive analysis of the legislative history of the Celler-Kefauver Antimerger Act, which concluded that Congress did have strong efficiency goals and did not mean to preclude an efficiencies defense in merger cases, *see* Muris, *supra* note 18. Muris presents no evidence whatsoever that Congress knew or cared about the allocative inefficiency effects of mergers.

Opponents of the Celler-Kefauver amendment naturally claimed that it might hurt corporate efficiency.[29] However, the view of the Amendment's proponents, and thus of the majority in Congress, was that the Amendment probably would help, not hurt, corporate efficiency by increasing competitive pressure.[30]

28. Congress' principal economic concern with mergers was instead that the merging firms would engage in supracompetitive pricing, thereby unfairly transferring (perhaps "exploiting" or "stealing" would be a better word?) wealth from consumers (purchasers).[31] This view of the legislative history is shared by many scholars,[32] and can be stated as an attempt by Congress to define the property right we today call "consumers' surplus" and to

---

29 For example, Rep. Goodwin stated: "By preventing harmless and reasonable mergers among small and medium-sized concerns, this bill... will foreclose the chance that they may by consolidation or acquisition ever approximate either the size or the efficiency that the big competitors have already achieved. Thus we will hurt small business and help big business." 95 CONG. REC. 11,487 (1949). *See also Corporate Mergers and Acquisitions: Hearings on H.R. 2734 Before a Subcomm. of the Senate Comm. on the Judiciary*, 81st Cong., 1st & 2d Sess. 206 (1950) (statement of George S. Eaton) [hereinafter cited as *Senate Hearings*]; *Amending Sections 7 and 11 of the Clayton Act: Hearings on H.R. 988, H.R. 1240. H.R. 2006, and H.R. 2734 Before Subcomm. No. 3 of the House Comm. on the Judiciary*, 81st Cong., 1st Sess. 45 (1949) (statement of Gilbert Montague). *See also id.* at 83 (statement of John M. Blair, assistant chief economist, FTC).

30 For example, Rep. Celler stated: "Bigness does not mean efficiency, a better product, or lower prices." 95 CONG. REC. 11,486 (1949). *See also* 95 CONG. REC. 11,495–98 (1949) (statement of Rep. Boggs) (quoting Judge Learned Hand); *Senate Hearings*, *supra* note 33, at 308 (statement of James L. Donelly). In addition, the legislative history reveals Congress' willingness to allow small firms to merge, at least in part, to enable them to achieve increased efficiencies. *See, e.g.*, 95 CONG. REC. 11,488 (1949) (statement of Rep. Celler). As noted in *supra* note 33, however, Rep. Goodwin, an opponent of the bill, said it did not allow small firms to merge.

31 For example, Rep. Bennett wanted legislation to protect "the consuming public from unfair exploitation." 95 CONG. REC. 11,506 (1949). Rep. Carroll accused certain companies of "maintaining high prices which injure the consumer," *id.* at 11,492, and called monopoly prices "outrageous prices," *id.*; *see also id.* at 11,492–94. Rep. Byrne quoted (with apparent approval) from an FTC report that stated: "'[U]nder competitive capitalism consumers are protected from high prices by the constant rivalry among numerous firms for a greater share of the market....'" *Id.* at 11,506 (quoting FED. TRADE COMM'N, THE MERGER MOVEMENT: A SUMMARY REPORT 68 (1948)). Rep. Patman complained: "You know what a monopoly always does. It will do what is in the best interest of the people who own the monopoly." *Id.* at 7989. Sen. Kilgore wanted to protect "consumers" and "buyers" against "unjust exploitation." *Senate Hearings*, *supra* note 33, at 180; *see also* 95 CONG. REC. 11,493 (1949) (statement of Rep. Yates). Similar statements permeate the Clayton Act's legislative history. Rep. Hamlin expressed his distaste for monopoly pricing in these terms:

> The only reason why trusts and combinations are declared illegal is because they are organized and operated for the express purpose of... more effectively exploiting the people by taking advantage of their necessities and controlling the price of these necessities to the consumers, as well as the purchase price which they have to pay for the raw material.

51 CONG. REC. 9556 (1914).

See also id. at 9265 (statement of Rep. Morgan); *id.* at 14,223 (statement of Rep. Thompson). These statements are analyzed in context in Lande, *supra* note 5, at 80–142 (arguing that Congress passed the antimerger laws, and the Sherman and FTC Acts, primarily to further wealth transfers from purchasers to firms with market power goals). *See also* the discussion of congressional goals in Mark Glick & Darren Bush, *Breaking Up Consumer Welfare's Antitrust Policy Monopoly*, SUFFOLK U. L. REV. (2023).

32 *See, e.g.*, Louis Kaplow, *The Accuracy of Traditional Market Power Analysis and a Direct Adjustment Alternative*, 95 HARV. L. REV. 1817, 1822–23 (1982) (Congress was concerned with wealth transfers from consumers to dominant firms); F. M. Scherer, *The Posnerian Harvest: Separating Wheat from Chaff*, 86 YALE L.J. 974, 979 (1977) (reviewing RICHARD A. POSNER, ANTITRUST LAW: AN ECONOMIC PERSPECTIVE (1976), and arguing that Congress was concerned at least as much with distributional effects as with efficiency); Eleanor M. Fox, *The Modernization of Antitrust: A New Equilibrium*, 66 CORNELL L. REV. 1140, 1146–55 (1981) (one purpose of the antitrust laws was to stop wealth transfers from consumers and small suppliers to trusts); Herbert Hovenkamp, *Antitrust Policy After Chicago*, 84 MICH. L. REV. 213, 250–53 (1985) (Congress was "really concerned with protecting consumers from unfavorable wealth transfers." *Id.* at 250); Robert G. Harris & Lawrence A. Sullivan, *Horizontal Merger Policy: Promoting Competition and American Competitiveness*, 31 ANTITRUST BULL. 871, 897 (1986) ("protecting consumers from exploitation and loss of income to producers" were Congress' objectives); John S. Wiley, *Antitrust and Core Theory*, 54 U. CHI. L. REV. 556, 587–88 (1987) (Congress cared more about distributive justice than economic efficiency); William E. Kovacic, *Public Choice and the Public Interest: Federal*

award this property right to consumers.³³ The majority of Congress was not concerned with preserving or enhancing corporate efficiency.

29. Although Congress enacted the Clayton Act to protect consumers from the exploitive effects of nascent market power, there is some small amount of evidence that it desired to accomplish this in a manner that did not unduly sacrifice corporate efficiencies because this could harm the public. The very limited evidence for this,³⁴ when analyzed in light of the general pro-competition, anti-monopoly goals of the antimerger laws, suggests that Congress thought a merger should be prohibited *despite* its potential gains in efficiency if that merger were likely to create a firm with market power that could adversely affect consumers.

30. These same conclusions hold for the 1950 Celler-Kefauver Act. Professor Derek Bok's seminal analysis of the law's legislative debates did not find in the legislative record a significant amount of evidence of a congressional concern for efficiency. He noted that "none of the justifications for mergers by big companies were accorded any significance by Congress. Efficiency, expansion, and the like were ignored or simply brushed aside in the deliberations. Even opponents of the bill did not seek to argue that the interests of large companies would be infringed unwisely or unfairly by the bill."³⁵ He therefore concluded that improved efficiency was not an important goal of the Celler-Kefauver Act:

> There is little basis for concluding that the achievement of lower costs as such should give rise to favored treatment under Section 7. The possibility of lower costs was brushed aside in the legislative deliberations and there is every reason to believe that Congress preferred the noneconomic advantages of deconcentrated markets to limited reductions in the cost of operations.³⁶

Trade Commission Antitrust Enforcement During the Reagan Administration, 33 ANTITRUST BULL. 467, 477–78 n.18 (1988) ("distributional concerns, not allocative efficiency, led Congress to pass [the antitrust statutes]"). More generally, Nobel Laureate George Stigler argues that policy-makers concentrate on wealth transfers, not on efficiency. *See* George Stigler, *Economists and Public Policy*, 6 REGUL. (1982), at 13.

33 The most logical explanation of congressional intent is that in passing the antitrust laws, Congress defined certain property rights or entitlements for the first time. In effect, Congress attempted to guarantee consumers the right to purchase competitively priced goods by declaring that consumers' surplus was the property of consumers. Congress condemned any mergers substantially likely to lead to supracompetitive pricing that would "unfairly" transfer this property to firms with market power; i.e., Congress in effect deemed supracompetitive pricing to constitute wealth stolen from purchasers. The most faithful way to implement this concern is to prevent mergers substantially likely to lead to higher prices or reduced choice or output.

34 The remarks of one senator indicate a desire to protect consumers and to encourage corporate efficiency in the belief that these benefits would be passed on to consumers: "The chief purpose of antitrust legislation is for the protection of the public, to protect it from extortion practiced by the trust, but at the same time not to take away from it any advantages of cheapness or better service which honest, intelligent cooperation may bring." 51 CONG. REC. 14,223 (1914) (remarks of Sen. Thompson). Acknowledging the possibility that antimerger legislation might sacrifice corporate efficiency, one senator nevertheless strongly condemned monopolies and trusts because they "divide our people into classes, breed discontent and hatred, and in the end riot, bloodshed, and French revolutions." *Id.* at 15,955 (remarks of Sen. Borah).

35 *See* Derek C. Bok, *Section 7 of the Clayton Act and the Merging of Law and Economics*, 74 HARV. L. REV. 226, 230–33, 307 (1960), and the sources cited therein.

36 *Id.* at 318 (citations omitted). *See also id.* at 236–37. *See also* Fisher et al., *supra* note 19, at 785–88 (1989).

31. Other commentators have argued that, when it amended section 7, Congress did have significant efficiency goals. They were not, however, able to point to evidence in the legislative history indicating that economic efficiency figured significantly in the debates leading to the 1950 amendment.[37]

III. Conclusion: There Should Not Be an Efficiency Rebuttal

32. The overwhelmingly dominant goal of the Clayton Act and its Celler-Kefauver amendment was to prevent the possible formation of market power because the merger would transfer wealth from purchasers to the firm acquiring market power.[38] This concern was so strong that Congress wanted to prevent the rise of this market power in its incipiency.[39] Possible efficiencies from mergers should not be permitted to thwart congressional intent.

---

37 Muris, *supra* note 18, at 393–402, provided four categories of evidence which he alleged showed that Congress desired that the prospects of increased efficiency should count in favor of mergers:
   1. Evidence from the legislative history of prior bills on the same subject that Congress chose not to enact. However, between 1943 and 1949, sixteen bills to amend the Clayton Act were introduced in Congress. *Id.* at 393. Quotations from the legislative record of a selected number of these bills provide no significant insight into the motivations of the Congress that, years later, passed the Celler-Kefauver Act.
   2. Section 7 permits mergers between relatively small firms. Such firms, however, are unlikely to lead to a firm with market or monopoly power and thus to be of concern to section 7.
   3. The "failing company" exception. The wealth redistribution and efficiency effects of this exception are complex and uncertain. Since the failing company exception can save the costs of bankruptcy proceedings, and the management best able to utilize the failing assets will often be a horizontal competitor, the failing company exception could be justified from an efficiency perspective. The exception also, however, has clear distributive effects. It could enable the stockholders and creditors of the acquired company to receive more for their assets. It could also cause a transfer of wealth to the acquiring company if, through the addition of the productive facilities of the failing company, it increased its market power. The failing company exception could also result in benefits to consumers, for without it there could be a short-term under-supply of the failing company's product. This could result in higher prices to consumers in the short term. Further, if a high level of industry instability increased the cost of capital to businesses in that industry, consumer prices could go up in the long term. Although Bok recognized that Congress had a number of motivations, he concluded that "Congress's general unconcern with efficiency would indicate that this factor cannot be accorded much importance in accounting for the exception." Bok, *supra* note 39, at 340 (footnote omitted). Further, the goals of an exception to an Act cannot necessarily be attributed to the rest of the Act.
   4. Muris quotes a discussion between Senator Kefauver and Senator O'Connor involving two newspapers that might want to save costs by having "an arrangement by which one plant would print both newspapers, with each one following its own editorial policy." Muris, *supra* note 18, at 400 (citing 96 CONG. REC. 16,456 (1950)). The discussion concluded that such a proposal would violate the law only where "'it would result in a substantial lessening of competition... It may well be that by effecting a better arrangement for a more profitable undertaking, in the manner described, competition would be stimulated rather than lessened.'" *Id.* at 401 (quoting Sen. O'Connor). Despite Muris' contention that this dialogue evidences an intent to allow efficiency defenses, the venture was to be allowed only if it did not result in a "substantial lessening of competition." Thus, the joint venture was not to be allowed, despite its efficiency-enhancing possibilities, if it might lead to a firm with market power.

38 *See* Fisher et al., *supra* note 19, at 785–88.

39 *See* Lande, *supra* note 5, and Glick & Bush, *supra* note 35.

Decoding the Meaning of "Any Section of the Country": The Pabst-Blatz Saga

PETER C. CARSTENSEN[*]

University of Wisconsin Law School

Abstract

The Pabst-Blatz merger case took over a decade to resolve (1959 to 1970). In the course of that time, the Antitrust Division's conception of how to define relevant geographic and product markets evolved. This study draws on a body of internal documents received through a freedom of information act request that track that process. Lacking any significant economic analysis and support, the initial approach was largely legalistic looking to where the merging competed without regard to whether that constituted what an economist would identify as an economically relevant market. But even at the earliest stage of investigation, there were suggestions that the choice of market areas needed an explanation. Three potentially relevant geographic markets were identified: Wisconsin, a three-state area (Wisconsin, Illinois, and Michigan), and a national market. It became apparent when the government sought to appeal its loss at the trial court level that the record provided little support for either of the two more localized markets. While the Court reversed the lower court decision and seemed to embrace a relaxed view of geographic market definition, the Division's own merger standards had moved to identifying the geographic scope of potential market power.

---

[*] Fred W. & Vi Miller Chair in Law Emeritus, University of Wisconsin Law School. I am indebted to Benjamin Willstein, UW Law '26, for able research and editorial assistance.

1. Section 7 does not refer to "markets." It condemns any combination "*in any line of commerce... in any section of the country...* [that] may... substantially... lessen competition, or... tend to create a monopoly."[1] The resulting question is: when two merging firms compete with each other in some geographic area, will the elimination of such competition constitute a potential substantial lessening of competition? Such a merger necessarily eliminates competition between those firms. Hence, if each firm does a significant volume of business in any area, i.e., a section of the country, that combination could constitute a potential substantial lessening of competition condemned by the statute. This approach would then focus on measures of sales volume that showed a substantial overlap between the parties.

2. In contrast, the analysis could be based on the economic concept of a market. This later approach focuses on defining a "geographic market" within which the parties compete that is sufficiently distinct from other areas such that it would constitute a domain in which market power could exist.[2] Today, merger analysis usually focuses on an economic analysis of the geographic and product market dimensions of a horizontal merger, but this focus was the result of an evolutionary process.

3. Internal agency records can contribute insight into the evolution of the understanding at the Antitrust Division of the meaning of "section of the country." This chapter is based in significant part on documents I received many years ago in response to a Freedom of Information Act (FOIA) request.[3] This use of internal Antitrust Division documents is similar to the study of the *Topco* case that Harry First and I did.[4] These internal memoranda relate to the merger of Pabst and Blatz breweries in 1958, which the Supreme Court condemned in 1966[5] and was finally resolved in the early 1970s. They provide insight into the evolution of the understanding at the Antitrust Division of the meaning of "section of the country."

4. These same memoranda reveal a significant gap in appreciating the implications of the "line of commerce" employed and the alternatives that

---

1   15 U.S.C. § 18 (emphasis added).

2   *See* U.S. Dep't of Just. & Fed. Trade Comm'n, Merger Guidelines 39–40 (2023), https://www.justice.gov/atr/merger-guidelines (providing definitions of markets).

3   The overall project sought to examine the Antitrust Division's enforcement actions and inactions with respect to the beer industry over the period from the mid-1950s to the early 1980s. This was a period of dramatic change in the industry, and the thesis of the project was that antitrust enforcement consistently failed to take account of this dynamic in making decisions. Having done a background article (*see* Peter C. Carstensen, *Antitrust Law and the Paradigm of Industrial Organization*, 16 U.C. Davis L. Rev. 487 (1983)) and a rough draft, I moved on to other topics and the project has languished. But, at least, it provides the materials for this exploration of the development of market analysis.

4   Peter C. Carstensen & Harry First, *Rambling Through Economic Theory: Topco's Closer Look*, *in* Antitrust Stories 171 (Dan Crane & Eleanor Fox eds., 2007).

5   United States v. Pabst Brewing Co., 384 U.S. 546 (1966).

might have been more economically relevant.[6] However, this chapter will focus primarily on the "section of the country" element because that is the issue that most clearly evolved during this prolonged litigation. Some reference to the line of commerce issue is, however, unavoidable.

5. Compared to current FOIA practices, it appears that I got a very generous portion of the internal documents reflecting the views of staff as well as some of the more formal documents used in connection with the decisions to sue, appeal, and settle the case. At the same time, it is unlikely that I have all the memoranda that were generated over the years that the Division dealt with this matter. The materials are, however, quite sufficient to give a picture of how the "section of the country" claim emerged and developed in this case.[7]

6. The central insight of this history is that in the 1950s and early 1960s, many antitrust lawyers thought in terms of legal concepts rather than economic ones. For some lawyers, it was sufficient to point to a substantial overlap in sales territories as establishing a section of the country. But others recognized that something approximating the economic definition of a market was essential to defining a relevant section of the country. Over the course of this case, that perspective came to dominate despite the problematic record made at the trial court.

7. This essay is divided into three stages: the investigation leading to the complaint, the trial, and the appeal. A brief epilogue summarizes the post-Supreme Court history and the emergence of a more consistent approach to market definitions. This history provides the basis for further reflection on the challenge of converting a legal term, "section of the country," into an economic one of a relevant geographic market for merger analysis.

I. From Investigation to Resolution

1. The Investigation of the Pabst-Blatz Merger

8. The information that Pabst was proposing to acquire Blatz appeared in the *Wall Street Journal* on July 14, 1958.[8] The two lawyers handling one of the two then-pending beer merger cases recommended that there be

---

6   The lawyers at various times recognized that the market for beer was divided between "popular" priced beer and "premium" beers, which were primarily the national brands. This distinction appeared from time to time in the analyses. It was never carefully addressed in terms of its competitive relevance except in terms of the need to protect small brewers of popular-priced beer from competition by large brewers that employed extensive advertising and were possibly much more efficient in their production and distribution. Indeed, distribution itself is an additional complicating factor since the underlying legal regulation of the industry requires the separation of production and distribution. *Cf.* Peter C. Carstensen & Richard Dahlson, *Vertical Restraints in Beer Distribution: A Study of the Business Justifications for and Legal Analysis of Restricting Competition,* 1986 Wis. L. Rev 1 (1986). Although not addressed directly until the Supreme Court briefing in *Pabst*, the challenge of having distribution in any area became a factor in explaining the use of regional or local markets for analysis.

7   Subsequent references to these memoranda and documents will provide the author, recipient, and data when in memo form. Other documents will be identified by title and date. All such documents are on file with the author.

8   Hammond, Ward to Reycraft, July 18, 1958. In that pre-Hard-Scott-Rodino era, the agencies got no formal notice of proposed mergers nor a period of time to review them. Hence, the *Wall Street Journal* was one of the most significant sources of merger information.

an investigation.⁹ They noted that both Pabst and Blatz were nationally known premium brands of beers.¹⁰ At the time, beer sales were largely from local or regional brewers and sold at "popular" prices. However, a handful of beers – notably Budweiser, Schlitz, Pabst, Miller, and Blatz – were "premium" beers sold at higher prices. These brands differentiated themselves through advertising, despite being basically indistinguishable from regional beers.¹¹ Of these, Schlitz, Budweiser, and Pabst were the most prominent and the only ones operating a national network of breweries.¹² Remaining brands, such as Miller and Blatz, that only had breweries in Milwaukee, Wisconsin, faced substantial transportation costs that probably consumed much of their price advantage.

9. If beers were separated into national and regional or local brands, then the acquisition of one of the national brands by another might raise more competitive concerns. The beer industry was changing. Many regional and local breweries were either closing or being acquired.¹³ The consumption of beer was moving out of the tavern and into the living room. This meant that cans and bottles came to dominate over kegs, which significantly altered the costs of packaging, and television advertising was a much more significant and costly factor.

10. An important path for survival of the regional and local breweries was to find a way to create a premium brand to avoid the price disadvantage they faced. This challenge was growing as Anheuser, Schlitz, and Miller added additional breweries. While, in retrospect, the status of the brands within the broader beer market might have provided a different focus for the case, the memo's suggestion that the merger's significance lay in its combination of two premium brands was not pursued.

11. The task of investigating the merger was passed on without, so far as appears, much direction to the Chicago Field Office. Only one lawyer seems to have conducted this review, which took over a year. The resulting memorandum treats all beer as in the same commodity market despite recognizing the price differential.¹⁴

12. With respect to geographic markets, the memorandum used market shares in Wisconsin, a three-state region including Wisconsin, Illinois, and

---

9   See United States v. Anheuser-Busch Inc., [1957–1958 Transfer Binder] Trade Reg. Rep. (CCH) ¶ 45,058 (S.D. Fla. 1958). That case challenged the acquisition of the leading brewer in Miami by Anheuser-Busch.

10 See supra note 8 ("The principal product of both is generally considered to be a 'premium beer'. ...").

11 There is no definitive list of "national" brands. The five listed above seem generally to fall into this category, and some other brands were also known nationally or nearly so, such as Ballentine, Rheingold, and Falstaff. As to Blatz, its status as a premium beer was questionable outside Wisconsin, but it was sold in 38 states, so the brand had a national presence.

12 For example, Pabst had breweries in Wisconsin, Illinois, New Jersey, and California.

13 See Hammond, Ward to Reycraft, supra note 8.

14 Hunt to Jinkinson, Aug. 10, 1959, at 7.

Michigan, and nationally as the basis for determining the level of competition between Pabst and Blatz.[15] The memo offers no explanation for the choices. The two brewers did have substantial shares in Wisconsin – in combination, about 24% of total sales in the state. Blatz ranked first and Pabst fourth, with Schlitz third, while Hamm's, a Minnesota brewer, ranked second with a 12% market share.

13. These shares were markedly different from those in Illinois or Michigan.[16] So Wisconsin was a plausible *prima facie* geographic market, but there is no explanation of why the shares of Wisconsin's beer sales were so different from the other two states. Moreover, several Wisconsin breweries sold as much of their beer in other states as Wisconsin, and a substantial amount of the beer sold in Wisconsin came from out-of-state breweries.[17] Indeed, Hamm's from Minnesota ranked second with a share nearly equal to Blatz's.[18]

14. The three-state market is harder to explain in any retrospective analysis, as is the decision to include those states and not others. Neither of those key decisions is explained in the memorandum itself. For example, Minnesota, the home of the second-largest brewer of beer sold in Wisconsin, was not included. In Illinois, Anheuser from Missouri had 14.5% and Schlitz from Wisconsin 16.2%, while Pabst had 5.4% and Blatz 2.4%.[19] Michigan had a different pattern, with in-state brewers having a combined share of over 52%, while Blatz had 5.7% and Pabst 1.4%.[20] When the three states were combined, Blatz had 5.8% and Pabst 5.5%, which gave the merged firm the second-largest volume of sales behind Stroh, which only had sales in Michigan, and Schlitz, which was the only other brewer with more than 10% in this three-state market.[21]

15. It appears that the lawyer doing the investigation had identified the states in which the bulk of Blatz's beer was sold, 68% according to this memo.[22] Nothing in the discussion undertakes to explain the differences in volume among the states. The report also states that Blatz was being sold at "popular" beer prices.[23] Finally, the national shares

---

15 *Id.* at 2–6.

16 *Id.*

17 *Id.* It appears that the Utah and Florida merger cases used state data. In the case of Utah, the only beer allowed was 3.2% alcohol, which is substantially below the usual alcohol content, and so was a distinct product. Utah was the primary place where such beer could be sold. Complaint ¶ 7, United States v. Lucky Lager Brewing Co., No. C-15-58 (D. Utah Feb. 18, 1958). The Florida case focused on a merger in Miami and the focus was on sales in that area, which was quite distant from other breweries in other states. Hammon, Ward to Reycraft, Oct. 2, 1959. Hence, it was more like a "market" as merger analysis came to understand the concept.

18 Hunt to Jinkinson, *supra* note 14, at 3.

19 *Id.*

20 *Id.* at 4.

21 *Id.* at 5.

22 *Id.* at 2.

23 *Id.* at 7.

were 3.1% for Pabst and 1.5% for Blatz.[24] The memorandum overall is negative on whether to challenge this merger.[25] It is clearly negative with respect to a national claim; not enthusiastic about the three-state area; and suggests that Wisconsin is the most likely to provide a plausible basis to challenge the merger.[26]

16. This memo, with a short, neutral cover memo from the chief of the Field Office, was sent to Washington.[27] The cover memo contradicted the staff statement about Blatz prices and reported that prices remained at the premium level after the merger. In August 1959, the Chicago Field Office was told to send the materials on the merger to D.C. so that it could be handled in conjunction with the Florida case by the lawyers in D.C.[28] Later that month, the head of the D.C. Special Trial Section sent a memo to the acting assistant attorney general (AAAG), Robert Bicks, recommending suing the merger.[29] The memo used a broad reading of lessening competition from a House Report and argued that the "substantial nature of these companies' sales competition in the area [Wisconsin]... show[s] that a competitor of substance has been eliminated."[30] The emphasis was on Wisconsin and the risk to smaller brewers: the "competitive advantage" from the merger "may... substantially lessen... the ability of the smaller breweries [in Wisconsin] to compete."[31] There was no need to wait for the resolution of the Florida case as the Chicago Office had suggested.[32]

17. At that time, the attorney general (AG) had to approve the filing of antitrust cases. A formal memorandum presented the recommendation to file suit.[33] It lists Wisconsin and the three-state area as the geographic markets and justifies them based on the two existing beer merger cases and two other decided merger cases that had used states as relevant sections of the country.[34] The competitive risk was that "the combined company has obtained the competitive advantages of expanded advertising and increased economies of large production."[35]

---

24 *Id.* at 6.

25 *Id.* at 9 ("It is recommended that the matter be dropped or... held in abeyance [pending the outcome of the pending beer merger cases].")

26 *Id.*

27 Jinkinson to Reycraft, Aug. 14, 1959.

28 Reycraft to Jinkinson, Aug. 19, 1959.

29 Reycraft to Bicks, Aug. 24, 1959.

30 *Id.* at 2.

31 *Id.* at 4.

32 *Id.*

33 Memorandum to the Attorney General, date stamped Sept. 18, 1959.

34 *Id.* at 5 (citing American Crystal Sugar Co. v. Cuban-American Sugar Co., 152 F. Supp. 387 (S.D.N.Y. 1957), and United States v. Bethlehem Steel Corp., 168 F. Supp. 576 (S.D.N.Y. 1958)).

35 Reycraft to Bicks, *supra* note 29.

18. The analysis focused on the potential for Pabst to combine its distribution with that of Blatz and then use Blatz as a popular-priced beer. The prediction was that Blatz distributors would be harmed by loss of a premium brand, which, in turn, would harm the popular-priced beers that they also distributed. Pabst distributors would have a further advantage by excluding existing Blatz distributors. Somehow, the combined distribution would also produce further economies for the distributors, although it was not clear what those would be.[36]

19. Critics of merger enforcement in this period have highlighted this kind of protectionist attitude as a serious misapplication of antitrust law. Indeed, contemporary merger policy viewed putative improved efficiency stemming from a merger as negative.[37] The claimed harms to smaller brewers could have been reconceptualized as involving the risks of foreclosure of distribution by dominant brewers using exclusive dealing and price discrimination.[38] The state regulation of this industry is constitutionally exempt from challenge as a burden on interstate commerce, which facilitated both exclusionary and exploitive conduct by major brewers.[39] It is, however, worth recalling that in this period, the Division and the Federal Trade Commission (FTC) were trying to figure out the implications of the revised section 7 and lacked any defined structure for such an analysis.

20. Once the AG approved the filing of the case, the Chicago Field Office demanded that it handle the case.[40] AAAG Bicks agreed.[41] This led to some advice to the Chicago Field Office from the two lawyers handling the Florida case: "As the Pabst complaint indicates, our present idea is that Wisconsin is... a separate section of the country and that the three-state area encompassing Wisconsin, Illinois, and Michigan is a similarly appropriate section of the country."[42]

21. They compared the market issues in the Florida case that they were handling with Pabst.

> There are certain additional problems, however, in the Pabst-Blatz situation... such as the fact that Wisconsin brewers have substantial markets outside the state. This is true not only of the national brewers such as Schlitz, but of smaller brewers, such as Gettleman and

---

36 *Id.* at 7.

37 *See* Brown Shoe Co., Inc. v. United States, 370 U.S. 294, 344 (1962) ("But we cannot fail to recognize Congress' desire to promote competition through the protection of viable, small, locally owned business. Congress appreciated that occasional higher costs and prices might result from the maintenance of fragmented industries and markets. It resolved these competing considerations in favor of decentralization.").

38 *Cf.* Carstensen & Dahlson, *supra* note 6.

39 *See id.* at 7–9.

40 Jinkinson to Bicks, Sept. 21, 1959.

41 Bicks to Jinkinson, Sept. 28, 1959.

42 Hammon, Ward to Reycraft, *supra* note 17, at 2.

Foxhead. *Limiting the area of effective competition to Wisconsin will require some sort of answer to this out-of-state local brewery shipment situation.*[43]

22. Thus, the issue of justifying Wisconsin as well as the three-state region as relevant sections of the country was explicitly identified to the Chicago lawyers who were taking over the case.

23. By putting the Chicago Field Office in charge of the *Pabst* case, direct supervision of the three beer merger cases was now dispersed among three different parts of the Antitrust Division, and each case involved a potential distinct use of state or local regions as the relevant section of the country. The San Francisco office was handling the Utah case, which involved the acquisition of the brewer with a dominant share of the state market by one of its substantial competitors.[44] Utah at the time only allowed beer with a maximum of 3.2% alcohol.[45] This is substantially lower than the standard beer alcohol content. This made Utah unique in the sense that to compete, a brewer had to produce and distribute a distinct type of beer. It was also the case, however, that the third and fourth largest sellers of such beer were out-of-state brewers. Thus, the issue might have been better framed around the sale of 3.2% beer in a larger region, where distribution in Utah would be essential to justify allocating resources to this type of product.

24. In the Florida case, the largest brewer nationally – Anheuser-Busch – was in the process of building a new brewery in central Florida. Anheuser had acquired American Brewing, which had its only brewery in Miami, where it had a very large volume. In addition, Schlitz, the second largest national brewer, like Anheuser, was building a large brewery in the state. The complaint alleged that the adverse competitive effects would occur in the state or "regions" of the state.[46] This reflected the lawyers' understanding that out-of-state breweries had a difficult time competing in the Miami area because of transportation costs. After the Schlitz and Anheuser breweries came online, these cost differences were likely to increase. Thus, there was *prima facie* plausibility to a regional beer market consisting of Florida in and around Miami.

25. Whether retaining the *Pabst* case in Washington would have made a difference in the development of the market analysis is unknowable. It is undeniable that the direct supervision of the beer merger litigation was dispersed and only coordinated at a fairly high level at the

---

43   *Id.* at 3 (emphasis added).

44   United States v. Lucky Lager, 209 F. Supp. 665, 667–68 (D. Utah 1962) (describing the complaint); *see also*, Complaint, *supra* note 17.

45   *See id.* ¶ 7.

46   The complaint itself is unavailable in publicly available sources, but the two government lawyers handling that case provided that description. *See* Hammond, Ward to Reycraft, *supra* note 8.

headquarters of the Division. Indeed, nothing in the available documents, with one exception noted earlier,[47] shows any concern during the period of the development of the *Pabst* case with respect to the justification of Wisconsin or the three-state area as appropriate sections of the country.

2. Pre-Trial Actions, and the Trial Court Decision

26. The Chicago Field Office filed the complaint on October 1, 1959, about 14 months after the merger had occurred and the Blatz brewery was closed. The complaint followed the earlier memorandum and listed Wisconsin and the three-state region as the relevant sections of the country based on the volume of the parties' beer sold in these areas.[48] The answer, filed some five and a half months later, denied that either Wisconsin or the three-state region were relevant sections of the country and that states did not constitute relevant sections of the country.[49]

27. This commenced a very slow process of discovery and motion practice that lasted until 1964. By late December 1959, the staff had completed a number of interviews, and follow-up data collection that showed that in the year following the merger, Pabst had continued to price Blatz as a premium beer in Wisconsin.[50] Wisconsin-based brewers, however, were concerned that Pabst would reduce the Blatz price to the popular level and consolidate distribution so that local brewers would be excluded as well as facing a popular-priced Blatz.[51] Implicit in this description is the assertion that the number of potential distributors was limited so that the loss of a current distributor could impose significant hardship on the brewer. Pabst was also now brewing Blatz at all its breweries and reportedly consolidating distribution of the two brands in single distributors outside Wisconsin.[52] In one of the few documents that addressed the product market, the memorandum asserted that, based on production technology, beer was beer.[53] The price differences were explained as a consequence of advertising.

---

47 *See id.*

48 *See* Complaint, *supra* note 17 ¶¶ 12–14. Subsequently, the government added the national beer market as another relevant section of the country based again on the areas in which the parties competed. *See* Pl. Response to Pre-Trial Order, Sept. 18, 1961. These materials come from the Transcript of Record, filed July 28, 1965, https://appliedantitrust.com/09_merger_guidelines/00_classic_cases/06_pabst/3_sc/pabst_us_transcript_record_index_print.pdf.

49 *See* Answer ¶¶ 13, 14, 16 in *id.*

50 Hoyt to Jinkinson, Dec. 29, 1959, 1 ("Blatz is still a premium price beer in the State of Wisconsin and is still a local price beer elsewhere in the United States, as it was just prior to the merger.").

51 *Id.* ("[B]reweries [in Wisconsin]... were greatly worried over the possibility of Blatz becoming a local price beer in Wisconsin. . . .").

52 *Id.* at 2.

53 *Id.* at 2–3.

28. This memorandum illustrates one dimension of this litigation that reflects a lack of economic sophistication. There were clear differences in price and a recognition that if a premium beer was discounted, it was likely to capture significant sales from existing popular beers. This suggests the potential for two product sub-markets in beer, as the initial memo recommending the investigation suggested. In this conception, the loss of Blatz as a premium brand could harm competition by reducing the options for distributors to have a premium brand in their product mix. In turn, the reduction in the number of distributors would reduce the market potential for popular beers. However, a subsequent memo reported that there was, in fact, little consolidation of distribution.[54] The government had sought a preliminary injunction to bar the termination of distributorship absent good cause but withdrew that request in February 1961. In approving this action, the Washington supervisor suggested that distributors could be used on the issue of market definition.[55]

29. Meanwhile, attention began to focus on the unique claim that Pabst was a failing or floundering firm that needed to acquire Blatz to survive. The core contribution of Blatz was its management, which Pabst obtained.[56]

30. Starting in April 1961 and lasting into November, there were extensive discussions of possible settlements.[57] They focused on Wisconsin and were framed in terms of whether there would be any divestiture.[58] In July, a Washington-based lawyer for Pabst proposed a settlement that did not involve any divestiture but instead would have allowed a reopening of the case if the combined Pabst/Blatz sales in Wisconsin reached 30%, which was above their combined share pre-merger.[59] Apparently, the case could also be reopened if the price of either beer was unreasonably low. The proposal also included a proposed ban on future acquisitions and some protections for existing distributors. The Chicago staff argued against this because "the principal impact of the acquisition was felt in Wisconsin" and Pabst could cut the price of Blatz in Wisconsin to the detriment of the smaller brewers.[60]

31. In November, the Chicago staff submitted a proposed consent decree that it favored.[61] It would limit Pabst combined sales to "one-third of the total beer sales in the State of Wisconsin," and give small brewers

---

54 Jinkinson to Reycraft, Feb. 16, 1961, at 2 ("[T]here have only been a small number of consolidations of Pabst and Blatz distributors.").

55 Reycraft to Jinkinson, Feb. 24, 1961 ("I suggest you… consider developing the distributor witnesses for purposes other than showing direct injury to them." These included "line of commerce," impact of mergers on competition, and "the geographic areas in which they… compete" to support the claim for the "section of the country… set forth in the complaint.").

56 *See* Reycraft to Long, Apr. 21, 1960; *see also*, Long, Hunt, Hoyt to Jinkinson, Aug. 21, 1961.

57 *See* Jinkinson to Reycraft, Apr. 6, 1961; Reycraft to Jinkinson, Apr. 18, 1961.

58 *See* Long, Hunt, Hoyt to Jinkinson, *supra* note 56.

59 *See* Williams to Jinkinson, July 25, 1961.

60 Long, Hunt, Hoyt to Jinkinson, *supra* note 56; *see also* Jinkinson to Williams, Aug. 28, 1961.

61 Jinkinson to Sklarsky, Nov. 7, 1961; in the FOIA materials is a draft consent decree dated Nov. 6, 1961.

a right to complain to the court for two years if they had objections to particular Pabst practices, although Pabst could excuse its conduct as meeting competition from other large brewers.[62]

32. It does not appear that this proposal had any traction. A 1963 memo reports that the Division's senior management decided in 1961 that the priority goal in any settlement would be divestiture of the Blatz brand "together with sufficient facilities or business to make the trademark assignment a valid one" and not its old brewery.[63] This, too, is consistent with a concern with a reduction in the number of premium brands.

33. There is a two-year gap in the file, with memos resuming in 1963. Again, they focus on potential settlement terms as well as how to respond to Pabst's "failing firm" claim.[64]

34. In January 1964, the case finally moved toward trial. Both sides submitted pre-trial briefs. The government's brief argued that "Wisconsin is a natural, logical, and relevant area in which to assess the effect of the Pabst-Blatz merger[;]"[65] the two beers were sold at "similar prices" in Wisconsin;[66] Wisconsin breweries produced substantially more beer than was consumed in the state, and "Wisconsin and every other State is made into a distinct market by the system of legal regulation of the beer industry[;]" and Wisconsin is the "area where the most intense competition took place between Pabst and Blatz prior to the merger... [and] is the most significant area for judging the competitive effects of their merger."[67]

35. The brief also relied on the fact that Pabst sold nearly 30% of its beer in the three-state area, while Blatz sold about two thirds of its volume in that region.[68] Moreover, the government argued that "Wisconsin and every other State is made into a distinct market by the system of legal regulation of the beer industry."[69] Finally, the brief also contended that the pricing of Blatz in Wisconsin compared to its price in other states showed that "Pabst has recognized Wisconsin as a unique market."[70] This is the one argument that links back to an economic definition of the market.

---

62 *Id.* at 4–5.

63 Burgess to Jinkinson, Aug. 2, 1963.

64 Pabst claimed that it was a failing firm in the late 1950s and that the acquisition of Blatz was essential to its survival. The central thesis was that it needed new and better management, which is what it got by buying its competitor. *See* Woolley to Jinkinson, June 17, 1963.

65 Government's Pre-Trial Brief at 11; the trial court level briefs are available at the Chicago Branch of the National Archives in the case file, United States v. Pabst Brewing Company et al. As noted *infra*, not all the briefs were retained.

66 *Id.*

67 *Id.* at 12.

68 *Id.*

69 *Id.* at 14.

70 *Id.*

36. The three-state market area was justified as allowing the court to "see the effects of the merger in a larger… segment of the national market."[71] However, no other economic facts were cited to justify the selection of these states.

37. Pabst's response was to assert that only the United States constituted a relevant market.[72] It alleged "[b]eer flows in and out of Wisconsin unimpeded by state lines thus precluding the contention that it alone is a relevant geographic market."[73] More than 25% of the beer consumed in Wisconsin came from out of state, while more than 75% of beer produced in the state was sold in other states.[74] The most relevant data cited showed that, in 1953, when the Milwaukee breweries were shut down by a strike, the amount of out-of-state beer sold in the state doubled.[75] Similar arguments were advanced against the three-state market.[76]

38. When the case came to trial in late January 1964, the government presented its case entirely through documents and excerpts from depositions, despite earlier statements that it would call a number of industry witnesses.[77] As soon as the government rested, Pabst moved to dismiss the case on the grounds that neither Wisconsin nor the three-state region constituted appropriate sections of the county for section 7 purposes.[78] The court paused the trial and ordered the parties to submit briefs.

39. The internal response to the motion rejected the national market claim and asserted that regional markets were where brewers competed.[79] If the price in a region declines, distant brewers cannot afford the costs of shipping beer into such a region.[80] There is no reference to any actual cost data, although later in the memo, the point is made that the major national brewers were building breweries around the country.[81] States are appropriate regions also because they have the power to regulate beer sales. Assertedly, they can exclude brewers, and so state lines may be "arbitrar[]y," but "they are nevertheless real."[82] Moreover, contrary

---

71   *Id.* at 15.

72   Trial Brief of Defendant Pabst Brewing Company. Filed Jan. 13, 1964, at 21.

73   *Id.* at 22 (emphasis in original omitted).

74   *Id.* at 22–23.

75   *Id.* at 24. Indeed, the volume in those two months constituted more than 60% of the total amount of beer brought into the state in that year. *Id* at 23.

76   *Id* at 24–26.

77   United States v. Pabst, 233 F. Supp. 475, 478–80 (E.D. Wis. 1964).

78   *See* Government's Brief in Opposition to Defendant's Motion to Dismiss, Feb. 24, 1964.

79   *See* Woolley to Jinkinson, Apr. 27, 1964 (evaluating Pabst's brief on the market issues).

80   *Id.* at 2.

81   *Id.* at 1.

82   *Id.* at 3.

40. In its brief, the government contended that "[t]he use of local areas to test a merger has become a well-established practice in Section 7 cases"[84] and that "Wisconsin is a market which 'corresponds [sic] to the economic realities' of this case."[85] The brief then recites the information about the percentage of Pabst and Blatz production sold in Wisconsin.[86] Additionally, Wisconsin was relevant as the "center of the beer industry."[87] The brief then stressed the significance of the state law regulations of competition in the industry.[88]

to the defendant's claims, state regulations vary substantially despite the fact that both Pabst and Blatz were sold in most states.[83]

41. The Pabst brief was not in the district court file, but it apparently tracked the arguments in the pre-trial brief.[89] The government's reply brief reiterated the most salient points of its initial brief, which included the assertion that "Wisconsin is the area... where the most intense competition between Pabst and Blatz existed before the merger."[90] At the subsequent oral argument, the judge expressed doubts about the merits of the government case.[91]

42. A few months later, he dismissed the case.[92] The decision held was that the government failed to prove that Wisconsin or the three-state area were sections of the country in which adverse competitive effects were possible.[93] In his view, there was only a national market for beer since any brewer could sell beer in any state. Moreover, most brewers, in fact, sold beer in multiple states. He also emphasized that the government had not presented witnesses to explain why state or regional areas were competitively distinct in any way that would justify their use as sections of the country.[94]

---

[83] Government's Brief in Opposition, *supra* note 78, at 4.

[84] *Id.* at 4.

[85] *Id.* at 5 (quoting from *Brown Shoe*, 370 U.S. at 337).

[86] *Id.* at 5–6.

[87] *Id.* at 7.

[88] *Id.* at 7–10.

[89] *See* Woolley to Jinkinson, *supra* note 79.

[90] Government's Reply Brief to Brief of Defendant Pabst Brewing Company in Support of its Motion to Dismiss, Mar. 30, 1964.

[91] Long to Sklarsky, May 5, 1964.

[92] United States v. Pabst, 233 F. Supp. 475 (E.D. Wis. 1964).

[93] *Id.* at 481–88 (rejecting both Wisconsin and the three-state region because out-of-area beer entered those regions and beer produced in those areas was shipped out of the areas).

[94] *Id.* at 495.

3. The Appeal

43. The Chicago staff immediately asked for an appeal.[95] At the time, appeals went directly to the Supreme Court, meaning the solicitor general of the Justice Department had to approve. The Chicago staff memo focused on Wisconsin as the primary market.[96] It contended that under the recent Supreme Court *Philadelphia National Bank* decision, the merger was presumptively illegal in Wisconsin.[97] "The Government's evidence makes it abundantly clear that Wisconsin was the area where competition was most intense between Pabst and Blatz and... the elimination of Blatz as a vital competitor in the brewing industry has been most severely felt."[98]

44. The concept advanced was that the area where these two firms compete is the relevant section of the country without regard to boundary issues, even though 80% of their beer was sold outside of Wisconsin.[99] Blatz beer did receive a higher price in Wisconsin than elsewhere, which supported the conclusion that Wisconsin was a distinct market.[100] The three-state section of the country was justified because it was distinctive in terms of sales or it was an area with "an appreciable segment" of the sales of the parties.[101]

45. The subsequent memo for the solicitor general recommending the case to the Supreme Court reframed these points.[102] Wisconsin was characterized as "concentrated" and the three-state area as "of sufficient commercial importance to qualify as a section of the country."[103] The case presented the question "whether the government may establish a relevant geographic market by showing *merely* that the two parties to the merger competed in a selected area and that that area is not of de minimis commercial significance."[104] The Court had signaled that "elaborate proof of market structure and market behavior is unnecessary in appropriate cases."[105] Hence, any area where the firms compete is a section of the country based on a quotation from *Philadelphia National Bank* about areas of "competitive overlap."[106]

---

95 Cusack to Long, Oct. 30, 1964; *see also* Long to Hummel, Oct. 30, 1964; Spivak to Files, Dec. 16, 1964.
96 Cusack to Long, Oct. 30, 1965, 4–11.
97 *Id.* at 3–4 citing United States v. Philadelphia National Bank, 374 U.S. 321 (1963).
98 *Id.* at 6.
99 *Id.* at 7–8.
100 *Id.* at 11.
101 *Id.* at 17.
102 Memorandum for the Solicitor General, Dec. 21, 1964.
103 *Id.* at 4, 5.
104 *Id.* at 9 (emphasis added).
105 *Id.*
106 *Id.* at 11.

46. The memo also stated the three-state area is also a section since "the area accounted for between [two thirds] and almost [three quarters] of Blatz's total sales and for about 30% of Pabst's total sales."[107] The memo also stressed increased concentration even though merger was not the primary cause. Thus, the focus was entirely on where the merging parties did business without any proposed criteria forthe economic uniqueness of either alleged market.

47. The reviewer in the solicitor general's office agreed that if Wisconsin were a geographic market, then the *Philadelphia Bank* inference would follow.[108] The statistical data for either the three-state region or a national one were "less favorable."[109] But the memo questioned the use of states as markets based only on the fact that each party had a substantial volume of business.[110] Particularly, the reviewer claimed there needed to be "at least some economic considerations which justify the selection of that particular area and its differentiation from contiguous areas surrounding it."[111] The reviewer noted that where product competition exists generally, there has to be a reason to segment a state or other local area:[112]

> Unfortunately, the record does not explain why it is that locally produced beers enjoy such an advantage on their home grounds – e.g., whether because of transportation costs, local good will, ease of dealing with local distributors, etc. ...It would be much better if we could establish that Wisconsin was an appropriate "section of the country" without drawing upon evidence of Pabst and Blatz sales in the state. Unfortunately, that is probably impossible on the present record.[113]

48. A senior lawyer in the office similarly saw significant problems with the lack of explanation for the use of states.[114] However, there were responses from the Chicago staff that argued the fact of state regulation justified the use of states.[115] Another staff member, who had some background in

---

107 *Id.* at 5.

108 Goodman to the Solicitor General, Jan. 8, 1965, at 1.

109 *Id.*

110 *Id.*

111 *Id.* at 2. There is a reference to a Senate report made in connection with the 1950 amendments to the Clayton Act's merger provisions that suggests: "alternative (a) a test of 'relative substantiality' and (b) a test of 'distinctiveness.' Either the proposed submarket must be substantial in relation to some larger market (presumably the total national market) or it must be marked by features which relevantly differentiate it and set it apart from other areas." *Id* at 3.

112 *Id.* at 2.

113 *Id.* at 5.

114 Friedman to the Solicitor General, Jan. 22, 1965, 1 ("Unfortunately, the present record does not contain any evidence to show the extent to which the sale and distribution of beer is conducted on a state-wide basis... and whether the companies treat the State as an administrative or operating unit.").

115 Long to Seibel, Feb. 23, 1965; Long to Seibel, Feb. 26, 1965.

statistics and economics,[116] equated markets with a place where transactions occur and that expands into an "area from which the customers come to buy a good at a given market or markets."[117] This approach focused on transportation costs to define areas in which it would be profitable to compete. This explanation used states as a method of aggregating local retail markets but without any focus on whether there is market power.[118]

49. The decision to appeal was made while William Orrick was the assistant attorney general (AAG). Donald Turner took over that position in June 1965. He had a PhD in economics and was perhaps the most prominent antitrust scholar of the times. The initial filing is a "jurisdictional statement" that explains to the Court why it should hear the case. Turner's name appears on the jurisdictional statement, which was filed on July 28, 1965,[119] but he likely had little oversight on its preparation.

50. The statement initially described the merger and provided market share information for the two purported markets.[120] "[B]oth [firms] had breweries in Milwaukee, [so] the actual loss to competition in that section of the country was much greater than revealed by figures for sales throughout the nation as a whole."[121] Because the firms had much of their sales in Wisconsin and the three-state area, the statement justified the use of these areas for testing the legality of the merger. "The government's evidence shows that in at least one section of the country the effect of the merger upon competition would be much more severe than anything suggested by the national figures."[122] The argument pointed to different sales volumes in different states to contend that more localized markets were relevant.[123] Particularly, the government said that "[i]n the present case the government offered compelling proof that the Pabst-Blatz merger will have markedly more serious anticompetitive consequences in Wisconsin and the tri-State region – areas conveniently served by the Milwaukee and Peoria Heights breweries,"[124] and "[e]specially in Wisconsin, but also throughout the three-State area of Wisconsin, Illinois and Michigan, the effect will be much greater because both companies sold large portions of the beer consumed in those areas."[125]

---

116 Elliott B. Woolley, *The Method of Minimized Areas as a Basis for Correlation Analysis*, 9 Econometrica 38 (1941).

117 Woolley to Sarbaugh, Mar. 3, 1965.

118 *Id.* at 5 (Pabst and Blatz served "local markets" "in which each was a substantial competitive factor, and in which their merger may substantially affect competition therein").

119 Jurisdictional Statement at 1.

120 *Id.* at 4–7.

121 *Id.* at 12.

122 *Id.* at 17.

123 *Id.* at 18.

124 *Id.* at 20–21.

125 *Id.* at 18.

51. The focus of the argument was on the percentage of beer volume coming from these breweries within Wisconsin or the three-state area. What is missing is any reference to evidence that explains why more distant breweries did not or could not sell in these areas when, as the record showed, a significant share of the volume was in fact provided by out-of-area breweries.

52. The brief conceded that out-of-area breweries that already sold in the areas could expand sales in response to higher prices in the areas. This means that Wisconsin was not "a perfect separate market," but it was a better option than the national market.[126] The brief also conceded that the record did not explain any particular barriers to entry into Wisconsin:

> The record does not show whether the predominance of local beers is due to price differences based upon transportation costs, to the good will and loyalty of Wisconsin consumers toward their local product, to the existence of established business relationships between Wisconsin brewers and distributors, or to some other factor or combination of factors. Whatever the reason, the fact is that Wisconsin was an extraordinarily self-sufficient area of beer supply.[127]

53. At the end of the brief, the government acknowledged that "[s]tate boundaries do not necessarily have intrinsic commercial significance... Nonetheless, State statistics often provide the most convenient and workable means for measuring the effect of a merger in a submarket, once the general area has been *selected upon economic grounds.*"[128]

54. One of Turner's innovations at the Antitrust Division was a program of having a PhD economist as a special economic assistant. The first special economic assistant was William S. Comanor, who was on leave from Harvard's economics department. In January 1965, presumably in connection with preparing the brief in chief, he sent a memo to Turner evaluating the market definition issues in the *Pabst* case.[129] The memo explains markets in terms of market power considerations: "[W]e are really concerned with the constraint placed on the behavior of firms located within Wisconsin, and with the three-state area, by those located without.... If... these constraints are inconsequential, then it is appropriate to limit our analysis to a more restricted area."[130] He also criticized the jurisdictional statement, which admitted that the record did not explain why local beers dominated Wisconsin.[131]

---

126 *Id.* at 23.
127 *Id.*
128 *Id.* (emphasis added).
129 Comanor to Turner, Jan. 26, 1966.
130 *Id.* at 3.
131 *Id.* at 3–4.

55. The brief on the merits, filed on March 1, 1966, took a more economic approach to the market definition issue.[132] The statement of facts focused primarily on Wisconsin, contending that the greatest share of beer sold in the state was produced in the state.[133] It pointed to the concentration of Blatz's sales in Wisconsin and the three-state region[134] and the change in the merged firm's market ranking and share in both markets.[135]

56. The argument advanced the claim that it only needed to show two factors to establish a relevant geographic market based on sales:

> Where the government relies on sales percentages as a basis for arguing that a horizontal merger adversely changed the structure of competition in a section of the country, it need only show (1) that both the acquired and acquiring firm made substantial sales to customers located in that section and (2) that there is reason to believe that sellers whose sales were not included in the market suffer from some disadvantage in competing with those whose sales were included.[136]

57. The government then declared that the record supported both claims.

> First, both Pabst and Blatz made substantial sales to customers located in the state at the time of the merger. Second, there are persuasive if not conclusive indications that the sellers actually selling in the state had a significant competitive edge over other beer producers who might have wanted to sell there.[137]

58. The differentiation of Wisconsin rested on "evidence that the effective distribution of beer requires the creation of brand allegiance which in turn requires intensive advertising and promotional efforts and the enlistment of Distributors who will be vigorous and effective in creating a market for the brand in the state or local area where penetration is desired."[138] This allowed the larger brewers to change different prices from those they charged in other areas.[139]

59. The brief on the merits identified the basis for a relevant section of the country based on evidence that the competition in the region was to some significant degree distinct from that in adjacent areas. It also marshaled

---

132 The brief is available at THE MAKING OF MODERN LAW: U.S. SUPREME COURT RECORDS AND BRIEFS, 1832–1978, https://www.gale.com/c/making-of-modern-law-us-supreme-court-records-and-briefs-1832-1978.
133 Comanor to Turner, *supra* note 129, at 4–6.
134 *Id.* at 8.
135 *Id.* at 11.
136 *Id.* at 15.
137 *Id.* at 16.
138 *Id.*
139 *Id.*

the modest evidence in the record to support this revised vision of the relevant market.

60. The defendants' brief argued that the only relevant market was national.[140] This essentially repeated the argument consistently made, starting with the pre-trial brief, that breweries sell in a national market. It also focused on the failure of the government to provide evidence that either Wisconsin or the three-state region was a market in the economic sense.

61. Edwin Zimmerman, the deputy assistant attorney general for antitrust, argued the case for the government in the Supreme Court on April 27, 1966. The transcript shows again a focus on Wisconsin. "For purposes of analysis, I propose to deal principally with the State of Wisconsin and deal with the facts in the record on that state."[141] But this analysis "can be easily applied to the three-State area, the other region in the case."[142] Consistent with the brief, the emphasis again was on the competitive implications of the region selected: "[T]he purpose of market definition, the necessary implication is that what we wish to know is whether other sellers are capable of providing direct restraints on the ability of the merging firm to raise price."[143] "[T]wo overlapping factors: one, locational advantages, and secondly, and more importantly, the sustained investment in advertising to create brand preferences and sustained attention to distributorship relationships" distinguished Wisconsin from adjacent areas.[144] Consequently, "companies not conveniently located, do not represent a direct competitive restraint upon those companies now selling in Wisconsin."[145] There were also references to price differences between Wisconsin and adjacent states for the same beer,[146] the role of state regulation, and some evidence that advertising was often done on a state-wide basis.[147] There is only a passing reference to the three-state market: "In the three-state area, we find an even greater concentration of sales of the two companies. We find persistence of market shares, and we find that the two companies again represented a substantial portion of the three-state area."[148]

---

140 Brief for Pabst Brewing Co., 42–62. United States v. Pabst Brewing Co., 384 U.S. 546 1966 WL 115448.

141 Tr.8. A copy of the original transcript is on file with the author and the citations herein are to that transcript. A different version of the same transcript is available at https://www.oyez.org/cases/1965/404.

142 *Id.* at 9.

143 *Id.* The point was elaborated to explain why the District of Columbia was unlikely to be a relevant section of the country: "In other words, to generalize, if other sellers can sell to consumers in the area as readily as those selling there, the definition of the District of Columbia as a geographic market 'is economically meaningless'." *Id.* at 10.

144 *Id.* at 11–12.

145 *Id.* at 12.

146 *Id.* at 20.

147 *Id.* at 19–20.

148 *Id.* at 25.

62. Both the brief on the merits and the oral argument shifted the focus of market definition away from concern only where the merging parties had sales and turned it toward whether the region or regions were distinct from a competitive perspective. How easily could those not selling at specific locations make their goods or services available to buyers in that location? The underlying business reality is that if prices were to increase sufficiently, entry from distant suppliers is, of course, increasingly likely.

63. The hard question is how much of a distinction is necessary to support the claim that the region is a relevant section of the country. Even on the relatively slim record made at trial, it would appear that a plausible case existed for Wisconsin. On the other hand, the three-state region remained unjustified because the set of competitors in each state was quite different, and nothing suggested that a strong competitor in one state had any particular advantage over brewers outside the three-state area in entering and competing in any of the states where it was not yet doing business.

4. Decision and Results

64. The Supreme Court announced its decision reversing the dismissal of the case on June 13.[149] The decision, written by Justice Black, took a very open-ended view of market definition: "[T]he Government [must] prove the merger may have a substantial anticompetitive effect somewhere in the United States. ..."[150] "Th[e] phrase does not call for the delineation of a 'section of the country' by metes and bounds... ."[151] The opinion then pointed to the market share of the parties in Wisconsin, the decline in the number of breweries in the state and nationally, and the increased share of beer produced by the largest brewers in Wisconsin and the nation.[152]

65. Only one sentence referred to the three-state region.[153] The conclusion was that "the evidence as to the probable effect of the merger on competition in Wisconsin, in the three-state area, and in the entire country was sufficient to show a violation of [section] 7 in each and all of these three areas."[154] Thus, based only on the government's evidence, the Court seems to have decided the merits of the case.

66. Justice White concurred based only on the national market, which implied his doubts about the merit of either of the more local market areas. Justice Fortas concurred with the result, but apparently not the opinion. Justice Harlan wrote a short concurrence that questioned the opinion's

---

149 United States v. Pabst Brewing Co., 384 U.S. 546, 553 (1966).
150 *Id.* at 549.
151 *Id.*
152 *Id.* at 550–51.
153 *Id.* at 551.
154 *Id.* at 552.

relaxed view of market definition. His position was that market definition required:

> [S]tudy of statistics and other evidence bearing upon market shares, market trends, number of competitors and the like. . . . All of this, taken in the context of a *prima facie* case, supports the proposition that Wisconsin is an identifiable "section of the country" presenting impediments to the entry of new competitors and insulating those already within the market. . . . [T]his means that those already within such a local market can engage in oligopolistic pricing or other practices without a very real threat that brewers operating in other areas could easily, and within a reasonably short time, enter the Wisconsin market as effective competitors of those already entrenched there.[155]

67. This concurrence reflected more accurately the position of the United States and the emerging analysis of geographic markets in antitrust analysis of mergers.

68. On remand, the district court judge found the merger anticompetitive in all three sections of the country.[156] He also rejected Pabst's failing firm defense.[157] The question of what remedy to impose remained unanswered until 1970. There was no Blatz brewery left to divest. The only asset was the Blatz trademark. To be useful, buyers needed to have the production capacity to provide the necessary volume of beer. Ultimately, the label was sold to Heileman, a significant and, at the time, a successful regional brewer with comparable brands, including a premium label, Old Style Lager, and a super-premium label, Special Export. At the end of the day, this litigation did little to protect the small regional brewers from competition.

69. While the remanded case was being prepared for litigation, the Division was at work on developing the first merger guidelines. Drafts were circulating among staff lawyers. The Chicago lawyers handling the *Pabst* case expressed concern:

> [W]e doubt that Wisconsin fits with the definition of a separate market as defined on page 5. There is little in the Record to indicate any monopoly power over prices by producers in that State and we are somewhat alarmed at the similarity between this definition and that of Professor Adelman given at the trial. . . .[158]

---

155 *Id.* at 555, 560–61.

156 United States v. Pabst Brewing Co., 296 F. Supp. 994, 999–1000 (E.D. Wis. 1969) ("[A]ny brewery attempting to expand its sales operations into those areas [Wisconsin, the three-state region] will experience certain difficulties. . . . To this extent, it can be said that Wisconsin and the three-state area, like any area, present barriers to new entrants into competition. . . . The probable effect of the acquisition of Blatz... may be substantially to lessen competition... in the... sale of beer in the continental United States, the State of Wisconsin and the three-state area. . . .").

157 *Id.* at 1002.

158 Long, Hoyt, Cusack, Berman & Woolley to Spivack (Dir. of Operations), May 16, 1967, at 2. Although the government did not use an economist in the earlier trial, it appears that Pabst did employ one to support its national market theory.

70. Director of Operations Spivack took the position that the state is defendable as a market although not necessarily monopoly power: "[F]or there to be any regional or local submarkets in beer there must be reasons... that give brewers selling within the area a non de minimus [sic] advantage over brewers not selling within the area."[159] Deputy AAG Zimmerman commented to Spivack that a market requires that the participants have an advantage over non-participants: "The real question is how substantial this power or advantage must be."[160]

II. Deciding What Constitutes a "Section of the Country"

71. The *Pabst* case should be seen in the context of the evolution of merger enforcement. The initial conception of "section of the country" rested on the location of where the parties made the bulk of their sales that overlapped. Hence, they competed in that region and so the merger would eliminate that competition. This concept rests on an application of statutory language in a literal, legal way.

72. This was particularly evident in the identification of the three-state region. There, market shares of the merging parties were different in each of the states but cumulatively identified much of Blatz's volume and a substantial share of Pabst sales. But this approach ignored the role of a Minnesota brewer, Hamm's, as the second-largest seller in Wisconsin as well as the great differences in shares of sales in the other two states, not only by Pabst and Blatz but also by all other brewers.

73. The defense appears to have relied only on a national market for beer as the section of the country. Again, its position, as shown in the briefing, is that brewers sold across state lines, and a number sold beer in many or all states. This, too, was a literalist approach to the geographic market issue, even if an economist working for the defendants supported the claim,[161] because it did not explain why volumes of sales were so different in different states or regions. A good example was Stroh's dominance in Michigan, but its total absence in either Wisconsin or Illinois.

74. The lack of sophisticated economic analysis available to antitrust lawyers until well into the 1960s is another significant factor. It appears that neither side used an economist to help with the analysis and presentation of their respective cases prior to the Supreme Court decision. As the Comanor memo shows, there were criteria that could, in turn, have

---

159 Spivak to Turner, May 19, 1967, at 2.

160 Zimmerman to Spivack, June 5, 1967.

161 *See* Long, Hoyt, Cusack, Berman & Woolley to Spivack, *supra* note 158.

focused the factual inquiry to support an economically coherent market definition.

75. On the government side, the staff attorneys seemed to have had a protectionist view with respect to small businesses.[162] At least, that is the way the documents present the concerns. These concerns could have been reframed in more economically informed ways to focus on the potential for mergers among dominant firms to have an exclusionary effect in the distribution process.

76. Another perspective on this case is that the lawyers handling the case at investigation and litigation simply failed to develop any explicit justification for Wisconsin or three-state market claims. In both the Utah and Florida cases, there were apparent reasons for the use of the state. In the case of Florida, parts of the state were plausible markets in terms of economic competition. Similarly, in the earlier cases that had relied in part at least on states as defining markets, the underlying judicial analysis pointed to reasons that justified the use of the state as approximations of markets. The Chicago-based lawyers, in contrast, relied on states in a kind of doctrinal way based on their use in the two other pending beer cases and at least a couple of other cases.

77. At several points – including crucially when the case was returned to Chicago – other lawyers reminded the staff that it was important to justify in some way the use of Wisconsin and the three-state region as distinct markets. There were also references to the problems of obtaining distribution and the costs of longer-distance shipping, but there was no effort to quantify or get other evidence to support these ideas. As a result, as the government conceded in its jurisdictional statement, it had not built a record to provide support for its market definitions except in the showing of sales volume.

78. The Comanor memo at the time of the writing of the brief to the Supreme Court is a useful marker showing the evolution of thinking about the geographic dimension of the market.[163] The analysis explicitly focused on whether competitors in a specific region had or could have some level of market power because those outside the region could not easily enter and compete.

---

162 In addition to creating the special economic assistant position, Turner also created an Evaluation Section whose mission was to review all proposed cases for their economic rationality and consistency with competition policy. I was a member of that section for my five years at the Division. The Section was controversial because for some observers it seemed to obstruct the bringing of cases. *See* MARK J. GREEN, BEVERLY C. MOORE, JR. & BRUCE WASSERSTEIN, THE CLOSED ENTERPRISE SYSTEM; RALPH NADER'S STUDY GROUP REPORT ON ANTITRUST ENFORCEMENT (1972). A review of the protectionist perspectives of the trial lawyers in the *Pabst* case illustrates why some greater review was essential to ensure that merger enforcement, in particular, was consistent with a broader policy of protecting competition and not competitors.

163 In an email exchange with Professor Comanor, he reported that he had no present recollection of this memo or its role in the development of the brief. It is also notable that Richard Posner is listed on this brief, unlike the jurisdictional statement.

79. Here is where the role of distributors would have been more salient. A new entrant would require finding a distributor as well as establishing an awareness of the brand among consumers. But it would be very difficult for a new entrant into distribution to survive with only a single, new brand to distribute. Even if prices increased in a region, such entry by brewers not already distributed in the area would be unlikely in the short to intermediate term. Thus, existing competing brewers in any region were somewhat insulated from new competition, as Justice Harlan pointed out in his concurrence.[164]

80. The brief on the merits in the Supreme Court subtly but significantly shifted away from the argument that any area where two parties competed was a relevant market. Instead, consistent with the Comanor memo, the brief pointed to the reasons why both the regional markets, but especially Wisconsin, were economically distinct. Moreover, by culling the record, some evidentiary support existed for those claims. The 1968 Merger Guidelines then embedded this market power-based concept of the section of the country in merger market analysis.[165]

III. Conclusion

81. In retrospect, Wisconsin seems to have approximated a market given that Pabst and Blatz received prices above cost, and so had the discretion to choose prices. Brewers not presently distributed in Wisconsin were unable to enter and compete despite those above-cost prices. The rationale for the three-state region collapses when any sort of economic market analysis is employed. Nothing in the records makes those three states a unique unit.

82. The evolution of the *Pabst* case illustrates the development of thinking about market definition. It moved from an unfocused description of where firms competed to an identification of the region(s) in which competitors operated with limited potential for out-of-area competitors to enter and compete effectively. In turn, this focused merger law more explicitly on the potential for actual impact on competition. It may be, however, that market definition itself as an econometric exercise has now become doctrinal rather than functional, and other tools can provide better measures of the appropriate power of the parties.[166]

---

164 *See supra* note 155.

165 U.S. Dep't of Just, 1968 Merger Guidelines, https://www.justice.gov/archives/atr/1968-merger-guidelines.

166 *See* Louis Kaplow, *Why (Ever) Define Markets*, 124 Harv. L. Rev. 437 (2010).

The Other Side of Market Definition

TADASHI SHIRAISHI[*]
University of Tokyo

Abstract

Most works on market definition focus on delineating the scope of relevant suppliers, while this article explores the side of customers. It examines how a relevant market is defined and shows that the delineation of customers logically precedes that of suppliers, although this process usually remains implicit. This article elaborates on the logical structure of market definition and articulates its implications for various competition law issues, including submarkets, green deals, exploitative abuse, and international applications.

---

[*] Professor, University of Tokyo, Graduate Schools for Law and Politics.

I. Thesis and Premises

1. Thesis

1. This article aims to describe the structure of market definition in competition law and explore the side of relevant customers. It examines how a relevant market is defined and shows that the delineation of customers logically precedes that of suppliers, although this process usually remains implicit. This article's elaborated and streamlined framework enables fundamental thoughts on market definition and competition law.

2. Definition of "Market Definition"

2. Before examining market definition, this article will define the concept of "market definition." Here, the term "define" refers to explaining the meaning of "market definition." This clarification is necessary because the term "definition" in "market definition" holds another meaning.

3. "Market definition" can be defined as determining the outer boundaries of the relevant market in a specific case. In this process, experts do not explain the meaning of "market." Instead, they describe the range of a market in each specific case.

4. In short, "market definition" is not an abstract elaboration of a general concept of "market" but a delineation of the scope of a specific market in a specific case.

5. There can be more than one relevant market in a specific case. "Market definition" is conducted for each relevant market.

6. A "relevant market" is a market where competition law addresses whether conduct generates anticompetitive effects.

3. Focusing on Suppliers' Competition for Simplicity

7. In some cases, competition law concerns competition by those who supply goods or services, and in other cases, it concerns competition by those who demand goods or services.

8. For simplicity, this article refers only to competition by those who supply. It is not because competition by those who demand is less critical. Such competition includes competition by firms for workers. However, competition on the supply side is discussed much more frequently.

9. Those who supply are called "suppliers," while, interestingly, there is no word such as "demander" in English. Those on the demand side are usually called "customers," "buyers," or "purchasers" in the context of competition law, including market definition. This article uses "suppliers" and "customers" for consistency unless legitimate materials use different terms.[1]

---

1   See *infra* note 4.

II. Prevailing Framework

1. Leading Materials

10. The established framework for market definition that has explicitly prevailed in competition law is described by the U.S. Merger Guidelines of 2023 ("U.S. Guidelines")[2] and the EU Market Definition Notice of 2024 ("EU Notice").[3] These documents are the leading materials in English regarding market definition in the first half of the 2020s.

2. The Core Principle: Demand Substitutability

11. The core principle in the prevailing framework is demand substitutability. This principle means that the suppliers in a relevant market are those considered as available from the customers' viewpoint. The principle regarding the side of suppliers is called "demand substitutability" because customers are on the demand side, where they can choose among suppliers on the supply side.[4]

12. This core principle has given rise to many tools, including the hypothetical monopolist test, also known as the small but significant and non-transitory increase in price (SSNIP) test, and its derivatives. However, these tools are secondary to the core principle itself.

3. Submarket for Targeted Customers

13. After exploring some units that they perceive essential,[5] the U.S. Guidelines and the EU Notice shift to the issue of targeted customers that may create a submarket.[6]

14. The leading materials endorse similar conditions for identifying a relevant submarket. According to the U.S. Guidelines, "the suppliers engaging in targeting must be able to set different terms for targeted customers than other customers" and "the targeted customers must not be likely to defeat a targeted worsening of terms by arbitrage (e.g., by purchasing indirectly from or through other customers)."[7]

15. From the perspective of this article, what is critical here is that the leading materials complete their exploration of the units they perceive as essential before shifting to the topic of targeted customers.

---

2   U.S. Dep't of Just. & Fed. Trade Comm'n, Merger Guidelines (Dec. 18, 2023).

3   *Commission Notice on the Definition of the Relevant Market for the Purposes of Union Competition Law*, 2024 O.J. (C/2024/1645).

4   Interestingly, the EU Notice consistently uses "suppliers" and "customers," whereas the U.S. Guidelines alternate between "suppliers" and "sellers," as well as between "customers," "buyers," and "purchasers." As a hypothesis, this could be due to the EU's constant need for translations between its official languages. This difference in accessibility might be a contributing factor to the "Brussels effect."

5   U.S. Guidelines §§ 4.3–4.3.C and EU Notice, paras. 1–83.

6   U.S. Guidelines § 4.3.D.1. and EU Notice, paras. 88 and 89.

7   U.S. Guidelines § 4.3.D.1. Similar conditions are found in the EU Notice, para. 88.

16. This article will incorporate the customer issue at the beginning of an elaborated and streamlined framework, which will be described in section III. 1.

4. Interim Summary

17. In the prevailing framework discussed above, most discussions on market definition focus on delineating the scope of suppliers. The core principle of demand substitutability primarily refers to the supply side.
18. In this prevailing framework, customers are rarely specified. Most discussions explicitly mention the details of suppliers while paying less attention to those of customers.
19. After completing the units it perceives as essential, the prevailing framework then explores the issue of targeted customers. Here, naturally, the customers receive enough attention.

III. Framework Elaborated and Streamlined

1. Delineation of the Customers Precedes

20. This article agrees with the outcome of most discussions on market definition, but it would like to elaborate on and streamline the essential items. Such elaboration and streamlining would facilitate effective discussions and systematic identification of unknown issues.
21. If the scope of the suppliers is delineated as the alternatives available to the customers, understanding the types of customers must be essential for understanding their preferences. Therefore, the delineation of customers must always precede that of suppliers.
22. If we logically streamline the process, it should follow the sequence below: (1) First, we delineate who the relevant customers are. (2) Then, we delineate the relevant suppliers that can be alternatives for these relevant customers.
23. Suppose we find a smaller segment of customers with unique preferences for certain suppliers.[8] In that case, we should return to the process in step (1), restart with such customers, and confirm their unique alternatives again in step (2). Such iterations are included in the process, shifting back and forth between (1) and (2). However, the streamlined framework with a logical sequence can be described as firstly (1) and then (2), as shown above.

---

[8] Unique preferences often arise due to product differentiation, while others emerge because some customers view a group of goods or services collectively. The relevant markets constituted by such groups of goods or services are referred to as "cluster markets" in traditional articles, such as Robert Pitofsky, *New Definitions of Relevant Market and the Assault on Antitrust*, 90 COLUM. L. REV. 1805, 1862–64 (1990). In contrast, the "cluster markets" discussed in U.S. Guidelines § 4.3.D.4. combine small markets for administrative convenience, as these small markets generate similar competition analyses.

24. In contrast, the core descriptions by the prevailing framework do not care about the side of customers specifically.

2. Definition of the Concept of "Market"

25. We frequently discuss "market definition," but the term "definition" in this context does not refer to the meaning of the concept of "market" but instead to the delineation of the scopes of relevant markets in specific cases. We seldom encounter a formal "definition" of the concept of "market." Neither the U.S. Guidelines nor the EU Notice explicitly describe it. The U.S. Guidelines state that "[a] relevant antitrust market is an area of effective competition,"[9] but it is a function, rather than a definition, of "market."

26. One of the rare examples of such a definition is found in section 2(4) of the Antimonopoly Act of Japan. The Act was enacted in 1947[10] and amended in 1949[11] to insert the definition as section 2(2). Current section 2(4), which is substantially the same as the original provision in 1949, is as follows:

> The term "competition" as used in this Act means a situation in which two or more enterprises ... engage in, or can engage in, either conduct listed in the following Items.
>
> (i) supplying the same or similar goods or services to the same demander,
>
> (ii) receiving supplies of the same or similar goods or services from the same supplier

27. This paragraph verbalizes the concept of "competition" and, in turn, the concept of "market" as the forum for such "competition." In a "market" for supplying goods or services, enterprises (suppliers) compete for demanders (item (i)), while in a "market" for receiving supplies of goods or services, enterprises (demanders) compete for suppliers (item (ii)). Item (ii) refers to demanders' competition for suppliers. Item (i) refers to ordinary competition by suppliers for demanders.

28. The framers of the 1949 Amendment were logical enough to rely on the term "demander." It covers everything from final consumers to big corporate customers such as Toyota when it purchases auto parts. The Japanese equivalent of the English term "demander" is not popular among Japanese people either, but this Japanese equivalent has taken root in competition law in Japan. For example, there are numerous instances of the Japanese term in the Annual Merger Case Reports by the Japan Fair

---

9   U.S. Guidelines § 4.3.

10 Act on Prohibition of Private Monopolization and Maintenance of Fair Trade (Act No. 54 of Apr. 14, 1947). On the enactment, *see* Harry First, *Antitrust in Japan: The Original Intent*, 9 PAC. RIM L. & POL'Y J. 1 (2000).

11 Act Amending the Act on Prohibition of Private Monopolization and Maintenance of Fair Trade (Act No. 214 of June 18, 1949).

Trade Commission (JFTC),[12] likely because the term is simple, logical, and indispensable for sound competition law analysis.

3. Supplementary Notes

A. *The Term "Consumer"*

29. As an alternative for the term "customer," we sometimes observe the term "consumer." The term "consumer" usually refers to natural persons who are the final customers of goods or services.

30. Meanwhile, some legitimate materials on competition law use the term "consumer" to cover corporate customers as well. For example, the European Commission's merger guidelines explain, "In the context of competition law, the concept of 'consumers' encompasses intermediate and ultimate consumers."[13] More thoroughly, the Guidelines on the Application of Article 81(3) of the Treaty, cited in the merger guidelines above, explain as follows:

> The concept of "consumers" encompasses all direct or indirect users of the products covered by the agreement, including producers that use the products as an input, wholesalers, retailers and final consumers, i.e. natural persons who are acting for purposes which can be regarded as outside their trade or profession. In other words, consumers within the meaning of Article 81(3) are the customers of the parties to the agreement and subsequent purchasers. These customers can be undertakings as in the case of buyers of industrial machinery or an input for further processing or final consumers as for instance in the case of buyers of impulse ice-cream or bicycles.[14]

31. The term "consumer" in this context is equivalent to the concept of "demander."[15]

32. However, most experts and learners are unaware of the definition of "consumer" described above. They usually use the term for natural persons as final customers. That is why this article avoids relying on the term "consumer."

33. Numerous public releases by competition authorities use the dual term "consumer" to legally refer to corporate customers and politically emphasize their contributions to the general public.

---

12 The Reports are published only in Japanese.

13 *Guidelines on the Assessment of Non-Horizontal Mergers under the Council Regulation on the Control of Concentrations between Undertakings*, 2008 O.J. (C 265) 6, para. 16 (footnote omitted). A similar description is found in *Guidelines on the Assessment of Horizontal Mergers under the Council Regulation on the Control of Concentrations between Undertakings*, 2004 O.J. (C 31) 5, n.105.

14 *Guidelines on the Application of Article 81(3) of the Treaty*, 2004 O.J. (C 101) 97, para. 84.

15 See *supra* section III.2.

B. *About the Ability to Identify the Targeted Customers*

34. In discussing targeted customers, the U.S. Guidelines and the EU Notice mention the conditions for finding an independent and small relevant market.

35. As one of the conditions that should be cumulatively established, the materials refer to the suppliers' ability to identify the targeted customers and set different terms for them.[16]

36. The author of this article doubts it. As long as such customers have unique preferences, we should admit the existence of such a relevant market, no matter whether the suppliers can identify such customers and set different terms for them.

37. The author of this article agrees that competition law violation is not usually established in such a situation. However, we should conclude that this is because we cannot establish anticompetitive effects in any relevant market rather than because we cannot find a relevant market.

38. If the suppliers cannot discriminate against the targeted customers, the suppliers usually have no choice but to offer competitive prices even to such customers. The suppliers want to retain customers who can switch to alternatives.

39. However, when the number of targeted customers is enormous or rapidly increasing, suppliers may be able to raise prices profitably even when they cannot distinguish the targeted segment from the larger mass.

40. In order to avoid missing such exceptional and significant false negatives and adequately enforce the law, we should find a relevant market for targeted customers ("submarket") even in such a situation. Most normal cases would not generate sufficient anticompetitive effects in such a relevant market, but we need such a relevant market to address exceptional cases that are critical from a competition law perspective.

41. An illustration comes from a judgment of the Supreme Court of Japan.

42. In the 2010 judgment in *NTT East*,[17] the relevant facts of which occurred between 2002 and 2004, the Court defined a relevant market for those customers who preferred internet connections via optical fibers, also known as fiber to the home (FTTH), because such customers were unsatisfied with the speed obtained from ADSL connections.

43. The carriers could not differentiate between those who distinctly preferred FTTH and those who could switch to ADSL.

44. That was why the report by Advocate General Yukito Okada emphasized that the number of customers who distinctly preferred FTTH was rapidly

---

16 The first condition cited in *supra* section II.3.
17 Nippon Telegraph and Telephone East Corp. v. Fair Trade Commission, Saikō Saibansho [Sup. Ct.] Dec. 17, 2010, Heisei 21 (gyo-hi) 348.

increasing. The report cited a textbook created by the author of this article that contended the necessity of finding a smaller relevant market even in such situations.[18]

45. In short, the *NTT East* judgment illustrates a tribunal finding a competition law violation by defining a relevant market for targeted customers even when the suppliers could not distinguish the targeted segment from the larger mass.

IV. Examples of Phenomena Explained by the Elaborated and Streamlined Framework

46. The elaborated and streamlined framework outlined above demonstrates that a relevant market consists not of a single layer but of two layers: the layer of relevant suppliers and the layer of relevant customers. In this market, one layer sells, while the other layer purchases, the relevant goods or services.

47. This framework clarifies and explains many phenomena, including the following examples.

1. Geographic Scope of the Layer of Relevant Customers

48. When the prevailing framework talks about the "geographic market definition," it usually implies that the geographic scope refers to that of suppliers. This implication is natural because the prevailing framework usually focuses on the layer of suppliers.

49. Nevertheless, there are two layers, even if one is usually unmentioned.

50. Because there are two layers, there can naturally be two different geographic scopes in a single relevant market. For example, the relevant customers might be found in a specific region, while the relevant suppliers could be located nationwide. Another example is a case where the relevant customers are domestic, while the relevant suppliers are worldwide. When we refer to a "worldwide market," we should clarify which layer extends worldwide.

2. Whether Justifications Contribute Within the Relevant Market

51. As environmental sustainability gains prominence, all experts know about justifications in competition law discussions. Even if conduct generates anticompetitive effects, it could be considered safe and legal when it is justified by factors such as the necessity of developing sustainable systems through so-called green deals.

---

18 SAIKOSAIBANSHO HANREI KAISETSU MINJIHEN HEISEI 22 vol. 2 (2014)(written by Advocate General Yukito Okada). Advocate generals in Japan are professional judges aged around 40 in the Japanese judiciary's career system.

52. Some experts and competition authorities insist that such justifications must contribute within the same relevant market. According to this view, collusive arrangements that contribute to the same market can be justified, while those that contribute to a different market cannot.

53. In this insistence, the crucial checkpoint is who the relevant customers are. For such experts and authorities, even if the conduct contributes to the same group of suppliers, the fact is insufficient to justify the anticompetitive effects. However, if the conduct contributes to the same group of customers, these experts and authorities are more likely to be satisfied.[19]

54. Although the author of this article disagrees with the "within the market" insistence, the critical issue here is the importance of the layer of customers.

3. Dominant Position and Superior Bargaining Position

55. In the context of exploitative abuse regulation,[20] some jurisdictions support the criterion of superior bargaining position rather than that of dominant position, which is explicitly required in article 102 of the Treaty on the Functioning of the European Union (TFEU).

56. Some supporters of the superior bargaining position standard also advocate for the label of "relative superiority." They do so to address the alleged violator's small market share. According to such experts, "relative superiority" suffices for allegations even if the market share is small.

57. This article suggests that the market share appears small because such a "market" includes irrelevant customers. Suppose the alleged violator enjoys "relative superiority" over specific customers. In that case, the alleged violator enjoys an "absolute superiority" in an adequately defined relevant market that includes only those relevant customers suffering from abusive conduct.

58. In such a well-defined relevant market with relevant customers, an issue that needs to be discussed arises: whether we should adopt the standard of "dominant position" or "superior bargaining position." This issue should be focused on, with the noise from irrelevant customers excluded.

4. International Application of Competition Law

A. *Elaboration of the Effects Doctrine*

59. In international application, also known as extraterritoriality, the effects doctrine has gained widespread acceptance in most jurisdictions, regardless of its name in each jurisdiction. It is implied that the "effects" arise in a

---

19 Examples include the guidelines of the U.K. Competition & Mkts Authority, Green Agreements Guidance: Guidance on the Application of the Chapter I Prohibition in the Competition Act 1998 to Environmental Sustainability Agreements (CMA 185, Oct. 12, 2023), paras. 5.20–5.23.

20 *See* Tadashi Shiraishi, *The Exploitative Abuse Prohibition: Activated by Modern Issues*, 62 ANTITRUST BULL. 737 (2017).

market within the jurisdiction that applies its competition law. However, the concept of "market within the jurisdiction" usually remains undefined.

60. The author of this article defines a "market within the jurisdiction" as a market in which the relevant customers are located within the jurisdiction's territory.[21]

61. This elaboration explains most cases of international application of competition law. Examples include the U.S. Supreme Court in *Empagran*,[22] which refused to recover treble damages for customers outside the U.S.

62. The elaboration also explains why the U.S. Department of Justice (DOJ) statement made in 1992[23] received criticism from many other competition authorities. In that statement, the DOJ attempted to clarify that U.S. law could be applied to cases where U.S. exporters were excluded from markets serving foreign customers.

B. *Cathode Ray Tube*

63. The Supreme Court of Japan in *Cathode Ray Tube*[24] provided an example for advanced studies of the effects doctrine as elaborated above. In this case, five competing groups of suppliers in Southeast Asia fixed prices of cathode ray tubes supplied to manufacturers of television sets in Southeast Asia. The JFTC issued cease and desist orders and imposed fines on suppliers of cathode ray tubes. The sole reason for the JFTC to justify its international application was that the affected manufacturers of television sets in Southeast Asia were subsidiaries of parent firms located in Japan.

64. The critical issue in this case was who the relevant customers were and where they were located. On the side of the customers were the physical purchasers of cathode ray tubes in Southeast Asia and their parent firms in Japan.

65. The Court rendered a judgment in favor of the JFTC, presenting a three-tier reasoning.

66. On the first tier, the Court established a basic proposition according to which conduct that affects the "Japanese economic order with free

---

[21] Tadashi Shiraishi, *Customer Location and the International Reach of National Competition Laws*, in 59 JAPANESE YEARBOOK OF INTERNATIONAL LAW 202 (2017).

[22] F. Hoffmann-La Roche Ltd. v. Empagran S.A., 542 U.S. 155 (2004).

[23] Department of Justice Policy Regarding Anticompetitive Conduct that Restricts U.S. Exports (Apr. 3, 1992). This statement was reprinted in 62 Antitrust & Trade Reg. Rep. (BNA) 483 (1992).

[24] Samsung SDI (Malaysia) v. Fair Trade Commission, Saikō Saibansho [Sup. Ct.] Dec. 12, 2017, Heisei 28 (gyo-hi) 233. Another group of suppliers, headed by MT Picture Display (MTPD) in Japan, also submitted its writ of certiorari, but the Supreme Court chose Samsung's to deliver the opinion. MTPD used to be a joint venture between Matsushita and Toshiba, and it was a 100% subsidiary of Panasonic when it received the JFTC Order. For details of the case up to the time of the Tokyo High Court judgments, *see* Shiraishi, supra note 21.

67. competition" can be scrutinized under the Antimonopoly Act of Japan. This proposition is a form of the effects doctrine.

67. On the second tier, the Court discussed when the "Japanese economic order with free competition" is affected. The Court stated that the "Japanese economic order with free competition" is affected when the affected market includes Japan. The Court also clarified that a typical example of a market that includes Japan is a market where customers are located in Japan.

68. On the third tier, after finding that the parent firms in Japan directed the business activities of their subsidiaries in Southeast Asia, the Court concluded that the affected customers included those parent firms in Japan. Depending on such findings, the Court stated that the relevant customers in the case were also located in Japan and that, in turn, the relevant market included Japan.

69. Again, the crucial factor in this case was the demand side of the relevant market. The supply side did not receive the spotlight. The parent firm of one of the five groups that created the cartel was headquartered in Japan,[25] but every expert recognized that this fact was irrelevant.[26]

V. Conclusion

70. In conclusion, a relevant market in the context of competition law consists of two layers: customers and suppliers. In other words, a relevant market consists of the relevant customers, the relevant suppliers, and the relevant products or services. The relevant customers rarely receive explicit mentions but play critical and fundamental roles in competition law discussions.

71. Japan has a classic case in which movie theater firms proposed a merger of sorts in 1950. The Tokyo High Court rendered a judgment in 1951[27] in favor of the JFTC decision that blocked the proposal. The merging firms argued that the relevant market covered the whole of Tokyo, while the JFTC defined a narrower relevant market that only covered the districts of Marunouchi and Yūrakuchō. The Tokyo High Court affirmed the JFTC decision, although it added Ginza to the two districts.

72. This judgment has long been a famous case in Japan. However, most commentaries have focused on the geographic coverage on the side of suppliers: all of the movie theaters in the whole of Tokyo or only those

---

25 *See supra* note 24.

26 The parents of the suppliers were located in Japan (MTPD), South Korea (two groups including Samsung), Taiwan, and Thailand. The Taiwanese group submitted a leniency application.

27 Toho v. Fair Trade Commission, Tōkyō Kōtō Saibansho [Tokyo High Ct.] Sept. 19, 1951, Showa 25 (gyo-na) 21.

in the two or three districts. However, from this article's perspective, readers of the judgment can see that the crucial focus was on the customers' side. The Court justified the small relevant market, stating that geographically concentrated movie theaters attracted specific customers who gathered in the three districts without comparing with theaters in other districts of Tokyo.

73. This analysis is an illustration of how an elaboration of a concept helps in understanding an unelaborated legendary case.

PART IV

Getting to First Place – Microsoft and Other Players

Two Cheers for the Revolving Door

STEPHEN CALKINS[*]
Wayne State University Law School

with

ERICA STRAUS[**]
Wayne State University Law School

Abstract

Where do top US government antitrust lawyers come from – and go to? The so-called "revolving door" has long been a familiar part of the process. In recent years and especially during the Biden Administration, this custom has attracted increased attention and concern. What are the facts? This chapter sets out, in detailed tables, the background and subsequent employment of top government antitrust lawyers. Many enforcers came from major law firms (FTC commissioners much less frequently than others) and leave for major law firms. (Although studied in less detail, top state antitrust enforcers are starting to transition to major law firms, too.) The concerns about the "revolving door" are obvious. The reality, however, is that government agencies need legal talent, and that talent is often found in law firms. Even during the Biden years, large numbers of private practitioners were

---

[*] Professor, Wayne State University Law School, and formerly general counsel to the FTC, commissioner on the Irish Competition and Consumer Protection Commission, and of counsel/special counsel to Covington. Much of the research for this paper was done by Ms. Straus, such that she deserves more than an acknowledgment. The author has discussed issues related to this paper with a large number of persons familiar with the issue but did not have a clear understanding about whether views would be attributed to them, so he does not cite particular views but thanks all those who shared thoughts with him. Persons consulted include William Baer, Deborah Feinstein, Harry First, Andrew Gavil, Benjamin Hendricks, Emily Myers, Diana Moss, John Newman, Carl Shapiro, Willard Tom, Spencer Waller, Chris White, Lawrence White, and Arthur Wilmarth.

[**] Wayne State University Law School, J.D. expected, 2026.

recruited. Moreover, a variety of experiences has to help a government agency–and agencies can benefit from having "alumni" who can communicate with the public and perhaps rotate back to work for a state or federal enforcer. This chapter gives only two cheers, however, because some worrisome issues remain. Career staff are invaluable, yet "revolving" can create tensions. Outsiders do bring a particular mindset. Of course top private-firm lawyers heading into the government will think of returning to the private sector, but it is striking that so many FTC commissioners leave for corporate law firms without having come from there. Moreover, the post-agency-employment rules could be tougher. Finally, the inevitable reality is that consulting has costs. Although the "revolving door" is both inevitable and beneficial in many ways, it is an issue deserving of regular attention.

> Small businesses and community groups can't afford to hire *high-priced FTC alumni with special access and connections* to push their agenda.[1]

> A key priority of mine is ensuring that the FTC is regularly hearing and learning from the broader public, including the consumers, workers, and honest businesses that we strive to protect. Guarding against insularity is a constant challenge for virtually all federal agencies, and ensuring that the FTC is accessible even to those who lack *well-heeled counsel or personal connections* is essential to our institutional credibility.[2]

1. Take a look at our honoree's CV.[3] Harry First had a clerkship, then worked two years at the Department of Justice (DOJ) Antitrust Division (Division), and then went into academia, teaching first at Toledo but spending most of his career at NYU with side visits to Japan. But for fourteen years, he was counsel to Loeb & Loeb, a position that ended only when he took on a two-year stint as chief of the Antitrust Bureau for the New York State Office of the Attorney General (AG).

2. Harry participated in antitrust's "revolving door."

3. In a small way, I was once a high-priced Federal Trade Commission (FTC) alumnus – for a while after serving as FTC general counsel, I was of counsel/special counsel at Covington (although my agreement limited me to four hours a week, and no one has ever accused me of being "well-heeled"). And I am still a proud (double) FTC alumnus, even if I have not accepted outside compensation since I became a member of the Irish Competition and Consumer Protection Commission in 2011.

---

1 Prepared Remarks of Commissioner Rohit Chopra Regarding New Procedures to Ensure the Right to Petition the FTC (Sept. 15, 2021), https://www.ftc.gov/system/files/documents/public_statements/1596344/p072104choprastatementpetitionrulemaking.pdf (emphasis added).

2 Remarks of Chair Lina M. Khan on Passage of New Procedures to Open Up Rulemaking Petitions to the Public (Sept. 15, 2021), https://www.ftc.gov/system/files/documents/public_statements/1596336/p072104khanstatementpetitionrulemaking.pdf (emphasis added).

3 https://its.law.nyu.edu/facultyprofiles/index.cfm?fuseaction=profile.full_cv&personid=19919.

4. Since both Harry and I have participated in this now-controversial practice, it seemed appropriate to use this opportunity to reflect on it. I have been intrigued to watch the so-called revolving door become a big issue.

5. And a big issue it has increasingly become.[4] The Revolving Door Project[5] is laser-focused on it. That project "was created in order to scrutinize executive branch appointees to ensure they use their office to serve the broad public interest, rather than to entrench corporate power or seek personal advancement." A related project, OpenSecrets,[6] follows "campaign contributions, lobbying data and analysis." Recently, the *Wall Street Journal* ran a three-part story, each time on a front page, about "The Hidden Life of Google's Secret Weapon" (former George Mason professor and FTC Commissioner Joshua Wright).[7] Back in 2018, the Roosevelt Institute issued a report that focused on the issue.[8] A contributor to that report and subsequently FTC commissioner, Rohit Chopra, in his then-new role as director of the Consumer Financial Protection Bureau (CFPB), wrote that that agency "must take steps to protect the public interest from the potential risks and misconduct associated with the 'revolving door.'"[9]

6. It has become routine that agency appointees are scrutinized from a "revolving door" perspective.[10] Progressive groups demanded that President Biden refrain from appointing lawyers with ties to Amazon, Apple, Facebook, and Google.[11] Google, in particular, has been a focus of revolving door critics.[12]

---

[4] The lengthy list of commentaries bemoaning the "revolving door" includes David Dayen, *Attacks on Lina Khan's Ethics Reveal Copious Amounts of Projection*, THE AMERICAN PROSPECT (June 23, 2023), https://prospect.org/economy/2023-06-23-attacks-lina-khans-ethics-reveal-projection/, and RICK CLAYPOOL, THE FTC'S BIG TECH REVOLVING DOOR PROBLEM (May 23, 2019), https://www.citizen.org/wp-content/uploads/ftc-big-tech-revolving-door-conflicts-report.pdf. For an attempt to quantify some of the good and bad effects, *see* Brian Wallheimer, Should We Stop the 'Revolving Door'?, CHI. BOOTH REV. (Aug. 7, 2017), https://www.chicagobooth.edu/review/should-we-stop-revolving-door.

[5] *About Us*, REVOLVING DOOR PROJECT, https://therevolvingdoorproject.org/about-us/.

[6] https://www.opensecrets.org.

[7] Brody Mullins, *The Hidden Life of Google's Secret Weapon: Joshua Wright cleared a path to domination for the world's biggest tech companies, keeping regulators at bay while juggling inappropriate relationships and skirting conflict-of-interest standards at every turn*, WALL ST. J., June 8–9, 2024, at C1, June 10, 2024, at A1, and June 11, 2024, at A1 (about former George Mason law professor/FTC Commissioner/Wilson Sonsini lawyer Joshua Wright).

[8] ROOSEVELT INST., UNSTACKING THE DECK: A NEW AGENDA TO TAME CORRUPTION IN WASHINGTON (May 2018), https://rooseveltinstitute.org/wp-content/uploads/2020/07/RI-Unstacking-the-Deck-201805.pdf.

[9] Rohit Chopra, *Ethics Guidance to Protect the Public Trust and Detect Revolving Door Misconduct*, CFPB BLOG (Nov. 19, 2021), https://www.consumerfinance.gov/about-us/blog/ethics-guidance-to-protect-public-trust-and-detect-revolving-door-misconduct/.

[10] *See, e.g.*, Press Release, Roosevelt Inst., Statement: Roosevelt Research Director Responds to New Leadership at FTC, Elevates Revolving Door, https://rooseveltinstitute.org/2018/09/26/statement-roosevelt-research-director-responds-to-new-leadership-at-ftc-elevates-revolving-door/ (criticizing the 2018 appointment of Gail Levine as deputy director for the Bureau of Competition); Alan Pyke, *Lawyer Who Repped Equifax Will Run Office That Investigates Equifax*, THINKPROGRESS (May 17, 2018), https://archive.thinkprogress.org/equifax-lawyer-payday-loans-ftc-conflict-bf3a9594d5bd/.

[11] https://www.economicliberties.us/wp-content/uploads/2021/01/Final_AntitrustAppointmentsLetter_1.18.docx.pdf.

[12] Tech Transparency Project, *Google's US Revolving Door* (Apr. 26, 2016), https://www.techtransparencyproject.org/articles/googles-revolving-door-us.

7. The issue came to the fore when Trump FTC Chair Joe Simons nominated Covington partner and former FTC (and Securities and Exchange Commission – SEC) lawyer Andrew Smith to serve as director of the Bureau of Consumer Protection (BCP).[13] Democratic-appointed FTC Commissioners Chopra and Rebecca Slaughter took the highly unusual step of dissenting from the appointment. Both expressed respect for Mr. Smith but worried about his ties to credit reporting company Equifax.[14] Then, when Biden won the election, critics concerned about the revolving door preemptively set out lists of "personnel minefields that Biden should *avoid* for any antitrust role" (naming Renata Hesse, Juan Arteaga, Steven Sunshine, and Sonia Pfaffenroth).[15] Progressives successfully lobbied for the appointment of Jonathan Kanter and Lina Khan,[16] and now the Revolving Door Project is celebrating these "trustbusters" and demanding that presidential candidates "be asked if they will keep these winners in office."[17]

8. The "revolving door" is not just an issue for the FTC and the Division, of course. Indeed, Wall Street's influence over financial regulators has been a major source of concern,[18] and government-wide ties to the tech industry have alarmed critics.[19] But this essay will limit its focus to the Division, the FTC, and state antitrust enforcers.

---

13 Unless otherwise indicated, all biographical information is from the appendices or LinkedIn, and space is saved by omitting individual citations.

14 Dissenting Statement of Commissioner Rebecca Kelly Slaughter Regarding the Appointment of the Director of the Bureau of Consumer Protection (May 16, 2018), https://www.ftc.gov/system/files/documents/public_statements/1379509/commission_slaughter_dissenting_statement_on_vote_for_bcp_director.pdf; Statement of Commissioner Rohit Chopra Regarding the Commission's Votes to Appoint Senior Leadership, https://www.ftc.gov/system/files/documents/public_statements/1379515/chopra_-_statement_on_senior_leadership_picks_5-16-18_2.pdf ("While Smith may not *technically* be prohibited from working on these matters [rulemakings and policy matters], his participation may raise the appearance of a conflict…") Fourteen months later, Equifax agreed to pay at least $575 million and committed to conducting relief, *see* https://www.ftc.gov/news-events/news/press-releases/2019/07/equifax-pay-575-million-part-settlement-ftc-cfpb-states-related-2017-data-breach.

15 Elias Alsbergas & Andrea Beaty, *Biden's Antitrust Minefield*, REVOLVING DOOR PROJECT (Jan. 16, 2021), https://therevolvingdoorproject.org/bidens-antitrust-minefield/; *see also* Ryan Grim & David Dayen, *Big Tech Critics Alarmed at Direction of Biden Antitrust Personnel*, THE AMERICAN PROSPECT (Jan. 18, 2021) (objecting to Hesse and Arteaga), https://prospect.org/cabinet-watch/big-tech-critics-alarmed-at-direction-of-biden-antitrust-per/.

16 Press Release, Open Markets, With Kanter, Khan, Wu, and the Rest of Biden's Trustbusting Team, We're Looking at a New Era of Democracy for All Americans, From the Bottom Up (July 20, 2021), https://www.openmarketsinstitute.org/publications/with-kanter-khan-wu-and-the-rest-of-bidens-trustbusting-team-were-looking-at-a-new-era-of-democracy-for-all-americans-from-the-bottom-up.

17 Revolving Door Project tweet, Aug 5, 2024, at 4:36 PM; https://therevolvingdoorproject.org/revolving-door-project-applauds-doj-antitrusts-win-against-google/ ("Today's decision [in *Google*] confirms that the Biden-Harris administration's bold decision to appoint trustbusters Jonathan Kanter and Lina Khan means that everyday Americans are better off. . . .").

18 *See* James Kwak, *Incentives and Ideology: Financial Regulation is Constrained by Politics as well as Bureaucracy*, 127 HARV. L. REV. F. 253 (2014); Arthur E. Wilmarth, *Turning a Blind Eye: Why Washington Keeps Giving in to Wall Street*, 81 U. CIN. L. REV. 1283 (2013).

19 *See Google's US Revolving Door*, TECH TRANSPARENCY PROJECT (Apr. 26, 2016), https://www.techtransparencyproject.org/articles/googles-revolving-door-us.

I. A Revolving Door? The Facts

9. Do large numbers of antitrust and consumer lawyers and economists work, at various points in their careers, in government and in the private sector? Absolutely. There are appended charts compiled largely by Wayne Law student Erica Straus showing leading figures at the antitrust agencies and their employment before and after government service. Roughly 75% of assistant attorneys generals (AAGs) and FTC Bureau of Competition (BC) directors arrived from major law firms, although this pattern does not hold for FTC commissioners.

II. Pre-Appointment Backgrounds

10. Of the 19 AAGs appointed (not as acting), Richard Nixon to date, 14 (74%) came with substantial service at a major law firm (Kanter, Delrahim, Baer, Varney, Barnett, Pate, James, Klein, Bingaman, Rill, McGrath, Litvack, Shenefield, and McLaren); three were law professors at the time of appointment (two (Baxter and Kauper) with a couple of early years at major law firms; one (Don Baker) with three years at Cornell after nine years at the Division); and one (Rick Rule) with only four years of experience, all at the Division. Seven of the 19 (Barnett, Pate, Klein, Rule, Ginsburg, Shenefield, and Baker) were promoted to AAG, and one (Paul McGrath) moved laterally from DOJ Civil. Six of the other 11 (55%) had had previous experience at the Division or the FTC (Kanter, Delrahim, Baer, Varney, James, and Litvack). One of the 19 (Anne Bingaman) also had experience in state enforcement, as a law school professor, and in her own law firm.

11. Of the 17 principal deputy AAGs over this period, 13 (76%) had substantial corporate law background (Murray, Nigro, Finch, Hesse, Meyer, Majoras, Melamed, Klein, Litan (also Brookings), Smith, Furth, B. Wilson, and Comegys). Four had backgrounds substantially at the Division (Mekki, Rule, Favretto, and Morrison), while others were promoted from positions in the Division.

12. Of the 20 FTC directors of the BC, 1970 to date, 15 (75%) came directly or indirectly from major national law firms (although two (Jeff Zuckerman and Tom Campbell) served only as associates before joining government), and two (Kevin Arquit and Alan Ward) came from smaller firms. Two (Holly Vedova and Perry Johnson) were career FTC lawyers. One (Tim Muris) went from the University of Miami to be director first of BCP and then BC. Fully ten of the 20 had served previously at the Division or the FTC (50%), not counting those who moved from an FTC position into director of BC (seven of the 20 so moved; of these, one (Jeff Schmidt) also boasted of earlier FTC experience, one (Ian Conner) earlier Division experience).

13. The pattern changes for FTC commissioners. Of the 14 modern FTC chairs (starting with Nixon's Miles Kirkpatrick), only six (43%) had significant ties to leading law firms (Simons, Majoras, Muris, Pitofsky, Engman, and Kirkpatrick); five (Steiger, Oliver, Miller, Pertschuk, and Collier) arrived from other government positions (Pertschuk with the Senate); two (Khan and Kovacic) were from academia without substantial corporate law consulting (Kovacic had a year of consulting before joining the FTC); one (Leibowitz) came from a trade association (four years) and Capitol Hill (nine years); and one (Miller) from consulting and advocacy. (And, yes, several held multiple positions.) Seven (50%) (Khan, Simons, Kovacic, Majoras, Muris, Pitofsky, and Collier) had previously served at the Division (Majoras) or the FTC before becoming a commissioner.

14. Non-chair FTC commissioners generally fit the pattern observed by Bill Kovacic in 1997: few young partners doing substantial antitrust and consumer protection work, and lots of nominees with ties to the Hill and the executive branch.[20] Of the 30 modern non-chair FTC commissioners (appointed 1970 to date), it is striking how relatively few came from partnerships in global law firms. I count only six (20%): Tom Rosch (Latham), Tom Leary (Hogan), Christine Wilson (O'Melveny and Kirkland, then two years at Delta Airlines), Stephen Nye (Sullivan, Jones and Archer), and perhaps Maureen Ohlhausen (three years at Wilkinson Barker Knauer after a year at a trade association and 11 years at the FTC), and Pamela Harbour (four years at Kaye Scholer after a career in state enforcement). (Mayo Thompson came from Texas law firm Royston Rayzor; Deborah Owen was managing partner at the McNair Law Firm after six years on Capitol Hill and the White House; David Dennison from Dennison, Wern & Turner; and George Douglas from five years as president of Southwest Econometrics.) Ten other commissioners had served as a global law firm or consulting firm associate before going into government or advocacy (Ferguson, Holyoak, Bedoya, Slaughter, Phillips, Chopra, Mozelle Thompson, Anthony, Owen, and Strenio).

15. Of the 30, 12 (40%) worked in the White House or elsewhere in the executive branch (not counting the FTC) (Chopra, McSweeny, Swindle, Mozelle Thompson, Anthony, Starek, Varney, Owen, Strenio, Machol, Bailey, and Dole); seven (23%) did substantial work on Capitol Hill even if not immediately before nomination (Ferguson, Bedoya, Slaughter, Phillips, Owen, Clanton, and Dixon); six worked in state government (Ferguson, Holyoak, Brill, Harbour, Mozelle Thompson, and Dennison); four others came from academic appointments (Wright, Yao, Calvani, and Pitofsky, with all but Yao also having consulting or of counsel

---

20 William E. Kovacic, *The Quality of Appointments and the Capability of the Federal Trade Commission*, 49 ADMIN. L. REV. 915, 937 (1997).

positions (Wright and Pitofsky with major firms; Calvani with a smaller one)). (Adding that three to the six who came from partnerships yields nine (30%).) Six of the 30 (20%) had previous experience at the FTC (C. Wilson, Ohlhausen, Rosch, Azcuenaga, Pitofsky, and Dixon, with Azcuenaga working exclusively at the FTC; one (McSweeny) had worked in the Division (McSweeny worked there after leaving the White House)). With 60% having substantial experience on the Hill or in the White House or elsewhere in the executive branch other than the FTC (and avoiding double-counting), one is reminded of Bill Kovacic's line: "The surest path to the Commission leads through Capitol Hill or the White House."[21]

III. Post-Service Destination

16. Although one can count the numbers in different ways, there is no question but that large numbers of these officials affiliated with major law firms or consulting firms after leaving government. AAGs and Bureau directors came from that background and returned to it, although fewer AAGs *went* to law firms than *came from* them. The striking point is that FTC chairs and commissioners, many of whom did not come from such firms, overwhelmingly affiliated with them after leaving government. This effect is particularly pronounced for FTC non-chair commissioners, where only 20% came from major law firms and consulting firms, but 85% of departing commissioners affiliated with one.

17. Of the 18 of those AAGs who moved on, 11 (61%) took positions at major law firms and one (Bill Baxter) returned to Stanford but served four years of counsel to Shearman & Sterling (so 67% counting him); three (James, Klein, and Bingaman) took positions with businesses (Klein also serving as chancellor of the New York City public schools); two (Ginsburg and McLaren) became federal judges; and one (Kauper) returned to the University of Michigan.

18. Of the 16 principal deputy AAGs who have moved on from government, 12 (75%) went to major law firms (Murray, Nigro, Finch, Hesse, Meyer, Melamed, Smith, Rule, Furth, Favretto, Morrison, and Comegys), three to corporations (Majoras (after chair of FTC), Klein (after AAG; also chancellor of NY schools), and B. Wilson); and one to Brookings, only later to affiliate with a law firm (Litan).

19. Of the 19 modern directors of BC who have moved on from that position, 15 (79%) went to major law firms, with another two going back to academia but also affiliating with a major law firm (Muris) or consulting

---

21 *Id.*

20. group (Tom Campbell, who later won elective office) (so 17 combined, or 89%). Al Dougherty became general counsel of May Department Stores, and Holly Vedova retired.

20. Of the 13 modern FTC chairs who have left the government, seven (54%) (Simons, Leibowitz, Muris, Pitofsky, Collier, Engman, and Kirkpatrick) served at least part-time with a global law firm, one (economist James Miller) with an economics consulting group (so 62% counting him), and one (Deborah Majoras) with Procter & Gamble. Two (conservative Daniel Oliver and liberal Michael Pertschuk) moved to advocacy institutes, and one (William Kovacic) returned simply to his academic position.

21. Of the 26 modern non-chair FTC commissioners (appointed 1970 to date) who have left the government and not retired, 19 (73%) became affiliated with corporate law firms (C. Wilson, Phillips, Ohlhausen, McSweeny, Brill, Wright, Rosch, Harbour, Leary, Swindle, Azcuenaga, Varney, Owen, Strenio, Calvani, Bailey, Clanton, Pitofsky, and Nye) and two with consulting groups (Yao and Douglas) (21 combined, or 81%); and one each signed on with a trade association (Starek), a major corporation (Dennison), and his own consulting group (Mozelle Thompson). One (Machol) became an author after leaving government, and one (Mayo Thompson) became an attorney in private practice. Three retired (Anthony, Dixon, and, after working in Bob Dole's campaign, Dole).

IV. State Enforcers

22. Our honoree went into government – state government – from academia and a law firm "counsel" arrangement. Later, then-Columbia law professor Scott Hemphill followed Harry's lead by heading the New York antitrust bureau from 2011 to 2012.[22] There is not a pronounced pattern of state AG chiefs coming from major law firms, but a number of state AG antitrust chiefs did, including for the states of Colorado (Bryn Williams, who came in 2023 from a year at the Division preceded by six years at major law firms); DC (Adam Gitlin, who came in 2022 after six and a half years at the Division and then four and a half years at Lieff Cabraser (leaving as a partner)); Illinois (Elizabeth Maxeiner, who joined that office in 2015 after seven years at Sidley Austin)); Massachusetts (William Matlack, who came from nine years at Sullivan & Worcester following nine years in state enforcement);[23] Minnesota (Elizabeth Odette (the newest chair of the National Association of Attorneys General (NAAG) Multistate

---

22 CV at https://its.law.nyu.edu/facultyprofiles/index.cfm?fuseaction=profile.full_cv&personid=40904.

23 Matthew L. Brown, *Matlack Named State Antitrust Head*, WORCESTER BUS. J. (May 5, 2008), https://www.wbjournal.com/article/matlack-named-state-antitrust-head.

23. Antitrust Task Force), who joined the office in 2020 after 15.5 years at Lockridge Grindal Nauen); New York (Elinor Hoffmann: Lord Day & Lord nine years; Coudert Brothers (partner) 16 years); and Tennessee (David McDowell: Antitrust Division three years, Harwell Howard Hyne Gabbert & Manner (shareholder) ten years).[24] Movement from leading firms into state enforcement can be found for other positions as well, such as Thomas Collin becoming Ohio's principal assistant attorney general for antitrust after 39.5 years at Thompson Hine, and Arthur Biller heading into the Colorado AG's Office in 1972 – where he is leading the big case challenging the *Kroger/Albertson* merger – after six and a half years at Willkie Farr and just over four years at national law firm Lewis Brisbois.

23. There has also been movement from state enforcers into major law firms. Public records indicate that of the 12 most recent chairs of the NAAG Multistate Antitrust Task Force to step down, five went to major law firms (Mike Brockmeyer, Lloyd Constantine (several years at McDermott Will then founding Constantine Cannon), Vic Domen, Robert Langer, and Kevin O'Connor) and one (Trish Conners) went to a law firm upon hitting retirement age; three (Sarah Allen, Tom Greene, and Laurel Price) went to the Division or the FTC; two (Kathleen Foote and Robert Hubbard) stayed in state enforcement (with Foote recently retiring); and one (Gwendolyn Cooley) recently stepped down from state enforcement but shows no signs of retiring.

24. The bottom line is that, yes, a large number of top enforcers come from major law firms (although FTC commissioners much less frequently than AAGs or BC Bureau directors) and leave for major law firms. And the above survey does not address the economists who come from and go to consulting firms, or the very large number of government lawyers who come from associate or partner positions at major firms or go to such firms when they leave the government. There is something of a "revolving door."

V. Concerns About the "Revolving Door"

25. Are there legitimate concerns about the revolving door? Of course. The many attacks on the revolving door are not just making up worries. As Judge Easterbrook wrote for the Seventh Circuit, "it creates a risk of conflict of interest, a risk that people who hope to move to the private sector will favor while in public employment those firms they think may offer rewards later, and after these employees switch to the private side they may exercise undue influence on those they leave behind (who may

---

24 Thanks to Emily Myers.

seek to follow the same path, or may just need some of the information the departing employee took with him)."[25]

26. We will revisit concerns later, but first, let's consider the benefits.

VI. In Defense of the "Revolving Door"

27. A critical reality is that the "revolving door" – at least some version of it – is inevitable; it is baked into our system. Highlighting concerns may prevent abuses, but it could also serve principally to discourage terrific candidates from being willing to serve. What enforcement agencies really need is talent, from wherever it comes – and talented lawyers from the private sector bring with them important benefits. Moreover, the public can gain from lawyers who serve in the government and then move on.

VII. Some Version of a "Revolving Door" Is Inevitable

28. FTC commissioners are appointed to terms capped at seven years, although few serve that long. Fifteen of the 20 chairs designated by the president have had terms shorter than four years, in part because a new president can designate a new person as chair. Since chairs nominate senior staff to political positions (meaning they can be removed), senior staff have relatively short terms. AAGs have relatively short terms, too. Look over the list in the appendix, and you will see lots of two- or three-year terms and a number of four-year terms, but none longer than that. Even when presidents serve eight years, their top staff members rarely do. And since AAGs change, so do the top staffers they appoint.

29. Given that top officials have relatively short terms, our competition system has a constant need to attract new top officials *and to have incumbents move on*. High-level officials need to *come* from somewhere and then *go* somewhere. Since these are law enforcement positions, the logical places from which to attract and to which to send these officials are law firms and, to a lesser extent, law schools (and, for where FTC commissioners come *from*, Congress and the executive branch).

---

[25] United States v. Medico Industries, Inc., 784 F.2d 840, 843 (7th Cir. 1986) (adding that "[o]n the other hand offering the opportunity to move from private to public employment and back again may enable the government to secure the services of skilled people who are unwilling to devote their careers to public service at current rates of pay. The government can hire people for less, and attract specially skilled agents, if it allows them to put their skills to use later for private employers.").

30. When Trump FTC Chair Joe Simons faced opposition to his nomination of a Covington partner as BCP Bureau director, he wrote forcefully as follows:

> The Commission has a long history of welcoming private sector experts into temporary government service. Many consumer protection and competition luminaries consider their time at the Commission to be a highlight of their careers. Regardless of which party enjoys political power, it is impossible to attract high caliber professionals to the FTC without encountering some conflicts. That is precisely why the agency has well-established processes for dealing with recusals, to ensure appropriate oversight and minimal disruption while strictly adhering to ethics rules.[26]

31. The very progressive Biden competition agencies serve as an illustration that movement from the private sector, including leading law firms, to and then from enforcement agencies is inevitable. To be sure, none of the current five FTC commissioners had substantial ties to major law firms (all but one (Holyoke) spent important time on Capitol Hill, a commonplace presidents look for FTC commissioners). But even though the progressives dominating modern debate are acutely sensitive to "revolving door" issues, a good number of important appointees have or had significant private law experience. This includes, most notably, AAG Jonathan Kanter, celebrated by progressives, who spent two years at the FTC, then 22 years in three leading law firms, 15 months at his own boutique, and then AAG. Other examples (some examples to the contrary are discussed below) include the following:

    – Laura Alexander, deputy director BC, Kirkland & Ellis (2008–2012); Cohen Milstein 2012–2020; advocacy organizations 2020–2024; FTC Feb. 2024 to date.

    – Hetal Doshi, deputy assistant attorney general, Feb. 2022 to date: seven years at major law firms plus a sabbatical year doing human rights; then seven years in a U.S. Attorney's Office.

    – Andrew Forman, deputy AAG: three years at Fried Frank; three years at FTC; 14 years at Cadwalader and Paul, Weiss (overlapping at all three firms with Jonathan Kanter).

    – Henry Liu, director of BC, 2023 to date: 15 years at Covington.

    – Kyle Mach, deputy director BC, Jan. 2024 to date: 18 years at Cravath and Munger Tolles.

---

26 Statement of Chairman Joe Simons on the Appointment of Senior Staff Leadership (May 16, 2018), https://www.ftc.gov/system/files/documents/public_statements/1379503/simons_-_senior_staff_appts_public_statement_5-16-18.pdf.

- Aviv Nevo, director of the FTC's Bureau of Economics, 2022 to date; senior advisor Cornerstone Research 2014–2022 (formerly academic appointments and two years at the Antitrust Division).

- Eric Posner, counsel to the AAG, Feb. 2022–Feb. 2023: of counsel at MoloLamken for three and a half years before, and again Jan. 2024 to date (also UChicago faculty).

32. But the most powerful demonstration that even progressive antitrust enforcers, very concerned about revolving door issues, have to recruit top people from leading law firms is provided by considering the leading lawyers litigating many of the Biden agencies' most high-profile cases.

33. Lead government attorneys in the following cases (see appendix) recently came to the government from the private sector:

- DOJ cases against:

  - ASSA ABLOY (Matthew Huppert and David Dahlquist)
  - Google (Ad Tech) (Julia Tarver Wood) (co-lead Aaron Teitelbaum came from Manhattan DA's Office and U.S. Attorney's Office)
  - JetBlue Airways (Edward Duffy) (co-lead Teitelbaum)
  - Live Nation Entertainment (Bonny Sweeney)
  - RealPage (Henry C. Su)
  - Visa (Edward Duffy)

- FTC cases against:

  - Amazon.com, Inc. (Edward Takashima)
  - IQVIA Holdings (Jennifer Fleury)
  - Meta Platforms Inc. (Abby Dennis)
  - Syngenta Crop Protection AG (Allyson Maltas)
  - Tempur Sealy International (Allyson Maltas, co-lead)
  - Tapestry, Inc. (Abby Dennis)

34. In addition, DOJ's lead attorney against Apple (Jonathan Lasken) spent five years at a corporate law firm, followed by three years at the Division, four at the FTC, and now two at the Division; its lead against Sugar Corporation (Brian Hanna) spent five years at a corporate law firm before joining the Division in 2015. Similarly, the lead in the big FTC monopoly case against Meta (Daniel Matheson) spent 11 years at corporate law firms before joining the FTC in 2016; the agency's co-lead attorney against Tempur Sealy (Stephen Rodger) spent nine years at Covington before joining the FTC in 2012; and three co-lead attorneys against Kroger spent

time in corporate law firms: nine years before joining the FTC in 2017 (James Weingarten); five years before joining in 2014 (Charles Dickinson); and three years after a six-year stint in the Division before joining the FTC in 2020 (Susan Musser). (Weingarten also was the lead FTC attorney in *FTC v. Microsoft Corp.* (N.D. Cal. 2023), and Musser was also the lead complaint counsel in the FTC's in-house merger case *Illumina/Grail*.)

35. (To be sure, some of the leading agency trial counsel did not have significant experience in private law firms. Prominent Biden-era cases led by career government lawyers include DOJ cases against Apple (co-lead Lorraine Van Kirk, seven years as a county counsel, a year at CFPB, then Division since 2022), Bertelsmann (John Read), Google (search) (Kenneth Dintzer), UnitedHealth Group (Bindi Bhagat), and American Airlines Group/JetBlue (William H. Jones II). (Dintzer moved, but from DOJ Antitrust (five years) to DOJ Civil, returning only for the *Google* case.) Similarly, the FTC's case against Novant Health was led by Nathan Brenner, a 2014 law school graduate who clerked, worked four years at the Division, and subsequently has worked at the Commission, and its case against U.S. Anesthesia Partners is being led by Kara Monahan, who came to the FTC in 2012 after a clerkship.)

36. The odds are overwhelming that many of these lawyers who came from leading law firms will move on to leading law firms. Some leading Biden-era lawyers already have, including Jennifer Fleury, who just rejoined Hogan,[27] James Weingarten, who recently joined Milbank,[28] Mark Seidman, head of the FTC merger "shop" responsible for groceries, who joined Weil Gotshal after an 18-year career at the FTC,[29] and David Schwartz, who worked at the FTC for over nine years (including leading the Amazon investigation) after a clerkship and four years at Quinn Emanuel, who became a partner at Bryan Cave in August 2024. And many others will do likewise. Few are nearing retirement age. Presidents even closely aligned with outgoing presidents want to appoint their own AAGs and FTC chairs, and both Kanter and Kahn have served what is normally considered full terms. A new AAG or chair will mean new top staff will replace the old top staff, who will move on even if they want to stay. And new top staff will want their own top litigators, so many of the Biden top litigators will also move on – and, yes, for many that will mean to law firms.

37. Some kind of movement is inevitable not only at the highest levels, but at almost every level. Large numbers of newly minted lawyers begin their

---

27 Press Release, Hogan Lovells, Hogan Lovells welcomes back FTC Deputy Chief Trial Counsel as Partner in Antitrust Practice (Oct. 15, 2024), https://www.hoganlovells.com/en/news/hogan-lovells-welcomes-back-ftc-deputy-chief-trial-counsel-as-partner-in-antitrust-practice.

28 News, Milbank, FTC Chief Trial Counsel James Weingarten Joins Milbank's Antitrust and Competition Group (June 17, 2024), https://www.milbank.com/en/news/ftc-chief-trial-counsel-james-weingarten-joins-milbanks-antitrust-and-competition-group.html.

29 News & Announcements, Weil, Weil Reinforces Leading Global Antitrust Group with Addition of FTC Veteran Mark Seidman (Sept. 4, 2024), https://www.weil.com/articles/weil-reinforces-leading-global-antitrust-group-with-addition-of-ftc-veteran-mark-seidman.

careers at corporate law firms – as did all four non-chair FTC commissioners. Maybe new lawyers want to earn money to pay off loans; maybe they want to experience practicing law at a high level; maybe they want to learn more about what parts of the legal world appeal to them. Regardless of why, it happens, and state and federal enforcement agencies would be shooting themselves in the foot if such experience disqualified applicants.

38. What, then, about agency lawyers who want to move on, whether to have a different legal experience or to change location or the nature of work, or even – this does happen – to earn greater income? The Biden-era lawyers listed above as recently leaving gave over 18 years to the FTC (Seidman); over nine years (Schwartz); seven and a half years (Weingarten); and two years (Fleury). Or consider Rick Dagen, who worked for a year at Venable, three years at the International Trade Commission, three years at Sidley Austin, then 23 years and eight months at the FTC before joining Axinn.[30] It is hard to argue that lawyers like these did not benefit the FTC. Requiring new hires to make a lifetime commitment would seriously harm recruiting. While perhaps at one time Americans went to a first employer and stayed there, retiring with a pension and a gold watch, that is no longer true. Today, Americans hold an average of 12.7 jobs by age 56, changing jobs more rapidly in younger years but still switching in their 40s and 50s.[31] In the legal profession globally, 54% of younger lawyers "are somewhat or highly likely to move to a new but comparable workplace," while 33% believe they "will be moving to a new legal profession."[32] It should not be surprising – indeed, it would seem desirable – that legal job changes include stints in federal and state governments.

39. Of course, saying that movement in and out of government is inevitable does not prove that it is desirable. The European Commission, for instance, has traditionally followed a career government lawyer model, and that has its own advantages. But the American model of movement in and out of government offers benefits not only in recruiting but in other ways as well.

VIII. What Is Needed Is Talent

40. Would the Justice Department have prevailed in the landmark *Microsoft* case had the legendary David Bois not been brought in to lead the effort? Were the FTC's lead lawyer George Cary and BC Bureau Director

---

[30] *See* News, Axinn, Longtime FTC Veteran Richard Dagen Joins Axinn (Jan. 7, 2014), https://www.axinn.com/media-229.html.

[31] Economic News Release, U.S. Bureau of Labor Statistics, Number of Jobs, Labor Market Experience, Marital Status, and Health for Those Born 1957–1964 (Aug. 22, 2023), https://www.bls.gov/news.release/nlsoy.nr0.htm.

[32] IBA, Legal Pol'y & Rsch. Unit, IBA Young Lawyers' Report (2022) at 18.

Bill Baer important to success in *FTC v. Staples, Inc.*?[33] Proving such things is a challenge, but one cannot deny that talent matters. The importance of attracting talent is shown simply by the remarkable number of leading Biden agency cases being led for the government by lawyers brought in from major law firms (see above). There are terrific career government lawyers – Mel Orlans was a great number two on the *Staples* case, for instance – but there are also terrific lawyers at leading private firms. Government enforcement needs talent. Indeed, when Bill Kovacic noted in 1997 the paucity of lawyers from major firms becoming FTC commissioners, it was a lament rather than a celebration.

IX. A Variety of Experiences Has to Help

41. It has to be an advantage for enforcers to know what they are up against. When defense lawyers claim that this or that request is impossibly burdensome, it helps to have been in their shoes. If you have been on the other side, you have a better understanding of how that side will function. As Doug Melamed wrote in a tweet, "I learned, after being in defense practice, govt enforcement, and in-house, that one is a much better lawyer for any side after having experience on, and thinking from the perspective of, all sides."[34] As one of the persons I interviewed mentioned, it is easier when you have "outsiders" to have your own "red team" and "blue team" to play out what is likely to transpire. (This cuts both ways, to be sure, but the judicial process works better when there is better lawyering, and government lawyers will do better if they know what to expect.)

42. Done right, newcomers can shake things up in a good way. This can apply to small procedures ("Why do we do it this way?") and to major policy changes. Think of the revised cartel leniency program under Anne Bingaman, and the modern merger guidelines under Bill Baxter. And many accomplishments deserve to share credits among career lawyers and participants in the "revolving door" (consider the FTC's impressive reverse-payment campaign that led to *FTC v. Actavis, Inc.*, for which IP competition guru Michael Carrier and I think credit should be shared by FTC Chair Jon Leibowitz and career lawyer Markus Meier).[35] New blood often is a good thing (and, of course, arrivals often mean departures).

---

33   970 F. Supp. 1066 (1997).

34   https://x.com/dougmelamed/status/1320033810025598977 (Oct. 24, 2020).

35   570 U.S. 136 (2013). Email permission to cite Carrier. *Actavis* was one of the few antitrust accomplishments to attract multiple votes when I surveyed the American Antitrust Institute's advisors' listserv for notable successes. *See also* Jean-Christophe Roda, *United States: The U.S. Supreme Court issues a landmark decision in relation to "reverse payment" settlements and rules that such agreements should be subject to "rule of reason" analysis (* Actavis*)*, CONCURRENCES no. 3-2013, art. no. 54214.

43. The Biden agencies have been unusually aggressive in attracting leaders with a variety of experiences. The four current FTC BC deputy Bureau directors include not only Kyle Mach from Cravath and Munger Tolles, but also:
    – Laura Alexander, a partner at leading plaintiffs' law firm Cohen Milstein after three years at Kirkland, and then four years at competition advocacy organizations;
    – Tara Isa Koslov, 27 years at the FTC in various positions after two and a half years at Vinson & Elkins;
    – Rahul Rao, four years as managing AAG in the Washington (State) AG's Office following time as a stay-at-home father, as a consultant, and seven years at global law firms.

44. (Former deputy directors include John Newman, who spent almost two years on leave from the University of Miami, having spent three years at the Division before joining academia.)

45. The five deputy AAGs (not counting the traditionally career criminal deputy) include corporate law firm (with a side trip to the FTC) alum Andrew Forman, but also:
    – Hetal Doshi, seven years at major law firms plus a sabbatical year doing human rights, then seven years in a U.S. Attorney's Office;
    – John W. Elias, 18 years at the DOJ (various roles) and the White House;
    – Michael Kades, 20 years at the FTC, including two years detailed to Capitol Hill, then four years at a competition advocacy organization;
    – Doha Mekki, three years and four months at Crowell & Moring, then nine years at the Division.

46. Moreover, the lead counsel in Biden-era cases (see appendix) include plenty of lawyers from corporate law firms, but also Bonny Sweeney, who has had a distinguished career as a partner at plaintiffs-oriented firms Milberg, Robbins Geller, and Hausfeld; and Henry Su, who was a partner at Fenwick & West and at Howrey, but also from 2017 to 2021 at more plaintiffs-focused Constantine Cannon.

X. Prior Government Experience Can Benefit the Public

47. Serving the public begets serving the public. Our honoree was better equipped and more likely to be interested in leading New York's antitrust program because he had started his post-clerkship career as an attorney in the Antitrust Division. I ended up as FTC general counsel in part because

I started my career as an FTC attorney advisor, and I would not have ended up serving as a commissioner in the Irish Competition and Consumer Protection Commission had I not served as general counsel. It is striking how many excellent lawyers serve the public and then later serve the public again.

48. The top people at the agencies overwhelmingly tend to have prior competition enforcement experience. Of the 19 AAGs appointed by Presidents Nixon through Biden, 15 had had previous government competition service, including the nine most recent (Kanter, Delrahim, Baer, Varney, Barnett, Pate, James, Klein, and Bingaman). Of the 20 FTC directors of the Bureau of Competition, 1970 to date, 14 had previous government service (Halverson in state enforcement), and six were elevated to the director position from other FTC service. Of the 14 modern-era FTC chairs (1970 to date), 12 had previous government service, most but not all of which involved competition enforcement. Bill Kovacic went from being an FTC staffer to a major law firm and to academia before returning to the FTC as general counsel, leaving, and coming back as a commissioner and then chair.

49. Even if former agency lawyers do not resume serving as agency lawyers, they may aid the competition system in other ways. Consider the following:

- After 28 years in private practice, much at Patterson Belknap, William Cavanaugh was appointed deputy AAG for civil matters during the Obama administration in 2009.[36] He later returned to Patterson Belknap but has been prominently aligned with the Biden Antitrust Division since he was appointed lead counsel in a state case against Google.[37]

- Daniel Francis served 10.5 years in global law firms, then three years at the FTC, rising to BC deputy director, then left for academia and is now assistant professor at NYU teaching antitrust.

- Adam Gitlin went from six and a half years at the Division to two years at the Brennan Center and four and a half years at plaintiffs-oriented Lieff Cabraser before becoming the antitrust chief for DC.

- Jay Himes went from 19 years at major private law firms to become antitrust bureau chief for NY, then 12.5 years at Labaton Sucharow, back to the NY AG's Office for just under two years, and is now an FTC administrative law judge.

---

[36] Press Release, U.S. Dep't of Just., Antitrust Division Senior Leadership Named (Apr. 22, 2009), https://www.justice.gov/opa/pr/antitrust-division-senior-leadership-named.

[37] Firm News, Patterson Belknap, Partner Bill Cavanaugh Represents Lead State Plaintiffs Colorado and Nebraska in Google Monopoly Search Lawsuit (Oct. 31, 2023), https://www.pbwt.com/news/partner-bill-cavanaugh-represents-lead-state-plaintiffs-colorado-and-nebraska-in-google-monopoly-search-lawsuit.

- Jon Leibowitz went from working on the Hill to working with a trade association to nine years as a commissioner (four as chair) of the FTC before becoming a partner at Davis Polk. After eight years there, however, he retired and, in October 2021, joined the Maryland Office of Attorney General part-time as a senior counsel.[38]

50. Of course, a critic could see someone being in government, then leaving, and then returning or taking a different government role as simply illustrating the revolving door. My view is that subsequent government service is made both more likely and more likely to be effective by previous government service, and that the public benefits from that. Persons who served in government competition enforcement often view themselves as agency alums with loyalty to their old agency, and they are more likely to answer the call when help is needed.

51. Moreover, the public can benefit from early government service independent of whether it leads to additional such service. Working in an agency can give one insights not available any other way. You really understand an agency when you have been part of that agency. The benefits to academic scholarship are obvious. This can be seen in the work of our honoree but in others, too. Spencer Waller's recent interest in merging consumer protection and competition[39] and John Newman's recent focus on the "second half of Clayton Act § 7"[40] are only two examples.

52. Our antitrust system depends on compliance. Competition is preserved when enforcers bring cases that send a message – and when private entities receive and respond to those messages. Former enforcers may well be attuned to those messages, understanding how to interpret them and help firms comply.

53. During investigations and proceedings, moreover, our competition system relies on private counsel. Preserving documents, producing documents, answering questions honestly – much of our system depends on respect for law enforcement, and experience in law enforcement can help make that work. At the most personal level, too, it can benefit agencies when they can call someone known to them who can make a commitment on which the enforcement agency can rely. Trust is an important part of the process.

---

[38] Press Release, Md. Off. of the Att'y Gen., Former FTC Chair Jon Leibowitz to Join Office of Attorney General (Oct. 14, 2021) https://www.marylandattorneygeneral.gov/press/2021/101421.pdf.

[39] Darren Bush & Spencer Weber Waller, *Using Consumer Protection Law to Achieve Competition Policy Goals* (U. Hous. L. Ctr. No. 2024-A-4, Mar. 13, 2024), https://papers.ssrn.com/sol3/papers.cfm?abstract_id=4714225.

[40] Robert H. Lande, John M. Newman & Rebecca Kelly Slaughter, *The Forgotten Anti-Monopoly Law: The Second Half of Clayton Act § 7* (U. Miami Legal Stud. Rsch Paper No. 4769563, Apr. 8, 2024), https://papers.ssrn.com/sol3/papers.cfm?abstract_id=4769563.

XI. The Missing Third Cheer

54. I do not pretend there are no legitimate issues related to the "revolving door." My guess is they are more acute where private parties seek government benefits such as contracts, licenses, and the like. But when the *Wall Street Journal* runs a three-part front-page story on "The Hidden Life of Google's Secret Weapon," no one can say the revolving door issue does not exist. And AAG Kanter recently delivered a high-profile address at the Fordham international antitrust conference in which he loudly cried that "[a]ll over the world, money earmarked specifically to discourage antitrust and competition law enforcement is finding its way into the expert community upon which we all depend... Conflicts of interest and capture have become so rampant and commonplace that it is increasingly rare to encounter a truly neutral academic expert." Kanter's is a different issue, but related.

55. *Do lawyers from or possibly going to the private sector litigate less vigorously?* I just do not see this happening. Heck, the best way to impress opposing counsel is to beat them at their own game. Moreover, anyone pulling punches would be noticed and called out.

56. *Are lawyers from the outside and/or likely to leave less likely to take risks?* Again, I do not see this happening. Every lawsuit is a risk, and yet government agencies file them even when led by persons from or possibly going to the private sector. Inevitably, one can wonder whether additional suits should have been filed – some big tech examples come to mind, and one wonders about *Live Nation/Ticketmaster* – but it is hard to put oneself into the shoes of decision-makers from years ago (just how trivial did Instagram seem at the time?). Was there an under-appreciation of the durability of big tech market power? Yes. But it is not clear that that was because of "revolving door" blinders.

57. *Do lawyers from outside the government bring their own mindset or worldview?* Of course, in big ways and small. When Miles Kirkpatrick came to the FTC, he changed it in part through the people he brought; when Jim Miller came to the FTC with his people, he changed it through them; and when Lina Khan came in with her new people, they changed it. Everyone has a worldview, and it makes a difference for better or worse. More generally, each new individual in a leadership position brings a worldview. A background in corporate law is different from a background in progressive (or conservative) advocacy, which is different from a background in plaintiffs' class action litigation.

58. *Can aspects of the "revolving door" process be uncomfortable?* Yes. Four issues come to mind.

59. First, the heart of the antitrust agencies is in the career staff, who carry with them expertise, institutional memory, and a deep understanding of

what is important. The "revolving door" inevitably creates tensions when new leaders parade in with new approaches and implicit or perhaps even explicit criticism of past approaches. Those new leaders constantly need to strive to work with and not against the career staff, which is overwhelmingly comprised of good people who want to perform well.

60. Second, the Commission's rules restricting former members and employees allow them freely to assist and advise private parties "behind-the-scenes" – drafting documents, suggesting strategy, and counseling on oral presentations – so long as the member/employee did not participate "personally and substantially" for the Commission in that proceeding or investigation, and so long as important nonpublic documents or information did not come to or be likely to have come to the individual.[41] That is true even if the matter "was pending under the employee's official responsibility" and even if the individual was a commissioner of a "senior employee" as defined. In those cases, there are stricter prohibitions on "darkening the door" of the agency during a "cooling off" period (one year for commissioners and "senior employees," and two years when a matter was pending under an official responsibility) – but one can accomplish an awful lot "behind the scenes."

61. Third, as noted above, new leaders come with a particular mindset. That is inevitable. An issue can arise, however, when the leadership as a whole shares the same mindset. Does that lead to excessive sticking with comfortable approaches? Most talented leaders will fight hard and take risks; the question is whether they will be excessively tied to traditional approaches. Change can be good and important. The Biden Commission's aggressive competition rulemaking challenge to non-compete clauses is something that traditional enforcers likely would not have done. (Of course, it may or may not work out, which remains to be seen.)

62. Fourth, it is a bit troubling that so many non-chair FTC commissioners move on to leading law firms without coming from there (often coming from the Hill, the White House or the executive branch). The many AAGs and Bureau directors who come from leading law firms and move on to leading law firms are not moving to a highly compensated position previously not enjoyed by them – but many non-chair commissioners are. As Kovacic wrote, their government positions provide "an opportunity to become better known, to acquire some substantive expertise, and to become knowledgeable about the process of competition and consumer protection policymaking," which would be "useful to someone who wishes to work in a law firm, a lobbying firm, or in a business organization."[42]

---

41 16 C.F.R. § 4.1(b).

42 Kovacic, *supra* note 20, at 948.

63. *Consulting, which can be part of a "revolving door," does have costs.*
64. For more than a dozen years, I have done no consulting. I have no clients. Before that, for about a dozen years, I was of counsel or special counsel to Covington, a global law firm (just as Harry was counsel to Loeb & Loeb). I did not give the firm a lot of time – my arrangement called for no more than four hours a week – but I had a connection to the firm.
65. Consulting had lots of benefits. When I needed an office in Washington, or San Francisco, or London, I could have one. I attended firm events and got to know some of the most talented lawyers going. I learned how a great law firm is run. I was exposed to fascinating legal issues and fact patterns (I even got an exam question or two), and I could practice the craft of lawyering. And, of course, I received compensation.
66. But consulting has costs. Today, reporters regularly call me because they know I am always willing to comment, freely speaking my mind without worrying about offending a firm's client. When a government official wants to bounce an idea off me, it is exhilarating to volunteer that I have no clients and speak only for myself. I regularly give presentations to state enforcers and federal judges, and I am totally free to opine on any brand-new development without checking with anyone. In scholarship, too, I can research and write whatever I want. If I see something that seems wrong, I can condemn it immediately on some social media platform without worrying whether a firm's client is involved. Moreover, I never have to worry about anyone wondering whether if I am criticizing this or that company it is because some rival company *wants* them criticized. I am a free person, and when I was counsel, I was not completely free.
67. The above discussion is focused on consulting (possibly but not necessarily a "revolving door" issue), not the kind of influence-peddling that was recently highlighted by AAG Kanter. I would have thought it goes without saying that any author should – and would – fully disclose any financial arrangements that might even arguably influence positions taken. That might not always be the case, however. I have experienced being contacted by a lawyer encouraging me to write a commentary about a legal issue affecting his clients – and, unless I misheard, suggesting that I could be compensated for doing so. I declined, but wondered how such an arrangement could be transparently disclosed without making the publication valueless. When one hears the occasional story about a law firm wanting to check an expert economics witness's publication before it is in "print," one wonders if there will be full disclosure. Maybe, then, there is less transparency than there should be, which, if true, would be a real problem.
68. That problem, however, is not a "revolving door" issue but a funding issue. Funding is a challenge. Our academic institutions, many the envy of the world, depend in significant part on philanthropy. Whenever an

individual or an entity becomes a major donor, the leadership of the institution inevitably will worry if such a donor is angered. If an academic institution agrees to accept funding for a chair in this or that specialty, well, there will be such a chair. Donors to an institute focused on free market issues expect free market research and scholarship, just as donors to an institute focused on civil rights expect a certain kind of research and scholarship.[43]

69. The general funding issue, as to which I do not have a fully developed view, can slide over into the "revolving door" issue when persons move into government from an academic program where they enjoyed the support of a specific institute. It is routine for academics going into government to return from where they came: I returned to Wayne State, Harry returned to NYU, Bob Pitofsky returned to Georgetown, Tom Kauper to Michigan, Don Turner to Harvard, Bill Baxter to Stanford, Spencer Waller to Loyola, John Newman to Miami, Eric Posner to Chicago, and so forth. The *Wall Street Journal* exposé on George Mason Professor/FTC Commissioner/George Mason Professor Joshua Wright – who had close ties to George Mason's Law and Economics Center – reported that "[s]everal companies Wright defended with his vote while on the FTC, including Google and Qualcomm, donated to the Law and Economics Center at George Mason University."[44] Reportedly, Google donated $200,000 to the center during Wright's first year at the FTC, and Allergan's foundation donated to the Center in 2015 after Wright had co-authored a November 2014 paper supporting a predecessor company.[45] As the Journal notes: "There are no rules prohibiting the contributions, and Wright wasn't required to report them." Heck, Wright might well not have known of the donations (although, had they been made in previous years, he might have guessed they would continue). I do not have easy answers for this conundrum, but it is clear that when someone entering government has close ties to an institution, there are particular reasons to be concerned that entities might donate to that institution with the hope of currying favor with that individual. (Ironically, this troubling issue arises only sometimes when academics enter government, and not when the more classic "revolving door" candidate from a major law firm enters.)

---

43 Full disclosure: When I was interim dean, I had a small role in helping create Wayne Law's Damon J. Keith Center for Civil Rights, *see Damon J. Keith Center*, WAYNE STATE U., https://law.wayne.edu/keith-center.

44 WALL ST. J., June 8–9, 2024, at C3.

45 *Id.* Allergan's predecessor company was Actavis, and FTC proceedings against it eventually resulted in the Supreme Court decision, FTC v. Actavis, Inc., 570 U.S. 136 (2013). Wright gave several speeches about *Actavis* (obviously a "hot topic" at the time), *see Joshua D. Wright: Former Commissioner*, FED. TRADE COMM'N, https://www.ftc.gov/about-ftc/commissioners-staff/joshua-d-wright. The presumably referenced article was eventually published as Bruce H. Kobayashi, Joshua D. Wright, Douglas H. Ginsburg & Joanna Tsai, Actavis *and Multiple ANDA Entrants: Beyond the Temporary Duopoly*, 29 ANTITRUST 89, 89 (Spring 2013). None of the speeches nor the article mentioned any donation to the Law and Economics Center.

XII. Concluding Observations

70. It is inevitable that talented lawyers will move in and out of government, and on balance it is a good thing. We would not want an enforcement system where lawyers had to choose, shortly after receiving a JD, whether to devote all of their lives or none of their lives to public enforcement. In the end, the public interest is to have talented lawyers working for the government, and that is more likely when lawyers can come and go.

71. At the same time, it is important to recognize and attempt to minimize costs.

72. One cost, somewhat perversely, comes from exaggerating the extent of any perceived problem. Many distinguished public servants have come from and/or gone to major law firms, and implying that doing so is unethical may do more harm (for instance, by discouraging the making or accepting of a good appointment) than good. To be sure, departing government lawyers should not suggest they are blessed with special influence (and they probably are not). It might help, in this connection, if the ethics rules were less permissive about departing lawyers' freedom almost immediately to give advice (subject to the limits discussed above) about influencing former associates "behind the scenes."[46]

73. The right approach is to err on the side of transparency. Any author or speaker with any direct or indirect financial interest ought to disclose it clearly. Disclosure should be sufficiently clear that there simply would not be interested-party-commissioned articles.

74. Another right approach is to recognize that persons coming into the government from anywhere – corporate law firms, Congress, advocacy groups, plaintiffs' law firms, academia, etc. – bring particular perspectives, such that those making selections should strive for diversity in backgrounds. The Biden administration, while not perfect, has impressively tapped plaintiffs' law firms as well as corporate law firms, and also public interest organizations, academia, and state enforcement. One hopes that future administrations will follow this lead. Ironically, it would also be good if future administrations tapped as FTC commissioners *more* partners in leading law firms, as well as economists and other experts (and state enforcers such as the two we have now), so as to shake up the pattern seen too regularly for FTC non-chair commissioners and achieve the excellence the agency deserves.

---

[46] Of course, there is a tradeoff between the ability to recruit talent and restricting what that talent does after *moving* on. For an argument that the FTC is too strict, *see* Lindsey Barrett, Laura M. Moy, Paul Ohm & Ashkan Soltani, *Illusory Conflicts: Post-Employment Clearance Procedures and the FTC's Technological Expertise*, 35 BERKELEY TECH. L.J. 793 (2020).

XIII. Appendix I: Lead Counsel in Biden-era Cases[47]

FTC Cases		
Case & Date Filed	**Lead Counsel**	**Employment History**
FTC et al. v. Amazon.com, Inc. (W.D. Wash. 2023)	Susan A. Musser *Co-Lead Attorney*	DOJ, *Trial Attorney*, 2011–17; Hogan Lovells, *Senior Associate*, 2017–20; FTC, *Senior Trial Counsel* (2020–22), *Deputy Chief Trial Counsel* (2022–24), *Chief Trial Counsel* (2024–present).
	Edward H. Takashima *Co-Lead Attorney*	Boies Schiller Flexner, *Associate* (2014–17), *Partner* (2017–22); FTC BC, *Attorney*, (2022–23), *Senior Trial Counsel* (2023–present).
Illumina Inc. (FTC Dkt. 9104) (2021)	Susan A. Musser *Lead Attorney*	*See above.*
FTC v. IQVIA Holdings Inc. et al. (S.D.N.Y. 2023)	Jennifer Fleury *Lead Attorney*	Hogan Lovells, *Associate* (c. 2012–15), *Senior Associate* (2015–20); DOJ, *Trial Attorney*, 2020–22; FTC BC, *Attorney & Deputy Chief Trial Counsel*, 2022–24; Hogan Lovells, *Partner*, 2024–present.
FTC et al. v. Kroger Company et al. (D. Or. 2024)	James H. Weingarten (Withdrawn: 6/12/14) *Co-Lead Attorney*	Williams & Connolly, *Associate*, 2008–17; FTC BC, *Attorney* (2017–19), *Senior Trial Counsel*, (2019–22), *Deputy Chief Trial Counsel* (2022–24), *Chief Trial Counsel* (2024); Milbank, *Partner*, 2024–present.
	Susan A. Musser *Co-Lead Attorney*	*See above.*
	Charles E. Dickinson *Co-Lead Attorney*	Hogan Lovells, *Associate*, 2009–14; FTC BC, *Attorney* (2014–present), *Counsel to the Director* (2021–22).
FTC v. Meta Platforms, Inc. (D.D.C. 2020)	Daniel J. Matheson *Lead Attorney*	WilmerHale/Axinn/Gibson Dunn, *Associate*, 2005–16; FTC, *Attorney* (2016–19), *Deputy Chief Trial Counsel* (2019–present).
FTC v. Meta Platforms Inc. et al. (N.D. Cal. 2022)	James H. Weingarten (Withdrawn: 6/6/24) *Lead Attorney*	*See above.*
	Abby L. Dennis *Lead Attorney*	Boies Schiller Flexner, *Associate* (2009–15), *Partner* (2016–21); FTC BC, *Senior Trial Counsel* (2021–23), *Deputy Assistant Director* (2023–present).

---

47 The names of the lead attorneys listed herein were gathered from various federal court filings, government press releases, and legal news sources. Similarly, the attorneys' employment histories were collected from LinkedIn profiles, legal news sources, and other publicly available databases. While the author has taken great care to verify these facts, certain details could not be fully confirmed and have been included in this study with due caution. Information is believed to be current as of October 20, 2024. [There has to be a cutoff date, and that's the one we used.]

FTC Cases		
Case & Date Filed	**Lead Counsel**	**Employment History**
FTC v. Microsoft Corporation et al. (N.D. Cal. 2023)	James H. Weingarten (Withdrawn: 6/7/24) *Lead Attorney*	*See above.*
FTC v. Novant Health, Inc. et al. (W.D.N.C. 2024)	Nathan Brenner *Lead Attorney*	DOJ Antitrust, *Trial Attorney*, 2016–20; FTC BC, *Attorney* (2020–22), *Senior Trial Counsel* (2022–24), *Deputy Chief Trial Counsel* (2024–present).
FTC et al. v. Syngenta Crop Protection AG et al. (M.D.N.C. 2022)	James H. Weingarten (Withdrawn: 6/12/24) *Lead Attorney*	*See above.*
	Allyson M. Maltas *Lead Attorney*	Latham & Watkins, *Associate* (2004–17), *Counsel* (2017–24); FTC, *Senior Trial Counsel*, 2024–present.
FTC v. Tapestry, Inc. et al. (S.D.N.Y. 2024)	Abby L. Dennis *Lead Attorney*	*See above.*
FTC v. Tempur Sealy International, Inc. et al. (S.D. Tex. 2024)	Allyson M. Maltas *Co-Lead Attorney*	*See above.*
	Stephen Rodger *Co-Lead Attorney*	Covington, *Associate*, 2003–12; FTC BC, *Attorney* (2012–22), *Deputy Assistant Director* (2022–present).
FTC v. U.S. Anesthesia Partners, Inc. et al. (S.D. Tex. 2023)	Kara L. Monahan *Lead Attorney*	FTC BC, *Deputy Assistant Director*, 2012–present.

Antitrust Division Cases		
Case & Date Filed	**Lead Counsel**	**Employment History**
U.S. et al. v. American Airlines Group Inc. et al. (D. Mass. 2021)	William H. Jones II *Lead Attorney*	DOJ Antitrust, *Trial Attorney* (1998–present); S. Judiciary Comm., *Antitrust Counsel*, 2002–03; U.S. Attorney's Offices, *Special Assistant U.S. Attorney*, 2010.
U.S. et al. v. Apple Inc. (D.N.J. 2024)	Jonathan H. Lasken *Co-Lead Attorney*	Hunton & Williams, *Associate*, 2010–15; DOJ Antitrust, *Appellate Attorney*, 2015–18; FTC, *Senior Trial Counsel*, 2018–22; DOJ Antitrust, *Senior Litigation Counsel* (2022–present), *Assistant Chief* (2022–present).
	Lorraine Van Kirk *Co-Lead Attorney*	County of Santa Clara, *Deputy County Counsel*, 2014–21; CFPB, *Senior Litigation Counsel*, 2021–22; DOJ Antitrust, *Senior Litigation Counsel*, 2022–present.

Antitrust Division Cases		
Case & Date Filed	**Lead Counsel**	**Employment History**
U.S. v. ASSA ABLOY AB et al. (D.D.C. 2022)	Matthew R. Huppert *Co-Lead Attorney*	Paul, Weiss, *Associate*, 2011–12; Kellogg Hansen, *Associate*, 2014–21; DOJ Antitrust, *Trial Attorney* (2021–23), *Litigation Counsel to the AAG* (2023–present).
	David E. Dahlquist *Co-Lead Attorney*	Winston & Strawn, *Associate* (2001–08), *Partner* (2009–22); DOJ Antitrust, *Senior Trial Counsel* (2022–24), *Acting Deputy Director* (2024–present).
U.S. v. Bertelsmann SE & CO. KGaA et al. (D.D.C. 2021)	John R. Read *Lead Attorney*	DOJ Antitrust, *Trial Attorney* (1994–present), *Chief* (after 2004).
U.S. et al. v. Google LLC (D.D.C. 2020)	Kenneth M. Dintzer *Lead Attorney*	DOJ Antitrust, *Trial Attorney*, 1992–97; DOJ Civil, *Trial Attorney* (1997–2003), *Senior Trial Attorney* (2003–07), *Assistant Director* (2007–14), *Deputy Branch Director* (2014–present); DOJ Antitrust, *Senior Trial Counsel*, 2020–24.
U.S. et al. v. Google LLC (E.D. Va. 2023)	Julia Tarver Wood *Co-Lead Attorney*	Paul, Weiss, *Attorney & Partner*, 1997–2023; DOJ Antitrust, *Senior Litigation Counsel*, 2023–present.
	Aaron M. Teitelbaum *Co-Lead Attorney*	Manhattan District Attorney's Office, *Assistant District Attorney*, 2015–18; U.S. Attorney's Offices, *Assistant U.S. Attorney*, 2018–22; DOJ Antitrust, *Senior Litigation Counsel*, 2022–present.
U.S. et al. v. JetBlue Airways Corporation et al. (D. Mass. 2023)	Edward W. Duffy *Co-Lead Attorney*	Vinson & Elkins, *Associate*, 2011–13; K&L Gates, *Associate*, 2013–16; Reed Smith, *Partner*, 2016–22; DOJ Antitrust, *Senior Trial Counsel*, 2022–present.
	Aaron M. Teitelbaum *Co-Lead Attorney*	See above.
U.S. et al. v. Live Nation Entertainment, Inc. et al. (S.D.N.Y. 2024)	Bonny Sweeney *Lead Attorney*	Foley Hoag, *Associate*, 1988–94; Milberg, *Partner*, 1996–2004; Robbins Geller, *Partner*, 2004–14; Hausfeld, *Partner*, 2015–22; DOJ Antitrust, *Senior Trial Counsel*, 2022–present.
U.S. et al. v. RealPage, Inc. (M.D.N.C. 2024)	Henry C. Su *Lead Attorney*	Williams Mullen, *Associate*, 1993–96; Hunton & Williams, *Senior Associate*, 1996–2001; Fenwick & West, *Senior Associate* (2001–03), *Partner* (2004–05); Howrey, *Partner*, 2005–11; FTC, *Attorney Advisor* (2011–13, 2015–17), *BC Trial Attorney* (2013–15, 2017); Constantine Cannon, *Trial Lawyer & Partner*, 2017–21; Bradley Arant, *Partner*, 2021–23; DOJ Antitrust, *Senior Litigation Counsel*, 2024–present.

Antitrust Division Cases		
Case & Date Filed	**Lead Counsel**	**Employment History**
U.S. et al. v. United-Health Group, Inc. et al. (D.D.C. 2022)	Bindi R. Bhagat *Lead Attorney*	DOJ Antitrust, *Trial Attorney*, 2012–present.
U.S. v. U.S. Sugar Corporation et al. (D. Del. 2022)	Brian Hanna *Lead Attorney*	McGuireWoods, *Litigation and Investigation Attorney*, 2010–15; DOJ Antitrust, *Trial Attorney*, 2015–present.
U.S. v. Visa Inc. (S.D.N.Y. 2024)	Edward W. Duffy *Lead Attorney*	See above.

XIV. Appendix II: Antitrust Division Employment Chart[48]

Assistant Attorneys General of the Antitrust Division		
Name & Tenure	**Prior Employment**	**Subsequent Employment**
Jonathan S. Kanter 2021–Present	FTC, *Attorney*, 1998–2000; Fried Frank, *Associate*, 2000–07; Cadwalader, *Partner*, 2007–16; Paul, Weiss, *Partner, Co-Chair*, 2016–20; The Kanter Law Group, *Founding Partner*, 2020–21.	
Makan Delrahim 2017–21	Patton Boggs, *Associate*, 1995–98; S. Judiciary Comm., *Staff, Chief Counsel*, 2000–03; DOJ Antitrust, *DAAG*, 2003–05; Brownstein Hyatt, *Partner*, 2005–17; The White House, *Deputy Counsel, Deputy Assistant*, 2017.	Latham & Watkins, *Partner*, 2022–present.
William J. Baer 2013–16	FTC, *Assistant General Counsel, Attorney Advisor, etc.*, 1975–80; FTC BC, *Director*, 1995–99; Arnold & Porter, *Associate* (1980–95), *Partner* (2000–12).	DOJ, *Acting AAG*, 2016–17; Arnold & Porter, *Partner*, 2017–20; Brookings, *Visiting Fellow*, 2020–present.
Christine A. Varney 2009–11	Pierson, Semmes & Finley, *Associate*, 1986–89; Executive Office of the President, *Cabinet Secretary*, 1993–94; FTC, *Commissioner*, 1994–97; Hogan & Hartson, *Associate* (1990–93), *Partner* (1997–2009).	Cravath, *Partner*, 2011–present.
Thomas O. Barnett 2005–08	Covington, *Associate, Partner, Vice Chair*, 1990–2004; DOJ Antitrust, *DAAG*, 2004–05.	Covington, *Partner*, 2009–present.

[48] The employment histories listed herein were compiled based on data gathered from hundreds of publicly available sources, including official press releases, congressional hearing transcripts, faculty biographies, newspaper archives, LinkedIn profiles, and curricula vitae. While the author has taken great care to verify employment positions and dates, certain details could not be fully confirmed and have been included in this study with due caution. Information is believed to be current as of October 20, 2024. [There has to be a cutoff date, and that's the one we used.]

Assistant Attorneys General of the Antitrust Division		
Name & Tenure	Prior Employment	Subsequent Employment
R. Hewitt Pate 2002–05	Hunton & Williams, *Associate, Partner*, 1990–2001; DOJ Antitrust, *DAAG*, 2001–02.	Hunton & Williams, *Partner*, 2005–09; Chevron, *VP, General Counsel*, 2009–present.
Charles A. James 2001–02	FTC BC, *Attorney, Advisor, Assistant*, 1979–85; DOJ Antitrust, *DAAG, Acting AAG*, 1991–92; Jones Day, *Associate* (1985–91), *Partner* (1993–2001).	Chevron, *VP, General Counsel, Executive VP*, 2002–10; ASU Law, *Adjunct Faculty*, after 2010.
Joel I. Klein 1996–2000	Rogovin, Stern & Huge, *Associate, Partner*, 1976–81; Onek, Klein & Farr, *Partner*, 1981–93; Office of White House Counsel, *Deputy Counsel*, 1993–95; DOJ Antitrust, *Principal DAAG*, 1995–96.	Bertelsmann, *Chairman, CEO, Chief U.S. Liaison Officer*, 2001–02; NYC Public Schools, *Chancellor*, 2002–10; News Corp., *Executive VP, CEO, etc.*, 2003–20; Oscar Health, *Chief Policy & Strategy Officer, Senior Advisor*, 2016–22; Retromer Therapeutics, *CEO*, 2020–present.
Anne K. Bingaman 1993–96	New Mexico AG's Office, *Attorney*, 1970–72; UNM Law, *Assistant Professor, Associate Professor*, 1972–76; Bingaman & Davenport, *Founding Partner*, 1977–82; Brown, Bain & Bingaman, *Partner*, 1982–84; Onek, Klein & Farr, *Partner*, 1984–85; Powell Goldstein, *Partner*, 1985–93.	LCI International, *Senior VP*, 1997–98; Valor Telecommunications, *Founder, Chairman, CEO*, 1998–2005; Soundpath Conferencing, *Founder*, 2003–08.
James F. Rill 1989–92	Collier Shannon, *Associate, Partner*, 1959–89.	Collier Shannon, *Partner*, 1992–2000; Howrey, *Senior Partner, Co-Chair*, 2000–11; Baker Botts, *Partner, Senior Counsel*, 2011–present.
Charles F. Rule 1986–89	DOJ Antitrust, *Special Assistant, DAAG, Acting DAAG, Principal DAAG*, 1982–86.	Covington, *Partner*, 1989–2001; Fried Frank, *Partner*, 2001–07; Cadwalader, *Partner*, 2007–16; Paul, Weiss, *Partner*, 2016–22; Rule Garza Howley, *Chair*, 2022–present.
Douglas H. Ginsburg 1985–86	Harvard Law, *Professor*, 1975–83; DOJ Antitrust, *DAAG*, 1983–84; OMB, *Administrator*, 1984–85.	NYU Law, *Professor*, 2011–13; D.C. Court of Appeals, *Judge, Chief Judge*, 1986–present; George Mason Law, *Professor, Institute Chair*, 2013–present.

Assistant Attorneys General of the Antitrust Division		
Name & Tenure	Prior Employment	Subsequent Employment
J. Paul McGrath 1983–85	Dewey Ballantine, *Associate, Partner*, 1965–81; DOJ Civil, *AAG*, 1981–83.	Dewey Ballantine, *Managing Partner, Chairman*, 1985–92; AlliedSignal, *General Counsel, Associate General Counsel*, 1992–94; FMC Corp., *Senior VP, General Counsel*, 1996–2000; American Standard Companies, *Senior VP, General Counsel, Secretary*, 2000–04.
William F. Baxter 1981–83	Stanford Law, *Assistant Professor*, 1956–58; Covington, *Member*, 1958–60; Stanford Law, *Professor*, 1960–98.	Stanford Law, *Professor*, 1960–98; Shearman & Sterling, *Of Counsel*, 1984–98.
Sanford M. Litvack 1980–81	DOJ Antitrust, *Trial Attorney*, 1959–61; Donovan, Leisure, *Attorney*, 1961–79.	Donovan, Leisure, *Managing Partner*, 1981–86; Disney, *VP, General Counsel*, 1991–2000; Dewey Ballantine, *Partner* (1986–91), *Of Counsel* (2000–02); Quinn Emanuel, *Partner*, 2003–04; Hogan Lovells, *Senior Counsel*, 2004–19; Chaffetz Lindsey, *Partner*, 2019–present.
John H. Shenefield 1977–79	Hunton & Williams, *Associate, Partner*, 1965–77; DOJ Antitrust, *DAAG*, 1977.	DOJ, *Associate AG*, 1979–81; Milbank, *Partner*, 1981–86; Morgan Lewis, *Partner, Counsel*, after 1986.
Donald I. Baker 1976–77	DOJ Antitrust, *Trial Attorney, Chief, DAAG*, 1966–75; Cornell Law, *Professor*, 1975–78.	Cornell Law, *Professor*, 1975–78; Jones Day, *Of Counsel, Partner* (1977–83), *Partner* (1991–94); Sutherland Asbill & Brennan, *Partner*, 1983–91; Baker & Miller, *Founding Partner*, 1994–present.
Thomas E. Kauper 1972–76	Sidley Austin, *Attorney*, 1962–64; Michigan Law, *Assistant Professor, Associate Professor, Professor*, 1964–2008.	Michigan Law, *Professor*, 1969–2008.
Richard W. McLaren 1969–72	Hodges Reavis, *Attorney*, 1946–49; Chadwell Keck, *Partner*, 1950–69.	U.S. District Court for the Northern District of Illinois, *Judge*, 1972–76.

Principal Deputy Assistant Attorneys General of the Antitrust Division		
Name & Tenure	**Prior Employment**	**Subsequent Employment**
Doha Mekki 2022–Present	Crowell & Moring, *Associate*, 2011–15; DOJ Antitrust, *Assistant Chief, Special Counsel, etc.*, 2015–22.	
Michael F. Murray 2020–21	Gibson Dunn, *Associate*, 2010–13; Jones Day, *Associate*, 2014–17; DOJ, *Associate Deputy AG*, 2017–18; DOJ Antitrust, *DAAG*, 2018–20.	Paul Hastings, *Partner, Chair*, 2021–present.
Bernard A. Nigro, Jr. 2019–20	Fried Frank, *Partner*, 1999–2003; FTC BC, *Deputy Director*, 2003–06; Willkie Farr, *Partner*, 2006–09; Fried Frank, *Partner, Chair*, 2009–17; DOJ Antitrust, *DAAG*, 2017–19.	Fried Frank, *Chair*, 2020–present.
Andrew C. Finch 2017–19	DOJ Antitrust, *Counsel*, 2003–05; Paul, Weiss, *Counsel, Partner*, 2005–17; DOJ Antitrust, *Acting AAG*, 2017.	Paul, Weiss, *Partner*, 2019–present.
Renata B. Hesse 2012–17	Brobeck, Phleger & Harrison, *Associate*, 1990–97; DOJ Antitrust, *Trial Attorney, Section Chief*, 1997–2006; Wilson Sonsini, *Member*, 2006–11: FCC, *Senior Counsel*, 2011–12; DOJ Antitrust, *Special Advisor, DAAG*, 2012.	DOJ Antitrust, *Acting AAG*, 2016–17; Sullivan & Cromwell, *Partner*, 2017–present.
David L. Meyer 2006–09	DOJ Antitrust, *Special Assistant*, 1987–89; Covington, *Partner, Vice Chair*, 1989–2006.	Morrison & Foerster, *Partner, Co-Chair*, 2009–20; Law Office of David L. Meyer, *Principal*, 2020–present.
Deborah P. Majoras 2002–04	Jones Day, *Associate, Partner*, 1991–2001; DOJ Antitrust, *DAAG*, 2001–04.	FTC, *Chairman*, 2004–08; Procter & Gamble, *Senior VP, CLO, etc.*, 2008–22.
A. Douglas Melamed 1996–2000	Wilmer, Cutler & Pickering, *Associate, Chair, Partner*, 1971–96.	DOJ Antitrust, *Acting AAG*, 2000–01; WilmerHale, *Partner, Co-Chair*, 2001–09; Intel, *Senior VP, General Counsel, etc.*, 2009–15; Stanford Law, *Visiting Professor, Professor*, 2014–23.
Joel I. Klein 1995–96	*See above.*	*See above.*

Principal Deputy Assistant Attorneys General of the Antitrust Division		
Name & Tenure	**Prior Employment**	**Subsequent Employment**
Robert E. Litan 1993–95	Arnold & Porter, *Associate*, 1979–82; Powell Goldstein, *Senior Associate, Partner, Of Counsel*, 1982–90; Brookings, *Senior Fellow, Director*, 1984–93.	OMB, *Associate Director*, 1995–96; Brookings, *VP, Director, etc.*, 1996–2012; Bloomberg Government, *Research Director*, 2012–14; Korein Tillery, *Of Counsel, Partner*, 2013–21; Berger Montague, *Shareholder*, 2021–present.
Alison L. Smith 1989–91	Vinson & Elkins, *Associate, Partner*, 1977–89.	Vinson & Elkins, *Partner*, 1991–2004; Dewey Ballantine, *Partner*, 2004–05; Haynes and Boone, *Partner*, 2005–10; McDermott Will & Emery, *Partner*, after 2010.
Charles F. Rule 1985–86	*See above.*	*See above.*
Helmut F. Furth 1982–85	Donovan, Leisure, *Associate, Partner*, 1955–78; Sullivan & Cromwell, *Of Counsel*, 1978–82.	Baity & Joseph, *Attorney*, after 1985; Patterson Belknap, *Partner*, until 1990; Davis Markel, *Partner*, after 1990; Bryan Cave, *Attorney*, after 1990.
Richard J. Favretto 1979–81	DOJ Antitrust, *Trial Attorney, Deputy Director, etc.*, 1966–79.	Mayer Brown, *Partner, Senior Counsel*, 1981–2023.
Hugh P. Morrison, Jr. 1976–78	DOJ Antitrust, *Chief, Acting AAG, etc.*, 1962–76.	Cahill Gordon & Reindel, *Partner*, until 1991.
Bruce B. Wilson 1972–76	Montgomery McCracken Walker, *Attorney*, 1962–69; DOJ Antitrust, *Chief, DAAG, etc.*, 1969–72.	DOJ Antitrust, *Staff*, 1976–79; Conrail, *Senior VP, General Counsel*, 1979–97.
Walker B. Comegys 1969–72	Goodwin, Procter & Hoar, *Associate, Partner*, 1954–69.	DOJ Antitrust, *Acting AAG*, 1972; Mintz Levin, *Partner*, 1972–75; Powers & Hall, *Partner, Director*, 1975–84; Law Offices of Walker B. Comegys, *Founder, Director*, 1984–98.

XV. Appendix III: FTC Employment Chart[49]

FTC Chairs		
Name & Tenure	**Prior Employment**	**Subsequent Employment**
Lina M. Khan 2021–Present	Open Markets Institute, *Legal Director*, 2017–18; FTC, *Legal Fellow*, 2018; H. Judiciary Comm., *Counsel*, 2019–20; Columbia Law, *Legal Fellow* (2018–19), *Associate Professor* (2020–21).	
Joseph J. Simons 2018–21	FTC BC, *Assistant, Assistant Director, etc.*, 1987–89; Wachtell Lipton, *Associate*, 1989–94; Collier Shannon, *Partner, Counsel*, 1994–98; Clifford Chance, *Partner*, 1998–2001; FTC BC, *Director*, 2001–03; Paul, Weiss, *Partner*, 2003–17.	Paul, Weiss, *Of Counsel*, 2021–present.
Jon D. Leibowitz 2009–13	Motion Picture Association of America, *VP*, 2000–04; FTC, *Commissioner*, 2004–09.	Davis Polk, *Partner*, 2013–21; Maryland Office of the AG, *Senior Counsel*, 2021–present.
William E. Kovacic 2008–09	FTC, *Attorney, Attorney Advisor*, 1979–83; Bryan Cave, *Associate*, 1983–86; George Mason Law, *Professor*, 1986–99; FTC, *General Counsel*, 2001–04; GW Law, *Professor*, 1999–2011; FTC, *Commissioner*, 2006–11.	GW Law, *Professor*, 1999–2011; FTC, *Commissioner*, 2006–11.
Deborah P. Majoras 2004–08	Jones Day, *Associate, Partner*, 1991–2001; DOJ Antitrust, *DAAG, Principal DAAG*, 2001–04.	Procter & Gamble, *Senior VP & General Counsel, CLO & Secretary, etc.*, 2008–22.
Timothy J. Muris 2001–04	FTC, *Assistant, Consultant*, 1974–77; Miami Law, *Assistant Professor, Associate Professor, Professor*, 1976–81; FTC, *BCP Director* (1981–83), *BC Director* (1983–85); OMB, *Executive Associate Director*, 1985–88; Collier Shannon, *Of Counsel*, 1988–2000; Howrey Simon, *Of Counsel*, 2000–01; George Mason Law, *Professor, Interim Dean, etc.*, 1988–present.	O'Melveny & Myers, *Of Counsel*, 2004–11; Kirkland & Ellis, *Of Counsel*, 2011–17; George Mason Law, *Professor*, 1988–present; Sidley Austin, *Senior Counsel*, 2017–present.

---

49 The employment histories listed herein were compiled based on data gathered from hundreds of publicly available sources, including official press releases, congressional hearing transcripts, faculty biographies, newspaper archives, LinkedIn profiles, and curricula vitae. While the author has taken great care to verify employment positions and dates, certain details could not be fully confirmed and have been included in this study with due caution. Information is believed to be current as of October 20, 2024. [There has to be a cutoff date, and that's the one we used.]

FTC Chairs		
Name & Tenure	**Prior Employment**	**Subsequent Employment**
Robert Pitofsky 1995–2001	Dewey Ballantine, *Attorney*, 1957–63; NYU Law, *Professor*, 1963–70; FTC, *BCP Director* (1970–73), *Commissioner* (1978–81); Arnold & Porter, *Of Counsel*, 1973–78, 1981–83, 1989–95; Georgetown Law, *Professor, Dean, etc.*, 1973–78, 1981–95.	Georgetown Law, *Professor*, after 2001; Arnold & Porter, *Of Counsel*, after 2001.
Janet D. Steiger 1989–95	Postal Rate Commission, *Commissioner, Chairman*, 1980–89.	FTC, *Commissioner*, 1995–97.
Daniel Oliver 1986–89	Hawkins Delafield, *Attorney*, 1967–70; Alexander & Green, *Attorney*, 1971–73, 1976–79; Rincon Communications, *President*, 1980–81; Dep't of Education, *General Counsel*, 1981–83; Dep't of Agric., *General Counsel*, 1983–86.	Education and Research Institute, *Board Chairman*, until present; Pacific Research Institute, *Director*, until present.
James C. Miller III 1981–85	Georgia State University, *Assistant Professor*, 1968–69; USDOT, *Senior Staff Economist*, 1969–72; Texas A&M, *Associate Professor*, 1972–74; Council of Economic Advisors, *Senior Staff Economist*, 1974–75; Council on Wage and Price Stability, *Assistant Director*, 1975–77; American Enterprise Institute, *Resident Scholar, Center Co-Director*, 1977–81; Economic Impact Analysts, *President, Board Chairman*, 1978–81; OMB, *Administrator*, 1981.	OMB, *Director*, 1985–88; Hagler Bailly, *Senior Advisor*, 2000–02; LECG, *Director*, 2002–03; CapAnalysis Group, *Chairman*, 2002–06; Husch Blackwell, *Senior Advisor*, after 2006; King & Spalding, *Senior Advisor*, until present.
Michael Pertschuk 1977–81	S. Commerce Comm., *Counsel, Chief Counsel, Staff Director*, 1964–68.	FTC, *Commissioner*, 1981–84; Advocacy Institute, *Co-Director*, 1984–2014.
Calvin J. Collier 1976–77	Kirkland & Ellis, *Attorney*, 1968–69; Dep't of Commerce, *Special Assistant, Deputy Under Secretary*, 1969–73; Dep't of Housing and Urban Development, *Program Director*, 1973; FTC, *General Counsel*, 1973–75; OMB, *Associate Director*, 1975–76.	Hughes Hubbard & Reed, *Partner*, 1978–88; Kraft Foods, *Senior VP, General Counsel, Secretary*, 1988–2004.
Lewis A. Engman 1973–75	Warner Norcross & Judd, *Associate, Partner*, 1961–70; White House Domestic Council, *Assistant Director*, 1971–73.	Warner Norcross & Judd, *Partner*, 1976–79; Pharmaceutical Manufacturers Association, *President*, 1979–84; Winston & Strawn, *Counsel, Partner*, 1984–93.

FTC Chairs		
Name & Tenure	**Prior Employment**	**Subsequent Employment**
Miles W. Kirkpatrick 1970–73	Morgan Lewis, *Associate, Partner*, 1944–68; ABA Antitrust Section, *Head*, 1968–69.	Morgan Lewis, *Chairman*, 1973–85.

FTC Commissioners (Non-Chair Positions)		
Name & Tenure	**Prior Employment**	**Subsequent Employment**
Andrew N. Ferguson 2024–Present	Covington, *Associate*, 2014–15; Bancroft, *Associate*, 2015–16; Sidley Austin, *Associate*, 2018; U.S. Senate, *Senior Special Counsel, Chief Counsel*, 2018–21; Virginia Office of the AG, *Solicitor General*, 2022–23.	
Melissa Holyoak 2024–Present	O'Melveny & Myers, *Associate*, 2003–08; KermaPartners, *Consultant*, 2008–10; Holland & Knight, *Manager*, 2010–11; Center for Class Action Fairness, *Senior Counsel*, 2012–20; Utah AG's Office, *Solicitor General*, 2020–23.	
Alvaro Bedoya 2022–Present	WilmerHale, *Associate*, 2007–09; S. Judiciary Comm., *Counsel, Chief Counsel*, 2009–14; Georgetown Law, *Clinic Director, Adjunct Professor, etc.*, 2014–22.	
Rebecca K. Slaughter 2018–Present	Sidley Austin, *Associate*, 2008–09; S. Judiciary Comm., *Counsel, Senior Counsel, Chief Counsel*, 2009–18.	FTC, *Acting Chair*, 2021.
Christine S. Wilson 2018–23	Collier Shannon, *Associate*, 1995–2000; Howrey Simon, *Senior Associate*, 2000–01; FTC, *Chief of Staff* (2001–02); *Consultant* (2003–04); O'Melveny & Myers, *Partner*, 2004–11; Kirkland & Ellis, *Partner*, 2011–16; Delta Air Lines, *Senior VP*, 2016–18.	EdenSpring Foundation, *Founder, President*, 2023–present; Freshfields, *Senior Advisor*, 2024–present.
Noah J. Phillips 2018–22	Cravath, *Associate*, 2006–10; Steptoe & Johnson, *Associate*, 2010–11; S. Judiciary Comm., *Counsel, Chief Counsel*, 2011–18.	Cravath, *Partner*, 2022–present.
Rohit Chopra 2018–21	Booz, Allen & Hamilton, *Consultant*, 2004–06; McKinsey & Company, *Associate*, 2008, 2009–10; CFPB, *Assistant Director, Student Loan Ombudsman*, 2010–15; Consumer Federation of America, *Senior Fellow*, 2017.	CFPB, *Director*, 2021–present.
Maureen K. Ohlhausen 2012–18	FTC, *Attorney, Attorney Advisor, etc.*, 1997–2008; Business Software Alliance, *Policy Counsel*, 2009; Wilkinson Barker Knauer, *Partner*, 2009–12.	FTC, *Acting Chair*, 2017–18; Baker Botts, *Partner*, 2018–24; Wilson Sonsini, *Partner*, 2024–present.

FTC Commissioners (Non-Chair Positions)		
Name & Tenure	**Prior Employment**	**Subsequent Employment**
Terrell McSweeny 2014–18	The White House, *Deputy Assistant, Policy Advisor*, 2009–12; DOJ Antitrust, *Chief Counsel*, 2012–14.	Covington, *Partner, Senior Of Counsel*, 2018–present.
Julie S. Brill 2010–16	Office of the Vermont AG, *Assistant Attorney General, Director, etc.*, 1988–2009; North Carolina Dep't of Just., *Senior Deputy Attorney General, Chief*, 2009–10.	Hogan Lovells, *Partner, Co-Director*, 2016–17; Microsoft, *CPO, Corporate VP, etc.*, 2017–present.
Joshua D. Wright 2013–16	LECG, *Consultant*, 1998–2002; George Mason Law, *Assistant Professor, Professor, etc.*, 2004–23; Charles River Associates, *Senior Consultant*, 2009–13.	Wilson Sonsini, *Senior Of Counsel*, 2016–19; George Mason Law, *Professor, Institute Executive Director*, 2004–23; Lodestar Law & Economics, *Founding Partner*, 2022–present.
J. Thomas Rosch 2006–13	McCutchen Doyle, *Associate, Partner*, 1965–73; FTC BCP, *Director*, 1973–75; McCutchen Doyle, *Partner*, 1975–93; Latham & Watkins, *Partner*, 1994–2006.	Latham & Watkins, *Of Counsel*, 2013–16.
Pamela J. Harbour 2003–10	Office of the New York State AG, *Assistant AG, Assistant First Deputy AG, etc.*, 1987–99; Kaye Scholer, *Partner*, 1999–2003.	Norton Rose Fulbright, *Partner*, 2010–13; BakerHostetler, *Partner*, 2013–14; Herbalife Nutrition, *Senior VP, Legal Officer*, 2014–21; Tupperware, *Independent Board Director*, 2021–present.
Thomas B. Leary 1999–2005	White & Case, *Associate, Partner*, 1958–71; General Motors, *Attorney-in-Charge, Assistant General Counsel*, 1971–82; Hogan & Hartson, *Partner*, 1983–99.	Hogan Lovells, *Of Counsel*, after 2006.
Orson G. Swindle III 1997–2005	Dep't of Agric., *State Director*, 1981–85; Dep't of Commerce, *Assistant Secretary*, 1985–89; U.S. Congress, *Candidate*, 1993–94, 1995–96.	Hunton & Williams, *Senior Policy Advisor*, 2005–09.
Mozelle W. Thompson 1997–2004	Skadden, *Associate*, 1982–90; New York State Agencies, *Acting Executive Director, Executive VP, General Counsel*, 1990–93; Dep't of the Treasury, *Deputy Assistant Secretary, Principal Deputy Assistant Secretary*, 1993–97.	Thompson Strategic Consulting, *CEO*, 2005–present.
Shiela F. Anthony 1997–2003	Dow, Lohnes & Albertson, *Associate*, 1985–93; DOJ Office of Legislative Affairs, *AAG*, 1993–95.	*Insufficient information available.*

Two Cheers for the Revolving Door

FTC Commissioners (Non-Chair Positions)		
Name & Tenure	**Prior Employment**	**Subsequent Employment**
Mary L. Azcuenaga 1984–98	FTC, *Litigation Attorney, Assistant General Counsel*, 1975–84.	Heller Ehrman, *Shareholder*, 1998–2008; Baker & McKenzie, *Partner*, 2008–11: *Independent Consultant*, 2011–present.
Roscoe B. Starek III 1990–97	Dep't of State, *Deputy Assistant Secretary, Legislative Counsel, etc.*, 1982–88; The White House, *Deputy Director, Deputy Assistant*, 1989–90.	Direct Marketing Association, *Senior VP*, after 1998; Wine and Spirits Wholesalers of America, *Senior VP*, after 2002.
Christine A. Varney 1994–97	Pierson, Semmes & Finley, *Associate*, 1986–89; Hogan & Hartson, *Associate*, 1990–93; Executive Office of the President, *Cabinet Secretary*, 1993–94.	Hogan & Hartson, *Partner*, 1997–2009; DOJ Antitrust, *AAG*, 2009–11: Cravath, *Partner*, 2011–present.
Dennis A. Yao 1991–94	Ford Motor Company, *Analyst, Chief Analyst*, 1977–79; UPenn, *Associate Professor, Professor, etc.*, 1983–2004.	LECG, *Principal*, 1994–2000; UPenn, *Lecturer, Professor, etc.*, 1983–2004; Harvard, *Professor*, 2004–present.
Deborah K. Owen 1989–94	Piper & Marbury, *Attorney*, 1977–79; H. Judiciary Comm., *Associate Counsel*, 1980–82; S. Judiciary Comm., *General Counsel*, 1983–85; White House Counsel's Office, *Associate Counsel*, 1985–86; McNair Law Firm, *Managing Partner*, 1986–89.	Arent Fox, *Partner*, after 1994.
Andrew J. Strenio Jr. 1986–91	Wald, Harkrader & Ross, *Attorney*, 1980; Council of Economic Advisors, *Staff Economist*, 1980–81; FTC BCP, *Attorney, Assistant Director*, 1982–84; ICC, *Commissioner*, 1984–85.	Fox, Bennett & Turner, *Partner*, 1991–94; Hunton & Williams, *Partner*, 1994–98; Powell Goldstein, *Partner*, 1998–2001; Sidley Austin, *Partner*, 2001–20.
Terry Calvani 1983–90	Vanderbilt Law, *Associate Professor, Professor, etc.*, 1974–83; Haskell Slaughter, *Of Counsel*, 1980–83.	FTC, *Acting Chair*, 1985–86; Pillsbury Winthrop, *Partner*, 1990–2002; Freshfields, *Of Counsel*, 2005–19; Brunswick Group, *Senior Advisor*, 2020–present.
Margot E. Machol 1988–89	Dep't of the Treasury, *Executive Assistant*, 1981–85; Council of Economic Advisors, *Special Assistant*, 1985–88.	Chesapeake Associates, *President*, 1990–2004; Millenium Challenge Corporation, *Chief of Staff*, 2004–06; HELP Commission, *Staff Director*, 2006–08.

FTC Commissioners (Non-Chair Positions)		
Name & Tenure	Prior Employment	Subsequent Employment
Patricia P. Bailey 1979–88	DOJ, *Attorney, Special Assistant*, 1977–79; Merit Systems Protection Board, *Attorney, Executive Legal Assistant*, 1979.	Squire, Sanders & Dempsey, *Partner*, after 1989.
George W. Douglas 1982–85	UNC, *Assistant Professor, Associate Professor, etc.*, 1965–76; Southwest Econometrics, *President*, 1976–82.	Southwest Econometrics, *President*, after 1985.
David A. Clanton 1976–83	U.S. Senate, *Staff Counsel, Legislative Assistant*, 1971–76.	FTC, *Acting Chair*, 1981; Buchanan Ingersoll, *Partner*, 1984–88; Baker McKenzie, *Partner, Senior Counsel*, 1988–2020.
Robert Pitofsky 1978–81	*See above.*	*See above.*
Paul R. Dixon 1961–81	FTC, *Trial Attorney*, 1938–42, 1945–57; S. Judiciary Comm., *Counsel, Staff Director*, 1957–61.	FTC, *Acting Chair*, 1976.
Elizabeth H. Dole 1973–79	White House Office of Consumer Affairs, *Deputy Director*, 1969–73.	Bob Dole's Vice-Presidential Campaign, *Staff*, 1979–80.
Stephen A. Nye 1974–78	Pillsbury, Madison & Sutro, *Attorney*, 1962–68; Competitive Capital Fund, *General Counsel*, 1968–70; Sullivan, Jones and Archer, *Partner*, 1970–74.	Howrey & Simon, *Partner*, 1978.
Mayo J. Thompson 1973–75	Royston Rayzor, *Associate, Senior Partner*, 1953–73.	*Private Practice*, after 1975.
David S. Dennison Jr. 1970–73	*Private Practice*, 1945–63; Ohio AG's Office, *Special Assistant*, 1951–56, 1963–68; Dennison, Wern & Turner, *Senior Partner*, 1963–70.	Wheeling-Pittsburgh, *VP-Secretary, General Counsel*, after 1974; *Private Practice*, until 2000.

Directors of the FTC's Bureau of Competition[50]		
Name & Tenure	Prior Employment	Subsequent Employment
Henry Liu 2023–Present	Covington, *Associate, Partner*, 2008–23.	
Holly Vedova 2021–23	FTC, *Attorney, Attorney Advisor*, 1990–2021.	
Ian R. Conner 2019–21	DOJ Antitrust, *Trial Attorney*, 2003–07; Hunton & Williams, *Associate*, 2007–11; Kirkland & Ellis, *Partner*, 2011–17; FTC BC, *Deputy Director*, 2017–19.	Latham & Watkins, *Partner*, 2021–present.

---

50 It is important to note that of the last 19 directors of the Bureau of Competition, only *three* have held the position for four or more years, reflecting relatively short tenures.

Directors of the FTC's Bureau of Competition[50]		
Name & Tenure	**Prior Employment**	**Subsequent Employment**
D. Bruce Hoffman 2017–19	FTC BC, *Associate Director, Deputy Director*, 2001–04; Hunton & Williams, *Partner, Chair*, 2005–17; Shearman & Sterling, *Partner*, 2017.	Cleary Gottlieb, *Partner*, 2020–present.
Deborah L. Feinstein 2013–17	Arnold & Porter, *Associate*, 1987–89; FTC, *Attorney Advisor, Assistant*, 1989–91; Arnold & Porter, *Associate, Partner*, 1991–2013.	Arnold & Porter, *Partner*, 2017–present.
Richard A. Feinstein 2009–13	DOJ Antitrust, *Trial Attorney, Acting Assistant Chief, etc.*, 1977–85; McKenna & Cuneo, *Associate, Partner*, 1986–98; FTC BC, *Assistant Director*, 1998–2001; Boies Schiller Flexner, *Partner*, 2001–09.	Boies Schiller Flexner, *Partner*, 2013–present.
Jeffrey Schmidt 2006–08	Pillsbury, Madison & Sutro, *Associate*, 1979–85; FTC, *Attorney Advisor*, 1985–87; Transora, *CLO, CAO*, 2001–03; Pillsbury Winthrop, *Partner*, 1987–2001, 2003–05; FTC BC, *Deputy Director*, 2005–06.	Linklaters, *Partner*, after 2008.
Susan A. Creighton 2003–05	Wilson Sonsini, *Partner*, 1987–2001; FTC BC, *Deputy Director*, 2001–03.	Wilson Sonsini, *Partner*, 2006–present.
Joseph J. Simons 2001–03	*See above.*	*See above.*
Richard G. Parker 1999–2001	O'Melveny & Myers, *Associate, Partner*, 1975–98; FTC BC, *Senior Deputy Director*, 1998–99.	O'Melveny & Myers, *Partner*, 2001–18; Gibson Dunn, *Partner*, 2018–23; Milbank, *Partner*, 2023–present.
William J. Baer 1995–99	FTC, *Assistant General Counsel, Attorney Advisor, etc.*, 1975–80; Arnold & Porter, *Associate, Partner*, 1980–95.	Arnold & Porter, *Partner*, 2000–12; DOJ Antitrust, *AAG*, 2012–16; DOJ, *Acting Associate AG*, 2016–17; Arnold & Porter, *Partner*, 2017–20; Brookings, *Visiting Fellow*, 2020–present.
Kevin J. Arquit 1989–92	Fish & Neave, *Associate*, 1978–82; Harris Beach & Wilcox, *Associate*, 1982–86; FTC, *Attorney Advisor, General Counsel*, 1986–89.	Clifford Chance, *Chair*, 1992–2002; Simpson Thacher & Bartlett, *Partner, Chair*, 2002–16; Weil, Gotshal & Manges, *Partner, Co-Chair*, 2016–19; Kasowitz Benson Torres, *Partner, Co-Chair*, 2019–21; JBS USA, *CLO*, 2021–24; Quinn Emanuel, *Partner, Co-Chair*, 2024–present.

Directors of the FTC's Bureau of Competition[50]		
Name & Tenure	**Prior Employment**	**Subsequent Employment**
Jeffrey I. Zuckerman 1986–89	Sullivan & Cromwell, *Associate*, 1974–81; DOJ Antitrust, *Special Assistant*, 1981–84; EEOC, *Chief of Staff*, 1984–86.	Curtis Mallet-Prevost, *Partner, Senior Counsel*, 1989–2017; The Zuckerman Law Group, *Managing Partner*, 2017–present.
Timothy J. Muris 1983–85	*See above.*	*See above.*
Thomas J. Campbell 1981–83	Winston & Strawn, *Attorney*, 1978–80; DOJ, *Executive Assistant*, 1981.	NERA, *Consulting Economist*, 1983–88; California State Senate, *Senator*, 1993–95; U.S. House of Representatives, *Congressman*, 1989–93, 1995–2001; Stanford Law, *Associate Professor, Professor*, 1983–2002; LECG, *Principal*, 1993–95, 2001–03; California Dep't of Fin., *Director*, 2004–05; UC Berkeley, *Business School Dean, Professor*, 2002–04, 2005–08; Berkeley Research Group, *Director, Consulting Economist*, 2009–present; Chapman University, *Dean, Professor, etc.*, 2009–present.
E. Perry Johnson 1980–81	FTC BC, *Assistant Director, Deputy Director, etc.*, 1974–80.	Bryan Cave, *Partner*, 1981–2020.
Alfred F. Dougherty, Jr. 1977–80	Hogan & Hartson, *Attorney*, 1970–74; FTC BC, *Assistant, Assistant Director, Deputy Director*, 1974–76; Hogan & Hartson, *Attorney*, 1976–77.	The May Department Stores Company, *Executive VP, General Counsel*, after 1981.
Owen M. Johnson, Jr. 1975–77	Kirkland & Ellis, *Associate, Partner*, 1963–70; FTC BC, Assistant Director, 1970–72; Hogan & Hartson, *Partner*, 1972–75.	Akin Gump, *Partner*, after 1977.
James T. Halverson 1973–75	Minnesota AG's Office, *Special Assistant AG*, 1967–71; Dorsey Marquart, *Attorney, Partner*, 1965–72; FTC, *Assistant General Counsel, Acting General Counsel*, 1972–73.	Shearman & Sterling, *Partner*, 1975–97; Steptoe & Johnson, *Partner*, 1997–2006; Jast Management, *CEO*, after 2003.
Alan S. Ward 1970–73	Hollabaugh, Jacobs & Ward, *Partner*, 1963–70; FTC BC, *Consultant*, 1970.	BakerHostetler, *Partner*, 1973–2001.

On Rabbis and Mentors

BARAK D. RICHMAN[*]
The George Washington University Law School

Abstract

This tribute to Harry First highlights his mentorship during my efforts to subject the Rabbinic Assembly to the antitrust laws. It is also a story in which the antitrust critique of the professions accidentally produced the deepest the lessons of professionalism.

---

[*] Alexander Hamilton Professor of Business Law, George Washington University; Senior Scholar, Clinical Excellence Research Center, Stanford University School of Medicine; Special Counsel for Competition Policy, Department of Health and Human Services, Office of the General Counsel. The author additionally thanks Clark Havighurst and Vicki Vossen for their frequent inspirations during this academic journey.

1. Although law schools and most lawyers tend to deify the concept of professionalism, antitrust scholars see it as a double-edged sword. What are promulgated to insiders as codes of ethics, outsiders see as barriers to entry and agreements to fix prices or output. And what professional schools promote as paradigms of Aristotelean morals and laudatory commitments to the public interest, skeptics critique as collusive rules designed to generate maximum wealth for a cartel. This skeptical view is best encapsulated by George Bernard Shaw's famous quip that "[a]ll professions are conspiracies against the laity."[1]

2. The truth, of course, is somewhere in the middle. Professional associations are notorious for self-congratulatory excess and mobilizing fiercely to advance their own authority. At the same time, they remain pillars of civil society: There is no denying that physicians exhibit a deep commitment to the welfare of their patients, lawyers show admirable devotion to their clients regardless of who is paying the bills, and scientists toil on behalf of cumulative knowledge and not just patent rights. Society continuously benefits from the persistence of noneconomic motivations that professionals exhibit and that professional schools inculcate.

3. The balance between the widely purported benefits of professionalism and their more subtle but very substantial costs has been a preoccupation for me. It is as much an academic fascination as a battle between my simultaneous tendencies to be cynical and idealistic. This journey began when I struggled with what I thought was excessive veneration for judges, it percolated when I became an outspoken critic of one of the nation's most sacred institutions, and it ended – or at least is now at a stasis – with some lessons on when reverence is appropriate and what one must do to deserve it. It is also a story about a young scholar pursuing an angry passion while learning from a patient and exceedingly wise mentor.

4. I will proceed chronologically, beginning with my background in economics and the study of medicine, then with my struggles with what I have called the "rabbinic cartel," and finally with the story's lessons for the current moment. Harry First appeared on the scene in Act II, and his presence has been felt thereafter.

I. Professionalism in Law and Medicine

1. The Political Science of Judges

5. Before attending law school, and before being introduced to the inside of the legal profession, I completed coursework in economics and studied under Pablo Spiller, one of the pioneers of positive political theory (PPT).[2]

---

[1] GEORGE BERNARD SHAW, THE DOCTOR'S DILEMMA (1909).

[2] My contribution to this literature, under Pablo Spiller's direction, is Mario Bergara, Barak Richman & Pablo T. Spiller, *Modeling Supreme Court Strategic Decision Making: The Congressional Constraint*, LEGIS. STUD. Q. (May 2003).

The principles of PPT rest on the premise that political actors maximize utility functions that are dictated by policy preferences.[3] Just like a market actor will maximize utility subject to budget constraints and preferences for consumption, political actors will exert effort and resources to achieve policy outcomes that advance their preferred ideals. PPT and its offshoots revolutionized political science, turning the field towards quantitative analytics and formal models, and dramatically changed the study of legislatures and agencies.[4] Legal scholars, however, were more resistant to PPT's treatment of judges as maximizers of naked policy preferences who effectively ignored the influence of judicial precedents, legal doctrines, and (almost) the entirety of what is taught in law school.[5]

6. As most know well, PPT's use of judicial "ideology," usually measured as the political ideology of a judge's appointing president, has enormous statistical power in predicting judicial decisions,[6] and the legal world now seems quite receptive to what political scientists call the attitudinal model and what PPT called judicial politics. But I was in the minority when I finished law school and entered the academy.[7] Judging is different, I was told. It is sacred. A judge is bound by and committed to the law – the judge is a professional, they could have said – and adheres to principles that are not captured from self-interested economic models.

7. At times, I felt I was the one-eyed man in the country of the blind.[8] I had no distaste for judges, but I was developing an intense distaste for the reverence of judges, and that distaste began to infuse other areas of my scholarship. On this domain, I was heavily influenced by Clark Havighurst (someone I genuinely revered) and his use of the antitrust laws to critically assess medical codes of ethics.[9] I found that antitrust critique of professional associations insightfully pierced the facades of the professions and the constituent individuals who wore cloaks of grandeur.

---

3   See https://en.wikipedia.org/wiki/Positive_political_theory (describing positive political theory as "the study of politics using formal methods such as social choice theory, game theory, and statistical analysis. . . . where the individuals/parties/nations involved in a given interaction are modeled as rational agents playing a game, guided by self-interest.").

4   For a sample of some of the most influential authors to use PPT, see https://weingast2023.sites.stanford.edu/mcnollgast.

5   For an example of a constructive but skeptical critique of PPT, see Ernest A. Young & Erin C. Blondel, *Does the Supreme Court Follow the Economic Returns? A Response to* A Macrotheory of the Court, 58 DUKE L.J. 1759 (2009).

6   See Andrew D. Martin, Kevin M. Quinn, Theodore W. Ruger & Pauline T. Kim, *Competing Approaches to Predicting Supreme Court Decision Making*, 2 PERSP. ON POL. 761 (Dec. 2004)

7   It is likely that the Supreme Court's intervention in *Bush v. Gore* and the continued politicization of the judiciary in the 20+ years since have changed prevailing perceptions of judges. *See* Linda Greenhouse, *Learning to Live with* Bush v. Gore, 4 GREEN BAG 2d 381 (2000–2001). For me, the issuance of *Bush v. Gore* during my 2L year only solidified my prior beliefs.

8   *Cf.* H. G. WELLS, THE COUNTRY OF THE BLIND (1904).

9   Clark Havighurst's voluminous and enormously influential scholarship spanned several decades. Among his most pioneering work were his edited volumes of LAW AND CONTEMPORARY PROBLEMS in 1970; *see Health Care: Part I*, 35 LAW AND CONTEMPORARY PROBLEMS 229 (Spring 1970) and *Health Care: Part II*, 35 LAW AND CONTEMPORARY PROBLEMS 667 (Autumn 1970). For a comprehensive list of Professor Havighurst's work, *see* https://law.duke.edu/fac/havighurst/bibliography.

2. "On Doctors and Judges"

8. When Mitu Gulati and Jack Knight joined the faculty of Duke Law School, I was no longer the lone employer of empirical tools and political science models in scrutinizing judicial behavior.[10] They, in collaboration with our dean (and former federal judge) David Levi, organized a conference designed to bring judges and scholars of judges – the studied alongside the studiers – in conversation with one another. They invited my participation, and I took the opportunity to explore deeper themes in the professions. In a conference in which judicial practice clashed with political science, my contribution, entitled "On Doctors and Judges," positioned my efforts in this way: "Relying on economics and sociology more than political science, I suggest that there is much to learn about judges from thinking about doctors."[11]

9. The piece began with a "superficial comparison":

> Both wear austere frocks of uniform color. Both publicly commit to solemn oaths before beginning service. Both are addressed by their professional titles to convey respect, even outside their workplace. Both are atop a strict hierarchy, in which their words receive the highest deference and their relationships with others are characterized by authority and control.[12]

10. It then invoked Kenneth Arrow's seminal 1963 article, "Uncertainty and the Welfare Economics of Medical Care,"[13] to offer an explanation behind the superficial similarities – or both professions' heavy reliance on superficialities.

> For Nobel Prize-winning economist Kenneth Arrow, these social symbols were – for doctors – more than mere ornaments. In a seminal 1963 article that gave birth to the field of health economics, Professor Arrow suggests that the social roles enjoyed by doctors, and the institutions and norms that characterize the doctor's position of authority and deference, arise to solve economic problems inherent in the delivery of healthcare. . . . Consequently, Arrow writes, nonmarket social institutions arise to improve upon the failure of the marketplace.

---

10 Both Knight and Gulati are giants in this field and were pioneers during its early stages. *See, e.g.*, LEE EPSTEIN & JACK KNIGHT, THE CHOICES JUSTICES MAKE (1997); Stephen J. Choi, Mitu Gulati & Eric A. Posner, *What Do Federal District Judges Want? An Analysis of Publications, Citations, and Reversals*, 28 J. L. ECON. & ORG. 518 (2012); Stephen J. Choi, Mitu Gulati & Eric A. Posner, *Judicial Evaluations and Information Forcing: Ranking State High Courts and Their Judges*, 58 DUKE L.J. 1313 (2009).

11 Barak Richman, *On Doctors and Judges*, 58 DUKE L.J. 1731, 1731 (2009).

12 *Id.*

13 Kenneth J. Arrow, *Uncertainty and the Welfare Economics of Medical Care*, 53 AM. ECON. REV. 941, 947, 949–51 (1963).

11. In the postscript to his article, Professor Arrow notes that "the medical profession is only one example" in which market mechanisms fail to insure against uncertainty and that "[a]ll professions share some of the same properties." Perhaps he had judges, and the courtroom, in mind.[14]

12. The upshot, for me, was that the professions relied on some Wizard of Oz bluster. The directive to society was "Pay no attention to the man behind the curtain,"[15] instead look at – and show deep reverence for – the pageantry. The more ornamental these nonmarket institutions appeared, the more I felt they needed penetration. The heart of my article was a call for scholars and professionals of all types to "bring their respective and different toolkits to engage constructively with each other," in particular to scrutinize "the powerful strain of professionalism in the judicial community," and that "the social scientist can, as an outsider, generate significant insights into the judicial process that academic and professional insiders cannot."[16]

II. The Rabbinate

13. Around the time I published "On Doctors and Judges," I was introduced to another group of professionals – rabbis – and to another code of ethics that served to solidify a professional cartel. I cannot remember whether I wrote of the "superficial comparison" – the austere frock, the constant invocation of professional titles, the social hierarchy and the severity of instructions – with rabbis in mind as well, but I was already predisposed to studying the third of the triumvirate with the same skepticism.

14. This new scholarly path proved to be intellectually invigorating, newsworthy, and additional fuel for my personal deeply skeptical, anti-establishment attitudes towards professional cartels. It was also what introduced me to the kindness, wisdom, and generous mentorship of Harry First.

---

14 Richman, *supra* note 11, at 1731–32 (footnotes omitted). The article continued:
> Similar nonmarket institutions and norms characterize the social relationships judges have with laypeople, and these institutions arguably arise to overcome similar problems of uncertainty. The social institutions and symbols that surround the judicial role – such as the robe, gavel, honorific title, and even the power to hold parties in contempt – sustain the authority that judges require to dispense the law. Individuals follow the law not just because of the threat of sanctions but also because of a strongly-felt social norm, a deep reverence for the law, and a widespread belief in the prudence and integrity of the presiding judge. Indeed, without such social norms, it would be difficult to employ enough policemen to force compliance with the law or enough bailiffs to bring order in the courtroom. The severity of a judge's decrees might even be compared to the severity of a doctor's instructions. Failure to adhere to either is associated not just with risking personal welfare but also with exhibiting questionable judgment. *Id.* at 1732–33.

15 https://www.youtube.com/watch?v=R2wGui_NHPA.

16 Richman, *supra* note 11, at 1741.

1. "That's an Antitrust Violation"

15. At my synagogue in Durham, North Carolina, our longtime rabbi announced his retirement; I found myself on the search committee for a new rabbi and was thus introduced to the underground institutions that guide American Judaism.

16. Our synagogue affiliated itself with what is called the Conservative Movement, an interconnected collection of institutions founded in the early 20th century that revolve around a centrist Jewish Theology.[17] Rabbis affiliated with the Conservative Movement are members of the Rabbinical Assembly (RA), which can be described as a professional association akin to the AMA. For example, the RA establishes standards of religious practice, crafts professional codes of conduct, manages credentialing, and offers an assortment of resources for its members.

17. Early in our search committee's process, I learned that the RA also plays an active role in the hiring of rabbis. At one committee meeting, our committee chair reported to us the rules governing rabbinic searches, as laid down to him by the RA's leadership: The RA requires synagogues to enroll exclusively in its search process, filters the selection of candidates the congregations may interview, and prohibits candidates and congregations from finding each other directly. Any Conservative rabbi who seeks a pulpit outside the RA's centralized process, and any congregation that interviews candidates from other movements, will be penalized. Rabbis in violation would be prevented from obtaining a pulpit, and congregations in violation would be denied access to RA rabbis.

18. We did not greet this news happily. Our congregation is an eclectic community that finds appeal in different Jewish denominations, and we would have preferred a broader search for our religious leader. It also did not sit well to be subject to dictates from an office in New York, and to learn that the rabbinate would sanction rabbis or congregations pursuing nontraditional paths. But before all that sunk in, I blurted out, "They can't do that. That's an antitrust violation."

19. My fellow committee members – none of whom were attorneys, few of whom had any familiarity with the antitrust laws, and all of whom were immersed in the self-contained world of institutional Judaism – carried on. We did our search according to the RA's rules, hired a rabbi, and called it a job well done. After we disbanded, I started a new research agenda.

---

[17] For a sampling of the Conservative Movement's history and orientation, *see* https://en.wikipedia.org/wiki/Conservative_Judaism.

2. The Sherman Act and the First Amendment

20. I started with an op-ed published in *The Forward*, a contemporary Jewish periodical with its roots in the Jewish socialist movement of the late 19th century. I targeted this decidedly non-antitrust publication to convey that my concern regarding the RA's hiring rules was not purely academic, but that I was targeting something harmful to American Judaism that was in need of reform.

21. My essay, "Rabbi Searches Are Tough, but Are They Illegal?" described the RA rules preserved as an effort to secure a lucrative market for senior rabbis at the expense of junior rabbis and innovative congregations.[18] I observed that the rules prevented interviewing candidates who graduated from independent seminaries, which are educational alternatives and threats to the seminary that dominates Conservative Judaism (and houses the RA's offices), and were aimed at achieving full employment for RA members rather than supporting the spiritual needs of congregants. I further noted that the centralization of power and suppression of innovative ideas are precisely the sort of entrenched dominance that the Sherman Act is designed to remedy.

22. Some personal theology inescapably entered my calculation as well. Conservative Judaism was once the largest denomination in America, at one point being home to 50% of America's Jews. But the movement was frequently and rightly criticized for being inattentive to members, and its numbers – and affection for it – began to sink sharply. I framed this in monopolistic terms:

23. The history of the Sherman Act reveals that concentrated power can be difficult to dislodge. This inflexibility also reveals a systemic tragedy within Conservatism, whose history includes efforts by centralized powers to resist valuable innovations that spread across America. Such a hierarchical structure of religious authority is antithetical to the American religious experience. It is appropriately targeted by the Sherman Act, which is designed to harness the benefits of an unfettered marketplace of ideas.[19]

24. And, recognizing that readers of *The Forward* cared more about the health of American Judaism than they did for compliance with the Sherman Act, I closed the piece with a call to action that I hoped would resonate:

> [R]ecognizing the illegality of the RA's placement practices forces us to confront many of Conservative Judaism's deepest challenges, including the critical importance of heeding the grassroots needs of

---

18 Barak Richman, *Rabbi Searches Are Tough, but Are They Illegal?*, FORWARD (Sept. 29, 2010), https://forward.com/opinion/131723/rabbi-searches-are-tough-but-are-they-illegal/.

19 *Id.*

Conservative Jews and the creativity of nontraditional congregations. Ultimately, conforming to the law will be good for congregations, good for the Conservative movement and it will be good for the RA as well.[20]

25. The op-ed triggered more writing. First came "Saving the First Amendment from Itself: Relief from the Sherman Act Against the Rabbinic Cartels,"[21] which was derived from what could be described as a legal brief. The abstract explains the title:

> America's rabbis currently structure their employment market with rules that flagrantly violate the Sherman Act. The consequences of these rules, in addition to the predictable economic outcomes of inflated wages for rabbis and restricted consumer freedoms for the congregations that employ them, meaningfully hinder Jewish communities from seeking their preferred spiritual leader. Although the First Amendment cannot combat against this privately-orchestrated (yet paradigmatic) restriction on religious expression, the Sherman Act can. Ironically, however, the rabbinic organizations implementing the restrictive policies claim that the First Amendment immunizes them from Sherman Act scrutiny, thereby claiming the First Amendment empowers them to do what the First Amendment was arguably designed to prevent. This essay evaluates this interesting intersection between the Sherman Act and the First Amendment, and it argues that the Sherman Act can, and must, be vigorously applied against the private rabbinic cartels.[22]

26. Can, and must. So I concluded in my first academic-cum-advocacy piece. And it was around this same time that I first met Harry First.

3. The Wisdom of a Rabbi

27. I forget what precisely engineered my first meeting with Harry First, but whatever brought me into the same room (probably a workshop at NYU?), I used that meeting as an excuse to share with him my early thinking on what could be called my crusade. I remember an early email he sent after I shared with him a draft of the "Saving" article – he wrote, "this reads more like a brief than an article. That's not necessarily a bad thing, but is it what you intended?" I said yes.

28. Harry generously recognized two things. First, this was an exercise in advocacy for me, and thus my overarching objective was to instigate

---

20 *Id.*

21 Barak Richman, *Saving the First Amendment from Itself: Relief from the Sherman Act Against the Rabbinic Cartels*, 39 Pepp. L. Rev. 1347 (2013).

22 *Id.* at 1741.

change. And second, critically, publications alone would not advance my agenda. He arranged a meeting with someone close to the RA and with a wealth of antitrust knowledge. The three of us had lunch, discussed the topic, and explored possible resolutions. In looking back at that meeting, I realize how young I must have appeared – or at least how young I acted. I was doctrinaire and outraged. Harry and his experienced colleague were reasoned and patient, simultaneously sympathetic and wise. There evidently is a difference between winning an argument and stimulating reform, and both sages reminded me that I wanted the latter, even to the exclusion of the former.

29. That afternoon continues to produce echoes for me. At one point, I was making a theological point – that Jewish law abhors cartels just like the common law – and Harry reminded me, "however right you may be, that is not your winning argument." He deftly nudged me to think practically, even as I was relentlessly uncompromising. And, in connecting me with his antitrust-familiar and RA-sympathetic colleague, he was implicitly encouraging me to capitalize on this diplomacy opportunity, to pose problems that can be solved with compromises rather than litigation, where halfway progress is a victory. He was probably asking me to use a skill set I did not yet have and may still not have. Often, the best lessons are learned long after the teaching was delivered.

4. Postscript

30. I kept writing and the RA kept resisting.[23] My next product, written with Harry's help, was an amicus brief for the Supreme Court's consideration in *Hosanna-Tabor Evangelical Lutheran Church and School v. EEOC*. The case considered the reach of what is called the "ministerial exception" and specifically whether employment laws that prohibited religious discrimination applied to a seminary's firing of one of its teachers. I worried that a broad ministerial exception would preclude enforcement not just of civil rights laws in religious contexts but also of the antitrust laws, and I argued that sustaining the Sherman Act would support, not suppress, the underlying religious interest in hiring clergy. The brief emphasized:

> Nothing is more central to a congregation's mission than finding the religious leader that best suits its spiritual needs. Petitioner put it best when, citing *McClure v. Salvation Army*, 460 F.2d 553, 558 (5th Cir. 1972), it argued that "[t]he relationship between an organized church and its ministers is its lifeblood." But an expansive ministerial exception that permits professional associations of clergy to implement

---

23 The high point of the battle was a profile in the *New York Times*, which described me as a "formidable foe" while reporting that the RA deemed me to be "the source of damage." Samuel G. Freedman, *Seeing and Battling a 'Cartel' in the Hiring of Rabbis*, N.Y. Times (Aug. 24, 2012).

otherwise-illegally restrictive placement policies is at cross purposes with this value.[24]

31. This led to another article,[25] and then another,[26] and then another.[27] The marginal value of each successive article was probably diminishing, at least from an advocacy perspective, even if each article took a different analytical tact and legal strategy to a thoroughly troubled institution. But I kept learning from each article, and perhaps the nature of the RA's enshrinement – and the manifold problems it both reflects and causes – might have been becoming more publicly apparent as well.

32. Today, the RA is a shell of its former self, at least as far as market power is concerned. The Conservative Movement is licking its wounds after four decades of decline – the most meaningful part of that observation is that it now recognizes that it has wounds to address – and not coincidentally, a new generation of leadership is now in charge. More importantly, from an antitrust perspective, there are now more ways to get a pulpit rabbinate. Both the growth of independent seminaries (those that the RA aimed to stifle) and the emergence of alternative mechanisms to find pulpit employment, such as Rabbis Without Borders, have reduced the RA's market share and market power. Sometimes legal and rhetorical action defeats a monopolist, and sometimes market forces do. I would like to think this was some combination of the two.[28]

33. Does this story end with both sides declaring victory? I can claim partial credit for nudging Conservative Judaism to accept the need for long-overdue reforms, and Conservative Movement leadership can satisfyingly say they retired without being sued. Perhaps an accidental détente, with reciprocal claims for success, is the end of the story?

34. Hardly. In writing now in the fall of 2024, I am not living in an easy moment for Judaism. The horrific events of October 7, 2023 and Israel's troublingly militaristic response have left little room for casual enjoyment of Jewish rites, and the American Jewish community (my circles, at least) is deeply divided

---

24 Harry First & Barak Richman, Amicus Brief of Antitrust Professors and Scholars, Hosanna Tabor Evangelical Lutheran Church and School v. Equal Employment Opportunity Commission, Et Al., No. 10-553, Supreme Court of the United States, https://papers.ssrn.com/sol3/papers.cfm?abstract_id=3039612 (citations omitted) 13.

25 Michael E. Helfand & Barak Richman, *The Challenge of Co-Religionist Commerce*, 64 Duke L.J. 769 (2015).

26 Barak Richman & Daniel Libenson, *Right-Skilling: Rabbis and the Rabbinic Role for a New Century*, in Keeping Faith in Rabbis: A Community Conversation on Rabbinic Education 30–46 (Hayim Herring & Ellie Roscher eds., 2014), https://papers.ssrn.com/sol3/papers.cfm?abstract_id=2772061.

27 Barak Richman, *Religious Freedom Through Market Freedom: The Sherman Act and the Marketplace for Religion*, 60 Wm & Mary L. Rev. 1523 (2019).

28 The *New York Times* closed its profile, noting: "For now, Mr. Richman has no plaintiff around whom to build a court case. . . . 'You need a Curt Flood,' he said, referring to the baseball player who successfully challenged the game's reserve clause. Then, referring to the Virginia State Bar case, he added, 'Or a Lew Goldfarb.'" *See* Freedman, *supra* note 23. I never did find a plaintiff, in large part because of the personal toll a rabbi-plaintiff would have assumed in challenging the professional association that would guide his professional career, and in part because the RA ultimately changed from within.

on what spiritual path to follow. There is enormous need for thoughtful leadership, and it is hard not to partially blame the RA establishment for, in demanding professional conformity, failing to nurture innovative leaders that may have been better suited for the current moment. But it may also be a time for me to realize that instead of demanding an old Jewish institution to change, likely beyond its capability, my energies may have been better spent contributing to new Jewish institutions that can guide us through these fraught modern times. A tragedy brings things into perspective.

III. Lessons from My Rabbi

35. "Rabbi" is a Hebrew word that literally means "my teacher." The word's colloquial meaning, which encompasses spiritual leader, community leader, and so much more, reflects Judaism's deep respect for learning and education. It is the teacher who is deified, not the high priest (the Cohen) or the political leader (the King).

36. Harry was and is my teacher, my rabbi. I first need to emphasize how rabbinic Harry was in these scholarly and – let's face it – spiritual struggles that drove me to the continued writings. Harry never indicated categorical support or opposition to what I wrote. He simply wanted to help me write and advance the argument better. He recognized that both I, as a young scholar, and the Jewish institutions that we shared are better off with an airing of the arguments. And he provided counsel by supporting me in playing the process out. He was encouraging education-by-doing, playing the teacher-as-coach, and shunning the imperial approach that so many professors *and rabbis* default to. I need to put it this way: Harry, as a rabbi, stands in stark contrast to the rabbis who ran the rabbinic cartel.

37. Harry also embodies the values of professionalism, the very canon that prompted my exercise in resistance, and in doing so he softened my attitudes toward that form of cooperative wisdom. Professionalism and professional associations are deeply, perhaps inevitably flawed, but they do contain an accumulation of collective experience, reflect some good intentions, and create institutional resistance to the excesses of both the market and political power. They also encourage generous people to pay it forward, something that Harry did and something I hope to emulate. It took a while, but Harry's patient lessons reminded me that complicated institutions are complicated, that flawed leaders are not all bad, and that constructive reform sometimes requires forging new pathways rather than targeting adversaries. I began this essay recognizing the double-edged nature of professionalism, but that is not how I would have begun this essay if I had written it 15 years ago. It is a tribute to Harry, and the good-natured lessons-by-example that he lives daily, that I have come around (partly) on professionalism itself.

Competition vs. Regulation

JONATHAN JACOBSON[*]
Wilson Sonsini Goodrich & Rosati

Abstract

Harry First is one of the great competition law thought leaders over the past few decades. He has championed aggressive, but thoughtful, enforcement both in his role as a sought-after professor at a great law school and as the Chief of New York's Antitrust Bureau. Harry has advocated for greater rulemaking and some regulation to reign in perceived excesses of "big tech," and we part company there. This paper traces the failed history of regulation in the U.S., and the rise of the consumer welfare standard (and its close variants) in its place. With the consumer welfare standard, we have witnessed enormous economic growth and innovation – in no small part attributable to the workings of "big tech." Now, however, heavy regulation in Europe and elsewhere, combined with a neo-Brandeisian approach is the U.S., threaten that growth – reducing and even removing many of the incentives that led to this great economic expansion. We should return to consumer welfare so that innovation can thrive.

---

[*] Member N.Y. Bar. Retired partner at Wilson Sonsini Goodrich & Rosati. Many thanks to Keith Klovers for very helpful comments – although all mistakes continue to be mine. Given my prior cases representing Google, I will not address the specific pending litigations against it. The cases on which I worked are addressed in my memoir, MY LIFE IN ANTITRUST (2024), *available at* https://www.wsgr.com/a/web/89YbdCjKoDr4dUfacfGkU4/jacobson-memoir.pdf.

38. Harry First stands as one of the competition greats of the past many years. His many students, his colleagues at NYU, and his past colleagues at the New York Attorney General's Antitrust Bureau will attest to his brilliance, his many insights, and his compassion. Harry has long championed aggressive antitrust enforcement, rulemaking, and even some regulation to cabin the market power of leading firms, especially in tech.[1] His views are largely in line with the current heads of the enforcement community, federal and state. Despite my deep admiration for Harry, we part company on some of these issues. This paper addresses the suggestion of regulation or rulemaking to "rein in" Big Tech.

39. The current hostility to Big Tech in some quarters is accompanied by a view that the current lodestar for competition analysis – the "consumer welfare" standard – should be discarded or at least revised. The arguments all boil down to "big is bad." And sometimes "big" firms do indeed have opportunities to behave very badly. Yet, in the almost 40 years in which the consumer welfare standard has prevailed, what have we seen? The greatest leap in innovation in world history, accompanied by enormous increases in U.S. GDP, especially compared to the rest of the world. And what is the suggested replacement for the consumer welfare standard? There is none, just a desire to make sure the remarkable successes of the "big tech" firms cannot be replicated again.

40. This short paper will discuss the history of agency regulation in the U.S., describe the current movement to abandon the consumer welfare standard, address the illogic of weakening or punishing the firms that have led the innovations we enjoy today, and then mention the few studies that have addressed these issues.

I. Regulation in the United States 1887–1980s

41. Regulatory agencies began in the United States. The first was the Interstate Commerce Commission (ICC), created in 1887 to regulate railroads and, later, other surface-based common carriers. Regulation was viewed as an effective way to resolve the interstices of otherwise unclear statutory commands and, in the case of the ICC, to make sure fares were not too far out of line. For many decades, regulation was favored with minimal controversy. The New Deal, following the Great Depression, led to the creation of many regulatory agencies, and there are roughly 100 at present. The most important today include the Food and Drug Administration (1906), the Federal Communications Commission (1934), and the Securities

---

[1] *See, e.g.*, Eleanor Fox & Harry First, *We Need Rules to Rein in Big Tech*, CPI ANTITRUST CHRON. (Oct. 2020); Harry First, *Antitrust and Regulatory Alternatives: How the Past Points the Way to the Future*, 11 J. ANTITRUST ENF'T. 173 (2023).

and Exchange Commission (1934). The very existence of regulatory agencies is being challenged today, however, by the right with what seems to be the support of at least some Justices on the Supreme Court.[2]

42. Congress created the Federal Trade Commission (FTC) in 1914, but although the Commission was eventually given rulemaking powers, it was and is essentially an enforcement agency rather than a "regulator." Its ability to make competition regulations is today in dispute and is one of the issues being litigated in connection with the FTC's 2024 rule against covenants not to compete.[3] The FTC's ability to set procedural rules, such as the contents of the Hart-Scott-Rodino (HSR) form, has more support.[4]

43. Antitrust enforcement became quite aggressive in the second New Deal under Thurman Arnold, with extensive successes in the motion picture industry and other fields of business. There was a push to go after vertical integration generally, but the Supreme Court rejected that argument in the 1948 *Paramount* case.[5] The courts occasionally pushed back on merger enforcement (as in the *Columbia Steel* case, also 1948),[6] but the Celler-Kefauver Act of 1950[7] amended section 7 of the Clayton Act and stopped all that. It made successful merger challenges much easier, and made clear that the Act would apply to vertical and conglomerate mergers as well as horizontal consolidations. Merger challenges abounded afterward, including challenges to what today would be viewed as trivial transactions. As Justice Stewart later pointed out, the "sole consistency … in litigation under § 7, [was that] the Government always wins."[8] That was true from 1950 all the way to 1974.[9]

---

2   *See* Loper Bright Enterprises v. Raimondo, 144 S. Ct. 2244 (2024), *see* Dion M. Bregman, Julie S. Goldemberg, Meaghan Kent, William R. Peterson & Stephanie L. Roberts, *The US Supreme Court Overrules the* Chevron *Doctrine Ending the Requirement for Courts to Defer to Agency Interpretation of Law* (Loper Bright / Raimondo), E-COMPETITIONS June 2024, art. no 119501, www.concurrences.com/119501.

3   *See* Bryan Koenig, *FTC, Challengers, Their Backers Vie for Noncompetes' Fate*, LAW360 (July 29, 2024), https://www.law360.com/articles/1862555/ftc-challengers-their-backers-vie-for-noncompetes-fate; David Minsky, *FTC Regroups After Noncompete Setbacks in Florida, Texas*, LAW360 (Aug. 23, 2024), https://www.law360.com/competition/articles/1872990/ftc-regroups-after-noncompete-setbacks-in-florida-texas.

4   The statute actually provides for broad rule-making powers. 15 U.S.C. § 57a(1):

Except as provided in subsection (h), the Commission may prescribe –

(A) interpretive rules and general statements of policy with respect to unfair or deceptive acts or practices in or affecting commerce (within the meaning of section 45(a)(1) of this title), and

(B) rules which define with specificity acts or practices which are unfair or deceptive acts or practices in or affecting commerce (within the meaning of section 45(a)(1) of this title), except that the Commission shall not develop or promulgate any trade rule or regulation with regard to the regulation of the development and utilization of the standards and certification activities pursuant to this section. Rules under this subparagraph may include requirements prescribed for the purpose of preventing such acts or practices.

5   United States v. Paramount Pictures, Inc., 334 U.S. 131 (1948).

6   United States v. Columbia Steel Co., 334 U.S. 495 (1948).

7   Pub. L. No. 81-899, 64 Stat. 1125 (1950).

8   United States v. Von's Grocery Co., 384 U.S. 270, 301 (1966) (Stewart, J., dissenting).

9   *See* United States v. Marine Bancorp., Inc., 418 U.S. 602 (1974).

44. Intense antitrust enforcement was in no way limited to mergers. Although horizontal cartel agreements (such as bid rigging, price fixing, and customer allocation) were and are considered without controversy as per se illegal, by the mid-1970s there were per se rules for things like vertical exclusive territories, tying arrangements, and resale pricing agreements. These rulings had the virtue of providing somewhat clear rules on what could or could not be done, but they lacked the flexibility to recognize and approve activities that would enhance competition. One example was the 1972 *Topco* decision,[10] where small grocers formed a co-op to produce private-label grocery products that the small grocers could not afford to produce on their own. Each member would have an exclusive territory in which its private-label products could compete against the large grocery chains. Exclusivity was necessary to induce the required investment. But the member grocers were technically "competitors," and the Supreme Court ruled that this was a horizontal division of territories and so illegal per se. Another example was the "nine no-nos,"[11] a string of intellectual property licensing practices that could be harmful but were just as likely to be benign. One example was package licensing. There were even some *criminal* prosecutions for price-cutting under section 3 of the Robinson-Patman Act.[12]

45. This rigid approach began to change in the mid-1970s. Prior aggressive enforcement was founded on the "structure-conduct-performance" paradigm, which held (and holds) that the more concentrated an industry's *structure*, the more the firms' *conduct* is likely to be lackluster (with less innovation and tacit collusion), such that the industry's *performance* would suffer. This focus on industry concentration naturally led to more intensive anti-merger enforcement as well as conduct rules designed to mitigate the effects of concentration. But pushback began. One main event was the 1974 Airlie House Conference, co-chaired by Eleanor Fox and Robert Pitofsky.[13] The research presented there suggested that concentration could be and very often was the result of intense and successful competition, not its opposite. At the same time, concerns were being expressed that the U.S.'s harsh competition rules were making the country less competitive internationally. Consumer electronics, long a U.S.-driven industry, was basically lost to Asia. Even automobile manufacturing, a source of so many U.S. jobs, was contracting due to competition from firms like Toyota and Mazda. The production of steel,

---

10 United States v. Topco Assocs., Inc., 405 U.S. 596 (1972).

11 *See* Deputy Assistant Att'y Gen. Bruce Wilson, Patent and Know-How License Arrangements: Field of Use, Territorial, Price and Quantity Restrictions (Nov. 1970). They were abandoned in 1981. *See* Deputy Assistant Att'y Gen. Abbott B. Lipsky, Remarks Before the American Bar Ass'n Antitrust Section: Current Antitrust Division Views on Patent Licensing Practices (Nov. 5–6, 1981).

12 *See* United States v. National Dairy Products Corp., 372 U.S. 29 (1963).

13 The papers presented are collected in INDUSTRIAL CONCENTRATION: THE NEW LEARNING (Harvey J. Goldschmid, H. Michael Mann & J. Fred Weston eds., 1974).

a field long dominated by the U.S., was becoming lost to Asia and Europe. Many worried that this trend would continue. Some blamed U.S. antitrust enforcement.[14] An irony was that by beating down large and successful U.S. companies, we inadvertently led to the creation of large and successful foreign companies.

46. The very aggressive U.S. antitrust rules of this period were enabled by the lack of any coherent standards. Antitrust was deemed to support multiple goals, such as "fairness," the preservation of small businesses, and the dispersion of economic power. Although this approach made it much easier to slap down large firms, it was internally inconsistent and hard to administer. As one example, small businesses can be well preserved by allowing them to fix prices and allocate customers. No one thinks that this would make any sense.

47. Chicago School writers, most prominently Robert Bork, proposed a single economics-based standard that Bork called "consumer welfare." And the Supreme Court used that verbiage (without the associated baggage) in 1979 in *Reiter v. Sonotone*.[15] It quickly became clear, however, that this was not *consumer* welfare; it was *total* welfare, including producers as well as consumers. Under total welfare, a practice that injured consumers (such as by raising prices) would be considered lawful if the profits of the suppliers increased by the same amount. Although none of the Chicagoans supported such a result, it was the logical outcome of a strict application of their approach. Chicagoans had more luck with vertical restraints, with the 1977 *Sylvania*[16] decision upholding (in the context of applying the rule of reason) vertical exclusive territories and, 30 years later, the *Leegin* decision overruling 88 years of vertical resale price maintenance precedents.[17] Bork was right in saying that the choice of legal or welfare standard would both drive outcomes and lead to greater consistency in administering antitrust law.

48. At the same time, there developed a broad consensus favoring deregulation. President Carter appointed Fred Kahn as his deregulation czar, and he and many others were able to reduce the level of regulation. The main concern was that regulation of prices meant higher prices and carried with it the danger of "regulatory capture," i.e., undue agency coziness with the regulated – with personnel often going in and out of the agencies to private companies or law firms. So, a pushback against heavy regulation began.

---

14 *E.g.*, Malcolm Baldridge, *Halting the LTV-Republic Steel Merger: How to Ruin an Entire Industry*, N.Y. TIMES, Mar. 11, 1984, at F2, *available at* https://www.nytimes.com/1984/03/11/business/business-forum-halting-the-ltvrepublic-steel-merger.html. Baldridge was commerce secretary at the time, and the *LTV-Republic* merger challenge by the Department of Justice (DOJ) was blocked at his instigation.

15 442 U.S. 330 (1979).

16 Continental T.V., Inc. v. GTE Sylvania, Inc., 433 U.S. 36 (1977).

17 Leegin Creative Leather Products, Inc., v. PSKS, Inc., 551 U.S. 877 (2007), *see* Peter J. Carney & Kristen J. McAhren, *The US Supreme Court Overturns Its Long-Standing Prohibition against Vertical Agreements between Manufacturers and Their Dealers Setting Minimum Resale Prices* (Leegin Creative), E-COMPETITIONS June 2007, art. no 38050.

One example was the replacement of the Civil Aeronautics Board with the Federal Aviation Administration. It remained important, of course, to maintain airline safety through regulation, but the change enabled greater competition among airlines with significant new entry by the likes of Jet Blue. Extras such as decent meals in coach declined or were eliminated, but airfare costs declined significantly. Another example was the 1995 abolition of the very first regulatory agency, the ICC, leading to wider opportunities in surface transportation. As Wilson and Klovers have explained, the overall outcome was that "[a]fter deregulation, prices fell, output expanded, and firms innovated."[18]

49. Consumer welfare got its true birth in the 1980s. "Post-Chicagoans," such as Steve Salop, developed an economic alternative focusing on what economists call "consumer surplus," but not in a wooden fashion.[19] The essence of this approach was the consideration of price and output effects, quality, and innovation. "Consumers" would include middlemen and others in a distribution chain. Basically, anything that increased market output (properly measured) was good. Reductions in output were bad. At the same time, Reagan's head of the Antitrust Division came out with revised Merger Guidelines in 1982. Despite a fear that the new Guidelines would rule out many otherwise sound merger challenges, the opposite proved true. The then-new Guidelines articulated and adopted the hypothetical monopolist test for defining markets,[20] which resulted in increasingly tiny markets and more merger challenges as a direct result. More broadly, the consumer welfare approach led to a consistent approach to the problems in issue and led to a remarkable consensus on antitrust standards for the first time. Until it did not.

II. The Current Movement

50. Most prominently in Europe, but increasingly in the U.S. too, the consumer welfare standard is being ignored or simply rejected in favor of an approach that condemns large tech companies from competing to gain sales. Hyperbole? Not really.

51. A key example is the iPhone. Apple has succeeded with a closed system in which apps, messages, and payments must be sourced from Apple only.

---

18 Christine Wilson & Keith Klovers, *The Growing Nostalgia for Past Regulatory Misadventures and the Risk of Repeating These Mistakes With Big Tech*, 8 J. ANTITRUST ENF'T. 10 (Mar. 2020), https://doi.org/10.1093/jaenfo/jnz029.

19 *E.g.*, Steven C. Salop, Avoiding Error in the Antitrust Analysis of Unilateral Refusals to Deal, Statement before the Antitrust Modernization Commission (Sept. 21, 2005), https://govinfo.library.unt.edu/amc/commission_hearings/pdf/Salop_Statement_Revised%209-21.pdf.

20 U.S. DEP'T OF JUST., 1982 Merger Guidelines § II.A, https://www.justice.gov/sites/default/files/atr/legacy/2007/07/11/11248.pdf.

The European Commission (EC) is trying to force Apple to allow third parties to have their own app downloads and payment systems. Apple today has a very secure platform, but the security is necessarily in doubt if third parties are given such broad access. Or take Amazon. Amazon uses the data it collects from sales on its site, including sales of third-party sellers, to improve its own offerings. Preventing Amazon from doing so would do little to help third-party sellers, but it would hamper Amazon's efforts to improve its own sales.

52. Europe has doubled (maybe quintupled) down on its attack on tech through the Digital Markets Act (DMA). The DMA imposes obligations and prohibitions on "gatekeepers" that provide "core platform services" and are designated as such by the Commission. To date, the designations are as follows:

    – U.S.-based Facebook: Facebook Marketplace, Facebook, Instagram, WhatsApp, Facebook Messenger, and Meta Ads

    – U.S.-based Google: Google Play, Google Maps, Google Shopping, Google Search, YouTube, Android, Chrome, and Alphabet's online advertising service

    – U.S.-based Amazon: Amazon Marketplace and Amazon Advertising

    – U.S.-based Apple: App Store, iOS, and Safari

    – U.S.-based Microsoft: LinkedIn and Windows PC OS

    – U.S.- or China-based ByteDance: TikTok

    – Netherlands-based Booking.com: online reservations

53. The level of protectionism is apparent. Booking.com was the very last of the designees; it is headquartered in Amsterdam. Everyone else is a U.S. company, save perhaps ByteDance, which can be considered either Chinese or U.S.-based. The consequences of a designation are horrific. "Gatekeepers" are barred from tactics that would increase their market shares on "core platform services," such as "self-preferencing." This approach would render it illegal for a firm to prefer its own properties on its own platform – again making competition itself illegal. Promoting your product over those of rivals used to be known as competition. Now, you must promote your competitors instead. I have called out this theory as especially absurd in a recent paper.[21]

54. There is a movement, hopefully now stopped, for similar treatment in the U.S. The American Innovation and Choice Online Act (AICOA), introduced in 2022 by Democratic and Republican sponsors, would impose obligations similar to the DMA on tech firms, but without the

---

[21] Jonathan Jacobson & Ada Wang, *Competition or Competitors? The Case of Self-Preferencing*, 38 ANTITRUST 13 (Fall 2023).

formal regulatory apparatus. It stalled and was not enacted. But the federal agencies and numerous state attorneys general are taking a similar approach, suing the large tech firms using theories that would have been laughed out of court not so very long ago. One of these is EU-styled "self-preferencing." Ugh.

55. Using competition rulemaking is less intrusive than relying on a regulatory agency. But how much less intrusive depends on the specific rules in issue. Rules such as AICOA's coming from legislative acts or agency action mitigate the problem of industry capture but would prevent competition just as effectively.

III. Potential Impact

56. The critical policy question is whether this new regulatory approach will improve the economy. On a theoretical level, the debate is quite similar to the age-old debate that began with Schumpeter and Arrow. Schumpeter famously was of the view that large firms with market power had more to spend on R&D and would contribute greater innovation than smaller firms. Arrow countered that greater innovation could be expected from small firms, as their survival was dependent on it. The debate rages today with no global answers. Both sides can point both to theory and anecdotal evidence supporting their position.[22]

57. In our present context, however, finding the answer is not difficult. The chief concern about large firms with market power is that they will no longer compete effectively, and that they will retard innovation and progress, choosing "the quiet life," as many have explained.[23] Here we *know* that is not the case. While that is what happened with Microsoft and Internet Explorer 5, we *know* that we will see amazing, continued innovation from Amazon, Apple, and Google. They demonstrate that every day. We hear that these firms have excluded rivals. That is half true. The untrue part is that these firms have adopted tactics designed to hinder rivals rather than enhance their own products or services. None of the cases contain a single such allegation that would survive scrutiny under current law. The true part is that entry or expansion in these markets is difficult. But that effect is attributable to competition. People do not want to enter these markets because there are no profits to be had. Nothing inhibits entry more than the improbability of making a dime.

---

22   *See* Jonathan Baker, *Beyond Schumpeter vs. Arrow: How Antitrust Fosters Innovation*, 74 ANTITRUST L.J. 575 (2007), https://digitalcommons.wcl.american.edu/cgi/viewcontent.cgi?article=2128&context=facsch_lawrev; Jonathan Jacobson, Merger Policy & Innovation, Presentation to the New York State Bar Association, Antitrust Section, Annual Meeting (Jan. 25, 1996), https://www.wsgr.com/PDFSearch/jacobson_merger.pdf.

23   The phrase dates back to J. R. Hicks, *Annual Survey of Economic Theory: The Theory of Monopoly*, 3 ECONOMETRICA 1 (1935) ("The best of all monopoly profits is a quiet life").

58. Digital competition today is often "diagonal" rather than vertical or horizontal. By that, we mean that a firm in one market may not compete directly with firms in another, separate market, but may need to innovate to avoid incursions from those other firms. Facebook and Amazon provide one of many good examples. The two do not compete directly, but Amazon must innovate to avoid incursions by Facebook and Facebook must innovate to avoid losing too many users to Amazon. Properly considered, this means they are in the same market, but even if they are not, their diagonal competition forces both to continue to innovate to maintain or expand their sales. This may not help their smaller rivals, but consumers surely benefit. The upshot is that there can be no reasonable fear that these firms will stop competing and enjoy the quiet life.

59. The argument is sometimes made that "yes, but in the long-term competition will thrive better if small firms can face an equal playing field." Sounds nice, right? But how do you level the playing field? Is it by making the smaller players better? Would that we could. No, leveling the playing field means handicapping successful firms, which would be crazy, the EC approach notwithstanding. Consider the EC requirement that Microsoft offer a version of Windows without Windows Media Player. Did that improve Windows? Of course not; it made it worse. Consumers and the economy generally would suffer if Apple had to deal with more malware by being forced to "open" the iPhone's system, or if Amazon could not promote itself as the most reliable seller and shipper. Knee-capping the firms that have provided the greatest enhancements to the economy makes no sense at all.

60. So, what is leading this push? It will be denied, but the driving force is a desire to protect competitors at the expense of competition. The only beneficiaries of the EC and current U.S. agency approach are firms that have failed to compete successfully without regulatory help. Consumers do not benefit from a rule of law that promotes an inferior outcome they choose to avoid.

61. Remedies are also problematic. How would it help consumers to force Amazon to promote third-party sellers over its own? Or, worse, to promote inferior methods of delivery over Prime? What would you advise Amazon to do?

IV. Empirical Evidence

62. There are almost no empirical analyses of the impact of regulation on competition and consumer welfare. The DMA is too new and the heavy regulation that prevailed from the 1940s through much of the 1970s in the U.S. is not especially relevant. But there is some recent scholarship.

63. One paper is Antitrust Platform Regulation and Entrepreneurship: Evidence from China, by Ke Rong, D. Daniel Sokol, Di Zhou and Feng Zhu The authors there studied the implementation of China's Anti-Monopoly Guidelines for the Platform Economy as a "quasi-natural experiment" to evaluate the effects of antitrust regulation on platform competition. The authors used a difference-in-differences approach to look at the impact on the degree of investment and the entry of startups in platform markets. They concluded: "The results show that the Platform Guidelines did not increase competition in these affected markets. Rather, competition weakened in these markets, with less venture capital investment flowing into them and fewer startups entering these markets."[24]

64. China's Anti-Monopoly Guidelines for the Platform Economy resulted in the designation of a number of "digital giants": Alibaba, Tencent, ByteDance, DiDi, Meituan, and JD. Several fines have been issued: Alibaba's amounted to some 4% of its total sales. The authors identified "41 industries that were deeply influenced by the affected platforms prior to platform antitrust regulation, along with 127 uninfluenced industries."[25] Their study analyzed the differences in the creation of startups and the level of research investment. The econometric results were that "the monthly number of investments in the affected industries is 26.73% lower than that in the other industries. Similarly… the monthly number of newly established companies in the affected industries is 18.72% lower than that in the other industries as a result of the platform antitrust policy."[26]

65. An April 2024 analysis of the effects of digital regulation in Europe by David Evans reached a similar result.[27] This was not econometrics, but Evans observed that "Europe has given birth to few leading digital businesses over [the past] three decades" in which U.S. and Chinese companies – China's before the new regulatory regime just discussed – created many dozens. He noted: "Of the 69 digital businesses worth $10 billion or more as of December 2023, Europe, which accounts for 21% of global GDP, had spawned just five [7%]: Spotify, Adyen, Revolut, Adevinta

---

[24] Ke Rong, D. Daniel Sokol, Di Zhou & Feng Zhu, Antitrust Platform Regulation and Entrepreneurship: Evidence from China (Harvard Bus. School Working Paper No. 24-039, Jan. 2024) at 1.

[25] *Id.* at 3.

[26] *Id.* at 9.

[27] David S. Evans, Why Europe Must End Its 30-Year Digital Winter to Ensure Its Long-Run Future (Apr. 18, 2024), https://ssrn.com/abstract=4799197 or http://dx.doi.org/10.2139/ssrn.4799197.

and Checkout.com. Together they account for less than 1% of the total value of the 69 businesses. None is based in Germany, France, Spain or Italy, the four largest EU economies."[28] In addition, "Private consumption inclusive of government social benefits in 2019 was substantially lower than the U.S.: 72% for Europe and 78% for the five largest economies (Germany, [the] U.K., France, Italy and Spain) as a percentage of the comparable metric for the U.S." Moreover, "[b]etween 1995 and 2019, private consumption inclusive of government social benefits declined, relative to the U.S., [by 8%] for the five largest economies and [by 13%] for the 15 members of the EU in 1995."[29]

66. These are just two analyses, understandable given how recently the heavy regulatory regimes began. And the economies studied are not identical to the U.S. But the conclusions are troubling. And there are no studies reaching a contrary result.[30]

V. Concluding Observations

67. The large Internet companies today are just that, large. But when we ask how they got there, it is difficult to see the current enforcement moves as anything other than punishing success. Apple invented the iPhone, the iPad, the Apple Watch, Apple TV, Oculus, and more. Amazon made shopping easier for hundreds of millions of consumers, and its amazing online delivery capabilities proved especially important during the pandemic. Google made it so easy to find stuff on the Internet that it became a verb, and constructed an advertising system that allows advertisers to provide and consumers to see the most relevant ads in nanoseconds. Each of the companies innovates every day and regards innovation as critical to their survival. The benefits to consumers have been monumental. They have been achieved, at least in the U.S., because a faithful application of the consumer welfare standard has made it possible – by avoiding interference and intervention absent evidence of actual or likely consumer harm.

68. Why in the world would we want to stop that?

---

28 Id. at 3.

29 Id. at 5.

30 There is a House subcommittee report: INVESTIGATION OF COMPETITION IN DIGITAL MARKETS, MAJORITY STAFF REPORT AND RECOMMENDATIONS, SUBCOMM. ON ANTITRUST, COM. & ADMIN. L. OF THE COMM. ON THE JUDICIARY (2020). But it does not purport to examine the economic effects of digital regulation on consumers.

Competition and Innovation: Incorporating a More Dynamic Perspective into Enforcement

WOLFGANG KERBER[*]
University of Marburg

SIMONETTA VEZZOSO[**]
Trento University

Abstract

This paper calls for a fundamental shift in competition policy towards a dynamic, innovation-oriented approach. It contends that the traditional competition economics approach, being too narrow, fails to capture competition as a knowledge-generating and experimentation-driven process. Drawing on insights from innovation research, strategic management theory, and evolutionary and complexity economics, the paper emphasizes that competitive processes are marked by parallel experimentation and mutual learning, where firm heterogeneity is essential for generating new knowledge and fostering innovation. The paper explores how competition law enforcement can target essential resources, assets, and capabilities for innovation while managing uncertainty and meeting legal standards of proof. It further examines challenges such as trade-offs between innovations and the emerging issue of the direction of innovation. Ultimately, the paper calls for the development of novel assessment frameworks and methodologies within an integrated policy context to foster a more dynamic, innovation-driven economy.

---

[*] Professor of Economics at the University of Marburg, Senior Professor at the University of Bonn; kerber@wiwi.uni-marburg.de.

[**] Senior Researcher, Adjunct Professor at the Department of Economics and Management of the University of Trento, simonetta.vezzoso@unitn.it.

Competition and Innovation:
Incorporating a More Dynamic Perspective into Enforcement

I. Towards More Innovation-Oriented Enforcement

1. Integrating more innovation and a dynamic approach into competition policy enforcement still poses significant challenges and resistance. Considering innovation from a dynamic perspective would necessarily imply that many of the concepts now established in competition policy should be significantly reconsidered. In fact, the traditional static notion of competition, which continues to play a central role in the enforcement of competition policy and shapes fundamental assessment concepts and methodologies, is inadequately equipped to address innovation effectively, especially in the context of the digitalization of the economy.[1]

2. For effectively enhancing competition enforcement, it is essential to adopt a broader approach that, in addition to traditional competition economics, also incorporates insights from interdisciplinary research into the dynamic and complex nature of innovation, and technological and economic evolution. This must lead to the development of innovation-specific assessment concepts and methods that are capable of complementing, and to some extent replacing, traditional static assessment frameworks.[2]

3. Although competition economics has increasingly analyzed innovation, there remains a risk of focusing exclusively on innovation incentives. This would overlook research showing that innovation, properly understood as the "successful development and application of new knowledge,"[3] is a very complex phenomenon, which in competition policy enforcement cannot be reduced to incentives to invest in R&D. Mergers, agreements and unilateral behaviors can also significantly impact innovation and the generation of new knowledge in ways that do not stem from a change of incentives. Mergers, for example, can also adversely affect innovation by reducing parallel experimentation among different R&D projects, which limits the exploration of new solutions and slows the development of new knowledge generation (see section II). Therefore, while the analysis of innovation incentives remains important, the overall

---

1 Cf. Harry First, *The Internet of Change: Foreword to the Symposium on the Google and Facebook Cases*, 67 ANTITRUST BULLETIN 3, 5 (2022): "If the internet is disrupting everything, why won't it disrupt antitrust law as well? Is it reasonable to expect that the economic models on which antitrust is built, and the policy goals on which antitrust has focused, will stay the same, unchanged by the economic disruption the Internet has unleashed. The answer to this rhetorical question must be 'no'."

2 Cf. Wolfgang Kerber, *Competition, Innovation, and Competition Law: Dissecting the Interplay*, in DYNAMIC MARKETS, DYNAMIC COMPETITION AND DYNAMIC ENFORCEMENT: THE IMPACT OF THE DIGITAL REVOLUTION AND GLOBALISATION ON COMPETITION LAW ENFORCEMENT IN EUROPE 33 (Damien Gerard, Bernd Meyring & Eric Morgan de Rivery eds., 2018); Wolfgang Kerber, *Towards a Dynamic Concept of Competition that Includes Innovation*, OECD, DAF/COMP/WD(2023)42 (8 June 2023).

3 For this definition of innovation, *see* OECD, *Competition, Patents and Innovation: Key Findings, Summary and Notes* 17 (OECD Roundtables on Competition Policy Papers No. 72, 2008), https://www.oecd.org/daf/competition/39888509.pdf.

effects on innovation should be considered as decisive in competition policy enforcement.[4]

4. Such an innovation-oriented enforcement of competition law requires a strong determination to maintain the preconditions for Schumpeterian competition through the use of an effective competition policy toolkit, which might have to extend beyond traditional antitrust law. It is important that such a dynamic approach does not lead to weaker enforcement of competition law, as some may fear.[5] On the contrary, protecting and enabling Schumpeterian competition with disruptive innovations might require proactive and vigorous competition law enforcement.

5. Achieving more innovation-oriented enforcement does not need to start from scratch, as a dynamic approach to competition has already been sufficiently developed to inform concrete implications for competition policy enforcement (II). An important key strategy of competition enforcement might be to analyze the effects of mergers, agreements and unilateral conduct on other companies' access to certain resources, specialized assets, and capabilities that are necessary for their innovation (III). Additionally, competition policy enforcers must also increasingly address trade-offs between different types of innovation (IV) and deal with concerns about the direction of innovation, because innovations, particularly in the digital economy, may not always yield positive effects for individuals and society due to market failures in selecting beneficial innovations (V).

II. Innovation Competition as a Knowledge-Generating Process of Experimentation with New Problem Solutions and Learning

6. There is a clear disconnect between the static models used in traditional competition economics and the phenomenon of competition as a rivalrous and dynamic process, as viewed by most competition scholars. In a dynamic view of the competitive process, the emphasis shifts from price competition to the efforts of enterprises to enhance their knowledge and develop better products and services, with the aim of attracting more customers, increasing market shares, and generating higher profits. Competing firms can be understood as testing their (usually diverse) hypotheses about how to better solve customer problems through a process of parallel experimentation. Market feedback helps these firms identify what might succeed and which errors to avoid. They learn from their own experiences

---

4 Cf. also OECD, *The Role of Innovation in Competition Enforcement* (OECD Roundtables on Competition Policy Papers No. 301, 2023), www.oecd.org/daf/competition/the-role-of-innovation-in-competition-enforcement-2023.pdf.

5 Cf. for instance Andrew P. McLean, *Innovation against Change*, 12 J. ANTITRUST ENF'T 378 (2024).

while also mutually benefiting from observing the successes and failures of their competitors. This knowledge-generating aspect of competition drives innovations that offer better solutions to the problems faced by individuals, firms, and society.

7. This dynamic concept of competition has deep roots in economic thought. The key economists who most notably provide a solid theoretical foundation for this dynamic approach are undoubtedly Joseph Schumpeter and Friedrich A. von Hayek. However, it is equally important to recognize contributions from other fields, including innovation research, evolutionary and complexity economics, empirical studies of industrial dynamics, and business and management research.[6]

8. Such a concept of competition as a knowledge-generating process aligns very well with the dynamic and rivalrous nature of competitive processes that antitrust enforcers often seek to preserve. The traditional argument that innovation constitutes the most effective form of competition is attributed to Schumpeter.[7] A defining feature of this dynamic approach is that competition is seen as a process of innovation and imitation. Firms push forward with new innovations, while others attempt to catch up or even leapfrog the initial innovators through imitation and their own innovation efforts. From this ongoing process, radical innovations can also emerge, leading to both the "destruction" and "creation" of markets and industries ("creative destruction"). The rivalrous element is particularly crucial within this concept, as the innovative advances by leading firms place competitive pressure on their lagging rivals, compelling them to innovate – or at least imitate – to remain competitive and capable of staying in the market.[8]

9. Clearly, dynamic concepts of competition, often referenced by competition enforcers and the judiciary, are all to some extent influenced by Schumpeter's vision of competition. It is, however, very problematic that competition economics interpreted Schumpeter's approach as a theory suggesting that a certain market structure – namely, monopoly – would lead to the largest incentives to innovate, thereby having the most positive effects on innovation. This interpretation has sparked a widespread

---

[6] *Cf.* J Gregory Sidak & David J. Teece, *Dynamic Competition in Antitrust Law*, 5 J. Competition L. & Econ. 581 (2009); Richard Nelson et al., Modern Evolutionary Economics: An Overview (2018); Kerber (2018), *supra* note 2; Nicolas Petit & David J. Teece, *Innovating Big Tech Firms and Competition Policy: Favoring Dynamic over Static Competition*, 30 Indus. & Corp. Change 1168 (2021); Kerber (2023), *supra* note 2; Nicolas Petit & Thibault Schrepel, *Complexity-minded Antitrust*, 33 J. Evol. Econ. 541 (2023); Alexandre de Streel & Pierre Larouche, *Disruptive Innovation and Antitrust* (GW Competition & Innovation Lab Working Paper Series No. 2024/24, 2024), https://ssrn.com/abstract=4906842.

[7] Joseph A. Schumpeter, The Theory of Economic Development: An Inquiry into Profits, Capital, Credit, Interest and the Business Cycle (1934); Joseph A. Schumpeter, Capitalism, Socialism and Democracy (1942).

[8] The rivalrous character of Schumpeterian competition has been recently emphasized by the "business stealing" approach. *See* Giulio Federico, Fiona Scott Morton & Carl Shapiro, *Antitrust and Innovation: Welcoming and Protecting Disruption*, 20 Innovation Pol'y & Econ. 125 (2020), and CMA, Merger Assessment Guidelines (CMA 129, Mar. 18, 2021) (partly based upon this approach).

debate framed as "Schumpeter vs. Arrow," where Schumpeter and Arrow represent opposing views on how static market structures impact innovation.[9] It is, however, very unclear whether such a static interpretation of market structures is compatible with Schumpeter's dynamic view of competition and the ensuing endogeneity of market structures.

10. In addition to Schumpeter, Hayek is undoubtedly a pioneer of a dynamic concept of competition as a knowledge-generating process. Central to his concept is the recognition of the knowledge problem and the characterization of competition as a discovery procedure for generating new knowledge through a trial-and-error process. Since no one knows *ex ante* the best solution to a problem, competition, as a process of parallel experimentation, can be viewed as a "procedure" for generating new knowledge. This underpins Hayek's famous defense of the market economy with decentralized decision-making, which enables better utilization of the dispersed knowledge in society. This reasoning can be extended to dispersed creative ideas for innovation, whose effective utilization depends on economic actors' ability to test them in market competition and learn from the outcomes of their economic and technological experiments.[10]

11. This Hayekian view of competition as a dynamic knowledge-generating process through trial and error aligns well with the findings of many empirical studies in management and industrial dynamics research, which emphasize the importance of firm heterogeneity. These studies have shown that the knowledge, capabilities, and other resources of firms can be not only highly heterogeneous but are also evolving over time in a dynamic world.[11] Recognizing this heterogeneity is crucial for competition enforcement, as it underpins the disruptive nature of competition ("maverick"). It allows firms to introduce vastly different solutions that can completely replace existing ones.

12. In a rapidly changing economy driven by new technologies, firms frequently face situations of "true uncertainty," as defined by Frank Knight.[12] The heterogeneity or diversity of firms implies that they do not react the same way to changes; rather, their reactions, particularly in terms of their innovation

---

9 *See* for this discussion Philippe Aghion et al., *Competition and Innovation: An Inverted-U Relationship*, 120 Q. J. Econ. 701 (2005); Michael L. Katz & Howard A. Shelanski, *Mergers and Innovation*, 74 Antitrust L.J. 1 (2007); Carl Shapiro, *Competition and Innovation: Did Arrow Hit the Bull's Eye?*, in The Rate & Direction of Inventive Activity Revisited 361 (Josh Lerner & Scott Stern eds., 2012); OECD, *Competition and Innovation: A Theoretical Perspective* 11 (OECD Roundtables on Competition Policy Papers No. 294, 2023).

10 Friedrich A. von Hayek, *The Meaning of Competition*, in Individualism and Economic Order 92 (1948); Friedrich A. von Hayek, *Competition as a Discovery Procedure*, in New Studies in Philosophy, Politics, Economics and the History of Ideas 179 (1978); Wolfgang Kerber, *Competition, Innovation and Maintaining Diversity Through Competition Law*, in Competition Policy and the Economic Approach: Foundations and Limitations 173, 176 (Josef Drexl, Wolfgang Kerber & Rupprecht Podszun eds., 2012).

11 For the heterogeneity of firms, *see* Richard R. Nelson, Why do Firms Differ, and How Does It Matter? 12 Strategic Mgmt. J. 61 (1991); Constance E. Helfat, *The Economic View of Strategic Management*, in Strategic Management: State of the Field and its Future 61, 62 (Irene M. Duhaime, Michael A. Hitt & Majorie A. Lyles eds., 2021).

12 Frank H. Knight, Risk, Uncertainty, and Profit 19 (1921).

activities, can vary significantly and take different directions. Here, the profound lack of knowledge about the future renders clear rational decision-making impossible.[13] As a consequence, in these "ill-defined" situations, competing firms, each with different knowledge, capabilities, and resources, will develop distinct perspectives on the existing opportunities and the most promising strategic options for innovation. This refers to decisions about whether to innovate, how much to invest, the direction of innovation, which opportunities to explore, and which paths to follow in the innovation process. It is precisely due to the heterogeneity of firms and the diversity of different innovation approaches that the competitive process can work effectively as an exploratory process of experimentation with new problem solutions.[14]

13. Both the Schumpeterian view of competition as a dynamic and rivalrous process of innovation and imitation and the Hayekian emphasis on the knowledge-generating effects of competition through trial-and-error processes unequivocally assign an important role to competition policy. While it is certainly part of the Schumpeterian concept of competition that an innovating firm may exploit temporary monopolies and market power, the key aspect is the preservation of an effective ongoing rivalrous process of competition that leads to a continuous and sustained stream of innovations. Therefore, effective and appropriate competition law, enforced decisively, is crucial for safeguarding the dynamic competitive process.[15] The conceptualization of competition as a process, the alleged enforcement's goal of preserving innovation competition, and the importance of assessing harm to innovation often appear in policy statements and decisions by competition authorities.[16] However, when a specific rationale for the alleged effects on innovation is presented in concrete enforcement cases, the economic perspective employed almost exclusively focuses on incentives to innovate.[17] What is then considered in the competition assessment is how those incentives change due to a transaction or specific behavior. Thus, for instance, the concern that emerged from the European Commission's analysis of the 2015 merger between Pfizer and Hospira was that post-merger, Pfizer's innovation incentives would have diminished, leading it to discontinue the development of a specific pharmaceutical for the treatment of auto-immune diseases.[18]

---

13 W. Brian Arthur, *Foundations of Complexity Economics*, 3 Nat. Rev. Phys. 136, 137 (2021).

14 *See* Stan J. Metcalfe, Evolutionary Economics and Creative Destruction (1998); Joseph Farrell, *Complexity, Diversity, and Antitrust*, 51 Antitrust Bull. 165 (2006); Kerber, *supra* note 10.

15 *See also* de Streel & Larouche, *supra* note 6, for a similar approach that uses the concept of "disruptive innovation" (Christensen) and asks how to ensure through antitrust policy "that it can happen and will not be thwarted by incumbent firms" (*id.* at 51).

16 *Cf.* for instance, Alexander Iken et al., *Non-Price Competition: EU Merger Control Framework and Case Practice*, 1 Competition Pol'y Brief 1 (Apr. 2024).

17 *Id.* at 2; for example, the "business stealing" approach focuses only on innovation incentives (Federico et al., *supra* note 8).

18 Case COMP/M.7559, Pfizer/Hospira, C(2015) 5639 final.

14. A dynamic view of competition, which also considers the knowledge-generating effects through parallel experimentation with a variety of new solutions and continuous learning, necessitates a significant expansion and redirection of the evaluative framework. From an economic perspective, it is not enough to assess only the effects on incentives for investing in R&D. The evaluation must also account for the effects of a merger or a specific behavior on the effectiveness of the process of knowledge generation through parallel experimentation with new innovations, market feedback and mutual learning among firms from the successes and failures of their competitors. If a merger reduces the number of parallel experiments, fewer diverse innovation solutions are tried out, leading to less market feedback and reduced mutual learning between firms from their experiences. This may result in a slowing down of the process of generating new knowledge. Equally important is the heterogeneity or diversity of the experimenting firms, as this influences the variety of new innovative solutions tested in dynamic competition processes. Greater diversity can foster broader and more creative exploration processes with different paths of innovation that might otherwise remain unexplored. Therefore, both the number and the diversity of firms play a crucial role.[19]

15. What are the implications for competition policy enforcement, specifically in merger cases? The positive effects of parallel experimenting firms for the generation of new knowledge introduce an additional theory of harm related to mergers, independent of those based on innovation incentives. For example, in the EU *Dow/DuPont* merger case, the European Commission's main reasoning was that reducing the number of competing firms in the crop protection industry would decrease the incentives to invest in R&D in the entire industry. This reasoning relied on emerging economic models about how mergers would affect the innovation incentives of the lower number of firms after the merger.[20] In contrast, a dynamic view of competition as a process of parallel experimentation would emphasize the loss of knowledge generation resulting from the merger. Fewer firms (with perhaps also less diversity) would engage in searching for innovative problem solutions through a process of parallel experimentation and mutual learning. These two theories of harm point to distinct negative effects on innovation through mergers, arising from two different mechanisms. It can be assumed that both are likely to be relevant in merger cases and, when considered together, may strengthen the argument for prohibiting a merger.

---

19 Cf. Kerber, *supra* note 10, at 182–188; for the importance of diversity for antitrust enforcement; *see also*, in particular, Farrell, *supra* note 14.

20 Case COMP/M.7932, Dow/DuPont, C(2017) 1946 final; for an overview of these models, *see* Ioannis Kokkoris & Tommaso Valletti, *Innovation Considerations in Horizontal Merger Control*, 16 J. COMPETITION L. & ECON. 220 (2020).

16. However, for both theories of harm, it can also be demonstrated that, under certain conditions, innovation efficiencies can exist, potentially forming the basis for an innovation defense of mergers.[21] Trade-offs between the two theories of harm may also exist. For example, in the *Dow/DuPont*[22] and *Bayer/Monsanto*[23] merger decisions, the European Commission reasoned that the closer the merging parties are in terms of innovation competition, along the dominant innovation path, the more likely the merger is to harm innovation.[24] This reasoning follows from the innovation incentive rationale, but from the perspective of knowledge generation through parallel experimentation with new problem solutions, mergers between highly heterogeneous firms may be much more problematic. Such mergers reduce diversity and therefore the variety of new experiments and the scope for exploring diverse innovation paths.[25]

17. As the examples just provided deriving from recent merger policy decisions demonstrate, much remains to be done to guide competition enforcement towards protecting competition as a knowledge-generating process. In this context, innovation can also be incremental, but the assessment should be oriented towards preserving innovation as a disruptive force, where there is high uncertainty regarding future outcomes of innovation efforts, as the aim is also to protect the mechanism from which future markets endogenously emerge.

18. Nonetheless, this does not imply that protecting current or potential innovation competition in identified product markets should be neglected, and various antitrust authorities have made this a clear priority in their enforcement actions. Thus, for instance, in the *Google/Enel X* case, the Italian competition authority carefully assessed the long-term implications of Google's behavior, preventing competitors from accessing significant user data streams that were necessary for their operations. It came to the conclusion that Google's behavior was abusive also because it stifled innovation and hindered the emergence of new (more privacy-friendly) products for which there was a latent user demand.[26] The number of cases in which this approach has been utilized by competition authorities

---

21   *See* Federico et al., *supra* note 8, at 133–35 (about innovation synergies); Kerber, *supra* note 10, at 185 (innovation efficiencies through mergers can also lead to more successful experiments, which might overcompensate the loss through a lower number of parallel experiments).

22   Case COMP/M.7932, Dow/DuPont, *supra* note 20.

23   Case COMP/M.8084, Bayer/Monsanto, C(2018) 1709 final.

24   *See also* Elias Deutscher & Stavros Makris, *Sustainability Concerns in EU Merger Control: From Output-Maximising to Polycentric Innovation Competition*, 11 J. ANTITRUST ENF'T 350, 370 (2023).

25   *See* in much more detail with regard to the *Dow/DuPont* merger case Wolfgang Kerber & Simonetta Vezzoso, Dow/Dupont: Another Step Towards a Proper Assessment Concept of Innovation Effects of Mergers (June 24, 2019) at 12–24, https://ssrn.com/abstract=3856885 (posted June 7, 2021).

26   Autorità Garante della Concorrenza e del Mercato [AGCM] [Italian Competition Authority] April 27, 2021, n. 29645, A529 Google/Compatibilità App Enel X Italia con Sistema Android Auto.

has been increasing in recent years, demonstrating a clear intent to move beyond an assessment limited to effects on prices and quantities.[27]

19. It must also be noted that due to constraints imposed by relevant legislation, competition authorities often hesitate to conduct a competition assessment that moves away from defining a market in traditional terms. As a result, the focus risks remaining at best limited to protecting incremental innovation. Indeed, a more dynamic approach has already been employed when competition enforcers have consciously moved away from the traditional definition of product markets and shifted their focus to what they term "innovation spaces." This approach has gained traction, particularly in EU merger control, starting with the *Dow/DuPont* case, and is now enshrined in the Commission Notice on the definition of the relevant market, which removes the need to define relevant markets in every instance.[28] This is clearly an important step in the right direction, but a dynamic analysis such as the one advocated here obviously requires much more.[29]

20. Also more aligned with a dynamic view of competition are those policy initiatives that, while extending beyond traditional antitrust tools, aim to keep markets open for innovators and, to some extent, promote the spillover effects of innovation in the economy. This type of objective particularly characterizes the Digital Markets Act (DMA),[30] which is applied within the European Union to designated gatekeepers. These gatekeepers are subject to a series of clearly defined obligations that include requirements regarding interoperability and access for third-party competitors and operators related to specific core platform services. Gatekeepers, with their entrenched market positions, not only have little incentive to develop or promote services that would result in displacing their current services,[31] but they also desire to control other innovations within their ecosystem that might displace their services. Therefore, the DMA aims to preserve third parties' innovation incentives by prohibiting specific practices that could negatively affect them.[32] This can also include providing access possibilities to the users of gatekeepers, which the latter might otherwise block, to enable more innovative services to be tried out. In particular, also

---

27 *See* Harry First, *Merger Policy for a Platform Economy*, 4 ZWeR 334, 364 (2023) (emphasizing the focus on harm to innovation instead of price-raising in six recent merger cases); OECD, *supra* note 4.

28 European Commission, Commission Notice on the Definition of the Relevant Market for the Purposes of Union Competition Law, 2024 O.J. (C), para. 92.

29 Kerber & Vezzoso, *supra* note 25.

30 Regulation (EU) 2022/1925 of the European Parliament and of the Council of 14 September 2022 on Contestable and Fair Markets in the Digital Sector and Amending Directives (EU) 2019/1937 and (EU) 2020/1828 (Digital Markets Act), 2022 O.J. (L 265) 1.

31 Richard J. Gilbert & A. Douglas Melamed, *Innovation Under Section 2 of the Sherman Act*, 84 ANTITRUST L.J. 1 (2021).

32 Jacques Crémer et al., *Fairness and Contestability in the Digital Markets Act*, 40 YALE J. REGUL. 973 (2023).

through the obligations that promote unbundling and interoperability, the DMA can enable more diverse firms to experiment with new problem solutions, and therefore contribute to the generation of new knowledge through a broader explorative process.[33] However, it remains to be seen whether, in terms of promoting dynamic competition as advocated here, targeted structural measures would have been more effective.[34]

III. The Key Role of Necessary Resources, Assets and Capabilities for Innovation as New Objects of Assessment in Competition Cases

21. Integrating a more dynamic perspective into competition law enforcement requires competition authorities to reconcile the inherent uncertainty of innovation processes in such competitive processes with the obligation to meet the standards of proof mandated by the applicable legislative framework. The analysis becomes particularly complex when dealing with radical innovations that lead to the creation of new markets, where the uncertainty and unpredictability of innovations appear hardly tractable. Although this uncertainty can explain the traditional cautiousness in dealing with innovation, ignoring innovation effects is clearly not an option in competition law enforcement. Therefore, it is necessary for policymakers and enforcers to develop effective strategies to deal with this knowledge problem.

22. While it is hard to predict innovations, we already know a lot about certain preconditions that must be met for firms to be capable of innovating in a specific field. These range from having patent portfolios regarding certain technologies to employing researchers with certain characteristics, having certain physical resources and, increasingly, access to specific types and quantities of data. Therefore, it can be a promising strategy for competition authorities to focus on the resources, assets, and capabilities that are necessary for innovation as key objects of competition analyses. For competition enforcement, this necessarily means that innovation-specific concepts and methods suitable for assessing resources, assets, and capabilities will need to be employed. In the following, we will show how such a strategy can be applied.

23. As already discussed in section II, the traditional approach to defining product markets often does not fit a dynamic view of competition with its focus on innovation. Instead, a different approach is needed to identify

---

33 *See also* the discussion about trade-offs between innovations within digital ecosystems in section IV.

34 Martin Watzinger & Monica Schnitzer, *The Breakup of the Bell System and Its Impact on US Innovation* (CEPR Discussion Paper No. DP17635, 2022).

which firms are in competition for innovating in a certain field or industry. Here, the innovation market approach already made an important contribution by directly analyzing (i) the parallel (overlapping) innovation activities of firms, and (ii) the resources, specialized assets, and capabilities that are necessary for innovating in a specific innovation space or industry.[35] For example, in the *Dow/DuPont* case, the European Commission conducted detailed innovation-specific assessments regarding necessary resources, assets and capabilities of firms in the crop protection industry. This was done to identify which of these firms are competitors, on the one hand, at the level of the entire industry and, on the other hand, at the level of the various specific innovation spaces (with already existing **R&D** projects), serving as an important first step of the competitive analysis. In this competition case, enforcers made a big step forward in developing a suitable innovation-specific assessment approach, which is much better compatible with a dynamic view of competition as a knowledge-generating process.[36]

24. Moreover, in the context of potential competition analyses, such as in the abandoned merger between Adobe and Figma, competition authorities would already routinely assess the ability to enter a market by assessing, for example, whether a potential competitor has sufficient relevant resources to enter, whether it could add to its capabilities either organically or through acquisition, etc.[37] The dynamic perspective on resources, assets, and capabilities advocated here, however, would not merely assess the ability to enter a specific market but rather focus on the capability to innovate within a specific field. In addition to the capabilities that firms possess, the resources they can draw upon – whether material (such as computing power) or intangible assets like patent portfolios and other types of intellectual property – are equally important. Depending on the various fields of innovation, different bundles of specific resources, assets, and capabilities will likely be necessary to innovate.

25. A disproportionately large concentration or even monopolization of certain critical resources, which are essential for innovation in a specific field, should be of particular concern for competition authorities. Especially relevant in the enforcement of competition law are behaviors, agreements, and mergers that result in the control of critical resources, assets, and capabilities for innovation, which might lead to the foreclosure of other firms. This can have direct negative effects on innovation processes.

---

35 *Cf.* Richard J. Gilbert & Steven C. Sunshine, *Incorporating Dynamic Efficiency Concerns in Merger Analysis: The Use of Innovation Markets*, 63 ANTITRUST L.J. 569 (1995); for an empirical analysis of the use of the innovation market approach in U.S. merger cases, *see* Benjamin. R Kern, Ralf Dewenter & Wolfgang Kerber, *Empirical Analysis of the Assessment of Innovation Effects in U.S. Merger Cases*, 16 J. INDUS. COMPETITION & TRADE 373 (2016).

36 Case COMP/M.7932, Dow/DuPont, *supra* note 20; Kerber & Vezzoso, *supra* note 25, at 25.

37 *See* Laura Corbett et al., Adobe/Figma: *Much Ado(be) About Nothing?*, 2 COMPETITION MERGER BRIEF 1 (Sept. 2024).

For example, in the merger case *Adobe/Figma*, the question could have been asked whether, through the acquisition of Figma, Adobe would have gained the ability to control critical resources for innovation, thereby hindering the capacity for experimentation in a specific field.

26. Similarly, in the area of unilateral conduct, particular concern should also be given to bundling strategies employed by dominant firms. Additionally, various types of agreements, including those related to the licensing of specific intellectual property, can aim to control the resources, assets and capabilities that other firms need to independently experiment and, potentially, innovate. Consequently, the analysis of the effects of such practices and strategies must necessarily consider the potential negative repercussions on innovation processes in a specific field.

27. The necessity to preserve innovation processes has become increasingly clear to competition enforcers over recent years. This was evident, for example, in the analysis made during the abandoned acquisition of Arm by Nvidia, where the enforcement focus was on preserving innovation races and protecting the inherent uncertainty about who may succeed on the merits. In particular, Arm's IP was considered a very important input in order to be able to participate in the innovation races taking place in nascent markets like the Internet of Things (IoT) and artificial intelligence (AI).[38] This inquiry, along with the formulation of applicable theories of harm, should not be reserved solely for so-called nascent markets in merger control, but instead routinely also explored in the many contexts where innovation competition is a significant dimension of rivalry among firms that should be carefully preserved.

28. A more dynamic perspective on competition enforcement necessarily extends to the crucial phase of remedies, which in the past has not always received the attention it deserves. In this regard, to reinvigorate innovation competition that has been stifled by particularly entrenched dominant positions, it will often be necessary to ensure that competitors have access to resources, assets (including intellectual property), and capabilities essential for innovation.[39] This approach is similar to what has already been implemented, for instance, in pharmaceutical sector mergers, where antitrust authorities aim to ensure that when the divestiture of R&D projects is deemed necessary, it includes the resources, assets, and capabilities necessary for innovation. In the remedial phase following the finding of an antitrust violation due to the abuse of a dominant position that has impeded the proper functioning of innovative processes, it will be crucial to ensure that conditions are restored in such a way that it is not past

---

[38] *Cf.* Press Release, CMA, CMA Finds Competition Concerns with NVIDIA's Purchase of Arm' (Aug. 20, 2021).

[39] Ketan Ahuja, *Promoting Innovation Ecosystems in Antitrust: A Framework for Antitrust Analysis Applied to Emerging AI Technologies*, ROOSEVELT INST. (June 27, 2024).

abuses but robust innovation competition that governs the evolution of products and services going forward. Similar reflections appear to characterize the broad remedial proposals from the Department of Justice (DOJ), following the finding by the District Court for the District of Columbia that Google is liable under section 2 of the Sherman Act for maintaining monopolies in U.S. general search services and U.S. general search text advertising. According to the DOJ, "the remedy must restore incentives for innovation and disruptive entry that Google's conduct has – for over a decade – diminished."[40]

29. Data access remedies for enabling more innovation do play an increasingly important role in the European Union. For instance, the German Federal Cartel Office imposed a far-reaching data-sharing remedy on the dominant German national railway company Deutsche Bahn, requiring non-discriminatory access to (exclusively controlled) real-time railway mobility data to new innovative mobility service providers, which without these data would be unable to offer their services in competition with the vertically integrated incumbent Deutsche Bahn. Opening this monopolistically controlled critical data set would allow new innovative service providers to develop and experiment with new multimodal mobility services.[41] Since, however, it is unclear whether competition law is the most suitable instrument for making more data available for innovation, the EU has enacted several regulatory solutions for mandatory data sharing with the objective of promoting more innovation and competition as part of its European strategy for data.[42]

30. This recommended strategy for enforcement, which emphasizes a greater focus on the analysis of resources, assets, and capabilities that are necessary for innovation in specific fields, also requires the development of new concepts and methods. These are needed to define the necessary resources, assets and capabilities and to operationalize such an enforcement approach so that it can be applied in a reliable way. Competition law enforcers have already experimented with developing new methods in specific cases, such as analyzing patent portfolios in the *Dow/DuPont* merger case. Particularly interesting are also attempts to seriously consider the assessment of firm capabilities necessary for innovation. There is a

---

[40] Executive Summary of Plaintiffs' Proposed Final Judgment at 5, United States v. Google, Case 1:20-cv-03010-APM (D.D.C. Nov. 20, 2024).

[41] Bundeskartellamt [BKartA] [Federal Cartel Office] June 26, 2023, decision B9-144/19; Niharika Parshurampuria, Laura Lehoczky-Deckers, Katharina Bongs & Andreas Reindl, *The German Competition Authority orders the national incumbent rail operator to make its real-time traffic data available to rivals (Deutsche Bahn)*, E-COMPETITIONS June 2023, art. no. 113149. *See also* a parallel data access case of the EU Commission against the Spanish national railway company Renfe, Case AT.40735, Jan. 17, *2024; see also* Pedro Callol, *The EU Commission accepts commitments made by the Spanish State-owned railway company to allay abuse of dominance concerns (Renfe)*, E-COMPETITIONS Jan. 2024, art. no. 116945.

[42] *Cf.* European Commission, *A European Strategy of Data*, COM(2020) 66 final (Feb. 19, 2020), the Second Payment Services Directive (opening bank account data), the Data Act with new data access and sharing rights with regard to IoT data, and specific data access and sharing obligations in the Digital Markets Act.

growing body of literature in competition policy research focused on innovation capabilities, which can draw insights from existing studies in the field of strategic management.[43] The analysis of innovation capabilities can also be very interesting for the formulation of an innovation defense in merger control, which, for example, also looks at the innovation potential of the merged firm.[44] However, we are likely still at an early stage in developing concepts and methods to enable a dynamic perspective in the enforcement of competition policy. Access to objective methods for analyzing these capabilities is essential to meet the standard of proof to which competition enforcers are held. Future revisions to the European Commission's Merger Guidelines should incorporate specific concepts and methods aimed at better orienting enforcement towards a more dynamic and innovation-focused approach.

IV. The Complex World of Multiple Innovations and the Problem of Trade-offs Between Innovations

31. In competition policy, the potential trade-off between price competition (static efficiency) and dynamic competition (innovation) has long been discussed. Echoing Schumpeter and others, we believe the benefits of innovation can be more important than losses through static inefficiencies.[45] This not only pertains to arguments that higher prices, resulting from temporary market power, should be accepted under certain conditions to incentivize medium- and long-term innovation activities, but also recognizes the benefits of engaging in experimentation with parallel but different research projects, despite the potential for R&D cost duplication from a static viewpoint.

32. Increasingly important, however, are trade-offs between innovations, which can arise in scenarios where innovations are not stand-alone innovations that can be developed, commercialized, and used independently of one another. Well-known, for example, is the phenomenon of cumulative innovations, where a trade-off exists between the incentives of a first innovator and the incentives of follow-on innovators.[46] Similarly, trade-offs regarding innovation incentives also occur if innovations are complementary to each other, meaning they can only be used and commercialized jointly. One important example is so-called complex products,

---

[43] Petit & Teece, *supra* note 6; Johann Peter Murmann & Fabian Vogt, *A Capabilities Framework for Dynamic Competition: Assessing the Relative Chances of Incumbents, Start-ups, and Diversifying Entrants*, 19 MGMT. & ORG. REV. 141 (2023).

[44] MARIO DRAGHI, THE FUTURE OF EUROPEAN COMPETITIVENESS, PART B: IN-DEPTH ANALYSIS AND RECOMMENDATIONS 299 (Sept. 2024).

[45] SCHUMPETER (1942), *supra* note 7; Petit & Teece, *supra* note 6, at 1173.

[46] *Cf.* SUZANNE SCOTCHMER, INNOVATION AND INCENTIVES 127–57 (2006).

such as smartphones, which incorporate hundreds or thousands of intellectual rights (IP)-protected technologies, because they require complex negotiation processes with high transaction costs to determine the royalties for the many IP right (IPR) holders involved. Since IP law has often been unable to resolve these problems on its own, competition law had to step in to enable innovation and competition in such situations. For example, competition law permits the formation of patent pools that reduce transaction costs, provided they include only complementary and/or essential IPRs.[47]

33. In all these case groups, complex conflicts and trade-offs emerge regarding the distribution of value from technologies to their IPR holders, affecting innovation incentives. Competition authorities have already been involved in evaluating the effects on IPR holders' innovation incentives against the impact on the innovation of complex products by manufacturers (royalty-stacking problem), or on the development of new technical standards (with standard-essential patents) with its manifold positive effects on efficiency and further innovations.[48]

34. Another example of an innovation trade-off in competition policy is the well-known EU decision from 2004, which sanctioned Microsoft for abusing its dominant position, notably through a "refusal to license."[49] This part of the decision revolved around access to IP-protected interface information to ensure compatibility between workgroup server operating systems and the Windows PC operating system. This case involved a trade-off between the effects of potential lower innovation incentives for Microsoft versus the effects of more incentives to innovate by providers of workgroup server operating systems. In its decision, the Commission used an explicit economic approach by asking which solution (mandatory access to interface information or not) would lead to more innovation overall.[50] However, this incentive balance test has not found further application in EU enforcement practice.

35. The UK competition authority discussed a trade-off between incentives to innovate with regard to a possible access remedy imposed on Google following its 2020 market investigation.[51] Although both the Commission in the *Microsoft* decision and the CMA in its report framed this argument as

---

47 *Cf.* Carl Shapiro, *Navigating the Patent Thicket: Cross Licenses, Patent Pools, and Standard-Setting*, *in* 1 INNOVATION POLICY AND THE ECONOMY 119 (Josh Lerner & Scott Stern eds., 2000); European Commission, *Guidelines on the Application of Article 101 of the Treaty on the Functioning of the European Union to Technology Transfer Agreements*, 2014 O.J. (C 89) 3 (section 4.4 Technology pools).

48 OECD, Licensing of IP Rights and Competition Law – Background Note by the Secretariat, DAF/COMP(2019)3 (Apr. 29, 2019).

49 Case COMP/C-3/37.792, Microsoft, C(2004)900 final.

50 *See* Simonetta Vezzoso, *The Incentives Balance Test in the EU Microsoft Case: A Pro Innovation "Economics-Based" Approach?*, 27 EUR. COMPETITION L. REV. 382 (2006).

51 CMA, ONLINE PLATFORMS AND DIGITAL ADVERTISING: MARKET STUDY FINAL REPORT (July 1, 2020), Appendix V: Assessment of Pro-Competition Interventions in General Search.

an innovation incentive trade-off, we would propose going a step further. We would also emphasize the additional positive innovation effects from the potential larger variety of workgroup server operating systems and search engines, respectively, that would be enabled by maintaining the openness of these markets to heterogeneous undertakings that can innovate in different directions. For instance, in the case of the access remedy discussed by the CMA, its concrete formulation should consider these additional innovation effects, specifically by facilitating access for diverse companies that explore differentiated innovation paths. The same applies to access obligations in the DMA, which should also aim to enhance these types of innovation effects and thereby promote contestability.

36. Serious trade-offs between different types of innovation can also potentially emerge in digital ecosystems, in which numerous firms can contribute complementary products and services to jointly create value for the customers of these ecosystems.[52] Often, a leading firm ("orchestrator") plays a key role in coordinating these complementary contributions by setting technical and commercial rules ("ecosystem governance"). However, a broad consensus among competition scholars exists about the ambivalent character of this orchestrator position: while the orchestrator's activities can significantly enhance the ecosystem's value, its power can also lead to anti-competitive behavior vis-à-vis the complementors.[53] This is particularly relevant for innovation, which may occur both at the level of the (architecture of the) ecosystem by the orchestrator and at the level of the many products and services within the ecosystem through the innovative activities of many firms. This can lead to direct conflicts between the orchestrator and these firms, as the ecosystem's architecture and rules can constrain their innovations, both technically and in terms of their business models. Not only can complementors be restricted in the volume and direction of their innovative efforts, but orchestrators can also benefit from their extensive monitoring of the innovative activities within their ecosystems and on their platforms. For example, they can readily identify which new apps launched by developers in their app store are successful and either copy them or otherwise use the data produced in an anti-competitive way, thereby depriving the complementing firms of their innovation benefits.[54]

---

[52] For the law & economics of digital ecosystems, *see* Michael G. Jacobides, Carmelo Cennamo & Annabelle Gawer, *Towards a Theory of Ecosystems*, 39 STRAT. MGMT. J. 2255 (2018); Nicolas Petit & David Teece, *Taking Ecosystems Competition Seriously in the Digital Economy: A (Preliminary) Dynamic Competition/Capabilities Perspective*, OECD, DAF/COMP/WD(2020)90 (Dec. 2, 2020); Georgios Petropoulos, *Competition Economics of Digital Ecosystems*, OECD, DAF/COMP/WD(2020)91 (Nov. 3, 2020); Michael G. Jacobides & Ioannis Lianos, Ecosystems and Competition Law in Theory and Practice, 30 INDUS. & CORP. CHANGE 1199 (2021); Philipp Hornung, *The Ecosystem Concept, the DMA, and Section 19a GWB*, 12 J. ANTITRUST ENF'T, 396, 406 (2024).

[53] *See* Petropoulos, *supra* note 52, at 5–7; Petit & Teece, *supra* note 52, at 5; Hornung, *supra* note 52, at 406.

[54] *See* Simonetta Vezzoso, *Competition Policy in a World of Big Data*, *in* RESEARCH HANDBOOK ON DIGITAL TRANSFORMATIONS 400 (F. Xavier Olleros & Majlinda Zhegu eds., 2016) for Amazon as another example of a platform orchestrator profiting off complementors' experiments with new offerings; Petropoulos, *supra* note 52, at 6.

37. In competition policy, questions arise about whether and to what extent the power of orchestrators to set certain types of rules and practices should be limited to protect the innovation incentives of the complementing firms and their freedom to innovate. This would allow for more experimentation with new innovations, although it could, conversely, impose certain restrictions on innovations at the ecosystem level. Along the same lines, the previously mentioned DMA already imposes several obligations on gatekeepers, aimed at preserving the innovation incentives and autonomy of business users. It also provides some protection against gatekeepers using data generated by these users on the platform to directly compete with them.

38. Overall, it is crucial that competition enforcers, in complex situations of multiple and interrelated innovations, may need to take decisions about balancing different types of innovation activities. This requires the development of assessment concepts and methods to address such trade-off issues appropriately.

V. The New Issue of the "Direction" of Innovation Processes and the Interplay with Other Policies

39. If competition authorities increasingly need to also address conflicts between the innovation activities of different firms and between different types of innovations, they are becoming engaged with questions about the direction of innovation activities. Traditionally, competition and antitrust policy do not ask this question, operating under the assumption that market selection works well, i.e., that only innovations with overall positive effects are successful in competition in markets, and/or that it is the task of other policies to deal with systematic distortions of the direction of innovation in markets.

40. However, in recent years, the issue of the "direction" or the "quality" of innovations has also increasingly entered competition and antitrust policy discussions.[55] Particularly pointed have been critiques of digital innovations, like social media, which are implicated in the spread of misinformation, addiction, and mental health concerns, posing significant risks to individuals, societal well-being, and democratic processes.[56]

---

55 *See* Maurice E. Stucke & Ariel Ezrachi, *Innovation Misunderstood*, 73 Am. U. L. Rev. 1941 (2024); Maurice E. Stucke & Ariel Ezrachi, How Big-Tech Barons Smash Innovation – and How to Strike Back 61 (2022); Viktoria H.S.E. Robertson & Klaudia Majcher, *Capturing Innovation for Antitrust Purposes*, Antitrust Chron. (Sept. 2023); Daron Acemoglu, *Distorted Innovation: Does the Market Get the Direction of Technology Right?*, 113 AEA Papers and Proc. 1 (2023); Juliane Mendelsohn & Lukas Breide, *Considering the Direction of Innovation in EU Merger Control*, 11 J. Responsible innovation 2425120 (2024). *See also* William J. Baumol, *Entrepreneurship: Productive, Unproductive, and Destructive*, 95 J. Pol. Econ. 893 (1990).

56 *See*, for example, Wim Naudé, *Destructive Digital Entrepreneurship* (Inst. for Lab. Econ. (IZA), Discussion Papers No. 16384, 2023), https://hdl.handle.net/10419/282610.

The direction of innovation has also become a focal topic within competition law, particularly as discussions expand to include additional objectives of competition policy, such as sustainability and industrial policy. These discussions prompt inquiries about whether competition authorities should also evaluate the effects of mergers, agreements, and unilateral conduct on innovations that have positive or negative effects on sustainability or the competitiveness of domestic firms (e.g., as part of EU and U.S. industrial policy strategies).[57] However, also from a more traditional economic perspective, new serious concerns about systematic distortions of innovation due to market failures have been raised, notably by the recent Nobel laureate Acemoglu.[58]

41. In the following, we will not engage in the broader issues surrounding innovation policy and the direction of innovation in society.[59] Instead, our focus will be on the much narrower question whether market competition works well in selecting superior innovations, i.e., those that better fulfill consumer preferences or address societal challenges. Specifically, can we rely on the selection function of the market to correctly distinguish between "better" and "worse" innovations? This question hinges on whether market feedback works well, ensuring that the "development and successful application of new knowledge" (OECD)[60] moves in the right direction.

42. Chicago economics, for example, traditionally assumes that only "efficient" solutions can survive in the market. However, it is not hard to show from an economic perspective that markets can suffer from a number of selection problems regarding new innovations. These problems can lead to certain types of innovations being profitable and successful in markets, despite having negative effects on consumers and/or society. Simple market failure problems can already explain some selection errors, such as product innovations with negative external effects on the environment like high CO_2 emissions persisting due to uninternalized external costs, while products and services with positive external effects (like, e.g., high-quality news publishing) are underprovided by markets. Well-known too are also selection problems related to new technologies due to various forms of path-dependent dynamic effects, such as dynamic economies of

---

[57] See Justus Haucap et al., Competition and Sustainability: Economic Policy and Options for Reform in Antitrust and Competition Law (2024); Klaudia Majcher & Viktoria H.S.E. Robertson, *The Twin Transition to a Green and Digital Economy: The Role for EU Competition Law*, in Research Handbook on Sustainability and Competition law 194 (Julian Nowag ed., 2024). For the discussion about a new industrial policy-oriented approach to competition policy in the EU, see Draghi, *supra* note 44, at 298–300, and Ursula von der Leyen, *Europe's Choice: Political Guidelines for the Next European Commission 2024–2029* (July 18, 2024) at 7.

[58] Acemoglu, *supra* note 55.

[59] See also Mariana Mazzucato, The Entrepreneurial State: Debunking Public vs. Private Sector Myths 23 (2013); OECD, *supra* note 9, at 23.

[60] See *supra* note 3.

scale and network effects. They can lead to lock-in effects in outdated, inefficient technologies, for example, technical standards.[61]

43. In digital markets, especially, a prominent market failure arises from consumer information and behavioral challenges. Consumers often find it difficult to assess product quality and the risks of providing personal data. This issue is compounded by "dark nudging," where large digital platforms can manipulate consumer choices using the extensive data they control. This manipulation leads to the danger of consumers making systematic errors in selecting innovative services that truly match their preferences.[62] Dark nudging can not only negatively impact consumers, but also systematically distort the markets' selection function. Therefore, this distortion can also undermine competition as a process of experimentation. If exploiting information asymmetries and manipulating consumer behavior are profitable business strategies, this encourages innovations that refine these manipulative strategies, steering innovation in the wrong direction.[63]

44. What conclusions can be drawn from this critical discussion about the direction of innovation, e.g., resulting from selection errors in markets, for the application of competition and antitrust law? Competition authorities should be aware of such problems and, in case of doubt, be cautious about how to balance the effects of certain innovations with other innovations and/or static price effects. They should not automatically assume that more and faster innovations are always welfare-enhancing. However, addressing all types of market failure problems cannot fall within the scope of competition policy. There are good reasons for a division of labor between different policies. Sustainability problems through negative external effects should be primarily solved by environmental policies, information and behavioral problems by consumer and data protection law.

45. In recent years, however, both discussion and enforcement in competition policy have shown that, in particular on digital markets and with regard to the large digital platforms and tech firms, competition problems and information and behavioral problems exist simultaneously. Solving certain competition problems might also require effective policy solutions for the problem of behavioral manipulation and dark nudging. It might therefore be necessary that competition authorities also take into

---

61 *See* W. Brian Arthur, *Competing Technologies, Increasing Returns, and Lock-In by Historical Events*, 99 ECON. J. 116 (1989); Joseph Farrell & Timothy Simcoe, *Four Paths to Compatibility*, *in* THE OXFORD HANDBOOK OF THE DIGITAL ECONOMY 34, 35 (Martin Peitz & Joel Waldfogel eds., 2012), as overview Wolfgang Kerber & Heike Schweitzer, *Interoperability in the Digital Economy*, 8 J. INTELL. PROP. INFO. TECH. & ELEC. COM. L. 39, 42–48 (2017).

62 *Cf.* Jamie Luguri & Lior Jacob Strahilevitz, *Shining a Light on Dark Patterns*, 13 J. LEGAL ANALYSIS 43 (2021).

63 *Cf.* Digital Regulation Project, *Consumer Protection for Online Markets and Large Digital Platforms* (Policy Discussion Paper No. 1, 2021) at 18 (about the use of machine learning for behavioral manipulation).

account information and behavioral problems, either in the remedies in competition cases or through more collaboration with other policies like consumer or data protection law.[64]

46. Such a broader enforcement approach can already be seen clearly in recent cases and developments in competition policy. One example is the increasing consideration of privacy effects and data protection law in the application of competition law, in the aftermath of the German *Facebook* case.[65] Another example is the DMA with its objectives of contestability and fairness. It also has rules against behavioral manipulation (dark nudging) of end users (as part of its anti-circumvention rules), because the legislator has recognized that "offering choices to the end-user in a non-neutral manner" by the gatekeepers can impede the effectiveness of the obligations for the gatekeepers also with regard to contestability and competition.[66]

47. In the digital economy, a dynamic approach to competition enforcement that focuses on innovation competition as a process of experimentation with new problem solutions should consider that competition and antitrust law is one policy within a bundle of related policies, such as IP, industrial policy, consumer and data protection law, as well as other (also new) policies and regulations, which together provide the framework for a dynamic innovative economy. It is important to understand the interplay between these policies, including their synergies and conflicts, as well as to develop concepts for a stronger integrative approach that transcends the traditional policy silos. Therefore, competition and antitrust policy should be open, including at the enforcement level, to collaborate more with other policies and their enforcement agencies.[67]

VI. Conclusions

48. Integrating much more innovation and a dynamic approach into the enforcement of competition law and antitrust policy is necessary and urgent for enabling and protecting innovation competition as a

---

64 *See* HEIKE SCHWEITZER ET AL., MODERNISIERUNG DER MISSBRAUCHSAUFSICHT FÜR MARKTMÄCHTIGE UNTERNEHMEN 99 (2018) (explicitly discussing the effects of the combination of market power and information manipulation power through the large tech firms as part of the "intermediation power" of digital platforms); Wolfgang Kerber, *Taming Tech Giants: The Neglected Interplay Between Competition Law and Data Protection (Privacy) Law*, 67 ANTITRUST BULL. 280 (2022).

65 BKartA, Feb. 15, 2019, decision B6-22/16; for the broader legal discussion: ERIKA M. DOUGLAS, DIGITAL CROSSROADS: THE INTERSECTION OF COMPETITION LAW AND DATA PRIVACY, REPORT TO THE GLOBAL PRIVACY ASSEMBLY DIGITAL CITIZEN AND CONSUMER WORKING GROUP (July 2021), https://papers.ssrn.com/sol3/papers.cfm?abstract_id=3880737; from an economic perspective, Wolfgang Kerber & Karsten K. Zolna, *The German Facebook Case: The Law and Economics of the Relationship between Competition and Data Protection Law*, 54 EUR. J. L. & ECON. 217 (2022).

66 *See* art. 13(4) and (6) DMA; *see also* Daniela Seeliger, *Article 13: Anti-circumvention*, in DIGITAL MARKETS ACT: ARTICLE-BY-ARTICLE COMMENTARY 306 (Rupprecht Podszun ed., 2024).

67 Inge Graef, Damian Clifford & Peggy Valcke, *Fairness and Enforcement: Bridging Competition, Data Protection, and Consumer Law*, 8 INT'L DATA PRIV. L. 200 (2018); Kerber, *supra* note 64, at 298–300.

knowledge-generating process in our fast-evolving digital economy. This requires a broader interdisciplinary approach, incorporating insights from innovation research, strategic management theory, and evolutionary and complexity economics, to move beyond the overly narrow traditional competition economics approach. Competition law enforcement must complement its traditional static assessment approach with additional new innovation-specific assessment concepts and methods, which are capable of focusing on the specific characteristics of innovation processes and the dynamics of the competitive process. Competition policy should focus much more on how to protect and enable competition as a dynamic innovative process of exploration and experimentation with new problem solutions.

High Prices and Pharmaceuticals

Michael A. Carrier[*]

Rutgers Law School

Abstract

For decades, Professor Harry First has shared his knowledge and keen insights across a vast expanse of antitrust doctrine, including state antitrust law, the Microsoft case, and remedies. In his article, "Excessive Drug Pricing as an Antitrust Violation," Professor First focuses on the problem of high prices in the pharmaceutical industry. In particular, he laments "the assumed inapplicability of Section 2 of the Sherman Act to a monopolist's excessive pricing."[1] My contribution to this collection focuses on two drugs that have received attention for their high prices: the EpiPen and Daraprim. Professor First discusses these examples, highlighting the companies' price increases and the lack of justification for this conduct. And he suggests a role for antitrust in challenging this activity. This chapter takes this suggestion to the next level by diving deeper into the conduct and uncovering antitrust violations. It finds that currently existing antitrust doctrine is adaptable enough to address the behavior. The chapter begins with the epinephrine-injecting EpiPen, for which Mylan engineered sustained price increases at the same time it engaged in a patent settlement, filed a "citizen petition," and entered into exclusive contracts with schools. And it continues with infection-treating Daraprim, for which the price rose 5,000% after the company restricted its distribution system and denied samples that generics needed to enter the market.

---

[*] Board of Governors Professor, Rutgers Law School. Copyright © 2025 Michael A. Carrier. Parts of this article are adapted from previous work.

[1] Harry First, *Excessive Drug Pricing as an Antitrust Violation*, 82 Antitrust L.J. 701, 705 (2019).

1. For decades, Professor Harry First has shared his knowledge and keen insights across a vast expanse of antitrust doctrine, including state antitrust law, the *Microsoft* case, and remedies. In his article, "Excessive Drug Pricing as an Antitrust Violation," Professor First focuses on the problem of high prices in the pharmaceutical industry. In particular, he laments "the assumed inapplicability of Section 2 of the Sherman Act to a monopolist's excessive pricing."[2]

2. My contribution to this collection focuses on two drugs that have received attention for their high prices: the EpiPen and Daraprim.[3] Professor First discusses these examples, highlighting the companies' price increases and the lack of justification for this conduct.[4] And he suggests a role for antitrust in challenging this activity.[5] This chapter takes this suggestion to the next level by diving deeper into the conduct and uncovering antitrust violations. It finds that currently existing antitrust doctrine is adaptable enough to address the behavior.

3. The chapter begins with the epinephrine-injecting EpiPen, for which Mylan engineered sustained price increases at the same time it engaged in a patent settlement, filed a "citizen petition," and entered into exclusive contracts with schools. And it continues with infection-treating Daraprim, for which the price rose 5,000% after the company restricted its distribution system and denied samples that generics needed to enter the market.

I. Pharmaceutical Case Study 1: EpiPen

4. Conduct related to Mylan's EpiPen threatens anticompetitive behavior through settlements, citizen petitions, and exclusive contracts.

1. Background

5. In the summer of 2016, Mylan found itself under fire for high EpiPen prices. Between 2009 and 2016, Mylan had raised the price of this lifesaving device, which delivers epinephrine to treat anaphylaxis shock, 15 times, resulting in an increase of more than 400%.[6] The medicine in an EpiPen

---

2 Harry First, *Excessive Drug Pricing as an Antitrust Violation*, 82 ANTITRUST L.J. 701, 705 (2019).

3 For another example, see Michael A. Carrier, *Higher Drug Prices from Anticompetitive Conduct: Three Case Studies*, 39 J. LEGAL MED. 151, 152–56 (2019) (discussing settlements and "product hopping" in connection with Cephalon's switch from sleep-disorder-treating Provigil to Nuvigil).

4 First, *supra* note 1, at 727–30, 733–36.

5 *Id.* at 730–36.

6 Sy Mukherjee, *How Mylan Got Away With Its Enormous Price Hike for the EpiPen*, FORTUNE (Aug. 23, 2016), http://fortune.com/2016/08/22/mylan-epipen-price-hike-monopoly/; Matt Egan, *How EpiPen Came to Symbolize Corporate Greed*, CNN MONEY (Aug. 29, 2016), XXX http://money.cnn.com/2016/08/29/investing/epipen-price-rise-history/.

costs only pennies per dose.[7] But a pack of two, which needs to be replaced each year, and which families buy in multiple quantities for various locations, costs more than $600.[8] The consequences of these prices are felt in all corners, as life-threatening allergies from peanuts, shellfish, and other substances affect 15 million Americans and 1 in 13 children.[9]

6. Although many reasons were offered for the price hike (such as a slow-moving FDA approval process[10] and convoluted distribution chain[11]), Mylan cleared the field of competitors through at least three potentially anticompetitive actions that exploited (i) the litigation process through settlement, (ii) the administrative process through citizen petitions, and (iii) the laws requiring auto-injectors in schools through exclusive contracts.

2. Settlement

7. The first activity involved settlement. In August 2009, Meridian Medical Technologies (a Pfizer subsidiary that manufactures the EpiPen) and King Pharmaceuticals (which acquired Meridian) sued Teva for patent infringement.[12] After a four-day bench trial in early 2012,[13] the parties settled in April 2012,[14] only weeks before post-trial briefings were due in late May 2012.[15] While the terms of the settlement are confidential, a Mylan press release confirms that Teva agreed to delay entering the market for more than three years, until June 2015.[16] During the period in which Teva could not enter the market, EpiPen prices more than doubled, from (roughly) $220 to $460.[17]

---

7   Letter from Jason Chaffetz (R-UT) & Elijah E. Cummings (D-MD) to Heather Bresch (Aug. 29, 2016), https://oversightdemocrats.house.gov/sites/evo-subsites/democrats-oversight.house.gov/files/documents/2016-08-29%20JC%20and%20EEC%20%20to%20Bresch-Mylan%20EpiPen%20Pricing.pdf (questioning price increase and commencing congressional investigation).

8   *Id.*

9   Mukherjee, *supra* note 5, at 1.

10 *See, e.g.*, Rand Paul, *Sen. Rand Paul: EpiPen Scandal Is a Perfect Example of Crony Capitalism*, TIME (Sept. 7, 2016), http://time.com/4482179/sen-rand-paul-epipen-scandal/.

11 Dan Mangan & Anita Balakrishnan, *Mylan CEO Bresch: 'No One's More Frustrated Than Me' About EpiPen Price Furor*, CNBC (Aug. 25, 2016), http://www.cnbc.com/2016/08/25/mylan-expands-epipen-cost-cutting-programs-after-charges-of-price-gouging.html.

12 Complaint, King Pharm., Inc. et al. v. Teva Parenteral Med. Inc. et al., No. 09-652-GMS (D. Del. Aug. 28, 2009), ECF No. 1.

13 Official Transcript of Trial, King Pharm., Inc. et al. v. Teva Parenteral Med. Inc. et al., No. 09-652-GMS (D. Del. July 25, 2012), ECF No. 150–54.

14 *See* Press Release, Mylan, Mylan and Pfizer Announce Epinephrine Auto-injector Settlement Agreement with Teva, (Apr. 26, 2012), https://investor.mylan.com/news-releases/news-release-details/mylan-and-pfizer-announce-epinephrine-auto-injector-settlement-0.

15 Proposed Order Regarding Post-Trial Submissions, King Pharm., Inc. et al. v. Teva Parenteral Med. Inc. et al., No. 09-652-GMS (D. Del. Apr. 12, 2012), ECF No. 146.

16 *Id.*

17 *See* Dan Mangan, *This Chart Shows Why Everyone's Angry About Soaring Price of Lifesaving EpiPen*, CNBC (Aug. 23, 2016), http://www.cnbc.com/2016/08/23/this-chart-shows-you-why-a-lot-of-people-are-angry-about-the-price-of-epipen.html (providing figures from July 2012 and May 2015).

8. One cannot know with certainty how the court would have decided the patent litigation. But ominous tea leaves on the patents' validity are revealed by the court's *Markman*[18] claim construction hearing, which signaled greater success for Teva than for the patent owners.[19] The settlement also was concerning, not just because it delayed a successful generic from the market, but also because of its effects on other, later-filing generics. The Hatch-Waxman Act awards 180 days of exclusivity to the first generic to challenge a brand firm's patent claiming that it is invalid or not infringed.[20] This period does not begin until the first-filing generic enters the market, in this case three years in the future. Because Teva was the first filer,[21] as a result of delaying Teva's entry into the market, Mylan and its partners delayed *all generics* that sought to file applications based on the EpiPen.[22]

9. Settlements of patent litigation threaten potential landmines of anticompetitive effects. The Supreme Court made clear in *FTC v. Actavis*[23] that a settlement by which a brand pays a generic to delay entering the market could have "significant adverse effects on competition" and violate the antitrust laws.[24] Although the *Actavis* decision post-dated the settlement, the parties likely were aware at the time they settled in April 2012 that potentially rigorous scrutiny was on the horizon.[25]

10. Because the terms of the settlement are confidential, it is not possible to know whether there was a transfer of consideration to Teva. But the generic-friendly claim construction bolstering Teva's leverage, together with the vast scale of the market, increased the likelihood that Meridian delayed Teva's entry through payment.

3. Citizen Petition

11. In addition to delayed-entry settlements, Mylan sought to forestall Teva's entry by employing a "citizen petition," which is meant to raise safety

---

18   *See generally* Markman v. Westview Instruments, Inc., 517 U.S. 370 (1996) (holding that claim construction is a matter of law and that judges are to construe the meaning of patent claims).

19   *See* Michael A. Carrier & Carl J. Minniti III, *The Untold EpiPen Story: How Mylan Hiked Prices by Blocking Rivals*, 102 CORNELL L. REV. ONLINE 53, 61–62 (2017).

20   21 U.S.C. § 355(j)(5)(B)(iv).

21   *Update: Teva and Antares's Generic Challenge to Epi-Pen*, SEEKING ALPHA (Feb. 23, 2012), http://seekingalpha.com/article/388681-update-teva-and-antaress-generic-challenge-to-epipen.

22   *See* Michael A. Carrier, *Payment After* Actavis, 100 IOWA L. REV. 7, 15 (2014).

23   570 U.S. 136 (2013). *See* Michael A. Carrier, *The US Supreme Court issues first ruling on antitrust legality of reverse-payment drug patent settlements (*Actavis*)*, E-COMPETITIONS June 2013, art. no. 53120.

24   570 U.S. at 148.

25   Oral Argument at 25, 36, 37, *In re* K-Dur Antitrust, et al., Nos. 10-2077, 10-2078, 10-2079, & 10-4571 (3d Cir. Dec. 12, 2011). *See* Carrier & Minniti, *supra* note 18, at 62 (describing how appeal would be heard by the Third Circuit and how settlement was signed shortly after that court's December 2011 oral argument in *In re K-Dur Antitrust Litigation*, in which judges expressed skepticism about arguments for minimal antitrust scrutiny).

12. concerns with the FDA but has been used by brand firms to delay generic entry. As I have shown, "citizen" petitions are filed mostly by brand firms, and are almost always (92%) denied.[26]

12. Mylan filed its citizen petition against Teva's abbreviated new drug application (ANDA or generic application) in January 2015.[27] A response from the FDA was anticipated no later than June 2015[28] – only weeks before Teva was permitted to enter the market pursuant to its settlement. As my study revealed, Mylan's petition appears to have been filed as a delay tactic to avoid generic approval and the loss of its overwhelming share of the market.[29]

13. Just as concerning, in May 2015, four months after filing the petition, Mylan filed a supplemental study asserting that patients would not be able to operate Teva's proposed device without retraining.[30] Experts explained, however, that Mylan's supplemental study "had a lot of problems" as it "lacked a control group; did not study the actual generic but a prototype instead; used a small number of participants; failed to provide them with proper instructions for use; and told participants to watch a video rather than actually use the Teva device."[31]

14. Shining even more light on the questionable petition and supplemental study is the timing. In a development of which the industry would be keenly aware, Teva filed its ANDA against the EpiPen in 2008.[32] And court documents show that Teva produced its ANDA filing in the course of litigation in September 2010.[33] This material included "detailed product descriptions, drawings, and instructions for use" for Teva's proposed generic.[34]

15. At the time, Mylan was working hand in hand with Meridian/King, with the former taking over Orange Book's sponsorship of the drug application and the latter targeting rivals in litigation. It thus seems exceedingly

---

26 Michael A. Carrier & Carl Minniti, *Citizen Petitions: Long, Late-Filed, and At-Last Denied*, 66 AM. U. L. REV 305, 333 (2016) (examining all 505(q) petitions (which ask the FDA to take action against a pending generic application) filed between 2011 and 2015).

27 Citizen Petition from Mylan Specialty, L.P., Docket No. FDA-2015-P-0181-0001 at *1 (posted on Jan. 16, 2015).

28 *See* 21 U.S.C. § 355(q)(1)(F) ("The Secretary shall take final agency action on a petition not later than 150 days after the date on which the petition is submitted.").

29 *See* Carrier & Minniti, *supra* note 25, at 350–51.

30 Supplement from Mylan Specialty, L.P., Docket No. FDA-2015-P-0181-0007 at *10 (posted on May 5, 2015).

31 Ed Silverman, *How Mylan Tried to Keep Teva from Selling a Generic EpiPen*, STAT (Aug. 31, 2016), https://www.statnews.com/pharmalot/2016/08/31/mylan-teva-generic-epipen/.

32 Larry Smith, *The Promise of the Antares Pipeline Is the Basis of My Buy Recommendation*, SMITH ON STOCKS (Jan. 25, 2012), https://smithonstocks.com/the-promise-of-the-antares-pipeline-is-the-basis-of-my-buy-recommendation-ais-2-40/.

33 Defendants' Brief in Support of their Motion to Dismiss at 6, King Pharm., Inc. v. Teva Parenteral Med. Inc., No. 09-652-GMS (D. Del., filed Dec. 13, 2010).

34 *Id.*

likely that Mylan would have been aware of Teva's ANDA in 2008 and aware of documents explaining Teva's product in 2010. In fact, it was Mylan that announced the settlement of the litigation, confirming its close connection to the case. This connection raises significant concerns that Mylan waited more than four years to file its citizen petition in 2015.

16. It is reasonable to conclude that Mylan's (i) filing of a petition years after invariably knowing about Teva's generic, (ii) filing of a petition calculated to delay entry after settlement, and (iii) late-filing of a supplemental study comprised a strategy to delay Teva's ANDA approval *beyond* the already-*delayed* agreed entry date of June 2015. Although the FDA is required to respond to petitions within 150 days, on numerous occasions the agency offers only an interim response explaining that it requires more time due to "complex issues raised" in the petition.[35] As a result, a strategy similar to the one Mylan used easily could have pushed a petition's disposition (and thus generic approval) past 150 days. For a billion-dollar drug product like the EpiPen, each day of delay meant an extra $3 million.

17. Parties filing petitions with government agencies often can rely on the immunity from the antitrust laws provided by the *Noerr-Pennington* doctrine, as "[t]hose who petition [the] government for redress are generally immune from antitrust liability."[36] But this defense is not absolute. In particular, there is a well-established "sham" exception, which could be satisfied in this case by Mylan's likely longstanding knowledge of Teva's generic, the timing of the petition in relation to the settlement, and the questionable nature of the supplemental study.[37] On a broader level, the petition could be viewed as an integral part of an overall scheme of monopolization, together with settlement and (as discussed immediately below) exclusive dealing.[38]

4. Exclusive Dealing

18. In addition to delaying *future* generic entry from Teva (and others waiting in line behind it) through settlement and petition, Mylan blocked *present* competitors through its program for distributing the EpiPen to schools.[39]

---

35 *E.g.*, Interim Response Letter from FDA CDER to Cubist Pharm., Inc., Docket No. FDA-2015-P-1595-0004 (Oct. 26, 2015).

36 Prof'l Real Estate Investors, Inc. v. Columbia Pictures Indus., Inc., 508 U.S. 49, 56 (1993).

37 *E.g.*, Tyco Healthcare Grp. v. Mutual Pharm. Co., 762 F.3d 1338, 1348 (Fed. Cir. 2014); *In re* DDAVP Direct Purchaser Antitrust Litig., 585 F.3d 677, 694 (2d Cir. 2009); *In re* Flonase Antitrust Litig., 795 F. Supp. 2d 300, 317 (E.D. Pa. 2011); *In re* Prograf Antitrust Litig., 2012 WL 293850, at *5 (D. Mass. Feb. 1, 2012).

38 *See, e.g.*, *In re* Neurontin Antitrust Litig., 2009 WL 2751029, at *15 (D.N.J. Aug. 28, 2009).

39 The New York Attorney General launched an antitrust investigation of this conduct. Press Release, N.Y. Att'y Gen., A. G. Schneiderman Launches Antitrust Investigation into Mylan Pharmaceuticals Inc., Maker of EpiPen (Sept. 6, 2016), https://www.naag.org/wp-content/uploads/2020/11/09-06-16-NY-Investigation-of-Mylan-EpiPen.pdf.

19. In November 2013, in response to a seven-year-old girl at a Virginia school dying from an allergic reaction to peanuts,[40] Congress passed the School Access to Emergency Epinephrine Act.[41] Under this law, the secretary of the Department of Health and Human Services is authorized to give preferential funding to states with schools that maintain an emergency supply of epinephrine for students.[42] The law has had a significant effect: 12 states require[43] and 37 encourage[44] schools to stock epinephrine.[45] This federal legislation has been supplemented by state laws that mandate that public schools obtain autoinjectors.[46]

20. On one hand, such an arrangement could increase access to a lifesaving device. But on the other, it could exclude competitors. As a condition of receiving discounted EpiPens,[47] schools were required to agree that they would "not in the next twelve (12) months purchase any products that are competitive to EpiPen® Auto-Injectors."[48] The language appeared in order forms in August 2014, June 2015, and April 2016,[49] and Mylan has admitted such a practice.[50]

21. In antitrust terms, this conduct offers a discount price based on exclusivity. As the leading treatise explains, such an arrangement "should generally be treated as no different from an orthodox exclusive-dealing arrangement."[51] Exclusive dealing case law stems from section 3 of the Clayton Act, which prohibits a "discount... or rebate... on the condition, agreement, or understanding that the... purchaser... shall not use or deal in the goods... of a

---

40 Cynthia Koons & Robert Langreth, *How Marketing Turned the EpiPen into a Billion-Dollar Business*, BLOOMBERG BUSINESSWEEK (Sept. 23, 2015), https://www.bloomberg.com/news/articles/2015-09-23/how-marketing-turned-the-epipen-into-a-billion-dollar-business.

41 Pub. L. No. 113-48, 127 Stat. 575 (2013) (42 U.S.C. § 280g(d)(1)(F)–(G)).

42 *Id.*

43 *School Access to Epinephrine Map*, FOOD ALLERGY RSCH. & EDUC., https://www.foodallergy.org/our-initiatives/advocacy/food-allergy-issues/school-access-epinephrine (last updated on June 30, 2022).

44 *Id.* Hawaii is the only state that does not require or allow schools to stock epinephrine.

45 Koons & Langreth, *supra* note 39.

46 *See* Aimee Nienstadt, *The Insufficiency of the Law Surrounding Food Allergies*, 36 PACE L. REV. 595, 611 (2016) (providing analysis on state epinephrine autoinjector laws). For a discussion of Mylan's role in the enactment of the 2013 Act, see Carrier & Minniti, *supra* note 18, at 67–68.

47 Ike Swetlitz & Ed Silverman, *Mylan May Have Violated Antitrust Law in its EpiPen Sales to Schools, Legal Experts Say*, STAT (Aug. 25, 2016), https://www.statnews.com/2016/08/25/mylan-antitrust-epipen-schools/ (noting that the "discounted price was $112.10," roughly "a quarter of the cost charged to pharmacies at the time").

48 *Id.*

49 *Id.*

50 FULL HOUSE COMM. ON OVERSIGHT & GOV'T REFORM, HEARING ON REVIEWING THE RISING PRICE OF EPIPENS (Sept. 21, 2016), at 46-47, https://www.govinfo.gov/content/pkg/CHRG-114hhrg24914/pdf/CHRG-114hhrg24914.pdf (in testimony to House Committee, Bresch responded to Representative Duckworth's question about whether "schools that purchased discounted EpiPens had to make any representation and warrants to Mylan that they would adhere to certain conditions in order to access the discount price" by conceding: "'For people that wanted to buy it at the discounted rate, yes'").

51 PHILLIP AREEDA & HERBERT HOVENKAMP, XI ANTITRUST LAW: AN ANALYSIS OF ANTITRUST PRINCIPLES AND THEIR APPLICATION ¶ 1807b, at 133 (3d ed. 2011).

competitor" where there is an adverse effect on competition.⁵² Exclusive dealing can also constitute monopolization under section 2 of the Sherman Act if the defendant has monopoly power.⁵³ The general concern with exclusive dealing arrangements is that they block competitors from the market and result in higher prices and lower output.

22. While it is unclear exactly how much of the market was foreclosed by these agreements, antitrust concern is presented by high entry barriers in the form of FDA approval (exacerbated by the agency's caution given potentially fatal consequences from misapplication) and a 400% surge from 15 price hikes between 2009 and 2016.

II. Pharmaceutical Case Study 2: Daraprim

23. A second type of behavior is revealed by Daraprim. This drug received attention for its 5,000% price increase. But that increase was possible only because of the earlier restriction of its distribution system.

1. Background

24. Notorious pharmaceutical entrepreneur Martin Shkreli made worldwide headlines in 2015. As CEO of Turing Pharmaceuticals, Shkreli obtained U.S. marketing rights to pyrimethamine (Daraprim) and quickly increased the price by 5,000%, from $13.50 to $750 per pill.⁵⁴ Pyrimethamine is a decades-old drug used primarily to treat toxoplasmosis, a fatal parasitic brain infection that usually occurs in patients with weakened immune systems, such as those with end-stage HIV infection.⁵⁵ At the time of the price increase, there were no patents or other forms of market exclusivity.

25. In addition to increasing the price, Turing initiated another less widely understood move – it changed the distribution scheme for the drug. Before its acquisition by Turing, pyrimethamine was available without restriction to patients seeking to fill prescriptions at local pharmacies and to hospitals seeking to stock the product for inpatient use. But in the months before the price hike, apparently as a condition of the sale to Turing, pyrimethamine was switched to a controlled distribution system called Daraprim Direct, in which prescriptions or supplies of the product could be obtained only from a single source: Walgreens Specialty Pharmacy.⁵⁶

---

52 15 U.S.C. § 14; *see id.*
53 15 U.S.C. § 2.
54 Andrew Pollack, *Drug Goes From $13.50 a Tablet to $750, Overnight*, N.Y. TIMES, Sept. 21, 2015, at B1.
55 Sara Fazio, *Toxoplasmosis*, NEW ENG. J. MED. BLOG (Feb. 23, 2012), https://web.archive.org/web/20120422103725/https://blogs.nejm.org/now/index.php/toxoplasmosis/2012/02/23/.
56 Andrew Pollack & Julie Creswell, *The Mercurial Man Behind the Drug Price Increase That Went Viral*, N.Y. TIMES, Sept. 23, 2015, at B1.

As a result, hospitals could no longer obtain the drug from a general wholesaler, and patients could no longer find it at a local pharmacy.

26. Instead, Turing required institutions and individuals to set up accounts through Daraprim Direct, and outpatients were only able to receive the drug by mail order.[57] Comments from Turing executives suggested that a primary goal of the Daraprim Direct system was to make it impossible for anyone other than registered clients to obtain the drug, including generic manufacturers wishing to obtain samples for use in bioequivalence studies needed to obtain FDA approval. This behavior could demonstrate monopolization, with the next two sections analyzing evidence of monopoly power and exclusionary conduct.

2. Monopoly Power

27. Monopoly power has been defined as "the power to control prices or exclude competition."[58] It can be shown in one of two ways, each of which appeared to be satisfied in the case of Daraprim. First, monopoly power can be proved indirectly by examining a defendant's market share along with barriers to entry that could entrench that market position.[59] Courts regularly hold that a 90% market share supports market power, with several courts finding a 75% share to be sufficient.[60]

28. Evidence that Turing has 100% of the relevant market is provided by the lack of effective, FDA-approved substitutes. Pyrimethamine is part of all widely accepted first-line therapeutic regimens for toxoplasmosis.[61] In fact, the American Society of Microbiology warned that the 5,000% price increase would "negatively impact both health care costs and individual patient treatments."[62] Regulatory barriers to entry cement the effect of this high market share, as generics can enter the U.S. market only after receiving FDA approval.

29. Second, monopoly power can be proved directly,[63] such as through observable effects on the market, for example, a price increase or output reduction.[64] Turing's conduct revealed both types of direct evidence.

---

57 *New Pyrimethamine Dispensing Program: What Pharmacists Should Know*, PHARM. TIMES (July 17, 2015), https://www.pharmacytimes.com/contributor/monica-v-golik-mahoney-pharmd-bcps-aq-id/2015/07/new-pyrimethamine-dispensing-program-what-pharmacists-should-know.

58 United States v. E.I. du Pont de Nemours & Co., 351 U.S. 377, 391 (1956).

59 HERBERT HOVENKAMP, FEDERAL ANTITRUST POLICY: THE LAW OF COMPETITION AND ITS PRACTICE ¶ 6.2b, at 359–60 (5th ed. 2016).

60 *Id.* ¶ 6.2a, at 357.

61 Fazio, *supra* note 54.

62 Memorandum from the Democratic Staff to Democratic Members of the Full House Comm. on Oversight & Gov't Reform 5 (Feb. 2, 2016), https://oversightdemocrats.house.gov/sites/evo-subsites/democrats-oversight.house.gov/files/documents/Memo%20on%20Turing%20Documents.pdf.

63 ABA SECTION OF ANTITRUST LAW, ANTITRUST LAW DEVELOPMENTS 69–70 (7th ed. 2012) (noting that "direct proof has provided the basis for findings of substantial anticompetitive effects in some prominent cases").

64 Broadcom Corp. v. Qualcomm Inc., 501 F.3d 297, 307 (3d Cir. 2007).

30. To begin, Turing significantly increased the price. Even though there was not an increase in the costs of producing pyrimethamine (which costs pennies per pill to manufacture[65]), Turing raised the price by 5,000%. In addition, it was able to maintain this increase despite public outrage and substantial attention from the press and politicians.[66] Given the barriers to entry imposed by obtaining FDA review, the high prices likely will be maintained for an extended period of time.[67]

31. Output reductions are another direct indicator of monopoly power. After pyrimethamine's price increase, hospitals complained that they were not able to obtain the drug,[68] with Turing's own press release conceding that hospitals and clinics "were having trouble accessing the product."[69]

32. In short, Turing appears to have monopoly power in engineering and maintaining a 5,000% price increase, preventing hospitals from obtaining pyrimethamine, and ensuring the absence of FDA-approved substitutes for the drug.

3. Exclusionary Conduct

33. To bring a successful monopolization claim, a plaintiff must show not only monopoly power but also exclusionary conduct. Courts often distinguish between the "willful acquisition or maintenance of [monopoly] power" and "growth or development as a consequence of a superior product, business acumen, or historic accident."[70] Such a test is easier to state than apply.

34. In determining whether Turing's refusal to provide samples constitutes exclusionary conduct, consideration of the regulatory background is essential. The Supreme Court in *Verizon Communications v. Trinko*[71] explained that "[a]ntitrust analysis must always be attuned to the particular structure and circumstances of the industry at issue."[72] In particular, courts must take "careful account" of "the pervasive federal and state regulation characteristic of the industry," and the analysis must "recognize and reflect the distinctive economic and legal setting of the regulated industry to which it applies."[73]

---

65 See Karthick Arvinth, *Daraprim: Generic Version of Drug Costs Less than £0.07 in India*, INT'L BUSINESS TIMES (Sept. 25, 2015), http://www.ibtimes.co.uk/like-drug-costs-less-0-07-india-1521144.

66 Pollack, *supra* note 53.

67 *See, e.g.*, Star Fuel Marts, LLC v. Sam's E., Inc., 362 F.3d 639, 654 (10th Cir. 2004).

68 Letter from Stephen B. Calderwood & Adaora Adimora to Tom Evegan & Kevin Bernier (Sept. 8, 2015), https://consumerist.com/consumermediallc.files.wordpress.com/2015/09/pyrimethamineletterfinal.pdf.

69 Press Release, Turing Pharmaceuticals, Important News about Daraprim® (pyrimethamine) (Sept. 18, 2015), https://web.archive.org/web/20150921232830/http://www.turingpharma.com/media/press-release?headline=important-news-about-daraprim%25c2%25ae-%28pyrimethamine%29.

70 United States v. Grinnell Corp., 384 U.S. 563, 570–71 (1966).

71 540 U.S. 398 (2004).

72 *Id.* at 411.

73 *Id.*

35. A central objective of the Hatch-Waxman Act is to encourage generic entry.[74] Congress sought to achieve this goal through several mechanisms, including formalizing the expedited pathway and allowing generics to experiment on brand drugs before the end of the patent term.[75] Most relevant for our purposes, the scheme allows generics to earn abbreviated approvals if they can show that their drugs are bioequivalent to the brand's drug.[76] But this crucial element of competition is possible only if the generic has access to the brand firm's samples.[77] Restricted distribution systems threaten this access.

36. Most prescription drugs are available through a standard pharmaceutical distribution chain: from manufacturer to wholesaler, then to retail or mail-order pharmacy, and then to consumer.[78] The goal is to distribute the drug as widely as possible, as widespread distribution tends to increase manufacturers' revenues by making drugs available to be prescribed to as many people as possible.

37. Drugs with limited distribution schemes, by contrast, are not available through standard retail or mail-order pharmacies. Instead, the manufacturer eliminates the wholesaler and distributes the drug only through specialty pharmacies it selects. Funneling sales through one wholesaler gives the manufacturer complete control over the distribution chain, which could block generics from obtaining samples they need to conduct bioequivalence studies and reach the market.

38. Restricting the typically expansive distribution scheme also tends to involve conduct that makes no sense other than stifling generic entry. The no-economic-sense analysis asks whether conduct allegedly maintaining a monopoly by excluding nascent competition "likely would have been profitable if the nascent competition flourished and the monopoly was not maintained."[79] Such conduct provides a simple way to determine whether a company's sole motive is to impair competition. If a firm undertakes

---

74 *See, e.g.*, Michael A. Carrier, *Unsettling Drug Patent Settlements: A Framework for Presumptive Illegality*, 108 Mich. L. Rev. 37, 41–43 (2009).

75 *See* 35 U.S.C. § 271(e)(1); Lilly & Co. v. Medtronic, Inc., 496 U.S. 661, 669-70 (1990) (allowing experimentation before end of patent term would prevent "unintended distortion" of patent laws that would extend "*de facto* monopoly"); Fed. Trade Comm'n, Generic Drug Entry Prior to Patent Expiration: An FTC Study 5 (2002), https://www.ftc.gov/sites/default/files/documents/reports/generic-drug-entry-prior-patent-expiration-ftc-study/genericdrugstudy_0.pdf.

76 Fed. Trade Comm'n, Generic Drug Entry, *supra* note 74, at 5; Lauren Battaglia, *Risky Conduct with Risk Mitigation Strategies? The Potential Antitrust Issues Associated with REMS*, Antitrust Health Care Chron. 26, 28 (Mar. 2013).

77 Aaron S. Kesselheim & Jonathan J. Darrow, *Hatch-Waxman Turns 30: Do We Need a Re-designed Approach for the Modern Era?*, 15 Yale J. Health Pol'y L. & Ethics 293, 340–41 (2015).

78 Kaiser Fam. Found., Follow the Pill: Understanding the U.S. Commercial Pharmaceutical Supply Chain (2005), https://www.kff.org/wp-content/uploads/2013/01/follow-the-pill-understanding-the-u-s-commercial-pharmaceutical-supply-chain-report.pdf.

79 Gregory J. Werden, *Identifying Exclusionary Conduct Under Section 2: The "No Economic Sense" Test*, 73 Antitrust L.J. 413, 415 (2006).

39. conduct that makes no economic sense, then its "anticompetitive intent" can be "unambiguously... inferred."[80]

39. In the regulatory context, and considering behavior that does not make business sense, the leading monopolization cases foreshadow liability. For example, in *Aspen Skiing Co. v. Aspen Highlands Skiing Corp.*,[81] the owner of three downhill skiing facilities failed to offer a justification for withdrawing from a joint ticketing arrangement with the owner of the only other facility in the area.[82] Just as the Supreme Court found liability where the defendant was "willing to sacrifice short-run benefits and consumer goodwill in exchange for a perceived long-run impact on its smaller rival,"[83] a generic that offers to purchase samples at the full retail price can claim that a brand refuses sales that would have been profitable.

40. In a second example, *Otter Tail Power Co. v. United States*,[84] the Supreme Court required a company to share electric power transmission with rivals. Similar to the facts in that case, in which the defendant was able to "sell [power] at wholesale to those towns that wanted municipal plants" but refused to sell "solely to prevent municipal power systems from eroding its monopolistic position," the brand in this context already is voluntarily selling the drug but restricting its distribution system so that it does not need to sell to others.[85]

41. The 2015 switch of pyrimethamine to a restricted distribution scheme as a condition of its sale to Turing threatened to result in fewer sales. Drug manufacturers typically have expansive distribution systems. Absent medical necessity, there is no reason to voluntarily restrict these systems. In this case in particular, with no recent safety concerns, there was no apparent rationale for limiting distribution 62 years after FDA approval.

42. If there were any doubt as to the reason for the change in the distribution system, it was dispelled by Turing itself. Jon Haas, the director of patient access, admitted that he "would block [a] purchase" of pyrimethamine if a generic sought to order the pill and conceded that Turing "would like to do [its] best to avoid generic competition" and was "certainly not going to make it easier" for the generics.[86] Turing's insistence on behavior that lacks rational business sense provides strong evidence of blocking rivals. This is a powerful illustration of exclusionary conduct that appears to violate the antitrust laws.

---

80   A. Douglas Melamed, *Exclusive Dealing Agreements and Other Exclusionary Conduct – Are There Unifying Principles?*, 73 ANTITRUST L.J. 375, 393 (2006).
81   472 U.S. 585 (1985).
82   *Id.*
83   *Id.* at 610–11.
84   410 U.S. 366 (1973).
85   *Id.* at 378.
86   Ed Silverman, *How Martin Shkreli Prevents Generic Versions of his Pricey Pill*, PHARMALOT (Oct. 5, 2015), http://pharmalot.com/how-martin-shkreli-prevents-generic-versions-of-his-pricey-pill/.

III. Conclusion

43. High prices raise crucial issues. In the pharmaceutical context, they can sometimes be addressed by focusing on the underlying conduct, which could violate antitrust law. Behavior that makes no sense other than by harming a competitor, that undercuts a regulatory regime, or that involves collusive conduct should not be protected. In targeting this behavior, antitrust scrutiny under long-established doctrine could lower drug prices. In focusing on such an important issue, Harry First deserves credit.

Microsoft v. Apple

JOHN B. KIRKWOOD[*]

Seattle University School of Law

Abstract

Harry First and Andy Gavil produced the definitive analysis of the Microsoft litigation, the massive effort to hold the tech giant responsible for its exclusionary behavior in the 1990s. Almost thirty years later, the Department of Justice brought a similar monopolization case against another tech giant, Apple. Relying on First's and Gavil's work, this chapter compares the Microsoft litigation to the case against Apple. The parallels are striking. Both complaints allege that a dominant firm in a dynamic, high-tech industry acquired monopoly power and preserved it through exclusionary conduct directed at cross-platform products – products that would work on the defendant's platform and on competing platforms. At the same time, the cases differ in significant ways. First, it may be harder to prove that Apple has monopoly power. Apple faces closer substitutes than Microsoft did, Apple's market shares are smaller, and Apple's profit margins, while high, are lower than Microsoft's enormous margin. Second, one of the principal exclusionary tactics Apple has used is a refusal to expose the APIs developers need to produce products that may undermine Apple's power. Unilateral refusals to deal, however, have rarely been held illegal since Trinko. Finally, unlike Microsoft, Apple has raised substantial procompetitive justifications for its conduct, claiming that its restrictions are necessary to protect the safety, security, and privacy of iPhone users. Given the adverse consequences for numerous iPhone users if Apple is correct, courts are likely to examine Apple's claims carefully. In short, while the case against Apple is strong, it is more challenging than the case against Microsoft.

---

[*] Professor of Law and William C. Oltman Professor of Teaching Excellence, Seattle University School of Law. Member of the American Law Institute; advisor to the American Antitrust Institute and the Loyola Consumer Antitrust Center; and past chair of the Antitrust Section of the Association of American Law Schools. I want to thank Kathryn Boling for her excellent comments.

I. Introduction

1. Harry First and Andy Gavil have written the definitive analysis of the *Microsoft* litigation,[88] the massive effort to hold the tech giant responsible for its exclusionary behavior in the 1990s. Spearheaded by the United States Department of Justice (DOJ), supported by numerous state attorneys general, and supplemented by private treble damage actions, this enforcement campaign found Microsoft liable for repeated acts of monopolization, restricted its future conduct, and required it to pay billions of dollars in settlements.[89]

2. Perhaps the most consequential effect of the litigation was not its immediate effect on Microsoft but the role it played in clearing the way for other firms to innovate and grow. It chastened Microsoft and prevented it from stifling the development of the other tech giants. Had the litigation not happened, Microsoft might have bundled its own search engine with Windows and insisted that computer makers pre-install no other search engine. Instead, computer manufacturers like Dell felt free to make Google their default search engine. Likewise, Microsoft might have suppressed Amazon by insisting that the only online commerce site on the desktop would be Microsoft's.

3. The litigation also allowed Apple to expand from a niche player to a major force. The *Microsoft* order "required Microsoft to make various APIs[90] available to third-party developers, including Apple. [Apple then] launched a cross-platform version of iTunes that was compatible with the Windows operating system. As a result, a much larger group of users could finally use the iPod and iTunes."[91] Apple's iPod sales boomed, enhancing its capacity to develop the iPhone.[92] Apple's subsequent success, however, may not simply reflect exceptionally clever innovation. Like Microsoft, Apple may have used anticompetitive conduct to fortify its position. Indeed, joined by fifteen states and the District of Columbia, the DOJ has recently filed a complaint accusing Apple of acquiring monopoly power and preserving it through exclusionary conduct.[93] Specifically, the complaint alleges that Apple has monopolized two smartphone markets: the "performance" smartphone market – the market for higher-performance

---

[88] Andrew I. Gavil & Harry First, The Microsoft Antitrust Cases: Competition Policy for the Twenty-First Century (2014) ("Microsoft Cases").

[89] *See generally id.*

[90] APIs (Application Programming Interfaces) are software code that allows an application (app) to instruct an operating system to perform specific functions.

[91] Complaint at 19, United States et al. v. Apple Inc., No. 2:24-cv-04055 (D.N.J. Mar. 21, 2024) ("Apple Complaint").

[92] *Id.* at 20.

[93] *See generally* Apple Complaint.

4. smartphones – and the all smartphone market. The plaintiffs assert that Apple has maintained its power by preventing developers from offering software and hardware that would make it easier for iPhone users to switch to a competing phone like Samsung's Galaxy or Google's Pixel.

4. In broad outlines, the complaint against Apple parallels the complaint against Microsoft. Both complaints allege that a dominant firm in a dynamic, high-tech industry has acquired monopoly power and preserved it through exclusionary conduct directed at cross-platform products – products that would work on the defendant's platform and on competing platforms. On a range of important issues, however, the two cases differ. The plaintiffs may face greater challenges in *Apple* proving monopoly power, showing that the alleged exclusionary conduct violates prevailing law, and rebutting the defendant's asserted justifications. While the case against Apple appears to be solid, it is likely to be more difficult to win than the case against Microsoft.

5. This chapter illuminates the case against Apple by comparing it to the case against Microsoft. Part II summarizes the two sets of enforcement actions. Part III describes their broad similarities, and Part IV, the heart of this chapter, identifies their differences.

II. The Cases against Microsoft and Apple

6. This part summarizes the plaintiffs' contentions in the two enforcement actions.

1. Microsoft

7. What provoked the federal and state complaints against Microsoft is by now quite familiar. CEO Bill Gates, alarmed at the rise of the internet, the success of a competing internet browser, Netscape Navigator, and the cross-platform potential of Netscape, decided to force computer makers and others to substitute Microsoft's browser, Internet Explorer, for Netscape Navigator.

8. Gates did not fear direct competition. Windows, the world's leading operating system for personal computers that used Intel microchips, had no serious rivals. IBM once offered an operating system for Intel-compatible personal computers, but IBM's system attracted far fewer apps than Windows, and IBM withdrew from the market. Apple had developed an operating system for its line of Mac computers but those computers were so different from Intel-compatible computers that courts excluded them from the relevant market.

9. Microsoft's chief concern was middleware like Netscape. Although Netscape did not market an operating system, its browser would work

on any personal computer operating system. Moreover, apps like word processing and spreadsheets could be written directly for Netscape; they did not have to be written for a particular operating system like Windows. As a result, if app developers wrote enough apps for Netscape, Microsoft would lose much of its competitive advantage. Users could access most of the apps they could obtain on Windows by downloading Netscape – and then they could purchase a cheaper operating system. As Gates famously put it, Netscape would turn operating systems into a commodity.

10. Determined to prevent this erosion of its monopoly power, Microsoft adopted a range of exclusionary conduct. One component was particularly blatant: Microsoft tied Internet Explorer to Windows, first contractually, then technologically. Initially, Microsoft insisted that computer makers agree to preinstall Internet Explorer with Windows. Later, Microsoft integrated the two technologically so that removing key Explorer files would reduce the functionality of Windows, effectively preventing anyone from stripping Explorer out of Windows.

11. In addition, Microsoft adopted three other types of exclusionary conduct.[94] First, Microsoft distributed Internet Explorer without charge, making it impossible for Netscape Navigator to earn revenue.[95] Second, Microsoft prevented computer makers from altering the initial boot-up sequence of Windows or the Windows desktop, leaving Internet Explorer as the only browser visible to users. While users could download Netscape Navigator, Microsoft correctly calculated that they were highly unlikely to do so. Finally, Microsoft gave preferences to internet access providers like AOL and content providers like Disney in return for which they agreed to promote Internet Explorer exclusively or more favorably.

12. This multi-pronged assault largely destroyed Netscape Navigator, vaulted Internet Explorer into the lead position in the browser market, and deterred app developers from writing apps for Netscape. As a result, Netscape's potential to become a cross-platform alternative to Windows was extinguished. Instead, freed from serious challengers, Microsoft continued to charge high prices and earn extraordinary profits. While it did not charge the short-term profit-maximizing price, it apparently did charge the long-run profit-maximizing price, which enabled it to earn a breathtaking 90% margin on Windows.

2. Apple

13. The first significant antitrust attack on Apple was not the recent government complaint but a private action brought by Epic Games. Epic focused on Apple's restrictions in the aftermarket – the market for iPhone apps.

---

94 See MICROSOFT CASES, *supra* note 1, at 64.

95 Microsoft's aim, in a notorious phrase, was to "cut off [Netscape's] air supply."

Epic contended that Apple violated the Sherman Act by (i) preventing app developers from distributing their apps to iPhone users except through the App Store, and (ii) forbidding app developers from steering users to any payment method other than Apple's own payment system. These two restrictions allegedly allowed Apple to charge monopoly fees on app transactions and earn lavish profits.

14. While the government complaint repeats these allegations,[96] they did not fare well in the courts. Neither the district court nor the Ninth Circuit agreed with Epic Games that these exclusionary practices violated the Sherman Act.[97] In contrast, European regulators and Europe's new Digital Markets Act have taken a much more aggressive approach. In response, Apple has begun to back off its restrictions. Apple recently told Epic that it can (i) offer a new gaming app store on the iPhone, (ii) open the store to other game makers, and (iii) charge a 12% commission on app transactions, a reduction of more than half from Apple's traditional 30% commission.[98] These concessions suggest that Apple is likely to agree to similar changes in response to the government action.

15. The government action is much broader than Epic's lawsuit. The federal and state plaintiffs claim not only that Apple has monopolized the distribution of iPhone apps but that Apple has monopolized the smartphone itself. In essence, the plaintiffs allege that the iPhone has given Apple monopoly power and that Apple has maintained that power by squelching the development of technologies that would make it easier for users to switch to a competing smartphone.

16. The DOJ and its allies allege that there are two relevant markets – performance smartphones and all smartphones – and that Apple possesses monopoly power in both markets. "Performance smartphones" are more expensive smartphones that perform at a higher level than basic, entry-level smartphones. The complaint asserts that Apple has a 70% share of performance smartphones and a 65% share of all smartphones. Barriers to entry are very high. Not only must a new entrant invest billions of dollars and attain a large scale to compete, but attaining a large scale is almost impossible because iPhone users rarely switch to a new phone. "Nearly 90 percent of iPhone owners in the United States replace their iPhone with another iPhone."[99] This stickiness is due partly to the high quality of iPhones and partly because the costs of switching to a rival phone are so high-costs that Apple's conduct has allegedly inflated.

---

[96] *See, e.g.*, Apple Complaint at 3, 21.

[97] *See* Epic Games, Inc. v. Apple, Inc., 67 F.4th 946 (9th Cir. 2023). *See also* Kyle Bates & Tae Kim, *The US Court of Appeals for the Ninth Circuit affirms that a Big Tech's anti-steering policies violate California's Unfair Competition Law (Epic Games / Apple)*, e-Competitions Apr. 2023, art. no. 114089.

[98] *See* Tripp Mickle, *Pressured, Apple Yields on App Store Restrictions*, N.Y. Times, Aug. 17, 2024, at B1, B4.

[99] Apple Complaint at 67.

17. The plaintiffs contend that Apple's "extraordinary profits"[100] confirm its monopoly power. "Apple's per-unit smartphone profit margins are far more than its next most profitable rival."[101] In addition, "Apple extracts fees from developers – as much as 30 percent when users purchase apps or make in-app payments."[102] The district court in *Epic* found that on those fees, Apple's *total* profit margins – its margins after taking account of *all* costs, fixed as well as variable – have exceeded 70% for more than a decade.[103]

18. According to the government complaint, Apple has maintained those exceptional margins not through the kinds of classic exclusion that Microsoft used – exclusive dealing and tying – but by restricting the adoption of technologies – both hardware and software – that would reduce the costs of switching from an iPhone to a competing phone. These tactics allegedly harm consumers and developers over the long term by depriving them of the benefits that greater competition would produce – lower prices, superior quality, and waves of new products. In addition, the plaintiffs contend that this conduct harms consumers and developers *in the short run* by degrading the quality of Apple's existing products. "Apple repeatedly chooses to make its products worse for consumers to prevent competition from emerging."[104]

19. The complaint identifies five types of software and hardware that Apple has allegedly suppressed:

    – Superapps. A superapp is an app that can serve as a platform for other apps, called mini-programs. It is a type of cross-platform software because it can work on both iPhones and Android phones. As a result, if Apple allowed superapps, iPhone users could move their superapps to a Samsung phone and maintain much of their smartphone functionality. The government alleges that this ease of switching explains Apple's lower market share in Asia, where superapps are "enormously popular."[105] According to the complaint, Apple effectively prohibits superapps through a variety of restrictions, including blocking their mini-programs from accessing Apple's in-app payment system, the only payment system Apple has permitted.

    – Cloud-Streaming Gaming Apps. These apps allow users to play computing-intensive games without computationally powerful

---

100 *Id.* at 8.

101 *Id.* at 69; *see also id.* at 7 ("Apple charges as much as $1,599 for an iPhone and earns high margins on each one, more than double those of others in the industry.").

102 *Id.*

103 *See* John B. Kirkwood, *The New Limits on Antitrust*, Fla. St. U. L. Rev. (forthcoming 2025) (discussing the evidence).

104 Apple Complaint at 8.

105 Apple Complaint at 30.

smartphone hardware. The apps are middleware, which means that game developers can write one streaming app for both iPhones and Android phones. It also means that users do not need an iPhone to play the game; they can use a less advanced and cheaper phone. But Apple has allegedly imposed such onerous restrictions on cloud-streaming gaming apps that no developer has been willing to write one for the iPhone. Today, there are none available in the App Store.

- Third-Party Messaging Apps. These apps send messages to iPhone users from other phones, but Apple allegedly refuses to allow these apps to access the tools they need to send messages that are equivalent in quality to messages sent from another iPhone. This assertedly discourages consumers from purchasing a competing phone. According to the complaint, Apple also signals that competing phones are inferior by depreciating the quality of messages sent from an iPhone to another phone.

- Smartwatches. The Apple Watch is compatible only with an iPhone. Users who think that Apple's watch is best must therefore purchase an iPhone. Apple's unwillingness to create a cross-platform smartwatch inhibits switching to competing phones. Moreover, while third-party smartwatches can work with an iPhone, Apple allegedly employs contractual restrictions and technological tools to degrade their performance, reinforcing consumers' reluctance to leave the Apple ecosystem.

- Digital Wallets. The plaintiffs assert that the "Apple Wallet is only available on the iPhone. Thus, switching to a different smartphone requires leaving behind the familiarity of an everyday app, setting up a new digital wallet, and potentially losing access to certain credentials and personal data stored in Apple Wallet."[106] Moreover, "if third-party developers could create cross-platform wallets, users transitioning away from the iPhone could continue to use the same wallet, with the same cards, IDs, payment histories, peer-to-peer payment contacts, and other information, making it easier to switch smartphones."[107]

20. In these five ways, in short, Apple allegedly restricts switching between iPhones and competing phones. Apple does this through contractual provisions in its agreements with developers and by refusing to allow developers access to the APIs developers would need to create cross-platform products. According to the plaintiffs, the consequence is to reinforce Apple's monopoly power over smartphones.

---

106 *Id.* at 43–44.
107 *Id.* at 44.

21. Apple asserts that its conduct is justified by the safety, security, and privacy that it produces for iPhone users. The plaintiffs assert that this justification is a pretext because Apple could provide the same level of user protection without its restrictions or could improve user protection by making different choices. The plaintiffs note that Apple does not insist on controlling the distribution of apps for its Mac personal computers, yet they provide a safe and secure environment. Moreover, "super apps or alternative app stores could offer users and their families a more curated selection of apps that better protect user privacy and security. Indeed, Apple allows enterprise and public sector customers to offer more curated app stores on employee iPhones because it better protects privacy and security."[108]

III. Parallels

22. The case against Apple parallels the case against Microsoft in important ways. Both cases allege that a large firm has monopolized a high-tech market through exclusionary behavior. And in both cases, the exclusion involved raising rivals' costs rather than predatory pricing. To be sure, Microsoft distributed Internet Explorer free of charge, but this zero price did not fit the ordinary predatory pricing model. It was not intended to enable Microsoft to charge a monopoly price for Internet Explorer once Netscape was destroyed, but to destroy Netscape in order to allow Microsoft to continue to charge a monopoly price for Windows. Microsoft's goal was to preserve monopoly profits on Windows, not create monopoly profits on Internet Explorer.

23. In both cases, moreover, the target of the exclusion was not a direct competitor but software or hardware that could strengthen direct competition. Netscape was not an operating system. It was middleware that might, if enough apps were written for it, stimulate the creation of cheaper or better operating systems. That was hardly assured. The apps available on Netscape would have to be sufficiently comparable to those available on Windows that users would be willing to switch. And new operating systems would have to be superior to Windows in functionality or price. That was plausible, but far from certain.

24. It was likely enough, though, that the courts held that Microsoft's exclusionary conduct constituted monopolization. Microsoft's behavior had made a significant contribution to the preservation of its monopoly power. At bottom, the D.C. Circuit affirmed liability not because of how it assessed the probabilities but because it concluded that the defendant was not entitled to stamp out a nascent but unproven competitor.

---

108 *Id.* at 56.

25. The court resolved the uncertainties against Microsoft, almost certainly because the court concluded that Microsoft's conduct, with one exception, was unjustified. It was raw exclusion and did not deserve to be protected.

25. The plaintiffs' case against Apple follows a similar approach.[109] The superapps, digital wallets, and other software and hardware that Apple allegedly suppresses do not compete directly with Apple's smartphone. Moreover, it is hardly certain that these products, if allowed to develop, would significantly increase competition with the iPhone. For example, could a cross-platform Android smartwatch be created that works as well as the Apple Watch? And if so, would consumers be more likely to select an Android phone initially or switch from an iPhone to an Android phone? And if more Android phones were bought, would the increase in competition be enough to drive down the price or improve the quality of iPhones?

26. The plaintiffs contend that the answer to these questions is yes. Had Apple not impeded the development of the five technologies, or restricted their access to the iPhone, competition between the iPhone and competing phones would have increased significantly and consumers and developers would have benefited materially. In short, in both *Microsoft* and *Apple*, the target of the defendant's exclusion was not a mature rival but multiple sources of *potential* competition.

27. And the likelihood that this potential competition would turn into actual competition was allegedly sufficient to warrant section 2 liability.

28. Likewise, in both cases the plaintiffs base their proof of monopoly power not only on the standard structural evidence but also on direct evidence of monopoly pricing. In both cases, the plaintiffs assert that the defendant commanded a dominant share of a relevant market protected by high entry barriers. Moreover, the defendant allegedly exploited that position by charging monopoly prices and earning monopoly profits. Microsoft's profit margin on Windows exceeded 90% for many years. The plaintiffs contend that Apple's smartphone prices are substantially above those of its next closest rival and that Apple earns extraordinary profit margins, considerably more than its closest competitor. On its App Store commission charges, as I noted earlier, Apple's profit margin exceeded 70% for at least a decade.[110]

29. Finally, in both enforcement actions, the plaintiffs are comparable: a federal agency and multiple state attorneys general. These collaborations make it more likely that the enforcement action will succeed.

---

109 *See id.* at 20 ("[A]fter launching the iPhone, Apple began stifling the development of cross-platform technologies on the iPhone, just as Microsoft tried to stifle cross-platform technologies on Windows.").

110 *See supra* note 16.

30. In major respects, then, the *Microsoft* case and the *Apple* complaint follow parallel tracks. Both challenge the conduct of a dominant firm in a dynamic, high-technology sector. Both contend that the dominant firm possessed monopoly power in a market surrounded by high entry barriers. And both contend that the conduct at issue helped preserve that power by excluding cross-platform software that could create or strengthen actual competition.

IV. Differences

31. In other respects, the cases differ. The evidence of monopoly power is not quite as strong in *Apple*. And the alleged exclusionary conduct may be harder to challenge, because the law may be less favorable and the asserted justifications may be harder to rebut.

1. Monopoly Power

32. Both cases present plausible definitions of the relevant market. In *Microsoft*, the plaintiffs alleged, and the courts found, that the relevant product market was Intel-compatible PC operating systems. In Apple, the plaintiffs assert two product markets: performance smartphones and all smartphones. Both market definitions easily meet the legal test for market definition: reasonable substitutability. There are no reasonable substitutes for the relevant products. But *within* the relevant markets, Apple faces closer substitutes than Microsoft did. Apple competes with two major firms – Samsung and Google – that offer branded Android smartphones. In contrast, Microsoft competed with only one major firm – IBM, which never attracted enough apps to make it a comparable rival and eventually dropped out.[111]

33. In consequence, the market shares in the two cases differ significantly. Judge Jackson found that Microsoft's market share exceeded 90% for "the last decade."[112] In contrast, the complaint alleges that Apple's market share is 70% in the performance smartphone market and 65% in the all smartphone market. Although these shares are large enough to make Apple a dominant firm in both markets, they fall short of the near-exclusive position Microsoft held.

34. Because of Microsoft's overwhelming market share, the absence of close substitutes, and virtually impenetrable barriers to entry, Microsoft's ability

---

111 *See* Microsoft Cases, *supra* note 1, at 79 ("IBM had invested 'tens of millions of dollars' to attract [developers] to write software for its Intel-compatible operating system, OS/2, but could attract only 2500 applications 'at its peak' and eventually withdrew from the market for operating systems because it couldn't compete effectively with Microsoft.") (quoting Judge Jackson's findings of fact).

112 *Id.* at 78.

to charge a price above marginal cost – the most common measure of monopoly power[113] – was enormous. As I noted earlier, Microsoft's margin was more than 90% for many years, meaning that its price was approximately *ten* times its marginal cost.[114] Apple's profit margin is likely to be lower. The complaint alleges that Apple realizes an "extraordinary" profit margin on the iPhone, but the complaint gives no specific figures,[115] suggesting that Apple's margin is less spectacular than Microsoft's. In contrast, the complaint suggests, and the *Epic* decision confirms, that Apple has substantial monopoly power in the aftermarket – the market for the distribution of iPhone apps.[116]

2. Exclusionary Conduct

35. Microsoft suppressed potential competitors through classic forms of exclusion – exclusive dealing and tying. Apple uses contractual restrictions and refusals to deal to block or degrade technologies that would make it easier for consumers to switch from an iPhone to a competing phone. In the case of cloud-streaming gaming apps, for example, Apple's contracts with game developers restrict the features that a developer can offer on a gaming app. Those restrictions are allegedly so severe that app developers have concluded it is not worthwhile to develop a cloud-streaming gaming app for the iPhone. In the case of third-party messaging apps, Apple refuses to expose the APIs a developer would need to create an app that performs as well as Apple's messaging service. As a result, switching from an iPhone to a Samsung phone would diminish the quality of cross-platform messaging.

36. While Apple's exclusionary conduct may have been as effective as Microsoft's, the legal standards controlling them are different. Apple's contractual restraints are subject to the rule of reason, just like Microsoft's exclusive dealing, but Apple's refusals to deal are governed by *Trinko*,[117] an opinion that greatly reduced successful attacks on unilateral refusals to deal. In *Trinko*, Justice Scalia emphasized that Verizon's refusals to deal had not been preceded by a period of voluntary cooperation.

---

113 *See* IIB Phillip E. Areeda, Herbert Hovenkamp & John L. Solow, Antitrust Law ¶ 502 (5th ed. 2021) ("[T]he degree of a monopolist's market power is commonly defined by the excess of its profit-maximizing price above its marginal cost.").

114 This margin may have measured the excess of Microsoft's price over its average variable cost rather than over its marginal cost. But in the software industry, average variable cost and marginal cost are low and nearly identical. *See* John B. Kirkwood, *Market Power and Antitrust Enforcement*, 98 B.U. L. Rev. 1169, 1174–75 (2018).

115 *See supra* notes 13–14.

116 For a full discussion of Apple's power in the aftermarket, *see* Kirkwood, *supra* note 16.

117 Verizon Commc'ns Inc. v. Law Offs. of Curtis V. Trinko, LLP, 540 U.S. 398 (2004). *See* Veronica Kayne, William J. Kolasky, Doug Melamed, Thomas Mueller, Ali Stoeppelwerth, Leon B. Greenfield, Robert B. Bell & James W. Lowe, *The US Supreme Court limits the antitrust liability in the telecommunications sector, affecting a competitor's access to a rival's network (*Verizon / Trinko*)*, e-Competitions Jan. 2004, art. no. 120421.

That has become a legal test. It is now frequently impossible to challenge a refusal to deal unless the defendant had previously cooperated with the plaintiff. Because Apple has never cooperated with developers by exposing the APIs they need, it is likely to be difficult to convince a court to hold that Apple's refusals to deal are illegal, no matter how anticompetitive they are.

37. The cases also diverge in the strength of the defendant's justifications. The courts readily dismissed Microsoft's attempts to advance procompetitive explanations for its practices. With respect to some conduct, Microsoft offered no procompetitive rationale at all. In other instances, the courts regarded Microsoft's justifications as trivial or frivolous. In only one instance did the D.C. Circuit rule that Microsoft's exclusionary conduct was warranted by the benefits it provided consumers.

38. In contrast, Apple advances more weighty justifications. Apple maintains that its restrictions – its contractual restraints and refusals to expose APIs – are necessary to protect the safety, security, and privacy of its phones. Absent those restrictions, Apple contends, users would experience more security breaches, their privacy would be violated more often, and their phones would malfunction more frequently. The potential adverse consequences for over a billion iPhone users would be considerable.

39. The DOJ and its co-plaintiffs assert that Apple's arguments do "not justify Apple's monopolistic and anticompetitive conduct"[118] because they are pretextual. In support, the plaintiffs make two points. First, Apple does not impose comparable restrictions on apps for its Mac computers. Instead, it "gives developers the freedom to distribute software directly to consumers on Mac without going through an Apple-controlled app store and without paying Apple app store fees. This still provides a safe and secure experience for Mac users."[119] Second, "many alternative technologies that Apple's conduct suppresses would enhance user security and privacy."[120] The plaintiffs will have to establish these points in the face of a withering defense from Apple. In *Epic Games*, Apple retained multiple security experts to show that there were, in fact, no less restrictive alternatives to its restraints.

V. Conclusion

40. *Microsoft* was an iconic government victory. The DOJ and multiple states confronted one of the largest firms in the world, in an evolving high-tech industry, and demonstrated that it had monopoly power, that its

---

118 Apple Complaint at 55.
119 *Id.* at 55–56.
120 *Id.* at 56.

exclusionary conduct helped cement that power, and that its conduct was, with one exception, bereft of procompetitive justification. This remarkable victory, chronicled so comprehensively and incisively by First and Gavil, continues to be a model of antitrust enforcement.

41. Federal and state enforcers have followed up this achievement with another monopolization case against a tech giant. In this instance, the defendant is Apple, even bigger and more valuable than Microsoft was in the 1990s, a font of innovation, and the creator of one of the most popular products in the world, the iPhone. In broad outline, moreover, the theory of the case is identical: Apple possesses monopoly power, it has deployed exclusionary conduct to maintain that power, and its conduct lacks procompetitive justification.

42. At a more detailed level, however, the case against Apple is more challenging. First, it may be harder to prove that Apple has monopoly power. Apple faces closer substitutes than Microsoft did, Apple's market shares are smaller, and Apple's profit margins, while high, are lower than Microsoft's enormous margin. Second, one of the principal exclusionary tactics Apple has used is a refusal to expose the APIs developers need to produce products that may undermine Apple's power. Unilateral refusals to deal, however, have rarely been held illegal since *Trinko*. Third, unlike Microsoft, Apple has raised substantial procompetitive justifications for its conduct, claiming that its restrictions are necessary to protect the safety, security, and privacy of iPhone users. Given the adverse consequences for numerous iPhone users if Apple is correct, courts are likely to examine Apple's claims carefully.

43. Despite these challenges, there is good reason to believe that the plaintiffs will prevail in *Apple*. But whatever the ultimate outcome, we are all indebted to Harry First and Andy Gavil for their pathbreaking and precise analysis of *Microsoft*. They have made it much easier to understand and appraise *Apple*.

What Have We Learned from the Scholarship Inspired by the Microsoft Saga?

JAMIE HA[*]
Econic Partners

D. DANIEL SOKOL[**]
USC Gould School of Law and Marshall School of Business

Abstract

This chapter examines the academic literature inspired by the Microsoft trial. It begins with a background of the case. Then, it differentiates across a number of different themes of the Microsoft case with a focus largely on the literature from peer-reviewed journals in economics, business, and law (specifically the Antitrust Law Journal). Then, we examine particular issues that are inspired by the case.

---

[*] Econic Partners.

[**] Carolyn Craig Franklin Chair in Law, and Professor of Law and Business at the Gould School of Law and Marshall School of Business (marketing department) at USC.

I. Background

1. This chapter examines the academic literature inspired by the Microsoft trial. It begins with a background of the case. Then, it differentiates across a number of different themes of the *Microsoft* case with a focus largely on the literature from peer-reviewed journals in economics, business, and law (specifically the *Antitrust Law Journal*). Then, we examine particular issues that are inspired by the case.

2. By focusing on peer-reviewed work, this chapter is able to address work that often has strong opinions but has been vetted from overclaiming and lack of substantiation that is endemic in traditional student-edited law reviews. Of course, there are also books that explore the Microsoft saga, most notably Lopatka and Page (2007)[1] and First and Gavil (2014).[2] These books are comprehensive accounts. Our chapter takes a different approach – one that synthesizes the existing literature to distill the salient features in the academic literature and then concludes with thoughts regarding today's tech-related antitrust cases.

3. In 1981, Microsoft released MS-DOS, which became the dominant operating system (OS) for Intel-compatible PCs when IBM pre-installed it on its machines. Microsoft expanded its software lineup by launching Internet Explorer (IE) in 1995 and bundling it with Windows 95 and 98. The Department of Justice (DOJ) filed an antitrust lawsuit, claiming this bundling violated the Sherman Act by restraining competition, particularly targeting Netscape Navigator, the dominant browser at the time. By 1999, Microsoft held 76% of the browser market, despite Netscape initially having 90%. Initially found guilty, the court ordered Microsoft to be split into two entities (operating systems and software applications) with conduct restrictions. However, the case concluded on appeal with Microsoft being required to share its application programming interface (API) with third parties and barred from exclusive deals, avoiding the breakup.

4. The case highlighted four key findings of Microsoft's antitrust violations:
   - Microsoft held market power in PC operating systems.
   - An "applications barrier to entry" reinforced this power.
   - Emerging middleware technologies threatened this barrier.
   - Microsoft engaged in exclusionary practices to maintain its dominance by targeting middleware providers.

---

[1] WILLIAM H. PAGE & JOHN E. LOPATKA, THE MICROSOFT CASE: ANTITRUST, HIGH TECHNOLOGY, AND CONSUMER WELFARE (2007).

[2] ANDREW I. GAVIL & HARRY FIRST, THE MICROSOFT ANTITRUST CASES: COMPETITION POLICY FOR THE TWENTY-FIRST CENTURY (2014).

5. Plaintiffs argued that Microsoft maintained its OS monopoly by limiting browser distribution opportunities for rivals like Netscape. The D.C. Circuit found that Microsoft's agreements with internet access providers (IAPs) helped ensure that most subscribers were offered IE as the default or only browser, preventing Netscape from gaining enough users to challenge Microsoft's dominance.

6. According to the court, Microsoft employed several anticompetitive tactics:
   – Requiring original equipment manufacturers (OEMs) to place IE on desktops, excluding other browsers.
   – Offering IAPs a customized IE Access Kit contingent on using IE.
   – Making deals with IAPs to favor IE in exchange for support.
   – Preventing easy uninstallation of IE from Windows Control Panel.
   – Featuring IAPs on the Windows desktop if they exclusively used IE.

7. These practices were seen as anticompetitive, as they incentivized OEMs and IAPs to prioritize IE, limiting Netscape's distribution and stifling competition.

8. The court of appeals also noted five specific activities violating section 2 of the Sherman Act:
   – Windows license restrictions preventing OEMs from distributing browsers other than IE.
   – Integrating IE into Windows to impair rival browser distribution.
   – Exclusive agreements with 14 of the top 15 IAPs to limit rival browsers.
   – Exclusive deals with independent software vendors (ISVs) and Apple affecting browser "usage share."
   – Anticompetitive actions related to Java, including deceptive practices and pressuring Intel to limit cross-platform Java support.

9. While the D.C. Circuit did not address Microsoft's refusal to license intellectual property to competitors, this issue was central in the European Commission's case against Microsoft, which focused on Windows Media Player bundling and withholding technical information on operating system communication.

10. A Technical Committee was established to monitor Microsoft's compliance with the final judgments, evaluate complaints, and propose remedies. This committee played a vital role in helping the DOJ and settling states oversee Microsoft's adherence to legal requirements, especially to prevent Microsoft from foreclosing competitive browsers and other middleware that could threaten its dominance in the OS market.

What Have We Learned from the Scholarship Inspired by the Microsoft Saga?

1. Overview of the Case

A. *Heiner (2012)*

11. Heiner[3] examines the effects of antitrust regulation on Microsoft, particularly whether the imposed remedies fostered competition in the software industry. The primary goal of the regulation was to prevent Microsoft from leveraging its dominance in the PC operating system market to gain advantages in other software areas, focusing on reducing the "applications barrier to entry" that limited competition with Windows. The remedies aimed to promote software development, ensure non-Microsoft programs could run on Windows, enhance interoperability, and prevent Microsoft from forming exclusive deals with manufacturers or developers. Microsoft was also required to disclose APIs and make technical information available to developers, enabling non-Microsoft middleware to run on Windows. This led to the growth of alternative software, including browsers like Chrome and Firefox. Additionally, the rise of the Internet and the proliferation of non-Windows devices, such as smartphones and tablets, transformed the market by allowing applications to run on various platforms, reducing dependency on Windows and challenging Microsoft's dominance. He argues that these shifts, combined with Microsoft's response to the remedies, enabled competitors like Google, Apple, and Amazon to build platforms that leveraged the internet as a primary platform, forcing Microsoft to adapt and embrace interoperability. Heiner concludes that the combined effect of legal remedies and market changes contributed to increased competition and innovation, eroding the application barrier that once protected Microsoft's monopoly and opening the software industry to more players.

B. *Hesse (2009)*

12. Hesse[4] outlines the *Microsoft* case, first highlighting the key factors that fueled public interest: it involved a widely used product, challenged Microsoft's dominance after smaller DOJ actions, and featured a complex battle between the government and a powerful corporation. The DOJ's ability to navigate the tech market and enforce antitrust laws despite Microsoft's resistance further added to the case's importance. Hesse examines the lessons from the case, particularly regarding section 2 antitrust remedies and the challenges in creating effective solutions for monopolistic behavior. The remedies aimed not only to stop Microsoft's illegal

---

[3] David A. Heiner, Microsoft: *A Remedial Success?*, 78 ANTITRUST L.J. 329 (2012), https://www.jstor.org/stable/43486983.

[4] Renata B. Hesse, *Section 2 Remedies and U.S. v. Microsoft: What Is to Be Learned?*, 75 ANTITRUST L.J. 847 (2009), https://www.jstor.org/stable/27897602.

conduct but also to address future competition threats. Key provisions included the disclosure of APIs under section III.D and the licensing of communication protocols under section III.E. While the API disclosures were successful due to Microsoft's experience in API documentation and its incentive to promote Windows, the section III.E licensing requirements were more challenging, as they required Microsoft to tackle the complex and unfamiliar task of licensing its server-client communication protocols, something it had no prior incentive to do. Hesse explains that section III.E stood out because it imposed an affirmative obligation that went beyond typical remedies, which usually require ceasing harmful activities rather than proactive measures like technology licensing. Despite its ambition, section III.E faced ongoing implementation challenges, raising concerns that it might not fully achieve its goals. Hesse concludes that creating conduct remedies for monopolistic practices is inherently challenging, as it requires balancing current and future competition concerns within the limits of antitrust enforcement.

C. *Crandall and Jackson (2011)*

13. Crandall and Jackson[5] examine three antitrust cases involving IBM, AT&T, and Microsoft in high-tech markets driven by innovation and technological change. They point out that major changes in the competitive landscape were driven more by technological innovation than by government antitrust actions in all three cases. They explain that this is partly because the government failed to predict how technology would evolve and thus could not create effective remedies for the rapidly changing high-tech industry. While the government sought divestitures to address competition concerns in these cases, only AT&T underwent this process, which Crandall and Jackson argue was unnecessary and costly. Regarding the *Microsoft* case, Crandall and Jackson highlight that consumers have actually benefited from Apple and Microsoft's increased bundling of software, appliances, and operating systems and argue that reducing Microsoft's incentives to innovate in its operating systems was inefficient. They further explain that instead of antitrust actions, Microsoft's dominance in desktop operating systems was challenged by three emerging technologies: smartphone operating systems, cloud computing, and virtual appliances. Conversely, they also acknowledge that mandated interconnection in both the *Microsoft* and *AT&T* cases had pro-competitive effects. Crandall and Jackson conclude by criticizing the government's static market definition that prioritized protecting competitors over benefiting consumers.

---

5   Robert W. Crandall & Charles L. Jackson, *Antitrust in High-Tech Industries*, 38 REV. INDUS. ORG. 319 (2011), https://doi.org/10.1007/s11151-011-9298-4.

D. *Fisher (2000)*

14. Fisher[6] compares the *IBM* and *Microsoft* cases, noting significant differences in their use of bundling and monopoly leveraging. He argues that IBM did not have monopoly power to protect, and its bundling actions were driven by consumer demand to ensure that computers functioned properly. As a result, despite IBM's bundling, an independent software industry emerged, demonstrating that competition was still possible. Fisher argues that if consumers had rejected IBM's bundle, its actions would have made market entry easier rather than creating higher barriers; thus, IBM's behavior was viewed as competitive, not monopolistic, since it lacked the power to prevent market entry. In contrast, Microsoft held a dominant position in operating systems (Windows) and used bundling to protect its monopoly. Microsoft bundled Internet Explorer (IE) with Windows at no extra cost, deliberately suppressing competition from Netscape by preventing its browser from becoming an alternative platform. Fisher highlights that Microsoft also targeted Java, a potential threat to its operating system monopoly, by creating a version of Java tied specifically to Windows, limiting its cross-platform functionality. The court found Microsoft's practices anticompetitive because they were not driven by profit-maximizing motives alone but were instead aimed at preserving its monopoly power. Therefore, Fisher concludes that Microsoft's actions were not about competing on the merits of its product but about protecting its dominant market position.

E. *John, Weiss, and Dutta (1999)*

15. John, Weiss, and Dutta[7] examine the distinct characteristics of technology-intensive (TI) markets and provide a framework for guiding marketing decisions. They break down the marketing process into four stages – served-market definition, product development, attracting customers, and retaining customers – to highlight the distinct decision-making challenges firms face in TI markets. They define TI markets as markets with products relying heavily on scientific and technical know-how, with durable products that drive repeat purchases through improvements rather than replacements. This makes managing customer expectations crucial, and they define three key customer expectations: the pace of improvements, the significance of improvements, and uncertainty about future advancements. They provide the following advice accordingly:
    – Marketers should balance the value of existing products with potential future offerings when guiding upgrade decisions.

---

6   Franklin M. Fisher, *The IBM and Microsoft Cases: What's the Difference?*, 90 AM. ECON. REV. 180 (2000). https://doi.org/10.1257/aer.90.2.180.

7   George John, Allen M. Weiss & Shantanu Dutta, *Marketing in Technology-Intensive Markets: Toward a Conceptual Framework*, 63 J. MKTG. 78 (1999), https://doi.org/10.2307/1252103.

- While significant improvements drive purchases, their anticipation can delay buying, making it essential to tailor marketing around expected advancements.
- Customer decisions are also heavily influenced by uncertainty as they navigate ongoing technological changes, and marketing strategies must account for these uncertainties to support migration effectively.

16. They also present a continuum for monetizing know-how, from selling raw knowledge to fully developed products, and discuss transfer rights (full ownership or restricted licenses) based on market uncertainty. Migration strategies – such as trade-ins or technical support – help manage transitions between product generations, retaining customers and reducing fears of obsolescence. In conclusion, the framework aims to help firms navigate the complexities of TI markets and encourages further empirical research.

F. *Fox (2002)*

17. Fox[8] outlines the evolution of U.S. antitrust law and contrasts it with global frameworks, particularly those of the European Union (EU), by exploring three key antitrust approaches: limiting output, protecting market dynamics, and shielding smaller firms. In the U.S., antitrust law mainly targets consumer harm through output or price changes, treating exclusionary actions as a form of exploitation. Conversely, the EU and other jurisdictions consider exclusionary practices anticompetitive even if prices are not directly impacted, as such practices distort market structures and hinder innovation. Some countries also focus on protecting smaller firms from larger competitors, though this can sometimes be seen as protectionist. Fox explains that U.S. antitrust shifted in the 1980s under the Chicago School of Economics, favoring larger firms and emphasizing measurable consumer harm like reduced output or higher prices. This shift introduced flexibility in applying output limitation standards, enabling action against exclusionary conduct even without directly reducing output. However, exclusionary practices without direct consumer harm became less likely to be prosecuted. Fox highlights this shift through Timothy Muris's perspective, which supports focusing on proven consumer harm, aligning with the Chicago School's emphasis on output and consumer welfare. To illustrate this debate, Fox examines Microsoft's bundling of its browser with Windows, which was ruled illegal in both the U.S. and EU, though with different reasoning. U.S. courts focused more on consumer harm, while the EU condemned Microsoft for limiting market openness, even without immediate price or output effects, raising broader questions about whether exclusionary

---

[8] Eleanor M. Fox, *What Is Harm to Competition? Exclusionary Practices and Anticompetitive Effect*, 70 ANTITRUST L.J. 371 (2002), https://www.jstor.org/stable/40843559.

conduct alone justifies antitrust violations. Fox also references the *GE/Honeywell* merger case to illustrate the divergence between U.S. and EU approaches. U.S. regulators approved the merger, focusing on short-term consumer benefits like lower prices through bundling, while the EU blocked it, citing concerns about long-term competition and increased dominance. This case shows how U.S. regulators prioritize consumer welfare and efficiency, while the EU seeks to preserve competitive market structures and prevent dominance. In conclusion, Fox argues that antitrust approaches vary globally, shaped by cultural and economic factors. While countries may define "harm to competition" differently, Fox suggests this diversity enriches global antitrust discussions, leading to more nuanced and effective competition policies.

G. Baker (2015)

18. Baker[9] argues that contemporary antitrust conservatives, influenced by Bork's ideas – where antitrust should target price-fixing, monopoly-creating mergers, and limited exclusionary conduct, while downplaying small mergers, vertical agreements, and tying arrangements – continue to use "error cost" analysis to justify minimal antitrust intervention. He challenges this approach, suggesting it exaggerates over-enforcement risks, downplays under-enforcement risks, and overestimates costs while underestimating benefits, due to flawed assumptions about markets and legal systems. Baker critiques five erroneous assumptions on markets by conservatives:

    – Conservatives argue markets self-correct through entry, but entry is not always easy or timely, as many firms maintain dominance by creating entry barriers.

    – They claim oligopolies self-correct without new competitors entering, but research shows oligopolies often raise prices and cartels can be long-lasting.

    – Monopolies allegedly encourage innovation, but competition often drives more innovation by pushing firms to improve.

    – Bork's "single monopoly profit" theory argues monopolists extract all possible profits, so further exclusionary conduct will not harm competition, but real-world scenarios show exclusionary conduct can further harm competition.

    – Business practices common in competitive markets, like tying or exclusive dealing, can harm competition when used by powerful firms, undermining strict antitrust enforcement.

---

9   Jonathan B. Baker, *Taking the Error Out of "Error Cost" Analysis: What is Wrong with Antitrust's Right*, 80 ANTITRUST L.J. 1 (2015), https://www.jstor.org/stable/26411520.

19. Moreover, Baker critiques conservatives' four flawed assumptions about antitrust institutions:
    - Conservatives claim erroneous rulings last longer than monopolies or cartels, but legal precedents can be corrected within similar timeframes.
    - They argue competitors manipulate institutions, leading to false positives, but courts can identify self-interested complaints, and rivals can help detect anticompetitive behavior.
    - Conservatives claim courts struggle to assess exclusionary conduct, but courts reliably distinguish between harmful and beneficial practices, as seen in price-fixing or market division cases.
    - Conservatives argue private lawsuits, like class actions, are costly and frivolous, but they are essential for deterring anticompetitive behavior and compensating victims. Recent Supreme Court decisions limiting private lawsuits risk weakening enforcement.

20. Baker concludes that while antitrust law has largely adopted Chicago School ideas, conservatives still push for further reforms using "error cost" analysis that exaggerates false positives and downplays enforcement benefits. These biases risk weakening antitrust rules, reducing deterrence, and undermining the system's effectiveness, making strong enforcement essential for maintaining competition and societal benefits.

H. *Page (2009)*

21. Page[10] examines the use of mandatory contracting remedies in antitrust cases, particularly focusing on the *Microsoft* antitrust cases in the U.S. and Europe, comparing the effectiveness of remedies such as forced disclosure of interoperability information and unbundling software. Section 2 of the Sherman Act violations often involve dominant firms refusing to deal with rivals to weaken competition, and while courts may order firms to offer contracts, mandatory contracting is rare due to the challenges of dictating business terms. In both the U.S. and European *Microsoft* cases, mandatory contracting remedies aimed to prevent Microsoft from using its dominance to harm competition. The remedies had some success, like improving consumer options, but also faced issues, such as creating unwanted products. For example, Microsoft was ordered to allow trading partners more freedom to distribute rival software like Sun's Java and media players without facing penalties. These remedies promoted competition by preventing Microsoft from penalizing OEMs, although financial factors may have influenced the

---

10 William H. Page, *Mandatory Contracting Remedies in the American and European* Microsoft *Cases*, 75 ANTITRUST L.J. 787 (2009), https://www.jstor.org/stable/27897600.

lack of preinstallation of other programs like Mozilla's Firefox. The U.S. courts also found that Microsoft had violated antitrust laws by restricting OEMs from hiding Internet Explorer (IE), which discouraged the installation of competing browsers. While Microsoft was required to revise licenses and allow OEMs to hide access to certain products, the courts did not force Microsoft to remove actual code. In Europe, Microsoft was required to release a version of Windows without Windows Media Player (WMP), though this version failed in the market due to a lack of demand. These outcomes suggest that mandatory remedies reducing product functionality are ineffective if consumers do not demand unbundled versions. Additionally, Microsoft was required to share APIs and license communication protocols to allow rivals' servers to interoperate with Windows, but this remedy proved costly and attracted few users. The European case raised concerns about competitors cloning Microsoft's technology, though courts found these risks justified. Overall, the effectiveness of these mandatory dealings was limited, and Page concludes that courts should be cautious in imposing such remedies without clear evidence of need, and the failure of more proactive measures shows that courts and plaintiffs may not be able to predict or foster competition better than the market itself.

I. *Packalen (2010)*

22. Packalen[11] examines how cooperation between monopolists in complementary markets affects consumer welfare, focusing on whether such cooperation can reduce competition. His model demonstrates that while cooperation can eliminate double marginalization, leading to lower prices, it can also reduce incentives for new firms to enter the market, ultimately harming competition and consumer welfare. He emphasizes that cooperation between complementary monopolists may block entry, even though it resolves pricing inefficiencies. Packalen explores scenarios where incumbents use price commitments or lower entry costs to influence new competitors, finding that non-cooperative behavior between monopolists can sometimes produce better outcomes for consumers than cooperative behavior. He challenges traditional views like Cournot's double-monopoly result, concluding that the benefits of cooperation depend on its effects on both entry deterrence and pricing efficiency. The paper contrasts cooperative and non-cooperative pricing models, showing that in cases of uncertain entry, non-cooperative strategies can yield higher consumer surplus. Packalen references real-world examples, like Intel's royalty-free intellectual property sharing, as ways firms induce entry in complementary markets to reduce reliance on dominant competitors. He highlights that studying complementary markets is crucial, especially in

---

11   Mikko Packalen, *Complements and Potential Competition*, 28 INT'L J. INDUS. ORG. 244 (2010), https://doi.org/10.1016/j.ijindorg.2009.08.005.

industries like computing, where complementary monopolies are common. The policy takeaway is that the impact of cooperation on entry inducement must be considered before allowing cooperation between complementary monopolists, with partial cooperation agreements, such as patent pools with independent licensing, offering significant competitive advantages.

J. Carrier (2011)

23. Carrier[12] proposes applying tort law principles, specifically factual and legal causation, to improve how courts address causation in monopolization and antitrust injury cases, which are often inconsistently handled. He highlights the challenge of determining what would have happened if a monopolist had not engaged in anticompetitive conduct, particularly in fast-moving markets like technology. For instance, in the *Microsoft* case, the court required only a reasonable connection between Microsoft's actions and its monopoly power, while in *Rambus*, the court demanded stricter proof that the standard-setting organization (JEDEC) would have chosen alternative technology if Rambus had disclosed its patents. Carrier argues that this higher threshold is unrealistic and limits enforcement, favoring the "reasonable connection" test from *Microsoft* over the restrictive "necessary predicate" standard from the Sixth Circuit, which demands proving the defendant's conduct was the sole cause of the injury. He suggests using tort law's more structured approach to factual causation (whether the harm would have occurred "but for" the defendant's actions) and legal causation (whether the harm falls within the risks the law seeks to prevent) to better assess antitrust causation. He suggests that this would be especially useful in high-technology markets, where innovation moves quickly and counterfactual predictions are difficult. He further suggests that instead of requiring certainty, courts should focus on whether there is a reasonable link between the conduct and the harm. Carrier emphasizes the importance of applying these causation principles to government cases and incorporating them into the burden-shifting process in antitrust law, ensuring a thorough examination of causation without imposing unreasonably high standards.

K. Baker (2016a)

24. Baker[13] explores how dominant firms use the "appropriability defense" to justify exclusionary practices, claiming that such actions are necessary to protect their R&D investments and encourage innovation. He

---

12 Michael A. Carrier, *A Tort-Based Causation Framework for Antitrust Analysis*, 77 ANTITRUST L.J. 991 (2011), https://www.jstor.org/stable/23075640.

13 Jonathan B. Baker, *Evaluating Appropriability Defenses for the Exclusionary Conduct of Dominant Firms in Innovative Industries*, 80 ANTITRUST L.J. 431 (2016), https://www.jstor.org/stable/26411527.

proposes a framework to evaluate whether this defense holds up, focusing on whether dominant firms would increase their own R&D efforts in response to rival innovation. By examining cases like *Microsoft*, *IBM*, and *Xerox*, Baker shows that limiting exclusionary conduct could boost overall industry innovation by encouraging both rivals and the dominant firm to invest more in R&D. In Microsoft's case, exclusionary behavior against Netscape and Java was meant to preserve its dominance in operating systems, but evidence suggested Microsoft would have continued innovating even if its competitors advanced. This challenges Microsoft's appropriability defense. Similarly, in IBM's case, courts accepted some of IBM's actions as legitimate, but Baker questions whether IBM would have increased its innovation efforts had its rivals been allowed to compete more freely in the peripherals market. The *Xerox* case demonstrates that antitrust enforcement, specifically the Federal Trade Commission's (FTC) intervention requiring Xerox to license its patents, spurred innovation from both Xerox and its competitors, undermining Xerox's claim that patent accumulation was needed to protect its R&D efforts. The article also highlights that a dominant firm is more likely to view rival R&D as a strategic complement if (i) the firm anticipates maintaining a high market share even if both it and its rivals innovate, and (ii) the firm expects to lose significant business if rivals innovate while it does not. These factors suggest that antitrust enforcement can encourage both dominant firms and their competitors to innovate more, thus challenging the validity of the appropriability defense. Baker argues that competition is overall a stronger driver of innovation than exclusionary practices, urging closer scrutiny of appropriability defenses and advocating for a shift in antitrust enforcement to promote competitive innovation.

L. *Fumagalli and Motta (2020)*

25. Fumagalli and Motta[14] extend Carlton and Waldman's (2002)[15] analysis of exclusionary tying by examining how monopolistic firms can use tying to deter entry into complementary markets, even when dominance in the primary market cannot be maintained. They argue that by tying complementary products, the incumbent sacrifices short-term profits but successfully excludes more efficient rivals from the complementary market, putting the incumbent in a strong position to capture part of the rivals' efficiency gains when they enter the primary market. They find that tying is a more effective exclusionary strategy than pure bundling, particularly when a significant proportion of consumers "single-home" (purchase only

---

14 Chiara Fumagalli & Massimo Motta, *Tying in Evolving Industries, When Future Entry Cannot Be Deterred*, 73 INT'L J. INDUS. ORG. 102567 (2020), https://doi.org/10.1016/j.ijindorg.2019.102567.

15 Dennis W. Carlton & Michael Waldman, *The Strategic Use of Tying to Preserve and Create Market Power in Evolving Industries*, 33 RAND J. ECON. 194 (2002), https://www.jstor.org/stable/3087430.

the incumbent's products). Exclusion becomes more likely in markets with economies of scale or network effects in the complementary market, reinforcing the anticompetitive impact of tying. They also explain that tying can have anticompetitive effects as markets evolve over time. When an incumbent monopolist in the primary market faces competition in the secondary (complementary) market, it generally has no incentive to exclude rivals unless entry into the secondary market could lead to future competition in the primary market. In such cases, tying acts as a defensive strategy to protect market power. Even when competition in the primary market is inevitable, tying deters entry into the secondary market by limiting rivals' sales and preventing them from covering entry costs, allowing the incumbent to maintain control over both markets. Tying, compared to bundling, is more flexible and profitable for excluding competitors because it lets the incumbent exploit economies of scale while keeping pricing control. Exclusion becomes more severe when fewer consumers "multi-home" or use multiple secondary products, and network externalities can further strengthen the exclusionary effects of tying. The authors use the *Genzyme* case, where tying reduced competition in homecare services and affected the drug market, to illustrate how tying can impact broader markets. Fumagalli and Motta suggest that tying can remain a powerful tool for incumbents even when future entry into the primary market is inevitable, allowing the incumbent to capture efficiency rents from future competitors. They also propose further exploration into how a monopolist's incentives to invest in product quality or production efficiency might change, focusing on dominating either the primary or complementary market depending on the relative efficiency of rivals. This dynamic demonstrates that tying is a robust strategy for exclusion in markets shaped by network effects, economies of scale, and evolving competition.

M. *Carlton and Waldman (2002)*

26. Carlton and Waldman[16] analyze how firms use tying to maintain or extend their monopoly power, focusing on two strategic uses: (i) preventing competition by deterring entry into both primary and complementary markets, and (ii) transferring monopoly power to newly emerging markets, especially in industries undergoing rapid technological change. They argue that tying can protect monopolists by making it harder for new competitors to enter either market, contrasting previous work on price discrimination or foreclosure. They demonstrate that by tying products, monopolists can reduce rivals' profits in complementary markets, making it more difficult for them to enter the primary market. Tying can also allow monopolists to transfer their dominance from one market to another as industries evolve.

---

16 *Id.*

27. In the *U.S. v. Microsoft* case, Carlton and Waldman illustrate how Microsoft bundled Internet Explorer with Windows to prevent competition in both the browser and operating system markets. By doing so, Microsoft made it difficult for Netscape and Java to gain market share and stifled the emergence of new competitors that could challenge its dominance in operating systems. They argue that Microsoft used tying not only to expand into the browser market but also to protect its monopoly in operating systems by preventing these products from becoming credible threats. Furthermore, they highlight three key insights from the analysis: first, tying can take the form of a "virtual tie" through pricing, as seen in Microsoft's low pricing for Internet Explorer; second, tying is especially effective in markets with network externalities, such as software; third, firms can employ tying flexibly, adjusting strategies without committing long-term. This flexibility makes tying a potent tool for deterring entry across multiple markets without requiring a firm to lock in its approach. While tying can enhance a monopolist's control over markets, Carlton and Waldman note that antitrust enforcement against this practice is challenging. Courts must balance the potential efficiencies gained from tying (such as product improvements) against the potential harm caused by reduced competition. In some cases, tying could even improve social welfare if it leads to greater innovation by monopolists. Carlton and Waldman suggest further research into tying's impact on rapidly changing industries, including its relevance in mergers between monopolists and complementary good producers. They highlight that tying is a powerful tool for dominant firms to preserve market power and deter competition, raising critical issues for antitrust policy.

2. The Role of Academic Economists

A. *Salinger (2011)*

28. Salinger[17] critiques Bruce Owen and Christopher Yoo's argument that antitrust laws alone can address content and distribution issues, negating the need for net neutrality rules. While he agrees that this does not justify a blanket ban on internet service providers (ISPs) integrating into content, he argues that the case for such a ban is more complex than it appears. Using the cable television industry as an example, he contrasts its content-delivery integration issues with those of Microsoft and Intel, where companies selling complementary products are constrained by the threat of competition. He suggests that the acquisition of a dominant content network by a large cable operator could warrant antitrust intervention, but this does not justify net neutrality's broad prohibition on ISP-content integration.

---

17 Michael Salinger, *Discussion of Papers by Bruce Owen and Christopher Yoo*, 38 REV. INDUS. ORG. 435 (2011), https://www.jstor.org/stable/23884988.

29. Salinger provides two reasons for caution: First, the tradeoff between the benefits and costs of vertical integration might differ for the Internet compared to cable. Second, net neutrality proposals also address ISP pricing flexibility, which is a more significant concern than content integration. He warns that restricting ISP pricing to limit congestion could cause distortions, especially if ISPs are vertically integrated into content. He concludes that while outright bans on ISP investment in content are unnecessary, such measures could be worth considering if they prevent harmful restrictions on ISP pricing flexibility.

B. *Brennan (2011)*

30. Brennan[18] shares his observations on the *IBM, AT&T, Microsoft*, and *Intel* cases, responding to the work by Crandall, Jackson, and Wright. While Crandall and Jackson argue that divestiture was not necessary and that behavioral and accounting regulations could have sufficed in the *AT&T* case, Brennan notes that such regulations were seen as intrusive and uncertain in the U.S. legal environment, making divestiture the preferable solution. He contrasts this with *Verizon v. Trinko* (2004), where regulation was deemed an effective substitute for antitrust action, signaling a shift in handling competition in regulated industries.

31. Regarding the *Microsoft* case, Brennan highlights the lack of a consistent theory of harm, supporting evidence, and an appropriate remedy, as seen in the *AT&T* case. He criticizes that the plaintiffs focused on Microsoft's operating system monopoly while providing evidence about browser practices, particularly blocking Netscape, and proposing a remedy better suited to Microsoft's Office applications. This led to a remedy focused on removing contracts that restricted Netscape's distribution, while the broader issue of future application platforms was overlooked. He further argues that the plaintiffs avoided the harder task of proving Netscape and Java as future competitors. As for *Intel*, Brennan critiques Wright's assumption that buyers are victims of monopolistic practices. In exclusion cases like Intel's, buyers often benefit from practices such as exclusive dealing and loyalty rebates, which provide discounts and incentives. Thus, rising stock prices do not necessarily reflect reduced anticompetitive behavior, as Wright suggests. Brennan concludes by emphasizing the complexity of evaluating competition in high-tech sectors. He notes that technological change can quickly make market power temporary or turn seemingly benign mergers into major issues, as demonstrated by Microsoft and Netscape in the 1990s. While antitrust should not be eased in favor of innovation, balancing it with other tools remains a challenge.

---

18 Timothy J. Brennan, *"High-Tech" Antitrust: Incoherent, Misguided, Obsolete, or None of the Above? Comments on Crandall-Jackson and Wright*, 38 REV. INDUS. ORG. 423 (2011), https://doi.org/10.1007/s11151-011-9296-6.

C. *Katz and Rogerson (2009)*

32. Katz and Rogerson[19] critique Iansiti and Richards' (2009)[20] claim that Microsoft's market power and the applications barrier to entry have significantly weakened due to IT ecosystem changes. They argue that these technological shifts are insufficient to conclude Microsoft's dominance has substantially declined, noting that many traditional applications still rely on Windows, especially in enterprise settings. They highlight that middleware has not replaced the operating system as the primary platform, and Internet Explorer's large market share continues to reinforce the applications barrier to entry, allowing Microsoft to potentially restrict compatibility or charge for the browser. They also note that Iansiti and Richards fail to consider the role of plug-ins in browser-based applications and Microsoft's ability to limit their compatibility.

33. Katz and Rogerson identify three potential competitive developments: widespread use of non-Microsoft middleware, hardware platforms like smart TVs and game consoles as PC substitutes, and emulator software for running Windows applications on non-Microsoft systems, noting that none has emerged as a serious threat to Microsoft's dominance. When considering whether the court should extend the remedy provisions on Microsoft, they emphasize the need to assess Microsoft's ongoing market power, the government's credibility in settlement negotiations, and the risk of moral hazard if the provisions are not extended. They suggest reviewing the effectiveness of measures like disclosures, oversight committees, and faster dispute resolution, while weighing the costs and benefits of extending them.

D. *Liebowitz and Margolis (2013)*

34. Liebowitz and Margolis[21] critique the concept of "lock-in" in economic markets, specifically challenging the claims made by Paul David (in his article "Clio and the Economics of QWERTY"[22]) and Brian Arthur (in his article "Competing Technologies, Increasing Returns, and Lock-In by Historical Events"[23]). They argue that while David's QWERTY story is commonly cited as empirical support for market inefficiency due to lock-in, his conclusions lack empirical support and are based on faulty assumptions.

---

19 Michael L. Katz & William P. Rogerson, *The Applications Barrier to Entry and Its Implications for the Microsoft Remedies: Comment on Iansiti and Richards*, 75 ANTITRUST L.J. 723 (2009), https://www.jstor.org/stable/27897597.

20 Marco Iansiti & Greg Richards, *Six Years Later: The Impact of the Evolution of the IT Ecosystem*, 75 ANTITRUST L.J. 705 (2009), https://www.jstor.org/stable/27897596.

21 Stan J. Liebowitz & Stephen E. Margolis, *The Troubled Path of the Lock-In Movement*, 9 J. COMPETITION L. & ECON. 125 (2013), https://doi.org/10.1093/joclec/nhs034.

22 75 AM. ECON. REV. 332 (1985), https://www.jstor.org/stable/1805621.

23 99 ECON. J. 116 (1989), https://www.jstor.org/stable/2234208.

They further criticize David and Arthur for abandoning empirical validation when challenged. They outline three degrees of path dependence to clarify when lock-in might actually lead to inefficiency:

- First-degree path dependence occurs when durable commitments turn out to be the best choice, with no inefficiency or regret;
- Second-degree path dependence arises when decisions are made with available information, but unforeseen events lead to less favorable outcomes, though no better choice could have been made at the time;
- Third-degree path dependence occurs when a better alternative is available but not chosen, making it the only form with policy relevance since the inefficiency can be corrected.

35. Liebowitz and Margolis demonstrate that market inefficiencies caused by lock-in are overstated and that third-degree path dependence is rare in functioning markets, as forces like entrepreneurship, advertising, and firm adoption typically prevent inefficiencies from persisting. They also highlight that while path dependence can happen, most first- and second-degree path dependence does not lead to market failure. They also introduce the concept of "remediability" to emphasize the importance of correcting inefficiencies through market forces or government intervention. Liebowitz and Margolis conclude that empirical validation is essential to support claims of market inefficiency due to lock-in, and caution against basing antitrust policies on path dependence theories without solid evidence. The relevance to the *Microsoft* case lies in the centrality of lock-in to the antitrust arguments, where regulators argued that Microsoft used its operating system monopoly to lock in users and developers, hindering competition from companies like Netscape. However, this paper challenges the validity of lock-in theories and highlights that market forces often mitigate such inefficiencies. This casts doubt on claims that Microsoft relied on lock-in to maintain its monopoly, weakening the antitrust arguments about Microsoft's market dominance and anticompetitive effects.

E. *Hylton and Wu (2020)*

36. Hylton and Wu[24] assess the welfare tradeoff between patent law and antitrust law by examining the costs associated with deviating from the ideal antitrust enforcement standard – whether toward excessive enforcement or inadequate enforcement. This tradeoff is quantified using the error-cost ratio, which represents the ratio between the costs of excessive enforcement (false-positive costs) and the costs of inadequate enforcement (false-negative costs). Hylton and Wu argue that this tradeoff should be

---

24 Keith N. Hylton & Wendy Xu, *Error Costs, Ratio Tests, and Patent Antitrust Law*, 56 Rev. Indus. Org. 563 (2020), https://www.jstor.org/stable/48734248.

a key consideration in shaping an optimal enforcement system. The ideal enforcement scenario occurs when antitrust regulations allow an innovating monopolist to recover its R&D costs while also preventing the firm from imposing unnecessary deadweight loss on society. Such regulation may not be the most effective means of protecting innovation incentives, especially given the high ratio of false-positive costs to false-negative costs. Therefore, efforts to expand antitrust regulation into areas traditionally governed by patent law should be carefully evaluated considering these associated error costs.

F. *Pleatsikas and Teece (2001)*

37. Pleatsikas and Teece[25] argue against the use of traditional antitrust methods of defining markets and market power in high-technology contexts. They assert that high technology is distinct from more mature industries for three reasons: competition is focused on performance rather than price, products are highly differentiated, and incumbents are frequently overthrown.

38. In their explanation of the inadequacies of traditional antitrust frameworks, the authors address the limitations of the *Horizontal Merger Guidelines* and the antitrust factors derived from *Brown Shoe*. Regarding the former, they posit that the "hypothetical monopolist test," the small but significant and non-transitory increase in price (SSNIP), and Herfindahl-Hirschman Index (HHIs) are often unreliable in high technology contexts, where heightened product differentiation makes competing products (and, therefore, markets) difficult to identify. Additionally, they assert that the rapid innovation seen in high technology is incompatible with the entry standards specified in the *Horizontal Merger Guidelines*: "entry within one year for uncommitted entrants and within two years for committed entrants." Lastly, Pleatsikas and Teece refute the effectiveness of eight factors *Brown Shoe* has established for defining markets, sparing only elasticity of demand. The authors offer alternative frameworks for defining markets and market power, highlighting the relevance of competitive activity, price responsiveness, and innovative activity – primarily R&D investments – in evaluating market power.

---

25 Christopher Pleatsikas & David Teece, *The Analysis of Market Definition and Market Power in the Context of Rapid Innovation*, INT'L J. INDUS. ORG. 665 (2001), https://doi.org/10.1016/S0167-7187(00)00088-6.

3. Contemporary Significance: Important Theoretical and Empirical Questions about Platform Markets

A. *Eisenmann, Parker, and Alstyne (2011)*

39. Eisenmann, Parker, and Alstyne[26] introduce the theory of "platform envelopment" as an alternative entry path for aspiring platform providers into platform markets where incumbents are protected by strong network effects and high switching costs. Platform envelopment allows attackers to recombine valuable resources like user bases into multi-platform bundles, reducing consumer heterogeneity and enabling lower bundle prices, defined as a "bundling discount." Bundling strategies like platform envelopment are highly effective in platform-mediated markets, as network effects amplify share gains for attackers using foreclosure strategies, while economies of scope reduce both variable and fixed costs compared to selling items separately. By leveraging shared user relationships and common components, firms can enter without relying on Schumpeterian innovation, while foreclosing a target's access to users and harnessing scale economies. They highlight that leverage in envelopment attacks can come from revenue gains through pricing power for a pure bundle sold to overlapping user groups or from bundling discounts where user overlap is limited. Cost-side leverage comes from economies of scope, with the dominant factor depending on the relationship between the platforms. Moreover, they propose a typology of envelopment attacks, classifying them as complements, weak substitutes, or functionally unrelated, and highlight that attacks succeed with high user overlap, price discrimination benefits, or significant economies of scope. For complements, price discrimination is limited due to positively correlated user valuations, making success reliant on high user overlap and bundling at a price close to the sum of separate optimal prices. Weak substitutes, which share some user overlap and have positively correlated demand, succeed when significant economies of scope allow for deep discounts despite overlapping functionalities. Even with limited user overlap, unrelated platforms can benefit from bundling through price discrimination, with success likely when user overlap and economies of scope are high. They conclude by urging more scholarly focus on platform-mediated networks, citing firms like Microsoft, Apple, and Google as serial platform envelopers.

---

26 Thomas Eisenmann, Geoffrey Parker & Marshall Van Alstyne, *Platform Envelopment*, 32 STRATEGIC MGMT. J. 1270 (2011), https://doi.org/10.1002/smj.935.

B. *Werden (2001a)*

40. Werden[27] examines whether Microsoft's pricing strategy for its Windows operating system aligns with pure monopolistic behavior. The analysis centers on the concept of derived demand, where the demand for Windows is shaped by the demand for PCs. He argues that the heterogeneity of PC demand, especially higher elasticity for low-end PCs, plays a key role in shaping the derived demand elasticity for Windows. This leads to a lower-than-expected monopoly price for two reasons: (i) it is impractical to differentiate Windows prices based on PC type, and (ii) price-sensitive low-end PCs disproportionately influence the elasticity of derived demand. As a result, raising Windows' price has a greater impact on demand for lower-priced PCs, keeping the monopoly price lower. Although Microsoft's pricing may appear lower than what a pure monopolist would set, Werden suggests that this pricing reflects competitive pressures, the inability to perfectly price discriminate, and strategic bundling with complementary products, rather than straightforward monopolistic pricing. Furthermore, Werden contrasts this with Schmalensee's model, which assumes a higher price for a monopolistic OS provider but overlooks factors like OS durability, piracy, and network effects that also shape pricing strategies. He concludes that Microsoft's pricing strategy reflects complexities of market dynamics, rather than clear-cut monopolistic behavior.

C. *Lenard (2019)*

41. Lenard[28] addresses the growing relevance of multisided platforms in antitrust policy, particularly in the context of data-driven platforms. He explains the complexity of defining market power in data-driven platforms, where data may act as a barrier to entry if there are no good substitutes for the data essential to a platform's success, and whether antitrust laws need to evolve to address these new realities. He argues that digitization through cloud computing and mobile apps has reduced switching costs, allowing users to switch platforms with minimal data loss, which weakens traditional network effects. He concludes that the availability of multiple data sources and the portability of digital data lessen these concerns in many consumer-facing platforms, suggesting that the market power of data-driven platforms may be overstated in some cases. A key issue he highlights is whether below-cost pricing strengthens a firm's competitive position by increasing its accumulation of data, or whether it is only profitable because it undermines rivals' ability to gather their own data. Lenard also highlights the tension between privacy regulation and competition, noting that while privacy laws aim to

---

27   Gregory J. Werden, *Microsoft's Pricing of Windows and the Economics of Derived Demand Monopoly*, 18 Rev. Indus. Org. 257 (2001), https://www.jstor.org/stable/41799001.

28   Thomas M. Lenard (2019), *Introduction to the* RIO *Special Issue on Antitrust and the Platform Economy*, 54 Rev. Indus. Org. 617 (2019), https://www.jstor.org/stable/48702967.

protect consumers, they can unintentionally entrench dominant platforms by limiting smaller firms' access to essential user data, thereby reducing their ability to compete effectively in data-driven markets. Lenard concludes that as these data-driven platforms grow more integral to the economy, ongoing research and updated antitrust approaches are necessary.

D. *Werden (2001b)*

42. Werden[29] explains that network effects, both direct and indirect, create significant barriers to entry in industries like the PC operating system market, allowing incumbents to maintain market power. He uses *Microsoft* as a case study, highlighting the "applications barrier to entry," where the feedback loop between users and developers reinforced Microsoft's dominance. He elaborates that factors like short product life cycles, consumer preference for widely supported OSs, and developers' reluctance to back new systems made it difficult for new entrants to challenge Microsoft. Additionally, Microsoft's position as both an OS provider and a major applications developer amplified these barriers. Sunk costs gave Microsoft a further advantage, as it had already incurred significant non-recoverable investments, while new entrants faced high upfront expenses with no guarantee of success. Furthermore, Werden contrasts the court's broad definition of barriers to entry – any factor that raises entrants' costs – with Stigler's narrower definition – barrier to entry must be a cost incurred by new entrants but not by incumbents – to explain that economies of scale or high capital requirements would not qualify as barriers under Stigler's definition. Werden concludes that while Stigler focused on long-term barriers, short- and medium-term barriers caused by network effects are also critical in antitrust analysis, and legal definitions of barriers to entry should evolve to account for these dynamics in high-tech markets.

E. *Stefanadis (2003)*

43. Stefanadis[30] argues that formal economic theory has largely overlooked the idea that industries with sunk costs can be contestable without long-term contracts, and examines whether they can still be contestable under short-term transactions, challenging the notion that only long-term contracts support contestability. The paper presents a formal model to explore this argument, based on two key assumptions: an infinite time horizon and differing transaction costs between short-term and long-term markets.

---

29   Gregory J. Werden, *Network Effects and Conditions of Entry: Lessons from the* Microsoft *Case*, 69 ANTITRUST L.J. 111 (2001), https://www.jstor.org/stable/40843512.

30   Christodoulos Stefanadis, *Sunk Costs, Contestability, and the Latent Contract Market*, 12 J. ECON. & MGMT. STRATEGY 119 (2003), https://doi.org/10.1111/j.1430-9134.2003.00119.x.

The model demonstrates that a class of equilibria exists where all transactions occur in the spot market, and the monopolist lowers its spot market prices to prevent potential customers from engaging in long-term contracts with potential entrants. Thus, the key test for contestability is the transaction costs in the latent contract market. If these costs are too high, the monopolist can charge monopoly prices without facing competition. If the costs are low, the market becomes contestable, and the mere threat of new entrants offering long-term contracts forces the monopolist to lower prices even without such contracts being signed. Additionally, Stefanadis demonstrates that an industry can be imperfectly contestable, where prices are restrained but not necessarily reduced to average cost. Contestability is shown to depend on the relative transaction costs between contract and spot markets, with perfect contestability only achieved when contract costs are not higher than spot market costs. Stefanadis emphasizes that while some markets may be contestable due to the threat of entry, this does not apply universally, and the argument of contestability might be used by monopolists to avoid antitrust action in some cases. He concludes that contestability must ultimately be determined empirically, but expressing monopolists' arguments through formal models can help evaluate their validity in antitrust cases.

F. Chen, Doraszelski, and Harrington (2009)

44. Chen, Doraszelski, and Harrington[31] analyze how strategic pricing by smaller firms prevents the installed base differential from growing to the point of incompatibility, neutralizing increasing returns and avoiding market dominance. One solution to the network effects dilemma – where consumer value increases as a single product dominates – is for multiple firms to offer compatible products. However, compatibility becomes less appealing to the larger firm as it loses its competitive advantage when installed bases differ. For compatibility to remain a long-term solution, two conditions must be met: firms must initially find compatibility in their interests, and they must have incentives to maintain it as their installed bases diverge. The smaller firm typically drives this dynamic through aggressive pricing, keeping the differential low enough for the larger firm to also choose compatibility, ensuring stability and allowing both firms to maintain significant market shares. Additionally, they examine three policy options in networked markets: laissez-faire (endogenous compatibility), mandatory compatibility, and prohibited compatibility, demonstrating that firms prefer mandatory compatibility when network effects are modest, while consumers prefer endogenous compatibility. When network effects are strong, firms still favor mandatory compatibility, but

---

31 Jiawei Chen, Ulrich Doraszelski & Joseph E. Harrington, Jr., *Avoiding Market Dominance: Product Compatibility in Markets with Network Effects*, RAND J. ECON. 455 (2009), https://doi.org/10.1111/j.1756-2171.2009.00073.x.

consumers lean toward prohibited compatibility. In conclusion, they show that endogenous compatibility prevents market dominance by stabilizing market shares over time. By keeping the installed base differential modest, smaller firms use aggressive pricing to maintain compatibility, which incentivizes larger firms to stay compatible as well. This dynamic ensures stability, allowing both firms to hold significant market shares in the long run.

G. *Heil and Langvardt (1994)*

45. Heil and Langvardt[32] explore how market signaling interacts with antitrust law and how competitive market signaling is a natural and essential part of competitive behavior. Market signaling refers to actions taken by firms to communicate their market intentions to competitors, such as through new product introductions, pricing changes, or strategic preannouncements. They outline key types of signals: hostility (when a product threatens competitors, sparking strong reactions), consequence (reflecting the perceived impact on competitors' performance), and commitment (demonstrating a firm's dedication to a market strategy). Preannouncement signals provide advance notice of actions, often in markets with high consumer switching costs. Under antitrust law, signaling can violate the Sherman Act section 1 when it leads to implicit agreements, such as price-fixing or market divisions, which restrain trade. Under section 2, signaling by dominant firms may be seen as monopolistic if it discourages competitors or delays consumer decisions. While signaling can raise antitrust concerns under Sherman Act sections 1 and 2 when it leads to implicit agreements or exclusionary tactics, they argue that signaling is primarily procompetitive despite these risks, enhancing market efficiency, promoting innovation, preventing destructive price wars, and improving resource allocation. They advise that marketing managers carefully navigate signaling to avoid antitrust violations, ensuring their actions promote competition and are not interpreted as attempts to collude or monopolize, and regulators should remain mindful of the fine line between healthy competitive signaling and behaviors that hinder market competition.

H. *Reddy, Evans, Nichols, and Schmalensee (2001)*

46. Reddy, Evans, Nichols, and Schmalensee[33] critique Werden's analysis of Microsoft's pricing strategy during the 1998 antitrust case and argue that even when accounting for the heterogeneity of computer demand,

---

32   Oliver P. Heil & Arien W. Langvardt, *The Interface between Competitive Market Signaling and Antitrust Law*. 58 J. Mktg. 81 (1994), https://doi.org/10.2307/1252312.

33   Bernard Reddy, David Evans, Albert Nichols & Richard Schmalensee, *A Monopolist Would Still Charge More for Windows: A Comment on Werden*, 18 Rev. Indus. Org. 263 (2001), https://www.jstor.org/stable/41799002.

Microsoft's pricing of Windows does not align with the government's claim that Windows operates as a monopoly protected by high entry barriers. By comparing Microsoft's actual Windows prices with the theoretical monopoly pricing, they reject the idea that Microsoft has fully exploited monopoly power. They also refute Werden's reliance on assumed parameter values that are inconsistent with real-world PC market data, particularly noting his confusion between local and global maxima. By focusing on global profit maximization and using more realistic parameters, they conclude that the impact of allowing heterogeneous demand segments on short-run monopoly pricing is minimal. They assert that the government's monopoly theory is resoundingly rejected by the data, and they emphasize the need for further research into the pricing strategies of software firms in network industries where constant competitive threats and potential displacement shape pricing behavior.

I. *Owen (2011)*

47. Owen[34] challenges the assumption that vertical integration is inherently anticompetitive by explaining that vertical integration often enhances efficiency through reduced transaction costs and improved coordination, making it generally pro-competitive. He highlights that almost every production process in the economy is vertically integrated to some degree, with shifts happening naturally as a response to changes in prices, technology, and institutions. Owen explains that competition between hierarchical organizations (which manage multiple production stages) and market-based transactions (where independent firms operate through contracts) improves economic efficiency, and the inherent imperfections in both systems make vertical integration a natural and effective response to economic pressures. Owen warns that because the distinction between firms and markets is often unclear, rigid regulations like net neutrality or broad antitrust measures could oversimplify these relationships and undermine welfare by discouraging efficient business practices. Similarly, preemptive regulations (like net neutrality) without evidence of harm can stifle innovation, reduce the benefits of vertical integration, and deter investment, making them unnecessary given the necessary protections already provided by existing antitrust laws. Moreover, Owen uses historical cases such as the *Bell System*, where AT&T's vertical integration was initially justified as a natural monopoly but ultimately resulted in welfare loss, to emphasize the importance of evidence before intervention. Owen concludes that because vertical integration is typically a response to external challenges that enhances efficiency rather than threatening competition

---

34 Bruce M. Owen, *Antitrust and Vertical Integration in "New Economy" Industries with Application to Broadband Access*, 38 REV. INDUS. ORG. 363 (2011), https://www.jstor.org/stable/23884984.

or consumers, preemptive regulatory restrictions could harm investment more than they benefit consumer welfare; thus, effective policy should rely on waiting for *ex post* evidence of harm before justifying interventions.

J. *Hall and Hall (2000)*

48. C. Hall and R. Hall[35] aim to quantify the impact of Microsoft's anticompetitive practices in the desktop operating system market, particularly regarding the Internet browser. Along with natural barriers protecting a product like Windows, they highlight the artificial barriers Microsoft created to maintain market dominance. They estimate the harm caused by these exclusionary practices and the potential consumer benefits if these artificial barriers to entry were removed. Using the Cournot model, they simulate competition, assuming the personal computer industry operates as a symmetric oligopoly. They argue that Microsoft keeps Windows' price below the monopoly level to deter competitors from developing their own operating systems, thereby preventing rivals from gaining market share. The model helps quantify both the harm to consumers and the gains from reducing these barriers by analyzing computer and operating system prices under various competitive scenarios. It demonstrates that if barriers to entry were removed, the price of computers and operating systems would decrease, benefiting consumers. Thus, they emphasize that if Microsoft's only offense was creating these barriers, the damages should reflect that impact, making harsher punishments like divestiture excessive and unnecessary. They also discuss the role of the Internet's openness in keeping entry costs low for new operating systems and warn that if Windows became the only system offering a good browsing experience, entry costs would increase. They propose that Microsoft's web browsers be required to support industry standards, ensuring rival browsers and software can function on Windows. They also suggest a framework to allow Microsoft Office to run on new systems, with Microsoft earning royalties, and propose rules to prevent Microsoft from favoring Windows through hardware changes or monopolizing the web-browsing experience to ensure fair competition.

K. *Crandall (2019)*

49. Crandall[36] explains why antitrust interventions, such as the divestiture of large internet giants, are often ineffective in promoting competition in modern digital markets. He notes that in landmark cases like *Standard*

---

35 Chris E. Hall & Robert E. Hall, *Toward a Quantification of the Effects of Microsoft's Conduct*, 90 AM. ECON. REV. 188 (2000), https://doi.org/10.1257/aer.90.2.188.

36 Robert W. Crandall, *The Dubious Antitrust Argument for Breaking Up the Internet Giants*, 54 REV. INDUS. ORG. 627 (2019), https://www.jstor.org/stable/48702968.

Oil, AT&T, and *Paramount Pictures*, divestitures failed to restore meaningful competition, as dominant firms retained control through common ownership, aggressive tactics, or external factors. Unanticipated competition from new services had a more significant impact on consumer welfare than antitrust decrees. Similarly, in the *Microsoft* case, competition thrived despite the company not being broken up, demonstrating that technological advancements rather than legal interventions drove competition. The rise of mobile operating systems from Apple and Google played a larger role in diminishing Microsoft's dominance than any antitrust actions. Furthermore, Crandall suggests that section 2 antitrust cases against companies like Amazon, Facebook, or Google would likely fail, particularly in the digital advertising market, because network effects and data advantages would persist even after a breakup. This supports his argument that structural remedies would not lead to long-term economic welfare improvements. Instead, technological innovation and natural market evolution are more effective in addressing market power in dynamic, tech-driven industries. Crandall concludes that policymakers should be cautious in using antitrust measures against today's digital giants, as these interventions may not resolve the root causes of their dominance.

II. What Have We Learned?

1. Impact on End Consumers

A. *Jacobson and Sher (2006)*

50. Jacobson and Sher[37] critique the "no economic sense" test in antitrust law, particularly regarding exclusive dealing under section 2 of the Sherman Act. They argue the test focuses too narrowly on whether a company's actions would be profitable without excluding competitors, ignoring the complexity of exclusive dealing, which often has legitimate pro-competitive benefits (e.g., dealer loyalty, preventing free riding, improving quality, economies of scale, and competitive bidding). Jacobson and Sher explain that exclusive dealing often has efficiency justifications, making it difficult to distinguish between the economic benefits for the defendant and the exclusionary impact on rivals; it remains profitable even when harming competitors. They highlight that the test overlooks two key issues: (i) some harmful practices cost little or nothing to the company, and (ii) excluding competitors can sometimes create efficiencies that benefit consumers. They further note that the test's focus on internal costs and benefits can lead to

---

[37] Jonathan M. Jacobson & Scott A. Sher, *"No Economic Sense" Makes No Sense for Exclusive Dealing*, 73 ANTITRUST L.J. 779 (2006), https://www.jstor.org/stable/40843693.

errors, such as missing harmful practices (false negatives) or condemning beneficial ones (false positives). They highlight the issue of false negatives with the *Microsoft*, *United Shoe*, and *Dentsply* cases, where the actions were exclusionary and profitable but did not require significant profit sacrifice, meaning they might not have been considered illegal under the "no economic sense" test. They use the *Joyce Beverages* case to highlight a false positive, where an arrangement benefiting competition could have been wrongly condemned. They conclude that antitrust law should focus on consumer harm, not just whether the company's conduct made economic sense. Furthermore, while acknowledging that adjustments to the test could improve outcomes, they argue against its broader use due to (i) courts potentially failing to apply necessary adjustments, (ii) increased complexity undermining simplicity and business certainty, and (iii) the test's continued failure to assess consumer impact. Instead, they advocate for the "rule of reason," which weighs whether the conduct has a net positive or negative effect on competition and consumer welfare. Under this standard, a plaintiff must first show the defendant has market power and that exclusive dealing harms competition. If a *prima facie* case is made, the defendant can provide efficiency justifications, which the court must balance against the competitive harm.

B. *Gisser and Allen (2001)*

51. Gisser and Allen[38] show that consumer welfare is higher when a single monopoly dominates both the operating system and applications markets, using Microsoft as an example. They argue that splitting Microsoft into separate companies would lead to higher prices and reduced welfare. They show that if another firm has the potential to monopolize an application market, consumers will benefit more if Microsoft, already an established monopoly in the operating system market, is also allowed to monopolize the application market. They further suggest that disallowing the bundling of Windows with Internet Explorer would be a better solution if consumer welfare is also considered. In addition, they use a model based on Cournot's theory of two goods in the production of a third composite good with fixed proportion to demonstrate separate monopolies yield higher prices and lower consumer welfare than a single integrated monopoly. They conclude that antitrust policies should reconsider the separation of monopolies when a single integrated monopoly could be more beneficial to consumers, specifically noting that allowing Microsoft to stay as a single entity could keep prices lower and avoid negative outcomes for consumers.

---

38 Micha Gisser & Mark S. Allen, *One Monopoly Is Better Than Two: Antitrust Policy and Microsoft*, 19 REV. INDUS. ORG. 211 (2001), https://www.jstor.org/stable/41799039.

2. Impact on Firms

A. *Sinitsyn (2016)*

52. Sinitsyn[39] explores the concept of complementary fit, which refers to how well a firm's products and strategies align with market demands and technological advancements. He examines how increasing complementarity between a firm's products affects pricing strategies and profitability. Firms enhance consumer perception of complementary products by using strategies like umbrella branding, visual similarity, shared accessories, improved connections, joint usage promotions, and adjusted warranties to encourage purchases from the same brand. Using a model with two firms offering complementary products where consumers can mix and match between the firms, Sinitsyn demonstrates that:

    – Increasing complementarity improves consumer perception and demand but also intensifies price competition, potentially reducing profits;
    – If complementarity significantly boosts demand, firms benefit, but if demand gains are small, intensified competition lowers profitability;
    – Reducing compatibility with a rival's products is never profitable, as consumers simply switch to the rival's matching bundle, intensifying competition and lowering profits for both firms;
    – Firms achieve the highest profits when they avoid making their own bundles more attractive, as mixed bundles reduce competition, whereas improving complementarity leads to smaller profits due to increased competition between matching bundles.

53. He concludes that while firms would benefit from agreeing not to enhance the fit between their complementary products, without enforcement, each firm might still be tempted to do so. Thus, firms must weigh the benefits of increased demand against the intensified price competition. If the demand boost is substantial, firms should adopt complementarity-enhancing strategies, recognizing that once one firm invests in complementarity, the other is likely to follow.

B. *Chemla (2003)*

54. Chemla[40] analyzes how competition among downstream firms affects an upstream firm's payoff and its incentive to vertically integrate when negotiating optimal contracts. He argues that upstream firms benefit from

---

[39] Maxim Sinitsyn, *Choosing the Quality of the Fit between Complementary Products*, 25 J. ECON. & MGMT. STRATEGY 161 (2016), https://doi.org/10.1111/jems.12136.

[40] Gilles Chemla, *Downstream Competition, Foreclosure, and Vertical Integration*, 12 J. ECON. & MGMT. STRATEGY 261 (2003), https://doi.org/10.1111/j.1430-9134.2003.00261.x.

promoting competition when downstream firms have high bargaining power, noting that partial integration can result in anticompetitive outcomes. He also explores how vertical integration can act as a barrier to entry and trigger strategic mergers or spin-offs. Using the *Microsoft* case, Chemla highlights the pros and cons of vertical separation, suggesting that a vertically separated Microsoft might promote competition in related markets to improve its bargaining position despite its dominant status. He demonstrates that a firm with significant market power might favor competition among trading partners to strengthen its negotiation position, and that this incentive could surpass that of a social planner. He also highlights that even when conditional contracts like exclusive dealing agreements are allowed, the firm may still promote competition to its advantage. Chemla summarizes that (i) the limits of a monopolist's incentive to extend power to vertically related segments should be better understood for competition policy, (ii) vertical integration and spin-offs may occur sequentially in response to market changes, and (iii) the secrecy of financial contracts affects upstream firm profits and competitive outcomes, additionally concluding that because integration can result in either monopolistic or competitive outcomes based on downstream firms' characteristics, careful contract evaluation when assessing competition levels is necessary.

C. Rajgopal, Srivastava, and Zhao (2023)

55. Rajgopal, Srivastava, and Zhao[41] analyze the profitability of digital technology firms, focusing on the limitations of traditional accounting measures like ARR (accounting rate of return) in assessing modern tech companies. They introduce the internal rate of return (IRR) as a better measure of profitability for firms heavily invested in intangibles, arguing that ARR is more suitable for firms with stable and mature operations where managers can accurately estimate items such as economic depreciation, and further demonstrate that ARR better explains contemporaneous stock returns for companies with mature business models and low intangible investments. However, for digital-tech firms that rely heavily on intangible investments, IRR provides a more accurate picture of economic profitability. Their study finds that digital giants such as Apple, Microsoft, Amazon, Alphabet, and Facebook consistently outperform other sectors based on IRR, showing much higher returns compared to traditional ROIC (return on invested capital) measures. Furthermore, while they find the digital tech sector to be the best-performing over time, they show that high IRRs cannot be attributed solely to anticompetitive

---

41 Shivaram Rajgopal, Anup Srivastava & Rong Zhao, *Do Digital Technology Firms Earn Excess Profits? Alternative Perspectives*, 98 Acct. Rev. 321 (2023), https://doi.org/10.2308/TAR-2021-0176.

practices or innovation. Instead, the evidence suggests that the success of these companies likely stems from a combination of both market power and genuine technological innovation. They acknowledge the limitations of IRR as a measure and highlight the need for further research to better understand profitability in tech companies, especially in refining measures like ROIC to account for intangible investments.

D. *Tanriverdi and Lee (2008)*

56. Tanriverdi and Lee[42] examine how software firms can boost performance by diversifying within their industry while leveraging network externalities. They find that in industries like software, related diversification across platforms and product markets complement each other, improving sales growth and market share when implemented together. However, implementing only market-related or platform-related diversification reduces growth. The study emphasizes the importance of network externalities, such as enhanced application quality and customer growth, which are best realized when diversification is coordinated across both platforms and products. They challenge traditional theories by showing that partial diversification can lead to negative outcomes, especially in industries with high network externalities. They suggest that industries like software, computing, and telecommunications should integrate diversification strategies to maximize synergies and long-term performance.

E. *Stremersch and Tellis (2002)*

57. Stremersch and Tellis[43] offer a comprehensive synthesis of bundling strategies, addressing key gaps in the literature by clearly defining bundling terms, identifying two key dimensions for classifying bundling strategies, and establishing legal evaluation rules. They propose a framework for determining the optimal bundling strategy in various contexts and address three major shortcomings in the literature: unclear definitions, lack of legal clarity, and the absence of an integrative framework for bundling's optimality. They define bundling as the sale of two or more separate products in one package, with the distinction between price bundling – offering products together at a discount without integration – and product bundling – integrating products into one package – having significant strategic implications. Price bundling is considered a short-term promotional tool, while product bundling adds long-term value. According to

---

42 Hüseyin Tanriverdi & Chi-Hyon Lee, *Within-Industry Diversification and Firm Performance in the Presence of Network Externalities: Evidence from the Software Industry*, 51 ACAD. MGMT. J. 381 (2008), https://doi.org/10.5465/amj.2008.31767300.

43 Stefan Stremersch & Gerard J. Tellis, *Strategic Bundling of Products and Prices: A New Synthesis for Marketing*, 66 J. MKTG. 55 (2002), https://doi.org/10.1509/jmkg.66.1.55.18455.

the rule of reason, bundling by a firm with market power may be illegal if it threatens competition without providing sufficient consumer benefits. In the *Microsoft* case, they believe that the lack of sufficient consumer benefit from simply bundling Internet Explorer with Windows, without true product integration, exemplified the importance of these distinctions. Stremersch and Tellis highlight how bundling strategies can be misunderstood, even by large firms, and argue that Microsoft could have avoided legal issues by investing in true product integration. Furthermore, they demonstrate that the *Microsoft* case illustrates the need for firms to balance the economic benefits of bundling with potential legal challenges, especially in high-tech markets, and suggest that firms with dominant market power should focus on value-added product bundling for long-term benefits, rather than relying on price bundling, which carries greater legal risks.

3. Impact on Competition

A. *Weiser (2009)*

58. Weiser[44] argues that antitrust courts struggle to address rapidly changing, complex issues related to platform and application conflicts due to their slow pace and lack of technical expertise. He proposes that antitrust law should not be the sole mechanism for resolving these issues and suggests a need for more creative approaches and collaboration with regulatory bodies. He discusses the challenges platform owners face in ensuring fair treatment of application developers, especially when they gain significant market power, and identifies three areas for government oversight: (i) leveling the playing field, (ii) preventing instability and lack of transparency in private agreements, and (iii) protecting independent innovation that benefits society. He further outlines three challenges for antitrust enforcers: (i) developing strong relationships with standard-setting bodies, (ii) determining when these bodies violate antitrust laws (e.g., *Rambus* case), and (iii) deciding if such bodies should enforce interoperability standards, as seen in the *Microsoft* case. Additionally, he draws on lessons from the *AT&T* and *Microsoft* antitrust cases to explain that while the *AT&T* case demonstrates how regulatory agencies can effectively assist courts, the *Microsoft* case highlights the difficulties of enforcement without a dedicated regulatory body. Weiser concludes that while standard-setting bodies help with interoperability, they often lag behind technological changes and face governance challenges, and suggests that future antitrust enforcement should learn from both cases to improve platform-application oversight.

---

44 Philip J. Weiser, *Regulating Interoperability: Lessons from* AT&T, Microsoft, *and Beyond*, 76 ANTITRUST L.J. 271 (2009), https://www.jstor.org/stable/40843709.

B. *Duque (2023)*

59. Duque[45] analyzes the impact of choice screens on Internet Explorer (IE) users by examining browser usage data. The study shows that IE's market share continued its downward trend even after Microsoft breached its obligation to display the choice screen, suggesting IE did not benefit from a "stickiness" effect. He suggests that policymakers should carefully define their objectives for forced choices, whether aiming for exposure, attention, or reducing the market share of a dominant player. He highlights that a key issue is inertia, where users stick with defaults due to factors like status quo bias, lack of attention, or loss aversion. Regarding IE's market share, two hypotheses emerge: (i) users would have chosen IE even with a forced choice, as they were satisfied with the browser; or (ii) IE benefited from inertia that prevented users from switching to their preferred alternative. In the IE case, despite the introduction of the choice screen, IE's market share was already declining both before and after the intervention, suggesting that inertia may not have been the dominant factor. Moreover, empirical data show the choice screen's impact on IE's market share was minimal, with the decline ranging from 1.4% to 2%, and likely driven more by other factors like the entry of Chrome into the market rather than the choice screen itself. Additionally, dissatisfied users had likely already switched to alternatives, as evidenced by Firefox's significant market share before the intervention, while satisfied or less informed users likely stuck with IE, demonstrating the limited impact of the choice screen. The study raises important questions about how far choice screens should go and whether overwhelming users with too many choices might be counterproductive. Duque suggests that in cases where users are indifferent or disengaged, random assignment to qualified options could be more effective, although this could risk assigning poor defaults to naïve users. Finally, as antitrust concerns over default applications resurface, Duque calls for more experimental data to fully understand the mechanisms behind default stickiness and how it affects competition in different contexts.

C. *Windrum (2004) – slightly different paper*

60. Windrum[46] examines Microsoft's strategy during the browser wars against Netscape, applying the Arthur model of technological lock-in to understand how Microsoft, initially a late entrant, managed to overtake Netscape's dominant market position. According to the standard lock-in model, Netscape, with its early market lead and the bandwagon effects of

---

[45] Omar Vasquez Duque, *Active Choice vs. Inertia? An Exploratory Assessment of the European Microsoft Case's Choice Screen*, 19 J. COMPETITION L. & ECON. 60 (2023), https://doi.org/10.1093/joclec/nhac009.

[46] Paul Windrum, *Leveraging Technological Externalities in Complex Technologies: Microsoft's Exploitation of Standards in the Browser Wars*, 33 RSCH. POL'Y 385 (2004), https://doi.org/10.1016/j.respol.2003.09.002.

its Navigator browser, should have maintained its dominance. However, Microsoft adopted a different approach by utilizing its control over the Windows operating system to bundle Internet Explorer (IE) with new PCs. He argues that this effectively eliminated initial setup costs for users, while Netscape users had to go through the additional step of downloading their software. However, Microsoft adopted a different approach by utilizing its control over the Windows operating system to bundle IE with new PCs. This effectively eliminated initial setup costs for users, while Netscape users incurred costs downloading their software. Microsoft's strategy of bundling IE and integrating Internet functionality directly into the operating system allowed the company to lower user switching costs and merge previously distinct markets, giving it significant leverage in the growing networked computing environment. Windrum argues that Microsoft's success cannot be fully explained by the traditional Arthur model, which overlooks factors like initial setup costs and the strategic advantages of cross-market linkages. He proposes extending the model through a coupled Polya Urn framework, which better accounts for the dynamics of browser competition and explains how Microsoft created a market monopoly by leveraging its operating system dominance.

D. *Choi and Stefanadis (2001)*

61. Choi and Stefanadis[47] show how tying complementary products can be used by an incumbent monopolist to deter market entrants, especially in high-tech sectors where significant R&D investments are needed. Tying is a profitable strategy when the incumbent's risk of being supplanted by low-cost entry in both components outweighs the benefits of entry in just one, which can reduce consumer and overall economic welfare. Tying discourages competitors from investing and innovating by making success in one product contingent on another. They argue that this dynamic was evident in the *Microsoft* case, where tying Internet Explorer to its operating system reinforced Microsoft's dominance and blocked entry. While the Chicago School argues that tying can offer efficiency benefits, Choi and Stefanadis demonstrate that in dynamic, risky industries, it often strengthens monopoly power. Their model highlights three distinctions from the Chicago School's fixed-sum argument: (i) the incumbent faces potential entry in all components, (ii) the incumbent initially holds a monopoly in both complementary components, and (iii) risky investment plays a key role. Their analysis showed that in a scenario where only potential entrants can invest in low-cost technology, tying by the incumbent discourages entrants from investing, lowering the probability

---

47 Jay Pil Choi & Christodoulos Stefanadis, *Tying, Investment, and the Dynamic Leverage Theory*, 32 RAND J. ECON. 52 (2001), https://www.jstor.org/stable/2696397.

of successful market entry and reducing competition. In an extended model allowing all players to invest in new products, the basic results hold: incumbents can invest in R&D to strengthen their position and gain a competitive edge despite having already incurred fixed costs. This underscores how tying in industries with high entry risks and R&D costs preserves monopoly power.

E. *Iansiti and Richards (2009)*

62. Iansiti and Richards[48] analyze the impact of recent trends in IT ecosystem competition, elaborating that consumers and developers are less dependent on Windows, and the applications barrier to entry has significantly reduced. The IT ecosystem had been dynamic and highly innovative since the consent decree of the *Microsoft* case, changing its competitive dynamics and leading to the rise of new applications, platforms, and business models. They note that these trends have led to the emergence of companies like Google, revitalized older companies like Apple, and transformed the competitive landscape around the Windows operating system. They identify three key internet-related trends that have reshaped the IT ecosystem: First, internet-centric applications have become widespread and integral to computing, replacing some traditional client-based functions while augmenting others, such as social networking and media sharing. Second, Web 2.0 platforms enable the creation and delivery of applications with rich functionality, similar to traditional client applications, while enhancing their capabilities with content and services delivered over the network. These platforms have a vast user base and reach, offering significant opportunities for developers and a variety of choices for consumers, thereby lowering the application barrier to entry for client operating systems. Third, new business models combining integrated advertising and low-cost internet software distribution have facilitated the development and commercialization of OS-agnostic software services and applications, resulting in the emergence of thousands of new applications on Web 2.0 platforms. They conclude by suggesting that analysis of Microsoft's competitive position after the consent decree should consider these substantial transformations.

F. *Gilbert (2000)*

63. Gilbert[49] argues that while exclusive dealing arrangements are not inherently illegal under U.S. antitrust law, they can harm competition by foreclosing market access to rivals. These contracts may offer short-term

---

48   *Supra* note 20.
49   Richard J. Gilbert, *Exclusive Dealing, Preferential Dealing, and Dynamic Efficiency*, 16 Rev. Indus. Org. 167 (2000) https://www.jstor.org/stable/41798913.

efficiency by stabilizing demand and reducing free riding but can hinder long-term dynamic efficiency by discouraging investment and innovation from potential competitors. The traditional "Chicago School" view suggests that exclusive dealing is procompetitive because buyers will agree to exclusivity only if it creates more surplus than alternatives. However, Gilbert highlights a critical flaw in this model when there are many uncoordinated buyers and no single customer believes that rejecting an exclusive offer will improve the market outcome, which leads to a foreclosure outcome where a firm with market power can lock up enough customers to make entry unprofitable for rivals. Gilbert further examines cases like Microsoft's preferential dealing – where contracts limited rivals' access to complementary products and raised their costs – and Waste Management – where long-term exclusive contracts foreclosed the market and prevented competitors from securing contracts – to highlight how exclusive dealing can restrict competition by making it more difficult for customers to switch to rivals. He also explains that renegotiable preferential dealing contracts can lead to short-term efficiency, although they often impose socially excessive penalties that reduce competitors' incentives to invest. In situations without renegotiation, sellers generally prefer imposing penalties over below-cost pricing unless they have a mechanism to recoup those losses, as below-cost pricing can erode profitability. Ultimately, Gilbert emphasizes the tradeoff between short-term contractual benefits and long-term impacts on competition, cautioning that exclusive dealing can undermine dynamic market efficiency.

G. *Besanko, Doraszelski, and Kryukov (2019)*

64. Besanko, Doraszelski, and Kryukov[50] explore the efficiency of dynamic competition, where price is used as an investment tool to improve future competitive positions. Using a learning-by-doing model, they compare the welfare implications of dynamic competition to a first-best planner solution. They find that dynamic competition generally leads to low deadweight loss, typically less than 10% of maximum industry value in most cases, which contrasts with traditional competition models where price does not serve as an investment. They break down deadweight loss into three components: pricing distortion, entry and exit distortion, and market structure distortion. The low deadweight loss occurs not because firms mimic the planner's solution but because different sources of deadweight loss offset each other. Even when there are deviations from the optimal planner's strategy, the overall impact on deadweight loss remains modest due to the balancing effects of learning-by-doing. They conclude that dynamic competition is

---

50 David Besanko, Ulrich Doraszelski & Yaroslav Kryukov, *How Efficient Is Dynamic Competition? The Case of Price as Investment*, 109 AM. ECON. REV. 3339 (2019), https://www.jstor.org/stable/26773266.

socially beneficial, and regulatory intervention should focus on preventing collusion or exclusionary practices, as antitrust actions may have limited benefits when dynamic competition promotes welfare.

H. *Peitz (2008)*

65. Peitz[51] examines bundling as a strategy used by dominant firms to block competition in differentiated product markets. He develops a theoretical model to show under what conditions bundling becomes the preferred strategy for incumbents and how it affects potential competitors' entry. The model suggests that bundling is often the best strategy for the incumbent, even if it does not prevent entry. While bundling yields minimal gains for the incumbent if the competitor enters, it significantly benefits the incumbent by blocking entry, which reduces competition and overall welfare. Although bundling can make products more appealing to a broader range of buyers, it can also be used as an anticompetitive tool to deter or eliminate competitors. Peitz argues that antitrust authorities should intervene if (i) bundling is the incumbent's preferred strategy, (ii) bundling significantly deters entry, and (iii) monopoly bundling reduces overall welfare compared to independent pricing. If these conditions are met, authorities should take action. The paper references previous studies showing that while bundling can increase welfare, in certain market conditions, it blocks entry and harms competition. The empirical analysis suggests that bundling can be used to prevent competition, particularly when incumbents leverage it to maintain market power. However, the effectiveness of bundling as an entry deterrent depends on specific market conditions and product characteristics. These findings offer a theoretical framework for when bundling should be considered anticompetitive and when antitrust intervention is necessary.

4. Impact on Innovation

A. *Baker (2016b)*

66. The antitrust concern with monopolization is not limited to prices but also includes a dominant firm's suppression of new technologies, products, and business models. Baker[52] evaluates the impact of antitrust intervention on innovation by demonstrating the difference in the effectiveness of intervention addressing exclusionary conduct before new products are developed (pre-innovation) and after new products are developed (post-innovation).

---

51 Martin Peitz, *Bundling May Blockade Entry*, 26 INT'L J. INDUS. ORG. 41 (2008), https://doi.org/10.1016/j.ijindorg.2006.09.005.

52 Jonathan B. Baker, *Exclusionary Conduct of Dominant Firms, R&D Competition, and Innovation*, 48 REV. INDUS. ORG. 269 (2016), https://doi.org/10.1007/s11151-015-9485-9.

The results show that pre-innovation interventions will encourage the dominant firm to invest more in R&D to escape competition and encourage its rival to invest less, while post-innovation interventions can either encourage or discourage R&D investment based on the firm's perceptions of each other's investments. Specifically, antitrust intervention on exclusionary conduct that increases R&D costs for dominant firms will increase rival firms' investments. However, the dominant firm's investment will only increase if the dominant firm views the rival's investment as a strategic complement. These findings are important for evaluating the validity of the dominant firm's claim that its exclusionary conduct is beneficial for innovation by encouraging more R&D investments.

B. *Page and Childers (2012)*

67. Page and Childers[53] analyze how antitrust law interacts with innovation in platform markets, focusing on the *Microsoft* and *Intel* cases. Both companies, part of the Wintel standard (Windows OS and Intel central processing units (CPUs)), maintained market dominance due to innovation and entry barriers. The government claimed that Microsoft and Intel sought to monopolize related markets – browsers for Microsoft and graphics processing units (GPUs) for Intel – by using product design to hinder competitors. Microsoft was accused of integrating its Internet Explorer browser into Windows in a way that made it difficult for users and OEMs to remove or replace it, which courts viewed as monopolistic behavior. Similarly, Intel allegedly excluded smaller CPU rivals like AMD and Via through contracts with manufacturers and limited interoperability for competitors' GPUs, a tactic referred to as "predatory innovation" by the FTC. Both cases raised concerns about platform owners integrating new functions to improve efficiency while also limiting innovation from competitors that rely on interoperability. Courts struggled to balance fostering innovation and preventing anticompetitive behavior. The *Microsoft* case highlighted the need for antitrust standards to assess whether practices harm competition and consumers, not just rivals. Remedies in both cases aimed to stop anticompetitive actions while allowing legitimate innovation, with the *Microsoft* case showing the importance of weighing consumer benefits like efficiency and enhanced products against competitive harms. This approach, applied later in *Intel*, demonstrated the evolving understanding of platform markets, where product design choices could harm competition but also needed careful assessment to avoid stifling innovation. Lessons from *Microsoft* influenced the FTC's handling of *Intel*, showing how antitrust enforcement adapted to better balance innovation and competition.

---

53 William H. Page and Seldon J. Childers, *Antitrust, Innovation, and Product Design in Platform Markets: Microsoft and* Intel, 78 Antitrust L.J. 363 (2012), https://www.jstor.org/stable/43486984.

C. Wu (2012)

68. Wu[54] argues that while price-related conduct is easier to address, innovation-centered competition enforcement is more critical. He emphasizes that innovation-centered antitrust policy should prioritize preventing the exclusion of innovators, as monopolists may find exclusion a cheaper alternative to innovation. He suggests that making exclusion costly is essential for promoting innovation and can be enforced through Sherman Act sections 1 or 2, FTC Act section 5, or by preventing mergers that allow larger firms to acquire or discourage innovative small firms. Wu suggests that to protect innovation, a firm approaching or newly achieving dominance should not face immediate intervention unless there is strong evidence of improper methods. He concludes that intervention should occur once the monopolist has recouped its investments, at which point the argument for forbearance to preserve innovation incentives should cease.

D. Choi (2004)

69. Choi[55] explores how tying arrangements impact innovation incentives. While traditional antitrust policy in the U.S. focused on price increases by dominant companies, he argues that this approach may not be suitable for the fast-evolving technology industry, and antitrust enforcement should prioritize maintaining a competitive market for innovation instead. Moreover, he suggests that what sets the *Microsoft* case apart from earlier antitrust cases on tying is its focus on the effects on innovation. In his analysis, Choi highlights that a key factor in evaluating welfare effects is the nature of R&D competition without bundling and the extent of product differentiation. He demonstrates that in an R&D model with horizontal product differentiation, tying can improve social welfare by reducing duplicative R&D efforts, but generally harms social welfare, as it leads to foreclosure in the innovation market.

E. *Thatchenkery and Katila (2023)*

70. Thatchenkery and Katila[56] explore how regulatory intervention against a dominant platform owner, like Microsoft, impacts innovation and profitability in enterprise infrastructure software. While dominant platforms are

---

54 Tim Wu, *Taking Innovation Seriously: Antitrust Enforcement if Innovation Mattered Most*, 78 ANTITRUST L.J. 313 (2012), https://www.jstor.org/stable/43486982.

55 Jay Pil Choi, *Tying and Innovation: A Dynamic Analysis of Tying Arrangements*, 114 ECON. J. 83 (2004), https://www.jstor.org/stable/3590035.

56 Sruthi Thatchenkery & Riitta Katila, *Innovation and Profitability Following Antitrust Intervention Against a Dominant Platform: The Wild, Wild West?*, 44 STRATEGIC MGMT. J. 943 (2023), https://doi.org/10.1002/smj.3470.

often viewed as harmful to innovation and customer choice, their analysis shows that antitrust actions can reduce competitive threats, creating new opportunities and spurring innovation, but can also lead to wasteful development and higher repositioning costs, ultimately lowering profitability (more patents, but fewer profits). More specifically, antitrust intervention positively impacts rival complementors' innovation by reducing perceived threats, but it negatively affects their profitability as firms pursue riskier, less efficient strategies. In addition, such intervention reduces the dominant platform's profitability by limiting practices like bundling, which leads to lower sales and profits. For example, antitrust intervention on Microsoft led to increased innovation among rivals, which adopted more diverse strategies. However, overall profitability for both rivals and the dominant platform declined, suggesting that weakening a dominant platform can make it more challenging for firms to succeed financially.

F. Lenard (2011)

71. Lenard[57] emphasizes that, unlike traditional antitrust enforcement that focuses on static efficiency, dynamic efficiency is more important for the high-tech sector. He explains that Schumpeterian analysis prioritizes dynamic efficiency over static efficiency, arguing that antitrust enforcement can undermine innovation by increasing scrutiny on market winners. Inappropriate antitrust actions can impose restrictions that discourage innovation, especially in early-stage technology markets where uncertainties make enforcement prone to mistakes, such as misdefining markets or entry conditions. On the other hand, delayed action can allow early entrants to entrench themselves and erect barriers to new competition. High-tech industries present unique challenges due to network effects, economies of scale, and a cost structure characterized by high upfront costs and low marginal costs. These factors make it difficult to distinguish between anticompetitive behavior that restricts output, and pro-competitive behavior that benefits consumers. Lenard cites the *Microsoft* case as a lesson in the complexity of antitrust enforcement, where even when authorities are confident in identifying anticompetitive behavior, long legal processes and the difficulty of crafting effective remedies can limit the impact of such cases. He also discusses key antitrust cases, including *Microsoft*, *Intel*, *IBM*, and *AT&T*, while addressing issues like vertical integration, net neutrality, and emerging technologies such as cloud computing. Lenard highlights how technological shifts, such as the rise of cloud computing, smartphones, and virtual appliances, have eroded Microsoft's dominance in desktop computing by weakening the network

---

57 Thomas M. Lenard, *Introduction: Antitrust and the Dynamics of Competition in High-Tech Industries*, 38 REV. INDUS. ORG. 311 (2011), https://www.jstor.org/stable/23884982.

effects it once controlled. He concludes that more empirical studies are needed to build greater confidence in antitrust policies, despite the inherent limitations of such research.

III. Conclusion

72. The *Microsoft*-inspired literature is vast. In this chapter, we highlight some of the themes that have emerged in legal/policy, economics, and business scholarship. We examine the impact of the case on consumers, competitors, and innovation. The lessons on *Microsoft* remain significant, but the literature, particularly the policy and theoretical work, remains mixed and largely depends on assumptions and framing. The empirical work suggests nuance is needed in addressing tech-related harms. While *Microsoft* seems to have been a good case, the lesson largely seems to be that a case must be carefully constructed with a good understanding of theories of harm, credible remedies, and a sense of how to address the ever-present threat of unforeseen consequences. Such lessons are particularly salient in the current antitrust tech litigation environment.

Reference

American Economic Review

- Besanko, D., et al. (2019). How Efficient Is Dynamic Competition? The Case of Price as Investment. *The American Economic Review*, *109*(9), 3339–64. https://www.jstor.org/stable/26773266

- Fisher, F. M. (2000). The IBM and Microsoft Cases: What's the Difference? *American Economic Review*, *90*(2), 180–83. https://doi.org/10.1257/aer.90.2.180

- Hall, C. E., & Hall, R. E. (2000). Toward a Quantification of the Effects of Microsoft's Conduct. *American Economic Review*, *90*(2), 188–91. https://doi.org/10.1257/aer.90.2.188

The Economic Journal

- Choi, J. P. (2004). Tying and Innovation: A Dynamic Analysis of Tying Arrangements. *The Economic Journal*, *114*(492), *83*–101. https://www.jstor.org/stable/3590035

- Dunham, W. R. (2006). The Determination of Antitrust Liability in *United States v. Microsoft*: The Empirical Evidence the Department of Justice Used to Prove Its Case. *Journal of Competition Law & Economics*, *2*(4), 549–671. https://doi.org/10.1093/joclec/nhl023

- Duque, O. V. (2023). Active Choice vs. Inertia? An Exploratory Assessment of the European Microsoft Case's Choice Screen. *Journal of Competition Law & Economics*, *19*(1), 60–74. https://doi.org/10.1093/joclec/nhac009

- Evans, D. S., Nichols, A. L., & Schmalensee, R. (2005). *United States v. Microsoft*: Did Consumers Win? *Journal of Competition Law & Economics*, *1*(3), 497–539. https://doi.org/10.1093/joclec/nhi016
  Journal of Competition Law & Economics
- Liebowitz, S. J., & Margolis, S. E. (2013). The Troubled Path of the Lock-In Movement. *Journal of Competition Law & Economics*, *9*(1), 125–52. https://doi.org/10.1093/joclec/nhs034

Antitrust Law Journal

- Baker, J. B. (2015). Taking the Error Out of "Error Cost" Analysis: What's Wrong with Antitrust's Right. *Antitrust Law Journal*, *80*(1), 1–38. https://www.jstor.org/stable/26411520
- Baker, J. B. (2016a). Evaluating Appropriability Defenses for the Exclusionary Conduct of Dominant Firms in Innovative Industries. *Antitrust Law Journal*, *80*(3), 431–62. https://www.jstor.org/stable/26411527
- Carrier, M. A. (2011). A Tort-Based Causation Framework for Antitrust Analysis. *Antitrust Law Journal*, *77*(3), 991–1016. https://www.jstor.org/stable/23075640
- Fox, E. M. (2002). What Is Harm to Competition? Exclusionary Practices and Anticompetitive Effect. *Antitrust Law Journal*, *70*(2), 371–411. https://www.jstor.org/stable/40843559
- Gilbert, R. J., & Tom, W. K. (2001). Is Innovation King at the Antitrust Agencies? The Intellectual Property Guidelines Five Years Later. *Antitrust Law Journal*, *69*(1), 43–86. https://www.jstor.org/stable/40843511
- Heiner, D. A. (2012). *Microsoft*: A Remedial Success? *Antitrust Law Journal*, *78*(2), 329–62, https://www.jstor.org/stable/43486983
- Hesse, R. B. (2009). Section 2 Remedies and *U.S. v. Microsoft*: What Is to Be Learned? *Antitrust Law Journal*, *75*(3), 847–69. https://www.jstor.org/stable/27897602
- Iansiti, M., & Richards, G. (2009). Six Years Later: The Impact of the Evolution of the IT Ecosystem. *Antitrust Law Journal*, *75*(3), 705–21. https://www.jstor.org/stable/27897596
- Jacobson, J. M., & Sher, S. A. (2006). "No Economic Sense" Makes No Sense for Exclusive Dealing. *Antitrust Law Journal*, *73*(3), 779–801. https://www.jstor.org/stable/40843693
- Katz, M. L., & Rogerson, W. P. (2009). The Applications Barrier to Entry and Its Implications for the *Microsoft* Remedies: Comment on Iansiti and Richards. *Antitrust Law Journal*, *75*(3), 723–38. https://www.jstor.org/stable/27897597
- Page, W. H. (2009). Mandatory Contracting Remedies in the American and European *Microsoft* Cases. *Antitrust Law Journal*, *75*(3), 787–809. https://www.jstor.org/stable/27897600
- Page, W. H., & Childers, S. J. (2012). Antitrust, Innovation, and Product Design in Platform Markets: *Microsoft* and *Intel*. *Antitrust Law Journal*, *78*(2), 363–95. https://www.jstor.org/stable/43486984

- Shapiro, C. (2009). *Microsoft*: A Remedial Failure. *Antitrust Law Journal, 75*(3), 739–72. https://www.jstor.org/stable/27897598

- Weiser, P. J. (2009). Regulating Interoperability: Lessons from *AT&T, Microsoft*, and Beyond. *Antitrust Law Journal, 76*(1), 271–305. https://www.jstor.org/stable/40843709

- Werden, G. J. (2001b). Network Effects and Conditions of Entry: Lessons from the *Microsoft* Case. *Antitrust Law Journal, 69*(1), 87–111. https://www.jstor.org/stable/40843512

- Wu, T. (2012). Taking Innovation Seriously: Antitrust Enforcement if Innovation Mattered Most. *Antitrust Law Journal, 78*(2), 313–28. https://www.jstor.org/stable/43486982

1. Antitrust Bulletin

- Auer, D., & Petit, N. (2015). Two-Sided Markets and the Challenge of Turning Economic Theory into Antitrust Policy. *The Antitrust Bulletin, 60*(4), 426–61. https://doi.org/10.1177/0003603X15607155

- Lumer, D. (2022). Divestiture: Doctrinal Development and Modern Application. *The Antitrust Bulletin, 67*(1), 146–81. https://doi.org/10.1177/0003603X211067122

2. Review of Industrial Organization

- Baker, J. B. (2016b). Exclusionary Conduct of Dominant Firms, R&D Competition, and Innovation. *Review of Industrial Organization, 48*, 269–87. https://doi.org/10.1007/s11151-015-9485-9

- Brennan, T. J. (2011). "High-Tech" Antitrust: Incoherent, Misguided, Obsolete, or None of the Above? Comments on Crandall-Jackson and Wright. *Review of Industrial Organization, 38*, 423–33. https://doi.org/10.1007/s11151-011-9296-6

- Crandall, R. W. (2019). The Dubious Antitrust Argument for Breaking Up the Internet Giants. *Review of Industrial Organization, 54*(4), 627–49. https://www.jstor.org/stable/48702968

- Crandall, R. W., & Jackson, C. L. (2011). Antitrust in High-Tech Industries. *Review of Industrial Organization, 38*, 319–62. https://doi.org/10.1007/s11151-011-9298-4

- Gilbert, R. J. (2000). Exclusive Dealing, Preferential Dealing, and Dynamic Efficiency. *Review of Industrial Organization, 16*(2), 167–84. https://www.jstor.org/stable/41798913

- Gisser, M., & Allen, M. S. (2001). One Monopoly Is Better Than Two: Antitrust Policy and Microsoft. *Review of Industrial Organization, 19*(2), 211–25. https://www.jstor.org/stable/41799039

- Hylton, K. N., & Xu, W. (2020). Error Costs, Ratio Tests, and Patent Antitrust Law. *Review of Industrial Organization, 56*(4), 563–91. https://www.jstor.org/stable/48734248

- Lenard, T. M. (2011). Introduction: Antitrust and the Dynamics of Competition in High-Tech Industries. *Review of Industrial Organization*, *38*(4), 311–17. https://www.jstor.org/stable/23884982
- Lenard, T. M. (2019). Introduction to the *RIO* Special Issue on Antitrust and the Platform Economy. *Review of Industrial Organization*, *54*(4), 617–26. https://www.jstor.org/stable/48702967
- Owen, B. M. (2011). Antitrust and Vertical Integration in "New Economy" Industries with Application to Broadband Access. *Review of Industrial Organization*, *38*(4), 363–86. https://www.jstor.org/stable/23884984
- Reddy, B., et al. (2001). A Monopolist Would Still Charge More for Windows: A Comment on Werden. *Review of Industrial Organization*, *18*(3), 263–68. https://www.jstor.org/stable/41799002
- Salinger, M. (2011). Discussion of Papers by Bruce Owen and Christopher Yoo. *Review of Industrial Organization*, *38*(4), 435–40. https://www.jstor.org/stable/23884988
- Werden, G. J. (2001a). Microsoft's Pricing of Windows and the Economics of Derived Demand Monopoly. *Review of Industrial Organization*, *18*(3), 257–62. https://www.jstor.org/stable/41799001

3. International Journal of Industrial Organization

- Fumagalli, C. & Motta, M. (2020). Tying in Evolving Industries, When Future Entry Cannot Be Deterred. *International Journal of Industrial Organization*, *73*, 102567. https://doi.org/10.1016/j.ijindorg.2019.102567
- Kretschmer, T. (2004). Upgrading and Niche Usage of PC Operating Systems. *International Journal of Industrial Organization*, *22*(8–9), 1155–82. https://doi.org/10.1016/j.ijindorg.2004.08.004
- Packalen, M. (2010). Complements and Potential Competition. *International Journal of Industrial Organization*, *28*(3), 244–53. https://doi.org/10.1016/j.ijindorg.2009.08.005
- Peitz, M. (2008). Bundling May Blockade Entry. *International Journal of Industrial Organization*, *26*(1), 41–58. https://doi.org/10.1016/j.ijindorg.2006.09.005
- Pleatsikas, C., & Teece, D. (2001). The Analysis of Market Definition and Market Power in the Context of Rapid Innovation. *International Journal of Industrial Organization*, *19*(5), 665–93. https://doi.org/10.1016/S0167-7187(00)00088-6

4. RAND Journal of Economics

- Carlton, D. W., & Waldman, M. (2002). The Strategic Use of Tying to Preserve and Create Market Power in Evolving Industries. *The RAND Journal of Economics*, *33*(2), 194–220. https://www.jstor.org/stable/3087430
- Chen, J., et al. (2009). Avoiding Market Dominance: Product Compatibility in Markets with Network Effects. *The RAND Journal of Economics*, *40*(3), 455–85. https://doi.org/10.1111/j.1756-2171.2009.00073.x

- Choi, J. P., & Stefanadis, C. (2001). Tying, Investment, and the Dynamic Leverage Theory. *The RAND Journal of Economics*, *32*(1), 52–71. https://www.jstor.org/stable/2696397

5. Journal of Economics and Management Strategy

- Chemla, G. (2003). Downstream Competition, Foreclosure, and Vertical Integration. *Journal of Economics & Management Strategy*, *12*(2), 261–29. https://doi.org/10.1111/j.1430-9134.2003.00261.x

- Sinitsyn, M. (2016). Choosing the Quality of the Fit between Complementary Products. *Journal of Economics & Management Strategy*, *25*(1), 161–78. https://doi.org/10.1111/jems.12136

- Stefanadis, C. (2003). Sunk Costs, Contestability, and the Latent Contract Market. *Journal of Economics & Management Strategy*, *12*(1), 119–38. https://doi.org/10.1111/j.1430-9134.2003.00119.x

6. Accounting Review

- Rajgopal, S., Srivastava, A., & Zhao, R. (2023). Do Digital Technology Firms Earn Excess Profits? Alternative Perspectives. *The Accounting Review*, *98*(4), 321–44. https://doi.org/10.2308/TAR-2021-0176

7. Journal of Marketing

- Heil, O. P., & Langvardt, A. W. (1994). The Interface between Competitive Market Signaling and Antitrust Law. *Journal of Marketing*, *58*(3), 81–96. https://doi.org/10.2307/1252312

- John, G., et al. (1999). Marketing in Technology-Intensive Markets: Toward a Conceptual Framework. *Journal of Marketing*, *63*, 78–91. https://doi.org/10.2307/1252103

- Stremersch, S., & Tellis, G. J. (2002). Strategic Bundling of Products and Prices: A New Synthesis for Marketing. *Journal of Marketing*, *66*(1), 55–72. https://doi.org/10.1509/jmkg.66.1.55.18455

8. Academy of Management Journal

- Tanriverdi, H., & Lee, C.-H. (2008). Within-Industry Diversification and Firm Performance in the Presence of Network Externalities: Evidence from the Software Industry. *The Academy of Management Journal*, *51*(2), 381–97. https://doi.org/10.5465/amj.2008.31767300

9. Strategic Management Journal

- Eisenmann, T., et al. (2011). Platform Envelopment. *Strategic Management Journal*, *32*(12), 1270–85. https://doi.org/10.1002/smj.935

- Thatchenkery, S., & Katila, R. (2022). Innovation and Profitability Following Antitrust Intervention Against a Dominant Platform: The Wild, Wild West? *Strategic Management Journal*. https://doi.org/10.1002/smj.3470

10. Research Policy

- Windrum, P. (2004). Leveraging Technological Externalities in Complex Technologies: Microsoft's Exploitation of Standards in the Browser Wars. *Research Policy*, *33*(3), 385–94. https://doi.org/10.1016/j.respol.2003.09.002

11. Web Source

- Department of Justice (DOJ), Antitrust Division. (n.d.). U.S. v. Microsoft: Court's Findings of Fact. https://www.justice.gov/atr/us-v-microsoft-courts-findings-fact#i

Concurrences
Antitrust Publications & Events

The Institute of Competition Law

The Institute of Competition Law is a publishing company, founded in 2004 by Dr. Nicolas Charbit, based in Paris, London and New York. The Institute cultivates scholarship and discussion about antitrust issues though publications and conferences. Each publication and event is supervised by editorial boards and scientific or steering committees to ensure independence, objectivity, and academic rigor. Thanks to this management, the Institute has become one of the few think tanks in Europe to have significant influence on antitrust policies.

Aim

The Institute focuses government, business and academic attention on a broad range of subjects which concern competition laws, regulations and related economics.

Boards

To maintain its unique focus, the Institute relies upon highly distinguished editors, all leading experts in national or international antitrust: Bill Kovacic, Mario Monti, Eleanor Fox, Laurence Idot, Frédéric Jenny, Ioannis Lianos, Richard Whish, etc.

Authors

4,000 authors, from 85 jurisdictions.

Partners

- Universities: University College London, King's College London, Queen Mary University, Paris Sorbonne Panthéon-Assas, etc.

- Law firms: Baker Botts, Cleary Gottlieb Steen & Hamilton, Baker McKenzie, Jones Day, Norton Rose Fulbright, Skadden Arps, White & Case, etc.

Events

Brussels, Dusseldorf, Hong Kong, London, Milan, New York, Oslo, Paris, Singapore, Warsaw and Washington DC.

Online version

Concurrences website provides all articles published since its inception.

Publications

The Institute publishes Concurrences Review, a print and online quarterly peer-reviewed journal dedicated to EU and national competitions laws. e-Competitions is a bi-monthly antitrust news bulletin covering 85 countries. The e-Competitions database contains over 30,000 case summaries from 4,000 authors.

Concurrences
Competition Laws Review

Concurrences Review

Concurrences is a print and online quarterly peer reviewed journal dedicated to EU and national competitions laws. It has been launched in 2004 as the flagship of the Institute of Competition Law in order to provide a forum for academics, practitioners and enforcers. Concurrences' influence and expertise has garnered contributions or interviews with such figures as Christine Lagarde, Bill Kovacic, Emmanuel Macron, Antonin Scalia and Magrethe Vestager.

CONTENTS

More than 15,000 articles, print and/or online. Quarterly issues provide current coverage with contributions from the EU or national or foreign countries thanks to more than 2,500 authors in Europe and abroad.

FORMAT

In order to balance academic contributions with opinions or legal practice notes, Concurrences provides its insight and analysis in a number of formats:
- Forewords: Opinions by leading academics or enforcers
- Interviews: Interviews of antitrust experts
- On-Topics: 4 to 6 short papers on hot issues
- Law & Economics: Short papers written by economists for a legal audience
- Articles: Long academic papers
- Case Summaries: Case commentary on EU and French case law
- Legal Practice: Short papers for in-house counsels
- International: Medium size papers on international policies
- Books Review: Summaries of recent antitrust books
- Articles Review: Summaries of leading articles published in 45 antitrust journals

BOARDS

The Scientific Committee is headed by Laurence Idot, Professor at Panthéon Assas University. The International Committee is headed by Frederic Jenny, OECD Competition Comitteee Chairman. Boards members include Douglas Ginsburg, Benoît Cœuré, Howard Shelanski, Richard Whish, Wouter Wils, etc.

ONLINE VERSION

Concurrences website provides all articles published since its inception, in addition to selected articles published online only in the electronic supplement.

WRITE FOR CONCURRENCES

Concurrences welcome spontaneous contributions. Except in rare circumstances, the journal accepts only unpublished articles, whatever the form and nature of the contribution. The Editorial Board checks the form of the proposals, and then submits these to the Scientific Committee. Selection of the papers is conditional to a peer review by at least two members of the Committee. Within a month, the Committee assesses whether the draft article can be published and notifies the author.

e-Competitions
Antitrust Case Laws e-Bulletin

e-Competitions Bulletin

CASE LAW DATABASE

e-Competitions is the only online resource that provides consistent coverage of antitrust cases from 85 jurisdictions, organized into a searchable database structure. e-Competitions concentrates on cases summaries taking into account that in the context of a continuing growing number of sources there is a need for factual information, i.e., case law.

- 30,000 case summaries
- 4,000 authors
- 85 countries covered
- 60,000 subscribers

SOPHISTICATED EDITORIAL AND IT ENRICHMENT

e-Competitions is structured as a database. The editors make a sophisticated technical and legal work on all articles by tagging these with key words, drafting abstracts and writing html code to increase Google ranking. There is a team of antitrust lawyers – PhD and judges clerks – and a team of IT experts. e-Competitions makes comparative law possible. Thanks to this expert editorial work, it is possible to search and compare cases by jurisdiction, legal topics or business sectors.

PRESTIGIOUS BOARDS

e-Competitions draws upon highly distinguished editors, all leading experts in national or international antitrust. Advisory Board Members include: Sir Christopher Bellamy, Ioanis Lianos (UCL), Eleanor Fox (NYU), Frédéric Jenny (OECD), Jacqueline Riffault-Silk (Cour de cassation), Wouter Wils (King's College London), etc.

LEADING PARTNERS

- Association of European Competition Law Judges: The AECLJ is a forum for judges of national Courts specializing in antitrust case law. Members timely feed e-Competitions with just released cases.

- Academics partners: Antitrust research centres from leading universities write regularly in e-Competitions: University College London, King's College London, Queen Mary University, etc.

- Law firms: Global law firms and antitrust niche firms write detailed cases summaries specifically for e-Competitions: Baker Botts, Baker McKenzie, Cleary Gottlieb Steen & Hamilton, Jones Day, Norton Rose Fulbright, Skadden, White & Case, etc.

Concurrences +
THE COMPETITION LAW PORTAL

21 years of archives
50,000 articles

4 DATABASES

Concurrences
Access to latest issue and archives

- 16,000 articles from 2004 to the present
- European and national doctrine and case law

e-Competitions
Access to latest issue and archives

- 30,000 case summaries from 1911 to the present
- Case law of 85 jurisdictions

Books
Access to all Concurrences books

- 85 e-Books available
- PDF version

Conferences
Access to the documentation of all Concurrences events

- 650 conferences (Brussels, Hong Kong, London, New York, Paris, Singapore and Washington, DC)
- 350 PowerPoint presentations, proceedings and syntheses
- 550 videos
- Verbatim reports

NEW

New search engine
Optimized results to save time

- Search results sorted by date, jurisdiction, keyword, economic sector, author, etc.

New modes of access
IP address recognition

- No need to enter codes: immediate access
- No need to change codes when your team changes: offers increased security and saves time

Mobility

- Responsive design: site optimized for tablets and smartphones